TURING 图灵原版数学·纟

A First Course in Stochastic Processes

随机过程初级教程

（英文版·第2版）

[美] Samuel Karlin
Howard M.Taylor 著

人民邮电出版社
北　京

图书在版编目（CIP）数据

随机过程初级教程：第 2 版：英文 / （美）卡林（Karlin, S.）（美）泰勒（Taylor, H. M.）著. —北京：人民邮电出版社，2007.10
（图灵原版数学 · 统计学系列）
ISBN 978-7-115-16598-5

Ⅰ. 随… Ⅱ. 卡… Ⅲ. 随机过程 — 教材 — 英文 Ⅳ. O211. 6

中国版本图书馆 CIP 数据核字（2007）第 112613 号

内容提要

本书系统论述随机过程的基本理论和方法，理论与实际应用并重. 书中主要内容有：马尔可夫链、连续时间马尔可夫链、更新过程、鞅论、布朗运动、分支过程和平稳随机过程. 本书涉及范围十分广泛，含有丰富的背景知识，深入浅出，不需要测度论作为预备知识.

本书可作为高等学校本科生和研究生的教材，也可作为工程技术人员的参考书

图灵原版数学 · 统计学系列

随机过程初级教程（英文版 · 第 2 版）

◆ 著 ［美］Samuel Karlin Howard M.Taylor
责任编辑 明永玲

◆ 人民邮电出版社出版发行 北京市崇文区夕照寺街 14 号
邮编 100061 电子函件 315@ptpress.com.cn
网址 http://www.ptpress.com.cn
北京隆昌伟业印刷有限公司印刷
新华书店总店北京发行所经销

◆ 开本：700 × 1000 1/16
印张：35.75
字数：586 千字 2007 年 10 月第 1 版
印数：1– 3 000 册 2007 年 10 月北京第 1 次印刷

著作权合同登记号 图字：01-2007-3376 号

ISBN 978-7-115-16598-5/O1

定价：69.00 元

读者服务热线：(010)88593802 印装质量热线：(010)67129223

PREFACE

The purposes, level, and style of this new edition conform to the tenets set forth in the original preface. We continue with our tack of developing simultaneously theory and applications, intertwined so that they refurbish and elucidate each other.

We have made three main kinds of changes. First, we have enlarged on the topics treated in the first edition. Second, we have added many exercises and problems at the end of each chapter. Third, and most important, we have supplied, in new chapters, broad introductory discussions of several classes of stochastic processes not dealt with in the first edition, notably martingales, renewal and fluctuation phenomena associated with random sums, stationary stochastic processes, and diffusion theory.

Martingale concepts and methodology have provided a far-reaching apparatus vital to the analysis of all kinds of functionals of stochastic processes. In particular, martingale constructions serve decisively in the investigation of stochastic models of diffusion type. Renewal phenomena are almost equally important in the engineering and managerial sciences especially with reference to examples in reliability, queueing, and inventory systems. We discuss renewal theory systematically in an extended chapter. Another new chapter explores the theory of stationary processes and its applications to certain classes of engineering and econometric problems. Still other new chapters develop the structure and use of diffusion processes for describing certain biological and physical systems and fluctuation properties of sums of independent random variables useful in the analyses of queueing systems and other facets of operations research.

The logical dependence of chapters is shown by the diagram below. Section 1 of Chapter 1 can be reviewed without worrying about details. Only Sections 5 and 7 of Chapter 7 depend on Chapter 6. Only Section 9 of Chapter 9 depends on Chapter 5.

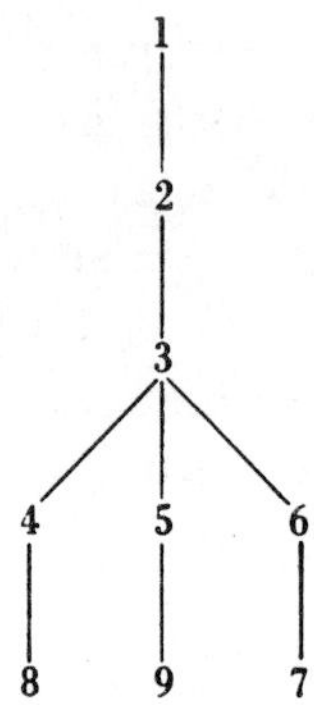

An easy one-semester course adapted to the junior–senior level could consist of Chapter 1, Sections 2 and 3 preceded by a cursory review of Section 1, Chapter 2 in its entirety, Chapter 3 excluding Sections 5 and/or 6, and Chapter 4 excluding Sections 3, 7, and 8. The content of the last part of the course is left to the discretion of the lecturer. An option of material from the early sections of any or all of Chapters 5–9 would be suitable.

The problems at the end of each chapter are divided into two groups. The first, more or less elementary; the second, more difficult and subtle.

The scope of the book is quite extensive, and on this account, it has been divided into two volumes. We view the first volume as embracing the main categories of stochastic processes underlying the theory and most relevant for applications. In *A Second Course* we introduce additional topics and applications and delve more deeply into some of the issues of *A First Course*. We have organized the edition to attract a wide spectrum of readers including theorists and practitioners of stochastic analysis pertaining to the mathematical, engineering, physical, biological, social, and managerial sciences.

The second volume of this work, *A Second Course in Stochastic Processes*, will include the following chapters: (10) Algebraic Methods in Markov Chains; (11) Ratio Theorems of Transition Probabilities and Applications; (12) Sums of Independent Random Variables as a Markov Chain; (13)

Order Statistics, Poisson Processes, and Applications; (14) Continuous Time Markov Chains; (15) Diffusion Processes; (16) Compounding Stochastic Processes; (17) Fluctuation Theory of Partial Sums of Independent Identically Distributed Random Variables; (18) Queueing Processes.

As noted in the first preface, we have drawn freely on the thriving literature of applied and theoretical stochastic processes. A few representative references are included at the end of each chapter; these may be profitably consulted for more advanced material.

We express our gratitude to the Weizmann Institute of Science, Stanford University, and Cornell University for providing a rich intellectual environment, and facilities indispensable for the writing of this text. The first author is grateful for the continuing grant support provided by the Office of Naval Research that permitted an unencumbered concentration on a number of the concepts and drafts of this book. We are also happy to acknowledge our indebtedness to many colleagues who have offered a variety of constructive criticisms. Among others, these include Professors P. Brockwell of La Trobe, J. Kingman of Oxford, D. Iglehart and S. Ghurye of Stanford, and K. Itô and S. Stidham, Jr. of Cornell. We also thank our students M. Nedzela and C. Macken for their assistance in checking the problems and help in reading proofs.

SAMUEL KARLIN
HOWARD M. TAYLOR

PREFACE TO FIRST EDITION

Stochastic processes concern sequences of events governed by probabilistic laws. Many applications of stochastic processes occur in physics, engineering, biology, medicine, psychology, and other disciplines, as well as in other branches of mathematical analysis. The purpose of this book is to provide an introduction to the many specialized treatises on stochastic processes. Specifically, I have endeavored to achieve three objectives: (1) to present a systematic introductory account of several principal areas in stochastic processes, (2) to attract and interest students of pure mathematics in the rich diversity of applications of stochastic processes, and (3) to make the student who is more concerned with application aware of the relevance and importance of the mathematical subleties underlying stochastic processes.

The examples in this book are drawn mainly from biology and engineering but there is an emphasis on stochastic structures that are of mathematical interest or of importance in more than one discipline. A number of concepts and problems that are currently prominent in probability research are discussed and illustrated.

Since it is not possible to discuss all aspects of this field in an elementary text, some important topics have been omitted, notably stationary stochastic processes and martingales. Nor is the book intended in any sense as an authoritative work in the areas it does cover. On the contrary, its primary aim is simply to bridge the gap between an elementary probability course and the many excellent advanced works on stochastic processes.

Readers of this book are assumed to be familiar with the elementary theory of probability as presented in the first half of Feller's classic *Introduction to Probability Theory and Its Applications.* In Section 1, Chapter 1 of my book the necessary background material is presented and the terminology and notation of the book established. Discussions in small print can be skipped on first reading. Exercises are provided at the close of each chapter to help illuminate and expand on the theory.

This book can serve for either a one-semester or a two-semester course, depending on the extent of coverage desired.

In writing this book, I have drawn on the vast literature on stochastic processes. Each chapter ends with citations of books that may profitably be consulted for further information, including in many cases bibliographical listings.

I am grateful to Stanford University and to the U.S. Office of Naval Research for providing facilities, intellectual stimulation, and financial support for the writing of this text. Among my academic colleagues I am grateful to Professor K. L. Chung and Professor J. McGregor of Stanford for their constant encouragement and helpful comments; to Professor J. Lamperti of Dartmouth, Professor J. Kiefer of Cornell, and Professor P. Ney of Wisconsin for offering a variety of constructive criticisms; to Dr. A. Feinstein for his detailed checking of substantial sections of the manuscript, and to my students P. Milch, B. Singer, M. Feldman, and B. Krishnamoorthi for their helpful suggestions and their assistance in organizing the exercises. Finally, I am indebted to Gail Lemmond and Rosemarie Stampfel for their superb technical typing and all-around administrative care.

SAMUEL KARLIN

CONTENTS

Chapter 1

ELEMENTS OF STOCHASTIC PROCESSES

Chapter 2

MARKOV CHAINS

Chapter 3

THE BASIC LIMIT THEOREM OF MARKOV CHAINS AND APPLICATIONS

Chapter 4

CLASSICAL EXAMPLES OF CONTINUOUS TIME MARKOV CHAINS

Chapter 5

RENEWAL PROCESSES

Chapter 6

MARTINGALES

Chapter 7

BROWNIAN MOTION

Chapter 8

BRANCHING PROCESSES

Chapter 9

STATIONARY PROCESSES

Appendix

REVIEW OF MATRIX ANALYSIS

Chapter 1

ELEMENTS OF STOCHASTIC PROCESSES

The first part of this chapter summarizes the necessary background material and establishes the terminology and notation of the book. It is suggested that the reader not dwell here assidously, but rather quickly. It can be reviewed further if the need should arise later.

Section 2 introduces the celebrated Brownian motion and Poisson processes, and Section 3 surveys some of the broad types of stochastic processes that are the main concern of the remainder of the book.

The last section, included for completeness, discusses some technical considerations in the general theory. The section should be skipped on a first reading.

1: Review of Basic Terminology and Properties of Random Variables and Distribution Functions

The present section contains a brief review of the basic elementary notions and terminology of probability theory. The contents of this section will be used freely throughout the book without further reference. We urge the student to tackle the problems at the close of the chapter; they provide practice and help to illuminate the concepts. For more detailed treatments of these topics, the student may consult any good standard text for a first course in probability theory (see references at close of this chapter).

The following concepts will be assumed familiar to the reader:

(1) A real random variable X.
(2) The distribution function F of X [defined by $F(\lambda) = \Pr\{X \leq \lambda\}$] and its elementary properties.
(3) An event pertaining to the random variable X, and the probability thereof.
(4) $E\{X\}$, the expectation of X, and the higher moments $E\{X^n\}$.
(5) The law of total probabilities and Bayes rule for computing probabilities of events.

The abbreviation r.v. will be used for "real random variables." A r.v.

X is called *discrete* if there is a finite or denumerable set of distinct values $\lambda_1, \lambda_2, \ldots$ such that $a_i \equiv \Pr\{X = \lambda_i\} > 0$, $i = 1, 2, 3, \ldots$, and $\sum_i a_i = 1$. If $\Pr\{X = \lambda\} = 0$ for every value of λ, the r.v. X is called *continuous*. If there is a nonnegative function $p(t)$, defined for $-\infty < t < \infty$ such that the distribution function F of the r.v. X is given by

$$F(\lambda) = \int_{-\infty}^{\lambda} p(t)\, dt,$$

then p is said to be the probability density of X. If X has a probability density, then it is necessarily continuous; however, examples are known of continuous r.v.'s which do not possess probability densities.

If X is a discrete r.v., then its mth moment is given by

$$E[X^m] = \sum_i \lambda_i^m \Pr\{X = \lambda_i\}$$

(where the λ_i are as earlier), if the series converges absolutely.

If X is a continuous r.v. with probability density $p(\cdot)$, its mth moment is given by

$$E[X^m] = \int_{-\infty}^{\infty} x^m p(x)\, dx,$$

provided the integral converges absolutely.

The first moment of X, commonly called the *mean*, is denoted by m_X or μ_X. The mth central moment of X is defined as the mth moment of the r.v. $X - m_X$ if m_X exists. The first central moment is evidently zero; the second central moment is called the *variance* (σ_X^2) *of* X. The *median* of a r.v. X is any value v with the property that $\Pr\{X \geq v\} \geq \frac{1}{2}$ and $\Pr\{X \leq v\} \geq \frac{1}{2}$.

If X is a random variable and g is a function, then $Y = g(X)$ is also a random variable. If X is a discrete random variable with possible values $x_1, x_2, \ldots$, then the expectation of $g(X)$ is given by

$$E[g(X)] = \sum_{i=1}^{\infty} g(x_i) \Pr\{X = x_i\} \tag{1.1}$$

provided the sum converges absolutely. If X is continuous and has the probability density function p_X then the expectation of $g(X)$ is computed from

$$E[g(X)] = \int g(x) p_X(x)\, dx. \tag{1.2}$$

The general formula, covering both the discrete and continuous cases is

$$E[g(X)] = \int g(x)\, dF_X(x) \tag{1.3}$$

where F_X is the distribution function of the random variable X. Technically speaking, the integral in (1.3) is called a Lebesgue-Stieltjes integral. We do not require knowledge of such integrals in this text but interpret (1.3) to signify (1.1) when X is a discrete random variable and to represent (1.2) when X possesses a probability density function p_X.

Let $F_Y(y) = \Pr\{Y \le y\}$ denote the distribution function for $Y = g(X)$. When X is a discrete random variable

$$E[Y] = \sum y_i \Pr\{Y = y_i\}$$
$$= \sum g(x_i) \Pr\{X = x_i\}$$

if $y_i = g(x_i)$ and provided the second sum converges absolutely. In general

$$E[Y] = \int y \, dF_Y(y)$$
$$= \int g(x) \, dF_X(x). \tag{1.4}$$

If X is a discrete random variable then so is $Y = g(X)$. It may be, however, that X is a continuous random variable while Y is discrete (the student should provide an example). Even so, one may compute $E[Y]$ from either form in (1.4) with the same result.

A. JOINT DISTRIBUTION FUNCTIONS

Given a pair (X, Y) of r.v.'s, their joint distribution function is the function F_{XY} of two real variables given by

$$F(\lambda_1, \lambda_2) = F_{XY}(\lambda_1, \lambda_2) = \Pr\{X \le \lambda_1, Y \le \lambda_2\}.$$

(The subscripts X, Y will usually be omitted unless there is possible ambiguity.)

The function $F(\lambda, +\infty) \equiv \lim_{\lambda_2 \to \infty} F(\lambda, \lambda_2)$ is a probability distribution function, called the *marginal distribution function* of X. Similarly, the function $F(+\infty, \lambda)$ is called the marginal distribution of Y. If it happens that $F(\lambda_1, +\infty) \cdot F(+\infty, \lambda_2) = F(\lambda_1, \lambda_2)$ for every choice of λ_1, λ_2, then the r.v.'s X and Y are said to be *independent*. A joint distribution function F_{XY} is said to possess a (joint) probability density if there exists a function $p_{XY}(s, t)$ of two real variables such that

$$F_{XY}(\lambda_1, \lambda_2) = \int_{-\infty}^{\lambda_2} \int_{-\infty}^{\lambda_1} p_{XY}(s, t) \, ds \, dt$$

for all λ_1, λ_2. If X and Y are independent, then $p_{XY}(s, t)$ is necessarily of the form $p_X(s)p_Y(t)$, where p_X and p_Y are the probability densities of the marginal distribution of X and Y, respectively.

The joint distribution function of any finite collection $X_1, \ldots, X_n$ of random variables is defined as the function

$$\begin{aligned} F(\lambda_1, \ldots, \lambda_n) &= F_{X_1,\ldots,X_n}(\lambda_1, \ldots, \lambda_n) \\ &= \Pr\{X_1 \leq \lambda_1, \ldots, X_n \leq \lambda_n\}. \end{aligned}$$

The distribution function

$$F_{X_{i_1},\ldots,X_{i_k}}(\lambda_{i_1}, \ldots, \lambda_{i_k}) = \lim_{\lambda_i \to \infty,\, i \neq i_1,\ldots,\, i_k} F(\lambda_1, \ldots, \lambda_n)$$

is called the marginal distribution of the random variables $X_{i_1}, \ldots, X_{i_k}$.

If $F(\lambda_1, \ldots, \lambda_n) = F_{X_1}(\lambda_1) \cdot \ \ldots \ \cdot F_{X_n}(\lambda_n)$ for all values of $\lambda_1, \lambda_2, \ldots, \lambda_n$, the random variables $X_1, \ldots, X_n$ are said to be independent.

A joint distribution function $F(\lambda_1, \ldots, \lambda_n)$ is said to have a probability density if there exists a nonnegative function $p(t_1, \ldots, t_n)$ of n variables such that

$$F(\lambda_1, \ldots, \lambda_n) = \int_{-\infty}^{\lambda_n} \cdots \int_{-\infty}^{\lambda_1} p(t_1, \ldots, t_n)\, dt_1 \cdots dt_n$$

for all real $\lambda_1, \ldots, \lambda_n$.

If X and Y are jointly distributed random variables having means m_X and m_Y, respectively, their covariance (σ_{XY}) is the product moment

$$\sigma_{XY} = E[(X - m_X)(Y - m_Y)].$$

If X_1 and X_2 are independent random variables having the distribution functions F_1 and F_2, respectively, then the distribution function F of the sum $X = X_1 + X_2$ is the *convolution* of F_1 and F_2:

$$\begin{aligned} F(x) &= \int F_1(x - y)\, dF_2(y) \\ &= \int F_2(x - y)\, dF_1(y). \end{aligned}$$

Specializing to the situation where X_1 and X_2 have the probability densities p_1 and p_2, the density function p of the sum $X = X_1 + X_2$ is the convolution of the densities p_1 and p_2:

$$\begin{aligned} p(x) &= \int p_1(x - y) p_2(y)\, dy \\ &= \int p_2(x - y) p_1(y)\, dy. \end{aligned}$$

B. CONDITIONAL DISTRIBUTIONS AND CONDITIONAL EXPECTATIONS

The conditional probability $\Pr\{A|B\}$ of the event A given the event B is defined by

$$\Pr\{A|B\}=\frac{\Pr\{A \text{ and } B\}}{\Pr\{B\}}, \quad \text{if} \quad \Pr\{B\}>0,$$

and is left undefined, or assigned an arbitrary value, when $\Pr\{B\}=0$. Let X and Y be random variables which can attain only countably many different values, say 1, 2, ... The *conditional distribution function* $F_{X|Y}(\cdot|y)$ of X given $Y=y$ is defined by

$$F_{X|Y}(x|y)=\frac{\Pr\{X\leq x,\ Y=y\}}{\Pr\{Y=y\}}, \quad \text{if} \quad \Pr\{Y=y\}>0,$$

and any arbitrary discrete distribution function whenever $\Pr\{Y=y\}=0$. This last prescription is consistent with the subsequent calculations invoked on conditional distribution functions.

Suppose X and Y are jointly distributed continuous random variables having the joint probability density function $p_{XY}(x, y)$. Then the conditional distribution of X given $Y=y$ is given by

$$F_{X|Y}(x|y)=\frac{\int_{\xi\leq x} p_{XY}(\xi, y)\, d\xi}{p_Y(y)}$$

wherever $p_Y(y)>0$, and with an arbitrary specification where $p_Y(y)=0$.

Note that $F_{X|Y}$ satisfies

(C.P.1) $F_{X|Y}(x|y)$ is a probability distribution function in x for each fixed y;

(C.P.2) $F_{X|Y}(x|y)$ is a function of y for each fixed x; and

(C.P.3) For any values x, y

$$\Pr\{X\leq x,\ Y\leq y\}=\int_{\eta\leq y} F_{X|Y}(x|\eta)\, dF_Y(\eta)$$

where $F_Y(\eta)=\Pr\{Y\leq\eta\}$ is the marginal distribution of Y. As noted earlier, in this book, the reader need only deal with the integral in (C.P.3) for the discrete and continuous versions. To wit, when Y is a continuous random variable having the probability density function $p_Y(y)$ the integral in (C.P.3) is computed as

$$\Pr\{X\leq x,\ Y\leq y\}=\int_{\eta\leq y} F_{X|Y}(x|\eta)p_Y(\eta)\, d\eta.$$

And when Y is discrete the formula is

$$\Pr\{X \leq x, Y \leq y\} = \sum_{\eta \leq y} F_{X|Y}(x|\eta) \Pr\{Y = \eta\}.$$

These three properties capture the essential features of conditional distributions. In fact, from (C.P.3) we obtain

$$\begin{aligned}\Pr\{X \leq x, Y = y\} &= \Pr\{X \leq x, Y \leq y\} - \Pr\{X \leq x, Y < y\} \\ &= \sum_{\eta \leq y} F_{X|Y}(x|\eta) \Pr\{Y = \eta\} - \sum_{\eta < y} F_{X|Y}(x|\eta) \Pr\{Y = \eta\} \\ &= F_{X|Y}(x|y) \Pr\{Y = y\}\end{aligned}$$

which then implies the definition $F_{X|Y}(x|y) = \Pr\{X \leq x, Y=y\}/\Pr\{Y=y\}$, at least where $\Pr\{Y = y\} > 0$.

In advanced work,* (C.P.1-3) is taken as the basis for the definition of conditional distributions. It can be established that such conditional distributions exist for arbitrary real random variables X and Y, and even for real random vectors $X = (X_1, \ldots, X_n)$ and $Y = (Y_1, \ldots, Y_n)$.

The application of (C.P.3) in the case $y = \infty$ produces the *law of total probability*

$$\begin{aligned}\Pr\{X \leq x\} &= \Pr\{X \leq x, Y \leq \infty\} \\ &= \int_{-\infty}^{+\infty} F_{X|Y}(x|y)\, dF_Y(y),\end{aligned}$$

which is one of the most fundamental formulas of probability analysis. When Y is discrete this relation becomes

$$\Pr\{X \leq x\} = \sum_{y} \Pr\{X \leq x | Y = y\} \Pr\{Y = y\}$$

and where Y has the probability density function $p_Y(y)$ we have

$$\Pr\{X \leq x\} = \int_{-\infty}^{+\infty} \Pr\{X \leq x | Y = y\} p_Y(y)\, dy.$$

When X and Y are jointly distributed continuous random variables,

* For more explication, including rigorous and intuitive discussions on conditional expectations the reader can consult Section 7, Chapter 6. These concepts play a fundamental role in the modern development of martingale theory.

we may define the *conditional density function* $p_{X|Y}(x|y)$ of X given $Y=y$ by

$$p_{X|Y}(x|y) = \frac{d}{dx} F_{X|Y}(x|y)$$

$$= \frac{p_{XY}(x, y)}{p_Y(y)}$$

at values y for which $p_Y(y) > 0$, and as a fixed arbitrary probability density function when $p_Y(y) = 0$.

Let g be a function for which the expectation of $g(X)$ is finite. The conditional expectation of $g(X)$ given $Y=y$ can be expressed in the form

$$E[g(X)|Y=y] = \int_x g(x)\, dF_{X|Y}(x|y).$$

When X and Y are jointly continuous random variables, $E[g(X)|Y=y]$ may be computed from

$$E[g(X)|Y=y] = \int g(x) p_{X|Y}(x|y)\, dx$$

$$= \frac{\int g(x) p_{XY}(x, y)\, dx}{p_Y(y)}, \quad \text{if} \quad p_Y(y) > 0, \tag{1.5}$$

and if X and Y are jointly distributed discrete random variables, taking the possible values $x_1, x_2, \ldots$, then the detailed formula reduces to

$$E[g(X)|Y=y] = \sum_{i=1}^{\infty} g(x_i) \Pr[X = x_i|Y=y]$$

$$= \frac{\sum_{i=1}^{\infty} g(x_i) \Pr\{X = x_i, Y=y\}}{\Pr\{Y=y\}}, \quad \text{if} \quad \Pr\{Y=y\} > 0.$$

In parallel with (C.P.1–3) we see that the conditional expectation of $g(X)$ given $Y=y$ satisfies

(C.E.1) $E[g(X)|Y=y]$ is a function of y for each function g for which $E[|g(X)|] < \infty$; and

(C.E.2) For any bounded function h we have

$$E[g(X)h(Y)] = \int E[g(X)|Y=y]h(y)\, dF_Y(y)$$

where F_Y is the marginal distribution function for Y.

Let us validate the latter formula in the continuous case.

We will stipulate that the set of values y for which $p_Y(y) > 0$ is an interval (a, b) where $-\infty \leq a < b \leq +\infty$. We first insert the appropriate probability density functions, and then substitute (1.5). This gives

$$
\begin{aligned}
\int E[g(X)|Y=y]h(y)\,dF_Y(y) &= \int_a^b E[g(X)|Y=y]h(y)p_Y(y)\,dy \\
&= \int_a^b \left(\int_{-\infty}^{+\infty} g(x)p_{X|Y}(x|y)\,dx\right)h(y)p_Y(y)\,dy \\
&= \int_a^b \left(\int_{-\infty}^{+\infty} g(x)\frac{p_{XY}(x,y)}{p_Y(y)}\,dx\right)h(y)p_Y(y)\,dy \\
&= \int_a^b \int_{-\infty}^{+\infty} g(x)h(y)p_{XY}(x,y)\,dx\,dy \\
&= E[g(X)h(Y)].
\end{aligned}
$$

In the last step we have used that $p_{XY}(x, y) > 0$ only when $a < y < b$.

The special case in (C.E.2) with $h(y) \equiv 1$ produces the formula expressing the *law of total probability* for expectations,

$$E[g(X)] = \int E[g(X)|Y=y]\,dF_Y(y),$$

which, when Y is discrete, becomes

$$E[g(X)] = \sum_{i=1}^{\infty} E[g(X)|Y=y_i]\Pr\{Y=y_i\}$$

and, when Y has a probability density function p_Y, becomes

$$E[g(X)] = \int E[g(X)|Y=y]p_Y(y)\,dy.$$

Since the conditional expectation of $g(X)$ given $Y-y$ is the expectation with respect to the conditional distribution $F_{X|Y}$, conditional expectations behave in many ways like ordinary expectations. In particular, if a_1 and a_2 are fixed numbers and g_1 and g_2 are given functions for which $E[|g_i(X)|] < \infty$, $i = 1, 2$, then

$$
\begin{aligned}
&E[a_1 g_1(X) + a_2 g_2(X)|Y=y] \\
&\qquad = a_1 E[g_1(X)|Y=y] + a_2 E[g_2(X)|Y=y].
\end{aligned}
$$

According to (C.E.1), $E[g(X)|Y=y]$ is a function of the real variable y. If we evaluate this function at the random variable Y, we obtain a random variable which we denote by $E[g(X)|Y]$. The basic property (C.E.2) then is stated for any bounded function h of y,

$$E[g(X)h(Y)] = E\{E[g(X)|Y]h(Y)\}.$$

When $h(y) = 1$ for all y, we get the law of total probability in the form

$$E[g(X)] = E\{E[g(X) | Y]\}.$$

The following list summarizes these and other properties of conditional expectations. Here, with or without affixes, X and Y are random variables, c is a real number, g is a function for which $E[|g(X)|] < \infty$, f is a bounded function and h is a function of two variables for which $E[|h(X, Y)|] < \infty$.

$$E[a_1 g(X_1) + a_2 g(X_2) | Y] = a_1 E[g(X_1) | Y] + a_2 E[g(X_2) | Y], \tag{1.6}$$

$$g \geq 0 \quad \text{implies} \quad E[g(X) | Y] \geq 0, \tag{1.7}$$

$$E[h(X, Y) | Y = y] = E[h(X, y) | Y = y], \tag{1.8}$$

$$E[g(X) | Y] = E[g(X)] \quad \text{if } X \text{ and } Y \text{ are independent}, \tag{1.9}$$

$$E[g(X) f(Y) | Y] = f(Y) E[g(X) | Y], \tag{1.10}$$

and

$$E[g(X) f(Y)] = E\{E[g(X) | Y] f(Y)\}. \tag{1.11}$$

As consequences of (1.6), (1.10) and (1.11), with either $g \equiv 1$ or $f \equiv 1$, we obtain,

$$E[c | Y] = c, \tag{1.12}$$

$$E[f(Y) | Y] = f(Y), \tag{1.13}$$

and

$$E[g(X)] = E\{E[g(X) | Y]\}. \tag{1.14}$$

C. INFINITE FAMILIES OF RANDOM VARIABLES

In dealing with an infinite family of random variables, a direct generalization of the preceding definitions involves substantial difficulties. We need to adopt a slightly modified approach.

Given a denumerably infinite family $X_1, X_2, \ldots$ of r.v.'s, their statistical properties are regarded as defined by prescribing, for each integer $n \geq 1$ and every set $i_1, \ldots, i_n$ of n distinct positive integers, the joint distribution function $F_{X_{i_1}, \ldots, X_{i_n}}$ of the random variables $X_{i_1}, \ldots, X_{i_n}$. Of course, some consistency requirements must be imposed upon the infinite family $F_{X_{i_1}, \ldots, X_{i_n}}$, namely, that

$$\begin{aligned} &F_{X_{i_1}, \ldots, X_{i_{j-1}}, X_{i_{j+1}}, \ldots, X_{i_n}}(\lambda_1, \ldots, \lambda_{j-1}, \lambda_{j+1}, \ldots, \lambda_n) \\ &\quad = \lim_{\lambda_j \to \infty} F_{X_{i_1}, \ldots, X_{i_n}}(\lambda_1, \ldots, \lambda_{j-1}, \lambda_j, \lambda_{j+1}, \ldots, \lambda_n) \end{aligned}$$

and that the distribution function obtained from

$$F_{X_{i_1}, X_{i_2}, \ldots, X_{i_n}}(\lambda_1, \lambda_2, \ldots, \lambda_n)$$

by interchanging two of the indices i_ν and i_μ and the corresponding variables λ_ν and λ_μ should be invariant. This simply means that the manner of labeling the random variables $X_1, X_2, \ldots$ is not relevant.

The joint distributions $\{F_{X_{i_1}, \ldots, X_{i_n}}\}$ are called the *finite-dimensional distributions* associated with $\{X_n\}_{n=1}^{\infty}$. In principle, all important probabilistic quantities of the variables $\{X_n\}_{n=1}^{\infty}$ can be computed in terms of the finite-dimensional distributions.

D. CHARACTERISTIC FUNCTIONS

An important function associated with the distribution function F of a r.v. X is its characteristic function $\phi(t)$ (abbreviated c.f.), where t is a real variable $-\infty < t < \infty$. We write it suggestively in the form

$$\phi(t) = \int_{-\infty}^{\infty} e^{it\lambda}\, dF(\lambda), \quad i = \sqrt{-1} \tag{1.15}$$

$$= E[e^{itX}].$$

Again the reader should interpret (1.15) symbolically. If F has a probability density function p, the characteristic function becomes

$$\phi(t) = \int_{-\infty}^{\infty} e^{it\lambda} p(\lambda)\, d\lambda.$$

When F is a distribution of a discrete r.v. X with possible values $\{\lambda_k\}_{k=0}^{\infty}$ and $\Pr\{X = \lambda_k\} = a_k$ $(k = 0, 1, \ldots)$, then (1.1) reduces to the series expression

$$\phi(t) = \sum_{k=0}^{\infty} e^{it\lambda_k} a_k.$$

Much of the importance of characteristic functions derives from the following three results:

(a) The relation between distribution functions and characteristic functions is one-to-one. Thus, knowing the characteristic function is synonomous to knowing the distribution function. The equation which expresses the distribution function in terms of its characteristic function is known as Levy's inversion formula; as we do not need it, we refer the reader to one of the references for a discussion of this matter.

(b) If $X_1, \ldots, X_n$ are independent r.v.'s, the characteristic function of their sum is the product of their characteristic functions. This simple result makes characteristic functions extremely expeditious for dealing with problems involving sums of independent random variables.

(c) When they are finite, the moments of a random variable may be determined by differentiating the characteristic function. The explicit relation is

$$E[X^k] = \frac{1}{i^k} \phi^{(k)}(0)$$

where $i = \sqrt{-1}$ and $\phi^{(k)}(t) = d^k\phi(t)/dt^k$ is the kth derivative of the c.f. $\phi(t)$.

The one-to-one correspondence between distribution functions and their characteristic functions is also preserved by various limiting processes. In fact, if F, F_1, F_2, ... are distribution functions such that $\lim_{n\to\infty} F_n(\lambda) = F(\lambda)$ for every λ at which F is continuous and $\phi_n(t)$ is the c.f. of F_n, then

$$\phi_n(t) = \int_{-\infty}^{\infty} e^{it\lambda}\, dF_n(\lambda) \to \phi(t) = \int_{-\infty}^{\infty} e^{it\lambda}\, dF(\lambda)$$

uniformly in every finite interval. Conversely, if ϕ_1, ϕ_2, ... are the characteristic functions of distribution functions F_1, F_2, ... and $\lim_{n\to\infty} \phi_n(t) = \phi(t)$ for every t, and $\phi(t)$ is continuous at $t = 0$, then $\phi(t)$ is the c.f. of a distribution function F and $\lim_{n\to\infty} F_n(\lambda) = F(\lambda)$ for every λ at which F is continuous. This result is known as Levy's convergence criterion.

E. GENERATING FUNCTIONS AND LAPLACE TRANSFORMS

For random veriables whose only possible values are the nonnegative integers, a function related to the characteristic function is the generating function, defined by

$$\begin{aligned} g(s) &= \sum_{k=0}^{\infty} p_k s^k \\ &= E[s^X], \end{aligned}$$

where

$$p_k = \Pr\{X = k\}.$$

Since by hypothesis $p_k \geq 0$ and $\sum_{k=0}^{\infty} p_k = 1$, $g(s)$ is defined at least for

$|s| \le 1$ (s is a complex variable) and is infinitely differentiable for $|s| < 1$. The generating function of a nonnegative integer valued random variable X is related to the characteristic function ϕ of X formally through a change of variable $s = e^{it}$:

$$\begin{aligned}\phi(t) &= E[e^{itX}]\\ &= E[(e^{it})^X]\\ &= g(e^{it}).\end{aligned}$$

Thus generating functions inherit the three basic properties of characteristic functions;

(a) A generating function determines the distribution function uniquely;

(b) The generating function of a sum of independent nonnegative integer valued random variables is the product of their generating functions; and

(c) The moments may be obtained through successive differentiation. The factorial moments are given by

$$E[X(X-1)\cdot\ldots\cdot(X-k)] = g^{(k+1)}(1),$$

where $g^{(k)}(s) = d^k g(s)/ds^k$ is the *kth* derivative of g. Hence

$$E[X] = g^{(1)}(1)$$

and

$$E[X^2] = g^{(2)}(1) + g^{(1)}(1).$$

We give an example of the use of generating functions in working with sums of independent random variables. Let $N, X_1, X_2, \ldots$ be independent nonnegative integer valued random variables and suppose we wish to determine the generating function $g_R(s)$ of the sum $R = X_1 + \cdots + X_N$, a sum of random variables with a random number of terms.

Let $g_N(s)$ be the generating function of N and suppose the X_i have the same distribution function with common generating function $g(s)$. Then, using (1.14) and (1.9),

$$\begin{aligned}g_R(s) &= E[s^R]\\ &= E[s^{X_1+\cdots+X_N}]\\ &= E\{E[s^{X_1+\cdots+X_N}|N]\}\\ &= \sum_{n=0}^{\infty} E[s^{X_1+\cdots+X_n}|N=n]\,\Pr\{N=n\}\\ &= \sum_{n=0}^{\infty} E[s^{X_1+\cdots+X_n}]\,\Pr\{N=n\}\end{aligned}$$

(since N and X_i are independent)

$$\begin{aligned}&= \sum_{n=0}^{\infty} g(s)^n\,\Pr\{N=n\}\\ &= E[g(s)^N]\\ &= g_N[g(s)].\end{aligned}$$

To sum up:

$$g_R(s) = g_N[g(s)].$$

Using the chain rule for differentiation we calculate

$$g'_R(s) = g'_N[g(s)] \cdot g'(s)$$

and setting $s = 1$ we can infer

$$E[R] = E[N] \cdot E[X].$$

In a similar fashion we calculate the variance of R, σ_R^2, given by

$$\sigma_R^2 = E[X]^2 \cdot \sigma_N^2 + E[N] \cdot \sigma_X^2,$$

where σ_N^2 and σ_X^2 are the variances of N and X, respectively. (See Elementary Problem 4.)

The following slight extension is also available. Let $X_1, X_2, \ldots$ be arbitrary independent identically distributed random variables (i.e., not necessarily integer valued), and let N be as above. Then

$$\phi_R(t) = g_N(\phi(t)),$$

where ϕ_R and g_N are the characteristic function and generating function of $R = X_1 + \cdots + X_N$ and N, respectively, and ϕ is the common characteristic function of the X_i.

When considering nonnegative r.v.'s it is more natural to replace the characteristic function by the Laplace transform of the distribution function. If the distribution F_X has a density p_X, the Laplace transform is defined as

$$\psi_X(s) = \int_0^\infty e^{-sx} p_X(x)\, dx.$$

This integral exists for a complex variable s, where $s = \sigma + it$, σ and t real, $\sigma \geq 0$. When s is purely imaginary, $s = it$, $\psi_X(s)$ reduces to the characteristic function $\phi_X(-t)$. For a discrete nonnegative r.v. the Laplace transform is defined as

$$\psi_X(s) = \sum_{n=0}^\infty e^{-s\lambda_n} \Pr\{X = \lambda_n\}.$$

As in the case of characteristic functions, if $X_1, X_2, \ldots, X_n$ are nonnegative independent r.v.'s then

$$\psi_{X_1 + \cdots + X_n}(s) = \prod_{k=1}^n \psi_{X_k}(s).$$

In the case of general distribution functions we write

$$\psi_X(s) = \int_0^\infty e^{-s\xi}\, dF_X(\xi)$$

for the Laplace transform.

As in the case of c.f.'s the Laplace transform uniquely determines the distribution function.

F. EXAMPLES OF DISTRIBUTION FUNCTIONS

Some elementary properties of several distribution functions are given in Tables I and II.

Two multivariate distributions of fundamental importance are:

(a) *Multivariate Normal*

Let σ_1, σ_2, m_1, m_2 and ρ be real constants subject to $\sigma_i > 0$, $i = 1, 2$ and $0 \leq |\rho| < 1$. Let

$$Q(x_1, x_2) = \frac{1}{1-\rho^2}\left\{\left(\frac{x_1 - m_1}{\sigma_1}\right)^2 - 2\rho\left(\frac{x_1 - m_1}{\sigma_1}\right)\left(\frac{x_2 - m_2}{\sigma_2}\right) + \left(\frac{x_2 - m_2}{\sigma_2}\right)^2\right\}.$$

If X_1 and X_2 are r.v.'s for which

$$\Pr\{X_1 \leq a, X_2 \leq b\} = \int_{-\infty}^{a}\int_{-\infty}^{b} \frac{1}{2\pi\sigma_1\sigma_2\sqrt{1-\rho^2}} \exp\left\{-\frac{1}{2}Q(x_1, x_2)\right\} dx_1\, dx_2$$

then X_1 and X_2 are said to have a *joint normal distribution*. It can be verified that $E[X_i] = m_i$ for $i = 1, 2$ and that the variance of X_i is σ_i^2. The covariance is given by

$$E[(X_1 - m_1)(X_2 - m_2)] = \rho\sigma_1\sigma_2$$

and ρ (a dimensionless variable) is called the *correlation coefficient*. The joint characteristic function is

$$\begin{aligned}\phi_{X_1, X_2}(t_1, t_2) &= E[e^{i(t_1X_1 + t_2X_2)}]\\ &= \exp\{i(t_1m_1 + t_2m_2) - \tfrac{1}{2}(t_1^2\sigma_1^2 + 2\rho t_1\sigma_1t_2\sigma_2 + t_2^2\sigma_2^2)\}.\end{aligned}$$

If X_1 and X_2 have a joint normal distribution then the conditional distribution of X_2 given $X_1 = x_1$ is also normal with probability density function

$$p_{X_2|X_1}(x_2|x_1) = \frac{1}{\sqrt{2\pi}\sigma} \exp\left[-\frac{1}{2}\left(\frac{x_2 - m}{\sigma}\right)^2\right], \quad -\infty < x_2 < \infty,$$

where

$$m = m_2 + \frac{\sigma_2}{\sigma_1}\rho(x_1 - m_1)$$

and

$$\sigma = \sigma_2\sqrt{1-\rho^2}.$$

TABLE I

Some Frequently Encountered Continuous Probability Distributions

Continuous distribution function	*Density, p(x)*	*Range of parameters*	*Characteristic Function* $\phi(t)$	*Mean*	*Variance*
Normal	$\frac{1}{\sqrt{2\pi}\sigma} \exp - \frac{(x-m)^2}{2\sigma^2}$ for $-\infty < x < \infty$	m real, $\sigma > 0$	$\exp\left[-\frac{\sigma^2 t^2}{2} + imt\right]$	m	σ^2
Exponential	$\lambda e^{-\lambda x}$ for $x > 0$	$\lambda > 0$	$\frac{\lambda}{\lambda - it}$	$\frac{1}{\lambda}$	$\frac{1}{\lambda^2}$
Gamma	$\frac{\lambda}{\Gamma(\alpha)} (\lambda x)^{\alpha-1} e^{-\lambda x}$ for $x > 0$	$\lambda > 0$, $\alpha > 0$	$\frac{\lambda^\alpha}{(\lambda - it)^\alpha}$	$\frac{\alpha}{\lambda}$	$\frac{\alpha}{\lambda^2}$
Uniform	$\frac{1}{b-a}$ for $a < x < b$	$a < b$	$\frac{e^{iub} - e^{iua}}{iu(b-a)}$	$\frac{a+b}{2}$	$\frac{(b-a)^2}{12}$
Beta with parameters p, q	$\frac{\Gamma(p+q)}{\Gamma(p)\Gamma(q)} x^{p-1}(1-x)^{q-1}$ for $0 < x < 1$	$p > 0$, $q > 0$	$\frac{\Gamma(p+q)}{\Gamma(p)\Gamma(q)} \int_0^1 e^{itx} x^{p-1}(1-x)^{q-1}\,dx$	$\frac{p}{p+q}$	$\frac{qp}{(p+q)^2(p+q+1)}$

Note: The gamma distribution with $\alpha = 1$ is the exponential distribution where the parameter λ occurs as a scale factor. The beta distribution of parameters $p = q = 1$ is the uniform distribution on (0, 1) sometimes abbreviated "uniform (0, 1)".

TABLE II

Some Frequently Encountered Discrete Probability Distributions

Discrete distribution function	*Probability Mass Function*	*Possible values of parameters*	*Generating function*	*Mean*	*Variance*
Poisson with parameter $\lambda > 0$	$\frac{e^{-\lambda}\lambda^n}{n!}$ for $n = 0, 1, 2, \ldots$	$\lambda > 0$	$e^{-\lambda+\lambda s}$	λ	λ
Binomial	$\binom{N}{n} p^n q^{N-n}$ for $n = 0, 1, \ldots, N$	$N = 1, 2, \ldots$ $0 < p < 1$ $q = 1 - p$	$(1 - p + ps)^N$	Np	Npq
Negative binomial (Pascal)	$\binom{\alpha + n - 1}{n} p^\alpha q^n$ for $n = 0, 1, 2, \ldots$	$\alpha > 0$ $0 < p < 1$	$\left(\frac{p}{1 - qs}\right)^\alpha$	$\frac{\alpha q}{p}$	$\frac{\alpha q}{p^2}$
Geometric	$p(1 - p)^n$ for $n = 0, 1, 2, \ldots$	$0 < p < 1$	$\frac{p}{1 - qs}$	$\frac{q}{p}$	$\frac{q}{p^2}$

Let $\|a_{ij}\|$ be an $n \times n$ symmetric positive definite matrix, let $\|b_{ij}\|$ be the inverse matrix of $\|a_{ij}\|$ and let $B = \det\|b_{ij}\|$ be the determinant of $\|b_{ij}\|$. Let m_i, $i = 1, \ldots, n$ be any real constants. The random variables $X_1, \ldots, X_n$ are said to have a joint normal distribution if they possess a probability density function of the form

$$p(x_1, \ldots, x_n) = \frac{\sqrt{B}}{(2\pi)^{n/2}} \exp\left\{-\frac{1}{2} Q(x_1, \ldots, x_n)\right\}, \qquad -\infty < x_i < \infty$$

where

$$Q(x_1, \ldots, x_n) = \sum_{i,\, j} (x_i - m_i) b_{ij} (x_j - m_j).$$

The joint characteristic function is

$$\begin{aligned}\phi(t_1, \ldots, t_n) &= E[\exp\{i \sum_{i=1}^{n} t_i X_i\}] \\ &= \exp\left\{i \sum_{i=1}^{n} t_i m_i - \frac{1}{2} \sum_{i=1}^{n} \sum_{j=1}^{n} t_i a_{ij} t_j\right\}.\end{aligned}$$

From this one can compute

$$E[X_i] = m_i \quad \text{for} \quad i = 1, \ldots, n$$

and

$$E[(X_i - m_i)(X_j - m_j)] = a_{ij},$$

which justifies the name *covariance matrix* for the matrix $\|a_{ij}\|$.

From the nature of the characteristic function it is easily checked that $X_1, \ldots, X_n$ have a joint normal distribution if and only if $Y = a_1 X_1 + \cdots + a_n X_n$ has a normal distribution for every choice of real numbers $a_1, \ldots, a_n$.

(b) *The Multinomial Distribution*

This is a discrete joint distribution of r variables in which only non-negative integer values $0, \ldots, n$ are possible. It is defined by

$$\Pr\{X_1 = k_1, \ldots, X_r = k_r\} = \begin{cases} \dfrac{n!}{k_1! \ldots k_r!} p_1^{k_1} \ldots p_r^{k_r} & \text{if} \quad k_1 + \cdots + k_r = n, \\ 0 \quad \text{otherwise,} & \end{cases}$$

where $p_i > 0$, $i = 1, \ldots, r$, and $\sum_{i=1}^{r} p_i = 1$.

The joint generating function is given by

$$\begin{aligned}g(s_1, \ldots, s_r) &= E[s_1^{X_1} \cdots s_r^{X_r}] \\ &= (p_1 s_1 + \cdots + p_r s_r)^n.\end{aligned}$$

G. LIMIT THEOREMS

A sequence $\{a_n\}$ of real numbers is said to converge to a real number a, written $\lim_{n\to\infty} a_n = a$, if for every positive ε there exists a number $N(\varepsilon)$ such that $|a_n - a| < \varepsilon$ for all $n > N(\varepsilon)$. There are several ways to generalize this concept to random variables. Let $Z, Z_1, Z_2, \ldots$ be jointly distributed random variables.

(a) *Convergence with probability one*

We say Z_n converges to Z with probability one if

$$\Pr\{\lim_{n\to\infty} Z_n = Z\} = 1.$$

In words, $\lim_{n\to\infty} z_n = z$ for a set of outcomes $Z = z, Z_1 = z_1, Z_2 = z_2, \ldots$ having total probability one.

(b) *Convergence in probability*

We say Z_n converges to Z in probability if for every positive ε

$$\lim_{n\to\infty} \Pr\{|Z_n - Z| > \varepsilon\} = 0,$$

or conversely, if for every positive ε

$$\lim_{n\to\infty} \Pr\{|Z_n - Z| \le \varepsilon\} = 1.$$

In words, by taking n sufficiently large, one can achieve arbitrarily high probability that Z_n is arbitrarily close to Z.

(c) *Convergence in quadratic mean*

We say Z_n converges to Z in quadratic mean if

$$\lim_{n\to\infty} E[|Z_n - Z|^2] = 0.$$

In words, by making n sufficiently large, one can ensure that Z_n is arbitrarily close to Z in the sense of mean square difference.

(d) *Convergence in distribution* (= *Convergence in law*)

Let $F(t) = \Pr\{Z \le t\}$ and $F_k(t) = \Pr\{Z_k \le t\}$, $k = 1, 2, \ldots$. We say Z_n converges in distribution to Z (or F_n converges in distribution to F) if

$$\lim_{n\to\infty} F_n(t) = F(t)$$

for all t at which F is continuous.

It can be proved that if Z_n converges to Z with probability one, then Z_n converges to Z in probability, and that this in turn implies that Z_n converges to Z in distribution. Thus convergence in distribution is the weakest form of convergence. In fact it can be shown that every family $\{F_\alpha\}$ of distribution functions contains a sequence $\{F_{\alpha_n}\}$ that converges to a function F at all t at which F is continuous (*the Helly-Bray Lemma*) but F may not be a proper distribution in that $F(\infty)$ may be less than one.

Many of the basic results of probability theory are in the form of limit theorems and we will mention a few here. (We do not state these results under the weakest possible hypotheses.)

Let $X_1, X_2, \ldots$ be independent identically distributed random variables with finite mean m. Let $S_n = X_1 + \cdots + X_n$ and let $\bar{X}_n = S_n/n$ be the sample mean.

Law of Large Numbers (Weak). $\bar{X}_n$ converges in probability to m. That is, for any positive ε

$$\lim \Pr\{|\bar{X}_n - m| > \varepsilon\} = 0.$$

Law of Large Numbers (Strong). $\bar{X}_n$ converges to m with probability one. That is

$$\Pr\{\lim_{n\to\infty} \bar{X}_n = m\} = 1.$$

Central Limit Theorem. Suppose each X_k has the finite variance σ^2. Let

$$\begin{aligned} Z_n &= \frac{S_n - nm}{\sigma\sqrt{n}} \\ &= \frac{1}{\sigma}(\bar{X}_n - m)\sqrt{n}, \end{aligned}$$

and let Z be a normally distributed random variable having mean zero and variance one. Then Z_n converges in distribution to Z. That is, for all real a,

$$\lim_{n\to\infty} \Pr\{Z_n \le a\} = \int_{-\infty}^{a} \frac{1}{\sqrt{2\pi}} e^{-u^2/2}\, du.$$

Borel-Cantelli Lemma. Let $A_1, A_2, \ldots$ be an infinite sequence of independent events. Then the event $\{A_i, \text{i.o.}\}$ (where i.o. stands for infinitely often), which is the occurrence of an infinite number of the A_i, is given by

$$\bar{A}_\infty = \{A_i, \text{i.o.}\} = \bigcap_{j=1}^{\infty} \bigcup_{i=j}^{\infty} A_i.$$

The Borel–Cantelli lemma states that the probability of $\bar{A}_\infty$ is zero or one, according to whether $\sum_{i=1}^{\infty} \Pr\{A_i\} < \infty$ or $\sum_{i=1}^{\infty} \Pr\{A_i\} = \infty$.

H. INEQUALITIES

There are a number of inequalities that play an important role in the analytic study of stochastic processes. We mention two here.

Chebyshev's Inequality. Let Z be a nonnegative random variable. Then for any positive number c

$$\Pr\{Z > c\} \leq \frac{1}{c} E[Z]. \tag{1.16}$$

Proof. Since Z is nonnegative,

$$E[Z] = \int_0^\infty z\, dF(z) \geq \int_c^\infty z\, dF(z)$$

$$\geq c \cdot \int_c^\infty dF(z) = c \Pr\{Z > c\},$$

which gives the inequality. If X is a random variable with mean μ and variance σ^2 and we apply (1.16) with $Z = (X - \mu)^2$ we obtain,

$$\Pr\{Z > \varepsilon^2\} = \Pr\{|X - \mu| > \varepsilon\} \leq \frac{\sigma^2}{\varepsilon^2}.$$

The Schwarz Inequality. Let X and Y be jointly distributed random variables having finite second moments. Then

$$(E[XY])^2 \leq E[X^2]\, E[Y^2].$$

Proof. For all real λ

$$0 \leq E[(X + \lambda Y)^2] = E[X^2] + 2\lambda E[XY] + \lambda^2 E[Y^2].$$

Considered as a quadratic function of λ, there is, then, at most one real root. Equivalently, the discriminant of the quadratic expression is nonpositive. That is

$$4(E[XY])^2 \leq 4E[X^2]E[Y^2]$$

which completes the proof.

2: *Two Simple Examples of Stochastic Processes*

The developments in this book are intended to serve as an introduction to various aspects of stochastic processes. The theory of stochastic processes is concerned with the investigation of the structure of families of random variables X_t, where t is a parameter running over a suitable index set T. Sometimes, when no ambiguity can arise we write $X(t)$ instead of X_t.

A *realization* or *sample function* of a stochastic process $\{X_t, t \in T\}$ is an assignment, to each $t \in T$, of a possible value of X_t. The index set t may correspond to discrete units of time $T = \{0, 1, 2, 3, \ldots\}$ and $\{X_t\}$ could then represent the outcomes at successive trials like the result of tossing a coin, the successive reactions of a subject to a learning experiment, or successive observations of some characteristic of a population, etc.

The values of the X_t may be one-dimensional, two-dimensional, or n-dimensional, or even more general. In the case where X_n is the outcome of the nth toss of a die, its possible values are contained in the set $\{1, 2, 3, 4, 5, 6\}$ and a typical realization of the process would be 5, 1, 3, 2, 2, 4, 1, 6, 3, 6, ... This is shown schematically in Fig. 1, where the ordinate for $t = n$ is the value of X_n. In this example, the random

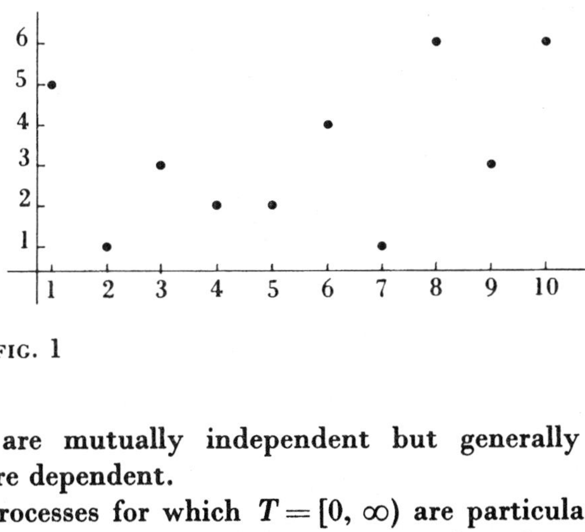

FIG. 1

variables X_n are mutually independent but generally the random variables X_n are dependent.

Stochastic processes for which $T = [0, \infty)$ are particularly important in applications. Here t can usually be interpreted as time.

We will content ourselves, for the moment, with a very brief discussion of some of the concepts of stochastic processes and two examples thereof; a summary of various types of stochastic processes is presented at the end of the chapter, while the examples themselves will be treated in greater detail in succeeding chapters.

Example 1. A very important example is the celebrated *Brownian motion process*. This process has the following characteristics:

(a) Suppose $t_0 < t_1 < \cdots < t_n$; then the increments $X_{t_1} - X_{t_0}, \ldots, X_{t_n} - X_{t_{n-1}}$ are mutually independent r.v.'s. (A process with this property is said to be a process with independent increments, and expresses the fact that the changes of X_t over nonoverlapping time periods are independent r.v.'s.)

(b) The probability distribution of $X_{t_2} - X_{t_1}$, $t_2 > t_1$, depends only on $t_2 - t_1$ (and not, for example, on t_1).

(c) $\Pr[X_t - X_s \leq x] = [2\pi B(t-s)]^{-1/2} \int_{-\infty}^{x} \exp[-u^2/2B(t-s)]\, du,$

$t > s$ (B is a positive constant).

Assume for each path that $X_0 = 0$. Note that $EX_t = 0$, $\sigma^2(X_t) = Bt$, where B is a fixed positive constant. It can be proved that, if $0 < t_1 < t_2 < \cdots < t_n < t$, then the conditional probability distribution of X_t, where the values of $X_{t_1}, \ldots, X_{t_n}$ are known, is given by (see Chapter 7)

$$\Pr\{X_t \leq x | X_{t_1} = x_1, \ldots, X_{t_n} = x_n\}$$
$$= [2\pi B(t-t_n)]^{-1/2} \int_{-\infty}^{x-x_n} \exp[-u^2/2B(t-t_n)]\, du.$$

The history of this process began with the observation by R. Brown in 1827 that small particles immersed in a liquid exhibit ceaseless irregular motions. In 1905 Einstein explained this motion by postulating that the particles under observation are subject to perpetual collision with the molecules of the surrounding medium. The analytical results derived by Einstein were later experimentally verified and extended by various physicists and mathematicians.

Let X_t denote the displacement (from its starting point, along some fixed axis) at time t of a Brownian particle. The displacement $X_t - X_s$ over the time interval (s, t) can be regarded as the sum of a large number of small displacements. The central limit theorem is essentially applicable and it seems reasonable to assert that $X_t - X_s$ is normally distributed. Similarly it seems reasonable to assume that the distribution of $X_t - X_s$ and that of $X_{t+h} - X_{s+h}$ are the same, for any $h > 0$, if we suppose the medium to be in equilibrium. Finally, it is intuitively clear that the displacement $X_t - X_s$ should depend only on the length $t - s$ and not on the time we begin observation.

The Brownian motion process (also called the Wiener process) has proved to be fundamental in the study of numerous other types of stochastic processes. In Chapter 7 we will discuss more fully an example of the one-dimensional Brownian motion process.

Example 2. Another basic example of a continuous time ($T = [0, \infty)$) stochastic process is the Poisson process. The sample function X_t counts the number of times a specified event occurs during the time period from 0 to t. Thus, each possible X_t is represented as a nondecreasing step function.

Figure 2 corresponds to a situation where the event occurred first at time t_1, then at time t_2, at time t_3, at time t_4, etc.; obviously the total

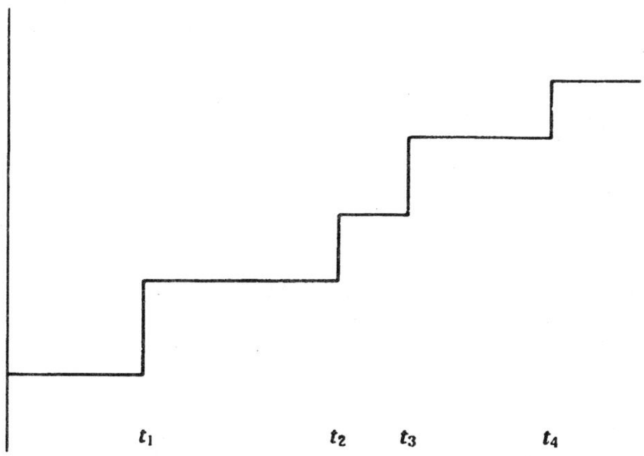

FIG. 2

number of occurrences of the event increases only in unit jumps, and $X_0 = 0$. Concrete examples of such processes are the number of x-rays emitted by a substance undergoing radioactive decay; the number of telephone calls originating in a given locality; the occurrence of accidents at a certain intersection; the occurrence of errors in a page of typing; breakdowns of a machine; and the arrival of customers for service. The justification for viewing these examples as Poisson processes is based on the concept of the law of rare events. We have a situation of many Bernoulli trials with small probability of success where the expected number of successes is constant. Under these conditions it is a familiar theorem that the actual number of events occurring follows a Poisson law. In the case of radioactive decay the Poisson approximation is excellent if the peroid of observation is very short with respect to the half-life of the radioactive substance.

We postulate that the numbers of events happening in two disjoint intervals of time are independent [see (a) above]. Analogously to (b), we also assume that the random variable $X_{t_0+t} - X_{t_0}$ depends only on t and not on t_0 or on the value of X_{t_0}. We set down the following further postulates, which are consistent with the intuitive descriptions given above:

I. The probability of at least one event happening in a time period of duration h is

$$p(h) = ah + o(h), \qquad h \to 0, \qquad a > 0$$

[$g(t) = o(t)$, $t \to 0$ is the usual symbolic way of writing the relation $\lim_{t\to 0} g(t)/t = 0$].

II. The probability of two or more events happening in time h is $o(h)$.

Postulate II is tantamount to excluding the possibility of the simultaneous occurrence of two or more events. In the concrete illustrations cited above, this requirement is usually satisfied.

Let $P_m(t)$ denote the probability that exactly m events occur in time t, i.e.,

$$P_m(t) = \Pr\{X_t = m\}, \qquad m = 0, 1, 2, \ldots .$$

The requirement II can be stated in the form

$$\sum_{m=2}^{\infty} P_m(h) = o(h),$$

and clearly

$$p(h) = P_1(h) + P_2(h) + \cdots .$$

Because of the assumption of independence,

$$P_0(t+h) = P_0(t)P_0(h) = P_0(t)(1 - p(h)),$$

and therefore

$$\frac{P_0(t+h) - P_0(t)}{h} = -P_0(t)\frac{p(h)}{h}.$$

But on the basis of Postulate I we know that $p(h)/h \to a$. Therefore, the probability $P_0(t)$ that the event has not happened during $(0, t)$ satisfies the differential equation

$$P_0'(t) = -aP_0(t),$$

whose well-known solution is $P_0(t) = ce^{-at}$. The constant c is determined by the initial condition $P_0(0) = 1$, which implies $c = 1$. Thus, $P_0(t) = e^{-at}$.

We will now calculate $P_m(t)$ for every m. It is easy to see that

$$P_m(t+h) = P_m(t)P_0(h) + P_{m-1}(t)P_1(h) + \sum_{i=2}^{m} P_{m-i}(t)P_i(h). \qquad (2.1)$$

By definition $P_0(h) = 1 - p(h)$. The requirement II implies that

$$P_1(h) = p(h) + o(h) \qquad \text{and}$$
$$\sum_{i=2}^{m} P_{m-i}(t)P_i(h) \le \sum_{i=2}^{m} P_i(h) = o(h), \qquad (2.2)$$

since obviously $P_k(t) \leq 1$. Therefore, with the aid of (2.2) we rearrange (2.1) into the form

$$\begin{aligned}P_m(t+h) - P_m(t) &= P_m(t)[P_0(h) - 1] + P_{m-1}(t)P_1(h) + \sum_{i=2}^{m} P_{m-i}(t)P_i(h) \\ &= -P_m(t)p(h) + P_{m-1}(t)P_1(h) + \sum_{i=2}^{m} P_{m-i}(t)P_i(h) \\ &= -aP_m(t)h + aP_{m-1}(t)h + o(h).\end{aligned}$$

Therefore

$$\frac{P_m(t+h) - P_m(t)}{h} \to -aP_m(t) + aP_{m-1}(t) \qquad \text{as} \quad h \to 0$$

and, formally, we get

$$P'_m(t) = -aP_m(t) + aP_{m-1}(t), \qquad m = 1, 2, \ldots, \tag{2.3}$$

subject to the initial conditions

$$P_m(0) = 0, \qquad m = 1, 2, \ldots .$$

In order to solve (2.3), we introduce the functions

$$Q_m(t) = P_m(t)e^{at}, \qquad m = 0, 1, 2, \ldots .$$

Substituting the above in (2.3) gives

$$Q'_m(t) = aQ_{m-1}(t), \qquad m = 1, 2, \ldots, \tag{2.4}$$

where $Q_0(t) \equiv 1$ and the initial conditions are $Q_m(0) = 0$, $m = 1, 2, \ldots$. Solving (2.4) recursively we obtain

$$\begin{aligned}
&Q'_1(t) = a \quad \text{or} \quad Q_1(t) = at + c && \text{so} \quad Q_1(t) = at \\
&Q_2(t) = \frac{a^2t^2}{2} + c && \text{so} \quad Q_2(t) = \frac{a^2t^2}{2!} \\
&\quad\vdots && \quad\vdots \\
& && Q_m(t) = \frac{a^mt^m}{m!}
\end{aligned}$$

Therefore

$$P_m(t) = \frac{a^mt^m}{m!} e^{-at}.$$

In other words, for each t, X_t follows a Poisson distribution with parameter at. In particular, the mean number of occurrences in time t is at.

Often the Poisson process arises in a form where the time parameter is replaced by a suitable spatial parameter. The following formal example illustrates this vein of ideas. Consider an array of points distributed in a space E (E is a Euclidean space of dimension $d \geq 1$). Let N_R denote the number of points (finite or infinite) contained in the region R of E. We postulate that N_R is a random variable. The collection $\{N_R\}$ of random variables, where R varies over all possible subsets of E, is said to be a homogeneous Poisson process if the following assumptions are fulfilled:

(i) The numbers of points in nonoverlapping regions are independent random variables.

(ii) For any region R of finite volume, N_R is Poisson distributed with mean $\lambda V(R)$, where $V(R)$ is the volume of R. The parameter λ is fixed and measures in a sense the intensity component of the distribution, which is independent of the size or shape. Spatial Poisson processes arise in considering the distribution of stars or galaxies in space, the spatial distribution of plants and animals, of bacteria on a slide, etc. These ideas and concepts will be further studied in Chapter 16.

3: *Classification of General Stochastic Processes*

The main elements distinguishing stochastic processes are in the nature of the *state space*, the *index parameter* T, and the dependence relations among the random variables X_t.

STATE SPACE S

This is the space in which the possible values of each X_t lie. In the case that $S = (0, 1, 2, \ldots)$, we refer to the process at hand as integer valued, or alternately as a discrete state process. If $S =$ the real line $(-\infty, \infty)$, then we call X_t a real-valued stochastic process. If S is Euclidean k space then X_t is said to be a k-vector process.

As in the case of a single random variable, the choice of state space is not uniquely specified by the physical situation being described, although usually one particular choice stands out as most appropriate.

INDEX PARAMETER T

If $T = (0, 1, \ldots)$ then we shall always say that X_t is a discrete time stochastic process. Often when T is discrete we shall write X_n instead of X_t. If $T = [0, \infty)$, then X_t is called a continuous time process.

We have already cited examples where the index set T is not one dimensional (spatial Poisson processes). Another example is that of waves in oceans. We may regard the latitude and longitude coordinates as the value of t, and X_t is then the height of the wave at the location t.

CLASSICAL TYPES OF STOCHASTIC PROCESSES

We now describe some of the classical types of stochastic processes characterized by different dependence relationships among X_t. In the examples, we take $T=[0, \infty)$ unless we state the contrary explicitly. For simplicity of exposition, we assume that the random variables X_t are real valued.

(a) *Process with Stationary Independent Increments*

If the random variables

$$X_{t_2}-X_{t_1}, X_{t_3}-X_{t_2}, \ldots, X_{t_n}-X_{t_{n-1}}$$

are independent for all choices of $t_1, \cdots, t_n$ satisfying

$$t_1 < t_2 < \cdots < t_n,$$

then we say that X_t is a process with *independent increments*. If the index set contains a smallest index t_0, it is also assumed that

$$X_{t_0}, X_{t_1}-X_{t_0}, X_{t_2}-X_{t_1}, \ldots, X_{t_n}-X_{t_{n-1}}$$

are independent. If the index set is discrete, that is, $T=(0, 1, \ldots)$, then a process with independent increments reduces to a sequence of independent random variables $Z_0=X_0$, $Z_i=X_i-X_{i-1}$ $(i=1, 2, 3, \ldots)$, in the sense that knowing the individual distributions of $Z_0, Z_1, \ldots$ enables one to determine (as should be fairly clear to the reader) the joint distribution of any finite set of the X_i. In fact,

$$X_i=Z_0+Z_1+\cdots+Z_i, \qquad i=0, 1, 2, \ldots.$$

If the distribution of the increments $X(t_1+h)-X(t_1)$ depends only on the length h of the interval and not on the time t_1 the process is said to have *stationary increments*. For a process with stationary increments the distribution of $X(t_1+h)-X(t_1)$ is the same as the distribution of $X(t_2+h)-X(t_2)$, no matter what the values of t_1, t_2 and h.

If a process $\{X_t, t\in T\}$, where $T=[0, \infty)$ or $T=(0, 1, 2, \ldots)$ has stationary independent increments and has a finite mean, then it is elementary to show that $E[X_t]=m_0+m_1 t$ where $m_0=E[X_0]$ and

$m_1 = E[X_1] - m_0$. A similar assertion holds for the variance:

$$\sigma_{X_t}^2 = \sigma_0^2 + \sigma_1^2 t$$

where

$$\sigma_0^2 = E[(X_0 - m_0)^2]$$

and

$$\sigma_1^2 = E[(X_1 - m_1)^2] - \sigma_0^2.$$

We will indicate the proof in the case of the mean. Let $f(t) = E[X_t] - E[X_0]$. Then for any t and s

$$\begin{aligned} f(t+s) &= E[X_{t+s} - X_0] \\ &= E[X_{t+s} - X_s + X_s - X_0] \\ &= E[X_{t+s} - X_s] + E[X_s - X_0] \\ &= E[X_t - X_0] + E[X_s - X_0] \end{aligned}$$

(using the property of stationary increments)

$$= f(t) + f(s).$$

The only solution, subject to mild regularity conditions, to the functional equation $f(t+s) = f(t) + f(s)$ is $f(t) = f(1) \cdot t$. We indicate the proof of the above statement assuming $f(t)$ differentiable, although much less would suffice. Differentiation with respect to t and independently in s verifies that

$$f'(t+s) = f'(t) = f'(s).$$

Therefore for $s = 1$, we find $f'(t) = \text{constant} = f'(1) = c$. Integration of this elementary differential equation yields $f(t) = ct + d$. But, $f(0) = 2f(0)$ implies $f(0) = 0$ and therefore $d = 0$ is necessary. The expression $f(t) = f(1)t$ for the case at hand is

$$E[X_t] - m_0 = (E[X_1] - m_0) \cdot t$$

or

$$E[X_t] = m_0 + m_1 t$$

as desired.

Both the Brownian motion process and the Poisson process have stationary independent increments.

(b) *Martingales*

Let $\{X_t\}$ be a real-valued stochastic process with discrete or continuous parameter set. We say that $\{X_t\}$ is a *martingale* if, $E[|X_t|] < \infty$ for all t, and if for any $t_1 < t_2 < \cdots < t_{n+1}$, $E(X_{t_{n+1}} | X_{t_1} = a_1, \ldots, X_{t_n} = a_n) = a_n$ for all values of $a_1, \cdots, a_n$. Martingales may be considered as appropriate models for fair games, in the sense that X_t signifies the amount of money that a player has at time t. The martingale property states, then, that the average amount a player will have at time t_{n+1}, given that he has amount a_n at time t_n, is equal to a_n regardless of what his past fortune has been. The reader can readily verify that the process $X_n = Z_1 + \cdots + Z_n$, $n = 1, 2, \ldots$, is a discrete time martingale if the Z_i are independent and have means zero. Similarly, if X_t, $0 \le t < \infty$ has independent increments whose means are zero, then $\{X_t\}$ is a continuous time martingale (see Elementary Problem 6).

Martingales are the subject matter of Chapter 6.

(c) *Markov Processes*

Roughly speaking, a *Markov process* is a process with the property that, given the value of X_t, the values of X_s, $s > t$, do not depend on the values of X_u, $u < t$; that is, the probability of any particular future behavior of the process, when its present state is known exactly, is not altered by additional knowledge concerning its past behavior. We should make it clear, however, that if our knowledge of the present state of the process is imprecise, then the probability of some future behavior will in general be altered by additional information relating to the past behavior of the system. In formal terms a process is said to be Markov if

$$\begin{aligned}\Pr\{a < X_t \le b | X_{t_1} = x_1, X_{t_2} = x_2, \ldots, X_{t_n} = x_n\} \\ = \Pr\{a < X_t \le b | X_{t_n} = x_n\}\end{aligned} \tag{3.1}$$

whenever $t_1 < t_2 < \cdots < t_n < t$.

Let A be an interval of the real line. The function

$$P(x, s; t, A) = \Pr\{X_t \in A | X_s = x\}, \qquad t > s, \tag{3.2}$$

is called the ***transition probability function*** and is basic to the study of the structure of Markov processes. We may express the condition (3.1) as follows:

$$\Pr\{a < X_t \le b | X_{t_1} = x_1, X_{t_2} = x_2, \ldots, X_{t_n} = x_n\} = P(x_n, t_n; t, A), \tag{3.3}$$

where $A = \{\xi | a < \xi \le b\}$. It may be proved that the probability distribution of

$$(X_{t_1}, X_{t_2}, \ldots, X_{t_n})$$

can be computed in terms of (3.2) and the initial distribution function of X_{t_1}. We will elaborate further on these concepts in our more detailed examination of discrete time, discrete state Markov processes (Chapter 2).

A Markov process having a finite or denumerable state space is called a *Markov chain*. A Markov process for which all realizations or sample functions $\{X_t, t \in [0, \infty)\}$ are continuous functions is called a *diffusion process*. The Poisson process is a continuous time Markov chain and Brownian motion is a diffusion process.

(d) *Stationary Processes*

A stochastic process X_t for t in T [here T could be one of the sets $(-\infty, \infty)$, $[0, \infty)$, the set of all integers, or the set of all positive integers] is said to be *strictly stationary* if the joint distribution functions of the families of random variables

$$(X_{t_1+h}, X_{t_2+h}, \ldots X_{t_n+h}) \quad \text{and} \quad (X_{t_1}, X_{t_2}, \ldots, X_{t_n})$$

are the same for all $h > 0$ and arbitrary selections $t_1, t_2, \ldots, t_n$ from T. This condition asserts that in essence the process is in probabilistic equilibrium and that the particular times at which we examine the process are of no relevance. In particular, the distribution of X_t is the same for each t.

A stochastic process X_t for $t \in T$ is said to be *wide sense stationary* or *covariance stationary* if it possesses finite second moments and if $\operatorname{Cov}(X_t, X_{t+h}) = E(X_t X_{t+h}) - E(X_t)E(X_{t+h})$ depends only on h for all $t \in T$. A stationary process that has finite second moments is covariance stationary. There are covariance stationary processes that are not stationary.

Stationary processes are appropriate for describing many phenomena that occur in communication theory, astronomy, biology, and sometimes economics and are discussed in more detail in Chapter 9.

A Markov process is said to have stationary transition probabilities if $P(x, s; t, A)$ defined in (3.2) is a function only of $t - s$. Remember that $P(x, s; t, A)$ is a conditional probability, given the present state. Therefore, there is no reason to expect that a Markov process with stationary transition probabilities is a stationary process, and this is indeed the case.

Neither the Poisson process nor the Brownian motion process is stationary. In fact, no nonconstant process with stationary independent increments is stationary. However, if $\{X_t, t \in [0, \infty)\}$ is Brownian motion or a Poisson process, then $Z_t = X_{t+h} - X_t$ is a stationary process for any fixed $h \geq 0$.

(e) *Renewal Processes.*

A renewal process is a sequence T_k of independent and identically distributed positive random variables, representing the lifetimes of some "units." The first unit is placed in operation at time zero; it fails at time T_1 and is immediately replaced by a new unit which then fails at time $T_1 + T_2$, and so on, thus motivating the name "renewal process." The time of the nth renewal is $S_n = T_1 + \cdots + T_n$.

A renewal counting process N_t counts the number of renewals in the interval $[0, t]$. Formally,

$$N_t = n \text{ for } S_n \leq t < S_{n+1}, \; n = 0, 1, 2, \ldots$$

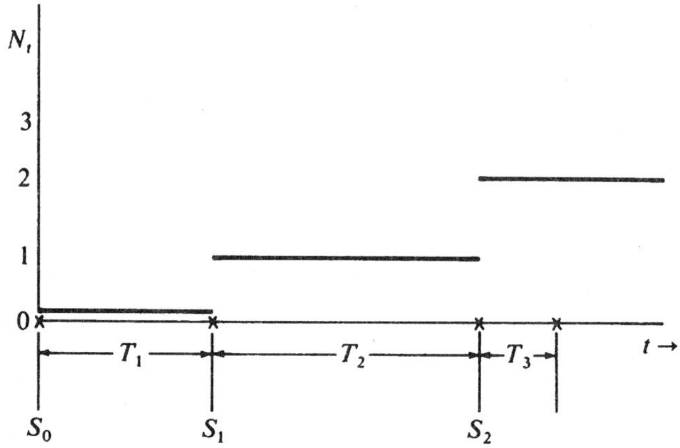

FIG. 3

Often the distinction is not made between the renewal process and the associated renewal counting process, and no real confusion results.

Renewal processes occur directly in many applied areas such as management science, economics, and biology. Of equal importance, often renewal processes may be discovered embedded in other stochastic processes that, at first glance, seem quite unrelated. Chapter 5 is devoted to renewal processes.

The Poisson process with parameter λ is a renewal counting process for which the unit lifetimes have exponential distributions with common parameter λ.

(f) *Point Processes*

Let S be a set in n-dimensional space and let $\mathscr{A}$ be a family of subsets of S. A *point process* is a stochastic process indexed by the sets $A \in \mathscr{A}$ and having the set $\{0, 1, \ldots, \infty\}$ of nonnegative integers as its state space. We think of "points" being scattered over S in some random manner, and of $N(A)$ as counting the number of points in the set A. Since $N(A)$ is a counting function there are additional requirements on each realization. For example, if A_1 and A_2 are mutually disjoint sets in $\mathscr{A}$ whose union $A_1 \cup A_2$ is also in $\mathscr{A}$, then we require

$$N(A_1 \cup A_2) = N(A_1) + N(A_2),$$

and if the empty set $\varnothing$ is in $\mathscr{A}$, then $N(\varnothing) = 0$.

Suppose S is a set in the real line (plane, 3 dimensional space) and for every subset $A \subset S$, let $V(A)$ be the length (respectively area, volume) of A. Then $\{N(A),\ A \subset S\}$ is a homogeneous *Poisson point process* of intensity $\lambda > 0$ if:

(i) For each $A \subset S$, $N(A)$ has a Poisson distribution with parameter $\lambda V(A)$, and

(ii) For every finite collection $\{A_1, \ldots, A_n\}$ of disjoint subsets of S, the random variables $N(A_1), \ldots, N(A_n)$ are independent.

Poisson point processes arise in considering the distribution of stars or galaxies in space, the planer distribution of plants and animals, of bacteria on a slide, etc. These ideas and concepts will be further studied in Chapter 16, Volume II.

Every Poisson process $\{X_t: t \in [0, \infty)\}$ defines a Poisson point process on $S = [0, \infty)$. In fact for an interval subset $A = (s, t]$, $s < t$, we use $N(A) = X_t - X_s$.

4: *Defining a Stochastic Process*

The distinguishing features of a stochastic process X_t are the relationships among the random variables, X_t, $t \in T$.

These relationships are specified by giving the joint distribution function of every finite family $X_{t_1}, \ldots, X_{t_n}$ of variables of the process. For the purposes of this book, a stochastic process may be considered as well defined once its state space, index parameter, and family of joint distributions are prescribed. However, in dealing with continuous parameter processes certain difficulties arise, which we illustrate by the following example.

Let U be a r.v. uniformly distributed on $[0, 1]$ and define X_t and Y_t as follows:

$$X_t = \begin{cases} 1 & \text{for } U = t, \\ 0 & \text{otherwise,} \end{cases}$$

and

$$Y_t \equiv 0, \qquad (t > 0).$$

A simple computation verifies that $\{X_t\}$ and $\{Y_t\}$ have the same finite dimensional distributions. However, obviously

$$\Pr\{X_t \le \tfrac{1}{2} \quad \text{for all } 0 \le t \le 1\} = 0$$

and

$$\Pr\{Y_t \le \tfrac{1}{2} \quad \text{for all } 0 \le t \le 1\} = 1,$$

which is a rather disconcerting state of affairs. To pinpoint the source of the difficulty we consider the following problem.

Suppose that $\{X_t, 0 \le t < \infty\}$, is a continuous parameter process, and we wish to evaluate $\Pr\{X_t \ge 0, 0 \le t \le 1\}$.

Let us consider the decreasing sequence of events

$$A_n = \{X_{t_i} \geq 0,\ t_i = i/2^n,\ i = 0, 1, \ldots, 2^n\},\ n = 1, 2, \ldots.$$

The probability of each A_n can be calculated in terms of the joint distribution function of the corresponding X_{t_i}, $i = 0, \ldots, 2^n$, and it would seem reasonable that we should take for $\Pr\{X_t \geq 0,\ 0 \leq t \leq 1\}$ the value $\lim_{n\to\infty} \Pr\{A_n\}$. However, that which seems reasonable is not necessarily free from inconsistencies. It is equally reasonable that we take $A_n' = \{X_{t_i} \geq 0,\ t_i = i/3^n,\ i = 0, 1, \ldots, 3^n\}$, and for $\Pr\{X_t \geq 0,\ 0 \leq t \leq 1\}$ the value $\lim_{n\to\infty} \Pr\{A_n'\}$, but it is by no means clear that $\lim_{n\to\infty} \Pr\{A_n\} = \lim_{n\to\infty} \Pr\{A_n'\}$, and in fact, the two limits need not be equal if no "smoothness" assumptions are made concerning the sample functions of the process. There are various sufficient conditions for the equality of the two limits: one of them is that $\lim_{\tau\to t} \Pr\{|X_t - X_\tau| \geq \varepsilon\} = 0$ for every $\varepsilon > 0$ and every t. With this condition, the problem can be formulated so that no inconsistency arises if we define $\Pr\{X_t \geq 0,\ 0 \leq t \leq 1\}$ as the common value of the two limits, and in fact, if $t_1, t_2, \ldots$ is any dense set of points in the interval $[0, 1]$, then $\Pr\{X_t \geq 0,\ 0 \leq t \leq 1\} = \lim_{n\to\infty} \Pr\{X_{t_i} \geq 0,\ i = 1, 2, \ldots, n\}$.

The nub of the matter is that while the axiom of total probability enables us to evaluate probabilities of events concerning a sequence of r.v.'s in terms of the probabilities of events involving finite and hence denumerable subsets of the sequence, the event $\{X_t \geq 0,\ 0 \leq t \leq 1\}$ involves a nondenumerable number of random variables. The details of this point are quite involved, and are well beyond the scope of the present book; the interested reader is referred to Doob,† Chapter 2. Some foundational questions which throw more light on these problems are discussed in Chapter 14.

Elementary Problems

1. Let X be a *nonnegative* discrete random variable with possible values $0, 1, 2, \ldots$. Show

$$E[X] = \sum_{n=0}^{\infty} \Pr\{X > n\} = \sum_{k=1}^{\infty} \Pr\{X \geq k\}.$$

Hint: Begin with $E[X] = \sum_{n=1}^{\infty} n \Pr\{X = n\} = \sum_{n=1}^{\infty} \sum_{k=1}^{n} \Pr\{X = n\}$.

† J. L. Doob, "Stochastic Processes," Wiley, New York, 1953.

2. Suppose a jar has n chips numbered $1, 2, \ldots, n$. A person draws a chip, returns it, draws another, returns it, and so on until he gets a chip which has been drawn before and then stops. Let X be the number of drawings required to accomplish this objective. Find the probability distribution of X.

Hint: It's easiest to first compute $\Pr\{X > k\}$.

Solution:

$$p(k) = (k-1)!\binom{n}{k-1}\frac{k-1}{n^k} \qquad \text{for} \quad k = 2, 3, \ldots, n+1.$$

3. Show that the expectation of the random variable X of Problem 2 is

$$E(X) = 2 + \left(1 - \frac{1}{n}\right) + \left(1 - \frac{1}{n}\right)\left(1 - \frac{2}{n}\right) + \cdots + \left(1 - \frac{1}{n}\right)\left(1 - \frac{2}{n}\right) \cdots\cdots \left(1 - \frac{n-1}{n}\right).$$

Hint: Use Elementary Problem 1.

4. The number of accidents occurring in a factory in a week is a random variable with mean μ and variance σ^2. The numbers of individuals injured in different accidents are independently distributed each with mean ν and variance τ^2. Determine the mean and variance of the number of individuals injured in a week.

Solution: $E(\text{injuries}) = \mu\nu$; $\quad \text{Var(injuries)} = \nu^2\sigma^2 + \mu\tau^2$.

5. The following experiment is performed. An observation is made of a Poisson random variable X with parameter λ. Then a binomial event with probability p of success is repeated X times and σ successes are observed. What is the distribution of σ?

Hint: Use the generating function for the random sum of random variables,

Solution: Poisson, with parameter λp.

6. Show that the sums $S_n = X_1 + \cdots + X_n$ of independent random variables X_n with zero mean form a martingale. Assume $E[|X_k|] < \infty$ for $k = 1, 2, \ldots$.

7. Prove that every stochastic process $\{X(t);\ t = 0, 1, \ldots\}$ with independent increments is a Markov process. (Remark: This is not true of stochastic processes $\{X(t);\ -\infty < t < \infty\}$.)

8. Consider a population of n couples where a boy is born to the ith couple with probability p_i and c_i is the expected number of children born to this couple. Assume p_i is constant with time for all couples and that sexes of successive children born to a particular couple are independent r.v's. Further, assume that no multiple births are allowed. The sex ratio is defined to be

$$S = \frac{\text{expected number of boys born in the population of } n \text{ couples}}{\text{expected number of children born in the population of } n \text{ couples}}.$$

Suppose $c_i = c$, $i = 1, 2, \ldots, n$. Find S.

Solution: $S \equiv S_0 = (\sum_{i=1}^{n} p_i)/n$.

9. If the parents of all couples decide to have children until a boy is born and then have no further children, show that

$$S = S_1 = \frac{n}{\sum_{i=1}^{n} \frac{1}{p_i}} \le S_0.$$

10. Suppose the parents of all couples decide that if their first child is a boy they will continue to have children until a girl is born and then have no further children. If their first child is a girl they will continue to have children until a boy is born and then have no further children. Compute S corresponding to this birth control behavior.

Solution:

$$S = S_2 = \frac{\left\{\sum_{i=1}^{n} 1/q_i - \sum_{i=1}^{n} p_i\right\}}{\sum_{i=1}^{n} [p_i q_i]^{-1} - n} \qquad \text{where} \quad q_i = 1 - p_i.$$

11. Suppose the parents of all children decide that if their first child is a boy they will continue to have children until a girl is born and then have no further children. If their first child is a girl they will have no further children. Compute S corresponding to this behavior.

Solution:

$$S = S_3 = 1 - \left[\frac{n}{\sum_{i=1}^{n} 1/q_i}\right].$$

12. Show that, depending on the value of $\{p_1, \ldots, p_n\}$, S_2 can satisfy either $S_2 \le S_0$ or $S_2 > S_0$, where S_0 is the sex ratio of Elementary Problem 8 and S_2 is the sex ratio of Elementary Problem 10.

13. Suppose that a child born to the ith set of parents in a population of n sets of parents has probability p_i of a birth disorder, $i = 1, 2, \ldots, n$. Assume that the birth of one affected child deters parents from further reproduction. Let $s =$ the number of offspring in a single family when no affected children are born. Assume that with respect to any given birth, p_i does not depend on preceding births. Show that

$$R_1 = \frac{\text{expected number of affected children}}{\text{expected total number of children born}} = \frac{\sum_{i=1}^{n} 1 - q_i^s}{\sum_{i=1}^{n} (1 - q_i^s)/p_i}.$$

(b) Assume that the birth of two affected children (but not one) will deter parents from further reproduction. Show that under this kind of selective limitation

$$R_2 = \frac{\sum_{i=1}^{n} \{2(1 - q_i^s) - sp_i q_i^{s-1}\}}{\sum_{i-1}^{n} \{[2(1 - q_i^s)/p_i] - sq_i^{s-1}\}}.$$

Problems

The following integrals may be useful in some of the problems, and are recorded here for future reference.

The gamma function is defined by

$$\Gamma(x) = \int_0^\infty \xi^{x-1} e^{-\xi}\, d\xi, \qquad x > 0.$$

For large x, $\Gamma(x) \sim \sqrt{2\pi}\, e^{-x} x^{x+1/2}$ (Stirling's formula). When $x = n$, an integer, $\Gamma(n) = (n-1)! = (n-1)(n-2) \ldots 2 \cdot 1$.

The Beta integral is given by

$$\frac{\Gamma(p)\Gamma(q)}{\Gamma(p+q)} = \int_0^1 x^{p-1}(1-x)^{q-1}\, dx$$

where $p > 0$, $q > 0$.

1. Let a, b, c be independent random variables uniformly distributed on (0, 1). What is the probability that $ax^2 + bx + c$ has real roots?

Answer: $(5 + 3 \log 4)/36$.

2. For each fixed $\lambda > 0$ let X have a Poisson distribution with parameter λ. Suppose λ itself is a random variable following a gamma distribution (i.e., with density

$$f(\lambda) = \begin{cases} \dfrac{1}{\Gamma(n)} \lambda^{n-1} e^{-\lambda}, & \lambda \geq 0, \\ 0, & \lambda < 0, \end{cases}$$

where n is a fixed positive constant). Show that now

$$\Pr\{X=k\}=\frac{\Gamma(k+n)}{\Gamma(n)\Gamma(k+1)}\left(\frac{1}{2}\right)^{k+n}, \qquad k=0,1,\ldots.$$

When n is an integer this is the negative binomial distribution with $p=\frac{1}{2}$.

3. For each given p let X have a binomial distribution with parameters p and N. Suppose N is itself binomially distributed with parameters q and M, $M \geq N$.

(a) Show analytically that X has a binomial distribution with parameters pq and M.

(b) Give a probabilistic argument for this result.

4. For each given p, let X have a binomial distribution with parameters p and N. Suppose p is distributed according to a beta distribution with parameters r and s. Find the resulting distribution of X. When is this distribution uniform on $x=0, 1, \ldots, N$?

Answer:

$$\Pr\{X=k\}=\binom{N}{k}\frac{\Gamma(r+s)\Gamma(k+r)\Gamma(N-k+s)}{\Gamma(r)\Gamma(s)\Gamma(N+r+s)};$$

$$\Pr\{X=k\}=1/(N+1) \qquad \text{when} \quad r=s=1.$$

5. (a) Suppose X is distributed according to a Poisson distribution with parameter λ. The parameter λ is itself a random variable whose distribution law is exponential with mean $=1/c$. Find the distribution of X.

(b) What if λ follows a gamma distribution of order α with scale parameter c, i.e., the density of λ is

$$c^{\alpha+1}\frac{\lambda^{\alpha}}{\Gamma(\alpha+1)}e^{-\lambda c}$$

for $\lambda>0$; 0 for $\lambda \leq 0$.

Answer:

$$\text{(a)} \quad \Pr\{X=k\}=\frac{c}{(c+1)^{k+1}};$$

$$\text{(b)} \quad \Pr\{X=k\}=\frac{\Gamma(k+\alpha+1)}{k!\Gamma(\alpha+1)}\left(\frac{1}{1+c}\right)^{k+\alpha+1}c^{\alpha+1}.$$

6. Suppose we have N chips marked 1, 2, ..., N, respectively. We take a random sample of size $2n+1$ without replacement. Let Y be the median of the random sample. Show that the probability function of Y is

$$\Pr\{Y=k\}=\frac{\binom{k-1}{n}\binom{N-k}{n}}{\binom{N}{2n+1}} \qquad \text{for} \quad k=n+1, n+2, \ldots, N-n.$$

Verify

$$E(Y)=\frac{N+1}{2} \qquad \text{and} \qquad \operatorname{Var}(Y)=\frac{(N-2n-1)(N+1)}{8n+12}.$$

7. Suppose we have N chips, numbered 1, 2, ..., N. We take a random sample of size n without replacement. Let X be the largest number in the random sample. Show that the probability function of X is

$$\Pr\{X=k\}=\frac{\binom{k-1}{n-1}}{\binom{N}{n}}\qquad \text{for}\quad k=n, n+1, \ldots, N$$

and that

$$EX=\frac{n}{n+1}(N+1),\qquad \operatorname{Var}(X)=\frac{n(N-n)(N+1)}{(n+1)^2(n+2)}.$$

8. Let X_1 and X_2 be independent random variables with uniform distribution over the interval $[\theta-\frac{1}{2}, \theta+\frac{1}{2}]$. Show that X_1-X_2 has a distribution independent of θ and find its density function.

Answer:

$$f_{X_1-X_2}(y)=\begin{cases}1+y, & -1\le y\le 0,\\ 1-y, & 0\le y<1,\\ 0\;, & |y|>1.\end{cases}$$

9. Let X be a *nonnegative* random variable with cumulative distribution function $F(x)=\Pr\{X\le x\}$. Show

$$E[X]=\int_0^\infty [1-F(x)]\,dx.$$

Hint: Write $E[X]=\int_0^\infty x\,dF(x)=\int_0^\infty \left(\int_0^x dy\right) dF(x)$.

10. Let X be a *nonnegative* random variable and let

$$X_c=\min\{X, c\}$$
$$=\begin{cases}X & \text{if}\quad X\le c\\ c & \text{if}\quad X>c\end{cases}$$

where c is a given constant. Express the expectation $E[X_c]$ in terms of the cumulative distribution function $F(x)=\Pr\{X\le x\}$.

Answer: $E[X_c]=\int_0^c [1-F(x)]\,dx$.

11. Let X and Y be jointly distributed discrete random variables having possible values 0, 1, 2, ... For $|s|<1$, $|t|<1$ define the joint generating function

$$\phi_{X,Y}(s,t)=\sum_{i,j=0}^{\infty} s^i t^j \Pr\{X=i, Y=j\}$$

and the marginal generating functions

$$\phi_X(s) = \sum_{i=0}^{\infty} s^i \Pr\{X = i\}$$

$$\phi_Y(t) = \sum_{j=0}^{\infty} t^j \Pr\{Y = j\}.$$

(a) Prove that X and Y are independent if and only if

$$\phi_{X,Y}(s, t) = \phi_X(s)\phi_Y(t) \quad \text{for all} \quad s, t.$$

(b) Give an example of jointly distributed random variables X, Y which are *not* independent, but for which

$$\phi_{X,Y}(t, t) = \phi_X(t)\phi_Y(t) \quad \text{for all} \quad t.$$

(This example is pertinent because $\phi_{X,Y}(t, t)$ is the generating function of the sum $X + Y$. Thus independence is sufficient but not necessary for the generating function of a sum of random variables to be the product of the marginal generating functions.)

12. Let $A_0, A_1, \ldots, A_r$ be $r + 1$ events which can occur as outcomes of an experiment. Let p_i be the probability of the occurrence of A_i $(i = 0, 1, 2, \ldots, r)$. Suppose we perform independent trials until the event A_0 occurs k times. Let X_i be the number of occurrences of the event A_i. Show that

$$\Pr\left\{X_1 = x_1, \ldots, X_r = x_r;\ A_0 \text{ occurs for the } k\text{th time at the } \left(k + \sum_{i=1}^{r} x_i\right)\text{th trial}\right\}$$

$$= \frac{\Gamma\left(k + \sum_{i=1}^{r} x_i\right)}{\Gamma(k) \prod_{i=1}^{r} x_i!} p_0^k \prod_{i=1}^{r} p_i^{x_i}. \tag{I}$$

13. Show that the probability generating function of the *negative multinomial distribution* (I) with parameters $(k; p_0, p_1, \ldots, p_r)$ is

$$\varphi(t_1, \ldots, t_r) = p_0^k\left(1 - \sum_{i=1}^{r} t_i p_i\right)^{-k}.$$

14. Consider vector random variable $\{X_0, X_1, \ldots, X_r\}$ following a *multinomial* distribution with parameters $(n; p_0, p_1, \ldots, p_r)$, and assume that n is itself a random variable distributed as a negative binomial with parameters $(k; \rho)$. Compute the joint distribution of $X_0, \ldots, X_r$.

15. Suppose that a lot consists of $m, n_1, \ldots, n_r$ items belonging to the 0th, 1st, ..., rth classes respectively. The items are drawn one-by-one without replacement until k items of the 0th class are observed. Show that the joint aistribution of the observed frequencies $X_1, \ldots, X_r$ of the 1st, ..., rth classes is

$$\Pr\{X_1 = x_1, \ldots, X_r = x_r\} = \left\{\binom{m}{k-1}\prod_{i=1}^{r}\binom{n_i}{x_i}\Big/\binom{m+n}{k+y-1}\right\} \cdot \frac{m-(k-1)}{m+n-(k+y-1)}$$

where

$$y = \sum_{i=1}^{r} x_i \quad \text{and} \quad n = \sum_{i=1}^{r} n_i.$$

16. *Continuation of Problem* 15 If $m \to \infty$ and $n \to \infty$ in such a way that $m/(m+n) \to p_0$ and $n_i/(m+n) \to p_i$, $i = 1, 2, \ldots, r$, show that the distribution of Problem 15 approaches the negative multinomial.

17. The random variable X_n takes the values k/n, $k = 1, 2, \ldots, n$, each with probability $1/n$. Find its characteristic function and the limit as $n \to \infty$. Identify the random variable of the limit characteristic function.

Answer:

(a) $\varphi_n(t) = (1 - e^{it}) \dfrac{1}{n} \cdot \dfrac{1}{\exp(-in^{-1}t) - 1}$,

(b) uniform (0, 1).

18. Using the central limit theorem for suitable Poisson random variables, prove that

$$\lim_{n\to\infty} e^{-n} \sum_{k=0}^{n} \frac{n^k}{k!} = \frac{1}{2}$$

***19.** The random variables X and Y have the following properties: X is positive, i.e., $P\{X > 0\} = 1$, with continuous density function $f(x)$, and $Y|X$ has a uniform distribution on $\{0, X\}$. Prove: If Y and $X - Y$ are independently distributed, then

$$f(x) = a^2 x e^{-ax}, \qquad x > 0, \quad a > 0.$$

***20.** Let U be gamma distributed with order p and let V have the beta distribution with parameters q and $p - q$ $(0 < q < p)$. Assume that U and V are independent. Show that UV is then gamma distributed with order q.

Hint:

$$\Pr\{UV \le x\} = \int_0^1 \left(\int_0^{x/\xi} e^{-\lambda}\lambda^{p-1}\, d\lambda\right) \frac{\xi^{q-1}(1-\xi)^{p-q-1}\, d\xi}{\Gamma(q)\Gamma(p-q)}.$$

Take Laplace transforms of both sides, interchange orders of integration, and then evaluate by expanding in suitable series of the form

$$(1+y)^{-\alpha-1} = \sum_{k=0}^{\infty} \binom{\alpha+k}{k} y^k.$$

***21.** Let X and Y be independent, identically distributed, positive random variables with continuous density function $f(x)$. Assume, further, that $U = X - Y$ and $V = \min(X, Y)$ are independent random variables. Prove that

$$f(x) = \begin{cases} \lambda e^{-\lambda x} & \text{for } x \geq 0, \\ 0 & \text{elsewhere,} \end{cases}$$

for some $\lambda > 0$. Assume $f(0) > 0$.

Hint: Show first that the joint density function of U and V is

$$f_{U,V}(u, v) = f(v)f(v + |u|).$$

Next, equate this with the product of the marginal densities for U, V.

22. Let X and Y be two independent, nonnegative integer-valued, random variables whose distribution has the property

$$\Pr\{X = x | X + Y = x + y\} = \frac{\binom{m}{x}\binom{n}{y}}{\binom{m+n}{x+y}}$$

for all nonnegative integers x and y where m and n are given positive integers. Assume that $\Pr\{X = 0\}$ and $\Pr\{Y = 0\}$ are strictly positive. Show that both X and Y have binomial distributions with the same parameter p, the other parameters being m and n, respectively.

23. (a) Let X and Y be independent random variables such that

$$\Pr\{X = i\} = f(i), \qquad \Pr\{Y = i\} = g(i),$$

where

$$f(i) > 0, \quad g(i) > 0, \quad i = 0, 1, 2, \ldots$$

and

$$\sum_{i=0}^{\infty} f(i) = \sum_{i=0}^{\infty} g(i) = 1.$$

Suppose

$$\Pr\{X = k | X + Y = l\} = \begin{cases} \binom{l}{k} p^k (1-p)^{l-k}, & 0 \leq k \leq l, \\ 0, & k > l. \end{cases}$$

Prove that

$$f(i) = e^{-\theta\alpha} \frac{(\theta\alpha)^i}{i!}, \qquad g(i) = e^{-\theta} \frac{\theta^i}{i!}, \qquad \alpha = 0, 1, 2, \ldots,$$

where $\alpha = p/(1-p)$ and $\theta > 0$ is arbitrary.

(b) Show that p is determined by the condition

$$G\left(\frac{1}{1-p}\right) = \frac{1}{f(0)}.$$

Hint: Let $F(s) = \sum f(i)s^i$, $G(s) = \sum g(i)s^i$. Establish first the relation

$$F(u)F(v) = F(vp + (1-p)u)G(vp + (1-p)u).$$

24. Let X be a nonnegative integer–valued random variable with probability generating function $f(s)=\sum_{n=0}^{\infty} a_n s^n$. After observing X, then conduct X binomial trials with probability p of success. Let Y denote the resulting number of successes.

(a) Determine the probability generating function of Y.
(b) Determine the probability generating function of X given that $Y=X$.

Solution: (a) $f(1-p+ps)$; (b) $f(ps)/f(p)$.

25. (Continuation of Problem 24) Suppose that for every p $(0<p<1)$ the probability generating functions of (a) and (b) coincide. Prove that the distribution of X is Poisson, i.e., $f(s)=e^{\lambda(s-1)}$ for some $\lambda>0$.

26. There are at least four schools of thought on the statistical distribution of stock price differences, or more generally, stochastic models for sequences of stock prices. In terms of number of followers, by far the most popular approach is that of the so-called "technical analysist", phrased in terms of short term trends, support and resistance levels, technical rebounds, and so on. Rejecting this technical viewpoint, two other schools agree that sequences of prices describe a random walk, when price changes are statistically independent of previous price history, but these schools disagree in their choice of the appropriate probability distributions. Some authors find price changes to have a normal distribution while the other group finds a distribution with "fatter tail probabilities", and perhaps even an infinite variance. Finally, a fourth group (overlapping with the preceding two) admits the random walk as a first-order approximation but notes recognizable second-order effects.

This exercise is to show a compatibility between the middle two groups. It has been noted that those that find price changes to be normal typically measure the changes over a fixed number of transactions, while those that find the larger tail probabilities typically measure price changes over a fixed time period that may contain a random number of transactions. Let Z be a price change. Use as the measure of "fatness" (and there could be dispute about this) the *coefficient of excess*

$$\gamma_2=[m_4/(m_2)^2]-3,$$

where m_k is the kth moment of Z about its mean.
Suppose on each transaction that the price advances by one unit, or lowers by one unit, each with equal probability. Let N be the number of transactions and write $Z=X_1+\cdots+X_N$ where the X_n's are independent and identically distributed random variables, each equally likely to be $+1$ or -1. Compute γ_2 for Z: (a) When N is a fixed number a, and (b). When N has a Poisson distribution with mean a.

27. Consider an infinite number of urns into which we toss balls independently, in such a way that a ball falls into the kth urn with probability $1/2^k$, $k=1, 2, 3, \ldots$. For each positive integer N, let Z_N be the number of urns which contain at least one ball after a total of N balls have been tossed. Show that

$$E(Z_N) = \sum_{k=1}^{\infty} [1 - (1 - 1/2^k)^N],$$

and that there exist constants $C_1 > 0$ and $C_2 > 0$ such that

$$C_1 \log N \leq E(Z_N) \leq C_2 \log N \qquad \text{for all } N.$$

Hint: Verify and use the facts:

$$E(Z_N) \geq \sum_{k=1}^{\log_2 N} \left[1 - \left(1 - \frac{1}{2^k}\right)^N\right] \geq C \log_2 N$$

and

$$1 - \left(1 - \frac{1}{2^k}\right)^N \leq N \frac{1}{2^k} \quad \text{and} \quad N \sum_{\log_2 N}^{\infty} \frac{1}{2^k} \leq C_2,$$

28. Let L and R be randomly chosen interval endpoints having an arbitrary joint distribution, but, of course, $L \leq R$. Let $p(x) = \Pr\{L \leq x \leq R\}$ be the probability the interval covers the point x, and let $X = R - L$ be the length of the interval. Establish the formula $E[X] = \int_{-\infty}^{\infty} p(x)\, dx$.

29. Let N balls be thrown independently into n urns, each ball having probability $1/n$ of falling into any particular urn. Let $Z_{N,n}$ be the number of empty urns after culminating these tosses, and let $P_{N,n}(k) = \Pr(Z_{N,n} = k)$.

Define $\varphi_{N,n}(t) = \sum_{k=0}^{n} P_{N,n}(k) e^{ikt}$.

(a) Show that

$$P_{N+1,n}(k) = \left(1 - \frac{k}{n}\right) P_{N,n}(k) + \frac{k+1}{n} P_{N,n}(k+1), \quad \text{for} \quad k = 0, 1, \ldots, n.$$

(b) Show that

$$P_{N,n}(k) = \left(1 - \frac{1}{n}\right)^N P_{N,n-1}(k-1) + \sum_{i=1}^{N} \binom{N}{i} \frac{1}{n^i} \left(1 - \frac{1}{n}\right)^{N-i} P_{N-i,n-1}(k).$$

(c) Define $G_n(t, z) = \sum_{N=0}^{\infty} \varphi_{N,n}(t) \frac{n^N}{N!} z^N$. Using part (b), show that $G_n(t, z) = G_{n-1}(t, z)(e^{it} + e^z - 1)$, and conclude that

$$G_n(t, z) = (e^{it} + e^z - 1)^n, \qquad n = 0, 1, 2, \ldots$$

NOTES

A colorful and rich introduction to probability theory and its applications is found in Feller [1]. Feller's book is limited in that it deals only with discrete probabilities.

The text by Gnedenko [2] also serves as an excellent introduction.

Another useful elementary text is that by Parzen [3].

The classic treatise on the subject of stochastic processes is that by Doob [4]. Doob's book serves indispensably for all researches concerned with stochastic processes.

Another outstanding book concerned with the structure of stochastic processes is the recent translation of Dynkin [5].

REFERENCES

1. W. Feller, "An Introduction to Probability Theory and Its Applications," Vol. 1, 2nd ed. Wiley, New York, 1957.
2. B. V. Gnedenko, "Theory of Probability." Chelsea, New York, 1962.
3. E. Parzen, "Modern Probability Theory and Its Applications." Wiley, New York, 1960.
4. J. L. Doob, "Stochastic Processes." Wiley, New York, 1953.
5. E. B. Dynkin, "Theory of Markov Processes." Academic Press, New York, 1965.

Chapter 2

MARKOV CHAINS

This chapter introduces Markov chains and should be included in every first course in stochastic processes. The precise definition of a Markov process (Example c, Section 3 of Chapter 1) might be reviewed at the start.

The reader should try to construct examples illustrating the properties *accessible*, *communicate*, *aperiodic*, *recurrent*, *transient* and *irreducible* discussed in Section 4.

Section 7 is only a page but could be omitted on first reading.

1: Definitions

A discrete time Markov chain $\{X_n\}$ is a Markov stochastic process whose state space is a countable or finite set, and for which $T = (0, 1, 2, \ldots)$. We may refer to the value of X_n as the outcome of the nth trial.

It is frequently convenient to label the state space of the process by the nonnegative integers $(0, 1, 2, \ldots)$, which we will do unless the contrary is explicitly stated, and it is customary to speak of X_n being in state i if $X_n = i$.

The probability of X_{n+1} being in state j, given that X_n is in state i (called a one-step transition probability), is denoted by $P_{ij}^{n,n+1}$, i.e.,

$$P_{ij}^{n,n+1} = \Pr\{X_{n+1} = j \mid X_n = i\}. \tag{1.1}$$

The notation emphasizes that in general the transition probabilities are functions not only of the initial and final state, but also of the time of transition as well. When one-step transition probabilities are independent of the time variable (i.e., of the value of n), we say that the Markov process has *stationary transition probabilities* (see the close of Section 3, Chapter 1). Since the vast majority of Markov chains that we shall encounter have stationary transition probabilities, we limit our discussion primarily to such cases.

In this case, $P_{ij}^{n,n+1} = P_{ij}$ is independent of n and P_{ij} is the probability that the state value undergoes a transition from i to j in one trial. It is customary to arrange these numbers P_{ij} as a matrix, that is, an infinite square array

$$\mathbf{P} = \left\| \begin{matrix} P_{00} & P_{01} & P_{02} & P_{03} & \cdots \\ P_{10} & P_{11} & P_{12} & P_{13} & \cdots \\ P_{20} & P_{21} & P_{22} & P_{23} & \cdots \\ \vdots & \vdots & \vdots & \vdots & \\ P_{i0} & P_{i1} & P_{i2} & P_{i3} & \cdots \\ \vdots & \vdots & \vdots & \vdots & \end{matrix} \right\|$$

and refer to $\mathbf{P} = \|P_{ij}\|$ as the Markov matrix or *transition probability matrix* of the process.

The $(i+1)$st row of $\mathbf{P}$ is the probability distribution of the values of X_{n+1} under the condition $X_n = i$. If the number of states is finite then $\mathbf{P}$ is a finite square matrix whose order (the number of rows) is equal to the number of states. Clearly, the quantities P_{ij} satisfy the conditions

$$P_{ij} \geq 0, \qquad i, j = 0, 1, 2, \ldots, \tag{1.2}$$

$$\sum_{j=0}^{\infty} P_{ij} = 1, \qquad i = 0, 1, 2, \ldots. \tag{1.3}$$

The condition (1.3) merely expresses the fact that some transition occurs at each trial. (For convenience, one says that a transition has occurred even if the state remains unchanged.)

The process is completely determined once (1.1) and the value (or more generally the probability distribution) of X_0 are specified. We shall now prove this fact.

Let $\Pr\{X_0 = i\} = p_i$. It is enough to show how to compute the quantities

$$\Pr\{X_0 = i_0, X_1 = i_1, X_2 = i_2, \ldots, X_n = i_n\}, \tag{1.4}$$

as any probability involving $X_{j_1}, \ldots, X_{j_k}$, $j_1 < j_2 < \cdots < j_k$, may be obtained, according to the axiom of total probability, by summing terms of the form (1.4).

By the definition of conditional probabilities we obtain

$$\begin{aligned} &\Pr\{X_0 = i_0, X_1 = i_1, X_2 = i_2, \ldots, X_n = i_n\} \\ &\quad = \Pr\{X_n = i_n \mid X_0 = i_0, X_1 = i_1, \ldots, X_{n-1} = i_{n-1}\} \\ &\quad\quad \cdot \Pr\{X_0 = i_0, X_1 = i_1, \ldots, X_{n-1} = i_{n-1}\}. \end{aligned} \tag{1.5}$$

Now by the definition of a Markov process,

$$\begin{aligned} &\Pr\{X_n = i_n \mid X_0 = i_0, X_1 = i_1, \ldots, X_{n-1} = i_{n-1}\} \\ &\quad = \Pr\{X_n = i_n \mid X_{n-1} = i_{n-1}\} = P_{i_{n-1}, i_n}. \end{aligned} \tag{1.6}$$

Substituting (1.6) into (1.5) gives

$$\Pr\{X_0 = i_0, X_1 = i_1, \ldots, X_n = i_n\}$$
$$= P_{i_{n-1}, i_n} \Pr\{X_0 = i_0, X_1 = i_1, \ldots, X_{n-1} = i_{n-1}\}. \tag{1.7}$$

If we proceed by induction (1.4) becomes

$$\Pr\{X_0 = i_0, X_1 = i_1, \ldots, X_n = i_n\} = P_{i_{n-1}, i_n} P_{i_{n-2}, i_{n-1}} \cdots P_{i_0, i_1} p_{i_0}. \tag{1.8}$$

2: *Examples of Markov Chains*

The importance of Markov chains lies in the large number of natural physical, biological, and economic phenomena that can be described by them. We now formulate several such examples.

A. SPATIALLY HOMOGENEOUS MARKOV CHAINS

Let ξ denote a discrete-valued random variable whose possible values are the nonnegative integers, $\Pr\{\xi = i\} = a_i$, $a_i \geq 0$, and $\sum_{i=1}^{\infty} a_i = 1$. Let $\xi_1, \xi_2, \ldots, \xi_n, \ldots$ represent independent observations of ξ.

We shall now describe two different Markov chains connected with the sequence of ξ_i's.

In each case the state space of the process coincides with the set of nonnegative integers.

(i) Consider the process X_n, $n = 0, 1, 2, \ldots$, defined by $X_n = \xi_n$, ($X_0 = \xi_0$ prescribed). Its Markov matrix has the form

$$\mathbf{P} = \begin{Vmatrix} a_0 & a_1 & a_2 & a_3 & \cdots \\ a_0 & a_1 & a_2 & a_3 & \cdots \\ a_0 & a_1 & a_2 & a_3 & \cdots \\ \vdots & & & & \end{Vmatrix}$$

Each row being identical plainly expresses the fact that the random variable X_{n+1} is independent of X_n.

(ii) Another important class of Markov chains arises from consideration of the successive partial sums η_n of the ξ_i, i.e.,

$$\eta_n = \xi_1 + \xi_2 + \cdots + \xi_n, \qquad n = 1, 2, \ldots$$

and, by definition, $\eta_0 = 0$. The process $X_n = \eta_n$ is readily seen to be a

Markov chain. We can easily compute its transition probability matrix as follows:

$$\begin{aligned}\Pr\{X_{n+1}=j\,|\,X_n=i\} &\\ &= \Pr\{\xi_1+\cdots+\xi_{n+1}=j\,|\,\xi_1+\cdots+\xi_n=i\}=\Pr\{\xi_{n+1}=j-i\}\\ &= \begin{cases} a_{j-i} & \text{for } j\geq i,\\ 0 & \text{for } j<i,\end{cases}\end{aligned}$$

where we have used the assumed independence of the ξ_i.

Schematically, we have

$$\mathbf{P}=\left\|\begin{matrix} a_0 & a_1 & a_2 & a_3 & a_4 & \cdots\\ 0 & a_0 & a_1 & a_2 & a_3 & \cdots\\ 0 & 0 & a_0 & a_1 & a_2 & \cdots\\ \vdots & & & & & \end{matrix}\right\|. \tag{2.1}$$

If the possible values of the random variable ξ are permitted to be the positive and negative integers, then the possible values of η_n for each n will be contained among the totality of all integers. Instead of labeling the states conventionally by means of the nonnegative integers, it is more convenient to identify the state space with the totality of integers, since the probability transition matrix will then appear in a more symmetric form. The state space consists then of the values $\ldots -2, -1, 0, 1, 2, \ldots$. The transition probability matrix becomes

$$\mathbf{P}=\left\|\begin{matrix} & \vdots & \vdots & \vdots & \vdots & \vdots & \\ \cdots & a_{-1} & a_0 & a_1 & a_2 & a_3 & \cdots\\ \cdots & a_{-2} & a_{-1} & a_0 & a_1 & a_2 & \cdots\\ \cdots & a_{-3} & a_{-2} & a_{-1} & a_0 & a_1 & \cdots\\ & \vdots & \vdots & \vdots & \vdots & \vdots & \end{matrix}\right\|,$$

where $\Pr\{\xi=k\}=a_k$, $k=0, \pm 1, \pm 2, \ldots$, and $a_k\geq 0$, $\sum_{k=-\infty}^{\infty} a_k=1$.

B. ONE-DIMENSIONAL RANDOM WALKS

In discussing random walks it is an aid to intuition to speak about the state of the system as the position of a moving "particle."

A one-dimensional random walk is a Markov chain whose state space is a finite or infinite subset $a, a+1, \ldots, b$ of the integers, in which the particle, if it is in state i, can in a single transition either stay in i or move to one of the adjacent states $i-1, i+1$. If the state space is taken as the nonnegative integers, the transition matrix of a random walk has the form

$$\mathbf{P} = \begin{Vmatrix} r_0 & p_0 & 0 & 0 & \cdots & & \\ q_1 & r_1 & p_1 & 0 & \cdots & & \\ 0 & q_2 & r_2 & p_2 & \cdots & & \\ & & \ddots & & & & \\ & & 0 & q_i & r_i & p_i & 0 \\ & & & \ddots & & & \ddots \end{Vmatrix}, \tag{2.2}$$

where $p_i > 0$, $q_i > 0$, $r_i \geq 0$, and $q_i + r_i + p_i = 1$, $i = 1, 2, \ldots$ $(i \geq 1)$, $p_0 \geq 0$, $r_0 \geq 0$, $r_0 + p_0 = 1$. Specifically, if $X_n = i$ then, for $i \geq 1$,

$$\Pr\{X_{n+1} = i + 1 \mid X_n = i\} = p_i: \qquad \Pr\{X_{n+1} = i - 1 \mid X_n = i\} = q_i$$

$$\Pr\{X_{n+1} = i \mid X_n = i\} = r_i,$$

with the obvious modifications holding for $i = 0$.

The designation "random walk" seems apt since a realization of the process describes the path of a person (suitably intoxicated) moving randomly one step forward or backward.

The fortune of a player engaged in a series of contests is often depicted by a random walk process. Specifically, suppose an individual (player A) with fortune k plays a game against an infinitely rich adversary and has probability p_k of winning one unit and probability $q_k = 1 - p_k$ $(k \geq 1)$ of losing one unit in each contest (the choice of the contest at each stage may depend on his fortune), and $r_0 = 1$. The process $\{X_n\}$, where X_n represents his fortune after n contests, is clearly a random walk. Note that once the state 0 is reached (i.e., player A is wiped out), the process remains in that state. This process is also commonly known as the "gambler's ruin."

The random walk corresponding to $p_k = p$, $q_k = 1 - p = q$ for all $k \geq 1$ and $r_0 = 1$ with $p > q$ describes the situation of identical contests with a definite advantage to player A in each individual trial. We shall prove in Chapter 3 that with probability $(q/p)^{x_0}$, where x_0 represents his fortune at time 0, player A is ultimately ruined (his entire fortune is lost), while with probability $1 - (q/p)^{x_0}$, his fortune increases, in the long run, without limit. If $p < q$ then the advantage is decidedly in favor of the house, and with certainty (probability 1) player A is ultimately ruined if he persists in playing as long as he is able to. The same (i.e., certainty of ultimate ruin) is true even if the individual games are fair, that is, $p_k = q_k = \frac{1}{2}$.

If the adversary, player B, also starts with a limited fortune y and player A has an initial fortune x (let $x + y = a$), then we may again consider the Markov chain process X_n representing player A's fortune. However, the states of the process are now restricted to the values $0, 1, 2, \ldots, a$. At any trial, $a - X_n$ is interpreted as player B's fortune. If we allow the possibility of neither player winning in a contest, the transition probability matrix takes the form

$$\mathbf{P} = \left\| \begin{matrix} 1 & 0 & 0 & 0 & \cdots & & \\ q_1 & r_1 & p_1 & 0 & \cdots & & \\ 0 & q_2 & r_2 & p_2 & \cdots & & \\ & & \ddots & & & & \\ & & & q_{a-1} & & r_{a-1} & p_{a-1} \\ 0 & \cdots & \cdots & 0 & & 0 & 1 \end{matrix} \right\| \tag{2.3}$$

Again $p_i(q_i)$, $i = 1, 2, \ldots, a-1$, denotes the probability of player A's fortune increasing (decreasing) by 1 at the subsequent trial when his present fortune is i, and r_i may be interpreted as the probability of a draw. Note that, in accordance with the Markov chain given in (2.3), when player A's fortune (the state of the process) reaches 0 or a it remains in this same state forever. We say player A is ruined when the state of the process reaches 0 and player B is ruined when the state of the process reaches a.

Random walks are not only useful in simulating situations of gambling but frequently serve as reasonable discrete approximations to physical processes describing the motion of diffusing particles. If a particle is subjected to collisions and random impulses, then its position fluctuates randomly, although the particle describes a continuous path. If the future position (i.e., its probability distribution) of the particle depends only on the present position, then the process $\{X_t\}$, where X_t is the position at time t, is Markovian. A discrete approximation to such a continuous motion corresponds to a random walk. A classical discrete version of Brownian motion (see Section 2 of Chapter 1) is provided by the symmetric random walk. By a symmetric random walk on the integers (say all the integers) we mean a Markov chain with state space the totality of all integers and whose transition probability matrix has the elements

$$P_{ij} = \begin{cases} p & \text{if } j = i+1, \\ p & \text{if } j = i-1, \\ r & \text{if } j = i, \\ 0 & \text{otherwise}, \end{cases} \qquad i, j = 0, \pm 1, \pm 2, \ldots,$$

where $p > 0$, $r \geq 0$, and $2p + r = 1$. Conventionally, "symmetric random walk" refers only to the case $r = 0$, $p = \frac{1}{2}$.

Motivated by consideration of certain physical models we are led to the study of random walks on the set of the nonnegative integers. We classify the different processes by the nature of the zero state. Let us fix attention on the random walk described by (2.2). If $p_0 = 1$, and therefore $r_0 = 0$, we have a situation where the zero state acts like a reflecting barrier. Whenever the particle reaches the zero state, the next transition automatically returns it to state one. This corresponds to the physical process where an elastic wall exists at zero, and the particle bounces off with no after-effects.

If $p_0 = 0$ and $r_0 = 1$ then 0 acts as an absorbing barrier. Once the particle reaches zero it remains there forever. If $p_0 > 0$ and $r_0 > 0$, then 0 is a partially reflecting barrier.

When the random walk is restricted to a finite number of states S, say $0, 1, 2, \ldots, a$, then both the states 0 and a independently and in any combination may be reflecting, absorbing, or partially reflecting barriers. We have already encountered a model (gambler's ruin, involving two adversaries with finite resources) of a random walk confined to the states S where 0 and a are absorbing [see (2.3)].

A classical mathematical model of diffusion through a membrane is the famous Ehrenfest model, namely, a random walk on a finite set of states whereby the boundary states are reflecting. The random walk is restricted to the states $i = -a, -a+1, \ldots, -1, 0, 1, \ldots, a$ with transition probability matrix

$$P_{ij} = \begin{cases} \dfrac{a-i}{2a}, & \text{if } j = i+1. \\[2ex] \dfrac{a+i}{2a}, & \text{if } j = i-1. \\[2ex] 0, & \text{otherwise.} \end{cases}$$

The physical interpretation of this model is as follows. Imagine two containers containing a total of $2a$ balls. Suppose the first container, labeled A, holds k balls and the second container B holds $2a-k$ balls. A ball is selected at random (all selections are equally likely) from among the totality of the $2a$ balls and moved to the other container. Each selection generates a transition of the process. Clearly the balls fluctuate between the two containers with a drift from the one with the larger concentration of balls to the one with the smaller concentration of balls. A physical system which in the main is governed by a set of restoring forces essentially proportional to the distance from an equilibrium position may sometimes be approximated by this Ehrenfest model.

The classical symmetric random walk in n dimensions admits the following formulation. The state space is identified with the set of all integral lattice points in E^n (Euclidean n space): that is, a state is an n-tuple

$\mathbf{k} = (k_1, k_2, \ldots, k_n)$ of integers. The transition probability matrix is defined by

$$P_{\mathbf{kl}} = \begin{cases} \dfrac{1}{2n} & \text{if } \sum_{i=1}^{n} |l_i - k_i| = 1. \\ 0 & \text{otherwise.} \end{cases}$$

Analogous to the one-dimensional case, the symmetric random walk in E^n represents a discrete version of n-dimensional Brownian motion.

C. A DISCRETE QUEUEING MARKOV CHAIN

Customers arrive for service and take their place in a waiting line. During each period of time a single customer is served, provided that at least one customer is present. If no customer awaits service then during this period no service is performed. (We can imagine, for example, a taxi stand at which a cab arrives at fixed time intervals to give service. If no one is present the cab immediately departs.) During a service period new customers may arrive. We suppose the actual number of arrivals in the nth period is a random variable ξ_n whose distribution function is independent of the period and is given by

$$\Pr\{k \text{ customers arrive in a service period}\} = \Pr\{\xi_n = k\} = a_k,$$

$$k = 0, 1, \ldots, \quad a_k \geq 0 \quad \text{and} \quad \sum_{k=0}^{\infty} a_k = 1. \tag{2.4}$$

We also assume the r.v.'s ξ_n are independent. The state of the system at the start of each period is defined to be the number of customers waiting in line for service. If the present state is i then after a lapse of one period the state is

$$j = \begin{cases} i - 1 + \xi & \text{if } i \geq 1, \\ \xi & \text{if } i = 0, \end{cases} \tag{2.5}$$

where ξ is the number of new customers having arrived in this period while a single customer was served. In terms of the random variables of the process we can express (2.5) formally as

$$X_{n+1} = (X_n - 1)^+ + \xi_n, \tag{2.6}$$

where $Y^+ = \max(Y, 0)$. In view of (2.4) and (2.5) the transition probability matrix may be trivially calculated and we obtain

$$\|P_{ij}\| = \left\| \begin{matrix} a_0 & a_1 & a_2 & a_3 & a_4 & \cdots \\ a_0 & a_1 & a_2 & a_3 & a_4 & \cdots \\ 0 & a_0 & a_1 & a_2 & a_3 & \cdots \\ 0 & 0 & a_0 & a_1 & a_2 & \cdots \\ 0 & 0 & 0 & a_0 & a_1 & \cdots \\ \vdots & & & & & \end{matrix} \right\| \tag{2.7}$$

It is intuitively clear that if the expected number of new customers, $\sum_{k=0}^{\infty} ka_k$, that arrive during a service period exceeds 1 then certainly with the passage of time the length of the waiting line increases without limit.

On the other hand, if $\sum_{k=0}^{\infty} ka_k < 1$ then we shall see that the length of the waiting line approaches an equilibrium (stationary state). If $\sum ka_k = 1$, a situation of gross instability develops. These statements will be formally elaborated after we have set forth the relevant theory of recurrence (see Section 5, Chapter 3).

D. INVENTORY MODEL

Consider a situation in which a commodity is stocked in order to satisfy a continuing demand. We assume that the replenishing of stock takes place at successive times $t_1, t_2, \ldots$, and we assume that the cumulative demand for the commodity over the interval (t_{n-1}, t_n) is a random variable ξ_n whose distribution function is independent of the time period,

$$\Pr\{\xi_n = k\} = a_k, \qquad k = 0, 1, 2, \ldots, \tag{2.8}$$

where $a_k \geq 0$ and $\sum_{k=0}^{\infty} a_k = 1$. The stock level is examined at the start of each period. An inventory policy is prescribed by specifying two nonnegative critical values s and $S > s$. The implementation of the inventory policy is as follows: If the available stock quantity is not greater than s then immediate procurement is done so as to bring the quantity of stock on hand to the level S. If, however, the available stock is in excess of s then no replenishment of stock is undertaken. Let X_n denote the stock on hand just prior to restocking at t_n. The states of the process $\{X_n\}$ consist of the possible values of the stock size

$$S, \quad S-1, \ldots, +1, \quad 0, \quad -1, \quad -2, \ldots,$$

where a negative value is interpreted as an unfulfilled demand for stock, which will be satisfied immediately upon restocking. According to the rules of the inventory policy, the stock levels at two consecutive periods are connected by the relation

$$X_{n+1} = \begin{cases} X_n - \xi_{n+1} & \text{if} \quad s < X_n \leq S, \\ S - \xi_{n+1} & \text{if} \quad X_n \leq s, \end{cases} \tag{2.9}$$

where ξ_n is the quantity of demand that arises in the nth period, based on the probability law (2.8). If we assume the ξ_n to be mutually independent, then the stock values $X_0, X_1, X_2, \ldots$ plainly constitute a Markov chain whose transition probability matrix can be calculated in accordance with the relation (2.9).

E. SUCCESS RUNS

Consider a Markov chain on the nonnegative integers with transition probability matrix of the form

$$\|P_{ij}\| = \begin{Vmatrix} p_0 & q_0 & 0 & 0 & \cdots \\ p_1 & 0 & q_1 & 0 & \cdots \\ p_2 & 0 & 0 & q_2 & \cdots \\ p_3 & 0 & 0 & 0 & \\ \vdots & & & & \end{Vmatrix}, \tag{2.10}$$

where $q_i > 0$, $p_i > 0$ and $q_i + p_i = 1$, $i = 0, 1, 2, \ldots$. The zero state plays a distinguished role here in that it can be reached in one transition from any other state, while state $i + 1$ can be reached only from state i.

This example is very easy to compute with and we will therefore frequently illustrate concepts and results in terms of it.

A special case of this transition matrix arises when one is dealing with success runs resulting from repeated trials each of which admits two possible outcomes, success (S) or failure (F). More explicitly, consider a sequence of trials with two possible outcomes (S) or (F). Moreover, suppose that in each trial, the probability of (S) is α and the probability of (F) is $\beta = 1 - \alpha$. We say a success run of length r happened at trial n if the outcomes in the preceding $r + 1$ trials, including the present trial as the last, were respectively, $F, S, S, \ldots, S$. Let us now label the present state of the process by the length of the success run currently under way. In particular, if the last trial resulted in a failure then the state is zero. Similarly, when the preceding $r + 1$ trials in order had the outcomes $F, S, S, \ldots, S$, the state variable would carry the label r. The process is clearly Markovian (since the individual trials were independent of each other) and its transition matrix has the form (2.10) where

$$p_n = \beta, \qquad n = 0, 1, 2, \ldots.$$

F. BRANCHING PROCESSES

Suppose an organism at the end of its lifetime produces a random number ξ of offspring with probability distribution

$$\Pr\{\xi = k\} = a_k, \qquad k = 0, 1, 2, \ldots, \tag{2.11}$$

where, as usual, $a_k \geq 0$ and $\sum_{k=0}^{\infty} a_k = 1$. We assume that all offspring act independently of each other and at the end of their lifetime (for simplicity, the lifespans of all organisms are assumed to be the same) individually have progeny in accordance with the probability distribution (2.11), thus propagating their species. The process $\{X_n\}$, where X_n is the population size at the nth generation, is a Markov chain.

In fact, the only relevant knowledge regarding the distribution of $X_{n_1}, X_{n_2}, \ldots, X_{n_r}, X_n, n_1 < n_2 < \cdots < n_r < n$, is the last known population count, since the number of the offspring is a function merely of the present population size. The transition matrix is obviously given by

$$P_{ij} = \Pr\{X_{n+1} = j \mid X_n = i\} = \Pr\{\xi_1 + \cdots + \xi_i = j\}, \qquad (2.12)$$

where the ξ's are independent observations of a random variable with probability law (2.11). The formula (2.12) may be reasoned simply as follows. In the nth generation the i individuals independently give rise to numbers of offspring $\{\xi_k\}_{k=1}^{i}$ and hence the cumulative number produced is $\xi_1 + \xi_2 + \cdots + \xi_i$.

If we use generating functions, then clearly the generating function of $\xi_1 + \xi_2 + \cdots + \xi_i$ is $[g(s)]^i$, where g is the generating function associated with ξ. (We are using the property of composition of generating functions in the case of sums of independent r.v.'s: see Section 1 of Chapter 1, page 12.) Hence, P_{ij} is simply the jth coefficient in the power series expansion of $[g(s)]^i$.

G. MARKOV CHAINS IN GENETICS

The following idealized genetics model was introduced by S. Wright to investigate the fluctuation of gene frequency under the influence of mutation and selection. We begin by describing a so-called simple haploid model of random reproduction, disregarding mutation pressures and selective forces. We assume that we are dealing with a fixed population size of $2N$ genes composed of type-a and type-A individuals. The make-up of the next generation is determined by $2N$ independent binomial trials as follows: If the parent population consists of j a-genes and $2N - j$ A-genes then each trial results in a or A with probabilities

$$p_j = \frac{j}{2N}, \qquad q_j = 1 - \frac{j}{2N},$$

respectively. Repeated selections are done with replacement. By this procedure we generate a Markov chain $\{X_n\}$ where X_n is the number of a-genes in the nth generation among a constant population size of $2N$ elements. The state space contains the $2N+1$ values $\{0, 1, 2, \ldots, 2N\}$.

The transition probability matrix is computed according to the binomial distribution as

$$\Pr\{X_{n+1}=k\,|\,X_n=j\}=P_{jk}=\binom{2N}{k}p_j^k q_j^{2N-k} \qquad (j,k=0,1,\ldots,2N). \tag{2.13}$$

For some discussion of the biological justification of these postulates we refer the reader to Fisher†.

Notice that states 0 and $2N$ are completely absorbing in the sense that once $X_n=0$ or $(2N)$ then $X_{n+k}=0$ or $(2N)$ respectively for all $k\geq 0$. One of the questions of interest is to determine the probability under the condition $X_0=i$ that the population will attain fixation, i.e., a pure population composed only of a-genes or A-genes. It is also pertinent to determine the rate of approach to fixation. We will examine such questions in our general analysis of absorption probabilities.

A more realistic model takes account of mutation pressures. We assume that prior to the formation of the new generation each gene has the possibility to mutate, that is, to change into a gene of the other kind. Specifically, we assume that for each gene the mutation a→A occurs with probability α_1, and A→a occurs with probability α_2. Again we assume that the composition of the next generation is determined by $2N$ independent binomial trials. The relevant value of p_j and q_j when the parent population consists of j a-genes are now taken to be

$$\begin{aligned} p_j &= \frac{j}{2N}(1-\alpha_1)+\left(1-\frac{j}{2N}\right)\alpha_2, \\ q_j &= \frac{j}{2N}\alpha_1+\left(1-\frac{j}{2N}\right)(1-\alpha_2). \end{aligned} \tag{2.14}$$

The rationale is as follows: We assume that the mutation pressures operate first, after which a new gene is determined by selecting at random from the population. Now the probability of selecting an a-gene after the mutation forces have acted is just $1/2N$ times the number of a-genes present: hence the average probability (averaged with respect to the possible mutations) is simply $1/2N$ times the average number of a-genes after mutation. But this average number is clearly $j(1-\alpha_1)+(2N-j)\alpha_2$, which leads at once to (2.14).

The transition probabilities of the associated Markov chain are calculated by (2.13) using the values of p_j and q_j given in (2.14).

† R. A. Fisher, "The Genetical Theory of Natural Selection," Oxford (Clarendon) Press, London and New York, 1962.

If $\alpha_1\alpha_2 > 0$ then fixation will not occur in any state. Instead, as $n \to \infty$, the distribution function of X_n will approach a steady state distribution of a random variable ξ where $\Pr\{\xi = k\} = \pi_k$ $(k = 0, 1, 2, \ldots, 2N)$ $(\sum_{k=0}^{n} \pi_k = 1, \pi_k > 0)$. The distribution function of ξ is called the steady state gene frequency distribution.

We return to the simple random mating model and discuss the concept of a selection force operating in favor of, say, a-genes. Suppose we wish to impose a selective advantage for a-genes over A-genes so that the relative number of offspring have expectations proportional to $1 + s$ and 1, respectively, where s is small and positive. We replace $p_j = j/2N$ and $q_j = 1 - j/2N$ by

$$p_j = \frac{(1+s)j}{2N+sj}, \qquad q_j = 1 - p_j,$$

and build the next generation by binomial sampling as before. If the parent population consisted of j a-genes, then in the next generation the expected population sizes of a-genes and A-genes, respectively, are

$$2N\frac{(1+s)\,j}{2N+sj}, \qquad 2N\frac{(2N-j)}{2N+sj}.$$

The ratio of expected population size of a-genes to A-genes at the $(n+1)$th generation is

$$\frac{1+s}{1}\cdot\frac{j}{2N-j} = \left(\frac{1+s}{1}\right)\left(\frac{\text{number of a-genes in the } n\text{th generation}}{\text{number of A-genes in the } n\text{th generation}}\right)$$

which explains the meaning of selectivity.

H. GENETIC MODEL II

The gene appears to be composed of a number of subunits, say for definiteness N. When a cell containing the gene prepares to split, each subunit doubles and each of the two cells receives a gene composed of the same number of subunits as before. One or more of the subunits may be in a mutant form. When doubling occurs it is assumed that mutant units produce mutant units and nonmutant units produce nonmutant units. Moreover, the subunits are assumed to be divided between the two new genes randomly as if by drawing from an urn. We shall trace a single line of descent rather than all the population as it multiplies. To describe the history of the line we consider a Markov chain whose state space is identified with the values $0, 1, 2, \ldots, N$. Then the gene is said to be in state i if its composition consists of i mutant subunits and $N-i$ normal subunits. The transition probabilities are computed by the formula

$$P_{ij}=\frac{\binom{2i}{j}\binom{2N-2i}{N-j}}{\binom{2N}{N}}. \tag{2.15}$$

The derivation of P_{ij} is as follows. Suppose the parent gene is in state i: then after doubling we obtain a totality of $2i$ mutant units and $2N-2i$ normal units. The nature of the daughter gene is formed by selecting an arbitrary N units from this collection. In accordance with the hypergeometric probability law, the probability that the daughter gene is in state j is given by (2.15).

The states $j=1,2,\ldots,N-1$ are called mixed, and states 0 and N will be called pure. State N is of interest in that a gene all of whose subunits are mutant may cause the death of its possessor, while state 0 implies that a gene of this type will produce no more of the mutant form. We will later determine the explicit probabilities that, starting from state i, the gene ultimately fixes in state 0 or state N.

3: *Transition Probability Matrices of a Markov Chain*

A Markov chain is completely defined by its one-step transition probability matrix and the specification of a probability distribution on the state of the process at time 0. The analysis of a Markov chain concerns mainly the calculation of the probabilities of the possible realizations of the process. Central in these calculations are the n-step transition probability matrices, $\mathbf{P}^{(n)}=\|P_{ij}^n\|$. Here P_{ij}^n denotes the probability that the process goes from state i to state j in n transitions. Formally,

$$P_{ij}^n=\Pr\{X_{n+m}=j\,|\,X_m=i\}. \tag{3.1}$$

Observe that we are dealing only with temporally homogeneous processes having stationary transition probabilities, since otherwise the left-hand side of (3.1) would also depend on m.

The Markovian assumption allows us to express (3.1) immediately in terms of $\|P_{ij}\|$ as stated in the following theorem.

Theorem 3.1. *If the one-step transition probability matrix of a Markov chain is* $\mathbf{P}=\|P_{ij}\|$, *then*

$$P_{ij}^n=\sum_{k=0}^{\infty}P_{ik}^rP_{kj}^s \tag{3.2}$$

for any fixed pair of nonnegative integers r and s satisfying $r+s=n$, where we define

$$P_{ij}^0=\begin{cases}1, & i=j,\\ 0, & i\neq j.\end{cases}$$

From the theory of matrices (see the appendix), we recognize relation (3.2) as just the formula for matrix multiplication, so that $\mathbf{P}^{(n)}=\mathbf{P}^n$; in other words, the numbers P_{ij}^n may be regarded as the entries in the matrix $\mathbf{P}^n$, the nth power of $\mathbf{P}$.

Proof. We carry out the argument in the case $n=2$. The event of going from state i to state j in two transitions can be realized in the mutually exclusive ways of going to some intermediate state k ($k=0, 1, 2, \ldots$) in the first transition and then going from state k to state j in the second transition.

Because of the Markovian assumption the probability of the second transition is P_{kj}, and that of the first transition is clearly P_{ik}. If we use the law of total probabilities Eq. (3.2) follows. The argument in the general case is identical.

If the probability of the process initially being in state j is p_j, i.e., the distribution law of X_0 is $\Pr\{X_0=j\}=p_j$, then the probability of the process being in state k at time n is

$$p_k^{(n)}=\sum_{j=0}^{\infty}p_jP_{jk}^n=\Pr\{X_n=k\}. \tag{3.3}$$

Besides determining the joint probability distributions of the process for all time, usually a formidable task, it is frequently of interest to find the asymptotic behavior of P_{ij}^n as $n\to\infty$. One might expect that the influence of the initial state recedes in time and that consequently, as $n\to\infty$, P_{ij}^n approaches a limit which is independent of i. In order to analyze precisely the asymptotic behavior of the process we need to introduce some principles of classifying states of a Markov chain.

4: *Classification of States of a Markov Chain*

State j is said to be ***accessible*** from state i if for some integer $n\geq 0$, $P_{ij}^n>0$: i.e., state j is accessible from state i if there is positive probability that in a finite number of transitions state j can be reached starting from state i. Two states i and j, each accessible to the other, are said to *communicate* and we write $i \leftrightarrow j$. If two states i and j do not communicate, then either

$$P_{ij}^n = 0 \qquad \text{for all} \quad n \geq 0$$

or

$$P_{ji}^n = 0 \qquad \text{for all} \quad n \geq 0$$

or both relations are true. The concept of communication is an equivalence relation.

(i) $i \leftrightarrow i$ (reflexivity), a consequence of the definition of
$P_{ij}^0 = \delta_{ij} = \begin{Bmatrix} 1, & i = j \\ 0, & i \neq j \end{Bmatrix}$.

(ii) If $i \leftrightarrow j$, then $j \leftrightarrow i$ (symmetry), from the definition of communication.

(iii) If $i \leftrightarrow j$ and $j \leftrightarrow k$, then $i \leftrightarrow k$ (transitivity).

The proof of transitivity proceeds as follows: $i \leftrightarrow j$ and $j \leftrightarrow k$ imply that there exist integers n and m such that $P_{ij}^n > 0$ and $P_{jk}^m > 0$. Consequently by (3.2) and the nonnegativity of each P_{rs}^t, we conclude that

$$P_{ik}^{n+m} = \sum_{r=0}^{\infty} P_{ir}^n P_{rk}^m \geq P_{ij}^n P_{jk}^m > 0.$$

A similar argument shows the existence of an integer ν such that $P_{ki}^\nu > 0$, as desired.

We can now partition the totality of states into equivalence classes. The states in an equivalence class are those which communicate with each other. It may be possible, starting in one class, to enter some other class with positive probability; if so, however, it is clearly not possible to return to the initial class, or else the two classes would together form a single class. We say that the Markov chain is *irreducible* if the equivalence relation induces only one class. In other words, a process is irreducible if all states communicate with each other.

To illustrate this concept, consider the transition probability matrix

$$\mathbf{P} = \left\| \begin{array}{cc:ccc} \frac{1}{2} & \frac{1}{2} & 0 & 0 & 0 \\ \frac{1}{4} & \frac{3}{4} & 0 & 0 & 0 \\ \hdashline 0 & 0 & 0 & 1 & 0 \\ 0 & 0 & \frac{1}{2} & 0 & \frac{1}{2} \\ 0 & 0 & 0 & 1 & 0 \end{array} \right\| = \left\| \begin{array}{cc} \mathbf{P}_1 & 0 \\ 0 & \mathbf{P}_2 \end{array} \right\|,$$

where $\mathbf{P}_1$ is an abbreviation for the matrix formed from the initial two rows and columns of $\mathbf{P}$, and similarly for $\mathbf{P}_2$. This Markov chain clearly divides into the two classes composed of states $\{1, 2\}$ and states $\{3, 4, 5\}$.

If the state of X_0 lies in the first class, then the state of the system thereafter remains in this class and for all purposes the relevant transition matrix is $\mathbf{P}_1$. Similarly, if the initial state belongs to the second class, then the relevant transition matrix is $\mathbf{P}_2$. This is a situation where we have two completely unrelated processes labeled together.

In the random walk model with transition matrix

$$\mathbf{P} = \left\| \begin{matrix} 1 & 0 & 0 & 0 \cdots\cdots & 0 & 0 & 0 \\ q & 0 & p & 0 \cdots\cdots & 0 & 0 & 0 \\ 0 & q & 0 & p \cdots\cdots & 0 & 0 & 0 \\ \vdots & & & & \vdots & \vdots & \vdots \\ 0 & \cdots\cdots & & & q & 0 & p \\ 0 & \cdots\cdots & & & 0 & 0 & 1 \end{matrix} \right\| \quad \begin{matrix} \textit{states} \\ 0 \\ 1 \\ 2 \\ \vdots \\ a-1 \\ a \end{matrix}$$

we have the three classes $\{0\}$, $\{1, 2, \ldots, a-1\}$, and $\{a\}$. This is an example where it is possible to reach the first class or third class from the second class, but it is not possible to return to the second class from either the first or the third class.

Direct inspection shows that the queueing Markov chain example C of Section 2 is irreducible when $a_k > 0$ for all k. Under the same condition we may easily verify that the inventory model (Example D) is irreducible: the success run Markov chain model (Example E) under the condition $q_i > 0$, $p_i > 0$, $(i = 0, 1, \ldots)$ is also irreducible.

PERIODICITY OF A MARKOV CHAIN

We define the period of state i, written $d(i)$, to be the greatest common divisor (g.c.d.) of all integers $n \geq 1$ for which $P_{ii}^n > 0$. [If $P_{ii}^n = 0$ for all $n \geq 1$ define $d(i) = 0$.] If in the random walk [see (2.2)] all $r_i = 0$, then every state has period two. If for a single state, i_0, $r_{i_0} > 0$, then every state now has period one, since regardless of the initial state j the system can reach state i_0 and remain in this state any length of time before returning to state j.

In a finite Markov chain of n states with transition matrix

$$\mathbf{P} = \left\| \overbrace{\begin{matrix} 0 & 1 & 0 & 0 & \cdots\cdots & 0 \\ 0 & 0 & 1 & 0 & \cdots\cdots & 0 \\ \vdots & & & & & \vdots \\ 0 & 0 & \cdots\cdots & & & 1 \\ 1 & 0 & 0 & \cdots\cdots & & 0 \end{matrix}}^{n} \right\|$$

each state has period n.

We state, without proof, three basic properties of the period of a state. (In this connection, consult Problems 2—4 of this chapter.)

Theorem 4.1. *If $i \leftrightarrow j$ then $d(i) = d(j)$.*

This assertion shows that the period is a constant in each class of communicating states.

Theorem 4.2. *If state i has period $d(i)$ then there exists an integer N depending on i such that for all integers $n \geq N$*

$$P_{ii}^{nd(i)} > 0.$$

This asserts that a return to state i can occur at all sufficiently large multiples of the period $d(i)$.

Corollary 4.1. *If $P_{ji}^{m} > 0$, then $P_{ji}^{m+nd(i)} > 0$ for all n (a positive integer) sufficiently large.*

A Markov chain in which each state has period one is called *aperiodic*. The vast majority of Markov chain processes we deal with are aperiodic. Random walks usually typify the periodic cases arising in practice. Results will be developed for the aperiodic case and the modified conclusions for the general case will be stated usually without proof. The industrious reader can easily supply the required formal proof.

5: Recurrence

Consider an arbitrary, but fixed, state i. We define for each integer $n \geq 1$,

$$f_{ii}^{n} = \Pr\{X_n = i, X_\nu \neq i, \nu = 1, 2, \ldots, n-1 \,|\, X_0 = i\}.$$

In other words, f_{ii}^{n} is the probability that, starting from state i, the first return to state i occurs at the nth transition. Clearly $f_{ii}^{1} = P_{ii}$ and f_{ii}^{n} may be calculated recursively according to

$$P_{ii}^{n} = \sum_{k=0}^{n} f_{ii}^{k} P_{ii}^{n-k}, \qquad n \geq 1, \tag{5.1}$$

where we define $f_{ii}^{0} = 0$ for all i. Equation (5.1) is derived by decomposing the event from which P_{ii}^{n} is computed according to the time of the first return to state i. Indeed, consider all the possible realizations of the process for which $X_0 = i$, $X_n = i$ and the first return to state i occurs at the kth transition. Call this event E_k. The events E_k $(k = 1, 2, \ldots, n)$ are clearly mutually exclusive. The probability of the event that the first return is at the kth transition is by definition f_{ii}^{k}. In the remaining $n - k$

transitions, we are dealing only with those realizations for which $X_n = i$. Using the Markov property, we have

$$\begin{aligned}\Pr\{E_k\} &= \Pr\{\text{first return is at } k\text{th transition } |X_0 = i\} \Pr\{X_n = i | X_k = i\} \\ &= f_{ii}^k P_{ii}^{n-k}, \qquad 1 \le k \le n,\end{aligned}$$

(recall that $P_{ii}^0 = 1$). Hence

$$\Pr\{X_n = i | X_0 = i\} = \sum_{k=1}^{n} \Pr\{E_k\} = \sum_{k=1}^{n} f_{ii}^k P_{ii}^{n-k} = \sum_{k=0}^{n} f_{ii}^k P_{ii}^{n-k},$$

since by definition $f_{ii}^0 = 0$.

We next introduce the related generating functions.

Definition. The generating function $P_{ij}(s)$ of the sequence $\{P_{ij}^n\}$ is

$$P_{ij}(s) = \sum_{n=0}^{\infty} P_{ij}^n s^n \qquad \text{for} \quad |s| < 1. \tag{5.2}$$

In a similar manner we define the generating function of the sequence $\{f_{ij}^n\}$ (for the definition of $\{f_{ij}^n\}$ when $i \neq j$, see immediately below Eq. (5.9))

$$F_{ij}(s) = \sum_{n=0}^{\infty} f_{ij}^n s^n \qquad \text{for} \quad |s| < 1. \tag{5.3}$$

Recall the property (see page 12 of Chapter 1)† that, if

$$A(s) = \sum_{k=0}^{\infty} a_k s^k \qquad \text{and} \quad B(s) = \sum_{l=0}^{\infty} b_l s^l, \tag{5.4}$$

then

$$A(s)B(s) = C(s) = \sum_{r=0}^{\infty} c_r s^r, \qquad \text{for} \quad |s| < 1, \tag{5.5}$$

where

$$c_r = a_0 b_r + a_1 b_{r-1} + \dots + a_r b_0 . \tag{5.6}$$

If we identify the a_k's with the f_{ii}^k's and the b_l's with the P_{ii}^l's, then comparing (5.1) with (5.6) we obtain

$$F_{ii}(s) P_{ii}(s) = P_{ii}(s) - 1 \qquad \text{for} \quad |s| < 1 \tag{5.7}$$

or

$$P_{ii}(s) = \frac{1}{1 - F_{ii}(s)} \qquad \text{for} \quad |s| < 1. \tag{5.8}$$

† $$\begin{aligned}A(s)B(s) &= \left(\sum_{k=0}^{\infty} a_k s^k\right)\left(\sum_{l=0}^{\infty} b_l s^l\right) \\ &= a_0 b_0 + (a_1 b_0 + b_1 a_0)s + (a_2 b_0 + a_1 b_1 + a_0 b_2)s^2 + \cdots \\ &= \sum_{k=0}^{\infty} s^k \left(\sum_{j=0}^{k} a_j b_{k-j}\right) = \sum_{k=0}^{\infty} c_k s^k.\end{aligned}$$

Subtracting the constant 1 in (5.7) is necessary since (5.1) is not valid for $n=0$.

By an argument analogous to that which led to (5.1), we obtain

$$P_{ij}^{n}=\sum_{k=0}^{n} f_{ij}^{k} P_{jj}^{n-k}, \qquad i\neq j,\ n\geq 0, \tag{5.9}$$

where f_{ij}^{k} is the probability that first passage from state i to state j occurs at the kth transition. Again we define $f_{ij}^{0}=0$ for all i and j. It follows from (5.9), if we refer to (5.5), that

$$P_{ij}(s)=F_{ij}(s)P_{jj}(s) \qquad \text{for} \quad |s|<1. \tag{5.10}$$

We say a state i is *recurrent* if and only if $\sum_{n=1}^{\infty} f_{ii}^{n}=1$. This says that a state i is recurrent if and only if, starting from state i, the probability of returning to state i after some finite length of time is one. A nonrecurrent state is said to be *transient*. We will prove a theorem that relates the recurrence or nonrecurrence of a state to the behavior of the n-step transition probabilities P_{ii}^{n}. Before proving the theorem, we need the following:

Lemma 5.1. (Abel).

(a) *If* $\sum_{k=0}^{\infty} a_k$ *converges, then*

$$\lim_{s\to 1-} \sum_{k=0}^{\infty} a_k s^k = \sum_{k=0}^{\infty} a_k = a \tag{5.11}$$

($\lim_{s\to 1-}$ means that s approaches 1 from values less than 1).

(b) *If* $a_k\geq 0$ *and* $\lim_{s\to 1-} \sum_{k=0}^{\infty} a_k s^k = a \leq \infty$, *then*

$$\sum_{k=0}^{\infty} a_k = \lim_{N\to\infty} \sum_{k=0}^{N} a_k = a.$$

Proof. (a) We will show that

$$\lim_{s\to 1-} \left|\sum_{k=0}^{\infty} a_k(s^k-1)\right| = 0. \tag{5.12}$$

Since $\sum_{k=0}^{\infty} a_k$ converges, for any $\varepsilon>0$ we can find an $N(\varepsilon)$ such that $|\sum_{k=N}^{N'} a_k|<\varepsilon/4$ for all $N'\geq N$. Choose such an N. Then write

$$\begin{aligned}\left|\sum_{k=0}^{\infty} a_k(s^k-1)\right| &= \left|\sum_{k=0}^{N} a_k(s^k-1)+\sum_{k=N+1}^{\infty} a_k(s^k-1)\right| \\ &\leq \left|\sum_{k=0}^{N} a_k(s^k-1)\right| + \left|\sum_{k=N+1}^{\infty} a_k(s^k-1)\right|.\end{aligned} \tag{5.13}$$

Now, for $0 \le s < 1$

$$\left|\sum_{k=0}^{N} a_k(s^k - 1)\right| \le MN|s^N - 1|, \tag{5.14}$$

where $M = \max_{0 \le k \le N} |a_k| < \infty$, so that for s sufficiently close to 1 we have

$$\left|\sum_{k=0}^{N} a_k(s^k - 1)\right| < \varepsilon/2.$$

To estimate $\sum_{k=N+1}^{\infty} a_k(s^k - 1)$ we sum by parts. This gives

$$\begin{aligned}\left|\sum_{k=N+1}^{\infty} a_k(s^k - 1)\right| &= \left|\sum_{k=N+1}^{\infty} (A_k - A_{k+1})(s^k - 1)\right| \\ &= \left|A_{N+1}(s^{N+1} - 1) + \sum_{k=N+2}^{\infty} A_k(s^k - s^{k-1})\right|,\end{aligned} \tag{5.15}$$

where

$$A_k = \sum_{r=k}^{\infty} a_r.$$

Obviously, (5.15) is bounded by

$$\frac{\varepsilon}{4}\,|(s^{N+1} - 1)| + \frac{\varepsilon}{4}\,s^{N+1} \le \frac{\varepsilon}{2}.$$

Putting these estimates together, we have

$$\left|\sum_{k=0}^{\infty} a_k(s^k - 1)\right| < \varepsilon,$$

provided s is sufficiently close to 1. ∎

(b) Since $\sum_{k=0}^{\infty} a_k s^k \le \sum_{k=0}^{\infty} a_k$ for $0 < s < 1$, the case $a = \infty$ is obvious. If $a < \infty$, then by our hypothesis

$$\sum_{k=0}^{\infty} a_k s^k < a < \infty \qquad \text{for} \quad 0 < s < 1.$$

Hence,

$$\sum_{k=0}^{n} a_k \le a \qquad \text{for all} \quad n.$$

Since $\sum_{k=0}^{n} a_k$ is a bounded monotone increasing function of n it has a finite limit, call it a'. But by part (a) of this lemma we may conclude that, $a = a'$. ∎

With this lemma we easily prove

Theorem 5.1. *A state i is recurrent if and only if*

$$\sum_{n=1}^{\infty} P_{ii}^n = \infty.$$

Proof. Assume i is recurrent, that is, $\sum_{n=1}^{\infty} f_{ii}^n = 1$. Then by Lemma 5.1(a)

$$\lim_{s\to 1-} \sum_{n=0}^{\infty} f_{ii}^n s^n = \lim_{s\to 1-} F_{ii}(s) = 1.$$

Thus from (5.8)

$$\lim_{s\to 1-} P_{ii}(s) = \lim_{s\to 1-} \sum_{n=0}^{\infty} P_{ii}^n s^n = \infty.$$

Appealing to Lemma 5.1(b), we have

$$\sum_{n=0}^{\infty} P_{ii}^n = \infty,$$

the desired result. To prove sufficiency, assume that state i is transient, that is, $\sum_{n=1}^{\infty} f_{ii}^n < 1$. Using Lemma 5.1(a) and consulting (5.8), we infer that

$$\lim_{s\to 1-} P_{ii}(s) < \infty.$$

Now appealing to Lemma 5.1(b), we have the result that $\sum_{n=1}^{\infty} P_{ii}^n < \infty$, contradicting our hypothesis and proving sufficiency. ∎

As an immediate consequence of Theorem 5.1 we obtain

Corollary 5.1. *If $i \leftrightarrow j$ and if i is recurrent then j is recurrent.*

Proof. Since $i \leftrightarrow j$ there exists $m, n \geq 1$ such that

$$P_{ij}^n > 0 \qquad \text{and} \qquad P_{ji}^m > 0.$$

Let $\nu > 0$. We obtain, by the usual argument (see page 60), $P_{jj}^{m+n+\nu} \geq P_{ji}^m P_{ii}^\nu P_{ij}^n$ and, on summing,

$$\sum_{\nu=0}^{\infty} P_{jj}^{m+n+\nu} \geq \sum_{\nu=0}^{\infty} P_{ji}^m P_{ii}^\nu P_{ij}^n = P_{ji}^m P_{ij}^n \sum_{\nu=0}^{\infty} P_{ii}^\nu .$$

Hence if $\sum_{\nu=0}^{\infty} P_{ii}^\nu$ diverges, then $\sum_{\nu=0}^{\infty} P_{jj}^\nu$ also diverges. ∎

This corollary proves that recurrence, like periodicity, is a class property: that is, all states in an equivalence class are either recurrent or nonrecurrent.

Remark. The expected number of returns to state i, given $X_0 = i$, is

$\sum_{n=1}^{\infty} P_{ii}^n$. Thus, Theorem 5.1 states that a state i is recurrent if and only if the expected number of returns is infinite.

6: Examples of Recurrent Markov Chains

Example 1. Consider first the one-dimensional random walk on the positive and negative integers, where at each transition the particle moves with probability p one unit to the right and with probability q one unit to the left $(p+q=1)$. Hence

$$P_{00}^{2n+1}=0, \qquad n=0,1,2,\ldots, \qquad \text{and} \qquad P_{00}^{2n}=\binom{2n}{n}p^nq^n=\frac{(2n)!}{n!n!}p^nq^n. \tag{6.1}$$

We appeal now to Stirling's formula,

$$n! \sim n^{n+\frac{1}{2}}e^{-n}\sqrt{2\pi}. \tag{6.2}$$

Applying (6.2) to (6.1) we obtain

$$P_{00}^{2n} \sim \frac{(pq)^n 2^{2n}}{\sqrt{\pi n}}=\frac{(4pq)^n}{\sqrt{\pi n}}.$$

It is readily verified that $p(1-p)=pq \leq \frac{1}{4}$ with equality holding if and only if $p=q=\frac{1}{2}$. Hence $\sum_{n=0}^{\infty} P_{00}^n=\infty$ if and only if $p=\frac{1}{2}$. Therefore, from Theorem 5.1, the one-dimensional random walk is recurrent if and only if $p=q=\frac{1}{2}$. Remember that recurrence is a class property. Intuitively, if $p \neq q$ there is positive probability that a particle initially at the origin will drift to $+\infty$ if $p>q$ (to $-\infty$ if $p<q$) without ever returning to the origin.

Example 2. We look now at the two-dimensional random walk in the full infinite plane. Let the probabilities of a transition one unit to the right, left, up, or down all be equal to $\frac{1}{4}$. We proceed to investigate recurrence of the state represented by the origin. Consider all paths whereby we move i units to the right, i units to the left, j units down, and j units up, where $2i+2j=2n$. We compute that

$$\begin{aligned} P_{00}^{2n+1} &= 0, & n&=0,1,2,\ldots,\\ P_{00}^{2n} &= \sum_{i,j,i+j=n}\frac{(2n)!}{i!i!j!j!}\left(\frac{1}{4}\right)^{2n}, & n&=1,2,3,\ldots. \end{aligned} \tag{6.3}$$

[The terms of (6.3) result from applying the multinomial distribution.] Multiplying numerator and denominator of (6.3) by $(n!)^2$ we obtain

$$P_{00}^{2n}=\left(\frac{1}{4}\right)^{2n}\binom{2n}{n}\sum_{i=0}^{n}\binom{n}{i}\binom{n}{n-i}.$$

But

$$\sum_{i=0}^{n} \binom{n}{i}\binom{n}{n-i} = \binom{2n}{n}$$

Hence,

$$P_{00}^{2n} = \left(\frac{1}{4}\right)^{2n} \binom{2n}{n}^2 .$$

Using Stirling's formula (6.2) again we obtain

$$P_{00}^{2n} \sim \frac{1}{\pi n}.$$

Hence, $\sum_{n=0}^{\infty} P_{00}^{n} = \infty$ and the state represented by the origin is again a recurrent state.

Example 3. We consider the symmetric random walk in three dimensions. By reasoning similar to the above we obtain

$$P_{00}^{2n+1} = 0, \qquad n = 0, 1, 2, \ldots,$$

$$P_{00}^{2n} = \sum_{i,j,0 \le i+j \le n} \frac{(2n)!}{i!i!j!j!(n-i-j)!\,(n-i-j)!} \left(\frac{1}{6}\right)^{2n}. \tag{6.4}$$

Multiplying numerator and denominator by $(n!)^2$ and factoring out a term $(\frac{1}{2})^{2n}$ gives

$$P_{00}^{2n} = \frac{1}{2^{2n}} \binom{2n}{n} \sum_{i,j,0 \le i+j \le n} \left[\frac{n!}{i!j!(n-i-j)!}\right]^2 \left(\frac{1}{3}\right)^{2n}, \tag{6.5}$$

$$P_{00}^{2n} \le c_n \frac{1}{2^{2n}} \binom{2n}{n} \frac{1}{3^n}, \tag{6.6}$$

where

$$c_n = \max_{i,j,0 \le i+j \le n} \left[\frac{n!}{i!j!(n-i-j)!}\right]. \tag{6.7}$$

Observe that we have used the fact that

$$\sum_{i,j,0 \le i+j \le n} \frac{n!}{i!j!(n-i-j)!} \left(\frac{1}{3}\right)^n = 1. \tag{6.8}$$

For large n the value of c_n is attained for $i = j \sim n/3$. We show this result as follows. Let i_0 and j_0 be the values of i and j which maximize the terms

$$\frac{n!}{i!j!(n-i-j)!} \qquad \text{where } 0 \le i + j \le n.$$

We may immediately write the four inequalities

$$\frac{n!}{j_0!(i_0-1)!(n-j_0-i_0+1)!} \le \frac{n!}{j_0!i_0!(n-j_0-i_0)!},$$

$$\frac{n!}{j_0!(i_0+1)!(n-j_0-i_0-1)!} \le \frac{n!}{j_0!i_0!(n-j_0-i_0)!},$$

$$\frac{n!}{(j_0-1)!i_0!(n-j_0-i_0+1)!} \le \frac{n!}{j_0!i_0!(n-j_0-i_0)!},$$

$$\frac{n!}{(j_0+1)!i_0!(n-j_0-i_0-1)!} \le \frac{n!}{j_0!i_0!(n-j_0-i_0)!}.$$

These inequalities reduce to

$$n-i_0-1 \le 2j_0 \le n-i_0+1,$$

$$n-j_0-1 \le 2i_0 \le n-j_0+1.$$

Hence for large n, $i_0 \sim n/3$ and $j_0 \sim n/3$. Inserting $i=j=n/3$ in (6.7), we obtain for (6.6)

$$P_{00}^{2n} \le \frac{n!}{(n/3)!(n/3)!(n/3)!(2)^{2n}3^n}\binom{2n}{n}. \tag{6.9}$$

If we use Stirling's formula the right-hand side of the inequality (6.9) is asymptotic to

$$\frac{3\sqrt{3}}{2\pi^{3/2}\,n^{3/2}}.$$

But if we sum these terms, we obtain

$$\sum_{n=1}^{\infty}\frac{3\sqrt{3}}{2\pi^{3/2}\,n^{3/2}} < \infty.$$

Hence $\sum_{n=1}^{\infty} P_{00}^n < \infty$ and by Theorem 5.1 the state represented by 0 is a transient state. Now, since recurrence is a class property and all states communicate we see that for the one- and two-dimensional symmetric random walks the particle will return with certainty to any state that it once occupied. However, in the three-dimensional symmetric random walk there is positive probability that once the particle leaves a state it never returns.

Example 4. Consider now the Markov chain which represents the success runs of binomial trials. The transition probability matrix is

$$\begin{Vmatrix} p_0 & 1-p_0 & 0 & 0 & \cdots\cdots\cdots & \\ p_1 & 0 & 1-p_1 & 0 & \cdots\cdots\cdots & \\ p_2 & 0 & 0 & 1-p_2 & \cdots\cdots & \\ \vdots & \vdots & & & & \\ p_r & 0 & \cdots\cdots\cdots & & 1-p_r & 0\cdots \\ \vdots & & & & \vdots & \vdots \end{Vmatrix} \qquad (0<p_i<1).$$

The states of this Markov chains all belong to the same equivalence class (any state can be reached from any other state). Since recurrence is a class property (see Corollary 5.1), we will investigate recurrence for the zeroth state. We compute that

$$\begin{aligned} f_{00}^1 &= p_0 = 1-(1-p_0), \\ f_{00}^n &= \left(\prod_{i=0}^{n-2}(1-p_i)\right)p_{n-1} \qquad \text{for} \quad n>1. \end{aligned} \tag{6.10}$$

Rewriting (6.10) we obtain

$$f_{00}^n = \prod_{i=0}^{n-2}(1-p_i)[1-(1-p_{n-1})], \qquad n>1,$$

$$f_{00}^n = (1-p_0)(1-p_1)\cdots(1-p_{n-2}) - (1-p_0)(1-p_1)\cdots(1-p_{n-1}), \qquad n>1.$$

Let

$$u_n = \begin{cases} (1-p_0)(1-p_1)\cdots(1-p_n), & n \geq 0, \\ 1, & n=-1. \end{cases}$$

Then if we sum the f_{00}^n's we have

$$\sum_{n=1}^{m+1} f_{00}^n = \sum_{n=1}^{m+1}(u_{n-2}-u_{n-1}) = (1-u_0)+(u_0-u_1)+\cdots+(u_{m-1}-u_m)$$

or

$$\sum_{n=1}^{m+1} f_{00}^n = 1-u_m. \tag{6.11}$$

To complete our argument we need the following:

Lemma 6.1. *If* $0<p_i<1$, $i=0,1,2,\ldots,$ *then* $u_m = \prod_{i=0}^m(1-p_i)\to 0$ *as* $m\to\infty$ *if and only if* $\sum_{i=0}^\infty p_i = \infty$.

Proof. Assume $\sum_{i=0}^\infty p_i=\infty$. Since the series expansion for $\exp(-p_i)$ is an alternating series with terms decreasing in absolute value, we can write

$$1 - p_i < 1 - p_i + \frac{p_i^2}{2!} - \frac{p_i^3}{3!} + \cdots = \exp(-p_i), \qquad i = 0, 1, 2, \ldots. \tag{6.12}$$

Since (6.12) holds for all i, we obtain $\prod_{i=0}^{m}(1-p_i) < \exp(-\sum_{i=0}^{m} p_i)$. But, by assumption,

$$\lim_{m\to\infty} \sum_{i=0}^{m} p_i = \infty; \qquad \text{hence} \quad \lim_{m\to\infty} \prod_{i=0}^{m} (1-p_i) = 0.$$

To prove necessity observe that from a straightforward induction

$$\prod_{i=j}^{m} (1-p_i) > (1 - p_j - p_{j+1} - \cdots - p_m)$$

for any j and all $m = j+1, j+2, \ldots$. Assume now that $\sum_{i=1}^{\infty} p_i < \infty$; then $0 < \sum_{i=j}^{\infty} p_i < 1$ for some $j > 1$. Thus

$$\lim_{m\to\infty} \prod_{i=j}^{m} (1-p_i) > \lim_{m\to\infty} (1 - \sum_{i=j}^{m} p_i) > 0,$$

which contradicts $u_m \to 0$. ∎

Returning to (6.11) and applying Lemma 6.1, we deduce that $\sum_{n=1}^{\infty} f_{00}^n = 1$ if and only if $\sum_{i=0}^{\infty} p_i = \infty$, or state 0 is recurrent if and only if the sum of the p_i's diverges.

We insert parenthetically the remark that, given any set $\{a_1, a_2, \ldots\}$, such that $a_i > 0$ and $\sum_{i=1}^{\infty} a_i \le 1$, we can exhibit a set of p_i's for which $f_{00}^n = a_n$ in the Markov chain discussed above. We let

$$f_{00}^1 = p_0 = a_1,$$

$$f_{00}^2 = (1-p_0)p_1 = a_2,$$

and then determine that

$$p_1 = \frac{a_2}{1-a_1}.$$

Set

$$f_{00}^3 = (1-p_0)(1-p_1)p_2 = a_3,$$

and this implies that

$$p_2 = \frac{a_3}{1-a_1-a_2}.$$

Proceeding in this manner we can derive an explicit set of p_i's satisfying $0 < p_i < 1$.

7: More on Recurrence

The next theorem shows that if recurrence is certain for a specified state, then the state will be occupied infinitely often with probability 1. We define

$$Q_{ii} = \Pr\begin{Bmatrix}\text{a particle starting in state } i \text{ re-}\\ \text{turns infinitely often to state } i\end{Bmatrix}$$

Theorem 7.1. *State i is recurrent or transient according to whether $Q_{ii} = 1$ or 0, respectively.*

Proof. Let Q_{ii}^N be defined as

$$Q_{ii}^N = \Pr\begin{Bmatrix}\text{a particle starting in state } i \text{ re-}\\ \text{turns to state } i \text{ at least } N \text{ times}\end{Bmatrix}$$

We can write

$$Q_{ii}^N = \sum_{k=1}^{\infty} f_{ii}^k Q_{ii}^{N-1} = Q_{ii}^{N-1} f_{ii}^*, \qquad \text{where} \quad f_{ii}^* = \sum_{k=1}^{\infty} f_{ii}^k.$$

The validity of this formula rests on decomposing the event of Q_{ii}^N according to the first return time. Proceeding recursively, we obtain

$$Q_{ii}^N = f_{ii}^* Q_{ii}^{N-1} = (f_{ii}^*)^2 Q_{ii}^{N-2} = \cdots = [f_{ii}^*]^{N-1} Q_{ii}^1.$$

But $Q_{ii}^1 = f_{ii}^*$ by definition. Hence

$$Q_{ii}^N = [f_{ii}^*]^N.$$

Since $\lim_{N\to\infty} Q_{ii}^N = Q_{ii}$, we have $Q_{ii} = 1$ or 0 according to whether $f_{ii}^* = 1$ or < 1, respectively, or equivalently, according to whether state i is recurrent or transient.

Theorem 7.2. *If $i \leftrightarrow j$ and the class is recurrent, then*

$$f_{ij}^* = \sum_{n=1}^{\infty} f_{ij}^n = 1.$$

We omit the simple proof.

We define the symbol Q_{ij} to be

$$\Pr\{\text{particle starting in state } i \text{ visits state } j \text{ infinitely often}\}.$$

An immediate consequence of Theorem 7.2 is

Corollary 7.1. *If $i \leftrightarrow j$ and the class is recurrent, then $Q_{ij} = 1$.*

Proof. It is easy to see that

$$Q_{ij} = f_{ij}^* Q_{jj}.$$

Since j is a recurrent state, by Theorem 7.1, $Q_{jj}=1$. By Theorem 7.2, $f_{ij}^*=1$, hence $Q_{ij}=1$. ■

Elementary Problems

1. Determine the transition matrix $\|P_{jk}\|$ for the following Markov chains:

(a) Consider a sequence of tosses of a coin with the probability of "heads" p. At time n (after n tosses of the coin) the state of the process is the number of heads in the n tosses minus the number of tails.

(b) N black balls and N white balls are placed in two urns so that each urn contains N balls. At each step one ball is selected at random from each urn and the two balls interchange. The state of the system is the number of white balls in the first urn.

(c) A white rat is put into the maze shown. The rat moves through the compartments at random, i.e., if there are k ways to leave a compartment he chooses each of these with probability $1/k$. He makes one change of compartment at each instant of time. The state of the system is the number of the compartment the rat is in.

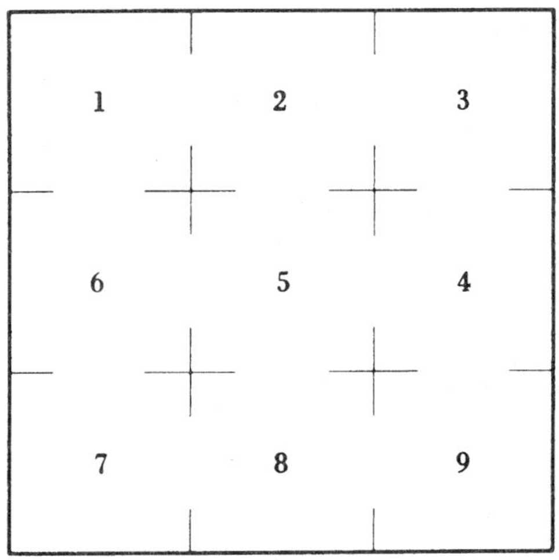

Solutions:

$$\text{(a)}\ P_{jk}=\Pr\left\{\begin{matrix}\text{number of heads minus number of tails}\\ =k\ \text{after}\ n+1\ \text{tosses}\,|\,\text{number of heads}\\ \text{minus number of tails}=j\ \text{after}\ n\ \text{tosses}\end{matrix}\right\}$$

$$=\begin{cases}p & \text{if}\quad k=j+1,\\ 1-p & \text{if}\quad k=j-1,\\ 0 & \text{otherwise,}\end{cases}$$

independent of n.

(b) $P_{jk} = \Pr\left\{\begin{matrix} k \text{ white balls in first urn after } n+1 \text{ interchanges} \mid j \\ \text{white balls in first urn after } n \text{ interchanges} \end{matrix}\right\}$

$$= \begin{cases} \left(\frac{j}{N}\right)^2 & \text{if } k = j-1, \quad j = 1, 2, \ldots, N, \\ 2\left(\frac{j}{N}\right)\left(\frac{N-j}{N}\right) & \text{if } k = j, \quad j = 0, 1, \ldots, N, \\ \left(1 - \frac{j}{N}\right)^2 & \text{if } k = j+1, \quad j = 0, 1, \ldots, N-1, \\ 0 & \text{otherwise,} \end{cases}$$

independent of n.

2. (a) Consider two urns A and B containing a total of N balls. An experiment is performed in which a ball is selected at random (all selections equally likely) at time t ($t = 1, 2, \ldots$) from among the totality of N balls. Then an urn is selected at random (A is chosen with probability p and B is chosen with probability q) and the ball previously drawn is placed in this urn. The state of the system at each trial is represented by the number of balls in A. Determine the transition matrix for this Markov chain.

(b) Assume that at time t there are exactly k balls in A. At time $t+1$ an urn is selected at random in proportion to its contents (i.e., A is chosen with probability k/N and B is chosen with probability $(N-k)/N$). Then a ball is selected from A with probability p or from B with probability q and placed in the previously chosen urn. Determine the transition matrix for this Markov chain.

(c) Now assume that at time $t+1$ a ball and an urn are chosen with probability depending on the contents of the urn (i.e., a ball is chosen from A with probability k/N or from B with probability $(N-k)/N$. Urn A is chosen with probability k/N or urn B is chosen with probability $(N-k)/N$). Determine the transition matrix of the Markov chain with states represented by the contents of A.

(d) Determine the equivalence classes in (a), (b), and (c).

Solution:

$$\text{(a)}\quad P_{ik} = \begin{cases} \frac{N-i}{N}p & \text{if } k = i+1, \\ \frac{i}{N}p + \frac{N-i}{N}q & \text{if } k = i, \qquad i = 0, 1, 2, \ldots, N. \\ \frac{i}{N}q & \text{if } k = i-1, \\ 0 & \text{otherwise,} \end{cases}$$

One equivalence class: $\{0, 1, 2, \ldots, N\}$.

$$\text{(b) } P_{ik} = \begin{cases} \dfrac{i}{N} q & \text{if } k = i+1, \\ \dfrac{i}{N} p + \dfrac{N-i}{N} q & \text{if } k = i, \qquad i = 1, 2, \ldots, N-1. \\ \dfrac{N-i}{N} p & \text{if } k = i-1, \\ 0 & \text{otherwise,} \end{cases}$$

$P_{ii} = 1$ if $i = 0$ and $i = N$. Equivalence classes are $\{0\}, \{N\}, \{1, 2, \ldots, N-1\}$.

$$\text{(c) } P_{ik} = \begin{cases} \dfrac{i^2}{N^2} + \dfrac{(N-i)^2}{N^2} & \text{if } k = i, \\ \dfrac{i(N-i)}{N^2} & \text{if } k = i+1 \text{ or } k = i-1, \\ 0 & \text{otherwise.} \end{cases}$$

Equivalence classes are $\{0\}, \{1, 2, \ldots, N-1\}, \{N\}$.

3. (a) A psychological subject can make one of two responses A_1 and A_2. Associated with these responses are a set of N stimuli $\{S_1, S_2, \ldots, S_N\}$. Each stimulus is conditioned to one of the responses. A single stimulus is sampled at random (all possibilities equally likely) and the subject responds according to the stimulus sampled. Reinforcement occurs at each trial with probability π $(0 < \pi < 1)$ independent of the previous history of the process. When reinforcement occurs, the stimulus sampled does not alter its conditioning state. In the contrary event the stimulus becomes conditioned to the other response. Consider the Markov chain whose state variable is the number of stimuli conditioned to response A_1. Determine the transition probability matrix of this M.C.

(b) A subject S can make one of three responses A_0, A_1, and A_2. The A_0 response corresponds to a guessing state. If S makes response A_1, the experiment reinforces the subject with probability π_1 and at the next trial S will make the same response. If no reinforcement occurs (probability $1 - \pi_1$), then at the next trial S passes to the guessing state. Similarly π_2 is the probability of reinforcement for response A_2. Again the subject remains in this state if reinforced and otherwise passes to the guessing state. When S is in the guessing state, he stays there for the next trial with probability $1 - c$ and with probabilities $c/2$ and $c/2$ makes responses A_1 and A_2 respectively. Consider the Markov chain of the state of the subject and determine its transition probability matrix.

Solutions: (a) $P_{ii} = \pi$; $P_{i,i+1} = ((N-i)/N)(1-\pi)$, $P_{i,i-1} = (i/N)(1-\pi)$, $P_{ij} = 0$ otherwise $(i, j = 1, 2, \ldots, N)$.

(b) $P_{00} = 1 - c$, $P_{0,1} = P_{0,2} = c/2$; $P_{10} = 1 - \pi_1$, $P_{11} = \pi_1$; $P_{20} = 1 - \pi_2$, $P_{22} = \pi_2$.

4. Determine the classes and the periodicity of the various states for a Markov chain with transition probability matrix

$$\text{(a)}\ \begin{Vmatrix} 0 & 0 & 1 & 0 \\ 1 & 0 & 0 & 0 \\ \frac{1}{2} & \frac{1}{2} & 0 & 0 \\ \frac{1}{3} & \frac{1}{3} & \frac{1}{3} & 0 \end{Vmatrix}, \qquad \text{(b)}\ \begin{Vmatrix} 0 & 1 & 0 & 0 \\ 0 & 0 & 0 & 1 \\ 0 & 1 & 0 & 0 \\ \frac{1}{3} & 0 & \frac{2}{3} & 0 \end{Vmatrix}.$$

5. Consider repeated independent trials of two outcomes S (success) or F (failure) with probabilities p and q, respectively. Determine the mean of the number of trials required for the first occurrence of the event SF (i.e., success followed by failure). Do the same for the event SSF and SFS.

6. The following sequential approach to estimating the size of a finite population, perhaps a wildlife population such as fish, is proposed. A member of the population is sampled at random, tagged and returned. Another is sampled, tagged and returned and so on, until a member is drawn that has been drawn before. When this occurs, say at trial T, we stop, (and possibly begin anew with a new kind of tag.) Based on the observed value of T we want to estimate the population size N.

Let X_n be the number of most recent successive untagged members observed without seeing a tagged one. Then $X_n = n$ for $n = 0, \ldots, T-1$ but $X_T = 0$, so that T is the first passage time $T = \min\{n \geq 1\colon X_n = 0\}$.

(a) For any fixed N, we claim that (X_n) is a success runs Markov chain. Specify the probabilities p_n and q_n.

(b) Compute $\Pr[T = t | X_0 = 0]$ for $t = 2, \ldots, N$. (See Elementary Problem 2 of Chapter 1.)

7. A component of a computer has an active life, measured in discrete units, that is a random variable T where $\Pr[T = k] = a_k$ for $k = 1, 2, \ldots$. Suppose one starts with a fresh component and each component is replaced by a new component upon failure. Let X_n be the age of the component in service at time n. Then (X_n) is a success runs Markov chain.

(a) Compute the probabilities p_i and q_i.

A "planned replacement" policy specifies replacing the component upon failure, or at time N, whichever occurs first. Then the time to replacement is $T^* = \min\{T, N\}$ where $T = \min\{n \geq 1\colon X_n = 0\}$.

(b) Compute $E[T^*]$ (See Elementary Problems 1, 2, and 3 of Chapter 1.)

8. Unknown to public health officials, a person with a highly contagious disease enters the population. During each period he either infects a new person which occurs with probability p, or his symptoms appear and he is discovered by public health officials, which occurs with probability $1 - p$. Compute the probability distribution of the number of infected but undiscovered people in the population at the time of first discovery of a carrier. Assume each infective behaves like the first.

Problems

1. Every stochastic $n \times n$ matrix corresponds to a Markov chain for which it is the one-step transition matrix. (By "Stochastic matrix" we mean $\mathbf{P} = \|P_{ij}\|$ with $0 \leq P_{ij} \leq 1$ and $\sum_j P_{ij} = 1$.) However, not every stochastic $n \times n$ matrix is the two-step transition matrix of a Markov chain. In particular, show that a 2×2 stochastic matrix is the two-step transition matrix of a Markov chain if and only if the sum of its principal diagonal terms is greater than or equal to 1.

2. Let $n_1, n_2, \ldots, n_k$ be positive integers with greatest common divisor d. Show that there exists a positive integer M such that $m \geq M$ implies there exist nonnegative integers $\{c_j\}_{j=1}^{k}$ such that

$$md = \sum_{j=1}^{k} c_j n_j .$$

(This result is needed for Problem 4 below.)

Hint: Let $A = \{n | n = c_1 n_1 + \cdots + c_k n_k, \{c_i\}$ nonnegative integers$\}$

$$\text{Let } B = \left\{ \begin{matrix} b_1 n_1 + \cdots + b_j n_j | n_1, n_2, \ldots, n_j \in A, \text{ and } b_1, \ldots, b_j \\ \text{are positive or negative integers} \end{matrix} \right\}.$$

Let d' be the smallest positive integer in B and prove that d' is a common divisor of all integers in A. Then show that d' is the greatest common divisor of all integers in A. Hence $d' = d$. Rearrange the terms in the representation $d = a_1 n_1 + \cdots + a_l n_l$ so that the terms with positive coefficients are written first. Thus $d = N_1 - N_2$ with $N_1 \in A$ and $N_2 \in A$. Let M be the positive integer, $M = N_2^2/d$. Every integer $m \geq M$ can be written as $m = M + k = N_2^2/d + k$, $(k = 0, 1, 2, \ldots)$, and $k = \delta N_2/d + b$ where $0 \leq b < N_2/d$ and $\delta = j$ when $j(N_2/d) \leq k < (j+1)N_2/d, j = 0, 1, 2, \ldots,$ so $md = N_2^2 + (\delta N_2/d + b)d = N_2(N_2 + \delta - b) + bN_1$.

3. Prove Theorem 4.1.
Hint: Let $P_{ii}^s > 0$, $P_{jj}^{n+s+m} \geq P_{ji}^n P_{ii}^s P_{ij}^m > 0$ for some $m > 0$ and $n > 0$. Since also $P_{ii}^{2s} > 0$, we have $P_{jj}^{n+2s+m} > 0$. Thus $d(j)$ divides $(n + 2s + m) - (n + s + m) = s$.

4. Prove Theorem 4.2 and Corollary 4.1.
Hint: By Problem 2 there exists N such that if $n \geq N$

$$P_{ii}^{nd(i)} = P_{ii}^{(c_1 n_1 + \cdots c_k n_k)} .$$

5. Given a finite aperiodic irreducible Markov chain, prove that for some n all terms of P^n are positive.

6. If j is a transient state prove that for all i

$$\sum_{n=1}^{\infty} P_{ij}^n < \infty .$$

Hint: Use relation (5.10).

7. Let a Markov chain contain r states. Prove the following:

(a) If a state k can be reached from j, then it can be reached in $r-1$ steps or less.

(b) If j is a recurrent state, there exists α $(0<\alpha<1)$ such that for $n>r$ the probability that first return to state j occurs after n transitions is $\leq \alpha^n$.

8. Consider a sequence of Bernoulli trials $X_1, X_2, X_3, \ldots$, where $X_n = 1$ or 0.

Assume

$$\Pr\{X_n = 1 | X_1, X_2, \ldots, X_{n-1}\} \geq \alpha > 0, \qquad n = 1, 2, \ldots.$$

Prove that

(a) $\Pr\{X_n = 1 \text{ for some } n\} = 1$,
(b) $\Pr\{X_n = 1 \text{ infinitely often}\} = 1$.

9. Let

$$\mathbf{P} = \begin{Vmatrix} 1-a & a \\ b & 1-b \end{Vmatrix}, \qquad 0 < a, \quad b < 1.$$

Prove

$$\mathbf{P}^n = \frac{1}{a+b}\begin{Vmatrix} b & a \\ b & a \end{Vmatrix} + \frac{(1-a-b)^n}{a+b}\begin{Vmatrix} a & -a \\ -b & b \end{Vmatrix}.$$

10. Consider a random walk on the integers such that $P_{i,i+1} = p$, $P_{i,i-1} = q$ for all integer i $(0 < p < 1, p+q=1)$. Determine P_{00}^n.

Answer:
$$P_{00}^{2m} = \binom{2m}{m} p^m q^m, \qquad P_{00}^{2m+1} = 0.$$

11. (Continuation) Find the generating function of $u_n = P_{00}^n$, i.e., determine $P(x) = \sum_{n=0}^{\infty} u_n x^n$.

Hint: Use the identity $\binom{2n}{n} = (-1)^n \binom{-\frac{1}{2}}{n} 2^{2n}$ where we define

$$\binom{a}{n} = \frac{a(a-1)\cdots(a-n+1)}{n!} \qquad \text{for any real } a.$$

Answer:
$$P(x) = (1-4pqx^2)^{-1/2}.$$

12. (Continuation) Determine the generating function of the recurrence time from state 0 to state 0.

Answer:
$$F(x) = 1 - \sqrt{(1-4pqx^2)}.$$

13. (Continuation) What is the probability of eventual return to the origin?

14. Suppose 2 distinguishable fair coins are tossed simultaneously and repeatedly. An account of the tallies of heads and tails are recorded. Consider the event E_n that at the nth toss the cumulative number of heads on both tallies are equal. Relate the event E_n to the recurrence time of a given state for a symmetric random walk on the integers.

15. Suppose $X_1, X_2, \ldots$ are independent with $\Pr\{X_k = +1\} = p$, $\Pr\{X_k = -1\} = q = 1 - p$ where $p \geq q$. With $S_0 = 0$, set $S_n = X_1 + \cdots + X_n$, $M_n = \max\{S_k: 0 \leq k \leq n\}$ and $Y_n = M_n - S_n$. If $T(a) = \min\{n: S_n = a\}$, show

$$\Pr\{\max_{0 \leq k \leq T(a)} Y_k < y\} = \begin{cases} \left(\dfrac{y}{1+y}\right)^a & \text{if } p = q = \dfrac{1}{2} \\ \left[\dfrac{\dfrac{p}{q} - \left(\dfrac{p}{q}\right)^{y+1}}{1 - \left(\dfrac{p}{q}\right)^{y+1}}\right]^a & \text{if } p \neq q. \end{cases}$$

Hint: The bivariate process (M_n, Y_n) is a random walk on the positive lattice. What is the probability that this random walk leaves the rectangle

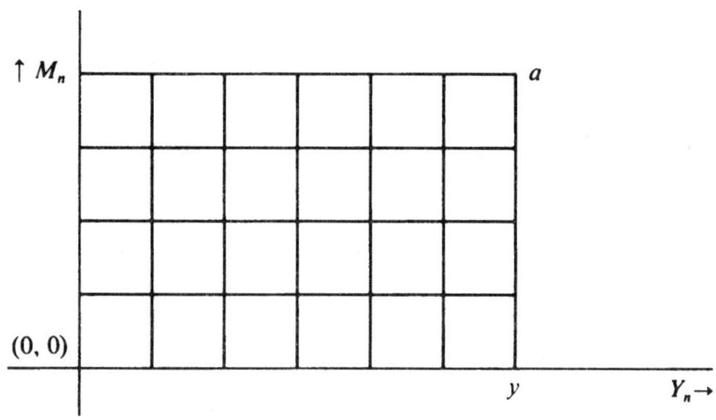

at the top?

16. (Continuation). Adding to the notation of Problem 15, let τ be the first time the partial sums S_n deviate y units from their maximum to date. That is, let $\tau = \min\{n: Y_n = y\}$. Show that $M_\tau = S_\tau + y$ has a geometric distribution $\Pr\{M_\tau \geq a\} = \theta^a$ for $a = 0, 1, \ldots$ and determine θ.

Hint: $M_\tau \geq a$ if and only if $\max_{0 \leq k \leq T(a)} Y_k < y$.

NOTES

Some aspects of the theory of Markov chains can be found in the last half of Feller [1].

The book by Kemeny and Snell [2] contains several enticing examples of Markov chains drawn from psychology, sociology, economics, biology, and elsewhere.

The most advanced treatment devoted to the analysis of the structure of Markov chains is that of Chung [3].

REFERENCES

1. W. Feller, "An Introduction to Probability Theory and Its Applications," Vol. 1, 2nd ed. Wiley, New York, 1957.
2. J. G. Kemeny and J. L. Snell, "Finite Markov Chains." Van Nostrand, Princeton, New Jersey, 1960.
3. K. L. Chung, "Markov Chains with Stationary Transition Probabilities." Springer-Verlag, Berlin, 1960.

Chapter 3

THE BASIC LIMIT THEOREM OF MARKOV CHAINS AND APPLICATIONS

The content of Sections 1–4 of this chapter is part of the standard apparatus of Markov chains that should be covered in every introductory course. However, the reader may wish to defer Section 2, a proof of the discrete renewal theorem, until Chapter 5 where renewal theory is covered in full generality.

The examples of Sections 5 and 6 are classical in the area of stochastic queueing models. Perhaps one of these sections might be skipped on first reading.

1: *Discrete Renewal Equation*

A key tool in the analysis of Markov chains is furnished by the following theorem.

Theorem 1.1. *Let $\{a_k\}$, $\{u_k\}$, $\{b_k\}$ be sequences indexed by $k = 0, \pm 1, \pm 2, \ldots$. Suppose that $a_k \geq 0$, $\sum a_k = 1$, $\sum |k|\, a_k < \infty$, $\sum k\, a_k > 0$, $\sum |b_k| < \infty$, and that the greatest common divisor of the integers k for which $a_k > 0$ is 1. If the renewal equation*

$$u_n - \sum_{k=-\infty}^{\infty} a_{n-k} u_k = b_n \qquad \text{for} \quad n = 0, \pm 1, \pm 2, \ldots$$

is satisfied by a bounded sequence $\{u_n\}$ of real numbers, then $\lim_{n\to\infty} u_n$ and $\lim_{n\to-\infty} u_n$ exist. Furthermore, if

$$\lim_{n\to-\infty} u_n = 0, \qquad \text{then} \qquad \lim_{n\to\infty} u_n = \frac{\sum_{k=-\infty}^{\infty} b_k}{\sum_{k=-\infty}^{\infty} k a_k} \tag{1.1}$$

In case $\sum_{k=-\infty}^{\infty} k a_k = \infty$, the limit relations are still valid provided we interpret

$$\frac{\sum_{k=-\infty}^{\infty} b_k}{\sum_{k=-\infty}^{\infty} k a_k} = 0.$$

The proof of this theorem in its general form as stated is beyond the scope of this book. Actually we will make use of this theorem only for the case where $\{a_k\}$, $\{u_k\}$, $\{b_k\}$ vanish for negative values of k, and $b_k \geq 0$. A proof of the theorem for this case is given in Section 2 below.

Remark 1.1. In the case where $a_{-k} = 0$, $b_{-k} = 0$, and $u_{-k} = 0$, for $k > 0$ the renewal equation becomes

$$u_n - \sum_{k=0}^{n} a_{n-k} u_k = b_n \qquad \text{for} \quad n = 0, 1, 2, \ldots .$$

Remark 1.2. (Reason for the term "renewal equation.") Consider a light bulb whose lifetime, measured in discrete units, is a random variable ξ, where

$$\Pr\{\xi = k\} = a_k \qquad \text{for} \quad k = 0, 1, 2, \ldots, \quad a_k > 0, \quad \sum_{k=0}^{\infty} a_k = 1.$$

Let each bulb be replaced by a new one when it burns out. Suppose the first bulb lasts until time ξ_1, the second bulb until time $\xi_1 + \xi_2$, and the nth bulb until time $\sum_{i=1}^{n} \xi_i$, where the ξ_i are independent identically distributed random variables each distributed as ξ. Let u_n denote the expected number of renewals (replacements) up to time n. If the first replacement occurs at time k then the expected number of replacements in the remaining time up to n is u_{n-k}, and summing over all possible values for k, we obtain

$$\begin{aligned} u_n &= \sum_{k=0}^{n} (1 + u_{n-k})\, a_k + 0 \sum_{k=n+1}^{\infty} a_k \\ &= \sum_{k=0}^{n} u_{n-k}\, a_k + \sum_{k=0}^{n} a_k \\ &= \sum_{k=0}^{n} a_{n-k}\, u_k + b_n, \end{aligned} \tag{1.2}$$

where

$$\sum_{k=0}^{n} a_k = b_n .$$

The reasoning behind (1.2) goes as follows. The term $1 + u_{n-k}$ is the expected number of replacements in time n if the first bulb fails at time k $(0 \leq k \leq n)$, the probability of this event being a_k. The second sum is the probability that the first bulb lasts a duration exceeding n time units. Taking account of the regenerative nature of the process, we may clearly evaluate u_n by decomposing the possible realizations by the event of the time of the first replacement.

The following theorem, the ergodic theorem for this particular case, describes the limiting behavior of P_{ij}^n as $n \to \infty$ for all i and j in the case of an aperiodic recurrent Markov chain. The proof is a simple application of the basic renewal limit theorem.

Theorem 1.2. (The basic limit theorem of Markov chains.)

(a) *Consider a recurrent irreducible aperiodic Markov chain. Let* $P_{ii}^n =$ *the probability of entering state* i *at the* nth *transition,* $n = 0, 1, 2, \ldots,$ *given that* $X(0) = i$ *(the initial state is* i*). By our earlier convention* $P_{ii}^0 = 1$. *Let* $f_{ii}^n =$ *probability of first returning to state* i *at the* nth *transition,* $n = 0, 1, 2, \ldots,$ where $f_{ii}^0 = 0$. *Thus*

$$P_{ii}^n - \sum_{k=0}^{n} f_{ii}^{n-k} P_{ii}^k = \begin{cases} 1 & \text{if } n = 0, \\ 0 & \text{if } n > 0. \end{cases}$$

[This is formula (5.1) of Chapter 2 derived earlier.] *Then*

$$\lim_{n\to\infty} P_{ii}^n = \frac{1}{\sum_{n=0}^{\infty} n f_{ii}^n}.$$

(b) *Under the same conditions as in* (a), $\lim_{n\to\infty} P_{ji}^n = \lim_{n\to\infty} P_{ii}^n$.

Proof. (a) Identify

$$\begin{aligned} u_n &= P_{ii}^n, \quad n \geq 0; \qquad u_n = 0, \quad n < 0; \\ a_n &= f_{ii}^n, \quad n \geq 0; \qquad a_n = 0, \quad n < 0; \end{aligned}$$

$$b_n = \begin{cases} 1 & n = 0, \\ 0 & n \neq 0; \end{cases}$$

and then apply Theorem 1.1.

(b) We use the recursion relation

$$P_{ji}^n = \sum_{v=0}^{n} f_{ji}^v P_{ii}^{n-v} \qquad i \neq j, \quad n \geq 0$$

[cf. formula (5.9) of Chapter 2]. More generally, let

$$y_n = \sum_{k=0}^{n} a_{n-k} x_k,$$

where

$$a_m \geq 0, \qquad \sum_{m=0}^{\infty} a_m = 1, \qquad \lim_{k\to\infty} x_k = c.$$

Under these circumstances we prove that $\lim_{n\to\infty} y_n = c$. In fact,

$$y_n - c = \sum_{k=0}^{n} a_{n-k} x_k - c \sum_{m=0}^{\infty} a_m = \sum_{k=0}^{n} a_{n-k}(x_k - c) - c \sum_{m=n+1}^{\infty} a_m.$$

For $\varepsilon > 0$ prescribed we determine $K(\varepsilon)$ so that $|x_k - c| < \varepsilon/3$ for all $k \geq K(\varepsilon)$.

$$y_n - c = \sum_{k=0}^{K(\varepsilon)} a_{n-k}(x_k - c) + \sum_{k=K(\varepsilon)+1}^{n} a_{n-k}(x_k - c) - c \sum_{m=n+1}^{\infty} a_m$$

and so

$$|y_n - c| \leq M \sum_{k=0}^{K(\varepsilon)} a_{n-k} + \frac{\varepsilon}{3} \sum_{h=K(\varepsilon)+1}^{n} a_{n-h} + |c| \sum_{m=n+1}^{\infty} a_m,$$

where

$$M = \max_{k \geq 0} |x_k - c|.$$

We choose $N(\varepsilon)$ so that $|c| \sum_{m=n+1}^{\infty} a_m < \varepsilon/3$ and

$$\sum_{k=0}^{K(\varepsilon)} a_{n-k} \equiv \sum_{m=n-K(\varepsilon)}^{n} a_m < \frac{\varepsilon}{3M} \qquad \text{for} \quad n \geq N(\varepsilon).$$

Then

$$|y_n - c| \leq \frac{\varepsilon}{3} + \frac{\varepsilon}{3} + \frac{\varepsilon}{3} = \varepsilon \qquad \text{for} \quad n \geq N(\varepsilon).$$

Now, setting

$$y_n = P_{ji}^n, \qquad a_n = f_{ji}^n, \qquad x_n = P_{ii}^n,$$

we have the desired result.

Remark 1.3. Let C be a recurrent class. Then $P_{ij}^n = 0$ for $i \in C$, $j \notin C$, and every n. Hence, once in C it is not possible to leave C. It follows that the submatrix $\|P_{ij}\|$, $i, j \in C$, is a transition probability matrix and the associated Markov chain is irreducible and recurrent. The limit theorem, therefore, applies verbatim to any aperiodic recurrent class.

Remark 1.4. If $a_n \to a$ as $n \to \infty$, it can be proved by elementary methods that

$$\lim_{n\to\infty} \frac{1}{n} \sum_{k=1}^{n} a_k = a. \tag{1.3}$$

Thus, if i is a member of a recurrent aperiodic class,

$$\lim_{n\to\infty} \frac{1}{n} \sum_{m=1}^{n} P_{ii}^m = \frac{1}{\sum_{n=0}^{\infty} n f_{ii}^n} = \frac{1}{m_i}, \tag{1.4}$$

where m_i is the mean recurrence time.

If i is a member of a recurrent periodic class with period d, one can show (see Problem 4 of Chapter 2) that $P_{ii}^m = 0$ if m is not a multiple of d (i.e., if $m \neq nd$ for any n), and that

$$\lim_{n\to\infty} P_{ii}^{nd} = \frac{d}{m_i}.$$

These last two results are easily combined with (1.3) to show that (1.4) also holds in the periodic case.

If $\lim_{n\to\infty} P_{ii}^n = \pi_i > 0$ for one i in an aperiodic recurrent class, then $\pi_j > 0$ for all j in the class of i. (The proof of this fact follows the method of Corollary 5.1 of Chapter 2 and will be omitted.) In this case, we call the class *positive recurrent* or *strongly ergodic*. If each $\pi_i = 0$ and the class is recurrent we speak of the class as *null recurrent* or *weakly ergodic*.

Theorem 1.3. *In a positive recurrent aperiodic class with states* $j = 0, 1, 2, \ldots,$

$$\lim_{n\to\infty} P_{jj}^n = \pi_j = \sum_{i=0}^{\infty} \pi_i P_{ij}, \qquad \sum_{i=0}^{\infty} \pi_i = 1$$

and the π's *are uniquely determined by the set of equations*

$$\pi_i \geq 0, \qquad \sum_{i=0}^{\infty} \pi_i = 1, \qquad \text{and} \qquad \pi_j = \sum_{i=0}^{\infty} \pi_i P_{ij}. \tag{1.5}$$

Any set $(\pi_i)_{i=0}^{\infty}$ satisfying (1.5) is called a *stationary probability distribution* of the Markov chain. We will expand on this concept in Chapter 11.

Proof. For every n and M, $1 = \sum_{j=0}^{\infty} P_{ij}^n \geq \sum_{j=0}^{M} P_{ij}^n$. Letting $n \to \infty$, and using Theorem 1.2, we obtain $1 \geq \sum_{j=0}^{M} \pi_j$ for every M. Thus, $\sum_{j=0}^{\infty} \pi_j \leq 1$. Now $P_{ij}^{n+1} \geq \sum_{k=0}^{M} P_{ik}^n P_{kj}$; if we let $n \to \infty$, we obtain $\pi_j \geq \sum_{k=0}^{M} \pi_k P_{kj}$. Next, since the left-hand side is independent of M, $M \to \infty$ gives

$$\pi_j \geq \sum_{k=0}^{\infty} \pi_k P_{kj}. \tag{1.6}$$

Multiplying by P_{ji}, then summing on j and using (1.6), yields $\pi_j \geq \sum_{k=0}^{\infty} \pi_k P_{kj}^2$ and then generally $\pi_j \geq \sum_{k=0}^{\infty} \pi_k P_{kj}^n$ for any n. Suppose strict inequality holds for some j. Adding these inequalities with respect to j, we have

$$\sum_{j=0}^{\infty} \pi_j > \sum_{j=0}^{\infty} \sum_{k=0}^{\infty} \pi_k P_{kj}^n = \sum_{k=0}^{\infty} \pi_k \sum_{j=0}^{\infty} P_{kj}^n = \sum_{k=0}^{\infty} \pi_k,$$

a contradiction. Thus, $\pi_j = \sum_{k=0}^{\infty} \pi_k P_{kj}^n$ for all n. Letting $n \to \infty$, since $\sum \pi_k$ converges and P_{kj}^n is uniformly bounded, we conclude that

$$\pi_j = \sum_{k=0}^{\infty} \pi_k \lim_{n\to\infty} P_{kj}^n = \pi_j \sum_{k=0}^{\infty} \pi_k \qquad \text{for every } j.$$

Thus, $\sum_{k=0}^{\infty} \pi_k = 1$ since $\pi_j > 0$ by positive recurrence.

Suppose $x = \{x_n\}$ satisfies the relations (1.5). Then

$$x_k = \sum_{j=0}^{\infty} x_j P_{jk} = \sum_{j=0}^{\infty} x_j P_{jk}^n,$$

and if we let $n \to \infty$ as before,

$$x_k = \sum_{j=0}^{\infty} x_j \lim_{n\to\infty} P_{jk}^n = \pi_k \sum_{j=0}^{\infty} x_j = \pi_k. \quad \blacksquare$$

Example. Consider the class of random walks whose transition matrices are given by

$$\mathbf{P} = \|P_{ij}\| = \begin{Vmatrix} 0 & 1 & 0 & \cdots\cdots \\ q_1 & 0 & p_1 & \cdots\cdots \\ 0 & q_2 & 0 & p_2 \cdots\cdots \\ \vdots & & & \end{Vmatrix}$$

(c.f. Example B, Chapter 2). This Markov chain has period 2. Nevertheless we investigate the existence of a stationary probability distribution, i.e., we wish to determine the positive solutions of

$$x_i = \sum_{j=0}^{\infty} x_j P_{ji} = p_{i-1}\, x_{i-1} + q_{i+1} x_{i+1}, \qquad i = 0, 1, \ldots, \tag{1.7}$$

under the normalization

$$\sum_{i=0}^{\infty} x_i = 1,$$

where $p_{-1} = 0$ and $p_0 = 1$, and thus $x_0 = q_1 x_1$. Using Equation (1.7) for $i = 1$, we could determine x_2 in terms of x_0. Equation (1.7) for $i = 2$ determines x_3 in terms of x_0, etc. It is immediately verified that

$$x_i = \frac{p_{i-1}\, p_{i-2} \cdots p_1}{q_i q_{i-1} \cdots q_1} x_0 = x_0 \prod_{k=0}^{i-1} \frac{p_k}{q_{k+1}}, \qquad i \geq 1,$$

is a solution of (1.7), with x_0 still to be determined. Now since

$$1 = x_0 + \sum_{i=1}^{\infty} x_0 \prod_{k=0}^{i-1} \frac{p_k}{q_{k+1}},$$

we have

$$x_0 = \frac{1}{1 + \sum_{i=1}^{\infty} \prod_{k=0}^{i-1} \frac{p_k}{q_{k+1}}}$$

and so

$$x_0 > 0 \quad \text{if and only if} \quad \sum_{i=1}^{\infty} \prod_{k=0}^{i-1} \frac{p_k}{q_{k+1}} < \infty .$$

In particular, if $p_k = p$ and $q_k = q = 1 - p$ for $k \geq 1$, the series

$$\sum_{i=1}^{\infty} \prod_{k=0}^{i-1} \frac{p_k}{q_{k+1}} = \frac{1}{p} \sum_{i=1}^{\infty} \left(\frac{p}{q}\right)^i$$

converges only when $p < q$.

2: *Proof of Theorem 1.1*

We prove Theorem 1.1 for the case where a_k, b_k, u_k all vanish when $k < 0$; b_k, $a_k \geq 0$ and $a_1 > 0$, $\sum_{k=0}^{\infty} a_k = 1$. The renewal equation then becomes

$$u_n - \sum_{k=0}^{n} a_{n-k} u_k = b_n \qquad \text{for} \quad n = 0, 1, 2, \ldots$$

or equivalently

$$u_n - \sum_{k=0}^{n} a_k u_{n-k} = b_n, \qquad n = 0, 1, 2, \ldots. \tag{2.1}$$

It is easily established inductively (by considering successive equations) that $u_k \geq 0$ for all k.

Since $\{u_n\}$ is by hypothesis a bounded sequence, $\lambda = \limsup_{n\to\infty} u_n$ is finite. Let $n_1 < n_2 < \cdots$ denote a subsequence for which $\lim_{j\to\infty} u_{n_j} = \lambda$. We prove that $\lim_{j\to\infty} u_{n_j - 1} = \lambda$ using the condition $a_1 > 0$. Suppose, to the contrary, that the last relation is not valid. It then follows from the definition of λ that there exists $\lambda' < \lambda$ such that $u_{n_j - 1} < \lambda'$ for an infinite number of j. We put $\varepsilon = [a_1(\lambda - \lambda')]/4$, $M = \sup_{n\geq 0} u_n$, and determine N such that

$$\sum_{k=0}^{n} a_k > 1 - \frac{\varepsilon}{M} \qquad \text{if} \quad n \geq N. \tag{2.2}$$

Let j be chosen so large that $n_j \geq N$ and

$$u_{n_j} > \lambda - \varepsilon, \qquad u_{n_j - 1} < \lambda' < \lambda, \qquad 0 \leq b_{n_j} < \varepsilon,$$
$$\text{and} \qquad u_n < \lambda + \varepsilon \qquad \text{for all} \quad n \geq n_j - N. \tag{2.3}$$

This is all possible by the very definition of λ and the determination of λ'.

From (2.1), (2.2), and (2.3), we have

$$u_{n_j} \le \sum_{k=0}^{n_j} a_k u_{n_j-k} + \varepsilon < \sum_{k=0}^{N} a_k u_{n_j-k} + M \sum_{k=N+1}^{n_j} a_k + \varepsilon$$

$$< \sum_{k=0}^{N} a_k u_{n_j-k} + 2\varepsilon \qquad \text{[use (2.2) and (2.3)]}$$

$$< (a_0 + a_2 + a_3 + \cdots + a_{N-1} + a_N)(\lambda + \varepsilon) + a_1\lambda' + 2\varepsilon \qquad \text{[use (2.3)]}$$

$$\le (1 - a_1)(\lambda + \varepsilon) + a_1\lambda' + 2\varepsilon < \lambda + 3\varepsilon - a_1(\lambda - \lambda') = \lambda - \varepsilon,$$

the last line resulting by the choice of ε. But this contradicts the first inequality in (2.3), and so $\lim_{j\to\infty} u_{n_j-1} = \lambda$.

Repeating the argument, we find that, for any integer $d \ge 0$,

$$\lim_{j\to\infty} u_{n_j-d} = \lambda. \tag{2.4}$$

Next, let $r_n = a_{n+1} + a_{n+2} + \cdots$; evidently $\sum_{k=0}^{\infty} ka_k = \sum_{n=0}^{\infty} r_n$, which is verified by summation by parts. (We do not postulate the convergence of the series $\sum r_n$.) Further, $a_1 = r_0 - r_1$, $a_2 = r_1 - r_2$, etc. Substituting into (2.1), we find

$$r_0u_n + r_1u_{n-1} + \cdots + r_nu_0 = r_0u_{n-1} + r_1u_{n-2} + \cdots + r_{n-1}u_0 + b_n, \qquad n = 1, 2, \ldots.$$

Setting $A_n = r_0u_n + \cdots + r_nu_0$, we may write this as

$$A_n = A_{n-1} + b_n, \qquad n = 1, 2, \ldots,$$

where $A_0 = r_0u_0 = (1 - a_0)u_0 = b_0$. It follows that $A_n = \sum_{i=0}^{n} b_i$. Now, since $r_n \ge 0$ and $u_n \ge 0$ for all n, we obtain for any fixed $N > 0$ and $j > 0$

$$r_0u_{n_j} + r_1u_{n_j-1} + \cdots + r_Nu_{n_j-N} \le A_{n_j} = \sum_{n=0}^{n_j} b_n.$$

Letting $j \to \infty$ leads to the relation $(r_0 + \cdots + r_N)\lambda \le \sum_{n=0}^{\infty} b_n$ or equivalently $\lambda \le \sum_0^\infty b_n \left(\sum_0^N r_n\right)^{-1}$.

Since $N > 0$ is arbitrary, it follows that

$$\lambda \le \frac{\sum_{n=0}^{\infty} b_n}{\sum_{n=0}^{\infty} r_n}. \tag{2.5}$$

Since $u_k \ge 0$ for all k, this proves the theorem in the case $\sum_{n=0}^{\infty} r_n = \infty$, for then $\lambda = \lim_{n\to\infty} u_n = 0$ as is clear from (2.5).

If $\sum_{n=0}^{\infty} r_n < \infty$, let $\mu = \liminf_{n\to\infty} u_n$. Reasoning as in the case of lim sup, we deduce that if $\lim_{j\to\infty} u_{n_j} = \mu$, then $\lim_{j\to\infty} u_{n_j-d} = \mu$ for each integer $d \geq 0$. We set $\sum_{n=N+1}^{\infty} r_n = g(N)$; then plainly $\lim_{N\to\infty} g(N) = 0$, and

$$\sum_{n=0}^{n_j} b_n \leq r_0 u_{n_j} + r_1 u_{n_j-1} + \cdots + r_N u_{n_j-N} + g(N)\cdot M.$$

Letting $j \to \infty$, we conclude that $\sum_{n=0}^{\infty} b_n \leq (r_0 + \cdots + r_N)\mu + g(N)M$.

Now, taking the limit as $N \to \infty$, we find

$$\sum_{n=0}^{\infty} b_n \leq \mu \sum_{n=0}^{\infty} r_n \qquad \text{or} \qquad \mu \geq \frac{\sum_{n=0}^{\infty} b_n}{\sum_{n=0}^{\infty} r_n}. \tag{2.6}$$

But (2.5) and (2.6), in conjunction, yield $\mu \geq \lambda$. On the other hand, by their definition $\mu \leq \lambda$. Thus $\mu = \lambda$, which means that $\lim_{n\to\infty} u_n$ exists and its value is

$$\lim_{n\to\infty} u_n = \frac{\sum_{n=0}^{\infty} b_n}{\sum_{n=0}^{\infty} r_n}.$$

For the case where $a_1 = 0$ but the greatest common divisor of those m for which $a_m > 0$ is 1, the proof can be carried through with the aid of Corollary 4.1 of Chapter 2 combined with the method above.

3: *Absorption Probabilities*

We have previously established (see Problem 6, Chapter 2) that if j is a transient state, then $P_{ij}^n \to 0$, and that if i, j are in the same aperiodic recurrent class, then $P_{ij}^n \to \pi_j \geq 0$. If i, j are in the same periodic recurrent class, the same conclusion holds if we replace P_{ij}^n by $n^{-1}\sum_{m=1}^{n} P_{ij}^m$. In order to complete the discussion of the limiting behavior of P_{ij}^n, it remains to consider the case where i is transient and j is recurrent.

If T is the set of all transient states, then consider

$$x_i^1 = \sum_{j\in T} P_{ij} \leq 1, \qquad i \in T,$$

and define recursively

$$x_i^n = \sum_{j\in T} P_{ij} x_j^{n-1}, \qquad n \geq 2, \quad i \in T.$$

Observe that x_i^n is just the probability that, starting from i, the state of the process stays in T for the next n transitions. Since $x_i^n \leq 1$ for all

$n \geq 1$ (they are probabilities), we may prove by induction that x_i^n is nonincreasing as a function of n. In fact

$$x_i^2 = \sum_{j \in T} P_{ij} x_j^1 \leq \sum_{j \in T} P_{ij} = x_i^1.$$

Now assuming that $x_j^n \leq x_j^{n-1}$ for all $j \in T$ we have

$$0 \leq x_i^{n+1} = \sum_{j \in T} P_{ij} x_j^n \leq \sum_{j \in T} P_{ij} x_j^{n-1} = x_i^n.$$

Therefore, $x_i^n \downarrow x_i$ i.e., x_i^n decreases to some limit x_i, and

$$x_i = \sum_{j \in T} P_{ij} x_j, \qquad i \in T. \tag{3.1}$$

It follows that if the only bounded solution of this set of equations is the zero vector $(0, 0, \ldots)$, then starting from any transient state absorption into a recurrent class occurs with probability one. In fact, it is clear that x_i $(i \in T)$ is the probability of never being absorbed into a recurrent class, starting from state i. Since this sequence is a bounded solution of (3.1) it follows that x_i is zero for all i.

Remark 3.1. If there are only a finite number of states, M, then there are no null states and not all states can be transient. In fact, since $\sum_{j=0}^{M-1} P_{ij}^n = 1$ for all n, it cannot happen that $\lim_{n\to\infty} P_{ij}^n = 0$ for all j.

The same argument restricted to recurrent classes shows that there are no null states. Let $C, C_1, C_2, \ldots$ denote recurrent classes. We define $\pi_i(C)$ as the probability that the process will be ultimately absorbed into the recurrent class C if the initial state is the transient state i. (Recall that once the process enters a recurrent class, it never leaves it.)

Let $\pi_i^n(C)$ = probability that the process will enter and thus be absorbed in C for the first time at the nth transition, given that the initial state is $i \in T$. Then

$$\begin{aligned} \pi_i(C) &= \sum_{n=1}^{\infty} \pi_i^n(C) \leq 1, \\ \pi_i^1(C) &= \sum_{j \in C} P_{ij}, \end{aligned} \tag{3.2}$$

$$\pi_i^n(C) = \sum_{j \in T} P_{ij} \pi_j^{n-1}(C), \qquad n \geq 2. \tag{3.3}$$

Rewriting (3.2) using (3.3) gives

$$\begin{aligned} \pi_i(C) = \pi_i^1(C) + \sum_{n=2}^{\infty} \pi_i^n(C) &= \pi_i^1(C) + \sum_{n=2}^{\infty} \sum_{j \in T} P_{ij} \pi_j^{n-1}(C) \\ &= \pi_i^1(C) + \sum_{j \in T} P_{ij} \sum_{n=2}^{\infty} \pi_j^{n-1}(C), \end{aligned}$$

$$\pi_i(C) = \pi_i^1(C) + \sum_{j \in T} P_{ij} \pi_j(C), \qquad i \in T. \tag{3.4}$$

Assuming the only *bounded* solution of the homogeneous set of equations

$$w_i = \sum_{j \in T} P_{ij} w_j, \qquad i \in T,$$

is the zero vector, then $\{\pi_i(C)\}$ is determined as the unique bounded solution of the system of equations (3.4). Moreover, either $\pi_i^1(C) > 0$ for some $i \in T$ or $\pi_i(C) = 0$ for every $i \in T$ and hence $\pi_i^n(C) = 0$ for all n.

Theorem 3.1. *Let $j \in C$ (C an aperiodic recurrent class). Then for $i \in T$, we have*

$$\lim_{n\to\infty} P_{ij}^n = \pi_i(C) \lim_{n\to\infty} P_{jj}^n = \pi_i(C)\pi_j .$$

Proof. Clearly $\pi_i^n(C) = \sum_{k \in C} \pi_{ik}^n(C)$ where $\pi_{ik}^n(C)$ represents the probability starting from state i of being absorbed at the nth transition into class C at state k. We have

$$\pi_i(C) = \sum_{\nu=1}^{\infty} \sum_{k \in C} \pi_{ik}^{\nu}(C) \le 1.$$

Therefore for any $\varepsilon > 0$ there exists a finite number of states $C' \subset C$ and an integer $N(\varepsilon) = N$ such that

$$\left|\pi_i(C) - \sum_{\nu=1}^{n} \sum_{k \in C'} \pi_{ik}^{\nu}(C)\right| < \varepsilon, \qquad \text{i.e.,} \quad \left|\sum_{\nu=1}^{\infty} \sum_{k \in C} \pi_{ik}^{\nu} - \sum_{\nu=1}^{n} \sum_{k \in C'} \pi_{ik}^{\nu}\right| < \varepsilon \tag{3.5}$$

for $n > N(\varepsilon)$. [Here we have abbreviated π_{ik}^{ν} for $\pi_{ik}^{\nu}(C)$.]

For $j \in C$ consider

$$P_{ij}^n - \sum_{\nu=1}^{n} \sum_{k \in C'} \pi_{ik}^{\nu} \pi_j .$$

Now by the usual recursion argument, which involves decomposing the events by the time of first entering some state in C, we obtain

$$P_{ij}^n = \sum_{\nu=1}^{n} \sum_{k \in C} \pi_{ik}^{\nu} P_{kj}^{n-\nu}, \qquad i \in T, \quad j \in C.$$

Combining these relations, we have

$$\begin{aligned}\left|P_{ij}^n - \left(\sum_{\nu=1}^{n} \sum_{k \in C'} \pi_{ik}^{\nu}\right)\pi_j\right| &= \left|\sum_{\nu=1}^{n} \sum_{k \in C'} \pi_{ik}^{\nu}(P_{kj}^{n-\nu} - \pi_j) + \sum_{\nu=1}^{n} \sum_{k \in C, k \notin C'} \pi_{ik}^{\nu} P_{kj}^{n-\nu}\right| \\ &\le \left|\sum_{\nu=1}^{N} \sum_{k \in C'} \pi_{ik}^{\nu}(P_{kj}^{n-\nu} - \pi_j)\right| \\ &\quad + \left|\sum_{\nu=N+1}^{n} \sum_{k \in C'} \pi_{ik}^{\nu}(P_{kj}^{n-\nu} - \pi_j)\right| + \sum_{\nu=1}^{n} \sum_{k \in C, k \notin C'} \pi_{ik}^{\nu} P_{kj}^{n-\nu}.\end{aligned}$$

But $P_{kj}^{n-\nu} \le 1$, $|P_{kj}^{n-\nu} - \pi_j| \le 2$, and $\lim_{n\to\infty} P_{kj}^{n-\nu} = \pi_j$ if C is aperiodic and $k \in C'$. Therefore, there exists $N' > N$ such that for $n > N'$, $|P_{kj}^{n-N} - \pi_j| < \varepsilon$ $(k \in C')$, so that for $n > N'$

$$\left|P_{ij}^n - \left(\sum_{\nu=1}^{n} \sum_{k \in C'} \pi_{ik}^\nu\right)\pi_j\right| \le \varepsilon + 2 \sum_{\nu=N+1}^{n} \sum_{k \in C'} \pi_{ik}^\nu + \sum_{\nu=1}^{n} \sum_{k \in C, k \notin C'} \pi_{ik}^\nu .$$

However, the choice of N and C' assures us that the right-hand side is $\le 4\varepsilon$. Then appealing to (3.5) and the above result, we obtain

$$|P_{ij}^n - \pi_i(C)\pi_j| \le 4\varepsilon + \varepsilon\pi_j \qquad \text{for} \quad n > N',$$

and therefore

$$\lim_{n\to\infty} P_{ij}^n = \pi_i(C)\pi_j. \quad \blacksquare$$

If C is periodic and $j \in C$, a similar proof may be used to show

$$\lim_{n\to\infty} \frac{1}{n} \sum_{m=1}^{n} P_{ij}^m = \pi_i(C)\pi_j .$$

We emphasize the fact that if i is a transient state and j is a recurrent state, then the limit of P_{ij}^n depends on both i and j. This is in sharp contrast with the case where i and j belong to the same recurrent class.

Example. (The gambler's ruin on $n+1$ states).

$$\begin{Vmatrix} 1 & 0 & 0 & 0 & \cdots & & & \\ q & 0 & p & 0 & \cdots & & & \\ 0 & q & 0 & p & \cdots & & & \\ \vdots & & & & & & & \\ & & & & \cdots & q & 0 & p \\ & & & & & 0 & 0 & 1 \end{Vmatrix}$$

We shall calculate $u_i = \pi_i(C_0)$ and $v_i = \pi_i(C_n)$, the probabilities that starting from i the process ultimately enters the absorbing (and therefore recurrent) states 0 and n, respectively. The system of equations (3.4) becomes

$$\begin{aligned} u_1 &= q \qquad + pu_2, \\ u_i &= qu_{i-1} + pu_{i+1}, \qquad 2 \le i \le n-2. \\ u_{n-1} &= qu_{n-2}, \end{aligned} \tag{3.6}$$

These are $n-1$ nonhomogeneous equations in $n-1$ unknowns. We try a solution of the form $u_r = x^r$. Substituting in the middle equations and removing common factors leads to

$$px^2 + q = x.$$

There are two solutions, $x=1$ and $x=q/p$. Thus the quantities $u_r=A+B(q/p)^r$, $r=1, 2, \ldots, n-1$, satisfy the middle equations of (3.6) for any values of A and B. We now determine A and B so that the first and last equations are fulfilled. (If $q=p$, the solution $x=1$ is a double root of $px^2+q=x$, and one then has to replace $(q/p)^r$ by r.) In the case $q \neq p$ this leads to the conditions

$$A+B\frac{q}{p}=q+p\left(A+B\frac{q^2}{p^2}\right)$$

or, simplifying,

$$A=1-B$$

and

$$A+B\left(\frac{q}{p}\right)^{n-1}=q\left(A+B\left(\frac{q}{p}\right)^{n-2}\right) \qquad \text{or} \qquad p^nA+q^nB=0.$$

Solving, we get

$$\mathrm{A}=\frac{q^n}{q^n-p^n}, \qquad B=\frac{-p^n}{q^n-p^n}.$$

Combining, we have

$$u_r=\frac{(q/p)^n-(q/p)^r}{(q/p)^n-1} \qquad \text{if } \frac{q}{p}\neq 1.$$

If $q=p$, we find similarly that $A=1$, $B=-1/n$ so that

$$u_r=\frac{n-r}{n} \qquad \text{when } p=q.$$

A similar calculation shows that

$$v_i=1-u_i,$$

which is to be expected, since it is evident that absorption into one of the classes C_0, C_n is certain.

Consider the gambler's ruin with an infinitely rich adversary. The equations for the probability of the gambler's ruin (absorption into 0) become

$$\begin{aligned} u_1 &= q \qquad +pu_2, \\ u_i &= qu_{i-1}+pu_{i+1}, \qquad i \geq 2. \end{aligned} \tag{3.7}$$

Again we find

$$u_i=A+B\left(\frac{q}{p}\right)^i \quad (q\neq p) \qquad \text{and} \qquad u_i=A+Bi \quad (q=p=\tfrac{1}{2})$$

If $q \geq p$ then the condition that u_i is bounded requires that $B=0$ and the first equation of (3.7) shows that $u_i \equiv 1$. If $q<p$ we find that $u_i=(q/p)^i$. In fact, a simple passage to the limit from the finite state gambler's ruin yields $u_1 = q/p$ and then it readily follows that $u_i = (q/p)^i$.

4: Criteria for Recurrence

We prove two theorems which will be useful in determining whether a given Markov chain is recurrent or transient and then we apply them to several examples.

Theorem 4.1. *Let $\mathfrak{P}$ be an irreducible Markov chain whose state space is labeled by the nonnegative integers. Then a necessary and sufficient condition that $\mathfrak{P}$ be transient (i.e., each state is a transient state) is that the system of equations*

$$\sum_{j=0}^{\infty} P_{ij} y_j = y_i, \qquad i \neq 0, \tag{4.1}$$

have a bounded nonconstant solution.

Proof. Let the transition matrix for $\mathfrak{P}$ be

$$\mathbf{P} = \|P_{ij}\| = \left\| \begin{matrix} P_{00} & P_{01} & \cdots \\ P_{10} & P_{11} & \cdots \\ \cdots & \cdots & \cdots \end{matrix} \right\|$$

and associate with it the new transition matrix

$$\tilde{\mathbf{P}} = \|\tilde{P}_{ij}\| = \left\| \begin{matrix} 1 & 0 & 0 & \cdots \\ P_{10} & P_{11} & P_{12} & \cdots \\ P_{20} & P_{21} & P_{22} & \cdots \\ \cdots & \cdots & \cdots & \cdots \end{matrix} \right\| \tag{4.2}$$

in which the zero state has been converted into an absorbing barrier while the transition probabilities governing the motion among the other states are unchanged. We denote the Markov chain with transition probability matrix (4.2) by $\tilde{\mathfrak{P}}$.

For the necessity, we shall assume that the process is transient and then exhibit a nonconstant bounded solution of (4.1).

Let $f_{i0}^* =$ probability of entering state 0 in some finite time, given that i is the initial state. Since the process $\mathfrak{P}$ is transient $f_{j0}^* < 1$ for some $j \neq 0$ or otherwise state 0 would be recurrent. (Prove this. Remember that all states in an irreducible Markov chain are simultaneously recurrent or nonrecurrent.) For the process $\tilde{\mathfrak{P}}$ clearly $\tilde{\pi}_0(C_0)=1$, $\tilde{\pi}_j(C_0)=f_{j0}^*<1$ for some $j\neq 0$, and $\tilde{\pi}_i(C_0)=\sum_{j=0}^{\infty}\tilde{P}_{ij}\tilde{\pi}_j(C_0)$ for all i. Hence $\tilde{\pi}_i(C_0)=\sum_{j=0}^{\infty}P_{ij}\tilde{\pi}_j(C_0)$ for $i\neq 0$ and thus $y_j=\tilde{\pi}_j(C_0)$ $(j=0,1,2,\ldots)$ is the desired bounded nonconstant solution.

Now assume that we have a bounded solution $\{y_i\}$ of (4.1). Then

$$\sum_{j=0}^{\infty}\tilde{P}_{ij}y_j=y_i \qquad \text{for all } i\geq 0,$$

and iterating we have for all $i\geq 0$ and all $n\geq 1$

$$\sum_{j=0}^{\infty}\tilde{P}_{ij}^n y_j=y_i.$$

If the chain is recurrent, then

$$\lim_{n\to\infty}\tilde{P}_{i0}^n=1,$$

and

$$\sum_{j\neq 0}\tilde{P}_{ij}^n y_j\leq M(1-\tilde{P}_{i0}^n)\to 0 \quad \text{as} \quad n\to\infty$$

where M is a bound for $\{y_j\}$. Hence

$$y_i=\sum_{j\neq 0}\tilde{P}_{ij}^n y_j+\tilde{P}_{i0}^n y_0\to y_0.$$

Thus $y_i=y_0$ for all i and $\{y_j\}$ is constant.

Theorem 4.2. *In an irreducible Markov chain a sufficient condition for recurrence is that there exists a sequence $\{y_i\}$ such that*

$$\sum_{j=0}^{\infty}P_{ij}y_j\leq y_i \qquad \text{for} \quad i\neq 0 \quad \text{with} \quad y_i\to\infty. \tag{4.3}$$

Proof. Using the same notation as in the previous theorem, we have

$$\sum_{j=0}^{\infty}\tilde{P}_{ij}y_j\leq y_i \qquad \text{for all } i.$$

Since $z_i=y_i+b$ satisfies (4.3), we may assume $y_i>0$ for all $i\geq 0$. Iterating the preceding inequality, we have

$$\sum_{j=0}^{\infty}\tilde{P}_{ij}^m y_j\leq y_i.$$

Given $\varepsilon > 0$ we choose $M(\varepsilon)$ such that $1/y_i \leq \varepsilon$ for $i \geq M(\varepsilon)$. Now

$$\sum_{j=0}^{M-1} \tilde{P}_{ij}^m y_j + \sum_{j=M}^{\infty} \tilde{P}_{ij}^m y_j \leq y_i$$

and so

$$\sum_{j=0}^{M-1} \tilde{P}_{ij}^m y_j + \min_{r \geq M} \{y_r\} \sum_{j=M}^{\infty} \tilde{P}_{ij}^m \leq y_i .$$

Since

$$\sum_{j=0}^{\infty} \tilde{P}_{ij}^m = 1$$

we have

$$\sum_{j=0}^{M-1} \tilde{P}_{ij}^m y_j + \min_{r \geq M} \{y_r\} \left(1 - \sum_{j=0}^{M-1} \tilde{P}_{ij}^m\right) \leq y_i .$$

As observed in the proof of the preceding theorem,

$$\lim_{n \to \infty} \tilde{P}_{ij}^n = 0 \qquad \text{for} \quad j \neq 0.$$

Thus, passing to the limit as $m \to \infty$, we obtain for each fixed i

$$\tilde{\pi}_i(C_0) y_0 + \min_{r \geq M} \{y_r\} (1 - \tilde{\pi}_i(C_0)) \leq y_i$$

or

$$1 - \tilde{\pi}_i(C_0) \leq \frac{1}{\min\limits_{r \geq M} \{y_r\}} (y_i - \tilde{\pi}_i(C_0) y_0) \leq \varepsilon K,$$

where

$$K = y_i - \tilde{\pi}_i(C_0) y_0 .$$

Since ε was arbitrary and $\tilde{\pi}_i(C_0) \leq 1$ we have $\tilde{\pi}_i(C_0) = 1$ for each i, proving the original process recurrent. ∎

5: *A Queueing Example*

Let us consider the queueing model discussed in Chapter 2 (Example C). The transition matrix is

$$\|P_{ij}\| = \left\| \begin{matrix} a_0 & a_1 & a_2 & a_3 & \cdots \\ a_0 & a_1 & a_2 & a_3 & \cdots \\ 0 & a_0 & a_1 & a_2 & \cdots \\ 0 & 0 & a_0 & a_1 & \cdots \\ \cdots & \cdots & \cdots & \cdots & \cdots \end{matrix} \right\|, \qquad \text{where} \quad a_k > 0 \quad \text{and} \quad \sum_{k=0}^{\infty} a_k = 1.$$

(Actually, in the subsequent analysis, we only use the properties $0 < a_0 < 1$ and $a_0 + a_1 < 1$ which guarantee that this Markov chain is irreducible.) If $\sum_{k=0}^{\infty} k a_k > 1$ we show that the system of equations $\sum_{j=0}^{\infty} P_{ij} y_j = y_i$, $i \neq 0$, admits a nonconstant bounded solution, and so by Theorem 4.1 the process will be transient. Letting $y_j = \xi^j$, the above system of equations takes the form

$$\sum_{j=0}^{\infty} P_{ij}\xi^j = \sum_{j=i-1}^{\infty} a_{j-i+1}\xi^j = \xi^i$$

or

$$\sum_{j=i-1}^{\infty} a_{j-i+1}\xi^{j-i+1} = \xi = \sum_{k=0}^{\infty} a_k \xi^k = f(\xi), \qquad i \neq 0.$$

Now $f(0) = a_0 > 0$ and $f(1) = \sum_{k=0}^{\infty} a_k = 1$, so that if $f'(1) = \sum_{k=0}^{\infty} k a_k > 1$ then there exists a ξ_0, $0 < \xi_0 < 1$, such that $f(\xi_0) = \xi_0$. This is easily seen from Fig. 1. The vector $y_j = \xi_0^j$, $i = 0, 1, \ldots$, is the desired bounded solution and is clearly nonconstant. If $\sum k a_k \leq 1$ then, applying Theorem 4.2 above with $y_j = j$, we have, provided $i \neq 0$,

$$\begin{aligned}
\sum_{j=0}^{\infty} P_{ij} j &= \sum_{j=i-1}^{\infty} a_{j-i+1} j \\
&= \sum_{j=i-1}^{\infty} a_{j-i+1}(j - i + 1) + i - 1 \\
&= \sum_{k=0}^{\infty} k a_k - 1 + i \\
&\leq i.
\end{aligned}$$

Therefore if $\sum k a_k \leq 1$, the process is recurrent.

In order to ascertain whether the process $\mathfrak{P}$ is null recurrent or positive recurrent we first deal with the following auxiliary problem of some independent interest.

Let $X_1, X_2, X_3, \ldots$ denote a sequence of independent identically distributed random variables taking on the values $-1, 0, 1, 2, \ldots$ with

$$\Pr\{X_i = k\} = b_k, \qquad k = -1, 0, 1, 2, \ldots, \quad b_{-1} > 0,$$

and let $S_n = X_1 + X_2 + \cdots + X_n$. Define Z as the value of n for which S_n first becomes negative and suppose that

$$\Pr\{Z = k\} = \gamma_k, \qquad k = 1, 2, 3, \ldots. \tag{5.1}$$

Let

$$U(s) = \sum_{k=0}^{\infty} \gamma_k s^k \qquad (\gamma_0 = 0) \tag{5.2}$$

denote the generating function of (5.1). If $T_n^{(r)} = r + S_n$ (r is a nonnegative integer), let $Z^{(r)}$ be the random variable equal to the first value of n for which $T_n^{(r)} < 0$. Since each $X_i \geq -1$ we infer easily that $Z^{(r)} = Z_1 + Z_2$

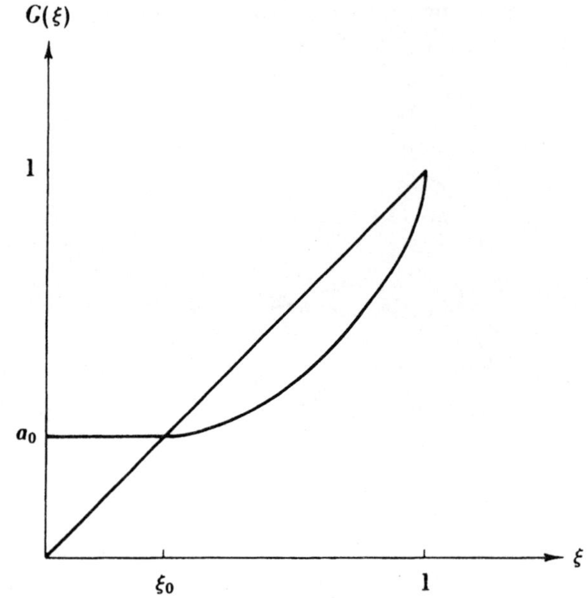

FIG. 1

$+ \cdots + Z_{r+1}$, where the Z_i are independent and identically distributed according to (5.1). The generating function of $Z^{(r)}$ is clearly $[U(s)]^{r+1}$. Let $\gamma_m^{(r+1)}$ denote the coefficient of s^m in $U(s)^{r+1}$.

Finally, we set

$$G(s) = \frac{b_{-1}}{s} + b_0 + b_1 s + b_2 s^2 + \cdots.$$

Our aim is to determine $U(s)$ in terms of $G(s)$. To this end we write the usual renewal relations

$$\gamma_1 = b_{-1}, \qquad \gamma_k = \sum_{j=0}^{\infty} b_j \gamma_{k-1}^{(j+1)}, \qquad k \geq 2. \tag{5.3}$$

The first of these relations is obvious. As for the second, the event $\{S_n \geq 0, n = 1, \ldots, k-1; S_k = -1\}$ is the union of the disjoint events $\{X_1 = j; X_2 + \cdots + X_n + j \geq 0, n = 2, \ldots, k-1; X_2 + \cdots + X_k + j = -1\}$, $j = 0, 1, \ldots$, whose probabilities are clearly equal to $b_j \gamma_{k-1}^{(j+1)}$, since the X_i are independent and identically distributed. By the law of total probabilities (5.3) results. Passing to generating functions on the basis of (5.3), we have

$$\begin{aligned}U(s) &= b_{-1}s + \sum_{n=2}^{\infty}\left(\sum_{j=0}^{\infty} b_j\gamma_{n-1}^{(j+1)}\right)s^n\\ &= b_{-1}s + s\sum_{j=0}^{\infty} b_j\left(\sum_{n=2}^{\infty}\gamma_{n-1}^{(j+1)}s^{n-1}\right)\\ &= b_{-1}s + s\sum_{j=0}^{\infty} b_j[U(s)]^{j+1}\\ &= b_{-1}s + sU(s)\left[G(U(s)) - \frac{b_{-1}}{U(s)}\right] \qquad \text{for} \quad 0 < s \le 1\\ &= sU(s)G(U(s)).\end{aligned}$$

Now $U(s)$ is continuous and strictly increasing for $s \in [0, 1]$, while $U(0) = 0$. Hence, for $0 < s \le 1$, $U(s)$ satisfies $G(U(s)) = 1/s$. But

$$G''(s) = \frac{2b_{-1}}{s^3} + 2b_2 + 6b_3 s + 12b_4 s^2 + \cdots > 0 \qquad \text{for} \quad s > 0,$$

so that $G(s)$ is a convex function, while from the definition of $G(s)$ it follows that $\lim_{s\downarrow 0} G(s) = +\infty$ and $G(1) = 1$. A glance at the figure below shows that the equation $G(x) = 1/s$ can have at most two positive solutions for each $s \in [0, 1]$. Since $\lim_{s\downarrow 0} U(s) = 0$ and $U(s)$ is strictly increasing in $[0, 1]$, we see that $U(s)$ must be the smaller of the two solutions of $G(x) = 1/s$, if there are two.

We now investigate the conditions under which $\sum_{k=0}^{\infty} \gamma_k = 1$ or <1; the following two cases arise.

Case 1. $G'(1) > 0$. $G'(1) > 0$ is equivalent to $b_{-1} < \sum_{n=0}^{\infty} nb_n$ and Fig.2 clearly shows that $U(1) = \sum_{k=0}^{\infty} \gamma_k = \xi_0 < 1$. Therefore the probability of the event $\{S_n \ge 0 \text{ for all } n\}$ is strictly positive.

Case 2. $G'(1) \le 0$. $G'(1) \le 0$ is equivalent to $b_{-1} \ge \sum_{n=0}^{\infty} nb_n$ and here we have $\sum_{k=0}^{\infty} \gamma_k = U(1) = 1$. Now, for $0 < s \le 1$, $G'(U(s))U'(s) = -1/s^2$ so that in Case 2, $U(s) \to 1$ when $s \to 1$ (see Figure 3). This implies that if $G'(1) < 0$, i.e., if

$$b_{-1} > \sum_{n=0}^{\infty} nb_n,$$

then

$$E(Z) = \sum_{n=0}^{\infty} n\gamma_n = U'(1) = \frac{-1}{G'(1)} < \infty,$$

and if $G'(1) = 0$, i.e., if

$$b_{-1} = \sum_{n=0}^{\infty} nb_n,$$

then

$$E(Z) = \sum_{n=0}^{\infty} n\gamma_n = U'(1) = \infty.$$

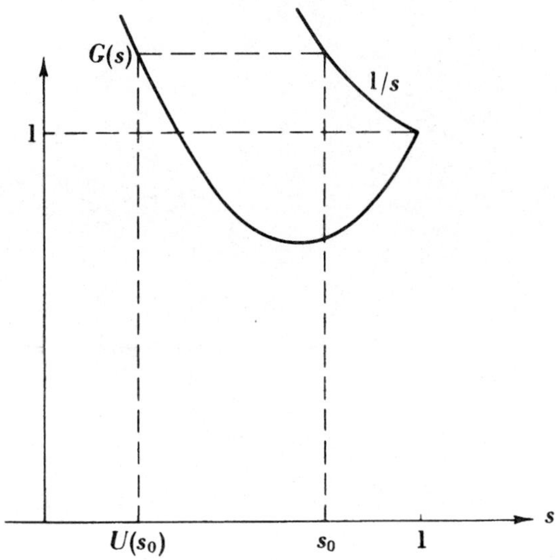

FIG. 2

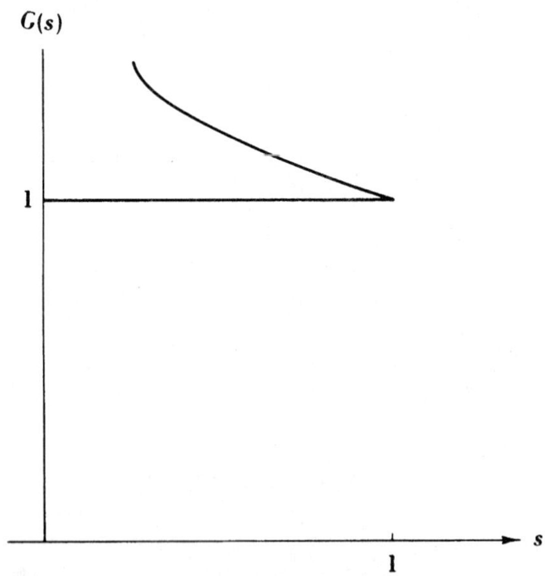

FIG. 3

Referring again to the queueing process, we identify the b's and the a's by $a_k = b_{k-1}$ and let Z_{ij} = length of time (number of transitions) required, starting in state i, to reach state $j < i$ for the first time. A little reflection reveals that $Z_{i,i-1}$ is precisely the random variable Z examined above whose generating function $U(s)$ was determined. Since

$$\sum_{i=0}^{\infty} a_i = 1,$$

we have

$$\left(b_{-1} > \sum_{n=0}^{\infty} nb_n\right) \leftrightarrow \left(a_0 > \sum_{n=0}^{\infty} na_{n+1}\right) \leftrightarrow \left(1 > \sum_{n=0}^{\infty} na_n\right)$$

and similarly

$$\left(b_{-1} = \sum_{n=0}^{\infty} nb_n\right) \leftrightarrow \left(a_0 = \sum_{n=0}^{\infty} na_{n+1}\right) \leftrightarrow \left(1 = \sum_{n=0}^{\infty} na_n\right).$$

Hence $E(Z_{i,i-1}) = \mu < \infty$ if $\sum_{n=0}^{\infty} na_n < 1$ and $E(Z_{i,i-1}) = \mu = \infty$ if $\sum na_n = 1$. Since we are permitted to move back only one step at a time (the process is "continuous" in this respect), we have

$$Z_{i,j} = Z_{i,i-1} + Z_{i-1,i-2} + \cdots + Z_{j+1,j}, \qquad j < i,$$

and therefore $E(Z_{i,j}) = (i-j)\mu$ and in particular $E(Z_{i,0}) = i\mu$.

Let us now consider the mean recurrence time of state zero. We notice first that the probability of the recurrence time equalling 1 is just a_0, the transition probability P_{00}. Now, the sample functions which start at 0 and first return to 0 in two or more transitions can be grouped according to the state i occupied at the first transition. The average recurrence time for such a group is precisely 1 plus the average time required to reach state 0 from state i. This decomposition, in conjunction with the Markov property, yields the following expression for the average recurrence time:

$$\begin{aligned}\sum_{n=0}^{\infty} nf_{00}^n &= E(\text{recurrence time}) \\ &= a_0 + \sum_{i=1}^{\infty} a_i[E(Z_{i,0}) + 1] = 1 + \sum_{i=1}^{\infty} a_i E(Z_{i,0}) \\ &= 1 + \sum_{i=1}^{\infty} i\mu a_i = 1 + \mu \sum_{i=0}^{\infty} ia_i.\end{aligned}$$

Thus

$$\sum_{n=0}^{\infty} nf_{00}^n < \infty \qquad \text{if} \quad \mu < \infty$$

i.e., provided

$$\sum_{i=0}^{\infty} ia_i < 1,$$

and

$$\sum_{n=0}^{\infty} nf_{00}^n = \infty \qquad \text{if } \mu = \infty,$$

or what is the same if

$$\sum_{i=0}^{\infty} ia_i = 1.$$

Summing up, we have

$$\sum_{n=0}^{\infty} na_n < 1 \Rightarrow \text{positive recurrent},$$

$$\sum_{n=0}^{\infty} na_n = 1 \Rightarrow \text{null recurrent}, \tag{5.4}$$

and

$$\sum_{n=0}^{\infty} na_n > 1 \Rightarrow \text{transient}.$$

These conclusions are rather intuitive. The expression $\sum_{n=0}^{\infty} na_n$ is the mean number of customers arriving during a service period. Thus, if $\sum_{n=0}^{\infty} na_n > 1$, then on an average more people arrive than are served in each period. Therefore, we could expect the waiting line to grow beyond all bounds. On the other hand, if $\sum_{n=0}^{\infty} na_n < 1$ then the state of the process approaches a stationary state. The evaluation of the stationary distribution is rather complicated (see Chapter 18).

6: Another Queueing Model

The state of the process is the length of the waiting line where, in each unit of time, one person arrives and k persons are served with probability $a_k > 0$, $k = 0, 1, 2, \ldots$ if there are at least k in the waiting line. The transition probability matrix may be easily evaluated as

$$\|P_{ij}\| = \left\| \begin{matrix} \sum_{i=1}^{\infty} a_i & a_0 & 0 & 0 & \cdots \\ \sum_{i=2}^{\infty} a_i & a_1 & a_0 & 0 & \\ \sum_{i=3}^{\infty} a_i & a_2 & a_1 & a_0 & \\ \vdots & \vdots & \vdots & \vdots & \end{matrix} \right\|$$

We show that there exists a stationary distribution if $\sum_{k=0}^{\infty} ka_k > 1$ so that in this case the process is positive recurrent. A stationary distribution is expected to exist since the average number of customers served is $\sum ka_k$ while a single new customer arrives.

Consider the equations $\sum_{i=0}^{\infty} \xi_i P_{ij} = \xi_j$ and let $\xi_i = \xi^i$. Then

$$\sum_{i=j-1}^{\infty} \xi^i a_{i-j+1} = \xi^j \qquad \text{for } j \geq 1; \qquad \text{i.e.,} \quad \sum_{i=j-1}^{\infty} \xi^{i-j+1} a_{i-j+1} = \xi,$$

which by a change of variable reduces to

$$\sum_{k=0}^{\infty} a_k \xi^k = \xi.$$

If ξ $(0 < \xi < 1)$ satisfies these equations, then for $j = 0$ we have

$$\begin{aligned}
\sum_{i=0}^{\infty} P_{i0} \xi^i &= \sum_{i=0}^{\infty} \left(\sum_{k=i+1}^{\infty} a_k \right) \xi^i \\
&= \sum_{k=1}^{\infty} \sum_{i=0}^{k-1} a_k \xi^i \qquad \text{(rearranging the order of summation)} \\
&= \sum_{k=1}^{\infty} a_k \left(\frac{1 - \xi^k}{1 - \xi} \right) = \frac{1}{1 - \xi} \left(1 - a_0 - \sum_{k=1}^{\infty} a_k \xi^k \right) \\
&= \frac{1}{1 - \xi} (1 - a_0 - (\xi - a_0)) = 1,
\end{aligned}$$

so that the equations are satisfied for $j = 0$ as well.

We consider $f(\xi) = \sum_{k=0}^{\infty} a_k \xi^k$. Since $f(0) = a_0 > 0$ and $f(1) = 1$, if $f'(1) = \sum_{k=0}^{\infty} ka_k > 1$ then there exists ξ_0 satisfying $0 < \xi_0 < 1$ and $f(\xi_0) = \xi_0$ (see Fig. 4). The values $\pi_i = (1 - \xi_0)\xi_0^i$, which sum to 1, are

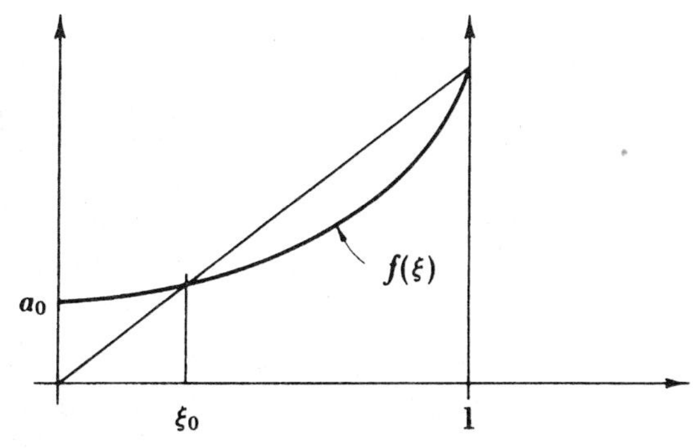

FIG. 4

therefore the stationary probabilities of the state of the process. In particular, the long-run probability that the line is empty is $1-\xi_0$.

Now the system of equations $\sum_{i=0}^{\infty} \xi_i P_{ij} = \xi_j$, $j \neq 0$, is identical with the system $\sum_{j=0}^{\infty} \tilde{P}_{ij}\xi_j = \xi_i$, $i \neq 0$, where the $\tilde{P}_{ij}$ are now the elements of the matrix from Section 5. In the case $\sum_{k=0}^{\infty} ka_k \leq 1$ the $\tilde{P}$ process (as we have seen) is recurrent and hence the latter system has no nonconstant bounded solution. Therefore, if $\sum ka_k \leq 1$ the system $\sum_{j=0}^{\infty} \eta_i P_{ij} = \eta_j$ admits no bounded solution and therefore, in particular, no stationary distribution exists so that the process is either null recurrent or transient. We now prove that the system of equations

$$\sum_{j=0}^{\infty} P_{ij} y_j = y_i, \qquad i \neq 0, \tag{6.1}$$

has a nonconstant bounded solution if and only if $\sum ka_k < 1$, so that the process will be transient if and only if $\sum ka_k < 1$, and therefore must be null recurrent in the case $\sum_{k=0}^{\infty} ka_k = 1$. Since (6.1) admits a constant solution we may let $y_0 = 0$. Then (6.1) reduces to

$$\begin{aligned}
a_2 y_0 + a_1 y_1 + a_0 y_2 &= y_1 \\
a_3 y_0 + a_2 y_1 + a_1 y_2 + a_0 y_3 &= y_2 \\
&\cdots\cdots\cdots \\
a_{n+1} y_0 + a_n y_1 + \quad \cdots \quad + a_1 y_n + a_0 y_{n+1} &= y_n \\
&\cdots\cdots\cdots
\end{aligned}$$

Multiplying the ith equation by s^{i+1} and summing, we obtain, after letting

$$Y(s) = \sum_{k=0}^{\infty} y_k s^k, \qquad A(s) = \sum_{k=0}^{\infty} a_k s^k,$$

and recognizing the convolution product, that

$$Y(s)A(s) - sa_0 y_1 = sY(s) \qquad \text{or} \qquad Y(s) = \frac{sa_0 y_1}{A(s) - s}, \tag{6.2}$$

provided $A(s) \neq s$. Since $A(0) = a_0$ and $A(1) = 1$, $A(s) = s$ for some s such that $0 < s < 1$ if $A'(1) = \sum_{k=0}^{\infty} ka_k > 1$. Therefore, $Y(s)$ cannot have bounded coefficients in this case since $Y(s)$ would then converge for every $s \in [0, 1)$. This implies that for $\sum_{k=0}^{\infty} ka_k > 1$ the process is recurrent.

From the strict convexity of $A(s)$, i.e., $A''(s) > 0$, it follows that $A(s) \neq s$ for $0 \leq s < 1$ if $A'(1) = \sum ka_k \leq 1$ (see Fig. 5). Consider the case $\sum ka_k \leq 1$:

$$A(s)-s=(1-s)\left[1-\frac{1-A(s)}{1-s}\right]$$

$$=(1-s)\left[1-(1-A(s))\sum_{k=0}^{\infty}s^k\right]$$

$$=(1-s)\left[1-\sum_{n=0}^{\infty}\left(1-\sum_{i=0}^{n}a_i\right)s^n\right]$$

(rearranging orders of summations)

$$=(1-s)\left[1-\sum_{n=0}^{\infty}\left(\sum_{i=n+1}^{\infty}a_i\right)s^n\right]$$

$$=(1-s)[1-W(s)],\qquad W(s)=\sum_{n=0}^{\infty}w_ns^n,$$

where

$$w_n=\sum_{i=n+1}^{\infty}a_i>0$$

and

$$\sum_{n=0}^{\infty}w_n=\sum_{n=0}^{\infty}\left(\sum_{i=n+1}^{\infty}a_i\right)=\sum_{k=0}^{\infty}ka_k\le 1.$$

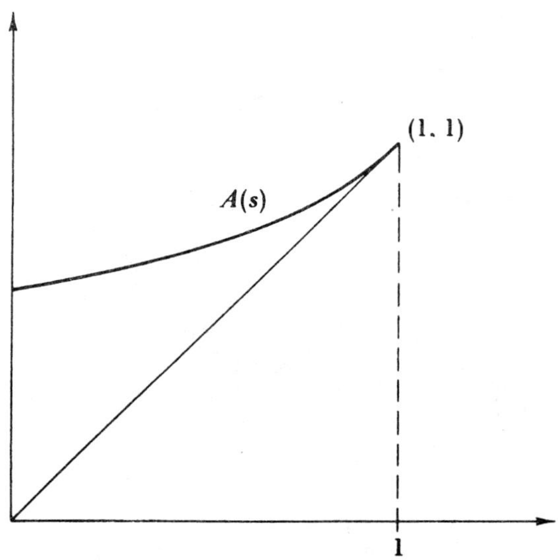

FIG. 5

Then

$$Y(s) = \frac{sa_0 y_1}{(1-s)[1-W(s)]}$$
$$= \frac{sa_0 y_1}{1-s}(1 + W(s) + (W(s))^2 + \cdots)$$
$$= sa_0 y_1 \frac{U(s)}{1-s} \qquad \text{where} \quad u_n \geq 0, \quad U(s) = \sum_{n=0}^{\infty} u_n s^n = \sum_{k=0}^{\infty} [W(s)]^k$$
$$= sa_0 y_1 V(s) \qquad \text{where} \quad v_n = \sum_{k=0}^{n} u_k, \quad V(s) = \sum_{n=0}^{\infty} v_n s^n,$$

i.e.,

$$V(s) = \frac{U(s)}{1-s}$$

Now

$$\left(W(1) = \sum ka_k < 1\right) \leftrightarrow \left(U(1) = \sum_{k=0}^{\infty} u_k < \infty\right),$$

since $U(1) = 1 + W(1) + (W(1))^2 + \cdots$, which is a convergent geometric series. Clearly $v_1 < v_2 < \cdots \to U(1)$, so that $Y(s) = sa_0 y_1 V(s)$ has bounded coefficients in its power series expansion if and only if $\sum ka_k < 1$. Therefore if $\sum ka_k < 1$ we may take $y_1 \neq 0$, $y_k = a_0 y_1 v_{k-1}$, and, retracing steps to Eq. (6.2) and equating coefficients, obtain a bounded nonconstant solution of (6.1). This implies that the process is transient. If $\sum ka_k = 1$ any solution of (6.1) is necessarily unbounded, implying the process is recurrent. To sum up, if

$\sum ka_k < 1$, the process is transient;

$\sum ka_k = 1$, the process is null recurrent;

$\sum ka_k > 1$, the process is positive recurrent.

7: *Random Walk*

We apply the recurrence criteria of Section 4 to the random walk induced by the Markov matrix

$$\|P_{ij}\| = \left\| \begin{matrix} r_0 & p_0 & 0 & 0 & \cdots \\ q_1 & r_1 & p_1 & 0 & \cdots \\ 0 & q_2 & r_2 & p_2 & \cdots \\ \vdots & \ddots & \ddots & \ddots & \end{matrix} \right\|$$

Let

$$\pi_0 = 1, \qquad \pi_n = \frac{p_0 p_1 \cdots p_{n-1}}{q_1 q_2 \cdots q_n}.$$

For the case $r_i \equiv 0$ it was shown (see the example of Section 1) that the random walk process at hand has a stationary distribution if and only if $\sum_{n=0}^{\infty} \pi_n < \infty$. Now consider the system of equations

$$\sum_{j=0}^{\infty} P_{ij} y_j = y_i, \qquad i \neq 0,$$

or

$$q_1 y_0 + r_1 y_1 + p_1 y_2 \qquad = y_1,$$

$$\cdots\cdots\cdots\cdots\cdots\cdots\cdots\cdots\cdots\cdots$$

$$q_n y_{n-1} + r_n y_n + p_n y_{n+1} = y_n.$$

$$\cdots\cdots\cdots\cdots\cdots\cdots\cdots\cdots\cdots\cdots$$

Inspection shows that the solutions span a two dimensional linear space. We can prescribe y_0 and y_1 arbitrarily and then all the other y_i are determined by these equations. Trivially $y_i \equiv 1$ is a solution. We show that $y_0 = 0, y_n = \sum_{i=0}^{n-1} 1/p_i \pi_i$, $n \geq 1$, is also a solution. For the first equation

$$q_1 y_0 + r_1 y_1 + p_1 y_2 = r_1 \left(\frac{1}{p_0}\right) + p_1 \left(\frac{1}{p_0} + \frac{q_1}{p_1 p_0}\right) = \frac{1}{p_0} = y_1.$$

For the nth equation we must show

$$q_n \left(\sum_{i=0}^{n-2} \frac{1}{p_i \pi_i}\right) + r_n \sum_{i=0}^{n-1} \frac{1}{p_i \pi_i} + p_n \sum_{i=0}^{n} \frac{1}{p_i \pi_i} = \sum_{i=0}^{n-1} \frac{1}{p_i \pi_i}.$$

Since $p_n + r_n + q_n = 1$ it suffices to verify that

$$q_n \sum_{i=0}^{n-2} \frac{1}{p_i \pi_i} + p_n \sum_{i=0}^{n} \frac{1}{p_i \pi_i} = (p_n + q_n) \sum_{i=0}^{n-1} \frac{1}{p_i \pi_i}.$$

But the left-hand side is just

$$(q_n + p_n) \sum_{i=0}^{n-1} \frac{1}{p_i \pi_i} - q_n \frac{1}{p_{n-1} \pi_{n-1}} + p_n \frac{1}{p_n \pi_n},$$

while

$$-q_n \frac{1}{p_{n-1} \pi_{n-1}} = \frac{-1}{(p_{n-1}/q_n) \pi_{n-1}} = \frac{-1}{\pi_n}$$

by the definition of π_n, which proves the assertion. Since the two solutions ($y_i \equiv 1$) and ($y_n = \sum_{i=1}^{n-1} 1/p_i \pi_i$) are clearly independent, the general

solution is $z_n = \alpha + \beta y_n$, and a nonconstant bounded solution of $\sum_{j=0}^{\infty} P_{ij} z_j = z_i$, $i \neq 0$, exists if and only if the y_n are bounded, i.e., $\sum_{i=0}^{\infty} 1/p_i \pi_i < \infty$.
Therefore, we have

$$\sum_{i=0}^{\infty} \frac{1}{p_i \pi_i} = \infty \Rightarrow \text{recurrent},$$

$$\sum_{i=0}^{\infty} \frac{1}{p_i \pi_i} = \infty \quad \text{and} \quad \sum_{i=0}^{\infty} \pi_i = \infty \Rightarrow \text{null recurrent},$$

$$\sum_{i=0}^{\infty} \frac{1}{p_i \pi_i} = \infty \quad \text{and} \quad \sum_{i=0}^{\infty} \pi_i < \infty \Rightarrow \text{positive recurrent},$$

$$\sum_{i=0}^{\infty} \frac{1}{p_i \pi_i} < \infty \Rightarrow \text{transient}.$$

Elementary Problems

1. A matrix $P = \|P_{ij}\|_{i,j=1}^{\infty}$ is called stochastic if

(i) $P_{ij} \geq 0$ for all i and $j = 1, 2, \ldots$

and

(ii) $\sum_{j=1}^{\infty} P_{ij} = 1$ for all $i = 1, 2, \ldots$.

A matrix P is called doubly stochastic if in addition to (i) and (ii) also

$$\sum_{i=1}^{\infty} P_{ij} = 1 \qquad \text{for all } j = 1, 2, \ldots .$$

Prove that if a finite irreducible Markov chain has a doubly stochastic transition probability matrix, then all the stationary probabilities are equal.

2. A Markov chain on states $\{0, 1, 2, 3, 4, 5\}$ has transition probability matrix

$$\text{(a)} \begin{Vmatrix} \frac{1}{3} & \frac{2}{3} & 0 & 0 & 0 & 0 \\ \frac{2}{3} & \frac{1}{3} & 0 & 0 & 0 & 0 \\ 0 & 0 & \frac{1}{4} & \frac{3}{4} & 0 & 0 \\ 0 & 0 & \frac{1}{5} & \frac{4}{5} & 0 & 0 \\ \frac{1}{4} & 0 & \frac{1}{4} & 0 & \frac{1}{4} & \frac{1}{4} \\ \frac{1}{6} & \frac{1}{6} & \frac{1}{6} & \frac{1}{6} & \frac{1}{6} & \frac{1}{6} \end{Vmatrix}, \qquad \text{(b)} \begin{Vmatrix} 1 & 0 & 0 & 0 & 0 & 0 \\ 0 & \frac{3}{4} & \frac{1}{4} & 0 & 0 & 0 \\ 0 & \frac{1}{8} & \frac{7}{8} & 0 & 0 & 0 \\ \frac{1}{4} & \frac{1}{4} & 0 & \frac{1}{8} & \frac{3}{8} & 0 \\ \frac{1}{3} & 0 & \frac{1}{6} & \frac{1}{6} & \frac{1}{3} & 0 \\ 0 & 0 & 0 & 0 & 0 & 1 \end{Vmatrix}$$

Find all classes. Compute the limiting probabilities $\lim_{n\to\infty} P_{5i}^n$ for $i = 0, 1, 2, 3, 4, 5$.

3. Consider a Gambler's ruin with initial fortune a and b $(a > 10, b > 10)$ for players I and II, respectively. Let $p\,(1-p)$ be the probability that I wins (loses) from II one unit each game. What is the probability that player I will achieve a fortune $a+b-3$ before his fortune dwindles to 5?

4. Let Y_n be the sum of n independent rolls of a fair die. Find

$$\lim_{n\to\infty} \Pr\{Y_n \text{ is a multiple of } 13\}.$$

5. Consider a Markov chain with transition probability matrix

$$P=\begin{bmatrix} p_0 & p_1 & p_2 & \cdots & p_m \\ p_m & p_0 & p_1 & \cdots & p_{m-1} \\ \vdots & \vdots & \vdots & & \vdots \\ p_1 & p_2 & p_3 & \cdots & p_0 \end{bmatrix}$$

where $0<p_0<1$ and $p_0+p_1+\cdots+p_m=1$. Determine $\lim_{n\to\infty} P_{ij}^n$, the stationary distribution.

6. Members of an indefinitely large population are either immune to a given disease or are susceptible to it. Let X_n be the number of susceptible members in the population at time period n and suppose $X_0=0$ and that in the absence of an epidemic $X_{n+1}=X_n+1$. Thus, in the absence of the disease, the number of susceptibles in the population increases in time, possibly owing to individuals losing their immunity, or to the introduction of new susceptible members to the population.

But in each period there is a constant but unknown probability p of a pandemic disease. When the disease occurs all susceptibles are stricken. The disease is non-lethal and confers immunity, so that if T is the first time of disease occurrence, then $X_T=0$.

Compute the stationary distribution for (X_n).

7. An airline reservation system has two computers only one of which is in operation at any given time. A computer may break down on any given day with probability p. There is a single repair facility which takes 2 days to restore a computer to normal. The facilities are such that only one computer at a time can be dealt with. Form a Markov chain by taking as states the pairs (x, y) where x is the number of machines in operating condition at the end of a day and y is 1 if a day's labor has been expended on a machine not yet repaired and 0 otherwise. The transition matrix is

From State ↓ \ To State →	(2, 0)	(1, 0)	(1, 1)	(0, 1)
(2, 0)	q	p	0	0
(1, 0)	0	0	q	p
(1, 1)	q	p	0	0
(0, 1)	0	1	0	0

where $p+q=1$. Find the stationary distribution in terms of p and q.

8. Consider a production line where each item has probability p of being defective. Assume that the condition of a particular item (defective or non-defective) does not depend on the condition of other items. The following sampling plan is used:

Initially every item is sampled as it is produced; this continues until i consecutive nondefective items are found. Then the sampling plan calls for sampling only one out of every r items at random until a defective one is found. When this happens the plan calls for reverting to 100% sampling until i consecutive nondefective items are found, etc.

State E_k $(k = 0, 1, \ldots, i)$ denotes that k consecutive nondefective items have been found in the 100% sampling portion of the plan, while state E_{i+1} denotes that the plan is in the second stage (sampling one out of r) and one or more nondefective items have been sampled in this stage. (Time m is considered to follow the mth observation for any m.) Then the sequence of states is a Markov chain with

$$P_{jk} = \Pr\left\{\begin{matrix}\text{in state } E_k \text{ after } m+1 \text{ observations} \mid \text{in state } E_j \\ \text{after } m \text{ observations}\end{matrix}\right\}$$

$$= \begin{cases} p & \text{if } k = 0, \quad j = 0, 1, \ldots, i, i+1, \\ 1-p & \text{if } k = j+1, \quad j = 0, 1, \ldots, i \text{ or } k = j = i+1, \\ 0 & \text{otherwise,} \end{cases}$$

for all m.

(a) Determine the stationary distribution.

(b) Determine the long run fraction of items that are inspected.

(c) Determine the average outgoing quality (AOQ), the long run fraction of defective items in the output of the sampling plan.

9. Sociologists often assume that the social classes of successive generations in a family can be regarded as a Markov chain. Thus, the occupation of a son is assumed to depend only on his father's occupation and not on his grandfather's. Suppose that such a model is appropriate and that the transition probability matrix is given by

		Son's Class		
		Lower	Middle	Upper
Father's Class	Lower	.40	.50	.10
	Middle	.05	.70	.25
	Upper	.05	.50	.45

For such a population, what fraction of people are middle class in the long run?

10. Suppose that the weather on any day depends on the weather conditions for the previous two days. To be exact, suppose that if it was sunny today and yesterday, then it will be sunny tomorrow with probability .8; if it was sunny today but cloudy yesterday, then it will be sunny tomorrow with probability .6; if it was cloudy today but sunny yesterday, then it will be sunny tomorrow with probability .4; if it was cloudy for the last two days, then it will be sunny tomorrow with probability .1.

Such a model can be transformed into a Markov chain provided we say that the state at any time is determined by the weather conditions during both that day and the previous day. We say the process is in

State (S, S) if it was sunny both today and yesterday,
State (S, C) if it was sunny yesterday but cloudy today,
State (C, S) if it was cloudy yesterday but sunny today,
State (C, C) if it was cloudy both today and yesterday.

Then the transition probability matrix is

		Today's State			
		(S, S)	(S, C)	(C, S)	(C, C)
	(S, S)	.8	.2		
Yesterday's	(S, C)			.4	.6
State	(C, S)	.6	.4		
	(C, C)			.1	.9

(a) Find the stationary distribution of the Markov chain.
(b) On what fraction of days in the long run is it sunny?

11. Consider a regular $2r+1$ polygon consisting of vertices $V_1, V_2, \ldots, V_{2r+1}$. Suppose that at each point V_k there is a nonnegative mass w_k^1 where $w_1^1 + \cdots + w_{2r+1}^1 = 1$. Obtain new masses $w_1^2, \ldots, w_{2r+1}^2$ by replacing the old mass at k by the arithmetic mean of neighboring masses, i.e.

$$w_k^2 = \tfrac{1}{2}(w_{k-1}^1 + w_{k+1}^1).$$

Do this transformation n times. Determine $\lim_{n\to\infty} w_k^n$.

Solution:

$$1/(2r+1), \text{ independent of } k.$$

12. Consider a light bulb whose life, measured in discrete units, is a random variable X where $\Pr[X=k]=p_k$ for $k=1, 2, \ldots$. If one starts with a fresh bulb and if each bulb is replaced by a new one when it burns out then u_n, the expected number of replacements up to time n, solves the equation

$$u_n = F_X(n) + \sum_{k=1}^{n} p_k u_{n-k}, \qquad n = 1, 2, \ldots$$

where $F_X(n) = \sum_{k\le n} p_k$.

In a large building it is often cheaper, on a per bulb basis, to replace all the bulbs, failed or not, than it is to replace a single bulb, due to economies of scale. A "block replacement policy" is a function of the block period N and calls for replacing bulbs as they fail during periods $0, 1, \ldots, N-1$, and then replacing all bulbs, failed or not, in period N. If C_1 is the per bulb block replacement cost and C_2 is the per bulb failure replacement cost it can be shown that the long run per bulb time average cost of such a policy is $[C_1 + C_2 u_{N-1}]/N$, which is the expected cost over a replacement cycle divided by the length of the cycle. (This result is formally proved in Chapter 5.)

(a) Based on intuition, note that u_n, the expected renewals up to time n, cannot converge but should grow unboundedly. What condition in Theorem 1.1 is violated in the renewal equation for u_n?

(b) Derive a renewal equation for $v_n = \Pr\{\text{a replacement is needed at time } n\}$. Note $v_n = u_n - u_{n-1}$ for $n = 1, 2, \ldots (u_0 = 0)$.

(c) If $p_1 = .4$, $p_2 = .3$, $p_3 = .2$ and $p_4 = .1$ compute and plot v_n for $n = 1, 2, \ldots, 10$. Compute $u_n = v_1 + \cdots + v_n$.

(d) If $C_1 = \$1$ and $C_2 = \$2$, determine the value for N that yields minimum cost.

Solution:

(b) $v_n = p_n + \sum_{k=1}^{n} p_{n-k} v_k, \qquad v_0 = p_0 = 0.$

(c)

$v_1 = .4000$	$v_6 = .4991$
$v_2 = .4600$	$v_7 = .5013$
$v_3 = .5040$	$v_8 = .5005$
$v_4 = .5196$	$v_9 = .4994$
$v_5 = .4910$	$v_{10} = .5002$

(d) $N^* = 2$.

Problems

1. Consider the following random walk:

$$P_{i,i+1} = p \qquad \text{with} \quad 0 < p < 1,$$
$$P_{i,i-1} = q = 1 - p \qquad \text{for} \quad i = 1, 2, \ldots, r-1,$$
$$P_{0,0} = P_{r,r} = 1.$$

Find $d(k) = E[\text{time to absorption into states 0 or } r \mid \text{initial state is } k]$.

Answer:

$$d(k) = \frac{k}{q-p} - \frac{r}{q-p}\frac{(1-(q/p)^k)}{1-(q/p)^r} \qquad \text{if } p \neq \tfrac{1}{2},$$
$$= k(r-k) \qquad \text{if } p = \tfrac{1}{2}.$$

2. Let $\mathbf{P} = \|P_{ij}\|$ be the transition probability matrix of an irreducible Markov chain and suppose $\mathbf{P}$ is idempotent (i.e., $\mathbf{P}^2 = \mathbf{P}$). Prove that $P_{ij} = P_{jj}$ for all i and j and that the Markov chain is aperiodic.

Hint: Use Theorem 1.2 for the averages $(1/m) \sum_{m=1}^{n} P_{ij}^m$.

3. Consider a finite Markov chain $\mathfrak{M}$ on the state space $\{0, 1, 2, \ldots, N\}$ with transition probability matrix $\mathbf{P} = \|P_{ij}\|_{i,j=0}^{N}$ consisting of three classes $\{0\}$,

$\{1, 2, \ldots, N-1\}$ and $\{N\}$ where 0 and N are absorbing states, both accessible from $k = 1, \ldots, N-1$, and $\{1, 2, \ldots, N-1\}$ is a transient class. Let k be a state satisfying $0 < k < N$. We define an auxiliary process $\mathfrak{M}$ called "the return process" by altering the first and last row of $\mathbf{P}$ so that $\tilde{P}_{0k} = \tilde{P}_{Nk} = 1$ and leave the other rows unchanged. The return process $\mathfrak{M}$ is clearly irreducible. Prove that the expected time until absorption u_k with initial state k in the $\mathfrak{M}$ process equals $1/(\pi_0 + \pi_N) - 1$ where $\pi_0 + \pi_N$ is the stationary probability of being in state 0 or N for the $\mathfrak{M}$ process.

Hint: Use the relation between stationary probabilities and expected recurrence times to states.

4. Consider a discrete time Markov chain with states $0, 1, \ldots, N$ whose matrix has elements

$$P_{ij} = \begin{cases} \mu_i, & j = i-1, \\ \lambda_i, & j = i+1, \qquad i, j = 0, 1, \ldots, N. \\ 1 - \lambda_i - \mu_i, & j = i, \\ 0, & |j - i| > 1, \end{cases}$$

Suppose that $\mu_0 = \lambda_0 = \mu_N = \lambda_N = 0$, and all other μ_i's and λ_i's are positive, and that the initial state of the process is k. Determine the absorption probabilities at 0 and N.

Answer: Define $\qquad \rho_0 = 1, \qquad \rho_i = \dfrac{\mu_1 \mu_2 \cdot \cdots \cdot \mu_i}{\lambda_1 \lambda_2 \cdot \cdots \cdot \lambda_i}$;

$$\Pr\{\text{absorption at } 0\} = 1 - \Pr\{\text{absorption at } N\} = \frac{\sum_{i=k}^{N-1} \rho_i}{\sum_{i=0}^{N-1} \rho_i}.$$

5. Under the conditions of Problem 4, determine the expected time until absorption.

6. Consider a Markov chain with the $N+1$ states $0, 1, \ldots, N$ and transition probabilities

$$P_{ij} = \binom{N}{j} \pi_i^j (1 - \pi_i)^{N-j}, \qquad 0 \le i, \ j \le N,$$

$$\pi_i = \frac{1 - e^{-2ai/N}}{1 - e^{-2a}}, \qquad a > 0.$$

Note that 0 and N are absorbing states. Verify that $\exp(-2aX_t)$ is a martingale [or, what is equivalent, prove the identity $E(\exp(-2aX_{t+1})|X_t) = \exp(-2aX_t)$], where X_t is the state at time t ($t = 0, 1, 2, \ldots$). Using this property show that the probability $P_N(k)$ of absorption into state N starting at state k is given by

$$P_N(k) = \frac{1 - e^{-2ak}}{1 - e^{-2aN}}.$$

Hint: Use the fact that absorption into one of the states 0 or N in finite time occurs with certainty and that the relations

$$E(\exp(-2aX_0)) = E(\exp(-2aX_n)) = P_N(k)\exp(-2aN) + (1 - P_N(k))$$

hold (justify this).

7. Consider a finite population (of fixed size N) of individuals of possible types A and a undergoing the following growth process. At instants of time $t_1 < t_2 < t_3 < \cdots$, one individual dies and is replaced by another of type A or a. If just before a replacement time t_n there are j A's and $N-j$ a's present, we postulate that the probability that an A individual dies is $j\mu_1/B_j$ and that an a individual dies is $(N-j)\mu_2/B_j$ where $B_j = \mu_1 j + \mu_2(N-j)$. The rationale of this model is predicated on the following structure: Generally a type A individual has chance $\mu_1/(\mu_1+\mu_2)$ of dying at each epoch t_n and an a individual has chance $\mu_2/(\mu_1+\mu_2)$ of dying at time t_n. (μ_1/μ_2 can be interpreted as the selective advantage of A types over a types.) Taking account of the sizes of the population it is plausible to assign the probabilities $\mu_1 j/B_j$ and $(\mu_2(N-j)/B_j)$ to the events that the replaced individual is of type A and type a, respectively. We assume no difference in the birth pattern of the two types and so the new individual is taken to be A with probability j/N and a with probability $(N-j)/N$. Consider the Markov chain $\{X_n\}$, where X_n is the number of A types at time t_n $(n = 1, 2, \ldots)$ with transition probabilities

$$P_{j,j-1} = \frac{\mu_1 j(N-j)}{B_j N}, \qquad P_{j,j+1} = \frac{\mu_2(N-j)j}{B_j N},$$

$$P_{jj} = 1 - P_{j,j-1} - P_{j,j+1}, \qquad P_{ij} = 0, \qquad \text{for } |i-j| > 1.$$

Find the probability that the population is eventually all of type a, given k A's and $(N-k)$ a's initially.

Hint: Show that the equations that determine the absorption probabilities can be reduced to a corresponding system of equations for absorption probabilities of a gambler's ruin random walk.

Answer:

$$\Pr\{\text{all } a\text{'s eventually left}\} = \frac{(\mu_1/\mu_2)^N - (\mu_1/\mu_2)^k}{(\mu_1/\mu_2)^N - 1}, \qquad \mu_1 \neq \mu_2,$$

$$= 1 - \frac{k}{N}, \qquad \mu_1 = \mu_2.$$

8. Let $\mathbf{P}$ be a 3×3 Markov matrix and define $\mu(\mathbf{P}) = \max_{i_1, i_2, j}[P_{i_1,j} - P_{i_2,j}]$ Show that $\mu(\mathbf{P}) = 1$ if and only if $\mathbf{P}$ has the form

$$\begin{pmatrix} 1 & 0 & 0 \\ 0 & p & q \\ r & s & t \end{pmatrix} \qquad (p, q \geq 0, p + q = 1; \quad r, s, t \geq 0, r + s + t = 1)$$

or any matrix obtained from this one by interchanging rows and/or columns.

***9.** If $\mathbf{P}$ is a finite Markov matrix, we define $\mu(\mathbf{P}) = \max_{i_1,i_2,j}(P_{i_1,j} - P_{i_2,j})$. Suppose $P_1, P_2, \ldots, P_k$ are 3×3 transition matrices of irreducible aperiodic Markov chains. Assume furthermore that for any set of integers α_i $(1 \le \alpha_i \le k)$, $i = 1, 2, \ldots, m$, $\prod_{i=1}^m \mathbf{P}_{\alpha_i}$ is also the matrix of an aperiodic irreducible Markov chain. Prove that, for every $\varepsilon > 0$, there exists an $M(\varepsilon)$ such that $m > M$ implies

$$\mu\left(\prod_{i=1}^{m} \mathbf{P}_{\alpha_i}\right) < \varepsilon \qquad \text{for any set } \alpha_i\ (1 \le \alpha_i \le k) \qquad i = 1, 2, \ldots, m.$$

***10.** If i is a recurrent state and X_k represents the state of the Markov chain at time k, then show that

$$\lim_{N\to\infty} \Pr\{X_k \ne i \quad \text{for} \quad n+1 \le k \le n+N | X_0 = i\} = 0.$$

If i is a positive recurrent state prove that the convergence in the above equation is uniform with respect to n.

***11.** Generalized Pólya Urn Scheme. In an urn containing a white and b black balls we select a ball at random. If a white ball is selected we return it and add α white and β black to the urn and if a black ball is selected we return it and add γ white and δ black, where $\alpha + \beta = \gamma + \delta$. The process is repeated. Let X_n be the number of selections that are white among the first n repetitions.

(i) If $P_{n,k} = \Pr\{X_n = k\}$ and $\varphi_n(x) = \sum_{k=0}^{n} P_{n,k} x^k$ establish the identity

$$\varphi_n(x) = \frac{(\alpha - \gamma)(x^2 - x)}{(n-1)(\alpha+\beta) + a + b} \varphi'_{n-1}(x) + \frac{\{x[(n-1)\gamma + a] + b + (n-1)\delta\}}{(n-1)(\alpha+\beta) + a + b} \varphi_{n-1}(x).$$

(ii) Prove the limit relation $E(X_n/n) \to \gamma/(\beta + \gamma)$ as $n \to \infty$.

Hint: Show that

$$\varphi'_n(1) = (\alpha - \gamma) \sum_{k=1}^{n} \frac{\varphi'_{k-1}(1)}{(k-1)(\alpha+\beta) + a + b} + \sum_{k=1}^{n} \frac{a + (k-1)\gamma}{(k-1)(\alpha+\beta) + a + b}$$

and deduce from this that $\varphi'_n(1)/n \to \gamma/(\beta + \gamma)$.

***12.** Under the conditions of Problem 11 prove

$$\lim_{n\to\infty} E\left[\left(\frac{X_n}{n}\right)^2\right] = \left(\frac{\gamma}{\beta+\gamma}\right)^2 \qquad \text{as} \quad n \to \infty$$

Hint: Determine a recursion relation for $\varphi''_n(1)$ as in (i) above.

***13.** Under the conditions of Problem 11 show that $X_n/n \to \gamma/(\beta+\gamma)$ in probability as $n \to \infty$.

***14.** Consider an irreducible Markov chain with a finite set of states $\{1, 2, \ldots, N\}$. Let $\|P_{ij}\|$ be the transition probability matrix of the Markov chain and denote by $\{\pi_j\}$ the stationary distribution of the process. Let $\|P_{ij}^{(m)}\|$ denote the m-step transition probability matrix. Let $\varphi(x)$ be a concave function on $x \geq 0$ and define

$$E_m = \sum_{j=1}^{N} \pi_j \varphi(P_{jl}^{(m)}) \qquad \text{with } l \text{ fixed.}$$

Prove that E_m is a nondecreasing function of m, i.e., $E_{m+1} \geq E_m$ for all $m \geq 1$.
Hint: Use Jensen's inequality.

***15.** Assume state 0 is positive recurrent. We take the initial state to be 0. Let $\{W_n\}$ $(n = 1, 2, \ldots)$ denote successive recurrence times which are of course independent and identically distributed random variables with finite mean and with a generating function $F(t) = \sum_{k=1}^{\infty} t^k \Pr\{W_1 = k\}$ $(|t| < 1)$. Define Y_n as the time of the last visit to state 0 before the time n. Show that

$$\sum_{n=0}^{\infty} t^n \sum_{j=0}^{n} x^j \Pr\{Y_n = j\} = \frac{(1 - F(t))}{(1-t)(1-F(xt))}.$$

Hint: Prove and use the relation $\Pr\{Y_n = j\} = \Pr\{W_1 + \cdots + W_{N_n} = j\} \cdot q_{n-j}$ where $q_i = \Pr\{W_1 > i\}$ and N_n is the number of visits to state 0 in the first n trials.

16. Fix the decreasing sequence of nonnegative numbers $1 = b_0 \geq b_1 \geq \cdots$ and consider the Markov chain having transition probabilities

$$P_{ij} = \begin{cases} \dfrac{b_j}{b_i}(\beta_i - \beta_{i+1}) & j \leq i \\[2ex] \dfrac{\beta_{i+1}}{\beta_i} & j = i+1 \\[2ex] 0 & \text{elsewhere,} \end{cases}$$

where $\beta_n = b_n/(b_1 + \cdots + b_n)$. Show that $P_{00}^n = 1/\sigma_n$ where $\sigma_n = b_1 + \cdots + b_n$. Thus the chain is transient if and only if $\sum \dfrac{1}{\sigma_n} < \infty$.

NOTES

The content of Sections 1–4 is part of the standard apparatus of Markov chains that is included in most books on the subject.

The examples of Section 5 are classical in the area of stochastic queueing models. For further refinements see, e.g., Takacs [1].

REFERENCE

1. L. Takacs, "Introduction to the Theory of Queues." Oxford Univ. Press, London and New York, 1962.

Chapter 4

CLASSICAL EXAMPLES OF CONTINUOUS TIME MARKOV CHAINS

Poisson and birth and death processes play a fundamental role in the theory and applications that embrace queueing and inventory models, population growth, engineering systems, etc. This chapter should be studied in every introductory course.

1: *General Pure Birth Processes and Poisson Processes*

The previous chapters were devoted to an elaboration of the basic concepts and methods of discrete time Markov chains. In this chapter we present a brief discussion of several important examples of continuous time, discrete state, Markov processes.

Specifically, we deal here with a family of random variables $\{X(t); 0 \leq t < \infty\}$ where the possible values of $X(t)$ are the nonnegative integers. We shall restrict attention to the case where $\{X(t)\}$ is a Markov process with stationary transition probabilities. Thus, the transition probability function for $t > 0$,

$$P_{ij}(t) = \Pr\{X(t+u) = j \mid X(u) = i\}, \qquad i, j = 0, 1, 2, \ldots, \tag{1.1}$$

is independent of $u \geq 0$.

It is usually more natural in investigating particular stochastic models based on physical phenomena to prescribe the so-called infinitesimal probabilities relating to the process and then derive from them an explicit expression for the transition probability function.

For the case at hand, we will postulate the form of $P_{ij}(h)$ for h small and, using the Markov property, we will derive a system of differential equations satisfied by $P_{ij}(t)$ for all $t > 0$. The solution of these equations under suitable boundary conditions gives $P_{ij}(t)$. We recall that the Poisson process introduced in Section 2, Chapter 1 was in fact treated from just this point of view.

By way of introduction to the general pure birth process we review briefly the axioms characterizing the Poisson process.

A. POSTULATES FOR THE POISSON PROCESS

The Poisson process has been considered in Section 2, Chapter 1, where it was shown that it could be defined by a few simple postulates. In order to define more general processes of a similar kind, let us point out various further properties that the Poisson process possesses. In particular, it is a Markov process on the nonnegative integers which has the following properties:

$$\text{(i)}\quad \Pr\{X(t+h)-X(t)=1\,|\,X(t)=x\}=\lambda h+o(h) \quad \text{as}\quad h\downarrow 0 \qquad (x=0,1,2,\ldots).$$

The precise interpretation of (i) is the relationship

$$\lim_{h\to 0+}\frac{\Pr\{X(t+h)-X(t)=1\,|\,X(t)=x\}}{h}=\lambda.$$

The $o(h)$ symbol means that if we divide this term by h then its value tends to zero as h tends to zero. Notice that the right-hand side is independent of x.

$$\text{(ii)}\quad \Pr\{X(t+h)-X(t)=0\,|\,X(t)=x\}=1-\lambda h+o(h) \qquad \text{as}\quad h\downarrow 0.$$

$$\text{(iii)}\quad X(0)=0.$$

These properties are easily verified by direct computation, since the explicit formulas for all the relevant probabilities are available.

B. EXAMPLES OF POISSON PROCESSES

(a) An illustrative example of the Poisson process is that of fishing. Let the random variable $X(t)$ denote the number of fish caught in the time interval $[0, t]$. Suppose that the number of fish available is very large, that the enthusiast stands no better chance of catching fish than the rest of us, and that as many fish are likely to nibble at one instant of time as at another. Under these "ideal" conditions, the process $\{X(t); t \geq 0\}$ may be considered to be a Poisson process. This example serves to point up the Markov property (the chance of catching a fish does not depend upon the number caught) and the "no premium for waiting" property, which is the most distinctive property possessed by the Poisson process. It means that the fisherman who has just arrived at the pier has as good a chance of catching a fish in the next instant of time as he who has been waiting for a bite for four hours without success.

(b) A less imaginative example is afforded by problems arising in the theory of counters. If $X(t)$ is the number of radioactive disintegrations detected by a Geiger counter in the time interval $[0, t]$, the process is Poisson as long as the half-life of the substance is large relative to t. This provision ensures that the chance for a disintegration per unit of time may be considered as constant over time.

(c) Poisson processes arise naturally in many models of queueing phenomena. In these examples most attention is placed upon the times at which $X(t)$ (= length of queue at time t) jumps rather than upon the values of $X(t)$ themselves. The fishing example (a) is of course a special waiting time example.

C. PURE BIRTH PROCESS

A natural generalization of the Poisson process is to permit the chance of an event occurring at a given instant of time to depend upon the number of events which have already occurred. An example of this phenomenon is the reproduction of living organisms (and hence the name of the process), in which under certain conditions—sufficient food, no mortality, no migration, etc.—the probability of a birth at a given instant is proportional (directly) to the population size at that time. This example is known as the Yule process.

Consider a sequence of positive numbers, $\{\lambda_k\}$. We define a pure birth process as a Markov process satisfying the postulates:

(i) $\Pr\{X(t+h)-X(t)=1|X(t)=k\}=\lambda_k h+o_{1,k}(h), \qquad (h\to 0+),$

(ii) $\Pr\{X(t+h)-X(t)=0|X(t)=k\}=1-\lambda_k h+o_{2,k}(h),$

(iii) $\Pr\{X(t+h)-X(t)<0|X(t)=k\}=0, \qquad (k\geq 0).$

As a matter of convenience we often add the postulate

(iv) $X(0)=0.$

With this postulate $X(t)$ does not denote the population size but, rather, the number of births in the time interval $[0, t]$.

Note that the left sides of (i) and (ii) are just $P_{k,k+1}(h)$ and $P_{k,k}(h)$, respectively (owing to stationarity), so that $o_{1,k}(h)$ and $o_{2,k}(h)$ do not depend upon t.

We define $P_n(t)=\Pr\{X(t)=n\}$, assuming $X(0)=0$.

In exactly the same way as for the Poisson process, we may derive a system of differential equations satisfied by $P_n(t)$ for $t \geq 0$, namely

$$\begin{aligned} P_0'(t) &= -\lambda_0 P_0(t), \\ P_n'(t) &= -\lambda_n P_n(t) + \lambda_{n-1} P_{n-1}(t), \qquad n \geq 1, \end{aligned} \tag{1.2}$$

with boundary conditions

$$P_0(0) = 1, \qquad P_n(0) = 0, \qquad n > 0.$$

Indeed, if $h > 0$, $n \geq 1$, then by invoking the law of total probabilities, the Markov property, and postulate (iii) we obtain

$$\begin{aligned} P_n(t+h) &= \sum_{k=0}^{\infty} P_k(t) \Pr\{X(t+h) = n | X(t) = k\} \\ &= \sum_{k=0}^{\infty} P_k(t) \Pr\{X(t+h) - X(t) = n-k | X(t) = k\} \\ &= \sum_{k=0}^{n} P_k(t) \Pr\{X(t+h) - X(t) = n-k | X(t) = k\}. \end{aligned}$$

Now for $k = 0, 1, \ldots, n-2$ we have

$$\begin{aligned} &\Pr\{X(t+h) - X(t) = n-k | X(t) = k\} \\ &\quad \leq \Pr\{X(t+h) - X(t) \geq 2 | X(t) = k\} \\ &\quad = o_{1,k}(h) + o_{2,k}(h) \end{aligned}$$

or

$$\Pr\{X(t+h) - X(t) = n-k | X(t) = k\} = o_{3,n,k}(h) \qquad k = 0, \ldots n-2.$$

Thus

$$\begin{aligned} P_n(t+h) = P_n(t)\,&[1 - \lambda_n h + o_{2,n}(h)] \\ &+ P_{n-1}(t)\,[\lambda_{n-1} h + o_{1,n-1}(h)] \\ &+ \sum_{k=0}^{n-2} P_k(t) o_{3,n,k}(h) \end{aligned}$$

or

$$\begin{aligned} P_n(t+h) - P_n(t) = P_n(t)&[-\lambda_n h + o_{2,n}(h)] \\ &+ P_{n-1}(t)[\lambda_{n-1} h + o_{1,n-1}(h)] + o_n(h), \end{aligned} \tag{1.3}$$

where, clearly, $\lim_{h \downarrow 0} o_n(h)/h = 0$ uniformly in $t \geq 0$ since $o_n(h)$ is bounded by the finite sum $\sum_{k=0}^{n-2} o_{3,n,k}(h)$ which does not depend on t.

Dividing by h and passing to the limit $h \downarrow 0$, we obtain the validity of the relations (1.2) where on the left-hand side we should, to be precise, write the right-hand derivative. However, with a little more care we can derive the same relation involving the left-hand derivative. In fact, from (1.3) we see at once that the $P_n(t)$ are continuous functions of t. Replacing

t by $t-h$ in (1.3), dividing by h, and passing to the limit $h \downarrow 0$, we find that each $P_n(t)$ has a left derivative which also satisfies Eq. (1.2).

The first equation of (1.2) can be solved immediately and yields

$$P_0(t) = \exp(-\lambda_0 t) > 0.$$

Define T_k as the time between the kth and the $(k+1)$st birth, so that

$$P_n(t) = \Pr\{\sum_{i=0}^{n-1} T_i \leq t < \sum_{i=0}^{n} T_i\}.$$

The random variables T_k are called the "waiting times" between births, and

$$S_k = \sum_{i=0}^{k-1} T_i = \text{the time at which the } k\text{th birth occurs.}$$

We have already seen that $P_0(t) = \exp(-\lambda_0 t)$. Therefore,

$$\Pr\{T_0 \leq z\} = 1 - \Pr\{X(z) = 0\} = 1 - \exp(-\lambda_0 z),$$

i.e., T_0 has an exponential distribution with parameter λ_0. It may be deduced from postulates (i)–(iv) that T_k, $k > 0$, also has an exponential distribution with parameter λ_k and that the T_i's are mutually independent (see Chapter 14 of Volume II, where a formal proof of this fact is given). Therefore, the characteristic function of S_n is given by

$$\varphi_n(w) = E\{\exp(iwS_n)\} = \prod_{k=0}^{n-1} E(\exp(iwT_k)) = \prod_{k=0}^{n-1} \frac{\lambda_k}{\lambda_k - iw}. \tag{1.4}$$

In the case of the Poisson process where $\lambda_k = \lambda$ for all k, we recognize from (1.4) that S_n is distributed according to a gamma distribution of order n with mean n/λ.

For a specific set of $\lambda_k \geq 0$ we may solve each equation of (1.2) by means of the integrating factor $\exp(\lambda_k t)$, obtaining

$$P_k(t) = \lambda_{k-1} \exp(-\lambda_k t) \int_0^t \exp(\lambda_k x)\, P_{k-1}(x)\, dx, \qquad k = 1, 2, \ldots,$$

which makes it clear that all $P_k(t) \geq 0$.

But there is still a possibility that

$$\sum_{n=0}^{\infty} P_n(t) < 1.$$

To assure the validity of the process, i.e., to determine criteria in order that $\sum_{n=0}^{\infty} P_n(t) = 1$ for all t, we must restrict the λ_k according to the following

$$\sum_{n=0}^{\infty} P_n(t) = 1 \leftrightarrow \sum_{n=0}^{\infty} \frac{1}{\lambda_n} = \infty. \tag{1.5}$$

The proof of this is given in Feller's book† and so is omitted here. The intuitive argument for this result is as follows: The time T_k between consecutive births is shown below to be exponentially distributed with a corresponding parameter λ_k. Therefore, the quantity $\sum_n 1/\lambda_n$ equals the expected time before the population becomes infinite. By comparison $1-\sum_{n=0}^{\infty} P_n(t)$ is the probability that $X(t)=\infty$.

If $\sum \lambda_n^{-1} < \infty$ then the expected time for the population to become infinite is finite. It is then plausible that for all $t>0$ the probability that $X(t) = \infty$ is positive.

D. THE YULE PROCESS

The Yule process is an example of a pure birth process that arises in physics and biology. Assume that each member in a population has a probability $\beta h + o(h)$ of giving birth to a new member in an interval of time length h ($\beta > 0$). Furthermore assume that there are $X(0) = N$ members present at time 0. Assuming independence and no interaction among members of the population, the binomial theorem gives

$$\Pr\{X(t+h)-X(t)=1|X(t)=n\}$$
$$=\binom{n}{1}[\beta h+o(h)][1-\beta h+o(h)]^{n-1}=n\beta h+o_n(h),$$

i.e., in this example $\lambda_n = n\beta$. The system of equations (1.2) in the case that $N = 1$ becomes

$$P_n'(t)=-\beta[nP_n(t)-(n-1)P_{n-1}(t)], \qquad n=1,2,\ldots,$$

under the initial conditions

$$P_1(0)=1, \qquad P_n(0)=0, \qquad n=2,3,\ldots$$

Its solution is

$$P_n(t)=e^{-\beta t}(1-e^{-\beta t})^{n-1} \qquad n\geq 1,$$

as may be verified directly.

The generating function may be determined easily by summing a geometric series. We have

$$f(s)=\sum_{n=1}^{\infty}P_n(t)s^n$$
$$=se^{-\beta t}\sum_{n=1}^{\infty}[(1-e^{-\beta t})s]^{n-1}=\frac{se^{-\beta t}}{1-(1-e^{-\beta t})s}.$$

† W. Feller, "An Introduction to Probability Theory and Its Applications," Vol. 1, 2nd ed. p. 406. Wiley, New York, 1957.

Let us return to the general case in which there are $X(0) = N$ members present at time 0. Since we have assumed independence and no interaction among the members, we may view this population as the sum of N independent Yule processes, each beginning with a single member. Thus, if we let

$$P_{Nn}(t) = \Pr\{X(t) = n | X(0) = N\}$$

and

$$f_N(s) = \sum_{n=N}^{\infty} P_{Nn}(t)s^n \tag{1.6}$$

we have

$$\begin{aligned} f_N(s) &= [f(s)]^N \\ &= \left[\frac{se^{-\beta t}}{1-(1-e^{-\beta t})s}\right]^N \\ &= (se^{-\beta t})^N \sum_{m=0}^{\infty} \binom{m+N-1}{m} (1-e^{-\beta t})^m s^m \\ &= \sum_{n=N}^{\infty} \binom{n-1}{n-N} (e^{-\beta t})^N (1-e^{-\beta t})^{n-N} s^n, \end{aligned}$$

where we have used the binomial series $(1-x)^{-N} = \sum_{m=0}^{\infty} \binom{m+N-1}{m} x^m$. According to (1.6), the coefficient of s^n in this expression must be $P_{Nn}(t)$. That is

$$P_{Nn}(t) = \binom{n-1}{n-N} e^{-N\beta t}(1-e^{-\beta t})^{n-N} \quad \text{for} \quad n = N, N+1, \ldots \tag{1.7}$$

2: *More about Poisson Processes*

In the previous section we derived the Poisson process from a set of assumptions that are approximated well in many practical situations. This process is often referred to as the completely random process, as it distributes points " at random " over the infinite interval $[0, \infty)$ in much the same way that the uniform distribution distributes points over a finite interval. In particular, the probability of an observation falling in a subinterval is a function of its length only and the number of events occurring in two disjoint time intervals are independent random variables.

Let us now examine the Poisson process a little more closely.

A. CHARACTERISTIC FUNCTION AND WAITING TIMES

We may write the characteristic function of $X(t)$ in a Poisson process as

$$\varphi_t(w) = E\{e^{iwX(t)}\} = \sum_{n=0}^{\infty} \frac{e^{-\lambda t}(\lambda t)^n e^{iwn}}{n!} = \exp[\lambda t(e^{iw} - 1)]$$

Thus

$$E(X(t)) = \lambda t, \qquad \mathrm{Var}(X(t)) = \lambda t.$$

In our discussion of the pure birth process we showed that

$$\Pr\{T_0 \leq z\} = 1 - \exp(-\lambda_0 z)$$

and mentioned that T_k follows an exponential distribution with parameter λ_k and that the T_k's are independent. For the Poisson process, however, $\lambda_k = \lambda$ for all k, so that the result becomes

Theorem 2.1. *The waiting times T_k are independent and identically distributed following an exponential distribution with parameter λ.*

The rigorous proof of this theorem will follow from the more general considerations of Chapter 14.

The definition of the process requires more than is present for the validity of this theorem. We need to assume that the time until the next change of $X(t)$ follows the same distribution laws from any start of measured time, not just if we measure from a previous change. This is simply the statement that

$$\Pr\{X(t_0 + \tau) - X(t_0) > 0\} = 1 - e^{-\lambda\tau},$$

which was derived in Section 1. This property can also be obtained in a more direct manner. Let $F(x) = \Pr\{X(t_0 + x) - X(t_0) > 0\}$ where t_0 is some time, depending perhaps on the history of the process up to that time, whose specification does not affect this probability.† Then

$$\begin{aligned} F(x+y) &= \Pr\{X(t_0 + x + y) - X(t_0) > 0\} \\ &= \Pr\{X(t_0 + y) - X(t_0) > 0\} + \Pr\{X(t_0 + y) - X(t_0) = 0\} \\ &\quad \times \Pr\{X(t_0 + x + y) - X(t_0 + y) > 0 | X(t_0 + y) - X(t_0) = 0\}. \end{aligned}$$

From the definition of $F(x)$, the independence of the increments of the

† The interpretation of this seemingly vague phrase will be given precision in our discussion of the concept of " Markov time "; see Chapter 14.

Poisson process, and the fact (which enters as an initial assumption in defining the Poisson process) that

$$\Pr\{X(t_0 + x) - X(t_0) > 0\}$$

is independent of t_0, we obtain the functional equation

$$F(x + y) = F(y) + [1 - F(y)]F(x).$$

The fact that this property characterizes the exponential distribution is the content of the following theorem.

Theorem 2.2. *If $F(x)$ is a distribution such that $F(0) = 0$ and $F(x) < 1$ for some $x > 0$, then $F(x)$ is an exponential distribution if and only if*

$$F(x + y) - F(y) = F(x)[1 - F(y)] \qquad \text{for all} \quad x, y \geq 0. \tag{*}$$

Proof. That the exponential distribution satisfies the condition follows directly by substitution. To show the converse, set $G(x) = 1 - F(x)$; then the condition (*) becomes

$$G(x + y) = G(x)G(y). \tag{2.1}$$

Obviously, $G(0) = 1$, $G(x)$ is nonincreasing, and for some $x > 0$, $G(x) > 0$. Suppose that $G(x_0) = 0$ for some $x_0 > 0$. From Eq. (2.1) it immediately follows that $G(x_0) = [G(x_0/n)]^n$ for every integer $n > 0$; hence $G(x_0/n) = 0$. But then (2.1) shows that $G(x) = 0$ for $x > x_0/n$. Since n is arbitrary, $G(x) = 0$ for all $x > 0$, contrary to hypothesis. Thus $G(x) > 0$ for every $x > 0$. Now for any integers m, $n > 0$ we deduce easily from (2.1) that $G(m/n) = [G(1)]^{m/n}$. Since $G(x)$ and $[G(1)]^x$ are both nonincreasing functions which coincide whenever x is rational, and $[G(1)]^x$ is continuous, it follows that $G(x) = [G(1)]^x = \exp(x \log G(1))$ for all $x > 0$. But $F(x)$ is a distribution, and so

$$\lim_{x \to \infty} G(x) = 1 - \lim_{x \to \infty} F(x) = 0,$$

which implies that $G(1) < 1$. Hence $G(x) = e^{-\lambda x}$, where

$$\lambda = -\log G(1) > 0. \quad \blacksquare$$

Another proof assuming that G is differentiable goes as follows: Observe that (2.1) implies

$$G'(x + y) = \frac{\partial}{\partial x} G(x + y) = G'(x)G(y),$$

$$G(x)G'(y) = \frac{\partial}{\partial y} G(x + y) = G'(x + y),$$

and therefore

$$G'(x) = aG(x), \tag{2.2}$$

where $a = G'(y_0)/G(y_0)$ for some y_0 where $G(y_0) \neq 0$. The solution of Eq. (2.2) is $G(x) = Ae^{ax}$ and $A = 1$ since $G(0) = 1 - F(0) = 1$. The parameter a is negative since $G(x) < 1$ for some $x > 0$.

B. UNIFORM DISTRIBUTION

The class of distributions that are connected with the Poisson process does not stop with the Poisson and exponential distributions. We shall show how the uniform and binomial distributions also arise.

Consider the times $\{S_i\}$ at which changes of $X(t)$ occur, i.e.,

$$S_i = \sum_{k=0}^{i-1} T_k.$$

We have the following result.

Theorem 2.3. *For any numbers s_i satisfying $0 \leq s_1 \leq s_2 \leq \cdots \leq s_n \leq t$,*

$$\Pr\{S_i \leq s_i,\ i = 1, \ldots, n \mid X(t) = n\}$$

$$= \frac{n!}{t^n} \int_0^{s_1} \cdots \int_{x_{n-2}}^{s_{n-1}} \int_{x_{n-1}}^{s_n} dx_n \cdots dx_1,$$

which is the distribution of the order statistics from a sample of n observations taken from the uniform distribution on $[0, t]$.†

Proof. The proof is an easy consequence of Theorem 2.1. In fact

$$\Pr\{S_1 \leq s_1, S_2 \leq s_2, \cdots, S_n \leq s_n,\ X(t) = n\}$$

$$= \Pr\{T_0 \leq s_1,\ T_0 + T_1 \leq s_2, \ldots, T_0 + \cdots + T_{n-1} \leq s_n,\ T_0 + \cdots + T_n > t\}$$

$$= \int_0^{s_1} \int_0^{s_2 - t_1} \int_0^{s_3 - (t_1 + t_2)} \cdots \int_0^{s_n - (t_1 + \cdots + t_{n-1})} \int_{t - (t_1 + \cdots + t_n)}^{\infty} \lambda^{n+1} e^{-\lambda(t_1 + \cdots + t_{n+1})}$$

$$\times\ dt_{n+1} \cdot \cdots \cdot dt_1$$

† This means the following. Take n independent observations of a random variable which is uniformly distributed over the interval $[0, t]$. Let $Y_1 \leq Y_2 \leq \cdots \leq Y_n$ denote these observations arranged in increasing order. Then the joint distribution of $Y_1, \ldots, Y_n$ is precisely the expression in the assertion of the theorem. The proof of this fact is quite simple, but a more complete discussion will be presented in Chapter 13 of Volume II.

$$= \lambda^{n+1} \int_0^{s_1} \int_0^{s_2 - t_1} \int_0^{s_3-(t_1+t_2)} \cdots \int_0^{s_n-(t_1+\cdots+t_{n-1})} e^{-\lambda(t_1+\cdots+t_n)}$$

$$\times \left[-\frac{1}{\lambda} \exp(-\lambda t_{n+1}) \right]_{t-(t_1+\cdots+t_n)}^{\infty} dt_n \cdot \cdots \cdot dt_1$$

$$= \lambda^n e^{-\lambda t} \int_0^{s_1} \int_0^{s_2 - t_1} \int_0^{s_3-(t_1+t_2)} \cdots \int_0^{s_n-(t_1+\cdots+t_{n-1})} dt_n \cdot \cdots \cdot dt_1 .$$

If we introduce the new variables

$$\begin{aligned} u_n &= t_1 + \cdots + t_n \\ u_{n-1} &= t_1 + \cdots + t_{n-1} \\ &\vdots \\ u_1 &= t_1 , \end{aligned}$$

the last expression becomes

$$\lambda^n e^{-\lambda t} \int_0^{s_1} \int_{u_1}^{s_2} \int_{u_2}^{s_3} \cdots \int_{u_{n-1}}^{s_n} du_n \cdot \cdots \cdot du_1 .$$

But

$$\Pr\{X(t) = n\} = e^{-\lambda t} \frac{(\lambda t)^n}{n!} ;$$

hence

$$\Pr\{S_1 \le s_1, S_2 \le s_2, \ldots, S_n \le s_n | X(t) = n\}$$

$$= \frac{\Pr\{S_1 \le s_1, \ldots, S_n \le s_n, X(t) = n\}}{\Pr\{X(t) = n\}}$$

$$= \frac{n!}{t^n} \int_0^{s_1} \int_{u_1}^{s_2} \cdots \int_{u_{n-1}}^{s_n} du_n \cdot \cdots \cdot du_1 .$$

C. BINOMIAL DISTRIBUTION

It follows from the properties of a Poisson process that for $u < t$ and $k < n$,

$$\Pr\{X(u) = k | X(t) = n\} = \Pr\{X(u) = k,\ X(t) - X(u) = n - k\} / \Pr\{X(t) = n\} \tag{2.3}$$

$$= \frac{(e^{-\lambda u} u^k / k!)[e^{-\lambda(t-u)}(t-u)^{n-k}/(n-k)!]}{e^{-\lambda t}(t^n/n!)} = \binom{n}{k} \frac{u^k (t-u)^{n-k}}{t^n}$$

A second example in which the binomial distribution plays a part may be given by considering two independent Poisson processes $X_1(t)$ and $X_2(t)$ with parameters λ_1 and λ_2.

$$\Pr\{X_1(t)=k|X_1(t)+X_2(t)=n\}=\frac{\Pr\{X_1(t)=k, X_2(t)=n-k\}}{\Pr\{X_1(t)+X_2(t)=n\}}$$

$$=\frac{[\exp(-\lambda_1 t)(\lambda_1 t)^k/k!][\exp(-\lambda_2 t)(\lambda_2 t)^{n-k}/(n-k)!]}{\exp[-(\lambda_1+\lambda_2)t](\lambda_1+\lambda_2)^n t^n/n!}$$

$$=\binom{n}{k}\left(\frac{\lambda_1}{\lambda_1+\lambda_2}\right)^k\left(\frac{\lambda_2}{\lambda_1+\lambda_2}\right)^{n-k}$$

3: A Counter Model

An interesting application of the Poisson process is the following problem. Electrical pulses with random amplitudes X_i arrive at random times t_i (i.e., according to a Poisson process) at a detector whose output for each pulse at time t is

$$X_i\exp[-\alpha(t-t_i)]_+=\begin{cases}0 & \text{for } t<t_i,\\ X_i\exp[-\alpha(t-t_i)] & \text{for } t>t_i;\end{cases}$$

that is, the amplitude impressed on the detector when the pulse arrives is X_i and its effect thereafter decays at an exponential rate. The detector is linear (i.e., additive) so if N_t pulses occur during the time epoch $[0, t]$ the output at time t is

$$\eta(t)=\sum_{i=1}^{N_t}X_i\exp[-\alpha(t-t_i)]_+.$$

A typical realization of this process has the shape shown in Fig. 1. We would like to know the distribution function of $\eta(t)$ for each t, or, equivalently, its characteristic function $\varphi_t(w)$.

We assume that the X_i are identically and independently distributed positive random variables with density function $h(x)$ and characteristic function

$$\psi(s)=\int_0^\infty e^{isx}h(x)\,dx.$$

Set

$$R(v;t)=\Pr\{\eta(t)\le v\}=\sum_{n=0}^{\infty}\Pr\{\eta(t)\le v|N_t=n\}\Pr\{N_t=n\}. \quad (3.1)$$

Of course $\Pr\{N_t = n\} = [(\lambda t)^n e^{-\lambda t}]/n!$, where λ is the intensity parameter of the Poisson process describing the arrival times of the pulses. From the result of Theorem 2.3 we know that, conditioned by the event $N_t = n$, i.e.,

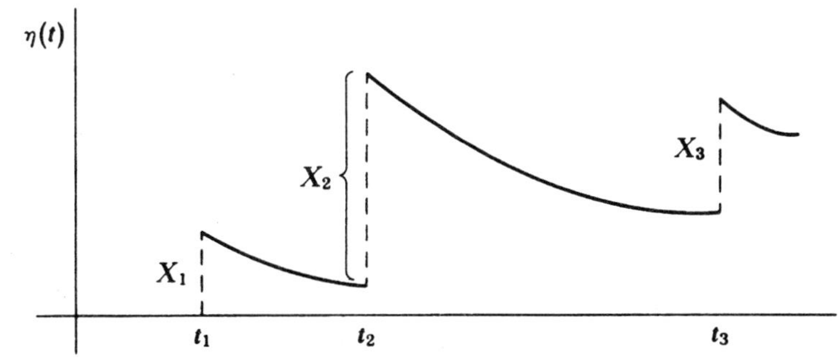

FIG. 1

that n pulses have arrived during the time interval $(0, t)$, the t_i are distributed like ordered observations from a uniform distribution on $(0, t)$. Let τ_i $(i = 1, 2, \ldots, N_t)$ denote independent uniformly distributed [on $(0, t)$] random variables whose values arranged in increasing order of magnitude are the t_j's.

Now let $Z_1, \ldots, Z_n$ be independent random variables, whose distributions are identical with that of the X_i, and which are also independent of the $\{\tau_i\}$. Consider the sum

$$\sum_{i=1}^{n} Z_i \exp[-\alpha(t - \tau_i)]_+ .$$

We define new random variables $Z_1', \ldots, Z_n'$ in accordance with

$$\begin{aligned}
Z_1' &= Z_j \quad \text{when} \quad \tau_j = \min(\tau_1, \ldots, \tau_n) = t_1 ,\\
Z_2' &= Z_j \quad \text{when} \quad \tau_j \text{ is the second smallest among the } \{\tau_i\} = t_2 ,\\
&\vdots \qquad\qquad \vdots\\
Z_n' &= Z_j \quad \text{when} \quad \tau_j = \max(\tau_1, \ldots, \tau_n) = t_n .
\end{aligned}$$

The ambiguity that occurs when two or more of the τ_i's are equal causes no trouble, as the probability of this event is zero. Then

$$\sum_{i=1}^{n} Z_i \exp[-\alpha(t - \tau_i)]_+ = \sum_{i=1}^{n} Z_i' \exp[-\alpha(t - t_i)]_+ ,$$

since the two sums differ only by a random rearrangement. Now since the Z_i are independent, identically distributed, and also independent of the τ_i, it is easily verified that the Z_i' are independent, their distributions coincide with the common distribution of the Z_i, and they are also independent of the τ_i. Being independent of the τ_i, the families $\{Z_i\}$ and $\{Z_i'\}$ are clearly independent of the t_i.

Since the Z_i' have all the properties required of the X_i, we can take

$$\eta(t) = \sum_{i=1}^{n} Z_i' \exp[-\alpha(t-t_i)]_+ = \sum_{i=1}^{n} Z_i \exp[-\alpha(t-\tau_i)]_+.$$

Let

$$Y_t(i) = Z_i \exp[-\alpha(t-\tau_i)]_+;$$

clearly for fixed t the $Y_t(i)$, $i=1, \ldots, n$ are independent and identically distributed random variables. Now define

$$\theta_t(s) = \int_0^\infty e^{isy} g_t(y, k)\, dy,$$

the characteristic function of $Y_t(k)$ where $g_t(y; k)$ is the density function of $Y_t(k)$. Since τ_k is uniformly distributed on $(0, t)$ and τ_k and Z_k are independent, we have

$$\begin{aligned}
\int_0^y g_t(u, k)\, du &= \Pr\{Y_t(k) \leq y\} \\
&= \Pr\{Z_k \exp[-\alpha(t-\tau_k)]_+ \leq y\} \\
&= \int_0^t \Pr\{Z_k \exp[-\alpha(t-\tau_k)]_+ \leq y \mid \tau_k = u\} \frac{du}{t} \\
&= \int_0^t \Pr\{Z_k \leq ye^{\alpha(t-u)}\} \frac{du}{t} \\
&= \frac{1}{t}\int_0^t H(ye^{\alpha(t-u)})\, du,
\end{aligned} \tag{3.2}$$

where H is the cumulative distribution function corresponding to the density h. Differentiating (3.2) gives

$$g_t(y; k) = \frac{1}{t}\int_0^t h(ye^{\alpha(t-u)})e^{\alpha(t-u)}\, du.$$

Therefore

$$\theta_t(s) = \int_0^\infty e^{isy} g_t(y; k)\, dy = \frac{1}{t}\int_0^t e^{\alpha(t-u)} \left(\int_0^\infty e^{isy} h(ye^{\alpha(t-u)})\, dy\right) du$$

$$= \frac{1}{t}\int_0^t du \int_0^\infty \exp[is(e^{-\alpha(t-u)}z)]h(z)\, dz \qquad \text{(if we make the change of variables } ye^{\alpha(t-u)} = z\text{)}$$

$$=\frac{1}{t}\int_0^t \psi(se^{-\alpha t}e^{\alpha u})\,du \qquad \text{(by the definition of } \psi)$$

$$=\frac{1}{t}\int_0^t \psi(se^{-\alpha v})\,dv \qquad \text{(if we put } v=t-u).$$

It follows that if $r(x;t)$ is the density function of $R(x,t)$ then

$$\varphi_t(w)=\int_0^\infty e^{iwx}r(x;t)\,dx$$

$$=\sum_{n=0}^\infty\left(\int_0^\infty e^{iwx}\frac{d}{dx}\Pr\{\eta(t)\le x|N_t=n\}\,dx\right)e^{-\lambda t}\frac{(\lambda t)^n}{n!}$$

[using (3.1)]

$$=\sum_{n=0}^\infty e^{-\lambda t}\frac{(\lambda t)^n}{n!}[\theta_t(w)]^n \qquad \text{(where we use the independence of the } Y_t(k)\text{, given the value of } N_t)$$

$$=\sum_{n=0}^\infty\frac{e^{-\lambda t}}{n!}\left(\lambda\int_0^t\psi(we^{-\alpha v})\,dv\right)^n$$

$$=\exp-\left\{\lambda\int_0^t[1-\psi(we^{-\alpha v})]\,dv\right\}.$$

By differentiating with respect to w we may compute moments of $\eta(t)$. For example,

$$E(\eta(t))=(-i)\frac{d}{dw}\varphi_t(w)\bigg|_{w=0}=\lambda(-i)\psi'(0)\cdot\int_0^t e^{-\alpha v}\,dv$$

$$=\lambda\cdot E(X_k)\frac{1-e^{-\alpha t}}{\alpha}.$$

4: Birth and Death Processes

One of the obvious generalizations of the pure birth processes discussed in Section 1 is to permit $X(t)$ to decrease as well as increase, for example, by the death of members. Thus if at time t the process is in state n it may, after a random waiting time, move to either of the neighboring states $n+1$ or $n-1$. The resulting "birth and death processes" can then be regarded as the continuous time analogs of random walks (Example B, Section 2, Chapter 2).

A. POSTULATES

As in the case of the pure birth processes we assume that $X(t)$ is a Markov process on the states 0, 1, 2, ... and that its transition probabilities $P_{ij}(t)$ are stationary, i.e.,

$$P_{ij}(t) = \Pr\{X(t+s) = j \mid X(s) = i\}.$$

In addition we assume that the $P_{ij}(t)$ satisfy

1. $P_{i,i+1}(h) = \lambda_i h + o(h)$ as $h \downarrow 0, \quad i \geq 0$
2. $P_{i,i-1}(h) = \mu_i h + o(h)$ as $h \downarrow 0, \quad i \geq 1$
3. $P_{i,i}(h) = 1 - (\lambda_i + \mu_i)h + o(h)$ as $h \downarrow 0, \quad i \geq 0$
4. $P_{ij}(0) = \delta_{ij}$.
5. $\mu_0 = 0, \lambda_0 > 0, \mu_i, \lambda_i > 0, i = 1, 2, \ldots$.

The $o(h)$ in each case may depend on i. The matrix

$$\mathbf{A} = \left\| \begin{matrix} -\lambda_0 & \lambda_0 & 0 & 0 \ldots \\ \mu_1 & -(\lambda_1+\mu_1) & \lambda_1 & 0 \ldots \\ 0 & \mu_2 & -(\lambda_2+\mu_2) & \lambda_2 \ldots \\ 0 & 0 & \mu_3 & -(\lambda_3+\mu_3) \ldots \\ \vdots & \vdots & \vdots & \vdots \end{matrix} \right\| \tag{4.1}$$

is called the *infinitesimal generator* of the process. The parameters λ_i and μ_i are called, respectively, the infinitesimal birth and death rates. In Postulates 1 and 2 we are assuming that if the process starts in state i, then in a small interval of time the probabilities of the population increasing or decreasing by 1 are essentially proportional to the length of the interval. Sometimes a transition from zero to some ignored state is allowed (see Section 7).

Since the $P_{ij}(t)$ are probabilities we have $P_{ij}(t) \geq 0$ and

$$\sum_{j=0}^{\infty} P_{ij}(t) = 1. \tag{4.2}$$

Using the Markovian property of the process we may also derive the Chapman–Kolmogorov equation

$$P_{ij}(t+s) = \sum_{k=0}^{\infty} P_{ik}(t) P_{kj}(s). \tag{4.3}$$

This equation states that in order to move from state i to state j in time $t+s$, $X(t)$ moves to some state k in time t and then from k to j in the remaining time s. This is the continuous time analog of formula (3.2) of Chapter 2.

So far we have mentioned only the transition probabilities $P_{ij}(t)$. In order to obtain the probability that $X(t) = n$ we must specify where the process starts or more generally the probability distribution for the initial state. We then have

$$\Pr(X(t) = n) = \sum_{i=0}^{\infty} q_i P_{in}(t),$$

where

$$q_i = \Pr\{X(0) = i\}.$$

B. WAITING TIMES

With the aid of the above assumptions we may calculate the distribution of the random variable T_i which is the waiting time of $X(t)$ in state i; that is, given the process in state i, what is the distribution of the time T_i until it first leaves state i? Letting

$$\Pr(T_i \geq t) = G_i(t)$$

it follows easily by the Markov property that as $h \downarrow 0$

$$G_i(t+h) = G_i(t)G_i(h) = G_i(t)(P_{ii}(h) + o(h)) = G_i(t)[1 - (\lambda_i + \mu_i)h] + o(h)$$

or

$$\frac{G_i(t+h) - G_i(t)}{h} = -(\lambda_i + \mu_i)G_i(t) + o(1),$$

so that

$$G_i'(t) = -(\lambda_i + \mu_i)G_i(t). \tag{4.4}$$

If we use the condition $G_i(0) = 1$ the solution of this equation is

$$G_i(t) = \exp[-(\lambda_i + \mu_i)t],$$

i.e., T_i follows an exponential distribution with mean $(\lambda_i + \mu_i)^{-1}$. The proof presented above is not quite complete, since we have used the intuitive relationship

$$G_i(h) = P_{ii}(h) + o(h)$$

without a formal proof. A rigorous proof of (4.4) will be given in Chapter 14 of Volume II.

According to Postulates 1 and 2, during a time duration of length h a transition occurs from state i to $i+1$ with probability $\lambda_i h + o(h)$ and from state i to $i-1$ with probability $\mu_i h + o(h)$. It follows intuitively that, given that a transition occurs at time t, the probability this transition is to state $i+1$ is $\lambda_i(\mu_i + \lambda_i)^{-1}$ and to state $i-1$ is $\mu_i(\mu_i + \lambda_i)^{-1}$. The rigorous demonstration of this result is beyond the scope of this book; however, comments on this problem and its intrinsic subtleties will be given later (see Chapter 14 of Volume II).

The description of the motion of $X(t)$ is as follows: The process sojourns in a given state i for a random length of time whose distribution function is an exponential distribution with parameter $(\lambda_i + \mu_i)$. When leaving state i the process enters either state $i+1$ or state $i-1$ with probabilities $\lambda_i(\mu_i+\lambda_i)^{-1}$ and $\mu_i(\mu_i+\lambda_i)^{-1}$, respectively. The motion is analogous to that of a random walk except that transitions occur at random times rather than at fixed time periods.

The traditional procedure for constructing birth and death processes is to prescribe the birth and death parameters $\{\lambda_i, \mu_i\}_{i=0}^{\infty}$ and to build the path structure by utilizing the above description concerning the waiting times and the conditional transition probabilities of the various states. We determine realizations of the process as follows. Suppose $X(0)=i$; the particle spends a random length of time (exponentially distributed with parameter $\lambda_i+\mu_i$) in state i and subsequently moves with probability $\lambda_i/(\mu_i+\lambda_i)$ to state $i+1$ and with probability $\mu_i/(\lambda_i+\mu_i)$ to state $i-1$. Next the particle sojourns a random length of time in the new state and then moves to one of its neighboring states, and so on. More specifically, we observe a value t_1 from the exponential distribution with parameter $(\mu_i+\lambda_i)$ which fixes the initial sojourn time in state i. Then we toss a coin with probability of heads $p_i=\lambda_i/(\lambda_i+\mu_i)$. If heads (tails) appears we move the particle to state $i+1$ $(i-1)$. In state $i+1$ we observe a value t_2 from the exponential distribution with parameter $(\lambda_{i+1}+\mu_{i+1})$ which fixes the sojourn time in the second state visited. If the particle at the first transition enters state $i-1$, the subsequent sojourn time t_2' is an observation from the exponential distribution with parameter $(\lambda_{i-1}+\mu_{i-1})$. After completing the second wait, a binomial trial is performed which chooses the next state to be visited, etc.

A typical outcome of these sampling procedures determines a realization. Its form could be

$$X(t)=\begin{cases} i, & 0<t<t_1, \\ i+1, & t_1<t<t_1+t_2, \\ i, & t_1+t_2<t<t_1+t_2+t_3, \\ \vdots & \\ \cdot & \end{cases}$$

Thus by sampling from exponential and binomial distributions appropriately, we construct typical sample paths of the process. Now it is possible to assign to this set of paths (realizations of the process) a probability measure in a consistent way so that $P_{ij}(t)$ is determined satisfying (4.2), (4.3), and the infinitesimal relations (p. 132). This result is rather deep and its rigorous discussion is beyond the level of this book. The process obtained in this manner is called the minimal process associated with the matrix **A**.

The above construction of the minimal process is fundamental since the infinitesimal parameters need not determine a unique stochastic process obeying (4.2), (4.3), and the postulates of page 132. In fact there could be several Markov processes which possess the same infinitesimal generator. This whole subject is rather complicated and we refer the reader to Chung.† In the special case of birth and death processes, a sufficient condition that there exists a unique Markov process with transition probability function $P_{ij}(t)$ for which the infinitesimal relations, (4.2) and (4.3) hold is that

$$\sum_{n=0}^{\infty} \pi_n \sum_{k=0}^{n} \frac{1}{\lambda_k \pi_k} = \infty, \tag{4.5}$$

where

$$\pi_0 = 1, \qquad \pi_n = \frac{\lambda_0 \lambda_1 \cdots \lambda_{n-1}}{\mu_1 \mu_2 \cdots \mu_n}, \qquad n = 1, 2, \ldots .$$

In most practical examples of birth and death processes the condition (4.5) is met and the birth and death process associated with the prescribed parameters is uniquely determined.

5: *Differential Equations of Birth and Death Processes*

As in the case of the pure birth and Poisson processes the transition probabilities $P_{ij}(t)$ satisfy a system of differential equations known as the *backward Kolmogorov differential equations*. These are given by

$$\begin{aligned} P'_{0j}(t) &= -\lambda_0 P_{0j}(t) + \lambda_0 P_{1j}(t), \\ P'_{ij}(t) &= \mu_i P_{i-1,j}(t) - (\lambda_i + \mu_i) P_{ij}(t) + \lambda_i P_{i+1,j}(t), \qquad i \geq 1, \end{aligned} \tag{5.1}$$

and the boundary condition $P_{ij}(0) = \delta_{ij}$.

To derive these we have from Eq. (4.3)

$$\begin{aligned} P_{ij}(t+h) &= \sum_{k=0}^{\infty} P_{ik}(h) P_{kj}(t) \qquad (5.2) \\ &= \mathrm{P}_{i,i-1}(h) P_{i-1,j}(t) + P_{i,i}(h) P_{ij}(t) + P_{i,i+1}(h) P_{i+1,j}(t) \\ &\qquad + \textstyle\sum_k' P_{ik}(h) P_{kj}(t), \end{aligned}$$

†K. L. Chung; "Markov chains with stationary transition probabilities." Springer-Verlag, Berlin, 1960.

where the last summation is over all $k \neq i-1, i, i+1$. Using postulates 1, 2, and 3 of Section 4 we obtain

$$\begin{aligned}\textstyle\sum_k' P_{ik}(h)P_{kj}(t) \leq \sum_k' P_{ik}(h) &= 1-[P_{i,i}(h)+P_{i,i-1}(h)+P_{i,i+1}(h)]\\ &= 1-[1-(\lambda_i+\mu_i)h+o(h)+\mu_i h+o(h)+\lambda_i h+o(h)]\\ &= o(h),\end{aligned}$$

so that

$$P_{ij}(t+h)=\mu_i hP_{i-1,j}(t)+(1-(\lambda_i+\mu_i)h)P_{ij}(t)+\lambda_i hP_{i+1,j}(t)+o(h).$$

Transposing the term $P_{ij}(t)$ to the left-hand side and dividing the equation by h, we obtain, after letting $h\downarrow 0$,

$$P'_{ij}(t)=\mu_i P_{i-1,j}(t)-(\lambda_i+\mu_i)P_{ij}(t)+\lambda_i P_{i+1,j}(t).$$

The above analysis is a special case of the derivation of the backward differential equations given in Chapter 14.

The backward equations are deduced by decomposing the time interval $(0, t+h)$, where h is positive and small, into the two periods

$$(0, h), \quad (h, t+h),$$

and examining the transitions in each period separately.

The equations (5.1) feature the initial state as the variable.

A different result arises from splitting the time interval $(0, t+h)$ into the two periods.

$$(0, t), \quad (t, t+h)$$

and adapting the preceding analysis. In this viewpoint, under more stringent conditions, we can derive a further system of differential equations

$$\begin{aligned}P'_{i0}(t)&=-\lambda_0 P_{i,0}(t)+\mu_1 P_{i,1}(t),\\ P'_{ij}(t)&=\lambda_{j-1}P_{i,j-1}(t)-(\lambda_j+\mu_j)P_{ij}(t)+\mu_{j+1}P_{i,j+1}(t), \qquad j\geq 1,\end{aligned} \tag{5.3}$$

with the same initial condition $P_{ij}(0)=\delta_{ij}$. These are known as the *forward Kolmogorov differential equations*. To do this we interchange t and h in Eq. (5.2) and under *stronger assumptions* in addition to Postulates 1, 2, and 3 it can be shown that the last term is again $o(h)$. The remainder of the argument is the same as before. The usefulness of the differential equations will become apparent in the examples which we study below.

A sufficient condition that (5.3) hold is that $(P_{kj}(h))/h = o(1)$ for $k \neq j$. $j-1, j+1$ where the $o(1)$ term apart from tending to zero is uniformly bounded with respect to k for fixed j as $h \to 0$. In this case it can easily be proved that $\sum_k' P_{ik}(t)P_{kj}(h)=o(h)$.

Before proceeding with some examples we discuss briefly the behavior of $P_{ij}(t)$ as t becomes large. It can be proved that the limits

$$\lim_{t\to\infty} P_{ij}(t) = p_j \tag{5.4}$$

exist and are independent of the initial state i and also that they satisfy the equations

$$\begin{aligned} -\lambda_0 p_0 + \mu_1 p_1 \qquad &= 0, \\ \lambda_{j-1}p_{j-1} - (\lambda_j + \mu_j)p_j + \mu_{j+1}p_{j+1} &= 0, \qquad j \geq 1. \end{aligned} \tag{5.5}$$

These equations are simply (5.3) where the left-hand side is set equal to zero. The convergence of $\sum_j p_j$ follows since $\sum_j P_{ij}(t) = 1$. If $\sum_j p_j = 1$ then the sequence $\{p_j\}$ is called a " stationary distribution." The reason for this is that p_j also satisfy

$$p_j = \sum_{i=0}^{\infty} p_i P_{ij}(t), \tag{5.6}$$

which tells us that if the process starts in state i with probability p_i then at any given time t it will be in state i with the same probability p_i. The proof of (5.6) follows from (4.3) and (5.4) if we let $t \uparrow \infty$ and use the fact that $\sum_{i=0}^{\infty} p_i < \infty$. The solution to (5.5) is obtained by induction. Letting

$$\pi_0 = 1, \qquad \pi_j = \frac{\lambda_0 \lambda_1 \cdot \cdots \cdot \lambda_{j-1}}{\mu_1 \mu_2 \cdot \cdots \cdot \mu_j}, \quad j \geq 1,$$

we have $p_1 = \lambda_0 \mu_1^{-1} p_0 = \pi_1 p_0$. Assuming that $p_k = \pi_k p_0$ for $k = 1, \ldots, j$ we obtain

$$\begin{aligned} \mu_{j+1} p_{j+1} &= (\lambda_j + \mu_j)\pi_j p_0 - \lambda_{j-1}\pi_{j-1} p_0 \\ &= \lambda_j \pi_j p_0 + (\mu_j \pi_j - \lambda_{j-1}\pi_{j-1}) p_0 \\ &= \lambda_j \pi_j p_0, \end{aligned}$$

and finally

$$p_{j+1} = \pi_{j+1} p_0.$$

In order that the sequence $\{p_j\}$ define a distribution we must have $\sum p_j = 1$. If $\sum \pi_k < \infty$ we see in this case that

$$p_j = \frac{\pi_j}{\sum \pi_k}, \qquad j = 0, 1, 2, \ldots.$$

If $\sum \pi_k = \infty$ then necessarily $p_0 = 0$ and the p_j are all zero. Hence, we do not have a limiting stationary distribution.

6: *Examples of Birth and Death Processes*

Example 1. *Linear Growth with Immigration.* A birth and death process is called a linear growth process if $\lambda_n = \lambda n + a$ and $\mu_n = \mu n$ with $\lambda > 0$, $\mu > 0$, and $a > 0$. Such processes occur naturally in the study of biological reproduction and population growth. If the state n describes the current population size, then the average instantaneous rate of growth is $\lambda n + a$. Similarly, the probability of the state of the process decreasing by one after the elapse of a small duration of time is $\mu nt + o(t)$. The factor λn represents the natural growth of the population owing to its current size while the second factor a may be interpreted as the infinitesimal rate of increase of the population due to an external source such as immigration. The component μn which gives the mean infinitesimal death rate of the present population possesses the obvious interpretation.

If we substitute the above values of λ_n and μ_n in (5.3) we obtain

$$\begin{aligned} P'_{i0}(t) &= -aP_{i0}(t) + \mu P_{i1}(t), \\ P'_{ij}(t) &= (\lambda(j-1) + a)P_{i,j-1}(t) - ((\lambda + \mu)j + a)P_{ij}(t) \\ &\qquad + \mu(j+1)P_{i,j+1}(t), \qquad j \geq 1. \end{aligned}$$

Now if we multiply the jth equation by j and sum, it follows that the expected value

$$EX(t) = M(t) = \sum_{j=1}^{\infty} jP_{ij}(t)$$

satisfies the differential equation

$$M'(t) = a + (\lambda - \mu)M(t),$$

with initial condition $M(0) = i$, if $X(0) = i$. The solution of this equation is

$$M(t) = at + i \qquad \text{if} \quad \lambda = \mu,$$

and

$$M(t) = \frac{a}{\lambda - \mu}\{e^{(\lambda-\mu)t} - 1\} + ie^{(\lambda-\mu)t} \qquad \text{if} \quad \lambda \neq \mu.$$

The second moment or variance may be calculated in a similar way. It is interesting to note that $M(t) \to \infty$ as $t \to \infty$ if $\lambda \geq \mu$, while if $\lambda < \mu$ the mean population size for large t is approximately

$$\frac{a}{\mu - \lambda}.$$

Example 2. *Queueing.* A queueing process is a process in which customers arrive at some designated place where a service of some kind is being rendered, for example, at the teller's window in a bank or beside the cashier at a supermarket. It is assumed that the time between arrivals, or inter-arrival time, and the time that is spent in providing service for a given customer are governed by probabilistic laws. The length of the queue at a given time t is represented by $X(t)$.

If we let $\lambda_i = \lambda$ for all i in the general birth and death process, the resulting process is a special simple case of a continuous time queueing process. The state of the system is then interpreted as the length of a queue for which the times between arrivals of the customers are independent random variables with an exponential distribution of parameter λ and for which the duration of the service time of the current customer is a random variable with an exponential distribution whose parameter, μ_n, may depend on the length of the line. At the completion of each service the line decreases by 1 and with each new arrival the line increases by 1. The classical case of a single-server queue corresponds to $\mu_i = \mu$, $i \geq 1$, i.e., each service follows the same exponential distribution with parameter μ independent of the length of the waiting line.

The classical telephone trunking model can be formulated as a queueing birth and death process with infinitely many servers, each of whose service time distribution has the same parameter μ, so that $\mu_i = i\mu$, $i \geq 1$. The rationale underlying this specification goes as follows: Suppose the queue consists of i individual customers; then since the number of servers is unlimited each customer is simultaneously receiving service. Now the length of service of each is independent of the others and distributed exponentially with parameter μ. It follows that the probability distribution of the time until at least one of the customers completes service (i.e., the length of time until the waiting line decreases by 1) is also exponentially distributed, but is now of parameter $i\mu$ (the student should prove this).

Besides the two special cases mentioned above it is possible to consider numerous other queueing models by appropriate specifications of the parameters μ_k. For example, a queue with n servers, each of whose service time has an exponential distribution with the same parameter μ, would correspond to $\mu_k = k\mu$ for $1 \leq k \leq n$, $\mu_i = n\mu$ for $i \geq n$.

For the single-server process with $\lambda < \mu$ the stationary distribution is easily calculated. In fact, in this case

$$\pi_n = \frac{\lambda_0 \lambda_1 \cdot \cdots \cdot \lambda_{n-1}}{\mu_1 \mu_2 \cdot \cdots \cdot \mu_n} = \left(\frac{\lambda}{\mu}\right)^n,$$

which, when normalized, results in

$$p_n = \frac{\mu - \lambda}{\mu} \left(\frac{\lambda}{\mu}\right)^n, \qquad n \geq 0,$$

i.e., a geometric distribution with mean $\lambda(\mu - \lambda)^{-1}$.

This gives us the answer to many problems involving stationarity. If the process has been going on a long time and $\lambda < \mu$, the probability of being served immediately upon arrival is

$$p_0 = \left(1 - \frac{\lambda}{\mu}\right).$$

We can also calculate the distribution of waiting time in the stationary case when $\lambda < \mu$. If an arriving customer finds n people in front of him, his total waiting time T, including his own service time, is the sum of the service times of himself and those ahead, all distributed exponentially with parameter μ, and since the service times are independent of the queue size, T has a gamma distribution of order $n+1$ with scale parameter μ

$$\Pr\{T \le t \mid n \text{ ahead}\} = \int_0^t \frac{\mu^{n+1}\tau^n e^{-\mu\tau}}{\Gamma(n+1)}\,d\tau. \tag{6.1}$$

By the law of total probabilities, we have

$$\Pr\{T \le t\} = \sum_{n=0}^{\infty} \Pr\{T \le t \mid n \text{ ahead}\} \cdot \left(\frac{\lambda}{\mu}\right)^n \left(1 - \frac{\lambda}{\mu}\right),$$

since $(\lambda/\mu)^n(1-\lambda/\mu)$ is the probability that in the stationary case a customer on arrival will find n ahead in line. Now, substituting from (6.1), we obtain

$$\begin{aligned}
\Pr\{T \le t\} &= \sum_{n=0}^{\infty} \int_0^t \frac{\mu^{n+1}\tau^n e^{-\mu\tau}}{\Gamma(n+1)} \left(\frac{\lambda}{\mu}\right)^n \left(1 - \frac{\lambda}{\mu}\right) d\tau \\
&= \int_0^t \mu e^{-\mu\tau} \left(1 - \frac{\lambda}{\mu}\right) \sum_{n=0}^{\infty} \frac{\tau^n \lambda^n}{\Gamma(n+1)}\, d\tau \\
&= \int_0^t \left(1 - \frac{\lambda}{\mu}\right) \mu \exp\left\{-\tau\mu\left(1 - \frac{\lambda}{\mu}\right)\right\} d\tau \\
&= 1 - \exp\left[-t\mu\left(1 - \frac{\lambda}{\mu}\right)\right],
\end{aligned}$$

which is also an exponential distribution.

If we wish to answer nonstationary questions, it is essential to determine $P_{ij}(t)$ for all t. This is a much harder problem but it has been solved. The details of this solution are beyond the scope of this book and we refer the interested student to any of the advanced books on queuing theory listed in the references.

For the telephone trunking problem with $\lambda_n = \lambda$ and $\mu_n = n\mu$ it is easily seen that

$$p_n = \frac{e^{-\lambda/\mu}(\lambda/\mu)^n}{n!},$$

which is the familiar Poisson distribution with mean λ/μ. As in Example 1, it is easy to show that

$$M(t) = \sum_{j=0}^{\infty} jP_{ij}(t)$$

satisfies the equation

$$M'(t) = \lambda - \mu M(t),$$

whose solution is

$$M(t) = \frac{\lambda}{\mu}(1 - e^{-\mu t}) + ie^{-\mu t}.$$

If we let $t \to \infty$, then $M(t) \to \lambda/\mu$, which is the mean value of the stationary distribution given above.

Example 3. *Some Genetic Models.* Consider a population consisting of N individuals which are either of gene type a or gene type A. The state of the process $X(t)$ represents the number of a-individuals at time t. We assume that the probability that the state changes during the time interval $(t, t + h)$ is $\lambda h + o(h)$ independent of the values of $X(t)$ and that the probability of two or more changes occurring in a time interval h is $o(h)$.

The changes in the population structure are effected as follows. An individual is to be replaced by another chosen randomly from the population; i.e., if $X(t) = j$ then an a-type is selected to be replaced with probability j/N and an A-type with probability $1 - j/N$. We refer to this stage as death. Next, birth takes place by the following rule. Another selection is made randomly from the population to determine the type of the new individual replacing the one that died. The model introduces mutation pressures which admit the possibility that the type of the new individual may be altered upon birth. Specifically, let γ_1 denote the probability that an a-type mutates to an A-type and let γ_2 denote the probability of an A-type mutating to an a-type.

The probability that the new individual added to the population is of type a is

$$\frac{j}{N}(1 - \gamma_1) + \left(1 - \frac{j}{N}\right)\gamma_2. \tag{6.2}$$

We deduce this formula as follows: The probability that we select an a-type and no mutation occurs is $(j/N)(1-\gamma_1)$. Moreover, the final type may be an a-type if we select an A-type which subsequently mutates into an a-type. The probability of this contingency is $(1-j/N)\gamma_2$. The combination of these two possibilities gives (6.2).

We assert that the conditional probability that $X(t+)-X(t)=1$, when a change of state occurs, is

$$\left(1-\frac{j}{N}\right)\left[\frac{j}{N}(1-\gamma_1)+\left(1-\frac{j}{N}\right)\gamma_2\right], \qquad \text{where} \quad X(t)=j. \tag{6.3}$$

In fact, the a-type population size can increase only if an A-type dies (is replaced). This probability is $1-(j/N)$. The second factor is the probability that the new individual is of type a as in (6.2).

In a similar way we find that the conditional probability that $X(t+)-X(t)=-1$ when a change of state occurs is

$$\frac{j}{N}\left[\left(1-\frac{j}{N}\right)(1-\gamma_2)+\frac{j}{N}\gamma_1\right], \qquad \text{where} \quad X(t)=j.$$

The stochastic process described is thus a birth and death process with a finite number of states† whose infinitesimal birth and death rates are

$$\lambda_j=\lambda\left(1-\frac{j}{N}\right)\left[\frac{j}{N}(1-\gamma_1)+\left(1-\frac{j}{N}\right)\gamma_2\right]$$

and

$$\mu_j=\lambda\frac{j}{N}\left[\frac{j}{N}\gamma_1+\left(1-\frac{j}{N}\right)(1-\gamma_2)\right],$$

respectively corresponding to an a-type population size j, $0\le j\le N$.

Although these parameters seem rather complicated, it is interesting to see what happens to the stationary measure $\{\pi_k\}_{k=0}^N$ if we let the population size $N\to\infty$ and the probabilities of mutation per individual γ_1 and γ_2 tend to zero in such a way that $\gamma_1 N\to\kappa_1$ and $\gamma_2 N\to\kappa_2$, where $0<\kappa_1$, $\kappa_2<\infty$. At the same time we shall transform the state of the process to the interval [0, 1] by defining new states j/N, i.e., the fraction of

† The definition of birth and death processes was given for an infinite number of states. The adjustments in the definitions and analyses for the case of a finite number of states is straightforward and even simpler and left to the reader.

a-types in the population. To examine the stationary density at a fixed fraction x, where $0 < x < 1$, we shall evaluate π_k as $k \to \infty$ in such a way that $k = [xN]$, where $[xN]$ is the greatest integer less than or equal to xN.

Keeping these relations in mind we write

$$\lambda_j = \frac{\lambda(N-j)}{N^2}(1-\gamma_1-\gamma_2)j\left(1+\frac{a}{j}\right), \qquad \text{where} \quad a = \frac{N\gamma_2}{1-\gamma_1-\gamma_2},$$

and

$$\mu_j = \frac{\lambda(N-j)}{N^2}(1-\gamma_1-\gamma_2)j\left(1+\frac{b}{N-j}\right), \qquad \text{where} \quad b = \frac{N\gamma_1}{1-\gamma_1-\gamma_2}.$$

Then

$$\begin{aligned}\log \pi_k &= \sum_{j=0}^{k-1} \log \lambda_j - \sum_{j=1}^{k} \log \mu_j \\ &= \sum_{j=1}^{k-1} \log\left(1+\frac{a}{j}\right) - \sum_{j=1}^{k-1} \log\left(1+\frac{b}{N-j}\right) + \log Na \\ &\quad - \log(N-k)k\left(1+\frac{b}{N-k}\right).\end{aligned}$$

Now using the expression

$$\log(1+x) = x - \frac{x^2}{2} + \frac{x^3}{3} - \cdots, \qquad |x| < 1,$$

it is possible to write

$$\sum_{j=1}^{k-1} \log\left(1+\frac{a}{j}\right) = a\sum_{j=1}^{k-1}\frac{1}{j} + c_k,$$

where c_k approaches a finite limit as $k \to \infty$. Therefore, using the relation

$$\sum_{j=1}^{k-1}\frac{1}{j} \sim \log k \qquad \text{as} \quad k \to \infty,$$

we have

$$\sum_{j=1}^{k-1} \log\left(1+\frac{a}{j}\right) \sim \log k^a + c_k \qquad \text{as} \quad k \to \infty.$$

In a similar way we obtain

$$\sum_{j=1}^{k-1} \log\left(1+\frac{b}{N-j}\right) \sim \log \frac{N^b}{(N-k)^b} + d_k \qquad \text{as} \quad k \to \infty,$$

where d_k approaches a finite limit as $k \to \infty$. Using the above relations we have

$$\log \pi_k \sim \log\left(C_k \frac{k^a(N-k)^b Na}{N^b(N-k)k}\right) \quad \text{as} \quad k \to \infty, \tag{6.4}$$

where $\log C_k = c_k + d_k$, which approaches a limit, say C, as $k \to \infty$. Notice that $a \to \kappa_2$ and $b \to \kappa_1$ as $N \to \infty$. Since $k = [Nx]$ we have, for $N \to \infty$,

$$\pi_k \sim C\kappa_2 N^{\kappa_2 - 1} x^{\kappa_2 - 1}(1-x)^{\kappa_1 - 1}.$$

Now from (6.4) we have

$$\pi_k \sim aC_k k^{a-1}\left(1 - \frac{k}{N}\right)^{b-1}.$$

Therefore

$$\frac{1}{N^a}\sum_{k=0}^{N-1} \pi_k \sim \frac{a}{N}\sum_{k=0}^{N-1} C_k \left(\frac{k}{N}\right)^{a-1}\left(1 - \frac{k}{N}\right)^{b-1}.$$

Since $C_k \to C$ as k tends to ∞ we recognize the right-hand side as the Riemann sum approximation of

$$\kappa_2 C \int_0^1 x^{\kappa_2 - 1}(1-x)^{\kappa_1 - 1}\,dx.$$

Thus

$$\sum_{i=0}^{N} \pi_i \sim N^{\kappa_2}\kappa_2 C \int_0^1 x^{\kappa_2 - 1}(1-x)^{\kappa_1 - 1}\,dx,$$

so that the resulting density on $[0, 1]$ is

$$\frac{\pi_k}{\sum \pi_i} \sim \frac{1}{N}\frac{x^{\kappa_2 - 1}(1-x)^{\kappa_1 - 1}}{\int_0^1 x^{\kappa_2 - 1}(1-x)^{\kappa_1 - 1}\,dx} = \frac{x^{\kappa_2 - 1}(1-x)^{\kappa_1 - 1}\,dx}{\int_0^1 x^{\kappa_2 - 1}(1-x)^{\kappa_1 - 1}\,dx},$$

since $dx \sim 1/N$. This is a beta distribution with parameters κ_1 and κ_2.

Example 4. *Logistic Process.* Suppose we consider a population whose size $X(t)$ ranges between two fixed integers N_1 and N_2 ($N_1 < N_2$) for all $t \geq 0$. We assume that the birth and death rates per individual at time t are given by

$$\lambda = \alpha(N_2 - X(t)) \qquad \text{and} \qquad \mu = \beta(X(t) - N_1),$$

and that the individual members of the population act independently of each other. The resulting birth and death rates for the population then become

$$\lambda_n = \alpha n(N_2 - n) \qquad \text{and} \qquad \mu_n = \beta n(n - N_1).$$

To see this we observe that if the population size $X(t)$ is n, then each of the n individuals has an infinitesimal birth rate λ so that $\lambda_n = \alpha n(N_2 - n)$. The same rationale applies in the interpretation of the μ_n.

Under such conditions one would expect the process to fluctuate between the two constants N_1 and N_2, since, for example, if $X(t)$ is near N_2 the death rate is high and the birth rate low and then $X(t)$ will tend toward N_1. Ultimately the process should display stationary fluctuations between the two limits N_1 and N_2.

The stationary distribution in this case is

$$p_{N_1+m} = \frac{c}{N_1+m}\binom{N_2-N_1}{m}\left(\frac{\alpha}{\beta}\right)^m, \qquad m = 0, 1, 2, \ldots, N_2 - N_1,$$

where c is an appropriate constant determined so that $\sum_m p_{N_1+m} = 1$. To see this we observe that

$$\begin{aligned}\pi_{N_1+m} &= \frac{\lambda_{N_1}\lambda_{N_1+1}\cdots\lambda_{N_1+m}}{\mu_{N_1+1}\mu_{N_1+2}\cdots\mu_{N_1+m}} \\ &= \frac{\alpha^m N_1(N_1+1)\cdot\cdots\cdot(N_1+m-1)(N_2-N_1)\cdot\cdots\cdot(N_2-N_1-m+1)}{\beta^m(N_1+1)\cdot\cdots\cdot(N_1+m)\,m!} \\ &= \frac{N_1}{N_1+m}\binom{N_2-N_1}{m}\left(\frac{\alpha}{\beta}\right)^m.\end{aligned}$$

7: *Birth and Death Processes with Absorbing States*

It is of importance to treat the case of birth and death processes where $\lambda_0 = 0$. This stipulation converts the zero state into an absorbing state. When a transition occurs from state 1, the particle moves to state 2 with probability $\lambda_1/(\lambda_1 + \mu_1)$ or it is trapped in state 0 with probability $\mu_1/(\lambda_1 + \mu_1)$. An important example of a birth and death process where 0 acts as an absorbing state is the linear growth process without immigration (cf. Example 1 of Section 6). In this case $\lambda_n = n\lambda$ and $\mu_n = n\mu$. Since growth of the population results exclusively from the existing population it is clear that when the population size becomes 0 it remains zero thereafter, i.e., 0 is an absorbing state.

A. PROBABILITY OF ABSORPTION INTO STATE 0

It is of interest to compute the probability of absorption into state 0 starting from state i ($i \geq 1$). This is not, *a priori*, a certain event since conceivably the particle (i.e., state variable) may wander forever among the states (1, 2, ...) or possibly drift to infinity.

Let u_i $(i = 1, 2, \ldots)$ denote the probability of absorption into state 0 from the initial state i. We can write a recursion formula for u_i by considering the possible states after the first transition. We know that the first transition entails the movements

$$i \to i+1 \qquad \text{with probability} \quad \frac{\lambda_i}{\mu_i + \lambda_i},$$

$$i \to i-1 \qquad \text{with probability} \quad \frac{\mu_i}{\mu_i + \lambda_i}.$$

We directly obtain

$$u_i = \frac{\lambda_i}{\mu_i + \lambda_i} u_{i+1} + \frac{\mu_i}{\mu_i + \lambda_i} u_{i-1}, \qquad i \geq 1, \tag{7.1}$$

where $u_0 = 1$. Another method for deriving (7.1) is to consider the "embedded random walk" associated with a given birth and death process. Specifically we examine the birth and death process only at the transition times. The discrete time Markov chain generated in this manner is denoted by $\{Y_n\}_{n=0}^{\infty}$, where $Y_0 = X_0$ is the initial state and Y_n $(n \geq 1)$ is the state at the nth transition. Obviously, the transition probability matrix has the form

$$\mathbf{P} = \left\| \begin{matrix} 1 & 0 & 0 & 0 & \cdots \\ q_1 & 0 & p_1 & 0 & \cdots \\ 0 & q_2 & 0 & p_2 & \cdots \\ \vdots & \vdots & & & \end{matrix} \right\|,$$

where

$$p_i = \frac{\lambda_i}{\lambda_i + \mu_i} = 1 - q_i \qquad (i \geq 1).$$

The probability of absorption into state 0 for the embedded random walk is the same as for the birth and death process since both processes execute the same transitions.

We turn to the task of solving (7.1) subject to the conditions $u_0 = 1$ and $0 \leq u_i \leq 1$ $(i \geq 1)$. Rewriting (7.1) we have

$$(u_{i+1} - u_i) = \frac{\mu_i}{\lambda_i}(u_i - u_{i-1}), \qquad i \geq 1.$$

Defining $v_i = u_{i+1} - u_i$, we obtain

$$v_i = \frac{\mu_i}{\lambda_i} v_{i-1}, \qquad i \geq 1.$$

Iteration of the last relation yields the formula

$$u_{i+1} - u_i = v_i = \left(\prod_{j=1}^{i} \frac{\mu_j}{\lambda_j}\right) v_0, \qquad i \geq 1.$$

Summing these equations from $i = 1$ to $i = m$ we have

$$u_{m+1} - u_1 = (u_1 - 1) \sum_{i=1}^{m} \left(\prod_{j=1}^{i} \frac{\mu_j}{\lambda_j}\right), \qquad m \geq 1. \tag{7.2}$$

Since u_m, by its very meaning, is bounded by 1 we see that if

$$\sum_{i=1}^{\infty} \left(\prod_{j=1}^{i} \frac{\mu_j}{\lambda_j}\right) = \infty \tag{7.3}$$

then necessarily $u_1 = 1$ and $u_m = 1$ for all $m \geq 2$. In other words, if (7.3) holds then ultimate absorption into state 0 is certain from any initial state. Suppose $0 < u_1 < 1$; then, of course,

$$\sum_{i=1}^{\infty} \left(\prod_{j=1}^{i} \frac{\mu_j}{\lambda_j}\right) < \infty.$$

Obviously, u_m is decreasing in m since passing from state m to state 0 requires entering the intermediate states in the intervening time. Furthermore, we claim that $u_m \to 0$ as $m \to \infty$. If we assume the contrary i.e., $u_m \geq \alpha > 0$ $(m \geq 1)$, a simple probabilistic argument implies that $u_m \equiv 1$ $(m \geq 1)$. (The student should supply a formal proof.) Now letting $m \to \infty$ in (7.2) permits us to solve for u_1; thus

$$u_1 = \frac{\sum_{i=1}^{\infty} \left(\prod_{j=1}^{i} \mu_j/\lambda_j\right)}{1 + \sum_{i=1}^{\infty} \left(\prod_{j=1}^{i} \mu_j/\lambda_j\right)}$$

and in addition we have

$$u_{m+1} = \frac{\sum_{i=m+1}^{\infty} \left(\prod_{j=1}^{i} \mu_j/\lambda_j\right)}{1 + \sum_{i=1}^{\infty} \left(\prod_{j=1}^{i} \mu_j/\lambda_j\right)}, \qquad m \geq 1.$$

In the special example of a linear growth birth and death process where $\mu_n = n\mu$ and $\lambda_n = n\lambda$, a direct calculation yields

$$\left.\begin{aligned} u_m &= \left(\frac{\mu}{\lambda}\right)^m && \text{when} \quad \mu < \lambda \\ u_m &= 1 && \text{when} \quad \mu \geq \lambda \end{aligned}\right\} \quad (m \geq 1).$$

B. MEAN TIME UNTIL ABSORPTION

Consider the problem of determining the mean time until absorption, starting from state m.

We assume that condition (7.3) holds so that absorption is certain. Notice that we cannot reduce our problem to a consideration of the embedded random walk since the actual time spent in each state is relevant for the calculation of the mean absorption time.

Let ω_i be the mean absorption time starting from state i (this could be infinite). Considering the possible states following the first transition and recalling the fact that the mean waiting time in state i is $(\lambda_i + \mu_i)^{-1}$ (it is actually exponentially distributed with parameter $\lambda_i + \mu_i$), we deduce the recursion relation

$$\omega_i = \frac{1}{\lambda_i + \mu_i} + \frac{\lambda_i}{\lambda_i + \mu_i}\,\omega_{i+1} + \frac{\mu_i}{\lambda_i + \mu_i}\,\omega_{i-1}, \qquad i \geq 1, \tag{7.4}$$

where by convention $\omega_0 = 0$. Letting $z_i = \omega_i - \omega_{i+1}$ and rearranging (7.4) leads to

$$z_i = \frac{1}{\lambda_i} + \frac{\mu_i}{\lambda_i} z_{i-1}, \qquad i \geq 1. \tag{7.5}$$

Iterating this relation gives

$$z_m = \frac{1}{\lambda_m} + \frac{\mu_m}{\lambda_m}\frac{1}{\lambda_{m-1}} + \frac{\mu_m \mu_{m-1}}{\lambda_m \lambda_{m-1}} z_{m-2}$$

and finally

$$z_m = \sum_{i=1}^{m} \frac{1}{\lambda_i} \prod_{j=i+1}^{m} \frac{\mu_j}{\lambda_j} + \left(\prod_{j=1}^{m} \frac{\mu_j}{\lambda_j}\right) z_0 .$$

(The product $\prod_{m+1}^{m} \mu_j/\lambda_j$ is interpreted as 1.)

In terms of ω_m we have

$$\omega_m - \omega_{m+1} = \sum_{i=1}^{m} \frac{1}{\lambda_i} \prod_{j=i+1}^{m} \frac{\mu_j}{\lambda_j} - \omega_1 \prod_{j=1}^{m} \frac{\mu_j}{\lambda_j}, \qquad m \geq 1. \tag{7.6}$$

It is more convenient to write

$$\sum_{i=1}^{m} \frac{1}{\lambda_i} \prod_{j=i+1}^{m} \frac{\mu_j}{\lambda_j} = \prod_{j=1}^{m} \frac{\mu_j}{\lambda_j} \sum_{i=1}^{m} \rho_i, \tag{7.7}$$

where

$$\rho_i = \frac{\lambda_1 \lambda_2 \cdot \cdots \cdot \lambda_{i-1}}{\mu_1 \mu_2 \cdot \cdots \cdot \mu_i} .$$

Then in terms of (7.7), the relation (7.6) becomes

$$\left(\prod_{j=1}^{m}\frac{\lambda_j}{\mu_j}\right)(\omega_m-\omega_{m+1})=\sum_{i=1}^{m}\rho_i-\omega_1. \tag{7.8}$$

Note that if $\sum_{i=1}^{\infty}\rho_i=\infty$, inspection of (7.8) reveals that necessarily $\omega_1=\infty$. Indeed, it is probabilistically evident that $\omega_m<\omega_{m+1}$ for all m and this property would be violated for m large if we assume to the contrary that ω_1 is finite.

Now suppose $\sum_{i=1}^{\infty}\rho_i<\infty$; then letting $m\to\infty$ in (7.8) gives

$$\omega_1=\sum_{i=1}^{\infty}\rho_i-\lim_{m\to\infty}\left(\prod_{j=1}^{m}\frac{\lambda_j}{\mu_j}\right)(\omega_m-\omega_{m+1}).$$

It is more involved but still possible to prove that

$$\lim_{m\to\infty}\left(\prod_{j=1}^{m}\frac{\lambda_j}{\mu_j}\right)(\omega_m-\omega_{m+1})=0$$

and then indeed

$$\omega_1=\sum_{i=1}^{\infty}\rho_i.$$

We summarize the discussion of this section in the following theorem:

Theorem 7.1. *Consider a birth and death process with birth and death parameters λ_n and μ_n, $n\ge 1$, where $\lambda_0=0$ so that 0 is an absorbing state.*

The probability of absorption into state 0 from the initial state m is

$$\begin{cases}\dfrac{\sum_{i=m}^{\infty}\left(\prod_{j=1}^{i}\mu_j/\lambda_j\right)}{1+\sum_{i=1}^{\infty}\left(\prod_{j=1}^{i}\mu_j/\lambda_j\right)} & \text{if } \sum_{i=1}^{\infty}\left(\prod_{j=1}^{i}\dfrac{\mu_j}{\lambda_j}\right)<\infty,\\[2ex] 1 & \text{if } \sum_{i=1}^{\infty}\left(\prod_{j=1}^{i}\dfrac{\mu_j}{\lambda_j}\right)=\infty.\end{cases} \tag{7.9}$$

The mean time to absorption is

$$\begin{cases}\infty & \text{if } \sum_{i=1}^{\infty}\rho_i=\infty,\\[2ex] \sum_{i=1}^{\infty}\rho_i+\sum_{r=1}^{m-1}\left(\prod_{k=1}^{r}\dfrac{\mu_k}{\lambda_k}\right)\sum_{j=r+1}^{\infty}\rho_j & \text{if } \sum_{i=1}^{\infty}\rho_i<\infty,\end{cases} \tag{7.10}$$

where $\rho_i=(\lambda_1\lambda_2\cdot\cdots\cdot\lambda_{i-1})/(\mu_1\mu_2\cdot\cdots\cdot\mu_i)$.

For the example of the linear growth birth and death process ($\lambda_n = n\lambda$, $\mu_n = n\mu$, and $\mu > \lambda$) the mean time ω_1 to absorption from state 1 is

$$\sum_{i=1}^{\infty} \rho_i = \frac{1}{\mu} \sum_{i=1}^{\infty} \frac{1}{i} \left(\frac{\lambda}{\mu}\right)^{i-1} = \frac{1}{\lambda} \sum_{i=0}^{\infty} \int_0^{\lambda/u} \xi^i \, d\xi = \frac{1}{\lambda} \int_0^{\lambda/u} \frac{1}{1-\xi} \, d\xi = -\frac{1}{\lambda} \log\left(1 - \frac{\lambda}{\mu}\right). \tag{7.11}$$

8: Finite State Continuous Time Markov Chains

A continuous time Markov chain X_t ($t > 0$) is a Markov process on the states 0, 1, 2, ... We assume as usual that the transition probabilities are stationary, i.e.,

$$P_{ij}(t) = \Pr\{X_{t+s} = j | X_s = i\}. \tag{8.1}$$

In this section we consider only the case where the state space S is finite, labeled as $\{0, 1, 2, \ldots, N\}$. Some aspects of the general, infinite state, continuous time, Markov chain are discussed in the following chapter.

The Markovian property asserts that $P_{ij}(t)$ satisfies

(a) $P_{ij}(t) \geq 0$,

(b) $\sum_{j=0}^{N} P_{ij}(t) = 1, \qquad i, j \in S$

(c) $P_{ik}(s+t) = \sum_{j=0}^{N} P_{ij}(s) P_{jk}(t) \qquad t, s \geq 0$ (Chapman–Kolmogorov relation),

and we postulate in addition that

(d) $\lim_{t \to 0+} P_{ij}(t) = \begin{cases} 1, & i = j, \\ 0, & i \neq j, \end{cases}$

holds.

If $\mathbf{P}(t)$ denotes the matrix $\|P_{ij}(t)\|_{i,j=0}^{N}$ then property (c) can be written compactly in matrix notation as

$$\mathbf{P}(t+s) = \mathbf{P}(t)\mathbf{P}(s), \qquad t, s \geq 0. \tag{8.2}$$

Property (d) asserts that $\mathbf{P}(t)$ is continuous at $t = 0$ since the fact $\mathbf{P}(0) = \mathbf{I}$ (= identity matrix) is implied by (8.2). It follows simply from (8.2) that $\mathbf{P}(t)$ is continuous for all $t > 0$. In fact if $s = h > 0$ in (8.2) then because of (d) we have

$$\lim_{h \to 0+} \mathbf{P}(t+h) = \mathbf{P}(t) \lim_{h \to 0+} \mathbf{P}(h) = \mathbf{P}(t)\mathbf{I} = \mathbf{P}(t). \tag{8.3}$$

On the other hand, for $t > 0$ and $0 < h < t$ we write (8.2) in the form

$$\mathbf{P}(t) = \mathbf{P}(t-h)\mathbf{P}(h). \tag{8.4}$$

But $\mathbf{P}(h)$ is near the identity when h is sufficiently small and so $\mathbf{P}(h)^{-1}$ [the inverse of $\mathbf{P}(h)$] exists and also approaches the identity $\mathbf{I}$. Therefore

$$\mathbf{P}(t) = \mathbf{P}(t) \lim_{h\to 0+} (\mathbf{P}(h))^{-1} = \lim_{h\to 0+} \mathbf{P}(t-h). \tag{8.5}$$

The limit relations (8.3) and (8.5) together show that $\mathbf{P}(t)$ is continuous. It is proved in Theorems 1.1 and 1.2 of Chapter 14 for the general, infinite state, continuous time, Markov chain that

$$\begin{aligned} &\lim_{h\to 0+} \frac{1-P_{ii}(h)}{h} = q_i, \\ &\lim_{h\to 0+} \frac{P_{ij}(h)}{h} = q_{ij}, \qquad i \neq j. \end{aligned} \tag{8.6}$$

exist, where $0 \le q_{ij} < \infty$ $(i \neq j)$ and $0 \le q_i \le \infty$, i.e., q_{ij} $(i \neq j)$ is always finite and q_i is defined but could be infinite. The possibility $q_i = \infty$ cannot occur in the case of a finite state, continuous time, Markov chain. In fact, starting with the relation

$$1 = P_{ii}(h) + \sum_{j=0,j\neq i}^{N} P_{ij}(h),$$

dividing by h, and letting h decrease to zero yields directly the relation

$$q_i = \sum_{j=0,j\neq i}^{N} q_{ij},$$

which shows that q_i is indeed finite.

Assuming that (8.6) has been verified we now derive an explicit expression for $P_{ij}(t)$ in terms of the infinitesimal matrix

$$\mathbf{A} = \left\| \begin{matrix} -q_0 & q_{01} & \cdots & q_{0N} \\ q_{10} & -q_1 & \cdots & q_{1N} \\ \vdots & & & \\ q_{N0} & q_{N1} & \cdots & -q_N \end{matrix} \right\|.$$

The limit relations (8.6) can be expressed concisely in matrix form:

$$\lim_{h\to 0+} \frac{\mathbf{P}(h)-\mathbf{I}}{h} = \mathbf{A}. \tag{8.7}$$

With the aid of this formula and referring to (8.2) we have

$$\frac{\mathbf{P}(t+h)-\mathbf{P}(t)}{h} = \frac{\mathbf{P}(t)[\mathbf{P}(h)-\mathbf{I}]}{h} = \frac{\mathbf{P}(h)-\mathbf{I}}{h}\mathbf{P}(t). \tag{8.8}$$

The limit on the right exists and this leads to the matrix differential equation

$$\mathbf{P}'(t) = \mathbf{P}(t)\mathbf{A} = \mathbf{A}\mathbf{P}(t), \tag{8.9}$$

where $\mathbf{P}'(t)$ denotes the matrix whose elements are $P'_{ij}(t)$.

The existence of $P'_{ij}(t)$ is obviously an immediate consequence of (8.7) and (8.8).

Equations (8.9) can be solved under the initial condition $\mathbf{P}(0) = \mathbf{I}$ by the standard methods of systems of ordinary differential equations† to yield the formula

$$\mathbf{P}(t) = e^{\mathbf{A}t} = \mathbf{I} + \sum_{n=1}^{\infty} \frac{\mathbf{A}^n t^n}{n!}. \tag{8.10}$$

In practical terms we determine the eigenvalues $\lambda_0, \lambda_1, \ldots, \lambda_N$ of $\mathbf{A}$ and a complete system of associated right eigenvectors $\mathbf{u}^{(0)}, \ldots, \mathbf{u}^{(N)}$ when possible (see the Appendix at the close of the book). Then we have the representation

$$\mathbf{P}(t) = \mathbf{U}\Lambda(t)\mathbf{U}^{-1}, \tag{8.11}$$

where $\mathbf{U}$ is the matrix whose column vectors are, respectively, $\mathbf{u}^{(0)}$, $\mathbf{u}^{(1)}, \ldots, \mathbf{u}^{(N)}$ and $\Lambda(t)$ is the diagonal matrix

$$\Lambda(t) = \begin{Vmatrix} \exp(\lambda_0 t) & 0 & \cdots & 0 \\ 0 & \exp(\lambda_1 t) & & 0 \\ \vdots & \vdots & \ddots & \vdots \\ 0 & 0 & \cdots & \exp(\lambda_N t) \end{Vmatrix}.$$

The rows of the matrix $\mathbf{U}^{-1}$ can also be identified as a complete system of left eigenvectors normalized to be biorthogonal to the $\{\mathbf{u}^{(i)}\}_{i=0}^{N}$.

Applications of (8.10) or (8.11) are implicit in Elementary Problems 7 and 13 of this chapter.

Elementary Problems

1. Let X_1 and X_2 be independent exponentially distributed random variables with parameters λ_1 and λ_2 so that

$$\Pr\{X_i > t\} = \exp\{-\lambda_i t\} \quad \text{for} \quad t \geq 0.$$

† E. A. Coddington, and N. Levinson, "Theory of Ordinary Differential Equations," Chapter 3. McGraw-Hill, New York, 1955.

Let

$$N = \begin{cases} 1 & \text{if} \quad X_1 < X_2, \\ 2 & \text{if} \quad X_2 \le X_1, \end{cases}$$

$$U = \min\{X_1, X_2\} = X_N,$$

$$V = \max\{X_1, X_2\},$$

and

$$W = V - U = |X_1 - X_2|.$$

Show

(a) $\Pr\{N=1\} = \lambda_1/(\lambda_1+\lambda_2)$ and $\Pr\{N=2\} = \lambda_2/(\lambda_1+\lambda_2)$.
(b) $\Pr\{U>t\} = \exp\{-(\lambda_1+\lambda_2)t\}$ for $t \ge 0$.
(c) N and U are independent random variables.
(d) $\Pr\{W>t|N=1\} = \exp\{-\lambda_2 t\}$ and
$\Pr\{W>t|N=2\} = \exp\{-\lambda_1 t\}$ for $t \ge 0$.
(e) U and $W = V - U$ are independent random variables.

2. Assume a device fails when a cumulative effect of k shocks occur. If the shocks happen according to a Poisson process with parameter λ find the density function for the life T of the device.

Solution:

$$f(t) = \begin{cases} \dfrac{\lambda^k t^{k-1} e^{-\lambda t}}{\Gamma(k)}, & t > 0, \\ 0, & t \le 0. \end{cases}$$

3. Let $\{X(t), t \ge 0\}$ be a Poisson process with intensity parameter λ. Suppose each arrival is "registered" with probability p, independent of other arrivals. Let $\{Y(t), t \ge 0\}$ be the process of "registered" arrivals. Prove that $Y(t)$ is a Poisson process with parameter λp.

4. Let $\{X(t), t \ge 0\}$ and $\{Y(t), t \ge 0\}$ be independent Poisson processes with parameters λ_1 and λ_2, respectively. Define $Z_1(t) = X(t) + Y(t)$, $Z_2(t) = X(t) - Y(t)$, $Z_3(t) = X(t) + k$, k a positive integer. Determine which of the above processes are Poisson and find λ.

5. Messages arrive at a telegraph office in accordance with the laws of a Poisson process with mean rate of 3 messages per hour.

(a) What is the probability that no message will have arrived during the morning hours (8 to 12)?
(b) What is the distribution of the time at which the first afternoon message arrives?

6. Let $X(t)$ be a homogeneous Poisson process with parameter λ. Determine the covariance between $X(t)$ and $X(t+\tau)$, $t > 0$ and $\tau > 0$, i.e., compute $E[(X(t) - E(X(t))(X(t+\tau) - EX(t+\tau))]$.

7. A continuous time Markov chain has two states labeled 0 and 1. The waiting time in state 0 is exponentially distributed with parameter $\lambda > 0$. The waiting time in state 1 follows an exponential distribution with parameter $\mu > 0$. Compute the probability $P_{00}(t)$ of being in state 0 at time t starting at time 0 in state 0.

Solution:

$$P_{00}(t) = \frac{\mu}{\lambda + \mu} + \frac{\lambda}{\lambda + \mu} e^{-(\lambda+\mu)t}.$$

8. In Elementary Problem 7 let $\lambda = \mu$ and define $N(t)$ to be the number of times the system has changed states in time $t \geq 0$. Find the probability distribution of $N(t)$.

Solution:

$$\Pr\{N(t) = n\} = e^{-\lambda t} \frac{(\lambda t)^n}{n!}.$$

9. Let $X(t)$ be a pure birth continuous time Markov chain. Assume that

$$\Pr\{\text{an event happens in } (t, t+h) | X(t) = \text{odd}\} = \lambda_1 h + o(h),$$
$$\Pr\{\text{an event happens in } (t, t+h) | X(t) = \text{even}\} = \lambda_2 h + o(h),$$

where $o(h)/h \to 0$ as $h \downarrow 0$. Take $X(0) = 0$. Find the following probabilities:

$$P_1(t) = \Pr\{X(t) = \text{odd}\}, \qquad P_2(t) = \Pr\{X(t) = \text{even}\}.$$

Hint: Derive the differential equations

$$P_1'(t) = -\lambda_1 P_1(t) + \lambda_2 P_2(t), \qquad P_2'(t) = \lambda_1 P_1(t) - \lambda_2 P_2(t)$$

and solve them.

Solution:

$$P_1(t) = \frac{\lambda_2}{\lambda_1 + \lambda_2}(1 - \exp\{-(\lambda_1 + \lambda_2)t\});$$

$$P_2(t) = \frac{\lambda_1}{\lambda_1 + \lambda_2} + \frac{\lambda_2}{\lambda_1 + \lambda_2} \exp\{-(\lambda_1 + \lambda_2)t\}.$$

10. Under the conditions of Elementary Problem 9 determine $E[X(t)]$.

Solution:

$$EX(t) = \frac{2\lambda_1\lambda_2}{\lambda_1 + \lambda_2} t + \frac{(\lambda_1 - \lambda_2)\lambda_2}{(\lambda_1 + \lambda_2)^2} [\exp\{-(\lambda_1 + \lambda_2)t\} - 1].$$

11. Suppose $g(t)$ is the conditional rate of failure of an article at time t, given that it has not failed up to time t, i.e., $\Pr\{\text{failure in time } (t, t+h) | \text{no failure up to time } t\} = g(t)h + o(h)$ as $h \downarrow 0$. Assume that $g(t)$ is positive and continuous on $(0, \infty)$. Find an expression for $F(t) = \Pr\{\text{failure at some time } \tau, \tau < t\}$ in terms of $g(\cdot)$.

Hint: Derive a differential equation for $F(t)$.

Solution: $F(t) = 1 - \exp[-\int_0^t g(\tau)\, d\tau]$.

12. Consider a variable time Poisson process, i.e., the occurrence of an event E during the time duration $(t, t+h)$ is independent of the number of previous occurrences of E and its probability is $\lambda(t)h + o(h)$ $(h \to 0)$. (Note that λ may now depend on t.)

(a) Prove that the probability of no occurrence of E during the time duration $[0, s]$ is

$$\exp\left(-\int_0^s \lambda(\xi)\, d\xi\right).$$

(b) Prove that the probability of k occurrences of E during the time duration $[0, s]$ is

$$\frac{1}{k!}\left(\int_0^s \lambda(\xi)\, d\xi\right)^k \exp\left(-\int_0^s \lambda(\xi)\, d\xi\right).$$

13. There are two transatlantic cables each of which can handle one telegraph message at a time. The time-to-breakdown for each has the same exponential distribution with parameter λ. The time to repair for each cable has the same exponential distribution with parameter μ. Given that at time 0 both cables are in working condition, find the probability that, if at time t two messages arrive simultaneously, they will find both cables operative.

Hint: This is a three-state continuous time, Markov chain.

Solution:

$$\frac{\mu^2}{(\lambda+\mu)^2} + \frac{\lambda^2 e^{-2(\lambda+\mu)t}}{(\lambda+\mu)^2} + \frac{2\lambda\mu}{(\lambda+\mu)^2} e^{-(\lambda+\mu)t}.$$

14. Consider the linear growth birth and death process $X(t)$ with parameters λ, μ and $a = 0$. Assume $X(0) = 1$. Find the distribution of the number of living individuals at the time of the first death.

Solution:

$$\Pr\{\text{number } k \text{ of births before the first death}\} = (\mu/(\mu+\lambda))(\lambda/(\lambda+\mu))^k.$$

15. Find the stationary distribution for the linear growth birth and death process when $\lambda < \mu$ (Example 1 of Section 6).

Solution:

$$p_n = \left(\frac{\lambda}{\mu}\right)^n \frac{(a/\lambda)((a/\lambda)+1)\cdot \cdots \cdot((a/\lambda)+n-1)}{n!}\left(1-\frac{\lambda}{\mu}\right)^{a/\lambda}.$$

16. A telephone exchange has m channels. Calls arrive in the pattern of a Poisson process with parameter λ; they are accepted if there is an empty channel, otherwise they are lost. The duration of each call is a r.v. whose distribution function is exponential with parameter μ. The lifetimes of separate calls are independent random variables. Find the stationary probabilities of the number of busy channels.

Solution:

$$p_n = \frac{(\lambda/\mu)^n(1/n!)}{\sum_{k=0}^{m} (\lambda/\mu)^k(1/k!)}, \qquad n = 0, 1, 2, \ldots, m.$$

17. We start observing a radioactive atom at time 0. It will decay and cease to be radioactive at a time t, $t > 0$, determined by the distribution

$$F(\tau) = \begin{Bmatrix} 0, & \tau < 0 \\ 1 - e^{-\lambda\tau}, & \tau \geq 0 \end{Bmatrix} = \Pr\{t \leq \tau\}.$$

Consider the state of the atom at time t as a random variable

$$x_t = \begin{cases} 0 & \text{if the atom is radioactive at time } t, \\ 1 & \text{if the atom is not radioactive at time } t. \end{cases}$$

The variables $\{x_t\}$ define a stochastic process.

Suppose that at time 0 we begin observing N independent radioactive atoms, represented in the above sense by x_t^i, $i = 1, 2, \ldots, N$. Let $X_t = \sum_{i=1}^{N} x_t^i$. Then $\{X_t\}$ is also a stochastic process. Show that for $t \ll 1/\lambda$ (t negligibly small compared with $1/\lambda$) and sufficiently large N, $\{X_t\}$ is very closely approximated by a Poisson process $Y(t)$ with parameter $\lambda N t$.

18. Suppose that in Problem 17 the approximation $t \ll \lambda^{-1}$ cannot be made. (i) Is the process a process with independent increments? (ii) Is it stationary? (iii) Does it have stationary transition probabilities? (iv) Is it a Markov process?

Solution: (i) Yes, (ii) no, (iii) yes, (iv) yes.

19. This problem attempts to relate the properties of the life history of a colonizing species to its chances for success, or more precisely, to the length of time it persists before going extinct.

Let $Z(t)$ be the population size at time t. We suppose $(Z(t);\ t \geq 0)$ evolves as a birth and death process with *individual* birth rate λ and *individual* death rate μ. By this we mean that each individual alive at time t gives birth to a new individual during the interval $(t, t + \Delta t)$ with probability (approximately) $\lambda(\Delta t)$, and dies during that interval with probability $\mu(\Delta t)$.

We want to construct a model that can be used to estimate the mean survival time of a population of such individuals, and we want the model to reflect the fact that all populations are limited in their maximum size by the carrying capacity of the environment, which we assume to be K individuals. Since all individuals have a chance of dying, all populations will surely go extinct if given enough time. We want to build into the model the properties of exponential growth (on the average) for small populations, as well as the ceiling K, beyond which the population cannot normally grow. There are any number of ways of approaching population size K and staying there at equilibrium. We will take the simple case where the birth parameters are

$$\lambda_i = \begin{cases} \lambda i & \text{for} \quad i = 0, \ldots, K-1 \\ 0 & \text{for} \quad i \geq K, \end{cases}$$

and the death parameters are $\mu_i = \mu i$ for $i = 0, 1, \ldots$.

In this model, compute the expected time to extinction, given the population begins with a single individual.

20. Suppose that we have a mechanism which can fail in two ways. Let the probability of the first type failure in the interval $(t, t+h)$ be $\lambda_1 h + o(h)$ and the probability of the second type failure in the interval $(t, t+h)$ be $\lambda_2 h + o(h)$. Upon failure, repair is performed whose duration is distributed as an exponetial random variable with parameter depending upon the type failure. Let μ_1 and μ_2 denote the respective parameters. Compute the probability that the mechanism is working at time t.

Solution:

$$\mathbf{P}(t) = e^{\mathbf{Q}t} \qquad \text{where} \quad \mathbf{Q} = \begin{Vmatrix} -(\lambda + \lambda_2) & \lambda_1 & \lambda_2 \\ \mu_1 & -\mu_1 & 0 \\ \mu_2 & 0 & -\mu_2 \end{Vmatrix}.$$

21. Compare the $M/M/1$ system for a first-come first-served queue discipline with one of last-come first-served type (for example, articles for service are taken from the top of a stack). How do the queue size, waiting time, and busy period distribution differ, if at all?

Solution: Queue size and busy period do not differ but the waiting time distributions differ. Why?

22. (Queuing with Balking) Customers, with independent and identically distributed service times, arrive at a counter in the manner of a Poisson process with parameter λ. A customer who finds the server busy joins the queue with probability $p (0 < p < 1)$. The service time distribution is exponential with parameter μ.

Formulate this model as a birth and death process.

Solution: $\lambda_n = \lambda p$; $\mu_n = \mu$.

23. Consider the $M/M/1$ system with queue discipline of last-come first-served type. Let $X(t)$ be the queue size at time t. Show that the process $\{X(t); t \geq 0\}$ is a birth and death process and determine its parameters.

Solution: $\lambda_n = \lambda$, $\mu_n = \mu$.

24. Under the condition that $X(0) = N = 1$, determine the mean and variance of the Yule process.

Solution:

$$E[X(t)] = e^{\lambda t}, \qquad \operatorname{Var}[X(t)] = e^{2\lambda t}(1 - e^{-\lambda t}).$$

Problems

1. Let $\{X(t), t \geq 0\}$ and $\{Y(t), t \geq 0\}$ be two independent Poisson processes with parameters λ_1 and λ_2, respectively. Define

$$Z(t) = X(t) - Y(t), \qquad t \geq 0.$$

This is a stochastic process whose state space consists of all the integers (positive, negative, and zero). Let

$$P_n(t) = \Pr\{Z(t) = n\}, \qquad n = 0, \pm 1, \pm 2, \ldots.$$

Establish the formula

$$\sum_{n=-\infty}^{\infty} P_n(t)z^n = \exp(-(\lambda_1 + \lambda_2)t) \exp(\lambda_1 zt + (\lambda_2/z)t), \qquad |z| \neq 0.$$

Compute $E(Z(t))$ and $E(Z(t)^2)$.

Answer: $E(Z(t))^2 = (\lambda_1 + \lambda_2)t + (\lambda_1 - \lambda_2)^2 t^2$.

2. Consider two independent Poisson processes $X(t)$ and $Y(t)$ where $E(X(t)) = \lambda t$ and $E(Y(t)) = \mu t$. Let two successive events of the $X(t)$ process occur at T and $T' > T$ so that $X(t) = X(T)$ for $T \leq t < T'$ and $X(T') = X(T) + 1$. Define $N = Y(T') - Y(T)$ = the number of events of the $Y(t)$ process in the time interval (T, T'). Find the distribution of N.

Answer:

$$\Pr\{N = m\} = \frac{\lambda}{\lambda + \mu}\left(\frac{\mu}{\lambda + \mu}\right)^m, \qquad m = 0, 1, 2, \ldots.$$

3. Consider a pure death process where $\mu_n = n\mu$ for $n = 1, 2, \ldots$, i.e., $P\{X(t+h) = j | X(t) = k\} = 0$ for $j > k$ and t and k positive. Assume an initial population of size i. Find $P_n(t) = P\{X(t) = n\}$, $EX(t)$, and $\operatorname{Var} X(t)$.

Answer:

$$P_n(t) = \binom{i}{n} e^{-n\mu t}(1 - e^{-\mu t})^{(i-n)},$$

$$EX(t) = ie^{-\mu t},$$

$$\operatorname{Var} X(t) = ie^{-\mu t}(1 - e^{-\mu t}).$$

4. Consider a Yule process with parameter β and initial state $N = 1$. Suppose the first individual is also subject to death, with the probability of death in the interval t to $t + h$, given that the individual is living at time t, being $\mu h + o(h)$. Compute the distribution of the number of offspring due to a single individual and his descendants at the time of death of the original parent.

Answer: Probability of a total of n offspring originating from a specified individual and of his line of descendants at the time of his death is

$$\int_0^\infty e^{-\beta t}(1-e^{-\beta t})^n \mu e^{-\mu t}\,dt = \frac{\mu}{\beta}\frac{\Gamma((\mu/\beta)+1)\Gamma(n+1)}{\Gamma(n+(\mu/\beta)+2)}.$$

5. Let $(X(t), Y(t))$ describe a stochastic process in two-dimensional space where $X(t)$ is a Poisson process with parameter λ_1 and $Y(t)$ is a Poisson process independent of $X(t)$ with parameter λ_2. Given that the process is in the state (x_0, y_0) at time $t=0$, $x_0+y_0<z$, what is the probability that it will intersect the line $x+y=z$ at the point (x, y)?

Answer:

$$\begin{cases} \dbinom{z-x_0-y_0}{x-x_0}\left(\dfrac{\lambda_1}{\lambda_1+\lambda_2}\right)^{x-x_0}\left(\dfrac{\lambda_2}{\lambda_1+\lambda_2}\right)^{y-y_0} & \text{for } x\geq x_0, y\geq y_0, \\ 0 & \text{otherwise.} \end{cases}$$

6. Consider a Poisson process with parameter λ. Let T be the time required to observe the first event, and let $N(T/\kappa)$ be the number of events in the next T/κ units of time. Find the first two moments of $N(T/\kappa)T$.

Answer:

$$E\left\{N\left(\frac{T}{\kappa}\right)T\right\}=\frac{2}{\lambda\kappa};\qquad E\left\{\left(N\left(\frac{T}{\kappa}\right)T\right)^2\right\}=\frac{6}{\lambda^2\kappa}+\frac{24}{\lambda^2\kappa^2}.$$

7. Consider n independent objects (such as light bulbs) whose failure time (i.e., lifetime) is a random variable exponentially distributed with density function $f(x, \theta)=\theta^{-1}\exp(-x/\theta)$, $x>0$; 0 for $x\leq 0$ (θ is a positive parameter). The observations of lifetime become available in order of failure. Let

$$X_{1,n}\leq X_{2,n}\leq\cdots\leq X_{r,n}$$

denote the lifetimes of the first r objects that fail. Determine the joint density function of $X_{i,n}$, $i=1, 2, \ldots, r$.

Answer:

$$f(x_1, x_2, \ldots, x_r)=r!\binom{n}{r}\frac{1}{\theta^r}\exp\left(-\frac{x_1+x_2+\cdots+x_{r-1}+(n-r+1)x_r}{\theta}\right).$$

8. In the preceding problem define $Y_{1,n}=X_{1,n}$ and

$$Y_{i,n}=X_{i,n}-X_{i-1,n}\qquad\text{for } 2\leq i\leq r.$$

Prove that $Y_{i,n}$ are mutually independent and find the distribution function of each.

Answer:

$$\Pr\{Y_{i,n}\leq y\}=1-\exp\left(-\frac{n-i+1}{\theta}y\right).$$

9. Consider a Poisson process of parameter λ. Given that n events happen in time t, find the density function of the time of the occurrence of the rth event $(r < n)$.

Answer:

$$p(x) = \begin{cases} \dfrac{n!}{(r-1)!(n-r)!} \dfrac{x^{r-1}}{t^r} \left(1 - \dfrac{x}{t}\right)^{n-r} & 0 < x < t, \\ 0, & \text{otherwise.} \end{cases}$$

10. Let $\mathfrak{M}$ be a continuous time birth and death process where $\lambda_n = \lambda > 0$, $n \geq 0$, $\mu_0 = 0$, $\mu_n > 0$, $n \geq 1$. Let $\pi = \sum_n \pi_n < \infty$, where $\pi_n = \lambda^n/(\mu_1 \mu_2 \cdot \cdots \cdot \mu_n)$ so that π_i/π is the stationary distribution of the process. Suppose the initial state is a r.v. whose distribution is the stationary distribution of the process. Prove that the number of deaths in $[0, t]$ has a Poisson distribution with parameter λt.

Hint: Let $a_k(t)$ be the probability that the number of deaths by time t is k. Derive the differential equation

$$a_k'(t) = -\lambda a_k(t) + \lambda a_{k-1}(t), \qquad k = 1, 2, \ldots.$$

11. The following defines one concept of a multivariate Poisson process in two dimensions. Let $(X(t), Y(t))$ be defined by $X(t) = \alpha(t) + \gamma(t)$, $Y(t) = \beta(t) + \gamma(t)$, where $\alpha(t)$, $\beta(t)$, and $\gamma(t)$ are three independent Poisson processes with parameters λ_1, λ_2, and λ_3, respectively. Find the generating function of the distribution of $(X(t), Y(t))$.

Answer:

$$\begin{aligned} &\sum \Pr\{X(t) = i, Y(t) = j\} x^i y^j \\ &\quad = \exp\{t(\lambda_1 x + \lambda_2 y + \lambda_3 xy - \lambda_1 - \lambda_2 - \lambda_3\}. \end{aligned}$$

12. Consider a Yule process $\{N_t, t \geq 0\}$ with birthrate λ and initial population of size 1. Find the distribution function of $N_t(x)$ = number of members of the population at time t of age less than or equal to x.

Hint: Condition on the value of N_{t-x}.

Solution:

$$\Pr\{N_t(x) = k\} = \frac{e^{-\lambda t}(1 - e^{-\lambda x})^k}{[1 - e^{-\lambda x} + e^{-\lambda t}]^{k+1}}.$$

13. Let $\{X_i(t); t \geq 0\}$, $i = 1, 2$, be two independent Yule processes with the same parameter λ. Let $X_i(0) = n_i$, $i = 1, 2$. Determine the conditional distribution of $X_1(t)$ given $X_1(t) + X_2(t) = N$ $(N \geq n_1 + n_2)$.

Answer:

$$\Pr\{X_1(t) = k | X_1(t) + X_2(t) = N\} = \frac{\dbinom{k-1}{n_1-1}\dbinom{N-k-1}{n_2-1}}{\dbinom{N-1}{n_1+n_2-1}} \qquad \text{for} \quad k \geq n_1.$$

14. Continuation of Problem 13.

Prove the limit distiibution relation

$$\lim_{t\to\infty} \Pr\left\{\frac{X_1(t)}{X_1(t)+X_2(t)} \le x\right\} = \frac{(n_1+n_2-1)!}{(n_1-1)!\,(n_2-1)!} \int_0^x y^{n_1-1}(1-y)^{n_2-1}\,dy.$$

Hint: Let $N\to\infty$ and $k\to\infty$ in such a way that $k/N\to y$ $(0<y<1)$. Then with the aid of Sterling's approximation establish the asymptotic relation

$$\lim_{\substack{\frac{k}{N}\to y,\ N\to\infty \\ k\to\infty}} \frac{\binom{k-1}{n_1-1}\binom{N-k-1}{n_2-1}}{\binom{N-1}{n_1+n_2-1}} = \frac{(n_1+n_2-1)!}{(n_1-1)!\,(n_2-1)!} y^{n_1-1}(1-y)^{n_2-1}$$

Use this to show that

$$\lim_{t\to\infty} \Pr\left\{y \le \frac{X_1(t)}{X_1(t)+X_2(t)} \le y+h\right\}$$

$$= \frac{(n_2+n_1-1)!}{(n_1-1)!\,(n_2-1)!} h y^{n_1-1}(1-y)^{n_2-1} + o(h).$$

15. A system is composed of N identical components; each independently operates a random length of time until failure. Suppose the failure time distribution is exponential with parameter λ. When a component fails it undergoes repair. The repair time is random, with distribution function exponential with parameter μ. The system is said to be in state n at time t if there are exactly n components under repair at time t. This process is a birth and death process. Determine its infinitesimal parameters.

16. In Problem 15, suppose that initially all N components are operative. Find the distribution $F(t)$ of the first time that there are two inoperative components.

Answer: The Laplace transform $\varphi(s)$ of $F(t)$ is

$$\varphi(s) = \frac{N(N-1)\lambda^2}{s^2 + s[(2N-1)\lambda+\mu] + N(N-1)\lambda^2}.$$

In the case $\lambda=\mu$,

$$1 - F(t) = \frac{\sqrt{N(N-1)}}{2}\{\exp[(-N+\sqrt{N})\lambda t] - \exp[(-N-\sqrt{N})\lambda t]\}.$$

17. Consider the following continuous version of the Ehrenfest model (see page 51, Chapter 2). We have $2N$ balls labeled 1, 2, 3, ..., $2N$. At time 0 each ball is equally likely to be placed in one of two urns. Subsequently, the balls independently undergo displacement randomly in time from one urn to the other by the following rules. A ball has a probability $\frac{1}{2}h + o(h)$ of changing urns during the time interval $(t, t+h)$ and probability $1-(h/2)+o(h)$ of remaining in the same urn during that interval. The movements over disjoint intervals of time are independent. Let $X(t)$ denote the number of balls in urn I at time t. Set

$$P_{jk}(t) = \Pr\{X(t) = k | X(0) = j\}, \qquad j, k = 0, 1, \ldots, 2N.$$

Establish the formula

$$g(t, s) = \sum_{k=0}^{2N} P_{jk}(t)s^k = 2^{-2N}[1 - e^{-t} + (1 + e^{-t})s]^j[1 + e^{-t} + (1 - e^{-t})s]^{2N-j}.$$

Hint: Define the random variables

$$X_i(t) = \begin{cases} 1 & \text{if the } i\text{th ball is in urn I at time } t, \quad \text{for } i = 1, 2, \ldots, 2N. \\ 0 & \text{otherwise,} \end{cases}$$

Then

$$X(t) = \sum_{i=1}^{2N} X_i(t).$$

Show that

$$\Pr\{X_i(t) = X_i(0)\} = \frac{1 + e^{-t}}{2}, \qquad i = 1, 2, \ldots, 2N.$$

18. For a linear growth birth and death process $X(t)$ with $\lambda = \mu$ (Example 1, Section 6), prove that

$$u(t) = \Pr\{X(t) = 0 | X(0) = 1\}$$

satisfies the integral equation

$$u(t) = \frac{1}{2}\int_0^t 2\lambda e^{-2\lambda\tau}\, d\tau + \frac{1}{2}\int_0^t 2\lambda e^{-2\lambda\tau}[u(t-\tau)]^2 d\tau.$$

Hint: Note that the waiting time to the first event (birth or death) is exponentially distributed with parameter 2λ.

19. (Continuation of Problem 18) Show that $u(t)$ satisfies the Ricatti differential equation

$$u'(t) + 2\lambda u(t) = \lambda + \lambda u^2(t), \qquad u(0) = 0.$$

20. (Continuation of Problem 19) Find $u(t)$.

Answer:

$$u(t) = \frac{\lambda t}{1 + \lambda t}.$$

21. (Continuation of Problem 20). Determine $\Pr\{X(t) = 0 | X(0) = 1, X(T) = 0\}$ for $0 < t < T$.

22. Consider a birth and death process with infinitesimal parameter λ_n, μ_n. Show that the expected length of time for reaching state $r + 1$ starting from state 0 is

$$\sum_{n=0}^{r} \frac{1}{\lambda_n \pi_n} \sum_{k=0}^{n} \pi_k$$

For the definition of π_n see Eq. (4.5).

Hint: Let T_n^* denote the elapsed time of first entering state $n+1$ starting from state n. Derive a recursion relation for $E(T_n^*)$.

23. The following problem arises in molecular biology. The surface of a bacterium is supposed to consist of several sites at which a foreign molecule may become attached if it is of the right composition. A molecule of this composition will be called acceptable. We consider a particular site and postulate that molecules arrive at the site according to a Poisson process with parameter μ. Among these molecules a proportion β is acceptable. Unacceptable molecules stay at the site for a length of time which is exponentially distributed with parameter λ. While at the site they prevent further attachments there. An acceptable molecule "fixes" the site preventing any further attachments. What is the probability that the site in question has not been fixed by time t?

Hint: Set the problem up as a three-state continuous time Markov chain for the site in question.

Answer: $$\frac{\beta\mu}{s_2 - s_1}\left[\left(1+\frac{\lambda}{s_1}\right)e^{s_1 t} - \left(1+\frac{\lambda}{s_2}\right)e^{s_2 t}\right]$$

where s_1, s_2 are the roots of $s^2 + s(\lambda+\mu) + \mu\beta\lambda = 0$.

24. Consider an infinitely many-server queue with an exponential service time distribution with parameter μ. Suppose customers arrive in batches with the interarrival time following an exponential distribution with parameter λ. The number of arrivals in each batch is assumed to follow the geometric distribution with parameter ρ $(0<\rho<1)$, i.e., $\Pr\{\text{number of arrivals in a batch has size } k\} = \rho^{k-1}(1-\rho)$ $(k=1,2,\ldots)$.
Formulate this process as a continuous time Markov chain and determine explicitly the infinitesimal matrix of the process.

25. Show for the $M/M/1$ queueing process in a stationary state that the distribution of time between successive departures has the same (exponential) distribution as the interarrival time distribution (see also Problem 10).

26. Let $\{X_i(t); t \geq 0\}$ $i=1,2$ be two independent Poisson processes with parameters λ_1 and λ_2 respectively. Let $X_1(0)=m$, $X_2(0)=N-1$, and $m<N$.
(a) Determine the probability that the X_2 process reaches N before the X_1 process does.
(b) Solve the same problem for $X_2(0)=n$ where $n<N$.

Answer: (*b*):

$$\sum_{r=0}^{N-m-1}\binom{N-n+r-1}{r}p^r q^{N-n}, \qquad p=\frac{\lambda_1}{\lambda_1+\lambda_2}$$

27. The following two birth and death processes (cf. Section 4, Chapter 4) can be viewed as models for queueing with balking.

(a) First consider a birth and death process with parameters

$$\lambda_n = \lambda q^n, \quad 0 < q < 1, \quad \lambda > 0 \quad (n = 0, 1, 2, \ldots),$$
$$\mu_n = \mu, \qquad \mu > 0,$$
$$\mu_0 = 0.$$

(b) Let the parameters be

$$\lambda_n = \frac{\lambda}{n+1}, \qquad \mu_n = \mu \qquad (n = 1, 2, \ldots),$$
$$\mu_0 = 0.$$

Determine the stationary distribution in each case.

Answer: (a) $p_m = p_0(\lambda/\mu)^m q^{m(m-1)/2}$ for $m \geq 1$. (b) $p_m = p_0(\lambda/\mu)^m(1/m!)$ for $m \geq 0$, whence $p_0 = e^{-\lambda/\mu}$.

28. Show for the $M/M/s$ system that the stationary queue size distribution $\{p_n, n = 0, 1, 2, \ldots\}$ is given by

$$p_0 = \left\{\frac{(s\rho)^s}{s!(1-\rho)} + \sum_{i=0}^{s-1} \frac{(s\rho)^i}{i!}\right\}^{-1}$$

$$p_n = \begin{cases} p_0 \dfrac{(s\rho)^n}{n!}, & 1 \leq n \leq s, \\[2ex] p_0\, \rho^n \dfrac{s^s}{s!}, & s < n < \infty, \end{cases}$$

where $\rho = \lambda/s\mu < 1$. Let $Q = \max(n - s, 0)$ $(n = 0, 1, 2, \ldots)$ be the size of the queue not including those being served. Show that

(i) $$\gamma = \Pr\{Q = 0\} = \frac{\sum_{i=0}^{s} (s\rho)^i/i!}{\sum_{i=0}^{s} [(s\rho)^i/i!] + [(s\rho)^s \rho/s!(1-\rho)]};$$

(ii) $E(Q) = (1 - \gamma)/(1 - \rho)$.

29. A system is composed of N machines. At most $M \leq N$ can be operating at any one time; the rest are "spares". When a machine is operating, it operates a random length of time until failure. Suppose this failure time is exponentially distributed with parameter μ.

When a machine fails it undergoes repair. At most R machines can be "in repair" at any one time. The repair time is exponentially distributed with parameter λ. Thus a machine can be in any of four states: (i) Operating, (ii) "Up", but not operating, i.e., a spare, (iii) In repair, (iv) Waiting for repair. There are a total of N machines in the system. At most M can be operating. At most R can be in repair.

Let $X(t)$ be the number of machines "up" at time t, either operating or spare. Then, (we assume) the number operating is $\min\{X(t), M\}$ and the number of spares is $\max\{0, X(t) - M\}$. Let $Y(t) = N - X(t)$ be the number of machines

" down". Then the number in repair is $\min\{Y(t), R\}$ and the number waiting for repair is $\max\{0, Y(t)-R\}$. The above formulas permit to determine the number of machines in any category, once $X(t)$ is known.

$X(t)$ is a birth and death process.

(a) Determine the birth and death parameters, λ_i and μ_i, $i=0, \ldots, N$.
(b) In the following special cases, determine π_j, the stationary probability that $X(t)=j$.
(a) $R=M=N$. (b) $R=1, M=N$.

30. (Continuation of Problem 29) (a) Determine the stationary distribution in the case $R<M=N$. (b) Let $X_{N,R}(\infty)$ denote a random variable having the stationary distribution in (a). Let $N\to\infty$, $R\to\infty$ but such that $N/R\to 1+\alpha$ where $\alpha>0$ is fixed. Determine normalizing constants a_N and b_N and a limiting distribution Φ for which

$$\lim_{N\to\infty} \Pr\left\{\frac{X_{N,R}(\infty)-a_N}{b_N}\leq x\right\}=\Phi(x).$$

(There are two cases (i) $\alpha>\lambda/\mu$ and (ii) $\alpha<\lambda/\mu$).

31. Consider a pure birth process having infinitesimal parameters $\lambda_n=\lambda n^2$, where $\lambda>0$ is fixed. Given that at time 0 there is a single particle, determine

$$P_\infty(t)=1-\sum_{k=1}^{\infty} P_k(t).$$

32. Let $X(t)$ be a Yule process starting at $X(0)=N$ and having birth rate β. Show

$$\Pr\{X(t)\geq n|X(0)=N\}=\sum_{k=n-N}^{n-1}\binom{n-1}{k}p^k q^{n-1-k}$$

where $q=1-p=e^{-\beta t}$.

NOTES

Poisson and birth and death processes play a fundamental role in the theory and applications that embrace queueing and inventory models, population growth, engineering systems, etc. Elementary discussions on Poisson and related processes can be found in all textbooks on stochastic processes.

The literature of queueing theory is voluminous. An elegant monograph reviewing this theory and its applications is that of Cox and Smith [1].

We also direct the student to the advanced books by Takács [2] and Riordan [3].

A compendium of results on queueing theory is contained in Saaty [4]. This reference also includes an extensive bibliography.

Applications to congestion theory and telephone trunking problems can be found in Syski [5].

Some special mathematical aspects of queueing theory are developed in the monograph by Beneš [6].

REFERENCES

1. D. R. Cox and W. L. Smith, "Queues." Methuen, London, 1961.
2. L. Takács, "Introduction to the Theory of Queues." Oxford Univ. Press, London and New York, 1962.
3. J. Riordan, "Stochastic Service Systems." Wiley, New York, 1962.
4. T. L. Saaty, "Elements of Queueing Theory with Applications." McGraw-Hill, New York, 1961.
5. R. Syski, "Congestion Theory." Oliver and Boyd, New York, 1960.
6. V. E. Beneš, "General Stochastic Processes in the Theory of Queues." Addison-Wesley, Reading, Massachusetts, 1963.

Chapter 5

RENEWAL PROCESSES

Renewal theory began with the study of stochastic systems whose evolution through time was interspersed with renewals, times when, in a statistical sense, the process began anew. Today, the subject is viewed as the general study of functions of independent, identically distributed, nonnegative random variables representing the successive intervals between renewals. The results are applicable in a wide variety of both theoretical and practical probability models.

The first six sections of this chapter are vital and should be included in every introductory course. Sections 7 and 8 are not difficult and will round out a basic knowledge of renewal theory if time permits their study. Section 9 offers a glimpse of a topic of some recent interest and may be omitted at first reading.

1: *Definition of a Renewal Process and Related Concepts*

A *renewal (counting) process* $\{N(t),\ t \geq 0\}$ is a nonnegative integer-valued stochastic process that registers the successive occurrences of an event during the time interval $(0, t]$, where the time durations between consecutive "events" are *positive, independent, identically distributed,* random variables (i.i.d.r.v.). Let the successive occurence times between events be $\{X_k\}_{k=1}^{\infty}$ (often representing the lifetimes of some units successively placed into service) such that X_i is the elapsed time from the $(i-1)$st event until the occurrence of the ith event. We write

$$F(x) = \Pr\{X_k \leq x\}, \qquad k = 1, 2, 3, \ldots,$$

for the common probability distribution of $\{X_k\}$. A basic stipulation for renewal processes is $F(0) = 0$, signifying that X_k are *positive* random variables. We refer to

$$S_n = X_1 + X_2 + \cdots + X_n, \qquad n \geq 1 \qquad (S_0 = 0, \text{ by convention}) \tag{1.1}$$

as the *waiting time* until the occurrence of the nth event. Note formally that

$$N(t) = \text{number of indices } n \text{ for which } 0 < S_n \leq t. \tag{1.2}$$

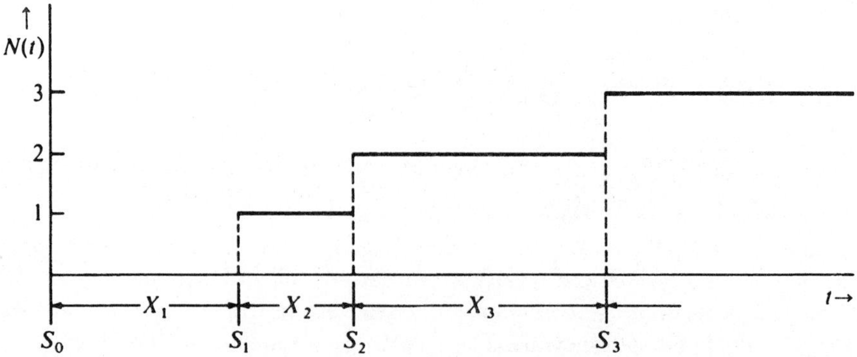

FIG. 1. The relation between the process of i.i.d.r.v's $\{X_n\}$ and the renewal counting process $N(t)$.

In common practice the counting process $\{N(t),\ t \geq 0\}$ and the partial sum process $\{S_n,\ n \geq 0\}$ are interchangeably called the "renewal process". The prototype physical renewal model involves successive replacements of light bulbs. A bulb is installed for service at time 0, fails at time X_1, and is then exchanged for a fresh bulb. The second bulb fails at time $X_1 + X_2$ and is replaced by a third bulb. In general, the nth bulb burns out at time $\sum_{i=1}^{n} X_i$ and is immediately replaced, etc. It is natural to assume that the successive lifetimes are statistically independent, with probabilistically identical characteristics in that

$$\Pr\{X_k \leq x\} = F(x).$$

Manifestly, $N(t)$ in this process records the number of renewals (light-bulb replacements) up to time t.

The principal objective of renewal theory is to derive properties of certain random variables associated with $\{N(t)\}$ and $\{S_n\}$ from knowledge of the interoccurrence distribution F. For example, it is of significance and relevance to compute the expected number of renewals for the time duration $(0, t]$:

$$E[N(t)] = M(t) \qquad \text{called the } \textit{renewal function}.$$

For this end, several pertinent relationships and formulas are worth recording. In principle, the probability law of $S_n = X_1 + \cdots + X_n$ can be calculated in accordance with the convolution formula

$$\Pr\{S_n \leq x\} = F_n(x),$$

where $F_1(x) = F(x)$ is assumed known or prescribed, and then

$$F_n(x) = \int_0^\infty F_{n-1}(x-y)\,dF(y) = \int_0^x F_{n-1}(x-y)\,dF(y).\dagger$$

We highlighted (1.2) earlier as the connecting link between the process $\{S_n\}$ and $\{N(t)\}$. The relation (1.2) can be expressed in the form

$$N(t) \geq k \qquad \text{if and only if} \quad S_k \leq t. \tag{1.3}$$

It follows instantly that

$$\begin{aligned}\Pr\{N(t) \geq k\} &= \Pr\{S_k \leq t\} \\ &= F_k(t), \qquad t \geq 0, \quad k = 1, 2, \ldots,\end{aligned} \tag{1.4}$$

and consequently

$$\begin{aligned}\Pr\{N(t) = k\} &= \Pr\{N(t) \geq k\} - \Pr\{N(t) \geq k+1\} \\ &= F_k(t) - F_{k+1}(t), \qquad t \geq 0, \quad k = 1, 2, \ldots.\end{aligned} \tag{1.5}$$

From the definition and taking cognizance of (1.4) and (1.5) we obtain

$$\begin{aligned}M(t) = E[N(t)] &= \sum_{k=1}^{\infty} k \Pr\{N(t) = k\} \\ &= \sum_{k=1}^{\infty} \Pr\{N(t) \geq k\} = \sum_{k=1}^{\infty} \Pr\{S_k \leq t\} = \sum_{k=1}^{\infty} F_k(t)\end{aligned}$$

(the third equality results after summation by parts. Consult also Elementary Problem 1, Chapter 1.) The convergence of the series

$$M(t) = \sum_{k=1}^{\infty} F_k(t) \tag{1.6}$$

will be verified formally in Section 4.

Problems 3, 16, and 17 concern the variance and higher moments of $N(t)$.

There are a number of other random variables of interest. Three of these are: the *excess life* (also called the excess random variable), the

† Here, and in what follows, our convention is to include the right endpoint in an integral over an interval, and omit the left. That is, $\int_a^b h(x)\,dG(x) = \int_{a+}^{b+} h(x)\,dG(x)$.

current life (also called the age random variable) and the *total life*, defined, respectively, by

$$\gamma_t = S_{N(t)+1} - t \qquad (\textit{excess or residual lifetime})$$
$$\delta_t = t - S_{N(t)} \qquad (\textit{current life or age random variable})$$
$$\beta_t = \gamma_t + \delta_t \qquad (\textit{total life}).$$

A pictorial description of these random variables is given in Figure 2. The fundamental significance of these random functions in the theory of renewal processes and their relevance for applications will be amply developed throughout this chapter.

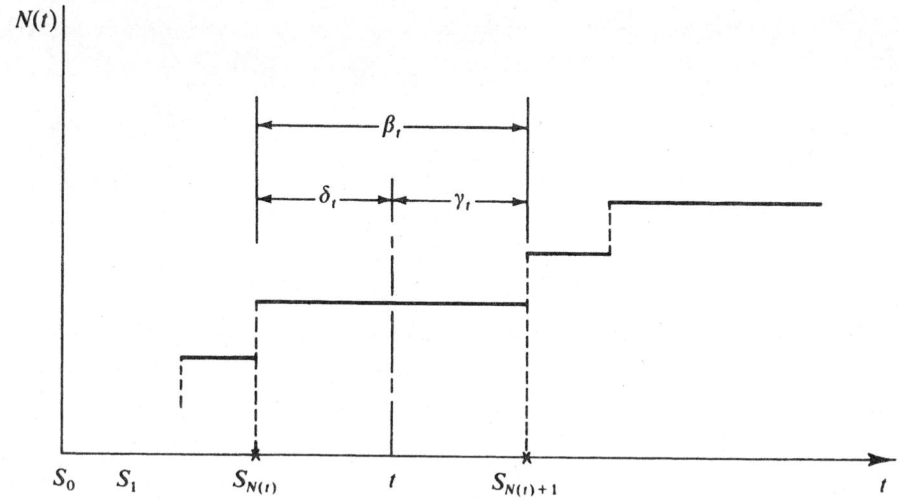

FIG. 2. The exess life γ_t, the current life δ_t, and the total life β_t.

2: *Some Examples of Renewal Processes*

The listing below points out the wide scope and diverse contexts in which renewal processes arise. Several of the examples will be studied in depth in later sections.

(a) *Poisson Processes*

A Poisson process $\{N(t), t \geq 0\}$ with parameter λ is a renewal counting process having the exponential interoccurrence distribution

$$F(x) = 1 - e^{-\lambda x}, \qquad x \geq 0,$$

as established in Theorem 2.1 of Chapter 4. This particular renewal process possesses a host of special features highlighted later in Section 3.

(b) *Counter Processes*

The times between successive electrical impulses or signals impinging on a recording device (counter) are often assumed to form a renewal process. Most physically realizable counters lock for some duration immediately upon registering an impulse and will not record impulses arriving during this dead period. Impulses are recorded only when the counter is freed (i.e., unlocked). Under quite reasonable assumptions, the sequence of events of the times of recorded impulses forms a renewal process, but it should be emphasized that the renewal process of recorded impulses is a *secondary* renewal process derived from the original renewal process comprised of the totality of all arriving impulses. Sections 3 and 7 elaborate the theory of counters concentrating on two kinds of locking mechanisms, the so-called counters of Types I and II.

(c) *Traffic Flow*

The distances between successive cars on an indefinitely long single-lane highway are often assumed to form a renewal process. So also are the time durations between consecutive cars passing a fixed location.

(d) *Renewal Processes Associated with Queues*

In a single-server queueing process there are imbedded many natural renewal processes. We cite two examples:

(i) If customer arrival times form a renewal process, then the times of the start of successive busy periods generate a second renewal process.

(ii) For the situation where the input process (the arrival pattern of customers) is Poisson, then the successive moments when the server passes from a busy to a free state determine a renewal process.

(e) *Inventory Systems*

In the analysis of most inventory processes it is customary to assume that the pattern of demands forms a renewal process. Most of the standard inventory policies induce renewal sequences, e.g., the times of replenishment of stock (see Section 8).

(f) *Renewal Processes Connected to Sums of Independent Random Variables*

(i) Let $\xi_1, \xi_2, \xi_3, \ldots$ be a sequence of real-valued (not necessarily positive) i.i.d. random variables. Assume $E(\xi_i) \geq 0$. Consider the process of partial sums $U_0 = 0$, $U_n = \xi_1 + \xi_2 + \cdots + \xi_n$, $n \geq 1$, whose values range over the real line. Define

$$S_1 = \inf\{n: U_n > 0\} \qquad \text{and} \qquad S_k = \inf\{n: U_n > U_{S_{k-1}}\}, \qquad k = 2, 3, \ldots,$$

$$X_1 = S_1 \qquad \text{and} \qquad X_k = S_k - S_{k-1}, \qquad k = 2, 3, \ldots .$$

It is clear that the sequence $X_1, X_2, X_3, \ldots$ constitutes a sequence of positive independent and identically distributed integer-valued random variables. The renewal process $S_m = X_1 + \cdots + X_m$, $m \geq 1$, can be interpreted as the successive times (indices) where U_n exceeds its previous maximum. In words, these form the sequence of successive new maxima.

(ii) The sequence $\{U_{S_m} - U_{S_{m-1}}\}_{m=1}^{\infty}$ also provides a sequence of i.i.d. positive random variables which therefore generate a renewal process. This example is of importance in the theory of fluctuations of sums of independent random variables (see Chapter 17 of Volume II.)

(g) *Renewal Processes in Markov Chains*

Let $Z_0, Z_1, \ldots$ be a recurrent Markov chain. Suppose $Z_0 = i$ and consider the times (elapsed number of generations) between successive visits to state i. Specifically,

$$X_1 = \min\{n > 0 : Z_n = i\},$$

and

$$X_{k+1} = \min\{n > X_k : Z_n = i\} - X_k, \qquad k = 1, 2, \ldots.$$

Since each of these times is computed from the same starting state i, the Markov property guarantees that $X_1, X_2, \ldots$ are i.i.d. and thus$\{X_k\}$ generates a renewal process. This fact permitted the application of renewal theory in Chapter 3 to prove the basic limit theorem for Markov chains.

(h) *Natural Embedded Renewal Processes*

Natural embedded renewal processes can be found in many diverse fields of applied probability including branching processes, insurance risk models, phenomena of population growth, evolutionary genetic mechanisms, engineering systems, econometric structures, and elsewhere.

3: *More on Some Special Renewal Processes*

A. THE POISSON PROCESS VIEWED AS A RENEWAL PROCESS

As mentioned earlier, the Poisson process with parameter λ is a renewal process whose interoccurrence times have the exponential distribution $F(x) = 1 - e^{-\lambda x}$, $x \geq 0$. The memoryless property of the exponential distribution (see p.125) serves decisively in yielding the explicit computation of a number of functionals of the Poisson renewal process.

(i) *The Renewal Function*

Since $N(t)$ has a Poisson distribution,

$$\Pr\{N(t) = k\} = \frac{(\lambda t)^k e^{-\lambda t}}{k!}, \qquad k = 0, 1, \ldots,$$

and

$$M(t) = E[N(t)] = \lambda t.$$

(ii) *Excess Life*

Observe that the excess life at time t exceeds x if and only if there are no renewals in the interval $(t, t + x]$ (Figure 3). This event has the same probability as that of no renewals in the interval $(0, x]$, since a Poisson process has stationary independent increments. In formal terms, we have

$$\begin{aligned}\Pr\{\gamma_t > x\} &= \Pr\{N(t + x) - N(t) = 0\} \\ &= \Pr\{N(x) = 0\} = e^{-\lambda x}.\end{aligned} \tag{3.1}$$

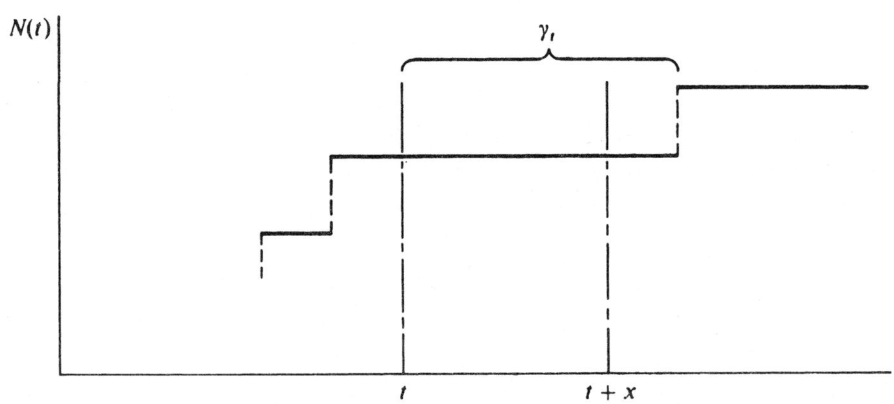

FIG. 3.

Thus, in a Poisson process, the excess life possesses the same exponential distribution

$$\Pr\{\gamma_t \le x\} = 1 - e^{-\lambda x}, \qquad x \ge 0 \tag{3.2}$$

as every life, another manifestation of the memoryless property of the exponential distribution.

Equation (3.2) can be written in the less explicit form

$$\Pr\{\gamma_t > x\} = 1 - F(x), \qquad x \ge 0, \quad t > 0. \tag{3.3}$$

We will see in Section 8 that this identity characterizes the Poisson process among all renewal processes.

(iii) *Current Life*

The current life δ_t, of course, cannot exceed t, while for $x < t$ the current life exceeds x if and only if there are no renewals in $(t - x, t]$, which again has probability $e^{-\lambda x}$. Thus the current life follows the truncated exponential distribution

$$\Pr\{\delta_t \le x\} = \begin{cases} 1 - e^{-\lambda x}, & \text{for} \quad 0 \le x < t, \\ 1, & \text{for} \quad t \le x. \end{cases} \tag{3.4}$$

It is convenient for later purposes to represent this formula in the guise

$$\Pr\{\delta_t \le x\} = \begin{cases} F(x), & x < t, \\ 1, & x \ge t. \end{cases} \tag{3.5}$$

It will be shown in Section 8 that this property of δ_t also characterizes the Poisson process.

(iv) *Mean Total Life*

Using the evaluation of Problem 9 of Chapter 1 for the mean of a nonnegative random variable, we have

$$\begin{aligned} E[\beta_t] &= E[\gamma_t] + E[\delta_t] \\ &= \frac{1}{\lambda} + \int_0^t \Pr\{\delta_t > x\}\, dx \\ &= \frac{1}{\lambda} + \int_0^t e^{-\lambda x}\, dx \\ &= \frac{1}{\lambda} + \frac{1}{\lambda}(1 - e^{-\lambda t}). \end{aligned}$$

Observe that the mean total life is significantly larger than the mean life $1/\lambda = E[X_k]$ of any particular renewal interval. A more striking expression of this phenomenon is especially revealed when t is large, where the process has been in operation for a long duration. Then the mean total life $E(\beta_t)$ is approximately twice the mean life. These facts appear at first paradoxical.

Let us reexamine the manner of the definition of the total life β_t with a view to explaining on an intuitive basis the above seeming discrepancy. First, an arbitary time point t is fixed. Then β_t measures the length of the renewal interval containing the point t. Such a procedure will tend with higher likelihood to favor a lengthy renewal interval rather than one of short duration. The phenomenon is known as *length-biased sampling* and occurs, well disguised, in a number of sampling situations.

(v) *Joint Distribution of* γ_t *and* δ_t

The joint distribution of γ_t and δ_t is determined in the same manner as the marginals. In fact, for any $x > 0$ and $0 < y < t$, the event $\{\gamma_t > x, \delta_t > y\}$ occurs if and only if there are no renewals in the interval $(t - y, t + x]$, which has probability $e^{-\lambda(x+y)}$. Thus

$$\Pr\{\gamma_t > x, \delta_t > y\} = \begin{cases} e^{-\lambda(x+y)}, & \text{if } x > 0, \quad 0 < y < t, \\ 0, & \text{if } y \geq t. \end{cases} \tag{3.6}$$

Observe that for the Poisson process γ_t and δ_t are independent, since their joint distribution factors as the product of their marginal distributions. That this property also characterizes the Poisson process among renewal processes is incorporated as Problem 25 at the close of the chapter.

B. REPLACEMENT MODELS

Let $X_1, X_2, \ldots$ represent the lifetimes of items (light bulbs, transistor cards, machines, etc.) that are successively placed in service, the next item commencing service immediately following the failure of the previous one. We stipulate that $\{X_i\}$ are independent and identically distributed positive random variables with finite mean $\mu = E[X_k]$. Since each item lasts, on the average, μ time units, we would expect to replace items over the long run at a mean rate of $1/\mu$ per unit time. That is, we would expect

$$\frac{1}{t} M(t) \to \frac{1}{\mu}, \qquad \text{as} \quad t \to \infty. \tag{3.7}$$

This is indeed the case, as will be demonstrated in Section 4.

In the long run, any replacement strategy that substitutes items prior to their failure will use more than $1/\mu$ items per unit time. Nonetheless, where there is some benefit in avoiding failure in service, and where units deteriorate, in some sense, with age, there may be an advantage in considering alternative replacement strategies.

An *age-replacement policy* calls for replacing an item upon failure or upon reaching age T, whichever occurs first. Arguing intuitively, we would expect the long-run fraction of failure replacements, items that fail before age T, will be $F(T)$, and the corresponding fraction of (conceivably less expensive) planned replacements will be $1 - F(T)$. A renewal interval for this modified age-replacement policy obviously follows a distribution law

$$F_T(x) = \begin{cases} F(x), & \text{for } x < T, \\ 1, & \text{for } x \geq T, \end{cases}$$

and the mean renewal duration is

$$\mu_T = \int_0^\infty \{1 - F_T(x)\}\, dx = \int_0^T \{1 - F(x)\}\, dx < \mu.$$

The same reasoning that led to (3.7) indicates that the long-run mean replacement rate is increased to $1/\mu_T$.

Now, let $Y_1, Y_2, \ldots$ denote the times between *actual successive failures.* The random variable Y_1 is composed of a random number of time periods of length T (corresponding to replacements not associated with failures), plus a last time period in which the distribution is that of a failure conditioned on failure before age T; that is, Y_1 has the distribution of $NT + Z$, where

$$\Pr\{N \geq k\} = \{1 - F(T)\}^k, \qquad k = 0, 1, \ldots,$$

and

$$\Pr\{Z \leq z\} = F(z)/F(T), \qquad 0 \leq z \leq T.$$

Hence,

$$\begin{aligned} E[Y_1] &= \frac{1}{F(T)} \{T[1 - F(T)] + \int_0^T (F(T) - F(x))\, dx\} \\ &= \frac{1}{F(T)} \int_0^T \{1 - F(x)\}\, dx. \end{aligned}$$

The sequence of random variables for interoccurrence times of the bona fide failures $\{Y_i\}$ generates a renewal process whose mean rate of failures per unit time in the long run is $1/E[Y_1]$. This inference again relies on a parallel reasoning to that leading to (3.7). Depending on F, the modified failure rate $1/E(Y_1)$ may possibly yield a lower failure rate than $1/\mu$, the rate when replacements are made only upon failure.

Block replacement policies are suggested when there are a number of units functioning in parallel at any one time, and where, because of economies of scale, it costs less per unit to refurbish all units simultaneously than to substitute for items individually. A *block replacement policy* calls for replacing items individually upon failure and all items at the block times $T, 2T, 3T, \ldots$. Accordingly, there is exactly one planned or block replacement every T units of time and, on the average, $M(T)$ failure replacements. Thus the total long-run replacements per unit time is $\{1+M(T)\}/T$, which may be compared to the corresponding figure for the other replacement strategies.

C. COUNTER MODELS

A counter is a device for detecting and registering instantaneous pulse-type signals. Familiar examples are the Geiger–Muller counter, which measures atmospheric cosmic radiation or source radiation, such as that emitted by a mass of radium. Another example is the electron multiplier.

All physically realizable counters are imperfect, incapable of detecting all signals that enter their detection chambers. After a particle or signal is registered, a counter must recuperate or renew itself in preparation for the next arrival. Signals arriving during the readjustment period, called *dead time* or *locked time*, are lost. We must distinguish between the *arriving* particles and the *recorded* particles. The experimenter observes only the particles recorded; from this he desires to infer the properties of the arrival process.

The particles or signals are assumed to arrive according to a renewal process with interarrival times $X_1, X_2, \ldots$, where $\Pr\{X_k \le x\} = F(x)$. Counter models are distinguished in the nature of the locking time mechanisms. We describe the two most common types.

Type I Counters

A particle arrives at time 0 and locks the counter for a dead time duration Y_1. The first particle to be registered is the first particle to arrive after time Y_1. With the registration of the particle, the counter is blocked for a time length, say Y_2. The next particle to be registered is that of the first arrival once the counter is freed. This process is repeated, where the successive locking times, denoted by $Y_1, Y_2, Y_3, \ldots$, are assumed independent with common distribution $\Pr\{Y_k \le y\} = G(y)$, and independent of the arrival process $\{X_k\}$.

Let Z_1 denote the elapsed time until the first signal is registered (not counting the one at the origin) and let Z_n, $n = 2, 3, \ldots$, be the elapsed time between the $(n-1)$st and nth registrations. Since the process starts afresh following each registration, $\{Z_k\}$ constitutes a renewal process. The action is diagrammed in Figure 4.

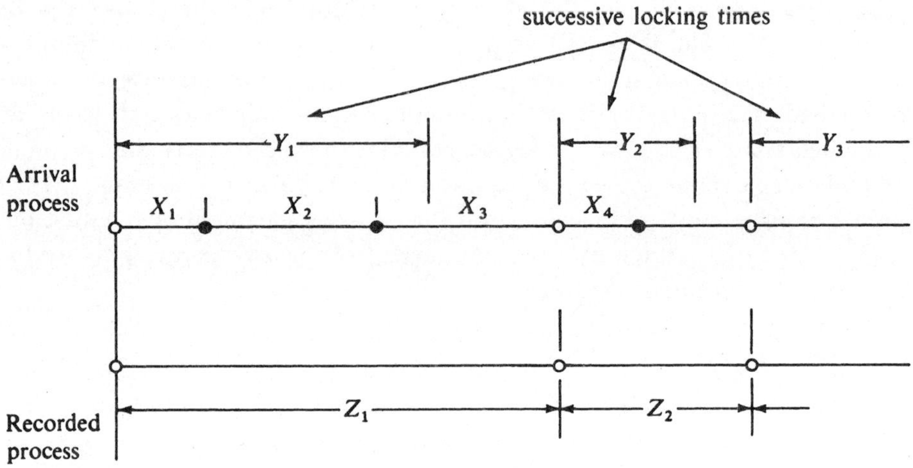

FIG. 4. A Type I Counter. ● denotes a lost signal and ○, a recorded signal.

Inspection of Figure 4 reveals that Z_1 is Y_1 plus the excess life at Y_1, or

$$Z_1 = Y_1 + \gamma_{Y_1} = S_{N(Y_1)+1},$$

where $S_k = X_1 + X_2 + \cdots + X_k$.

Since the $\{X_n\}$ and $\{Y_n\}$ processes are independent, invoking the law of total probability we obtain

$$\Pr\{Z_1 \le z\} = \int_0^z \Pr\{y + \gamma_y \le z \mid Y_1 = y\}\, dG(y)$$

$$= \int_0^z \{1 - A_{z-y}(y)\}\, dG(y),$$

where $A_x(t) = \Pr\{\gamma_t > x\}$.

An explicit formula for $A_x(t)$ is available (later) in Equation (6.1), so that the distribution of the time duration between counts in a Type I counter is completely specified.

In the long run, the mean rate per unit of time of recorded particles will be $1/E[Z_1]$, while the similar rate for arriving particles is $1/E[X_1]$. We will show later that the long-run fraction of recorded particles among the totality of all arriving particles is $E[X_1]/E[Z_1]$.

When the arrival process is Poisson, with mean λ, the memoryless property of the interoccurrence exponential distribution tells us that γ_t follows an exponential distribution, independent of t. Thus in this Poisson case

$$\Pr\{Z_1 \leq z\} = \int_0^z G(z-y)\lambda e^{-\lambda y}\,dy. \tag{3.8}$$

Type II Counters

Here the locking mechanism is more complicated. As before, an incoming signal is registered if and only if it arrives when the counter is free. Previously, however, only recorded particles induced the counter to lock. For Type II counters, every arriving signal can prolong the dead period of the counter, the associated locking times being added concurrently. For example, suppose the first particle locks the counter for a time duration σ_1 and a second pulse arrives at time $\tau < \sigma_1$ and independently engenders a locking time of extent σ_2; then the counter is next free at time σ_1 or $\tau + \sigma_2$, whichever occurs last assuming no additional particle arrivals prior to then. A typical realization of the process is diagrammed in Figure 5.

As with the Type I counter, let Z_n be the time between the $(n-1)$st and nth *recorded* pulses. Again $\{Z_k\}$ is a renewal process.

This counter process is quite difficult to analyze in general. We present a few results under the assumption that the arrival pattern is Poisson with rate λ.

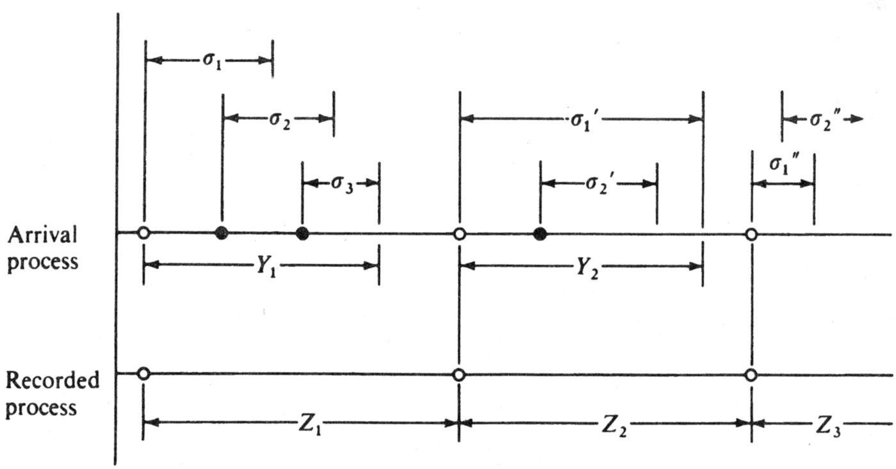

FIG. 5. A Type II counter. ● denotes a lost signal and ○, a recorded signal.

Let $p(t)$ be the probability that the counter is free at time t. We claim

$$p(t) = \exp\left\{-\lambda \int_0^t [1 - G(y)]\, dy\right\}, \tag{3.9}$$

where $G(y) = \Pr\{\sigma_k \le y\}$. To derive this formula, recall from Theorem 2.3 of Chapter 4 that, given n occurrences of a Poisson process in the interval $(0, t]$, the distribution of the occurrence times is the same as that of n *independent* random variables taken from a uniform distribution on $(0, t]$. The counter is free at time t if and only if all dead periods (i.e., locking times) engendered by these n signals have terminated before time t. The probability is $G(t-y)$ that a dead period commencing at time y will end before time t. Conditional that a signal impinges during the time interval $(0, t]$, its actual arrival time has a uniform distribution. The requirement that its induced dead period is culminated prior to time t therefore has probability $\int_0^t G(t-y)\, dy/t$. Since the locking times are assumed independent and independent of the arrival process, we have

$$\Pr\{\text{counter free at time } t \mid n \text{ signals in } (0, t]\}$$

$$= \left\{\int_0^t G(t-y) \frac{1}{t}\, dy\right\}^n.$$

But the number of signals arriving during the time interval $(0, t]$ has a Poisson distribution with mean λt. Invoking the law of total probabilities, we obtain

$$\begin{aligned} p(t) &= \sum_{j=0}^{\infty} \left\{\int_0^t G(t-y) \frac{1}{t}\, dy\right\}^j \frac{(\lambda t)^j e^{-\lambda t}}{j!} \\ &= \exp\left\{-\lambda t\left[1 - \int_0^t G(t-y) \frac{1}{t}\, dy\right]\right\} \\ &= \exp\left\{-\lambda \int_0^t [1 - G(y)]\, dy\right\}, \end{aligned}$$

and formula (3.9) is confirmed.

Continuing with our assumption of a Poisson stream of signals, $p(t)$ can be related to $M_R(t)$, the mean number of recorded signals in $(0, t]$. We claim

$$\frac{dM_R(t)}{dt} = \lambda p(t). \tag{3.10}$$

To prove this contention the following facts are relevant:

The probability of a signal appearing in the interval $(t, t+h]$ is $\lambda h + o(h)$. By definition, the probability of finding the counter free during this same short time period is $p(t) + o(h)$. Therefore, up to terms of order $o(h)$, $\lambda h p(t)$ is the probability of a recorded arrival in $(t, t+h]$. Since the probability of more than one signal in an interval $(t, t+h]$ is of order less than h as $h \downarrow 0$, we have

$$M_{\mathrm{R}}(t+h) = M_{\mathrm{R}}(t) + \lambda h p(t) + o(h),$$

where $o(h)$ incorporates all the negligible terms. Then

$$\frac{dM_{\mathrm{R}}(t)}{dt} = \lim_{h \downarrow 0} \frac{M_{\mathrm{R}}(t+h) - M_{\mathrm{R}}(t)}{h} = \lambda p(t),$$

which gives (3.10).

Note that $M_{\mathrm{R}}(0) = 0$, by its meaning. Now combining (3.9) and (3.10) and integrating yields

$$M_{\mathrm{R}}(t) = \int_0^t \lambda \exp\left\{-\lambda \int_0^s [1 - G(y)]\, dy\right\} ds. \tag{3.11}$$

4: Renewal Equations and the Elementary Renewal Theorem

A. THE RENEWAL FUNCTION

In Section 1 we derived a formula for the mean number of counts in $(0, t]$. Explicitly,

$$M(t) = E[N(t)] = \sum_{j=1}^{\infty} F_j(t), \tag{4.1}$$

where

$$F_j(t) = \Pr\{S_j \le t\}, \qquad t \ge 0.$$

Because of its far-reaching significance and relevance beyond its interpretation as a mean number of counts, $M(t)$ has been ascribed the special name, ***the renewal function***.†

Our initial task will be to show that $M(t)$ for each $t > 0$ is finite. To this end, first we infer, on the basis of the definition and monotonic nature of $F_j(x)$, the inequality

$$F_n(t) = \int_0^t F_{n-m}(t - \xi)\, dF_m(\xi) \le F_{n-m}(t) F_m(t), \qquad 1 \le m \le n-1.$$

† Recent authors tend to include the renewal that takes place at the origin and define the renewal function to be $1 + M(t) = E[1 + N(t)] = \sum_{n=0}^{\infty} F_n(t)$ where $F_0(t) = 1$ for $t \ge 0$ and 0 elsewhere. While this definition slightly simplifies some formulas, it calls more heavily on the Lebesgue–Stieltjes theory of integration than does the more traditional definition that we use.

In particular, for any integers k, r, and n, we have

$$F_{nr+k}(t) \leq F_{(n-1)r+k}(t) F_r(t).$$

Direct iteration leads to the relations

$$F_{nr+k}(t) \leq [F_r(t)]^n F_k(t), \qquad 0 \leq k \leq r-1. \tag{4.2}$$

In light of (4.2), we see that the series $M(t) = \sum_{k=1}^{\infty} F_k(t)$ for any t, where $F_r(t) < 1$, converges, indeed at least geometrically fast.

Since X_i are positive random variables, so that $F(0+) = 0$, and accordingly $F(t_0) < 1$ for some positive t_0, we infer inductively that for each $t > 0$ there must exist r fulfilling $F_r(t) < 1$. This fact is intuitive from probability considerations and equivalent to the statement that the partial sums S_n, sums of positive i.i.d.r.v.'s, increase to infinity with probability one.

Two important consequences emerge from the preceding discussion, which are now displayed for easy reference:

For any fixed t,

$$F_n(t) \to 0, \qquad \text{as} \quad n \to \infty \text{ (at least geometrically fast)}, \tag{4.3}$$

and

$$M(t) < \infty, \qquad \text{for all} \quad t.$$

Manifestly, $M(t)$ by its meaning (or from inspection of the formula (4.1)) is a nondecreasing function of t. Moreover, it readily can be checked that $M(t)$ is continuous from the right (since each $F_k(t)$ has this property and the series converges uniformly on finite intervals). Thus $M(t)$ is endowed with the characteristics of a distribution function apart from the exception that $M(\infty) = \lim_{t \to \infty} M(t) \neq 1$ (actually, $M(\infty) = \infty$). Nonetheless, it will be meaningful to write expressions of the type $\int a(t-y)\, dM(y)$, to be interpreted in a manner parallel to $\int a(t-y)\, dF(y)$, where F is a distribution function. In particular, in the common case in which M is differentiable with $m(t) = dM(t)/dt$, the integral $\int a(t-y)\, dM(y)$ reduces to $\int a(t-y) m(y)\, dy$.

At this point it is useful to generalize the notion of convolution to apply to any two increasing functions. Let A and B be nondecreasing functions, continuous from the right, with $A(0) = B(0) = 0$. *Define the convolution, denoted* $A * B$, by

$$A * B(t) = \int_0^t B(t-y)\, dA(y), \qquad t \geq 0. \tag{4.4}$$

Since $B(0) = 0$, we have $B(t-y) = \int_0^{t-y} dB(z)$. Inserting this in (4.4) and changing the order of integration produces

$$\begin{aligned} A * B(t) &= \int_0^t \left\{\int_0^{t-y} dB(z)\right\} dA(y) \\ &= \int_0^t \left\{\int_0^{t-z} dA(y)\right\} dB(z) \\ &= B * A(t), \end{aligned}$$

so that $*$ is a commutative operation.

We next show that the renewal function $M(t)$ satisfies the equation

$$M(t) = F(t) + \int_0^t M(t-y)\, dF(y), \qquad t \geq 0,$$

or, in convolution notation,

$$M(t) = F(t) + F * M(t), \qquad t \geq 0. \tag{4.5}$$

This identity will be validated invoking the *renewal argument*, which proceeds by conditioning on the time X_1 of the first renewal and counting the expected number of renewals thereafter. Manifestly, the probabilistic structure of events begins anew after the moment X_1, and consequently

$$E[N(t)|X_1 = x] = \begin{cases} 0, & \text{if } x > t, \\ 1 + M(t-x), & \text{if } x \leq t. \end{cases}$$

In words, there are no renewals in $(0, t]$ if the first lifetime X_1 exceeds t. On the other hand, where $X_1 = x < t$ there is the renewal engendered at time x plus, on the average, $M(t-x)$ further renewals occurring during the time interval extending from x to t. Applying the law of total probability yields

$$\begin{aligned} M(t) &= E[N(t)] \\ &= \int_0^t E[N(t)|X_1 = x]\, dF(x) \\ &= \int_0^t \{1 + M(t-x)\}\, dF(x) \\ &= F(t) + \int_0^t M(t-x)\, dF(x), \end{aligned}$$

and relation (4.5) is established.

Much of the power of renewal theory derives from the preceding method of reasoning that views the dynamic process starting anew at the occurrence of the first "event."

Renewal Equations

An integral equation of the form

$$A(t) = a(t) + \int_0^t A(t-x)\,dF(x), \qquad t \geq 0, \tag{4.6}$$

is called a renewal equation. The prescribed (or known) functions are $a(t)$ and the distribution function $F(t)$, while the undetermined (or unknown) quantity is $A(t)$.

Without ambiguity, we will employ the notation $B * c(t)$ for convolution of a function $c(t)$ (assumed reasonably smooth and bounded on finite intervals) with an increasing right-continuous function $B(t)$, $B(0) = 0$, to stand for

$$B * c(t) = \int_0^t c(t-\tau)\,dB(\tau). \tag{4.7}$$

Where $B'(t) = b(t)$ exists, then (4.7) reduces to

$$B * c(t) = \int_0^t c(t-\tau)b(\tau)\,d\tau,$$

provided this integral is well defined in the ordinary sense. Some elementary properties of $B * c$ are listed for ready reference leaving their straightforward validations to the student:

(i) $\max_{0 \leq t \leq T} |(B * c)(t)| \leq \max_{0 \leq t \leq T} |c(t)| \cdot B(T)$ (consult also (4.11) below);

(ii) $B * c_1 + B * c_2 = B * (c_1 + c_2)$;

(iii) If B_1 and B_2 are increasing, then (4.8)

$$B_1 * (B_2 * c) = (B_1 * B_2) * c.$$

Comparing (4.6) with (4.5) reveals that the renewal function $M(t)$ satisfies a renewal equation in which $a(t) = F(t)$. The following theorem affirms that the solution of an arbitrary renewal equation can be represented in terms of the renewal function.

Theorem 4.1. *Suppose a is a bounded function. There exists one and only one function A bounded on finite intervals that satisfies*

$$A(t) = a(t) + \int_0^t A(t-y)\,dF(y). \tag{4.9}$$

This function is

$$A(t) = a(t) + \int_0^t a(t-x)\, dM(x), \tag{4.10}$$

where $M(t) = \sum_{k=1}^{\infty} F_k(t)$ *is the renewal function.*

Proof. We verify first that A specified by (4.10) fulfills the requisite boundedness properties and indeed solves (4.9). Because a is a bounded function and M is nondecreasing and finite, for every T, it follows that

$$\begin{aligned}\sup_{0 \le t \le T} |A(t)| &\le \sup_{0 \le t \le T} |a(t)| + \int_0^T \left\{ \sup_{0 \le y \le T} |a(y)| \right\} dM(x) \\ &= \sup_{0 \le t \le T} |a(t)| \{1 + M(T)\} < \infty, \end{aligned} \tag{4.11}$$

establishing that the expression (4.10) is bounded on finite intervals. To check that $A(t)$ of (4.10) satisfies (4.9), we have

$$\begin{aligned} A(t) &= a(t) + M * a(t) \\ &= a(t) + \left(\sum_{k=1}^{\infty} F_k \right) * a(t) \\ &= a(t) + F * a(t) + \sum_{k=2}^{\infty} F_k * a(t) \\ &= a(t) + F * \left\{ a(t) + \left(\sum_{k=1}^{\infty} F_k \right) * a(t) \right\} \qquad \text{(since } F_k = F * F_{k-1} \text{ and using (4.8))} \\ &= a(t) + F * A(t). \end{aligned}$$

To complete the proof of Theorem 4.1 it remains to certify the uniqueness of A. This is done by showing that any solution of the renewal equation (4.9), bounded in finite intervals, is represented by (4.10).

Note for this end that the renewal equation (4.9) is suited to successive approximations by repeatedly substituting the expression for $A(t)$ into the right-hand side of (4.9) and expanding appropriately. We carry out this program using the convolution notation. Accordingly, we write (4.9) in the abbreviated form

$$A = a + F * A$$

and substitute for A on the right to get

$$\begin{aligned} A &= a + F * (a + F * A) \\ &= a + F * a + F * (F * A) \\ &= a + F * a + F_2 * A \qquad \text{(recall the identification } F_2 = F * F). \end{aligned}$$

Reliance on the properties of (4.8) has been tacitly implemented. We iterate this procedure, securing the equation

$$\begin{aligned} A &= a + F * a + F_2 * (a + F * A) \\ &= a + F * a + F_2 * a + F_3 * A = \cdots \\ &= a + \left(\sum_{k=1}^{n-1} F_k\right) * a + F_n * A. \end{aligned}$$

Next, observe that

$$\begin{aligned} |F_n * A(t)| &= \left| \int_0^t A(t-y)\, dF_n(y) \right| \\ &\le \left\{ \sup_{0 \le y \le t} |A(t-y)| \right\} \times F_n(t). \end{aligned}$$

Since A is assumed bounded in finite intervals, and $\lim_{n\to\infty} F_n(t) = 0$ (consult (4.3)), it follows that $\lim_{n\to\infty} |F_n * A(t)| = 0$ for every fixed t. Similarly, since a is bounded, we obtain

$$\lim_{n\to\infty} \left(\sum_{k=1}^{n-1} F_k\right) * a(t) = \left(\sum_{k=1}^{\infty} F_k\right) * a(t) = M * a(t).$$

Thus

$$\begin{aligned} A(t) &= a(t) + \lim_{n\to\infty} \left\{ \sum_{k=1}^{n-1} F_k * a(t) + F_n * A(t) \right\} \\ &= a(t) + M * a(t), \end{aligned}$$

and the general solution A of (4.9) acquires the representation (4.10). The uniqueness proof of Theorem 4.1 is complete. ∎

With the help of Theorem 4.1 we will prove the important relation

$$\begin{aligned} E[S_{N(t)+1}] &= E[X_1 + X_2 + \cdots + X_{N(t)+1}] \\ &= E[X_1] \cdot E[N(t) + 1] \\ &= E[X_1] \cdot [M(t) + 1] \end{aligned} \tag{4.12}$$

At first glance, this identity perhaps resembles an identity derived in Chapter 1 affirming the property that if $X_1, X_2, X_3, \ldots$ are independent identically distributed random variables and N is an integer-valued random variable independent of the X_i's, the equation $E[X_1 + \cdots + X_N] = E[X_1] \cdot E[N]$ prevails provided all mean values exist. The crucial difference in the present context is that the number of summands $N(t) + 1$ is *not* independent of the summand contributions themselves. For example, recall that in the Poisson discussion of Section 3, the total life β_t, the last summand involved in $S_{N(t)+1}$, has a mean that approached twice the unconditional mean for t large. For this reason, it is *not* correct, in particular, that $E[S_{N(t)}]$ can be evaluated as the product of $E[X_1]$ and $E[N(t)]$. In view of these cautionary comments, identity (4.12) is more intriguing and remarkable. (It is actually a special case of what is known as the Wald identity; in this connection see Chapter 6 on martingales.)

To derive (4.12) we will use a renewal argument to establish a renewal equation for

$$A(t) = E[S_{N(t)+1}].$$

As usual, we condition on the time of the first renewal $X_1 = x$, and distinguish two contingencies: the first where $x > t$ so that $N(t) = 0$ and $S_{N(t)+1} = x$, and the second where $x \leq t$. A direct interpretation of the quantities involved readily validates the equation

$$E[S_{N(t)+1} | X_1 = x] = \begin{cases} x, & \text{if } x > t, \\ x + A(t-x), & \text{if } x \leq t. \end{cases}$$

Next, invoking the law of total probability yields

$$\begin{aligned} A(t) &= E[S_{N(t)+1}] \\ &= \int_0^\infty E[S_{N(t)+1} | X_1 = x] \, dF(x) \\ &= \int_0^t [x + A(t-x)] \, dF(x) + \int_t^\infty x \, dF(x) \\ &= \int_0^\infty x \, dF(x) + \int_0^t A(t-x) \, dF(x) \\ &= E[X_1] + \int_0^t A(t-x) \, dF(x). \end{aligned}$$

Thus $A(t) = E[S_{N(t)+1}]$ satisfies a renewal equation for which $a(t) =$ the constant $E[X_1]$. Theorem 4.1 states that

$$\begin{aligned} A(t) &= a(t) + \int_0^t a(t-x) \, dM(x) \\ &= E[X_1] + \int_0^t E[X_1] \, dM(x) \\ &= E[X_1] \times [1 + M(t)], \end{aligned}$$

which completes the proof of (4.12).

Observe that the excess life $\gamma_t = S_{N(t)+1} - t$ has

$$E[\gamma_t] = E[X_1] \cdot [1 + M(t)] - t. \tag{4.13}$$

At several occasions in Section 3 the intuitive result $M(t)/t \to 1/\mu$ as $t \to \infty$, where $\mu = E[X_1]$ was applied. We are now in a position to prove this important fact, commonly referred to as the *elementary renewal* theorem.

Theorem 4.2. *Let $\{X_i\}$ be a renewal process with $\mu = E[X_1] < \infty$. Then*

$$\lim_{t\to\infty} \frac{1}{t} M(t) = \frac{1}{\mu}.$$

Proof. It is always the case that $t < S_{N(t)+1}$. Combined with Eq. (4.12), we have

$$t < E[S_{N(t)+1}] = \mu[1 + M(t)],$$

and therefore

$$\frac{1}{t} M(t) > \frac{1}{\mu} - \frac{1}{t}.$$

It follows that

$$\liminf_{t\to\infty} \frac{1}{t} M(t) \geq \frac{1}{\mu}. \tag{4.14}$$

To establish the opposite inequality, let $c > 0$ be arbitrary, and set

$$X_i^c = \begin{cases} X_i, & \text{if } X_i \leq c, \\ c, & \text{if } X_i > c, \end{cases}$$

and consider the renewal process having lifetimes $\{X_i^c\}$.

Let S_n^c and $N^c(t)$ denote the waiting times and counting process, respectively, for this truncated renewal process generated by $\{X_i^c\}$. Since the random variables X_i^c are uniformly bounded by c, it is clear that $t + c \geq S_{N^c(t)+1}^c$, and therefore

$$t + c \geq E[S_{N^c(t)+1}^c] = \mu^c[1 + M^c(t)],$$

where

$$\mu^c = E[X_i^c] = \int_0^c \{1 - F(x)\}\, dx,$$

and

$$M^c(t) = E[N^c(t)].$$

Obviously $X_i^c \le X_i$ entails $N^c(t) \ge N(t)$, and therefore $M^c(t) \ge M(t)$. It follows that

$$t + c \ge \mu^c[1 + M(t)],$$

and by rearrangement

$$\frac{1}{t} M(t) \le \frac{1}{\mu_c} + \frac{1}{t}\left(\frac{c}{\mu^c} - 1\right).$$

Hence

$$\limsup_{t\to\infty} \frac{1}{t} M(t) \le \frac{1}{\mu^c}, \qquad \text{for any} \quad c > 0. \tag{4.15}$$

Since

$$\lim_{c\to\infty} \mu^c = \lim_{c\to\infty} \int_0^c [1 - F(x)]\, dx$$

$$= \int_0^\infty [1 - F(x)]\, dx = \mu,$$

while the left-hand side of (4.15) is fixed, we deduce

$$\limsup_{t\to\infty} \frac{1}{t} M(t) \le \lim_{c\to\infty} \frac{1}{\mu^c} = \frac{1}{\mu}. \tag{4.16}$$

Inequalities (4.14) and (4.16) in conjunction imply

$$\lim_{t\to\infty} \frac{1}{t} M(t) = \frac{1}{\mu},$$

and the proof of the theorem is complete. ■

5: The Renewal Theorem

The subject of this section involves one of the most basic theorems in applied probability. The renewal theorem can be regarded as a refinement of the asymptotic relation $M(t) \sim t/\mu$, $t \to \infty$, established in Theorem 4.2.

It can be interpreted as a differentiated form of the limit formula $\lim_{t\to\infty} M(t)/t = 1/\mu$. More explicitly, subject to certain mild conditions on $F(x)$, the renewal theorem asserts that for any $h > 0$

$$M(t + h) - M(t) \to \frac{h}{\mu}, \qquad \text{as} \quad t \to \infty. \tag{5.1}$$

In words, the expected number of renewals in an interval of length h is approximately h/μ, provided the process has been in operation for a long duration. The statement of Theorem 5.1, appearing in a different formulation but equivalent to (5.1), provides the optimum setting for application of the renewal theorem. Another perspective on the renewal theorem emphasizes its value in ascertaining the asymptotic character of solutions of renewal equations.

The proof of the renewal theorem is lengthy and demanding. We will omit the details and refer to Feller [1] for comprehensive details. However, its statement will be given with care so that the student can understand its meaning and be able to apply it unhesitatingly without ambiguity. Throughout the later sections, numerous applications will be forthcoming, and the implications of the basic renewal theorem will accordingly be well recognized. For the precise statement, we need several preliminary definitions. (The reader concerned only with application can read the remainder of this section cursorily.)

Definition 5.1. A point α of a distribution function F is called *a point of increase* if for every positive ε

$$F(\alpha+\varepsilon)-F(\alpha-\varepsilon)>0.$$

A distribution function is said to be *arithmetic* if there exists a positive number λ such that F exhibits points of increase exclusively among the points $0, \pm\lambda, \pm 2\lambda, \ldots$. The largest such λ is called the *span* of F.

A distribution function F that has a continuous part is not arithmetic. The distribution function of a discrete random variable having possible values 0, 1, 2, ... is arithmetic with span 1.

Definition 5.2. Let g be a function defined on $[0, \infty)$. For every positive δ and $n = 1, 2, \ldots$, let

$$\underline{m}_n = \min\{g(t) : (n-1)\delta \le t \le n\delta\},$$
$$\bar{m}_n = \max\{g(t) : (n-1)\delta \le t \le n\delta\},$$
$$\underline{\sigma}(\delta) = \delta \sum_{n=1}^{\infty} \underline{m}_n, \qquad \text{and} \qquad \bar{\sigma}(\delta) = \delta \sum_{n=1}^{\infty} \bar{m}_n.$$

Then g is said to be *directly Riemann integrable* if both series $\underline{\sigma}(\delta)$ and $\bar{\sigma}(\delta)$ converge absolutely for every positive δ, and the difference $\bar{\sigma}(\delta) - \underline{\sigma}(\delta)$ goes to 0 as $\delta \to 0$.

Every monotonic function g which is absolutely integrable in the sense that

$$\int_0^{\infty} |g(t)|\,dt < \infty \tag{5.2}$$

is directly Riemann integrable, and this is the most important case for our purposes. Manifestly, all finite linear combinations of monotone functions satisfying (5.2) are also directly Riemann integrable.

Theorem 5.1. (The Basic Renewal Theorem). *Let F be the distribution function of a positive random variable with mean μ. Suppose that a is directly Riemann integrable and that A is the solution of the renewal equation*

$$A(t) = a(t) + \int_0^t A(t-x)\,dF(x). \tag{5.3}$$

(i) *If F is not arithmetic, then*

$$\lim_{t\to\infty} A(t) = \begin{cases} \dfrac{1}{\mu}\displaystyle\int_0^\infty a(x)\,dx, & \text{if } \mu < \infty, \\ 0, & \text{if } \mu = \infty. \end{cases}$$

(ii) *If F is arithmetic with span λ, then for $0 \le c < \lambda$,*

$$\lim_{n\to\infty} A(c+n\lambda) = \begin{cases} \dfrac{\lambda}{\mu}\displaystyle\sum_{n=0}^\infty a(c+n\lambda), & \text{if } \mu < \infty, \\ 0, & \text{if } \mu = \infty. \end{cases}$$

There is a second form of the theorem, equivalent to that just given, but expressed more directly in terms of the renewal function. Let $h > 0$ be given, and examine the special prescription of

$$a(y) = \begin{cases} 1, & \text{if } 0 \le y < h, \\ 0, & \text{if } h \le y, \end{cases}$$

inserted in (5.3). In this example, for $t > h$, because of (4.10), we have

$$\begin{aligned} A(t) &= a(t) + \int_0^t a(t-x)\,dM(x) \\ &= \int_{t-h}^t dM(x) \\ &= M(t) - M(t-h), \end{aligned}$$

and $\mu^{-1}\int_0^\infty a(x)\,dx = h/\mu$. If F is not arithmetic, we may conclude on the basis of the renewal theorem that

$$\lim_{t\to\infty}[M(t) - M(t-h)] = h/\mu, \tag{5.4}$$

with the convention $h/\mu = 0$ when $\mu = \infty$.

The following converse prevails. Theorem 5.1 can be deduced from the fact of (5.4) by approximating a directly Riemann integrable function with step functions. The formal statement of the second form of the renewal theorem follows.

Theorem 5.2. *Let F be the distribution function of a positive random variable with mean μ. Let $M(t) = \sum_{k=1}^{\infty} F_k(t)$ be the renewal function associated with F. Let $h > 0$ be fixed.*

(i) *If F is not arithmetic, then*

$$\lim_{t\to\infty} [M(t+h) - M(t)] = h/\mu.$$

(ii) *If F is arithmetic, the same limit holds, provided h is a multiple of the span λ.*

We conclude this section by recovering Theorem 4.2, the elementary renewal theorem, namely,

$$\lim_{t\to\infty} \frac{1}{t} M(t) = \frac{1}{\mu}, \tag{5.5}$$

as a corollary of Theorem 5.2. To this end, set $b_n = M(n+1) - M(n)$. Then stipulating F to be not arithmetic, Theorem 5.2 tells us that $b_n \to 1/\mu$ as $n \to \infty$, so that also the average of b_n converges to the same limit. Thus

$$\lim_{n\to\infty} \frac{1}{n} \sum_{k=0}^{n-1} b_k = \lim_{n\to\infty} \frac{1}{n} \sum_{k=0}^{n-1} [M(k+1) - M(k)] = \lim_{n\to\infty} \frac{1}{n} M(n) = \frac{1}{\mu}.$$

Now for an arbitrary $t > 0$, let $[t]$ denote the largest integer not exceeding t. Cognizance of the monotone nature of $M(t)$ allows the facts of

$$\frac{[t]}{t}\frac{M([t])}{[t]} \le \frac{M(t)}{t} \le \frac{[t]+1}{t}\frac{M([t]+1)}{[t]+1}.$$

Since $t^{-1}M(t)$ is trapped by functions converging to μ^{-1}, (5.5) ipso facto follows. If F is arithmetic with span λ, we set $b_n = M[(n+1)\lambda] - M(n\lambda)$ and use an entirely parallel argument.

6: *Applications of the Renewal Theorem*

(a) *Limiting Distribution of the Excess Life*

Let $\gamma_t = S_{N(t)+1} - t$ be the excess life at time t and for a fixed $z > 0$, set

$$A_z(t) = \Pr\{\gamma_t > z\}.$$

We employ the renewal argument to establish a renewal equation for A_z in the usual way by conditioning on the time $X_1 = x$ of the first renewal. We obtain (we encourage the student to draw a picture)

$$\Pr\{\gamma_t > z | X_1 = x\} = \begin{cases} 1, & \text{if } x > t + z, \\ 0, & \text{if } t + z \geq x > t, \\ A_z(t - x), & \text{if } t \geq x > 0. \end{cases}$$

Then by the law of total probability,

$$\begin{aligned} A_z(t) &= \int_0^\infty \Pr\{\gamma_t > z | X_1 = x\}\, dF(x) \\ &= 1 - F(t + z) + \int_0^t A_z(t - x)\, dF(x). \end{aligned} \tag{6.1}$$

Theorem 4.1 yields

$$A_z(t) = 1 - F(t + z) + \int_0^t \{1 - F(t + z - x)\}\, dM(x).$$

To obtain a limiting distribution, we assume

$$\mu = E[X_1] = \int_0^\infty \{1 - F(x)\}\, dx < \infty.$$

Then

$$\int_0^\infty \{1 - F(t + z)\}\, dt = \int_z^\infty \{1 - F(y)\}\, dy < \infty,$$

and $\{1 - F(t + z)\}$ being monotonic, is directly Riemann integrable as a function of t with z fixed. Applying the renewal theorem yields

$$\lim_{t \to \infty} \Pr\{\gamma_t > z\} = \lim_{t \to \infty} A_z(t) = \mu^{-1} \int_z^\infty \{1 - F(y)\}\, dy, \qquad z > 0, \tag{6.2}$$

which displays the asymptotic distribution of the excess life.

Limiting distributions for the current life δ_t and the total life β_t can be deduced from the result of (6.2). Observe, with the aid of Fig. 6, we can directly corroborate the equivalence of the sets of events

$$\{\gamma_t \geq x \text{ and } \delta_t \geq y\} \qquad \text{if and only if} \quad \{\gamma_{t-y} \geq x + y\}. \tag{6.3}$$

It follows that

$$\begin{aligned} \lim_{t \to \infty} \Pr\{\delta_t \geq y, \gamma_t \geq x\} &= \lim_{t \to \infty} \Pr\{\gamma_{t-y} \geq x + y\} \\ &= \mu^{-1} \int_{x+y}^\infty \{1 - F(z)\}\, dz, \end{aligned} \tag{6.4}$$

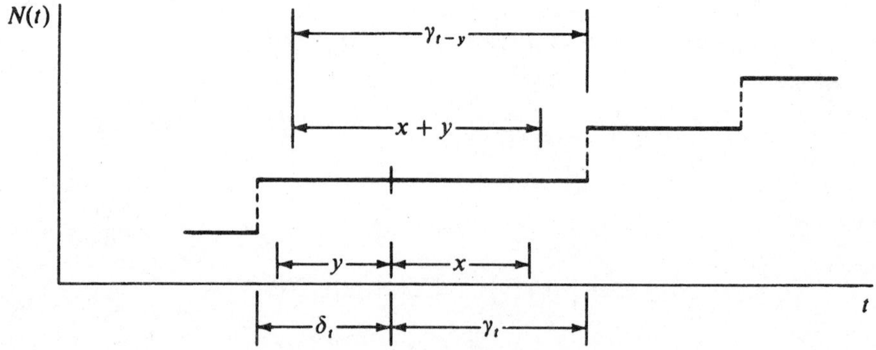

FIG. 6. Shows $\{\delta_t \geq y \text{ and } \gamma_t \geq x\}$ if and only if $\{\gamma_{t-y} \geq x + y\}$.

exhibiting the limiting joint distribution of $\{\delta_t, \gamma_t\}$. In particular,

$$\lim_{t\to\infty} \Pr\{\delta_t \geq y\} = \lim_{t\to\infty} \Pr\{\delta_t \geq y, \gamma_t \geq 0\}$$

$$= \mu^{-1} \int_y^\infty \{1 - F(z)\}\, dz. \tag{6.5}$$

The limiting distribution of $\beta_t = \delta_t + \gamma_t$ can be extracted from the limit formula (6.4). However it is equally quick to proceed via the renewal argument. We will be brief. Define

$$K_x(t) = \Pr\{\beta_t > x\}.$$

Conditioning on the time of the first renewal event, we have

$$\Pr\{\beta_t > x | X_1 = y\} = \begin{cases} 1, & \text{if } y > \max(x, t), \\ K_x(t-y), & \text{if } y \leq t, \\ 0, & \text{otherwise.} \end{cases}$$

The law of total probabilities produces the renewal equation

$$K_x(t) = 1 - F(\max(x, t)) + \int_0^t K_x(t-y)\, dF(y).$$

Application of the renewal theorem furnishes the limit law

$$\lim_{t\to\infty} \Pr\{\beta_t > x\} = \lim_{t\to\infty} K_x(t) = \frac{1}{\mu} \int_0^\infty [1 - F(\max(x, \tau))]\, d\tau$$

$$= \frac{1}{\mu} \int_x^\infty \xi\, dF(\xi), \tag{6.6}$$

where the last equality emanates from easy manipulations of the first integral together with integration by parts. Accordingly, we have established that the limiting distribution of the total life is

$$\lim_{t\to\infty} \Pr\{\beta_t \leq x\} = \frac{1}{\mu} \int_0^x \xi \, dF(\xi) = G(x).$$

When F has a density f, then the density of G is obviously $xf(x)/\mu$.

It is of interest to relate the mean of $G(x)$ with that of $F(x)$. Consider

$$\int_0^\infty x \, dG(x) = \frac{1}{\mu} \int_0^\infty x^2 \, dF(x), \tag{6.7}$$

and let us compare this quantity with μ, the mean length of an arbitrary renewal interval. Note that the Schwarz inequality (see Chapter 1) implies

$$\int_0^\infty x^2 \, dF(x) \geq \mu^2 = \left(\int_0^\infty x \, dF(x)\right)^2, \tag{6.8}$$

with strict inequality prevailing unless F is a degenerate distribution. The relation of (6.8) tells us that the mean limiting total life of the object in current operation strictly exceeds an ordinary mean lifetime. This fact is, of course, consistent with the analogous calculations done for the Poisson case (Section 3), which involved a mean total life exceeding the mean lifetime by a factor of 2. The inequality of (6.8) affirms the innate bias associated with sampling the lifetime interval that contains a prescribed point.

(b) *Asymptotic Expansion of the Renewal Function*

Suppose F is a nonarithmetic distribution with a finite variance σ^2. Under these assumptions we will determine the second term in the asymptotic expansion of $M(t)$ by proving

$$\lim_{t\to\infty} \{M(t) - \mu^{-1}t\} = \frac{\sigma^2 - \mu^2}{2\mu^2}.$$

Additional embellishments of the asymptotic behavior of $M(t)$ for t large can be ascertained employing parallel methods, where the existence of higher moments of F are stipulated.

Define

$$\begin{aligned} H(t) &= M(t) + 1 - \mu^{-1}t \\ &= E[N(t) + 1] - \mu^{-1}t \\ &= \mu^{-1}\{E[S_{N(t)+1}] - t\} \qquad \text{(by (4.12))} \\ &= \mu^{-1}E[\gamma_t] \qquad \text{(by (4.13))}. \end{aligned}$$

Once again, appeal to the renewal argument, conditioning on the time $X_1 = x$ of the first renewal, will provide a renewal equation for $H(t)$. Direct enumeration of cases leads to

$$E[\gamma_t | X_1 = x] = \begin{cases} x - t, & \text{if } x \geq t, \\ \mu H(t - x), & \text{if } x < t. \end{cases}$$

Invoking the law of total probability yields

$$\begin{aligned} \mu H(t) &= \int_0^\infty E[\gamma_t | X_1 = x]\, dF(x) \\ &= \int_t^\infty (x - t)\, dF(x) + \mu \int_0^t H(t - x)\, dF(x). \end{aligned}$$

Now

$$\begin{aligned} \int_t^\infty (x - t)\, dF(x) &= \int_0^\infty y\, dF(t + y) \\ &= \int_0^\infty \{1 - F(t + y)\}\, dy \end{aligned}$$

is a monotonic function of t, and expressing $1 - F(t + y) = \int_{t+y}^\infty dF(z)$ and interchanging the orders of integration leads to

$$\begin{aligned} &\int_0^\infty \left\{ \int_0^\infty [1 - F(t + y)]\, dy \right\} dt \\ &= \int_0^\infty \int_0^\infty \int_{t+y}^\infty dF(z)\, dy\, dt \\ &= \int_0^\infty \int_t^\infty \left\{ \int_0^{z-t} dy \right\} dF(z)\, dt \\ &= \int_0^\infty \int_t^\infty (z - t)\, dF(z)\, dt \\ &= \int_0^\infty \int_0^z (z - t)\, dt\, dF(z) \\ &= \frac{1}{2} \int_0^\infty z^2\, dF(z) = \frac{1}{2}(\sigma^2 + \mu^2) < \infty. \end{aligned}$$

Thus the renewal theorem implies

$$\lim_{t\to\infty} \mu H(t) = \mu^{-1}\tfrac{1}{2}(\sigma^2 + \mu^2),$$

or

$$\begin{aligned}\lim_{t\to\infty} \{M(t) - \mu^{-1}t\} &= \lim_{t\to\infty} \{H(t) - 1\} \\ &= \frac{\sigma^2 + \mu^2}{2\mu^2} - 1 \\ &= \frac{\sigma^2 - \mu^2}{2\mu^2},\end{aligned}$$

as was to be shown.

7: *Generalizations and Variations on Renewal Processes*

A. DELAYED RENEWAL PROCESSES

We continue to assume that $\{X_k\}$ are all independent positive random variables, but only $X_2, X_3, \ldots$ (*from the second on*) are identically distributed with distribution function F, while X_1 has possibly a different distribution function G. Such a process is called a *delayed renewal process.* We have all the ingredients for an ordinary renewal process except that the initial time to the first renewal has a distribution different from that of the other interoccurence times.

One way in which a delayed renewal process arises is when the component in operation at time $t = 0$ is not new. For example, suppose that the time origin is taken y time units after the start of an ordinary renewal process. Then the time to the first renewal after the origin in the delayed process will have the distribution of the excess life at time y of an ordinary renewal process.

As previously, let $S_0 = 0$ and $S_n = X_1 + \cdots + X_n$, and let $N(t)$ count the number of renewals up to time t. But now it is essential to distinguish between the mean number of renewals in the delayed process

$$M_D(t) = E[N(t)],$$

and the renewal function associated with the distribution F,

$$M(t) = \sum_{k=1}^{\infty} F_k(t).$$

Conditioning on the time of the first renewal, noting

$$E[N(t)|X_1 = x] = \begin{cases} 0, & \text{if } x > t, \\ 1 + M(t - x), & \text{if } x \le t. \end{cases}$$

and following with implementation of the law of total probability gives

$$\begin{aligned} M_D(t) &= \int_0^\infty E[N(t)|X_1 = x]\, dG(x) \\ &= \int_0^t \{1 + M(t-x)\}\, dG(x) \\ &= G(t) + \int_0^t M(t-x)\, dG(x) \\ &= G(t) + \int_0^t G(t-x)\, dM(x). \end{aligned} \tag{7.1}$$

Manifestly, Eq. (7.1) displays $M_D(t)$ as the solution of the renewal equation [compare with (4.9) and (4.10)]

$$M_D(t) = G(t) + \int_0^t M_D(t-x)\, dF(x). \tag{7.2}$$

We will show that $M_D(t)$ obeys the renewal theorem, assuming that F is a nonarithmetic distribution. (An analogous approach works in the arithmetic case.) From (7.1) we recall, for any $t > 0$,

$$M_D(t) = G(t) + \int_0^t M(t-x)\, dG(x),$$

and in particular, for $t > h$,

$$M_D(t-h) = G(t-h) + \int_0^{t-h} M(t-h-x)\, dG(x).$$

Agreeing that $M(x) = 0$ for $x < 0$, the difference of these equations becomes

$$M_D(t) - M_D(t-h) = G(t) - G(t-h) + \int_0^t \{M(t-x) - M(t-h-x)\}\, dG(x).$$

It is convenient to decompose the integral into two sections, viz.,

$$\int_0^{t/2} \{M(t-x) - M(t-h-x)\}\, dG(x) + \int_{t/2}^t \{M(t-x) - M(t-h-x)\}\, dG(x).$$

Since $\lim_{t\to\infty} \{M(t-x) - M(t-h-x)\} = h/\mu$, the first integral converges to h/μ, while the second converges to zero, since $\{M(t-x) - M(t-h-x)\}$, being convergent, is a bounded function of x. Of course, $G(t)-G(t/2)\to 0$ as $t\to\infty$, so that, in summary,

$$\lim_{t\to\infty}[M_D(t)-M_D(t-h)]=h/\mu.$$

B. STATIONARY RENEWAL PROCESSES

A delayed renewal process for which the first life has the distribution function

$$G(x)=\mu^{-1}\int_0^x\{1-F(y)\}\,dy$$

is called a stationary renewal process. We are attempting to model a renewal process that began indefinitely far in the past, so that the remaining life of the item in service at the origin has the limiting distribution of the excess life in an ordinary renewal process. We recognize G as this limiting distribution.

It is anticipated that such a process exhibits a number of stationary or time-invariant properties. We will content ourselves with showing that, for a stationary renewal process,

$$M_D(t)=E[N(t)]\equiv t/\mu, \tag{7.3}$$

and

$$\Pr\{\gamma_t^D\le x\}=G(x),$$

for all t. Thus, what is in general only an asymptotic renewal relation becomes an identity, holding for all t, in a stationary renewal process.

Recall from Eq. (7.2) that $M_D(t)$ satisfies the renewal equation

$$M_D(t)=G(t)+\int_0^t M_D(t-x)\,dF(x), \tag{7.4}$$

and since the solution to such an equation is unique (modulo suitable boundedness restrictions, see Theorem 4.1), we need merely check that $M_D(t)\equiv t/\mu$ satisfies (7.4). We have

$$\begin{aligned}G(t)+\int_0^t M_D(t-x)\,dF(x)&=\mu^{-1}\int_0^t\{1-F(x)\}\,dx+\mu^{-1}\int_0^t(t-x)\,dF(x)\\&=\mu^{-1}t+\mu^{-1}\left\{\int_0^t(t-x)\,dF(x)-\int_0^t F(y)\,dy\right\}\\&=\mu^{-1}t\end{aligned}$$

since the part in braces vanishes as can be checked by performing an integration by parts. The identity $M_D(t)\equiv t/\mu$ is hereby confirmed.

We will follow the same procedure to validate the equation $\Pr\{\gamma_t^{\mathrm{D}} \le x\} = G(x)$ for all x, where γ_t^{D} is the excess life in the delayed (stationary) renewal process. Let

$$A_x^{\mathrm{D}}(t) = \Pr\{\gamma_t^{\mathrm{D}} > x\}, \qquad \text{and} \qquad A_x(t) = \Pr\{\gamma_t > x\},$$

where γ_t is the excess life in an ordinary renewal process. The standard renewal argument leads to

$$A_x^{\mathrm{D}}(t) = 1 - G(t+x) + \int_0^t A_x(t-y)\, dG(y),$$

or

$$A_x^{\mathrm{D}}(t) = 1 - G(t+x) + G * A_x(t). \tag{7.5}$$

The renewal equation

$$A_x(t) = 1 - F(t+x) + F * A_x(t)$$

appeared earlier, in our deliberations of Section 6. By virtue of Theorem 4.1, the solution can be represented in the form

$$A_x(t) = a_x(t) + M * a_x(t), \tag{7.6}$$

where

$$a_x(t) = 1 - F(t+x).$$

Inserting (7.6) into (7.5) and citing the formula $M_{\mathrm{D}}(t) = G(t) + G * M(t)$ (this comes out directly from the definitions involved), we obtain

$$\begin{aligned} A_x^{\mathrm{D}}(t) &= 1 - G(t+x) + G * a_x(t) + G * M * a_x(t) \\ &= 1 - G(t+x) + M_{\mathrm{D}} * a_x(t) \\ &= 1 - G(t+x) + \int_0^t a_x(t-y)\, dM_{\mathrm{D}}(y). \end{aligned}$$

Now $a_x(t-y) = 1 - F(t+x-y)$ and $M_{\mathrm{D}}(y) \equiv y/\mu$, so that $dM_{\mathrm{D}}(y) = \mu^{-1}\, dy$. Then

$$\begin{aligned} A_x^{\mathrm{D}}(t) &= 1 - G(t+x) + \mu^{-1} \int_0^t \{1 - F(t+x-y)\}\, dy \\ &= 1 - G(t+x) + \mu^{-1} \int_x^{t+x} \{1 - F(u)\}\, du \\ &= 1 - G(t+x) + G(t+x) - G(x) \\ &= 1 - G(x), \end{aligned}$$

as was to be shown.

C. CUMULATIVE AND RELATED PROCESSES

Suppose associated with the ith unit or lifetime interval is a second random variable Y_i ($\{Y_i\}$ identically distributed) in addition to the lifetime X_i. We allow X_i and Y_i to be dependent, but assume that the pairs (X_1, Y_1), (X_2, Y_2), ... are independent. We use the notation $F(x) = \Pr\{X_i \leq x\}$, $G(y) = \Pr(Y_i \leq y\}$, $\mu = E[X_i]$, and $\nu = E[Y_i]$.

A number of problems of practical and theoretical interest have a natural formulation in these terms.

I. *Renewal Processes Involving Two Components to Each Renewal Interval*

Suppose that

$$Y_i \text{ represents a portion of the duration } X_i.$$

Figure 7 illustrates the model. In Fig. 7 we have depicted the Y portion occurring at the beginning of the interval, but this is not essential for the results that follow.

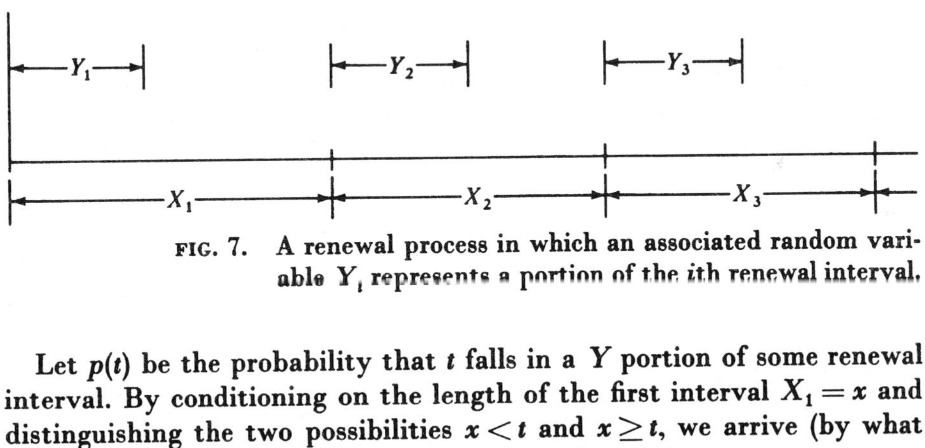

FIG. 7. A renewal process in which an associated random variable Y_i represents a portion of the ith renewal interval.

Let $p(t)$ be the probability that t falls in a Y portion of some renewal interval. By conditioning on the length of the first interval $X_1 = x$ and distinguishing the two possibilities $x < t$ and $x \geq t$, we arrive (by what is now a routine methodology) at the renewal equation

$$p(t) = \Pr\{t \text{ is covered by } Y_1\} + \int_0^t p(t - \xi)\, dF(\xi).$$

Let

$$I_{Y_1}(t) = \begin{cases} 1, & \text{if } Y_1 \text{ covers } t, \\ 0, & \text{if } Y_1 \text{ does not cover } t. \end{cases}$$

Then

$$\Pr\{t \text{ is covered by } Y_1\} = E[I_{Y_1}(t)],$$

and

$$\int_0^\infty \Pr\{t \text{ is covered by } Y_1\}\,dt = \int_0^\infty E[I_{Y_1}(t)]\,dt$$

$$= E\left[\int_0^\infty I_{Y_1}(t)\,dt\right]$$

$$= E[Y_1] = \nu,$$

since the totality of points covered by Y_1 is Y_1. Now applying the renewal theorem, we conclude that if F is nonarithmetic and $\Pr\{t$ is covered by $Y_1\}$ is directly Riemann integrable, then

$$\lim_{t\to\infty} p(t) = \mu^{-1}\int_0^\infty \Pr\{t \text{ is covered by } Y_1\}\,dt$$

$$= \nu/\mu. \tag{7.7}$$

Here are some concrete examples.

(a) *A Replacement Model*

Consider a replacement model in which replacement is not instantaneous. Let Y_i be the operating time and Z_i the lag period preceding installment of the $(i+1)$st operating unit. (The delay in replacement can be conceived as a period of repair of the service unit.) We assume that the sequence of times between successive replacements $X_k = Y_k + Z_k$, $k = 1, 2, \ldots$, constitutes a renewal process. Then $p(t)$, the probability that the system is in operation at time t, converges to $E[Y_1]/E[X_1]$, provided the distribution of X_k is nonarithmetic.

(b) *A Queuing Model*

If arrivals to a queue follow a Poisson process, then the successive times X_k from the commencement of the kth busy period to the start of the next busy period form a renewal process. (A busy period is an uninterrupted duration when the queue is not empty.) Each X_k is composed of a busy portion Z_k and an idle portion Y_k. Then $p(t)$, the probability that the queue is empty at time t, converges to $E[Y_1]/E[X_1]$.

(c) *A Counter Problem*

Let X_k, $k = 1, 2, \ldots$, denote the sequence of times between successive recorded particles in a counter and let Y_k represent the dead (blocked) time during the X_k renewal period. Then $p(t)$, the probability that the counter is blocked at time t, converges to $E[Y_1]/E[X_1]$.

II. *Cumulative Processes*

Interpret Y_i as a cost or value, etc., associated with the ith renewal cycle. A class of problems with natural setting in this general context of pairs (X_i, Y_i), where X_i generates a renewal process, will now be considered. Interest here focuses on the so-called *cumulative process*

$$W(t) = \sum_{k=1}^{N(t)+1} Y_k,$$

the accumulated costs or what-have-you up to time t (assuming transactions are made at the beginning of a renewal cycle). By conditioning on the time $X_1 = x$ until the first renewal, and examining the two possibilities $x > t$ and $x \le t$, we secure for $A(t) = E[W(t)]$ the renewal equation

$$A(t) = E[Y_1] + \int_0^t A(t-x)\,dF(x).$$

An appeal to Theorem 4.1 yields the formula

$$\begin{aligned} A(t) &= E[Y_1] + \int_0^t E[Y_1]\,dM(x) \\ &= E[Y_1][1 + M(t)]. \end{aligned}$$

It follows immediately that, where F is nonarithmetic and $h > 0$, then

$$\lim_{t\to\infty}[A(t) - A(t-h)] = E[Y_1]h/\mu,$$

and in any case,

$$\lim_{t\to\infty}\frac{1}{t}A(t) = E[Y_1]/\mu.$$

This justifies the interpretation of $E[Y_1]/\mu$ as a long-run mean cost, value, etc., per unit time, an interpretation that was used repeatedly in the examples of Section 3.

Here are some examples of cumulative processes.

(a) *Replacement Models*

Suppose Y_i is the cost of the ith replacement. Let us suppose that under an age-replacement strategy (see Example B, Section 3) a planned replacement at age T costs c_1 dollars, while a failure replaced at time $x < T$ costs c_2 dollars. If Y_k is the cost incurred at the kth replacement cycle, then

$$Y_k = \begin{cases} c_1 & \text{with probability} \quad 1 - F(T), \\ c_2 & \text{with probability} \quad F(T), \end{cases}$$

and $E[Y_k] = c_1[1 - F(T)] + c_2 F(T)$. Since the expected length of a replacement cycle is

$$E[\min\{X_k, T\}] = \int_0^T [1 - F(x)]\, dx,$$

we have that the long-run cost per unit time is

$$\frac{c_1[1 - F(T)] + c_2 F(T)}{\int_0^T [1 - F(x)]\, dx},$$

and in any particular situation a routine calculus exercise or recourse to numerical computation produces the value of T that minimizes the long-run cost per unit time.

Under a block replacement policy, there is one planned replacement every T units of time and, on the average, $M(T)$ failure replacements, so the expected cost is $E[Y_k] = c_1 + c_2 M(T)$, and the long-run mean cost per unit time is $\{c_1 + c_2 M(T)\}/T$.

(b) *Counter Models*

In a counter model (see Example C, Section 3), let Y_k be the number of unregistered signals that arise during the period X_k between the $(k-1)$st and kth recorded signals. Then the long-run mean number of uncounted particles per unit time is $E[Y_1]/E[X_1]$.

(c) *Risk Theory*

Suppose claims arrive at an insurance company according to a renewal process with interoccurrence times $X_1, X_2, \ldots$. Let Y_k be the magnitude of the kth claim. Then $W(t) = \sum_{k=0}^{N(t)+1} Y_k$ represents the cumulative amount claimed up to time t, and the long-run mean claim rate is

$$\lim_{t\to\infty} \frac{1}{t} E[W(t)] = E[Y_1]/E[X_1].$$

D. TERMINATING RENEWAL PROCESSES

Suppose we allow the possibility of infinite interoccurrence times in a renewal process. Such a process is called a *terminating* renewal process, since the renewals cease at the first infinite interoccurrence time. The situation is diagrammed in Fig. 8.

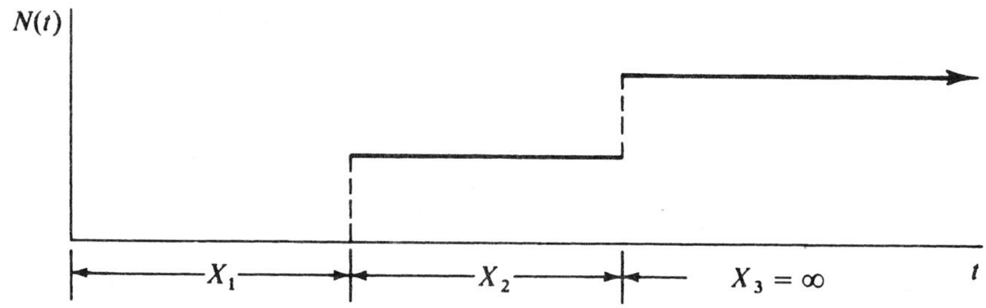

FIG. 8.

Let $L = F(\infty) = \Pr\{X_k < \infty\} < 1$ and $1 - L = \Pr\{X_k = \infty\} > 0$. Then the total number of renewals in all time, denoted by $N(\infty)$, is a finite-valued random variable and follows the geometric probability law

$$\Pr\{N(\infty) \geq k\} = L^k, \qquad k = 0, 1, 2, \ldots,$$

with

$$E[N(\infty)] = \sum_{k=1}^{\infty} \Pr\{N(\infty) \geq k\}$$
$$= L/(1 - L).$$

The realizations of the termination process still have the property $N(t) \geq k$ if and only if $S_k \leq t$, so that

$$\Pr\{N(t) \geq k\} = \Pr\{S_k \leq t\} = F_k(t),$$

and

$$M(t) = E[N(t)] = \sum_{k=1}^{\infty} F_k(t) < \sum_{k=1}^{\infty} L^k = L/(1 - L).$$

Moreover, the renewal argument continues to work, entailing the equation

$$M(t) = F(t) + \int_0^t M(t - x)\, dF(x).$$

However, the renewal theorem is *not* automatically applicable owing to the fact that F is not a proper probability distribution function. Fortunately, there is often a way to overcome this lacuna. Suppose that

$$g(s) = \int_0^{\infty} e^{sx}\, dF(x)$$

is a finite function of s for $s \geq 0$. Then g will be continuous and $g(0) = L < 1$ and $\lim_{s \to \infty} g(s) = \infty$, implying the existence of a unique positive value $s_0 = \lambda > 0$, for which

$$g(\lambda) = \int_0^{\infty} e^{\lambda x}\, dF(x) = 1.$$

Define $\hat{F}(t) = \int_0^t e^{\lambda x}\, dF(x)$. Then $\hat{F}(t)$ is nondecreasing and $\lim_{t\to\infty} \hat{F}(t) = 1$, showing that $\hat{F}$ is a proper distribution function. Now consider a renewal equation of the form

$$A(t) = a(t) + \int_0^t A(t-x)\, dF(x).$$

Set $\hat{A}(t) = e^{\lambda t} A(t)$, $\hat{a}(t) = e^{\lambda t} a(t)$, and verify

$$\begin{aligned}\hat{A}(t) &= e^{\lambda t} A(t)\\ &= e^{\lambda t} a(t) + \int_0^t e^{\lambda(t-x)} A(t-x) e^{\lambda x}\, dF(x)\\ &= \hat{a}(t) + \int_0^t \hat{A}(t-x)\, d\hat{F}(x),\end{aligned}$$

indicating that $\hat{A}$ satisfies a renewal equation now involving a proper distribution function, to which the renewal theorem can be applied. As a specific example, consider $A(t) = M(\infty) - M(t) = L/(1-L) - M(t)$. Equivalently, $A(t) = E[N(\infty) - N(t)]$ is the mean number of indices n for which $t < S_n < \infty$. We now develop a renewal equation satisfied by $A(t)$. In fact, we have

$$E[N(\infty) - N(t) | X_1 = x] = \begin{cases} 1 + L/(1-L), & \text{if } x > t, \\ A(t-x), & \text{if } 0 < x \le t. \end{cases}$$

It follows, using the law of total probabilities, that

$$\begin{aligned}A(t) &= \int_0^\infty E[N(\infty) - N(t) | X_1 = x]\, dF(x)\\ &= \{L - F(t)\}/(1-L) + \int_0^t A(t-x)\, dF(x).\end{aligned}$$

Next check that

$$\hat{a}(t) = e^{\lambda t}\{L - F(t)\}/(1-L)$$

is directly Riemann integrable. Note also

$$\begin{aligned}\int_0^\infty \hat{a}(t)\, dt &= \frac{1}{1-L} \int_0^\infty e^{\lambda t}\{L - F(t)\}\, dt\\ &= \frac{1}{1-L} \int_0^\infty e^{\lambda t} \int_t^\infty dF(x)\, dt\end{aligned}$$

$$= \frac{1}{1-L} \int_0^\infty \int_0^x e^{\lambda t}\, dt\, dF(x)$$

$$= \frac{1}{1-L} \int_0^\infty \frac{(e^{\lambda x} - 1)}{\lambda}\, dF(x)$$

$$= \frac{1}{1-L} \frac{(1-L)}{\lambda} = \frac{1}{\lambda}.$$

Thus

$$\lim_{t\to\infty} \hat{A}(t) = \lim_{t\to\infty} e^{\lambda t}[M(\infty) - M(t)]$$

$$= \left\{\lambda \int_0^\infty x e^{\lambda x}\, dF(x)\right\}^{-1}$$

We conclude that $M(t)$ approaches $M(\infty) = L/(1 - L)$ exponentially fast at rate λ.

E. ALTERNATING AND MARKOV RENEWAL PROCESSES

An *alternating renewal process* is a sequence $Y_1, Y_2, \ldots$ of independent random variables, where

$$\begin{array}{ll} Y_1, Y_{r+1}, Y_{2r+1}, \ldots & \text{have distribution function } F_1, \\ Y_2, Y_{r+2}, Y_{2r+2}, \ldots & \text{have distribution function } F_2, \\ \vdots & \\ Y_r, Y_{2r}, Y_{3r}, \ldots & \text{have distribution function } F_r. \end{array}$$

We think of a system passing successively through states 1, 2, ..., r, 1, 2, ..., r, 1, 2, ..., and sojourning a random time period during each visit to each state.

Let $p_i(t)$ be the probability that the system is in state i at time t. From relation (7.7) of Part C, we infer

$$\lim_{t\to\infty} p_i(t) = \mu_i/(\mu_1 + \cdots + \mu_r),$$

where

$$\mu_i = E[Y_i] < \infty, \qquad i = 1, \ldots, r,$$

provided the distribution $F = F_1 * F_2 \cdots * F_r$ is nonarithmetic.

A *Markov renewal* or *semi-Markov* process passes through states 1, ..., r according to a Markov chain having transition probability matrix $P = \|P_{ij}\|_{i,j=1}^r$. The time spent in state i, given that the next state is j, has distribution function F_{ij}, and, conditioned on the sequence of states, all sojourn times are assumed independent. The unconditional distribution function of the sojourn time in a state i is $F_i(t) = \sum_{j=1}^{r} P_{ij} F_{ij}(t)$, which is postulated to have a finite mean μ_i. Assume that the Markov chain is irreducible and recurrent, with stationary distribution given by $\pi_j = \sum_i \pi_i P_{ij}$.

Suppose the process starts in a fixed state i, and let a state k be prescribed. Call the duration between one visit to state i and the next an *i-cycle*. The sequence of times between these successive visits to state i forms a renewal process. From relation (7.7) and assuming at least one F_i is not arithmetic, the probability $p_k(t)$ of being in state k at time t converges to the mean time spent in state k during an i-cycle divided by the mean duration of an i-cycle. By the law of total probability, the mean time in state k during an i-cycle is the product of μ_k times the mean number of visits to k in the intervening time between successive visits to state i. The second factor depends only on the discrete-time Markov chain of state visits and therefore is necessarily proportional to π_k. It follows that

$$\lim_{t \to \infty} p_k(t) = c\pi_k \mu_k,$$

when c is a constant of proportionality. Since these probabilities necessarily sum to 1, $c = 1/(\pi_1 \mu_1 + \cdots + \pi_r \mu_r)$.

F. CENTRAL LIMIT THEOREM FOR RENEWALS

Theorem 7.1. *Let $\{X_n\}$ be a renewal process for which $\mu = E[X_1] < \infty$ and $\sigma^2 = E[(X_1 - \mu)^2] < \infty$. Then*

$$\lim_{t \to \infty} \Pr\left\{\frac{N(t) - t/\mu}{\sqrt{t\sigma^2/\mu^3}} < x\right\} = \Phi(x),$$

where

$$\Phi(x) = \frac{1}{\sqrt{2\pi}} \int_{-\infty}^{x} \exp(-\tfrac{1}{2}u^2)\, du$$

is the normal integral.

Proof. The proof rests on the central limit theorem for $S_n = X_1 + \cdots + X_n$ and the basic identity of realizations of the process in the form $\{N(t) < n\}$ if and only if $\{S_n > t\}$.

Let x be fixed and let $n \to \infty$ and $t \to \infty$ in such a way that

$$\lim_{\substack{t \to \infty \\ n \to \infty}} \frac{t - n\mu}{\sigma\sqrt{n}} = -x.$$

Then, by the usual central limit theorem,

$$\lim_{\substack{t\to\infty\\ n\to\infty}} \Pr\{S_n > t\} = \lim_{\substack{t\to\infty\\ n\to\infty}} \Pr\left\{\frac{S_n - n\mu}{\sigma\sqrt{n}} > -x\right\} = 1 - \Phi(-x) = \Phi(x).$$

But then

$$\begin{aligned}\Phi(x) &= \lim_{\substack{t\to\infty\\ n\to\infty}} \Pr\{S_n > t\}\\ &= \lim_{\substack{t\to\infty\\ n\to\infty}} \Pr\{N(t) < n\}\\ &= \lim_{\substack{t\to\infty\\ n\to\infty}} \Pr\left\{\frac{N(t) - t/\mu}{\sqrt{t\sigma^2/\mu^3}} < \frac{n - t/\mu}{\sqrt{t\sigma^2/\mu^3}}\right\}\\ &= \lim_{t\to\infty} \Pr\left\{\frac{N(t) - t/\mu}{\sqrt{t\sigma^2/\mu^3}} < x\right\},\end{aligned}$$

since $(n - t/\mu)/\sqrt{t\sigma^2/\mu^3} \to x$ as $t \to \infty$, $n \to \infty$ in such a manner that $(t - n\mu)/\sqrt{n\sigma^2} \to -x$. ■

The preceding analysis was conducted in a formal manner and needs tightening. The student may try to supply the epsilonics.

G. RUIN IN RISK THEORY

Let $N(t)$ be the number of claims incurred by an insurance company over the time interval $(0, t]$. Assume $N(t)$ is a Poisson process with parameter λ. Assume, moreover, that the magnitudes of the successive claims $Y_1, Y_2, Y_3, \ldots$ are independent identically distributed random variables having distribution function $G(x)$. Let the inflow of cash (premiums, investments, etc.) be c dollars per unit time and suppose the initial capital of the company is z. Then at time t, the cash balance is

$$\Gamma(t) = z + ct - \sum_{i=1}^{N(t)} Y_i,$$

where Y_i is the magnitude of the ith successive claim. It is of interest to ascertain the probability of continual solvency as a function of z. That is, we wish to determine

$$R(z) = \Pr\left\{z + ct - \sum_{i=1}^{N(t)} Y_i > 0, \text{ for all } t\right\} \tag{7.8}$$

$$= \text{probability of no ruin with initial capital } z.$$

We apply the renewal argument conditioning on the time T_1 of the first Poisson event. Together with the law of total probabilities, we obtain

$$R(z)=\int_0^\infty \Pr\left\{z+ct-\sum_{i=1}^{N(t)} Y_i>0 \text{ for all } t \mid T_1=\tau\right\}\lambda e^{-\lambda\tau}\,d\tau. \tag{7.9}$$

But another conditioning on the value of Y_1 entails

$$\Pr\left\{z+ct-\sum_{i=1}^{N(t)} Y_i>0 \text{ for all } t \mid T_1=\tau\right\}$$
$$=\int_0^\infty \Pr\left\{z+ct-\sum_{i=1}^{N(t)} Y_i>0 \text{ for all } t \mid Y_1=y,\ T_1=\tau\right\} dG(y). \tag{7.10}$$

The process $\Gamma(t)$ renews itself immediately after time τ holding the new initial capital $z+c\tau-y$, given $T_1=\tau$, $Y_1=y$. Therefore,

$$\Pr\left\{z+ct-\sum_{i=1}^{N(t)} Y_i>0 \text{ for all } t \mid Y_1=y,\ T_1=\tau\right\}=R(z+c\tau-y). \tag{7.11}$$

Of course, $R(u)=0$ for $u<0$.

The facts of (7.10) and (7.11) implemented into (7.9) produce the integral equation

$$R(z)=\int_0^\infty\left(\int_0^{z+c\tau} R(z+c\tau-y)\,dG(y)\right)\lambda e^{-\lambda\tau}\,d\tau.$$

A change of variables $t=z+c\tau$ in the outer integral and rearrangement gives

$$R(z)e^{-\lambda z/c}=\frac{\lambda}{c}\int_z^\infty\left(\int_0^t R(t-y)\,dG(y)\right)e^{-\lambda t/c}\,dt.$$

The representation assures that $R(z)$ is differentiable, and differentiation yields

$$e^{-\lambda z/c}\left[R'(z)-\frac{\lambda}{c}R(z)\right]=-\frac{\lambda}{c}e^{-\lambda z/c}\int_0^z R(z-y)\,dG(y),$$

or, equivalently,

$$R'(z)=\frac{\lambda}{c}R(z)-\frac{\lambda}{c}\int_0^z R(z-y)\,dG(y).$$

Integrating both sides with respect to z gives

$$R(w) - R(0) = \frac{\lambda}{c}\int_0^w R(z)\,dz - \frac{\lambda}{c}\int_0^w \left(\int_0^z R(z-y)\,dG(y)\right) dz.$$

Interchanging the orders of integration and then a change of variable $\xi = z - y$ leads to

$$R(w) = R(0) + \frac{\lambda}{c}\int_0^w R(z)\,dz - \frac{\lambda}{c}\int_0^w \left(\int_0^{w-y} R(\xi)\,d\xi\right) dG(y).$$

Define $S(x) = \int_0^x R(\xi)\,d\xi$. Next perform an integration by parts to obtain

$$R(w) - R(0) = \frac{\lambda}{c} S(w) - \frac{\lambda}{c}\left\{S(w) - \int_0^w R(w-y)[1-G(y)]\,dy\right\},$$

or

$$R(w) = R(0) + \frac{\lambda}{c}\int_0^w R(w-y)[1-G(y)]\,dy.$$

These manipulations have produced a renewal equation with an improper density $(\lambda/c)[1 - G(y)]$, since

$$\int_0^\infty \frac{\lambda}{c}[1-G(y)]\,dy = \frac{\lambda}{c}E[Y_1] = \frac{\lambda}{c}\mu.$$

If $\lambda\mu/c > 1$, it is certain that $R(z) = 0$ (why?). (Note that $\lambda\mu$ is the expected outflow per unit time servicing claims, while c is the rate of income.) Assume henceforth the case $\lambda\mu/c < 1$. With $a(w) = R(0)$, Theorem 4.1 continues to apply in this degenerate case to inform us

$$R(w) = a(w) + \int_0^w a(w-y)\,dM(y) = R(0)[1 + M(w)],$$

and since $M(w)$ corresponds to a terminating renewal process

$$\lim_{w\to\infty} M(w) = L/(1-L) = \frac{\lambda\mu/c}{1-\lambda\mu/c}$$

whence

$$\lim_{w\to\infty} R(w) = \frac{R(0)}{1-(\lambda\mu/c)}.$$

But $R(\infty) = 1$ (why?), and we obtain

$$R(0) = 1 - \frac{\lambda\mu}{c}.$$

More precise asymptotic relations can be achieved by refining the analysis.

8: More Elaborate Applications of Renewal Theory

A. A GENETIC MODEL WITH MUTATION

Consider a finite population of constant size N and label the individuals by $j = 1, \ldots, N$. This comprises the first generation in an evolutionary process subject to certain natural selection effects and mutation pressures. We now delimit the nature and order of the forces governing the process.

Each individual of the population is endowed with a characteristic called "fitness." Loosely speaking, fitness is a measure of the individual's innate relative advantage in contributing offspring to the succeeding generation. Let w_k^1 denote the fitness of the kth individual of the first generation. Determine

$$u_k = \frac{w_k^1}{\sum_{j=1}^{N} w_j^1}, \qquad k = 1, 2, \ldots, N, \tag{8.1}$$

which connotes the relative fitness value of the kth individual. The next generation of progeny is formed by performing N independent random samplings following a multinomial distribution with probability vector (8.1). Thus an offspring carries the fitness value w_k^1 of his parental type and will be selected with probability u_k. Manifestly, individuals of high fitness value compared to the others have concordahtly larger relative fitness values and manifestly have greater chance of propagating their own kind.

This multinomial reproduction procedure bears a population of offspring carrying fitness values

$$\tilde{w}^2 = (\tilde{w}_1^2, \tilde{w}_2^2, \ldots, \tilde{w}_N^2). \tag{8.2}$$

(Each of the values $\tilde{w}_i^2$ is, of course, one of the $\{w_k^1\}$. The type of an individual will be identified with his fitness.)

The vector $\tilde{w}^2$ does not yet comprise the mature population of the second generation. We will introduce the possibilities of mutation, so that an offspring can undergo a spontaneous change in fitness value. The precise assumption concerning the effects of the mutation changes is as follows: We suppose that $\{V_i^j;\ i=1, \ldots, N, j=2, \ldots\}$ is a rectangular array of independent, identically distributed positive random variables, and then let

$$\begin{aligned} w_1^2 &= \tilde{w}_1^2 V_1^2, \\ w_2^2 &= \tilde{w}_2^2 V_2^2, \\ &\vdots \\ w_N^2 &= \tilde{w}_N^2 V_N^2. \end{aligned}$$

The vector $(w_1^2, \ldots, w_N^2)$ represents the fitnesses of mature individuals in the second generation. The above procedure is repeated, sequentially producing successive N-dimensional vectors that depict the evolution of the population through the changes of the fitness vector $w^k = (w_1^k, \ldots, w_N^k)$, and the relative fitness vector $u^k = (u_1^k, \ldots, u_N^k)$ [the superscript indicates the generation number counting from the initial specified population of (8.1)]. The probability law governing the determination of w^{k+1} from w^k and u^k in line with the formation of w^2 from w^1 goes as follows: Sample N independent values from among $w_1^k, w_2^k, \ldots, w_N^k$ with probabilities u_i^k of choosing w_i^k, $i = 1, 2, \ldots, N$. Denote the resulting vector by $\tilde{w}^{k+1} = (\tilde{w}_1^{k+1}, \ldots, \tilde{w}_N^{k+1})$. Mutation changes then transform $\tilde{w}^{k+1}$ to w^{k+1} through multiplication by the positive random variables V_i^{k+1} in the explicit manner

$$w_i^{k+1} = \tilde{w}_i^{k+1} V_i^{k+1}, \qquad i = 1, 2, \ldots, N.$$

Finally, determine the relative fitness vector u^{k+1} by the rule

$$u_i^{k+1} = \frac{w_i^{k+1}}{\sum_{j=1}^{N} w_j^{k+1}}, \qquad i = 1, 2, \ldots, N.$$

The evolutionary process can be realized by the path of the point w^k, $k = 1, 2, \ldots$, traversed in N-dimensional space.

The relative fitness u^k is the projection of the random vector w^k onto the N-dimensional simplex

$$\Delta_N = \{x = (x_1, \ldots, x_N) : x_i \geq 0 \text{ and } x_1 + \cdots + x_N = 1\}.$$

Figure 9 illustrates the projection when $N = 3$. As generations pass, u^k describes the relative fitness point moving about the simplex Δ_N. It is natural to inquire concerning the long-run statistical behavior of u^k.

Define $T(0)$ as the elapsed number of generations (i.e., the smallest $k - 1$) until all components of $\tilde{w}^k$ coincide. Such a generation is called a *generation of equal components*.

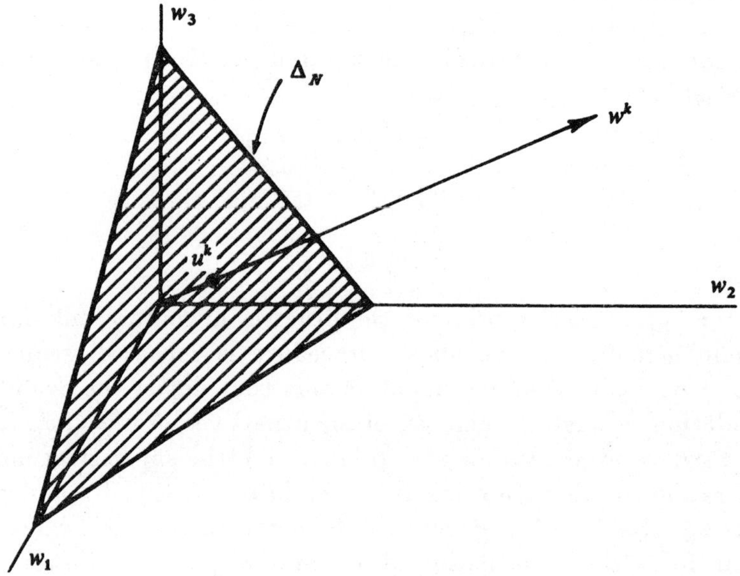

FIG. 9. u^k is the projection of w^k onto the simplex Δ_N.

Lemma 8.1. $\Pr\{T(0) < \infty\} = 1$. *In fact*, $E[T(0)] \leq N^N$.

Proof. Let $w^1 = (w_1^1, \ldots, w_N^1)$ be the fitnesses in the first generation. One way in which $T(0) = 1$ can occur is if the progeny population has

$$\tilde{w}_k^2 = w_\nu^1, \qquad \text{for all } k,$$

where

$$w_\nu^1 = \max\{w_1^1, \ldots, w_N^1\}.$$

This event clearly occurs with probability at least $\alpha = (1/N)^N$. Thus $\Pr\{T(0) = 1\} \geq \alpha$ and $\Pr\{T(0) > 1\} \leq 1 - \alpha$.

The same estimate applies for the transitions from the second to the third generation. Consequently, we have

$$\Pr\{T(0) > 2 | T(0) > 1\} \leq 1 - \alpha,$$

and

$$\Pr\{T(0) > 2\} \leq (1 - \alpha)^2.$$

By a direct induction, we deduce $\Pr\{T(0) > k\} \leq (1 - \alpha)^k$, so that $E[T(0)] \leq 1/\alpha = N^N$. ■

Let $T(0) + T(1)$ be the first generation time exceeding $T(0)$ that has equal components, and define $T(0) + \cdots + T(k)$ to be the first generation of equal components after $T(0) + \cdots + T(k-1)$. The key observation is that *the process of* $\{u^k\}$ *starts afresh at the generation times* $T(0)$, $T(0)+T(1)$, $\cdots$, and therefore this sequence of positive integer-valued random variables forms a renewal process. To see why this is so, let $\tilde{w}$ be the common fitness value at generation $T(k)$. Then all components of $\tilde{w}^{T(k)+1}$ have value $\tilde{w}$, and the jth component of $w^{T(k)+1}$ is $\tilde{w}V_j^{T(k)+1}$. The influence and relevance of $\tilde{w}$ disappears at the next step, because the multinomial probabilities are, in accordance with (8.1),

$$u_j = \frac{\tilde{w}V_j^{T(k)+1}}{\sum_{i=1}^{N} \tilde{w}V_i^{T(k)+1}} = \frac{V_j^{T(k)+1}}{\sum_{i=1}^{N} V_i^{T(k)+1}}, \qquad j = 1, 2, \ldots, N,$$

independent of $\tilde{w}$. Hence, following every generation of equal components, the process is determined solely by the independent identically distributed set of mutation multipliers of random variables. It follows that the sequence $T(0)$, $T(1)$, ..., induces a delayed renewal process.

Let $N(t)$ denote the renewal counting process induced by $\{T(k)\}$ and let $S_k = T(0) + \cdots + T(k-1)$ with $S_0 = 0$. Choose a generation time m. Then $S_{N(m)}$ is the last generation time prior to m where all the premutation fitnesses are the same. What is the distribution of the relative fitness $u^m = (u_1^m, \ldots, u_N^m)$?

At time $S_{N(m)}$ the relative fitnesses have equal components $1/N$. Consider

$$\delta_m = m - S_{N(m)},$$

the number of generations elapsed between $S_{N(m)}$ and m. The effect of mutation followed by the multinomial selection process over one generation can be summarized by a transition distribution function Γ:

$$\begin{aligned}\Gamma(z_1, \ldots, z_N; \eta_1, \ldots, \eta_N) = \Pr\{&\text{a relative fitness of} \\ &(\eta_1, \ldots, \eta_N) \text{ changes to } (\eta_1', \ldots, \eta_N') \text{ where} \\ &\eta_k' \le z_k,\ k = 1, \ldots, N\}.\end{aligned}$$

Hence

$$\begin{aligned}&\Pr\{u_k^m \le z_k,\ k = 1, \ldots, N \mid \delta_m = 1\} \\ &\quad = \Gamma\left(z_1, \ldots, z_N; \frac{1}{N}, \ldots, \frac{1}{N}\right).\end{aligned}$$

The result of k generations of the reproduction process with mutation and sampling selection effects starting from a generation of equal components can be expressed formally as

$$\begin{aligned}&\Pr\{u_j^m \le z_j,\ j = 1, \ldots, N \mid \delta_m = k\} \\ &\qquad = \Gamma^{(k)}\left(z_1, \ldots, z_N; \frac{1}{N}, \ldots, \frac{1}{N}\right),\end{aligned}$$

where $\Gamma^{(k)}$ stands for the iterated k-fold transition distribution induced from the transformation Γ.

The law of total probabilities provides us with the representation

$$\Pr\{u_j^m \le z_j, j=1, \ldots, N\} = \sum_{k=1}^{m} \Pr\{\delta_m = k\}\Gamma^{(k)}\left(z_1, \ldots, z_N; \frac{1}{N}, \ldots, \frac{1}{N}\right)$$

$$+ \Pr\{T(0) \ge m\}\Gamma^{(m+1)}(z_1, \ldots, z_N; u_1^1, \ldots, u_N^1). \tag{8.3}$$

Now the limiting distribution of current life associated with the renewal process $\{T(k)\}_{k=1}^{\infty}$ asserts that

$$\lim_{n\to\infty} \Pr\{\delta_n = k\} = \frac{1 - \Pr\{T(1) \le k\}}{E[T(1)]} \qquad \text{[a special case of (6.5)]}$$

Applying this fact in (8.2) leads to the result

$$\lim_{m\to\infty} \Pr\{u_j^m \le z_j, j=1, \ldots, n\}$$

$$= \sum_{k=1}^{\infty} \left\{\frac{1 - \Pr\{T(1) \le k\}}{E[T(1)]}\right\}\Gamma^{(k)}\left(z_1, \ldots, z_N; \frac{1}{N}, \ldots, \frac{1}{N}\right).$$

(The student should justify interchange of limit with sum; it is easy.)

This final relation describes the limiting behavior of relative fitness in the evolving population and, in fact, provides an explicit formula for the stationary distribution.

B. A BRANCHING PROCESS

Suppose at time $t = 0$ there is a single organism that lives a random time T_0, taken from a distribution F. At the end of its life, it produces j new organisms with probability p_j, $j = 1, 2, \ldots$. Each new organism lives and produces independently of the other members of the population and with the corresponding identical distributions governing all actions. Let $m = \sum jp_j$ be the mean of the offspring distribution. Let $M(t)$ denote the mean number of organisms living at time t. Using the law of total probability plus a renewal argument conditioning on the outcome after the death of the initial parent (see Chapter 8 for more details), we obtain

$$M(t) = 1 - F(t) + \sum_{j=1}^{\infty} p_j \int_0^t jM(t-x)\,dF(x)$$

$$= 1 - F(t) + m\int_0^t M(t-x)\,dF(x). \tag{8.4}$$

Except for the factor m, Eq. (8.4) presents a renewal equation. When $m > 1$, we can transform (8.4) into a proper renewal equation. Let β be such that $\int_0^\infty e^{-\beta x}\, dF(x) = 1/m$. There exists a unique such $\beta > 0$, since $\int_0^\infty e^{-\lambda x}\, dF(x)$ is a strictly decreasing continuous function of λ, taking the value 1 for $\lambda = 0$ and approaching zero as $\lambda \to \infty$.

Define

$$\hat{F}(t) = m \int_0^t e^{-\beta x}\, dF(x),$$

$$\hat{M}(t) = e^{-\beta t} M(t),$$

and

$$g(t) = e^{-\beta t}[1 - F(t)].$$

Multiply Eq. (8.4) by $e^{-\beta t}$ to get

$$e^{-\beta t} M(t) = e^{-\beta t}[1 - F(t)] + \int_0^t e^{-\beta(t-x)} M(t-x) m\, e^{-\beta x}\, dF(x),$$

which written in the new notation has the form

$$\hat{M}(t) = g(t) + \int_0^t \hat{M}(t-x)\, d\hat{F}(x).$$

Straightforward verifications guarantee that $g(t)$ is directly Riemann integrable, so that, if F is nonarithmetic, by the renewal theorem,

$$\lim_{t\to\infty} \hat{M}(t) = \frac{\int_0^\infty g(x)\, dx}{\int_0^\infty x\, d\hat{F}(x)}.$$

Now $\int_0^\infty g(t)\, dt = (m-1)/\beta m$, so

$$\lim_{t\to\infty} e^{-\beta t} M(t) = \frac{m-1}{\beta m^2 \int_0^\infty x e^{-\beta x}\, dF(x)},$$

and, asymptotically, $M(t)$ increases exponentially at the rate $e^{\beta t}$. The parameter β is known as the Malthusian rate of growth of the population.

C. INVENTORY THEORY

A shopkeeper keeps a certain quantity of stock on hand. When the stock runs low, he places an order to replenish his supplies. The inventory policy in operation is assumed to be of (s, S) type. (This is in common practice.) Specifically, two levels $s < S$ are prescribed. Suppose the stock is originally at level S. A period length is also specified, and the stock level at the end of each period is checked. If at the close of a period, the stock level falls below s, a requisition (or order) is placed to return the level of stock up to S ready for dispensation at the start of the next period.

Let X_i be the quantity of demand accumulated during the ith period. We assume that $X_1, X_2, \ldots,$ are independent identically distributed positive random variables with distribution function F. Let $N(t)$ be the corresponding renewal counting process. Clearly $N(S-s)+1$ is the number of demand periods elapsed until the first order for refill is placed, at which time the stock level is again S. A little reflection reveals that we are dealing with two renewal processes; the first is the demand process and the second is the refill process.

Let the number of demand periods between the $(i-1)$st and the ith stock refill be θ_i. Then $\{\theta_i\}$ is a discrete (integer-valued) renewal process with mean $E(\theta_i) = 1 + M(S-s)$, and

$$\Pr\{\theta_i = k\} = F_{k-1}(S-s) - F_k(S-s). \tag{8.5}$$

Let W_n be the stock level at the end of the nth demand period. Define G_n to be the conditional distribution

$$G_n(x) = \Pr\{S - x \le W_n | s \le W_n\}.$$

This is the distribution of the stock level at the close of the nth period, knowing that the level has not fallen below s. This distribution is calculated by conditioning on δ_n, the number of demand periods since the last stock refill where the stock level was S. (Recall that by assumption at time 0 the stock quantity is S.) We get

$$\begin{aligned} G_n(x) &= \sum_{j=1}^{\infty} \Pr\{\delta_n = j\} \Pr\{X_1 + \cdots + X_j \le x | X_1 + \cdots + X_j \le S - s\} \\ &= \sum_{j=1}^{\infty} \Pr\{\delta_n = j\} \left(\frac{F_j(x)}{F_j(S-s)}\right). \end{aligned} \tag{8.6}$$

But from (8.5)

$$\Pr\{\theta_1 \le j\} = 1 - F_j(S-s). \tag{8.7}$$

Hence, by appeal to the limit theorem for the excess random variable of the renewal process $\{\theta_i\}$ [see (6.2)] and by virtue of (8.7), we deduce

$$\lim_{n\to\infty} \Pr\{\delta_n = j\} = \frac{1}{E[\theta_1]} \Pr\{\theta_1 > j\} = \frac{F_j(S-s)}{E[\theta_1]}$$

$$= \frac{F_j(S-s)}{1+M(S-s)}. \tag{8.8}$$

Using the above result in (8.6), we may conclude

$$\lim_{n\to\infty} \Pr\{S-x \leq W_n | s \leq W_n\} = \lim_{n\to\infty} \sum_{j=1}^{\infty} \Pr\{\delta_n = j\} \frac{F_j(x)}{F_j(S-s)}$$

$$= \frac{M(x)}{1+M(S-s)},$$

which gives the limiting distribution of stock level in periods in which a requisition order is not pending.

D. CHARACTERIZATIONS OF THE POISSON PROCESS

The Poisson process is a very special renewal process. This section offers some characterizations of the Poisson process as a special process within the class of renewal processes. For this objective we will exploit several of the limit theorems of Section 6.

Let $\{X_k\}$ be a renewal process with $E[X_k] = \mu < \infty$, and $F(x) = \Pr\{X_k \leq x\}$. Assume $F(0) = 0$. Define

$$F_t(x) = \begin{cases} F(x), & \text{for } 0 \leq x < t, \\ 1, & \text{for } t < x. \end{cases}$$

[compare to (3.5)]. Of course, $F_t(x)$ is the distribution function for $\min\{X_k, t\}$.

Theorem 8.1. (a) *If there exists a sequence $\{t_j\}$, where $t_j \to \infty$ as $j \to \infty$, and for which the current life δ_t satisfies*

$$F_{t_j}(x) = \Pr\{\delta_{t_j} \leq x\}, \qquad \text{for all } x,$$

then F is an exponential distribution.

(b) *If there exists a sequence $\{t_j\}$, where $t_j \to \infty$ as $j \to \infty$, and for which*

$$F(x) = \Pr\{\gamma_{t_j} \leq x\}, \qquad \text{for all } x,$$

[compare with (3.3)] *then F is exponential.*

Proof. We will demonstrate only (a) since (b) is quite similar. By the result of (6.5), the limiting distribution of the current life δ_t is

$$\lim_{t\to\infty} \Pr\{\delta_t > y\} = \mu^{-1} \int_y^\infty \{1 - F(z)\}\, dz.$$

Letting t increase along t_j with due account of the hypothesis of the theorem, we derive the functional equation

$$1 - F(y) = \mu^{-1} \int_y^\infty \{1 - F(z)\}\, dz.$$

The right-hand side is clearly differentiable in y, yielding the elementary first-order differential equation

$$\frac{d}{dy}\{1 - F(y)\} = -\frac{1}{\mu}\{1 - F(y)\},$$

whose solution, subject to $F(0) = 0$, is

$$1 - F(y) = e^{-\lambda y}, \qquad \lambda = 1/\mu,$$

The proof is complete. ■

Theorem 8.2. *Suppose, for some* $t_0 > 0$,

$$\Pr\{\delta_t \le x\} = F_t(x), \qquad 0 \le t < t_0,\ x \ge 0.$$

Then, for some $\lambda > 0$, $F(x) = 1 - e^{-\lambda x}$ *for* $0 \le x < t_0$.

Proof. For $0 \le x \le t$, we have

$$\begin{aligned}
\Pr\{\delta_t \le x\} &= \sum_{j=1}^\infty \Pr\{\delta_t \le x \quad \text{and} \quad N(t) = j\} \\
&= \sum_{j=1}^\infty \Pr\{t - x < S_j \le t \quad \text{and} \quad S_{j+1} > t\} \\
&= \sum_{j=1}^\infty \int_{t-x}^t [1 - F(t-y)]\, dF_j(y) \\
&= \int_{t-x}^t [1 - F(t-y)]\, dM(y).
\end{aligned}$$

Thus, by hypothesis, for $0 \le x \le t < t_0$,

$$F(x) = \int_{t-x}^t [1 - F(t-y)]\, dM(y), \tag{8.9}$$

and

$$\frac{1}{x} F(x) = \frac{1}{x} \int_{t-x}^t [1 - F(t-y)]\, dM(y). \tag{8.10}$$

The function $M(t)$ is finite, right continuous, and nondecreasing and thus possesses a finite derivative $M'(t)$ for infinitely many t dense in any $(0, t_0]$ interval. Choose such a $t = \tau$ for wich $M'(\tau) < \infty$. Then (8.10) has a limit as x decreases to zero at $t = \tau$, and

$$F'(0) = [1 - F(0)]M'(\tau) = M'(\tau).$$

But the left-hand side of (8.10) is independent of t. Thus the limit on the right must exist for all t, and

$$F'(0) = M'(t), \qquad \text{for all} \quad t < t_0 .$$

Let $\lambda = F'(0)$, so that $M(t) = \lambda t$. We substitute this into (8.9) to obtain

$$F(x) = \int_{t-x}^{t} [1 - F(t-y)]\lambda \, dy.$$

We may now differentiate in x to obtain

$$dF(x)/dx = -\lambda[1 - F(x)], \qquad 0 \leq x < t_0 ,$$

or $F(x) = 1 - e^{-\lambda x}$, $0 \leq x < t_0$, as claimed. ∎

9: *Superposition of Renewal Processes*

In this section we will establish, under certain conditions, that the superposition of indefinitely many uniformly sparse renewal processes tends to a Poisson process. The following Theorem 9.1 can serve to give a meaningful rationale for the Poisson assumption in a variety of circumstances, just as the central limit theorem provides justification for the widespread postulate of the normal distribution in representing certain random variables.

Several other results pertaining to the superposition of renewal processes are also highlighted, lending a glimpse into a currently popular area of research.

For each integer $n = 1, 2, \ldots$, and for each $i = 1, \ldots, k_n$, where $k_n \to \infty$ as $n \to \infty$, let $N_{ni}(t)$ be a renewal counting process with interoccurrence time distribution $F_{ni}(t)$. The collection $\{N_{ni}(t);\, n = 1, 2, \ldots, i = 1, \ldots, k_n\}$ constitutes a triangular array of stochastic processes. *For every n, we assume the processes $\{N_{n1}(t)\}, \ldots, \{N_{nk_n}(t)\}$ are independent.*

By the *superposition process* $N_n(t)$, we mean the aggregate counting process

$$N_n(t) = \sum_{i=1}^{k_n} N_{ni}(t), \qquad t \geq 0.$$

The superposition process is *not*, in general, a *renewal* counting process because the interoccurrence times are not independent and certainly not identically distributed. In fact, the distribution of the intervals between "events" is complicated and in general intractable.

Definition 9.1. The triangular array $\{N_{ni}(t)\}$ is called infinitesimal if for every $t \geq 0$

$$\lim_{n\to\infty} \max_{1\leq i\leq k_n} F_{ni}(t) = 0. \tag{9.1}$$

Prior to the main theorem we give a preliminary lemma.

Lemma 9.1. *Let $\{N_{ni}(t)\}$ be an infinitesimal array with interoccurrence distribution $\{F_{ni}(t)\}$. Let $F_{ni}^{*j}(t)$ denote the j-fold convolution of $F_{ni}(t)$. Suppose for some finite nondecreasing function $c(t)$ that*

$$\limsup_{n\to\infty} \sum_{i=1}^{k_n} F_{ni}(t) \leq c(t), \qquad \text{for all} \quad t. \tag{9.2}$$

Then

$$\text{(a)} \quad \lim_{n\to\infty} \sum_{i=1}^{k_n} \sum_{j=2}^{\infty} [F_{ni}(t)]^j = 0,$$

$$\text{(b)} \quad \lim_{n\to\infty} \sum_{i=1}^{k_n} \sum_{j=2}^{\infty} F_{ni}^{*j}(t) = 0,$$

and

$$\text{(c)} \quad \lim_{n\to\infty} \sum_{i=1}^{k_n} F_{ni}^{*j}(t) = 0, \qquad \text{uniformly in} \quad j = 2, 3, \ldots.$$

Proof. We prove only (a); (b) and (c) follow easily by virtue of the inequality $F_{ni}^{*j}(t) \leq [F_{ni}(t)]^j$ [cf. (4.2)]. Let

$$A_n(t) = \sum_{i=1}^{k_n} \sum_{j=2}^{k_n} [F_{ni}(t)]^j.$$

Let $\varepsilon > 0$ and $t > 0$ be given. Since $\{F_{ni}(t)\}$ are infinitesimal, there exists n_0 such that

$$F_{ni}(t) \leq \varepsilon, \qquad \text{for} \quad i = 1, \ldots, k_n,$$

whenever $n \geq n_0$. Then for $n \geq n_0$ and increasing along the limit superior in (9.2), we have

$$A_n(t) \leq \sum_{i=1}^{k_n} \sum_{j=2}^{\infty} \varepsilon^{j-1} F_{ni}(t)$$

$$=\frac{\varepsilon}{1-\varepsilon}\sum_{i=1}^{k_n}F_{ni}(t)$$

$$\leq 2\frac{\varepsilon c(t)}{1-\varepsilon}.$$

Since $\varepsilon > 0$ is arbitrary, we conclude

$$\limsup_{n\to\infty} A_n(t) = 0,$$

as was to be shown. ■

Theorem 9.1. *Let $\{N_{ni}(t)\}$ be an infinitesimal array of renewal processes with superposition $N_n(t)$. Then*

$$\lim_{n\to\infty} \Pr\{N_n(t) = j\} = \frac{e^{-\lambda t}(\lambda t)^j}{j!}, \qquad j = 0, 1, 2, \ldots, \tag{9.3}$$

if and only if

$$\lim_{n\to\infty}\sum_{i=1}^{k_n} F_{ni}(t) = \lambda t. \tag{9.4}$$

Proof. (1) *Necessity*. Suppose (9.3) is true. For $j = 0$ we obtain

$$\lim_{n\to\infty} \Pr\{N_n(t) = 0\} = e^{-\lambda t},$$

or, equivalently,

$$\lim_{n\to\infty} [-\log \Pr\{N_n(t) = 0\}] = \lambda t.$$

Recalling that $N_{n,1}(t), \ldots, N_{n,k_n}(t)$ are nonnegative independent random variables by assumption, it follows that

$$-\log \Pr\{N_n(t) = 0\} = -\log \prod_{i=1}^{k_n} \Pr\{N_{ni}(t) = 0\}$$

$$= -\sum_{i=1}^{k_n} \log[1 - F_{ni}(t)].$$

Expanding in the Taylor series

$$-\log[1 - F_{ni}(t)] = \sum_{j=1}^{\infty} \frac{1}{j}[F_{ni}(t)]^j$$

gives

$$\lambda t = \lim_{n\to\infty} [-\log \Pr\{N_n(t) = 0\}]$$

$$= \lim_{n\to\infty}\left\{\sum_{i=1}^{k_n} F_{ni}(t) + \sum_{i=1}^{k_n}\sum_{j=2}^{\infty}\frac{1}{j}[F_{ni}(t)]^j\right\}.$$

The second sum is nonnegative, so that

$$\limsup_{n\to\infty} \sum_{i=1}^{k_n} F_{ni}(t) \le \lambda t,$$

and we may appeal to Lemma 9.1 to conclude that the second sum vanishes in the limit. Thus

$$\lambda t = \lim_{n\to\infty} \sum_{i=1}^{k_n} F_{ni}(t),$$

which is (9.4) as was desired to be shown.

(2) *Sufficiency*. Suppose (9.4) holds. The proof will consist of an induction on m to show

$$\lim_{n\to\infty} \Pr\{N_n(t) = m\} = e^{-\lambda t} \frac{(\lambda t)^m}{m!}, \qquad m = 0, 1, \ldots.$$

Step 1: $m = 0$. Using the same Taylor series argument as above

$$\Pr\{N_n(t) = 0\} = \prod_{i=1}^{k_n} [1 - F_{ni}(t)]$$

$$= \exp\left[-\sum_{i=1}^{k_n} F_{ni}(t) - \sum_{i=1}^{k_n} \sum_{j=2}^{\infty} \frac{[F_{ni}(t)]^j}{j}\right].$$

By virtue of assumption (9.4) and Lemma 9.1, the limit of the exponent is $-\lambda t$. Thus the limit relation

$$\lim_{n\to\infty} \Pr\{N_n(t) = 0\} = \exp\{-\lambda t\},$$

is confirmed.

Step 2: The induction step. Let m be given and suppose we have shown

$$\lim_{n\to\infty} \Pr\{N_n(t) = m - 1\} = \frac{e^{-\lambda t}(\lambda t)^{m-1}}{(m-1)!}.$$

We need an extension. Let $s_1, \ldots, s_r$ be a finite set of indices. Then, since the array is infinitesimal, it is correct that

$$\lim_{n\to\infty} \prod_{\substack{j=1 \\ j \ne s_1, \ldots, s_r}}^{k_n} [1 - F_{nj}(t)] = e^{-\lambda t}, \tag{9.5}$$

and, for each fixed r, the limit is uniform over the indices $s_1, \ldots, s_r$. Now

$$\Pr\{N_n(t) = m\} = P_n(t) + Q_n(t),$$

where

$$P_n(t) = \Pr\{N_n(t) = m \text{ and } N_{ni}(t) \leq 1,\ i = 1, \ldots, k_n\},$$

and

$$Q_n(t) = \Pr\{N_n(t) = m \text{ and } N_{ni}(t) \geq 2, \text{ for some } i\}.$$

We claim $Q_n(t) \to 0$ as $n \to \infty$. In fact, for any $\varepsilon > 0$

$$\begin{aligned} Q_n(t) &\leq \sum_{i=1}^{k_n} \Pr\{N_{ni}(t) \geq 2\} \\ &\leq \sum_{i=1}^{k_n} [F_{ni}(t)]^2 \\ &\leq \varepsilon \sum_{i=1}^{k_n} F_{ni}(t), \end{aligned}$$

if n is sufficiently large so that $F_{ni}(t) \leq \varepsilon$. Thus, using the hypothesis we have

$$\limsup_{n \to \infty} Q_n(t) \leq \varepsilon \lambda t,$$

and since ε is arbitrary, we have shown $Q_n(t) \to 0$ as $n \to \infty$. It remains to evaluate the limit of $P_n(t)$. Let $I(m)$ be all possible combinations $(i_1, \ldots, i_m)$ with $1 \leq i_j \leq k_n$. Then

$$\begin{aligned} P_n(t) &= \Pr\{N_n(t) = m \text{ and } N_{ni}(t) \leq 1,\ i = 1, \ldots, k_n\} \\ &= \sum_{I(m)} \Pr\{N_{ni_1}(t) = 1, \ldots, N_{ni_m}(t) = 1 \\ &\qquad \text{and } N_{ni}(t) = 0, \text{ for } i \notin I(m)\} \\ &= \frac{1}{m} \sum_{i=1}^{k_n} \Pr\{N_{ni}(t) = 1,\ N_n(t) - N_{ni}(t) = m - 1, \\ &\qquad \text{and } N_{nj}(t) \leq 1,\ j = 1, \ldots, k_n\} \\ &= \frac{1}{m} \sum_{i=1}^{k_n} \{F_{ni}(t) - F_{ni}^{*2}(t)\} R_{ni}(t) \end{aligned}$$

(the independence assumption on $N_{ni}(t)$ comes into play here) where

$$R_{ni}(t) = \Pr\{N_n(t) - N_{ni}(t) = m - 1,\ N_{nj}(t) \leq 1,\ j = 1, \ldots, k_n,\ j \neq i\}.$$

But by the induction step and (9.5), $R_{ni}(t) \to e^{-\lambda t}(\lambda t)^{m-1}/(m-1)!$ uniformly in i as $n \to \infty$. Thus

$$
\begin{aligned}
\lim_{n\to\infty} P_n(t) &= \lim_{n\to\infty} \frac{1}{m} \sum_{i=1}^{k_n} \{F_{ni}(t) - F_{ni}^{*2}(t)\} R_{ni}(t) \\
&= \lim_{n\to\infty} \frac{1}{m} \sum_{i=1}^{k_n} F_{ni}(t) e^{-\lambda t}(\lambda t)^{m-1} -/(m\,1)! \\
&= e^{-\lambda t}(\lambda t)^m/m!
\end{aligned}
$$

as was to be shown. ∎

Example 1. Suppose $F(t)$ is a distribution function for which $F(0) = 0$ and $F'(0) = \lambda > 0$. Let

$$F_{ni}(t) = F(t/n), \qquad i = 1, \ldots, n,$$

and, for all n, let $N_{ni}(t)$, $i = 1, \ldots, n$, be independent renewal counting processes with interoccurrence distribution F_{ni}. Then $N_{ni}(t)$ is a triangular array. Furthermore, since

$$\lim_{n\to\infty} \max_{1\le i\le n} F_{ni}(t) = \lim_{n\to\infty} F(t/n) = 0,$$

the array is infinitesimal. To verify (9.4) we compute

$$
\begin{aligned}
\lim_{n\to\infty} \sum_{i=1}^{n} F_{ni}(t) &= \lim_{n\to\infty} nF(t/n) \\
&= t \lim_{n\to\infty} \frac{F(t/n)}{t/n} \\
&= \lambda t.
\end{aligned}
$$

Hence, the distribution of the superposition $N_n(t)$ converges to the Poisson process.

We end this section with two characterizations of the Poisson process involving composition of renewal processes. A sum of two independent Poisson processes persists as a Poisson process with the rate parameters merely adding. We will show that in essence only the Poisson process, among renewal processes, possesses this property.

Theorem 9.2. *Let $N_1(t)$ and $N_2(t)$ be two independent renewal processes with the same interoccurrence distribution F having mean μ. Let $N(t) = N_1(t) + N_2(t)$. If $N(t)$ is also a renewal process, then $N_1(t)$, $N_2(t)$, and $N(t)$ are all Poisson.*

Proof. Let H be the interoccurrence distribution for $N(t)$. Then

$$\begin{aligned}1 - H(x) &= \Pr\{N(x) = 0\}\\ &= \Pr\{N_1(x) = 0,\ N_2(x) = 0\}\\ &= [1 - F(x)]^2.\end{aligned}$$

Let $\gamma_1(t)$, $\gamma_2(t)$, and $\gamma(t)$ be the excess life at time t for the processes N_1, N_2, and N, respectively. Then, because the processes N_1 and N_2 are composed, we necessarily have

$$\gamma(t) = \min\{\gamma_1(t),\ \gamma_2(t)\},$$

and

$$\Pr\{\gamma(t) > x\} = [\Pr\{\gamma_1(t) > x\}]^2.$$

Letting $t \to \infty$ and using the asymptotic distribution of excess life given in (6.5), we obtain

$$\frac{1}{\nu}\int_x^\infty [1 - H(y)]\,dy = \frac{1}{\mu^2}\left\{\int_x^\infty [1 - F(y)]\,dy\right\}^2, \tag{9.6}$$

where $\nu = \int_0^\infty [1 - H(y)]\,dy$. Both sides are differentiable† with respect to x, and earlier we noted $1 - H(x) = [1 - F(x)]^2$. Differentiating (9.6) gives

$$\frac{1}{\nu}[1 - F(x)]^2 = \frac{1}{\nu}[1 - H(x)] = \frac{2}{\mu^2}\left\{\int_x^\infty [1 - F(y)]\,dy\right\}[1 - F(x)],$$

or

$$1 - F(x) = \frac{2\nu}{\mu^2}\int_x^\infty [1 - F(y)]\,dy.$$

Letting $G(x) = 1 - F(x)$ this becomes, after differentiation,

$$\frac{dG(x)}{dx} = -\frac{2\nu}{\mu^2}G(x),$$

whose solution subject to $G(0) = 1$ is

$$G(x) = 1 - F(x) = e^{-\lambda x},$$

where $\lambda = 2\nu/\mu^2$, as desired. Thus, both $N_1(t)$ and $N_2(t)$ are Poisson, and, of course, then so must be their sum $N(t)$. ■

Theorem 9.3. *Let $N_1(t)$ be a Poisson process with parameter μ. Let $N_2(t)$ be a renewal process having a finite mean interoccurrence time and suppose N_1*

† This is immediate if F is continuous. The general case requires further argument.

and N_2 are independent. If $N(t) = N_1(t) + N_2(t)$ defines a renewal process, then $N_2(t)$ must also be Poisson.

Proof. We use the same technique as in Theorem 9.2. Suppose N_1, N_2, and N have interoccurrence distributions $1 - e^{-t/\mu}$, $G(t)$, and $H(t)$, respectively. Then

$$1 - H(t) = \{1 - G(t)\}e^{-t/\mu}, \tag{9.7}$$

and

$$\frac{1}{\mu_H}\int_x^\infty [1 - H(y)]\,dy = \frac{e^{-x/\mu}}{\mu_G}\int_x^\infty [1 - G(y)]\,dy,$$

where μ_H and μ_G are the means of H and G, respectively.
Differentiation leads to

$$\frac{\mu_G}{\mu_H}[1 - H(x)] = e^{-x/\mu}[1 - G(x)] + \frac{1}{\mu}e^{-x/\mu}\int_x^\infty [1 - G(y)]\,dy,$$

which, with (9.7), gives

$$[1 - G(x)]\left[\frac{\mu_G}{\mu_H} - 1\right] = \frac{1}{\mu}\int_x^\infty [1 - G(y)]\,dy. \tag{9.8}$$

Let

$$\lambda = \mu\left[\frac{\mu_G}{\mu_H} - 1\right], \qquad \text{and} \qquad F(x) = 1 - G(x).$$

Then differentiation of (9.8) gives

$$-\lambda\, dF(x)/dx = F(x),$$

or

$$F(x) = e^{-x/\lambda}, \qquad x \geq 0,$$

and

$$G(x) = 1 - e^{-x/\lambda}, \qquad x \geq 0,$$

as was to be shown. ■

Elementary Problems

1. If $\Pr\{X_i = 1\} = \frac{1}{3}$, $\Pr\{X_i = 2\} = \frac{2}{3}$, compute

$$\Pr\{N(1) = k\}, \qquad \Pr\{N(2) = k\}, \qquad \Pr\{N(3) = k\}.$$

2. A patient arrives at a doctor's office. With probability 1/5 he receives service immediately, while with probability 4/5 his service is deferred an hour. After an hour's wait again with probability 1/5 his needs are serviced instantly or another delay of an hour is imposed and so on.

(a) What is the waiting time distribution of the first arrival?

(b) What is the distribution of the number of patients who receive service over an 8-hr period assuming the same procedure is followed for every arrival and the arrival pattern is that of a Poisson process with parameter 1.

3. The weather in a certain locale A consists of rainy spells alternating with spells when the sun shines. Suppose that the number of days of each rainy spell is Poisson distributed with parameter 2 and a sunny spell is distributed according to a geometric distribution with mean 7 days. Assume that the successive random durations of rainy and sunny spells are statistically independent variables. In the long run, what is the probability on a given day that it will be raining?

4. The random lifetime of an item has distribution function $F(x)$. What is the mean remaining life of an item of age x?

Solution:

$$e(x) = E[X - x | X > x] = \frac{\int_x^\infty \{1 - F(t)\}\, dt}{1 - F(x)}.$$

5. If $f(x)$ is a probability density function associated with a lifetime distribution function $F(x)$, the *hazard rate* is the function $r(x) = f(x)/[1 - F(x)]$. Show that the replacement age T^* that minimizes the long run mean cost per unit time

$$\theta(T) = \frac{c_1[1 - F(T)] + c_2 F(T)}{\int_0^T [1 - F(x)]\, dx}$$

must satisfy

$$r(T^*) \times \int_0^{T^*} [1 - F(x)]\, dx - F(T^*) = \frac{c_1}{c_2 - c_1}.$$

6. Cars arrive at a gate. Each car is of random length L having distribution function $F(\xi)$. The first car arrives and parks against the gate. Each succeeding car parks behind the previous one at a distance that is random according to a uniform distribution [0, 1]. Consider the number of cars N_x that are lined up within a total distance x of the gate. Determine

$$\lim_{x \to \infty} E[N_x]/x,$$

for $F(\xi)$ a degenerate distribution of length c, and also for the case $F(\xi) = 1 - e^{-\xi}$.

Solution: $2/(1 + 2c)$ and $2/3$.

7. At the beginning of each day customers arrive at a taxi stand at times of a renewal process with distribution law $F(x)$. Assume an unlimited supply of cabs, as at an airport. Suppose each customer pays a random fee at the station following the distribution law $G(x)$, $x > 0$.

(i) Write an expression for the sum of money collected by the station by time t of the day.

(ii) Determine the limit expectation

$$\lim_{t\to\infty} E[\text{the money collected over an initial interval of time } t]/t.$$

8. Consider a counter of Type II, where the locking time with each pulse arrival is of fixed length of τ units. Assume pulses arrive according to a Poisson process with parameter λ. Determine the probability, $p(t)$, that the counter is free at time t.

Solution:

$$p(t) = \begin{cases} e^{-\lambda t}, & t < \tau, \\ e^{-\lambda\tau}, & t \geq \tau. \end{cases}$$

Problems

1. Find $\Pr\{N(t) \geq k\}$ in a renewal process having lifetime density

$$f(x) = \begin{cases} \rho e^{-\rho(x-\delta)}, & \text{for } x > \delta, \\ 0, & \text{for } x \leq \delta, \end{cases}$$

where $\delta > 0$ is fixed.

2. Throughout its lifetime, itself a random variable having distribution function $F(x)$, an organism produces offspring according to a nonhomogenous Poisson process with intensity function $\lambda(u)$. Independently, each offspring follows the same probabilistic pattern, and thus a population evolves. Assuming

$$1 < \int_0^\infty \{1 - F(u)\}\lambda(u)\, du < \infty,$$

show that the mean population size $m(t)$ asymptotically grows exponentially at rate $r > 0$, where r uniquely solves

$$1 = \int_0^\infty e^{-ru}\{1 - F(u)\}\lambda(u)\, du.$$

Hint: Develop a renewal equation for $B(t)$, the mean number of individuals born up to time t, and from this infer that $B(t)$ grows exponentially at rate r. Then express $m(t)$ in terms of $B(u)$ for $u \leq t$.

3. Show that $\lim_{t \to \infty} V(t)/t = \sigma^2/\mu^3$, where $V(t)$ is the variance of a renewal process $N(t)$ and μ and $\sigma^2 < \infty$ are the mean and variance, respectively, of the interarrival distribution.

4. For a renewal process with distribution $F(x)$ compute

$$p(t) = \Pr\{\text{number of renewals in } (0, t] \text{ is odd}\}.$$

Obtain this explicitly for a Poisson process with parameter λ and also explicitly when $F(t) = \int_0^t xe^{-x}\, dx$.

5. Breaks and recombinations occur along the length of a pair of chromosomes according to a Poisson process with parameter λ. To illustrate suppose breaks occur at points t_1 and t_2

then the recombined chromosomes have the form

Determine the probability that a point B whose original distance from the location A is l will remain connected with A on the same chromosome after recombination.

6. Show that the renewal function corresponding to the lifetime density

$$f(x) = \lambda^2 xe^{-\lambda x}, \qquad x \geq 0,$$

is

$$M(t) = \tfrac{1}{2}\lambda t - \tfrac{1}{4}(1 - e^{-2\lambda t}).$$

7. Let c_1 be the planned replacement cost and c_2 the failure cost in a block replacement model. Using the long-run mean cost per unit time formula $[c_1 + c_2 M(T)]/T$, show that the cost minimizing block replacement time T^* satisfies

$$e^{-2\lambda T^*}(1 + 2\lambda T^*) = 1 - (4c_1/c_2),$$

where $c_2 > 4c_1$, and the lifetime density is that of Problem 6.

8. Let $X_1, X_2, \ldots,$ be i.i.d. uniformly distributed on (0, 1). Define $N_k =$ the index n satisfying $X_1^k + X_2^k + \cdots + X_n^k \leq 1 < X_1^k + \cdots + X_{n+1}^k$ (the kth powers). Determine

$$\lim_{k \to \infty} E(N_k)/k.$$

Hint: Establish and use the identity $E(S_{N_k+1}) = E(N_k + 1)E(X_1^k)$, where $S_r = X_1^k + \cdots + X_r^k$, $r = 1, 2, \ldots$.

9. Determine the distribution of the total life β_t of the Poisson process.

Answer: $\Pr\{\beta_t \le x\} = 1 - [1 + \lambda \min\{t, x\}]e^{-\lambda x}$,

10. Show that the age $\{\delta_t; t \ge 0\}$ in a renewal process, considered as a stochastic process, is a Markov process, and derive its transition distribution function

$$F(y; t, x) = \Pr\{\delta_{s+t} \le y | \delta_s = x\}.$$

11. Suppose $A(t)$ solves the renewal equation $A(t) = a(t) + \int_0^t A(t-y)\, dF(y)$, where $a(t)$ is a bounded nondecreasing function with $a(0) = 0$. Establish that $\lim_{t\to\infty} A(t)/t = a^*/\mu$, where $a^* = \lim_{t\to\infty} a(t)$ and $\mu < \infty$ is the mean of $F(x)$.

12. Consider a system that can be in one of two states: "on" or "off." At time zero it is "on." It then serves before breakdown for a random time T_{on} with distribution function $1 - e^{-t\lambda}$. It is then off before being repaired for a random time T_{off} with the same distribution function $1 - e^{-t\lambda}$. It then repeats a statistically independent and identically distributed similar cycle, and so on. Determine the mean of $W(t)$, the random variable measuring the total time the system is operating during the interval $(0, t)$.

13. Successive independent observations are taken from a distribution with density function

$$f(x) = \begin{cases} xe^{-x}, & x \ge 0, \\ 0, & x \le 0, \end{cases}$$

until the sum of the observations exceeds the number t. Let $N + 1$ be the number of observations required. Prove that

$$\Pr\{N = n\} = \frac{t^{2n+1}e^{-t}}{\Gamma(2n+2)} + \frac{t^{2n}e^{-t}}{\Gamma(2n+1)}.$$

14. A renewal process is an integer-valued stochastic process that registers the number of points in $(0, t]$, when the interarrival times of the points are independent, identically distributed random variables with common distribution function $F(x)$ for $x \ge 0$ and zero elsewhere, and F is continuous at $x = 0$. A modified renewal process is one where the common distribution function $F(x)$ of the interarrival times has a jump q at zero. Show that a modified renewal process is equivalent to an ordinary renewal process, where the numbers of points registered at each arrival are independent identically distributed random variables, $R_1, R_2, \ldots$, with distribution

$$\Pr\{R_i = n\} = pq^{n-1}, \qquad n = 1, 2, \ldots,$$

for all $i = 1, 2, \ldots$, where $p = 1 - q$.

15. Consider a renewal process with underlying distribution function $F(x)$. Let W be the time when the interval duration from the preceding renewal event first exceeds $\xi > 0$ (a fixed constant). Determine an integral equation satisfied by

$$V(t) = \Pr\{W \le t\}.$$

Calculate $E[W]$. (Assume an event occurs at time $t = 0$.)

16. Consider a renewal process $N(t)$ with associated distribution function $F(x)$. Define $m_k(t) = E[N(t)^k]$. Show that $m_k(t)$ satisfies the renewal equation

$$m_k(t) = z_k(t) + \int_0^t m_k(t-\tau)\, dF(\tau), \qquad k = 1, 2, \ldots,$$

where

$$z_k(t) = \int_0^t \sum_{j=0}^{k-1} \binom{k}{j} m_j(t-\tau)\, dF(\tau).$$

Hint: Use the renewal argument.

17. (Continuation of Problem 16). By induction show that

$$z_k(t) = (-1)^{k-1}[F(t) - \tbinom{k}{1} m_1(t) + \cdots + (-1)^k \tbinom{k}{k-1} m_{k-1}(t)].$$

18. Consider a stochastic process $X(t)$, $t \ge 0$, which alternates in 2 states A and B. Denote by $\xi_1, \eta_1, \xi_2, \eta_2, \ldots$, the successive sojourn times spent in states A and B, respectively, and suppose $X(0)$ is in A. Assume $\xi_1, \xi_2, \ldots$, are i.i.d.r.v.'s with distribution function $F(\xi)$ and $\eta_1, \eta_2, \ldots$, are i.i.d.r.v.'s with distribution function $G(\eta)$. Denote by $Z(t)$ and $W(t)$ the total sojourn time spent in states A and B during the time interval $(0, t)$. Clearly $Z(t)$ and $W(t)$ are random variables and $Z(t) + W(t) = t$. Let $N(t)$ be the renewal process generated by $\xi_1, \xi_2, \ldots$. Define

$$\theta(t) = \eta_1 + \eta_2 + \cdots + \eta_{N(t)}.$$

Prove

$$P\{W(t) \le x\} = P\{\theta(t-x) \le x\},$$

and express this in terms of the distributions F and G.

Answer:

$$\Pr\{W(t) \le x\} = \sum_{n=0}^{\infty} G_n(x)[F_n(t-x) - F_{n+1}(t-x)],$$

where G_n and F_n are the usual convolutions.

19. Consider a renewal process with distribution $F(x)$. Suppose each event is erased with probability $1-q$. Expand the time scale by a factor $1/q$. Show that the resulting sequence of events constitutes a renewal process where the distribution function of the time between events is

$$\sum_{n=1}^{\infty}(1-q)^{n-1}qF_n(x/q)=F(x;q),$$

where F_n as usual denotes the n-fold convolution of F.

20. (Continuation of Problem 19). In the preceding problem let $\phi(s)$ be the Laplace transform of $F(x)$. Determine the Laplace transform of $F(x;q)$.

Answer:

$$\phi(s;q)=\frac{q\phi(sq)}{1-(1-q)\phi(sq)}.$$

21. (Continuation of Problem 20). If F has two moments, prove that

$$\phi(s;q)\to\frac{\lambda}{\lambda+s}, \qquad \text{as} \quad q\to 0+, \quad \text{for all} \quad s, \quad \operatorname{Re} s\geq 0,$$

where $\lambda^{-1}=\int_0^\infty x\,dF(x)$.

22. (Continuation of Problem 21). Appealing to the convergence theorem, Chapter 1, p. 11, prove that

$$F(x;q)\to 1-e^{-\lambda x}, \qquad \text{as} \quad q\to 0+.$$

23. Consider a renewal process with interarrival distribution $G_0(x)$. Suppose each event is kept with probability q and deleted with probability $1-q$, and then the time scale is expanded by a factor $1/q$ (see Problem 19). Show that the mean interarrival time is the same for the original and the new process. Repeat the above operation of deletion and scale expansion to obtain a sequence of renewal processes with interarrival distribution given by $G_{(n)}(x)$ after n such transformations of the process. In all these operations q is held fixed. Show that if $0<q<1$, then

$$\lim_{n\to\infty}G_{(n)}(x)=1-e^{-x\mu},$$

where $\mu=\int_0^\infty\{1-G_{(0)}(\xi)\}\,d\xi$.

Answer: Set

$$\phi_0(s)=\int_0^\infty e^{-s\xi}\,dG_0(\xi), \qquad \phi_i(s)=\int_0^\infty e^{-s\xi}\,dG_{(i)}(\xi).$$

Establish by induction that

$$\phi_n(s)=\frac{q^n\phi_0(sq^n)}{1-(1-q^n)\phi_0(sq^n)}.$$

Now letting $n \to \infty$ leads to the same result as in Problems 20–22.

24. Consider a triangular array of identically distributed renewal processes $N_{ni}(t), 1 \le i \le n$, where the interarrival times have a distribution $F(t)$ with mean μ. Consider the nth row of the array. In each process of this row, retain an event with probability $1/n$ and discard the event with probability $1-(1/n)$. This operation is applied independently to all events. Denote the new array of renewal processes obtained by this deletion operation by $N_{ni}^*(t)$. Next form the superposition of composed processes,

$$N_n^*(t) = \sum_{j=1}^{n} N_{nj}^*(t), \qquad 1 \le n < \infty.$$

Show that

$$\lim_{n\to\infty} \Pr[N_n^*(t) = j] = \frac{e^{-t/\mu}}{j!}(t/\mu)^j,$$

if and only if $F(t) = 1 - e^{-t/\mu}$. In other words, the superpositions converge to a Poisson process if and only if all original renewal component processes were Poisson.

Answer: Verify first that the modified array $N_{nj}^*(t)$ is infinitesimal, i.e., show that

$$\lim_{n\to\infty}\left[\sup_{1\le j\le n} F_{nj}^*(t)\right] = 0,$$

where $F_{ni}^*(t)$ is the interarrival distribution for the transformed process $N_{ni}^*(t)$. Indeed, paraphrasing the argument of Problem 19 gives,

$$\begin{aligned} F_{ni}^*(t) &= \sum_{j=1}^{\infty}\left(1-\frac{1}{n}\right)^{j-1}\frac{1}{n}F_j(t) \\ &\le \frac{1}{n}\sum_{j=1}^{\infty}F_j(t) \le \frac{1}{n}\sum_{j=1}^{\infty}[F(t)]^j \\ &\le \frac{1}{n}\frac{F(t)}{1-F(t)}. \end{aligned}$$

Where $F(t) < 1$, then manifestly $\lim_{n\to\infty}[\sup_{1\le i\le n} F_{ni}^*(t)] = 0$, while if $F(t) = 1$, we can determine an appropriate j such that $F_j(t) < 1$, and a similar estimate can be made.

Next apply the superposition Theorem 9.1,

$$\begin{aligned} \lim_{n\to\infty}\sum_{i=1}^{n} F_{ni}^*(t) &= \lim_{n\to\infty}\sum_{j=1}^{\infty}\left(1-\frac{1}{n}\right)^{j-1} F_j(t) \\ &= \sum_{j=1}^{\infty} F_j(t) \\ &= M(t) \quad \text{the renewal function} \\ &= t/\mu, \end{aligned}$$

which is equivalent to $F(t) = 1 - e^{-t/\mu}$.

25. Given a renewal process with finite mean, suppose the excess life γ_t and current life δ_t are independent random variables for all t. Establish that the process is Poisson.

Hint: Use the limit theorem of Section 5 on the identity

$$\Pr\{\delta_t > x, \gamma_t > y\} = \Pr\{\delta_t > x\}\Pr\{\gamma_t > y\},$$

to derive a functional equation for

$$v(x) = \frac{1}{\mu}\int_x^\infty [1 - F(\xi)]\, d\xi,$$

and deduce thereby that $1 - F(\xi) = e^{-\xi/\mu}$.

26. (a) Assume orders for goods arrive at a central office according to a Poisson process with parameter λ. Suppose to fill each order takes a random length of time following a distribution $F(\xi)$. The number of workers available is infinite, so that all orders are handled without delay. Let $W(t)$ represent the number of orders requested but not yet filled by time t. Find

$$\lim_{t\to\infty} \Pr\{W(t) \le k\}.$$

(b) Let $V(t)$ be the length of time required to fulfill all current orders given that at time 0 there are no unfilled orders. Determine the probability distribution of $V(t)$, i.e., find

$$\Pr\{V(t) < y\} = F(y, t).$$

Hint: Write out a recursion relation for $F(y, t)$ by conditioning on the time of the arrival of the first order.

27. The Laplace transform $g^*(\theta)$, $\theta > \theta$, of a continuous function $g(x)$, $x \ge 0$, is defined by $g^*(\theta) = \int_0^\infty e^{-\theta x} g(x)\, dx$. Establish the formula

$$m^*(\theta) = \frac{f^*(\theta)}{1 - f^*(\theta)},$$

for a renewal process having lifetime density $f(x)$, where $m(t) = dM(t)/dt$ is the derivative of the renewal function. Compute $m^*(\theta)$ when

$$\text{(i)}\quad f(x) = \lambda e^{-\lambda x}, \qquad x \ge 0,$$
$$\text{(ii)}\quad f(x) = x e^{-x}, \qquad x \ge 0.$$

28. Show that the limiting distribution as $t \to \infty$ of age δ_t in a renewal process has mean $(\sigma^2 + \mu^2)/2\mu$, where σ^2 and μ are the variance and mean, respectively, of the interoccurrence distribution.

29. Let δ_t be the age or current life in a renewal process in which the mean and variance of the interoccurrence distribution are μ and σ^2, respectively. Prove

$$\lim_{t\to\infty} \frac{1}{t}\int_0^t \delta_\tau\, d\tau = (\sigma^2 + \mu^2)/2\mu.$$

30. Let $X_1, X_2, \ldots,$ be the interoccurrence times in a renewal process. Suppose $\Pr\{X_k = 1\} = p$ and $\Pr\{X_k = 2\} = q = 1 - p$. Verify that

$$E[N_n] = \frac{n}{1+q} - \frac{q^2}{(1+q)^2} + \frac{q^{n+2}}{(1+q)^2}, \qquad n = 2, 4, \ldots,$$

where N_n is the number of renewals up to (discrete time) n.

REFERENCE

1. W. Feller, "An Introduction to Probability Theory and Its Applications," Vol. II. Wiley, New York, 1966.

Chapter 6

MARTINGALES

Stochastic processes are characterized by the dependence relationships among their variables. The martingale property expresses a relation that occurs in numerous contexts and has become a basic tool in both theoretical and applied probability. It is used for calculating absorption probabilities, analyzing the path structure of continuous time processes, deriving inequalities for stochastic processes, analyzing sequential decision and control models, and for a multitude of other purposes.

Martingale theory requires extensive use of conditional expectations. We suggest the reader review the properties of conditional expectation listed in Chapter 1 before continuing.

1: Preliminary Definitions and Examples

We initiate the formulation of the martingale concept with undoubtedly its earliest version, which although dated bears historical interest.

Definition 1.1. A stochastic process $\{X_n;\ n=0, 1, \ldots\}$ is a martingale if, for $n=0, 1, \ldots,$

$$\text{(i)}\quad E[|X_n|]<\infty,$$

and

$$\text{(ii)}\quad E[X_{n+1}|X_0, \ldots, X_n]=X_n.$$

Let X_n be a player's fortune at stage n of a game. The martingale property captures one notion of a game being fair in that the player's fortune on the next play is, on the average, his current fortune and is not otherwise affected by the previous history. In fact, the name "martingale" derives from a French acronym for the gambling strategy of doubling ones bets until a win is secured. At the present time, martingale theory has such broad scope and diverse domains of applications in general probability theory and mathematical analysis that to think of it purely in terms of gambling would be unduly restrictive and misleading.

A more general and pertinent definition follows. (In Section 7 we will elaborate the most up-to-date formulation.) Unless stated explicitly to the contrary, all random variables encountered are assumed to be real valued.

Definition 1.2. Let $\{X_n; n=0, 1, \ldots\}$ and $\{Y_n; n=0, 1, \ldots\}$ be stochastic processes. We say $\{X_n\}$ is a martingale with respect to $\{Y_n\}$ if, for $n=0, 1, \ldots,$

$$\text{(i)} \quad E[|X_n|]<\infty, \tag{1.1}$$

and

$$\text{(ii)} \quad E[X_{n+1}|Y_0, \ldots, Y_n]=X_n. \tag{1.2}$$

It is useful to think of $(Y_0, \ldots, Y_n)$ as the information or history up to stage n. Thus, in the gambling context, this history could include more information than merely the sequence of past fortunes $(X_1, \ldots, X_n)$ as, for example, the outcomes on plays in which the player did not bet. Actually, there is no desire to restrict Y_k to being a real random variable. In general, it well may be a finite- or even infinite-dimensional vector. Whenever the particular sequence $\{Y_n\}$ is not vital or is evident from the context, we will suppress reference to it and say only "$\{X_n\}$ is a martingale".

The history determines X_n in the sense that X_n is a function of $Y_0, \ldots, Y_n$, i.e., knowledge of the values of $Y_0, Y_1, \ldots, Y_n$ determines the values of X_n. Note from (1.2) that X_n is the particular function

$$X_n=E[X_{n+1}|Y_0, \ldots, Y_n]$$

of $Y_0, \ldots, Y_n$. From the property of conditional expectation, viz.,

$$E[g(Y_0, \ldots, Y_n)|Y_0, \ldots, Y_n]=g(Y_0, \ldots, Y_n), \tag{1.3}$$

we infer that

$$E[X_n|Y_0, \ldots, Y_n]=X_n,$$

and invoking the law of total probability, now yields

$$\begin{aligned} E[X_{n+1}] &= E\{E[X_{n+1}|Y_0, \ldots, Y_n]\} \\ &= E[X_n], \end{aligned}$$

so that, by induction,

$$E[X_n]=E[X_0], \qquad \text{for all} \quad n.$$

SOME EXAMPLES

These examples were selected to demonstrate the immense variety and relevance of martingale processes. We start with some important concrete cases and later add more general constructions.

(a) *Sums of Independent Random Variables*

Let $Y_0 = 0$ and $Y_1, Y_2, \ldots$ be independent random variables with $E[|Y_n|] < \infty$ and $E[Y_n] = 0$ for all n. If $X_0 = 0$ and $X_n = Y_1 + \cdots + Y_n$ for $n \geq 1$, then $\{X_n\}$ is a martingale with respect to $\{Y_n\}$. We check (1.1) from

$$E[|X_n|] \leq E[|Y_1|] + \cdots + E[|Y_n|] < \infty,$$

and verify (1.2) from

$$\begin{aligned} E[X_{n+1}|Y_0, \ldots, Y_n] &= E[X_n + Y_{n+1}|Y_0, \ldots, Y_n] \\ &= E[X_n|Y_0, \ldots, Y_n] + E[Y_{n+1}|Y_0, \ldots, Y_n] \\ &= X_n + E[Y_{n+1}] \qquad \text{(because of the independence assumption on } \{Y_i\}) \\ &= X_n \qquad \text{(since } E[Y_m] = 0 \text{ by stipulation.)} \end{aligned}$$

(b) *More General Sums*

Suppose $Z_i = g_i(Y_0, \ldots, Y_i)$ for some arbitrary sequences of random variables Y_i and functions g_i. Let f be a function for which

$$E[|f(Z_k)|] < \infty, \qquad \text{for} \quad k = 0, 1, \ldots.$$

Let a_k be a bounded function of k real variables. Then

$$X_n = \sum_{k=0}^{n} \{f(Z_k) - E[f(Z_k)|Y_0, \ldots, Y_{k-1}]\} a_k(Y_0, \ldots, Y_{k-1})$$

defines a martingale with respect to $\{Y_n\}$. (By convention, $E[f(Z_k)|Y_0, \ldots, Y_{k-1}] = E[f(Z_k)]$ when $k = 0$.) Since a_k is bounded, say,

$$|a_k(y_0, \ldots, y_{k-1})| \leq A_k, \qquad \text{for all} \quad y_0, \ldots, y_{k-1},$$

we have

$$E[|X_n|] \leq 2 \sum_{k=0}^{n} A_k E[|f(Z_k)|] < \infty.$$

Let $B_k = \{f(Z_k) - E[f(Z_k)|Y_0, \ldots, Y_{k-1}]\} a_k(Y_0, \ldots, Y_{k-1})$. Then citing (1.3) we see that

$$E[B_k|Y_0, \ldots, Y_{k-1}] = 0.$$

Thus,

$$\begin{aligned} E[X_n|Y_0, \ldots, Y_{n-1}] &= E[X_{n-1}|Y_0, \ldots, Y_{n-1}] + E[B_n|Y_0, \ldots, Y_{n-1}] \\ &= X_{n-1}, \end{aligned}$$

which establishes the martingale property.

(c) *The Variance of a Sum as a Martingale*

Let $Y_0 = 0$ and $Y_1, Y_2, \ldots,$ be independent identically distributed random variables with $E[Y_k] = 0$ and $E[Y_k^2] = \sigma^2$, $k = 1, 2, \ldots.$ Let $X_0 = 0$ and

$$X_n = \left(\sum_{k=1}^{n} Y_k\right)^2 - n\sigma^2.$$

Then $E[|X_n|] \le 2n\sigma^2 < \infty$, and

$$\begin{aligned} E[X_{n+1}|Y_0, \ldots, Y_n] &= E\left[\left(Y_{n+1} + \sum_{k=1}^{n} Y_k\right)^2 - (n+1)\sigma^2 | Y_0, \ldots, Y_n\right] \\ &= E\left[Y_{n+1}^2 + 2Y_{n+1}\sum_{k=1}^{n} Y_k + \left(\sum_{k=1}^{n} Y_k\right)^2 \right. \\ &\qquad \left. - (n+1)\sigma^2 | Y_0, \ldots, Y_n\right] \\ &= X_n + E[Y_{n+1}^2 | Y_0, \ldots, Y_n] \\ &\qquad + 2E[Y_{n+1}|Y_0, \ldots, Y_n]\left(\sum_{k=1}^{n} Y_k\right) - \sigma^2 \\ &= X_n. \end{aligned}$$

Thus $\{X_n\}$ is a martingale with respect to $\{Y_n\}$.

(d) *Right Regular Sequences and Induced Martingales for Markov Chains*

There is a routine and highly productive way of discovering martingales in association with Markov processes. Let $Y_0, Y_1, \ldots,$ represent a Markov chain process governed by the transition probability matrix $P = \|P_{ij}\|$. Let f be a bounded right regular sequence for P, that is, $f(i)$ is nonnegative and satisfies

$$f(i) = \sum_{j} P_{ij} f(j). \tag{1.4}$$

(See also Chapter 11, Volume II.) Set $X_n = f(Y_n)$. Then $E[|X_n|] < \infty$ since f is bounded, and

$$\begin{aligned} E[X_{n+1}|Y_0, \ldots, Y_n] &= E[f(Y_{n+1})|Y_0, \ldots, Y_n] \\ &= E[f(Y_{n+1})|Y_n] \qquad \text{(by the Markov property)} \\ &= \sum_{j} P_{Y_n, j} f(j) \end{aligned}$$

$$\left(\text{since } E[f(Y_{n+1})|Y_n = i] = \sum_j P_{ij} f(j)\right)$$

$$\begin{aligned} &= f(Y_n) \qquad \text{[in accordance with (1.4)]} \\ &= X_n. \end{aligned}$$

Many martingales that at first glance seem unrelated actually arise in this manner, or in the generalization that is our next example.

(e) *Martingales Induced by Eigenvectors of the Transition Matrix*

Probably the most widespread method of forming martingales is covered by this example (see Elementary Problems 8, 15, 18, 19, 21, and 23). Let $Y_0, Y_1, \ldots$ be a Markov chain having transition probability matrix $P = \|P_{ij}\|$. A vector f is a right *eigenvector* of P if for some λ, called the *eigenvalue*,

$$\lambda f(i) = \sum_j P_{ij} f(j), \qquad \text{for all} \quad i.$$

If f is a right eigenvector of P for which $E[|f(Y_n)|] < \infty$ for all n, then

$$X_n = \lambda^{-n} f(Y_n)$$

is a martingale, since

$$\begin{aligned} E[X_{n+1} | Y_0, \ldots, Y_n] &= E[\lambda^{-n-1} f(Y_{n+1}) | Y_0, \ldots, Y_n] \\ &= \lambda^{-n}\lambda^{-1} E[f(Y_{n+1}) | Y_n] = \lambda^{-n}\lambda^{-1} \sum_j P_{Y_n, j} f(j) \\ &= \lambda^{-n} f(Y_n) = X_n. \end{aligned}$$

More generally, suppose $Y_0, Y_1, \ldots$ is a discrete-time Markov process governed by the transition distribution function

$$F(y|z) = \Pr\{Y_{n+1} \le y | Y_n = z\}. \tag{1.5}$$

If

$$E[|f(Y_n)|] < \infty, \qquad \text{for all} \quad n,$$

and

$$\lambda f(y) = \int f(z)\, dF(z|y), \qquad \text{for all} \quad y,$$

then $X_n = \lambda^{-n} f(Y_n)$ is a martingale.

The subsequent examples amply demonstrate the power and versatility of this technique for producing martingales.

(f) *A Branching Process*

Let $\{Y_n\}$ specify a branching process (Chapter 2, Section 2, Example F) and suppose that the mean of the progeny distribution is $m < \infty$. Then $X_n = m^{-n} Y_n$ is a martingale. In order to validate this claim we designate by $Z^{(n)}(j)$ the number of progeny produced by the jth existing parent in the nth generation. Then

$$Y_{n+1} = Z^{(n)}(1) + \cdots + Z^{(n)}(Y_n),$$

where $Z^{(n)}(i)$, $i = 1, 2, \ldots, Y_n$ are independent and identically distributed.

Manifestly

$$E[Y_{n+1}|Y_n] = Y_n E[Z^{(n)}(1)] = mY_n,$$

so that m is an eigenvalue for the function $f(y) = y$. It follows that $X_n = m^{-n} Y_n$ is a martingale as asserted.

(g) *Wald's Martingale*

Let $Y_0 = 0$ and suppose $Y_1, Y_2, \ldots$ are independent identically distributed random variables having a finite *moment generating function* $\phi(\lambda) = E[\exp\{\lambda Y_k\}]$ existing for some $\lambda \neq 0$. Then $X_0 = 1$ and $X_n = \phi(\lambda)^{-n} \exp\{\lambda(Y_1 + \cdots + Y_n)\}$ determines a martingale with respect to $\{Y_n\}$, because the function $f(y) = e^{\lambda y}$ is an eigenfunction for the Markov process of partial sums $S_n = Y_1 + \cdots + Y_n$, and the associated eigenvalue is $\phi(\lambda)$. Indeed, in line with (1.5), the transition distribution function in the case at hand is

$$P\{S_{n+1} \leq y | S_n = x\} = G(y - x),$$

where G is the common distribution function of Y_k.

Now we can calculate $E[f(S_{n+1})|S_n = x]$, executing an obvious change of variable, to obtain

$$\int e^{\lambda y}\, d_y G(y - x) = e^{\lambda x} \int e^{\lambda \xi}\, dG(\xi) = e^{\lambda x}\phi(\lambda),$$

and this identity clearly validates the claim made before.

As an illustration suppose $Y_1, Y_2 \ldots$ are independent and normally distributed with mean zero and variance σ^2. Then

$$\phi(\lambda) = E[\exp\{\lambda Y_1\}] = \exp\{\tfrac{1}{2}\lambda^2\sigma^2\}$$

and

$$X_n = \exp\left\{\lambda(Y_1 + \cdots + Y_n) - \frac{n}{2}\lambda^2\sigma^2\right\}.$$

For the choice $\lambda = \mu/\sigma^2$, where μ is an arbitrary constant, we get

$$X_n = \exp\left\{\frac{\mu}{\sigma^2}(Y_1 + \cdots + Y_n) - \frac{n\mu^2}{2\sigma^2}\right\}.$$

This martingale appears again in Example (j).

(h) *Generalization of the Eigenvector Argument*

Let $Y_0, Y_1, \ldots$ be arbitrary random variables but having finite absolute means $E[|Y_n|] < \infty$. Suppose, for $n = 0, 1, 2, \ldots$,

$$E[Y_{n+1}|Y_0, \ldots, Y_n] = a_n + b_n Y_n, \qquad b_n \neq 0. \tag{1.6}$$

Let $l_{n+1}(z)$ be the linear function $l_{n+1}(z) = a_n + b_n z$, whose inverse is $l_{n+1}^{-1}(y) = (y - a_n)/b_n$, and let $L_n(y) = l_1^{-1}(l_2^{-1}(\cdots(l_n^{-1}(y)\cdots)))$. Then $X_n = kL_n(Y_n)$ is a martingale, for any constant k, because

$$\begin{aligned}\frac{1}{k}E[X_{n+1}|Y_0, \ldots, Y_n] &= E[L_{n+1}(Y_{n+1})|Y_0, \ldots, Y_n] \\ &= L_{n+1}\{E[Y_{n+1}|Y_0, \ldots, Y_n]\} && \text{(since } L_{n+1} \text{ is a linear function of its argument)} \\ &= L_{n+1}(l_{n+1}(Y_n)), && \text{by (1.6)} \\ &= L_n(Y_n) = \frac{1}{k}X_n.\end{aligned}$$

To illustrate concretely, let Y_0 be uniformly distributed over [0, 1], and given Y_n, suppose Y_{n+1} is uniformly distributed on $[Y_n, 1]$. Then $X_n = 2^n[1 - Y_n]$ is a martingale. We check directly:

$$\begin{aligned}E[X_{n+1}|Y_0, \ldots, Y_n] &= 2^{n+1}[1 - E[Y_{n+1}|Y_n]] \\ &= 2^{n+1}[1 - \tfrac{1}{2}(1 + Y_n)] \\ &= 2^n(1 - Y_n) = X_n.\end{aligned}$$

(i) *An Urn Scheme*

Here is another example of the generalized eigenvector argument. The model has application in the study of growth processes.

Consider an urn that at stage 0 contains one red and one green ball. A ball is drawn at random from the urn and it and one more of the same color are then returned. The experiment is repeated indefinitely. Let X_n be the fraction of red balls at stage n, and let $Y_n = (n+2)X_n$ be the number of red balls. Then $\{X_n\}$ is a martingale with respect to $\{Y_n\}$. We have that, given $Y_n = k$,

$$Y_{n+1} = \begin{cases} k+1, & \text{with probability } k/(n+2), \\ k, & \text{with probability } 1 - k/(n+2). \end{cases}$$

Hence

$$E[Y_{n+1}|Y_n = k] = \frac{(k+1)k + k(n+2-k)}{n+2} = k(n+3)/(n+2).$$

That is,

$$E[Y_{n+1}|Y_n] = b_n Y_n,$$

where $b_n = (n+3)/(n+2)$. Then, using the notation of (h), $l_n(z) = b_{n-1}z$, $l_n^{-1}(y) = z/b_{n-1}$, and

$$L_n(y) = \frac{y}{b_0 b_1 \cdots b_{n-1}} = \frac{2}{3} \cdot \frac{3}{4} \cdots \frac{n+1}{n+2} y = \frac{2}{n+2} y.$$

Thus

$$X_n = \frac{1}{2} L_n(Y_n) = \frac{1}{n+2} Y_n$$

is a martingale.

(j) *Likelihood Ratios*

Let $Y_0, Y_1 \ldots$ be independent, identically distributed random variables, and let f_0 and f_1 be probability density functions. A stochastic process of fundamental importance in the theory of testing statistical hypotheses is the sequence of likelihood ratios

$$X_n = \frac{f_1(Y_0) f_1(Y_1) \cdots f_1(Y_n)}{f_0(Y_0) f_0(Y_1) \cdots f_0(Y_n)}, \qquad n = 0, 1, \ldots.$$

To assure the definition, assume $f_0(y) > 0$ for all y. Since $Y_0, Y_1, \ldots$ are independent,

$$E[X_{n+1} | Y_0, \ldots, Y_n] = E\left[X_n \frac{f_1(Y_{n+1})}{f_0(Y_{n+1})} \middle| Y_0, \ldots, Y_n\right] = X_n E\left[\frac{f_1(Y_{n+1})}{f_0(Y_{n+1})}\right].$$

When the common distribution of the Y_k's has f_0 as its probability density function, $\{X_n\}$ is a martingale with respect to $\{Y_n\}$. To confirm this claim, we need only verify

$$E\left[\frac{f_1(Y_{n+1})}{f_0(Y_{n+1})}\right] = 1.$$

But

$$E\left[\frac{f_1(Y_{n+1})}{f_0(Y_{n+1})}\right] = \int \left\{\frac{f_1(y)}{f_0(y)}\right\} f_0(y)\, dy = \int f_1(y)\, dy = 1,$$

as desired.

As an example, suppose f_0 is the normal density with mean zero and variance σ^2, and f_1 is normal with mean μ and variance σ^2. Then

$$\frac{f_1(y)}{f_0(y)} = \exp\left\{\frac{2\mu y - \mu^2}{2\sigma^2}\right\},$$

and

$$X_n = \exp\left\{\frac{\mu}{\sigma^2}(Y_1 + \cdots + Y_n) - \frac{n\mu^2}{2\sigma^2}\right\}.$$

This martingale occurred earlier in Example (g).

Martingales constructed from likelihood ratios have many uses in evaluating the properties of sequential procedures for hypothesis testing.

(k) *Doob's Martingale Process*

Let $Y_0, Y_1, \ldots$ be an arbitrary sequence of random variables and suppose X is a random variable satisfying $E[|X|] < \infty$. Then

$$X_n = E[X \mid Y_0, \ldots, Y_n]$$

forms a martingale with respect to $\{Y_n\}$, called *Doob's process*. First

$$\begin{aligned} E[|X_n|] &= E\{|E[X \mid Y_0, \ldots, Y_n]|\} \\ &\le E\{E[|X| \mid Y_0, \ldots, Y_n]\} \\ &= E[|X|] < \infty. \end{aligned}$$

Second and last, by the law of total probability for conditional expectations,†

$$\begin{aligned} E[X_{n+1} \mid Y_0, \ldots, Y_n] &= E\{E[X \mid Y_0, \ldots, Y_{n+1}] \mid Y_0, \ldots, Y_n\} \\ &= E[X \mid Y_0, \ldots, Y_n] = X_n. \end{aligned}$$

(l) *Radon–Nikodym Derivatives*

Suppose Z is a uniformly distributed random variable on $[0, 1)$, and define the random variables Y_n by setting

$$Y_n = k/2^n,$$

for the unique k (depending on n and Z) that satisfies

$$\frac{k}{2^n} \le Z < \frac{k+1}{2^n}.$$

† The law of total probability for conditional expectation extends the usual law by introducing further conditioning on a random variable Z. The law states $E[X \mid Z] = E\{E[X \mid Y, Z] \mid Z\}$, valid whenever $E[|X|] < \infty$. The student should supply a proof.

Notice how Y_n provides increasingly more information about Z as n increases. Indeed, $Y_n \le Z < Y_n + (\frac{1}{2})^n$ so that Y_n determines the first n bits in Z's terminating binary expansion.

Let f be a bounded function on [0, 1] and form the difference quotient

$$X_n = 2^n\{f(Y_n + 2^{-n}) - f(Y_n)\}.$$

We claim that $\{X_n\}$ is a martingale with respect to $\{Y_n\}$. First observe that Z, conditional on $Y_0, \ldots, Y_n$, has a uniform distribution on $[Y_n, Y_n + 2^{-n})$, and thus Y_{n+1} is equally likely to be Y_n or $Y_n + 2^{-(n+1)}$ Thus

$$\begin{aligned} E[X_{n+1}|Y_0, \ldots, Y_n] &= 2^{n+1}E[f(Y_{n+1} + 2^{-(n+1)}) - f(Y_{n+1})|Y_0, \ldots, Y_n] \\ &= 2^{n+1}\{\tfrac{1}{2}[f(Y_n + 2^{-(n+1)}) - f(Y_n)] \\ &\quad + \tfrac{1}{2}[f(Y_n + 2^{-n}) - f(Y_n + 2^{-(n+1)})]\} \\ &= 2^n\{f(Y_n + 2^{-n}) - f(Y_n)\} = X_n. \end{aligned}$$

Note that

$$X_n = \frac{f(Y_n + 2^{-n}) - f(Y_n)}{2^{-n}}$$

is approximately the derivative of f at Z. In fact, under quite general conditions it can be shown that the sequence $\{X_n\}$ of approximate derivatives converges with probability one to a random variable $X_\infty = X_\infty(Z)$, called the Radon–Nykodym derivative of f evaluated at Z, and that $X_n = E[X_\infty|Y_0, \ldots, Y_n]$ (see the close of Section 7). Thus martingale properties find alliance and relevance in the theory of differentiation of functions and indeed in numerous other facets of mathematical analysis.

PREVIEW OF RESULTS

The next section treats generalizations where the martingale equality is replaced by an inequality. Following that, we deal with the two major results of martingale theory, the *optional sampling theorem* and the *martingale convergence theorem*, including a diversity of applications of these theorems.

The optional sampling theorem tells us that, under quite general circumstances, whenever X_n is a martingale, then $X_{T_n} = Z_n$ also constitutes a martingale for a collection of randomly selected times $\{T_n\}$, which form an increasing sequence of "Markov times." A Markov time T has the property that the event $\{T = n\}$ is determined only by the history $(Y_0, \ldots, Y_n)$ up to stage n. The optional sampling (or stopping) theorem finds frequent application in sequential decision problems and in deriving inequalities and estimates of probabilities of various events associated with certain stochastic processes.

Martingale convergence theorems provide general conditions under which a martingale X_n will converge to a limit random variable X_∞ as n increases. These theorems are of value for analyzing the path structure of processes and in determining the asymptotic distribution of a variety of functionals of quite general stochastic processes.

2: *Supermartingales and Submartingales*

For many purposes it is desirable to have available a more general concept, built around an inequality.

Definition 2.1. Let $\{X_n, n = 0, 1, \ldots\}$ and $\{Y_n, n = 0, 1, \ldots\}$ be stochastic processes. Then $\{X_n\}$ is called a supermartingale with respect to $\{Y_n\}$ if, for all n,

$$\begin{aligned} &\text{(i)} \quad E[X_n^-] > -\infty, \quad \text{where} \quad x^- = \min\{x, 0\},\\ &\text{(ii)} \quad E[X_{n+1}|Y_0, \ldots, Y_n] \leq X_n,\\ &\text{(iii)} \quad X_n \quad \text{is a function of} \quad (Y_0, \ldots, Y_n). \end{aligned} \tag{2.1}$$

We call $\{X_n\}$ a submartingale with respect to $\{Y_n\}$ if, for all n,

$$\begin{aligned} &\text{(i)} \quad E[X_n^+] < \infty, \quad \text{where} \quad x^+ = \max\{0, x\},\\ &\text{(ii)} \quad E[X_{n+1}|Y_0, \ldots, Y_n] \geq X_n,\\ &\text{(iii)} \quad X_n \quad \text{is a function of} \quad (Y_0, \ldots, Y_n). \end{aligned} \tag{2.2}$$

As we did with martingales, we will omit mention of $\{Y_n\}$ when it is either not important or else evident from the context which particular sequence $\{Y_n\}$ is involved.

The third stipulation in each definition states that X_n must be determined by the history up to time n, or equivalently, the information available to time n includes the value of X_n. As noted earlier, the determination is automatically satisfied in the martingale case with the requisite expression of X_n as a function of $\{Y_i\}_{i=0}^n$ being

$$X_n = E[X_{n+1}|Y_0, \ldots, Y_n]. \tag{2.3}$$

In the super- and submartingale cases, the martingale equality is replaced by an inequality. Therefore the requirement that X_n be determined by $(Y_0, \ldots, Y_n)$ must be explicitly imposed. We will sometimes indicate this functional relation by writing

$$X_n = X_n(Y_0, \ldots, Y_n).$$

Note that $\{X_n\}$ is a supermartingale with respect to $\{Y_n\}$ if and only if $\{-X_n\}$ is a submartingale. Similarly, $\{X_n\}$ is a martingale with respect to $\{Y_n\}$ if and only if $\{X_n\}$ is both a submartingale and a supermartingale. By this means, statements about supermartingales can be transcribed into equivalent statements concerning both submartingales and martingales. This will save us substantial writing, since often a proof in only one of the three cases need be given.

Example. Let $\{Y_n\}$ be a Markov chain having the transition probability matrix $P = \|P_{ij}\|$. If f is a right superregular sequence for P (i.e., a nonnegative sequence satisfying $\sum_j P_{ij} f(j) \le f(i)$ for all i), then $X_n = f(Y_n)$ defines a supermartingale with respect to Y_n. The proof of this assertion paraphrases the analysis of Example (d), Section 1.

There is, of course, a parallel correspondence between submartingales and subregular sequences [nonnegative sequences $f(i)$ for which $f(i) \le \sum_j P_{ij} f(j)$], provided we assume $E[f(Y_n)] < \infty$.

Jensen's Inequality. A function ϕ defined on an interval I is said to be *convex* if for every $x_1, x_2 \in I$ and $0 < \alpha < 1$, we have

$$\alpha\phi(x_1) + (1-\alpha)\phi(x_2) \ge \phi(\alpha x_1 + (1-\alpha)x_2). \tag{2.4}$$

A straightforward induction commencing from (2.4) proves

$$\sum_{i=1}^{m} \alpha_i \phi(x_i) \ge \phi\left(\sum_{i=1}^{m} \alpha_i x_i\right), \tag{2.5}$$

valid for all $x_1, x_2, \ldots, x_m \in I$ and $\alpha_i \ge 0$, $\sum_{i=1}^{m} \alpha_i = 1$. If ϕ is twice differentiable, then ϕ is convex if and only if $d^2\phi/dx^2 \ge 0$ for all x. Thus, convexity is often easy to verify. If X is a random variable that takes the value x_i with probability α_i ($i = 1, 2, \ldots, m$), then Eq. (2.5) can be succinctly written in the form

$$E[\phi(X)] \ge \phi(E[X]). \tag{2.6}$$

Jensen's inequality states that (2.6) prevails for all real random variables X whenever ϕ is convex on $(-\infty, \infty)$. Inequality (2.6) can be viewed as a continuous integrated version of (2.5). The same is true for conditional expectations: Thus, if ϕ is convex, we have

$$E[\phi(X) | Y_0, \ldots, Y_n] \ge \phi(E[X | Y_0, \ldots, Y_n]). \tag{2.7}$$

With these facts in hand we provide some ways of constructing submartingales from martingales.

Lemma 2.1. *Let $\{X_n\}$ be a martingale with respect to $\{Y_n\}$. If ϕ is a convex function for which $E[\phi(X_n)^+] < \infty$ for all n, then $\{\phi(X_n)\}$ is a submartingale with respect to $\{Y_n\}$. In particular, $\{|X_n|\}$ is always a submartingale and $\{|X_n|^2\}$ is a submartingale whenever $E[X_n^2] < \infty$ for all n.*

Proof. We need only show the submartingale inequality, the other properties being rather easily demonstrated. Using Jensen's inequality, we have

$$\begin{aligned} E[\phi(X_{n+1})|Y_0, \ldots, Y_n] &\geq \phi(E[X_{n+1}|Y_0, \ldots, Y_n]) \\ &= \phi(X_n). \quad \blacksquare \end{aligned}$$

Here is a similar result whose proof is omitted.

Lemma 2.2. *Let $\{X_n\}$ be a submartingale with respect to $\{Y_n\}$. If ϕ is a convex and increasing function, then $\phi(X_n)$ is a submartingale, provided $E[\phi(X_n)^+] < \infty$.*

(Note that less is demanded of $\{X_n\}$, merely a submartingale, but more of ϕ in that ϕ is increasing besides convex.)

Thus, for example, if $\{X_n\}$ is a submartingale and

$$\tilde{X}_n = \begin{cases} X_n, & \text{if } X_n > -c, \\ -c, & \text{if } X_n \leq -c, \end{cases} \tag{2.8}$$

where c is fixed, then $\{\tilde{X}_n\}$ is a submartingale for which $E[|\tilde{X}_n|] < \infty$ for all n, and as a special case, $\{X_n^+\}$ is a submartingale whenever $\{X_n\}$ is.

ELEMENTARY PROPERTIES

We include both the supermartingale and the martingale results in a single statement, the hypothesis and conclusion for the supermartingale being enclosed in parentheses. (The corresponding results for submartingales are derived by passing from $\{X_n\}$ to $\{-X_n\}$.)

(a) If $\{X_n\}$ is a (super) martingale with respect to $\{Y_n\}$, then

$$E[X_{n+k}|Y_0, \ldots, Y_n](\leq) = X_n, \qquad \text{for every} \quad k \geq 0. \tag{2.9}$$

Proof. We proceed by induction. By definition, (2.9) is correct for $k = 1$. Suppose (2.9) holds for k. Then

$$\begin{aligned} E[X_{n+k+1}|Y_0, \ldots, Y_n] &= E\{E[X_{n+k+1}|Y_0, \ldots, Y_n, \ldots, Y_{n+k}]|Y_0, \ldots, Y_n\} \\ &(\leq) = E\{X_{n+k}|Y_0, \ldots, Y_n\} \\ &(\leq) = X_n. \end{aligned}$$

(b) If $\{X_n\}$ is a (super) martingale, then for $0 \leq k \leq n$

$$E[X_n](\leq) = E[X_k](\leq) = E[X_0]. \tag{2.10}$$

Proof. Using (2.9) we take expectations in

$$E[X_n | Y_0, \ldots, Y_k](\leq) = X_k,$$

to conclude

$$E[X_n] = E\{E[X_n | Y_0, \ldots, Y_k]\}(\leq) = E[X_k].$$

The case $E[X_k](\leq) = E[X_0]$ uses the same argument. ∎

(c) Suppose $\{X_n\}$ is a (super) martingale with respect to $\{Y_n\}$ and that g is a (nonnegative) function of $Y_0, \ldots, Y_n$ for which the expectations that follow exist. Then

$$E[g(Y_0, \ldots, Y_n)X_{n+k} | Y_0, \ldots, Y_n](\leq) = g(Y_0, \ldots, Y_n)X_n. \tag{2.11}$$

Proof. Since $g(Y_0, \ldots, Y_n)$ is determined by $(Y_0, \ldots, Y_n)$, using a basic property of conditional expectation we have

$$\begin{aligned} E[g(Y_0, \ldots, Y_n)X_{n+k} | Y_0, \ldots, Y_n] &= g(Y_0, \ldots, Y_n)E[X_{n+k} | Y_0, \ldots, Y_n] \\ &(\leq) = g(Y_0, \ldots, Y_n)X_n. \end{aligned}$$

(For the supermartingale case $(\leq)$ we need $g \geq 0$.) ∎

A SEQUENTIAL DECISION MODEL

Consider a system with a finite number S of states, labeled by the integers 1, 2, ..., S. Periodically, say once a day, we observe the current state of the system, and then choose an action from a set containing a finite number A of possible actions, labeled 1, 2, ..., A. As a joint result of the current state s and the chosen action a, two things happen: (i) we receive an immediate income $i(s, a)$; and (ii) the system moves to a new state, where the probability of a particular state s' being attained is determined by a known function $q = q(s' | s, a)$. Our problem is to ascertain the policy for choosing actions that maximize the total expected income over an N period horizon.

Let $S_0, A_0, S_1, \ldots, A_{N-2}, S_{N-1}, A_{N-1}$ describe the sequence of alternating states and acts. A policy π is a set of functions $\pi_0, \ldots, \pi_{N-1}$, where π_n prescribes the act A_n as a function of the observed history $S_0, A_0, \ldots, A_{n-1}, S_n$. That is, if policy π is used, then

$$A_n = \pi_n(S_0, A_0, \ldots, A_{n-1}, S_n).$$

The expected reward under policy π as a function of the initial state $S_0 = s$ is

$$I(\pi, s) = E\left[\sum_{k=0}^{N-1} i(S_k, A_k)\right]$$

We want to choose π so as to maximize $I(\pi, s)$.

Define the functions $f_0, \ldots, f_N$ recursively backwards according to

$$f_N(s) = 0, \qquad \text{for all} \quad s, \tag{2.12}$$

and, for $n = 1, 2, \ldots, N$,

$$f_{n-1}(s) = \max_a \left\{ i(s, a) + \sum_{s'} f_n(s') q(s' | s, a) \right\}. \tag{2.13}$$

Then

$$X_n = \sum_{k=1}^{n} \{ f_k(S_k) - E[f_k(S_k) | S_0, A_0, \ldots, S_{k-1}, A_{k-1}] \}$$

defines a martingale with respect to $\{Y_n\} = \{(S_n, A_n)\}$ by Example (b) of Section 1. Thus

$$E[X_n] = 0. \tag{2.14}$$

Now (2.13) implies

$$f_{n-1}(s) \geq i(s, a) + \sum_{s'} f_n(s') q(s' | s, a), \qquad \text{for all} \quad s \text{ and } a,$$

so that, in particular,

$$\begin{aligned} f_{k-1}(S_{k-1}) &\geq i(S_{k-1}, A_{k-1}) + \sum_{s'} f_k(s') q(s' | S_{k-1}, A_{k-1}) \\ &= i(S_{k-1}, A_{k-1}) + E[f_k(S_k) | S_0, A_0, \ldots, S_{k-1}, A_{k-1}], \end{aligned} \tag{2.15}$$

and this holds no matter what policy is used. We substitute into (2.14) to conclude

$$\begin{aligned} 0 = E[X_N] &= E\left[\sum_{k=1}^{N} \{ f_k(S_k) - E[f_k(S_k) | S_0, A_0, \ldots, S_{k-1}, A_{k-1}] \}\right] \\ &\geq E\left[\sum_{k=1}^{N} \{ f_k(S_k) + i(S_{k-1}, A_{k-1}) - f_{k-1}(S_{k-1}) \}\right] \\ &= E\left[\sum_{k=0}^{N-1} i(S_k, A_k) + f_N(S_N) - f_0(S_0)\right]. \end{aligned}$$

That is,

$$E[f_0(S_0)] \geq E\left[\sum_{k=0}^{N-1} i(S_k, A_k)\right].$$

If $S_0 = s$, then this says, for any policy π,

$$f_0(s) \geq I(\pi, s).$$

In words, no policy can achieve an expected reward that exceeds $f_0(s)$. Thus, if we exhibit a policy π^* satisfying

$$f_0(s) = I(\pi^*, s),$$

then this policy is manifestly optimal. For each s, let

$$\pi_{n-1}^*(S_0, A_0, \ldots, A_{n-2}, s)$$

be the action that maximizes the right-hand side of (2.13). That is, if $A_{k-1}^* = \pi_{k-1}^*(S_0, A_0^*, \ldots, S_{k-1})$, then (2.15) reduces to the equality

$$f_{k-1}(S_{k-1}) = i(S_{k-1}, A_{k-1}^*) + E[f_k(S_k)|S_0, A_0^*, \ldots, S_{k-1}, A_{k-1}^*].$$

Continuing the same argument as before, we further obtain the equality

$$E[f_0(S_0)] = E\left[\sum_{k=0}^{N-1} i(S_k, A_k^*)\right]$$

or

$$f_0(s) = I(\pi^*, s).$$

Thus π^*, the policy that in state $S_{n-1} = s$ at stage $n - 1$ selects the action that maximizes the right-hand side of (2.13), is optimal.

3: *The Optional Sampling Theorem*

Consider a fair game in which on each play a dollar is won or lost with equal probability. We let $Y_1, Y_2, \ldots$ be independent identically distributed random variables with $\Pr\{Y_k = +1\} = \Pr\{Y_k = -1\} = \frac{1}{2}$. Let $X_n = Y_1 + \cdots + Y_n$ be the player's net gain at stage n. We know $E[X_n] = 0$, the mean net gain is zero. But the player need not play forever, nor need he predetermine a particular time n for stopping. Rather, he might let the choice of when to stop be determined depending on how the game evolves. For example he might try to stop when ahead.

Let T be the time the player ends his play and let X_T be his net gain then. We know $E[X_n] = 0$ for all n, but is it necessarily true that $E[X_T] = 0$? Can the player stop when ahead? The answer is "yes," but there are a number of qualifications.

First, we must outlaw clairvoyance and require that the choice of when to stop depends only on the information observed to date. That is, we require that the event that the player stops on the nth turn depends only on $Y_0, \ldots, Y_n$. A random variable T that satisfies this requirement for every n is called a *Markov time*, or sometimes a *stopping time* or *random variable independent of the future* (with respect to $\{Y_n\}$). We will give a crisper definition shortly.

Even with this restriction, we can achieve $E[X_T] > 0$! For example, $T = \min\{n : X_n = 1\}$ is a Markov time, since $\{T = n\}$ if and only if $Y_1 + \cdots + Y_k < 1$ for $k < n$, and $Y_1 + \cdots + Y_n = 1$. Since the random walk is recurrent, $T < \infty$, and $X_T \equiv 1$, so that $E[X_T] = 1 > 0$.

It is the purpose of this section to examine this matter more closely and in more generality. We will show that the Markov time T defined above has a number of adverse properties and, in a very real sense, is not physically realizable. For example, the mean of T is infinite, and indefinitely large losses occur, on the average, before stopping, so that a player would need an infinite fortune to adopt this strategy successfully.

On the other hand, under quite general conditions $E[X_T] = E[X_0]$ for a martingale, whenever T is a Markov time with finite expectation, and this conclusion has applications far beyond the gambling setup.

MARKOV TIMES

Markov times occur in many contexts. Here is an example of their use in Markov chains. Suppose i is a recurrent state in a Markov chain $\{Y_n\}$. We want to show

$$\Pr\{Y_n \text{ returns to } i \text{ at least twice}\} = 1.$$

Since i is recurrent we know

$$\Pr\{Y_n \text{ returns to } i \text{ at least once}\} = \Pr\{T_i < \infty\} = 1,$$

where $T_i = \min\{n \geq 1 : Y_n = i\}$ is the time of first return to i. We have, using the Markov property,

$$\begin{aligned}\Pr\{\text{return to } i \text{ at least twice}\} &= \Pr\{T_i < \infty\}\Pr\{\text{return after } T_i | T_i < \infty\}\\ &= \Pr\{T_i < \infty\}\Pr\{T_i < \infty | Y_0 = i\}\\ &= 1 \times 1 = 1.\end{aligned}$$

There is something that needs more discussion here. Why is the probability of returning to i after time T_i the same as the probability of ever returning to i? Here is a more detailed proof that shows where the Markov property is used and what attributes of the random time T_i make this possible. We note

$$
\begin{aligned}
&\Pr\{\text{return after } T_i \mid T_i = k\}\\
&\quad = \Pr\{Y_{k+n} = i, \text{ for some } n = 1, 2, \ldots \mid Y_j \neq i, j = 1, \ldots, k-1; Y_k = i\}\\
&\quad = \Pr\{Y_{k+n} = i, \text{ for some } n = 1, 2, \ldots \mid Y_k = i\}\\
&\qquad \text{(By the Markov property)}\\
&\quad = \Pr\{Y_n = i, \text{ for some } n = 1, 2, \ldots \mid Y_0 = i\}\\
&\qquad \text{(Using the fact of stationary transition probabilities)}\\
&\quad = \Pr\{T_i < \infty \mid Y_0 = i\} = 1.
\end{aligned}
$$

Thus

$$
\begin{aligned}
&\Pr\{T_i < \infty \text{ and return after } T_i\}\\
&\quad = \sum_{k=1}^{\infty} \Pr\{\text{return after } T_i \mid T_i = k\} \Pr\{T_i = k\}\\
&\quad = \sum_{k=1}^{\infty} 1 \times \Pr\{T_i = k\} = 1.
\end{aligned}
$$

The key is that the event $\{T_i = k\}$ is the same as the event $\{Y_j \neq i$, for $j = 1, \ldots, k-1;\ Y_k = i\}$ and, in particular, depends only on $(Y_0, \ldots, Y_k)$.

Definition 3.1. *A random variable T is called a Markov time with respect to $\{Y_n\}$ if T takes values in $\{0, 1, \ldots, \infty\}$ and if, for every $n = 0, 1, \ldots,$ the event $\{T = n\}$ is determined by $(Y_0, \ldots, Y_n)$. By "determined" we mean the indicator function of the event $\{T = n\}$ can be written as a function of* $Y_0, \ldots, Y_n$, i.e., we can decide whether $T = n$ or $T \neq n$ from knowledge of the values of the process $Y_0, Y_1, \ldots, Y_n$ only up to time n. *We signify this by writing*

$$
\begin{aligned}
I_{\{T=n\}} &= I_{\{T=n\}}(Y_0, \ldots, Y_n)\\
&= \begin{cases} 1, & \text{if } T = n,\\ 0, & \text{if } T \neq n. \end{cases}
\end{aligned}
$$

We often omit mention of $\{Y_n\}$ and say only "T is a Markov time." If T is a Markov time, then for every n the events $\{T \le n\}$, $\{T > n\}$, $\{T \ge n\}$, and $\{T < n\}$ are also determined by $(Y_0, \ldots, Y_n)$. In fact, we have

$$
I_{\{T \le n\}} = \sum_{k=0}^{n} I_{\{T=k\}}(Y_0, \ldots, Y_k),
$$

$$
I_{\{T > n\}} = 1 - I_{\{T \le n\}}(Y_0, \ldots, Y_n),
$$

and so on.

Conversely, if for every n, the event $\{T \le n\}$ is determined by $\{Y_0, \ldots, Y_n\}$, then T is a Markov time. Or, if for every n, the event $\{T > n\}$ is determined by $(Y_0, \ldots, Y_n)$, then T is a Markov time. (But see Problem 20.)

If $\{X_n\}$ is a martingale with respect to $\{Y_n\}$, then for every n, X_n is determined by $(Y_0, \ldots, Y_n)$. It follows that every Markov time with respect to $\{X_n\}$ is also a Markov time with respect to $\{Y_n\}$. The same statement holds for supermartingales and submartingales, of course.

Some Examples of Markov Times

(a) The fixed (that is, constant) time $T \equiv k$ is a Markov time. For all $Y_0, Y_1, \ldots$, we have

$$I_{\{T=n\}}(Y_0, \ldots, Y_n) = \begin{cases} 0, & \text{if } n \neq k, \\ 1, & \text{if } n = k. \end{cases}$$

(b) The first time the process $Y_0, Y_1, \ldots$ reaches a subset A of the state space is a Markov time. That is, for

$$T(A) = \min\{n : Y_n \in A\},$$

we have

$$I_{\{T(A)=n\}}\{Y_0, \ldots, Y_n\} = \begin{cases} 1, & \text{if } Y_j \notin A, \quad \text{for } j = 0, \ldots, n-1, \quad Y_n \in A, \\ 0, & \text{otherwise.} \end{cases}$$

(c) More generally, for any fixed k, the kth time the process visits a set A is a Markov time. However, the *last* time a process visits a set is *not* a Markov time. To determine whether or not a particular visit is the last, the entire future must be known.

ELEMENTARY PROPERTIES

(a) If S and T are Markov times, then so is $S + T$. We have

$$I_{\{S+T=n\}} = \sum_{k=0}^{n} I_{\{S=k\}} I_{\{T=n-k\}}.$$

(b) The smaller of two Markov times S, T, denoted

$$S \wedge T = \min\{S, T\},$$

is also a Markov time. This is clear because of the relation

$$I_{\{S \wedge T > n\}} = I_{\{S>n\}} I_{\{T>n\}}.$$

Thus, if T is a Markov time, then so is $T \wedge n = \min\{n, T\}$, for any fixed $n = 0, 1, \ldots$.

(c) If S and T are Markov times, then so is the larger $S \vee T = \max\{S, T\}$, since

$$I_{\{S \vee T \le n\}} = I_{\{S \le n\}} I_{\{T \le n\}}.$$

OPTIONAL SAMPLING THEOREM*

Suppose $\{X_n\}$ is a martingale and T is a Markov time with respect to $\{Y_n\}$. We will establish later

$$E[X_0] = E[X_{T\wedge n}] = \lim_{n\to\infty} E[X_{T\wedge n}].$$

If $T < \infty$, then $\lim_{n\to\infty} X_{T\wedge n} = X_T$; actually $X_{T\wedge n} = X_T$ whenever $n > T$. *Thus, whenever we can justify the interchange of limit $n \to \infty$ and expectation*, we can deduce the important identity

$$E[X_0] = \lim_{n\to\infty} E[X_{T\wedge n}] \overset{?}{=} E[\lim_{n\to\infty} X_{T\wedge n}] = E[X_T]. \tag{3.1}$$

We will later offer several conditions where, indeed, this interchange is legitimate.

Lemma 3.1. *Let $\{X_n\}$ be a (super) martingale and T a Markov time with respect to $\{Y_n\}$. Then for all $n \geq k$,*

$$E[X_n I_{\{T=k\}}](\leq) = E[X_k I_{\{T=k\}}]. \tag{3.2}$$

Proof. By the law of total probability and (2.9),

$$\begin{aligned} E[X_n I_{\{T=k\}}] &= E\{E[X_n I_{\{T=k\}}(Y_0, \ldots, Y_k)| Y_0, \ldots, Y_k]\} \\ &= E\{I_{\{T=k\}} E[X_n | Y_0, \ldots, Y_k]\} \\ (\leq) &= E\{I_{\{T=k\}} X_k\}. \quad \blacksquare \end{aligned}$$

Lemma 3.2. *If $\{X_n\}$ is a (super) martingale and T a Markov time, then for all $n = 1, 2, \ldots$*

$$E[X_0](\geq) = E[X_{T\wedge n}](\geq) = E[X_n]. \tag{3.3}$$

Proof. Using Lemma 3.1,

$$\begin{aligned} E[X_{T\wedge n}] &= \sum_{k=0}^{n-1} E[X_T I_{\{T=k\}}] + E[X_n I_{\{T\geq n\}}] \\ &= \sum_{k=0}^{n-1} E[X_k I_{\{T=k\}}] + E[X_n I_{\{T\geq n\}}] \qquad [X_T = X_k \text{ when } T = k] \\ (\geq) &= \sum_{k=0}^{n-1} E[X_n I_{\{T=k\}}] + E[X_n I_{\{T\geq n\}}] \qquad [\text{on the basis of } (3.2)] \\ &= E[X_n]. \end{aligned}$$

* Referred to also as the *optional stopping theorem.*

For a martingale, $E[X_n]=E[X_0]$, which completes the proof in this case. For a supermartingale, we have shown $E[X_{T\wedge n}]\ge E[X_n]$ and have yet to establish $E[X_0]\ge E[X_{T\wedge n}]$. We will do this assuming $E[|X_n|]<\infty$, for all n. The general case may be obtained by truncation, along the lines suggested in the remark following Lemma 2.2.

The sequence defined by

$$\tilde{X}_n=\sum_{k=1}^{n}\{X_k-E[X_k|Y_0,\ldots,Y_{k-1}]\}$$

is a martingale ($\tilde{X}_0=0$) [cf. Example (b) of Section 1]. Thus,

$$\begin{aligned}0&=E[\tilde{X}_{T\wedge n}]\\&=E\left[\sum_{k=1}^{T\wedge n}\{X_k-E[X_k|Y_0,\ldots,Y_{k-1}]\}\right]\\&\ge E\left[\sum_{k=1}^{T\wedge n}\{X_k-X_{k-1}\}\right]=E[X_{T\wedge n}]-E[X_0],\end{aligned}$$

and consequently

$$E[X_0]\ge E[X_{T\wedge n}],$$

which completes the proof. ■

We return to the matter of justifying an interchange of limit and expectation as $n\to\infty$ in (3.1). The most general conditions that guarantee this operation are that the random variables $\{X_{T\wedge n}\}$ be *uniformly integrable* in the sense that

$$\lim_{a\to\infty}\sup_{n\ge 0}E[|X^a_{T\wedge n}|]=0,$$

where

$$X^a_{T\wedge n}=\begin{cases}0, & \text{if } |X_{T\wedge n}|<a,\\ X_{T\wedge n}, & \text{if } |X_{T\wedge n}|\ge a,\end{cases}$$

and that $T<\infty$. We skip to conditions not quite so general, but still covering a number of cases of importance.

Lemma 3.3. *Let W be an arbitrary random variable satisfying $E[|W|]<\infty$, and let T be a Markov time for which $\Pr\{T<\infty\}=1$. Then*

$$\lim_{n\to\infty}E[WI_{\{T>n\}}]=0, \tag{3.4}$$

and

$$\lim_{n\to\infty}E[WI_{\{T\le n\}}]=E[W]. \tag{3.5}$$

Proof. We reduce the problem to one involving elementary convergence properties of series having nonnegative terms. First,

$$
\begin{aligned}
E[|W|] &\geq E[|W|I_{\{T\leq n\}}] \\
&= \sum_{k=0}^{n} E[|W| \big| T=k] \Pr\{T=k\} \qquad \text{(law of total probabilities)} \\
&\xrightarrow[n\to\infty]{} \sum_{k=0}^{\infty} E[|W| \big| T=k] \Pr\{T=k\} \\
&= E[|W|].
\end{aligned}
$$

Hence

$$\lim_{n\to\infty} E[|W|I_{\{T\leq n\}}] = E[|W|],$$

and

$$\lim_{n\to\infty} E[|W|I_{\{T>n\}}] = 0.$$

Next, observe

$$
\begin{aligned}
0 &\leq |E[W] - E[WI_{\{T\leq n\}}]| \\
&= |E[WI_{\{T>n\}}]| \\
&\leq E[|W|I_{\{T>n\}}] \to 0,
\end{aligned}
$$

which completes the proof. ■

The following theorem, the optional sampling theorem for dominated martingales, is a direct consequence.

Theorem 3.1. *Suppose $\{X_n\}$ is a martingale and T is a Markov time. If $\Pr\{T<\infty\}=1$ and $E[\sup_{n\geq 0}|X_{T\wedge n}|]<\infty$, then*

$$E[X_T] = E[X_0].$$

Proof. Set $W=\sup_{n\geq 0}|X_{T\wedge n}|$. Starting with the decomposition

$$X_T = \sum_{k=0}^{\infty} X_k\, I_{\{T=k\}} = \sum_{k=0}^{\infty} X_{T\wedge k} I_{\{T=k\}},$$

valid by virtue of the assumption $\Pr\{T<\infty\}=1$, we find that $|X_T|\leq W$, and therefore $E[|X_T|]\leq E[W]<\infty$, so that the expectation of X_T is defined. We need only show $\lim_{n\to\infty} E[X_{T\wedge n}] = E[X_T]$. We have

$$
\begin{aligned}
|E[X_{T\wedge n}] - E[X_T]| &\leq E[|(X_{T\wedge n} - X_T)|I_{\{T>n\}}] \\
&\leq 2E[WI_{\{T>n\}}].
\end{aligned}
$$

But $\lim_{n\to\infty} E[WI_{\{T>n\}}]=0$ by Lemma 3.3. With reference to (3.3) the proof is complete. ■

Corollary 3.1. *Suppose $\{X_n\}$ is a martingale and T is a Markov time with respect to $\{Y_n\}$. If*

(i) $$E[T]<\infty,$$

and there exists a constant $K<\infty$, for which

(ii) $$E[|X_{n+1}-X_n| \,|\, Y_0, \ldots, Y_n] \le K, \qquad \text{for} \quad n<T,$$

then $E[X_T]=E[X_0]$.

Proof. Define $Z_0=|X_0|$ and $Z_n=|X_n-X_{n-1}|$, $n=1, 2, \ldots$, and set

$$W=Z_0+\cdots+Z_T.$$

Then $W\ge|X_T|$, and

$$\begin{aligned} E[W] &= \sum_{n=0}^{\infty}\sum_{k=0}^{n} E[Z_k I_{\{T=n\}}] \\ &= \sum_{k=0}^{\infty}\sum_{n=k}^{\infty} E[Z_k I_{\{T=n\}}] \\ &= \sum_{k=0}^{\infty} E[Z_k I_{\{T\ge k\}}]. \end{aligned}$$

Observe that $I_{\{T\ge k\}}=1-I_{\{T\le k-1\}}$ is a function only of $\{Y_0, \ldots, Y_{k-1}\}$, and from (ii) the inequalities $E[Z_k|Y_0, \ldots, Y_{k-1}]\le K$ hold if $k\le T$. Hence

$$\begin{aligned} \sum_{k=0}^{\infty} E[Z_k I_{\{T\ge k\}}] &= \sum_{k=0}^{\infty} E\{E[Z_k I_{\{T\ge k\}}|Y_0, \ldots, Y_{k-1}]\} \\ &= \sum_{k=0}^{\infty} E\{I_{\{T\ge k\}} E[Z_k|Y_0, \ldots, Y_{k-1}]\} \\ &\le K\sum_{k=0}^{\infty} \Pr\{T\ge k\} \\ &\le K(1+E[T])<\infty. \end{aligned}$$

Thus $E[W]<\infty$. Since $|X_{T\wedge n}|\le W$ for all n by the definition of W, the result follows from Theorem 3.1. ■

Theroem 3.2. *(Optional Stopping Theorem). Let $\{X_n\}$ be a martingale and T a Markov time. If*

$$\text{(i)} \qquad \Pr\{T < \infty\} = 1,$$

$$\text{(ii)} \qquad E[|X_T|] < \infty,$$

$$\text{(iii)} \qquad \lim_{n \to \infty} E[X_n I_{\{T > n\}}] = 0,$$

then $E[X_T] = E[X_0]$.

Proof. We emphasize that (ii) must be assumed and is *not* a consequence of $E[|X_n|] < \infty$ for all n.

We write, for all n,

$$\begin{aligned} E[X_T] &= E[X_T I_{\{T \le n\}}] + E[X_T I_{\{T > n\}}] \\ &= E[X_{T \wedge n}] - E[X_n I_{\{T > n\}}] + E[X_T I_{\{T > n\}}]. \end{aligned}$$

Now $E[X_{T \wedge n}] = E[X_0]$ by Lemma 3.1, and $\lim_{n \to \infty} E[X_n I_{\{T > n\}}] = 0$ by assumption (iii). Lastly, we use Lemma 3.3 with $W = X_T$ and assumption (ii) to infer $\lim_{n \to \infty} E[X_T I_{\{T > n\}}] = 0$. Thus

$$E[X_T] = \lim_{n \to \infty} E[X_{T \wedge n}] = E[X_0],$$

as was to be shown. ∎

Here are some sample consequences of this fundamental theorem.

Corollary 3.2. *Suppose $\{X_n\}$ is a martingale and T is a Markov time. If*

$$\text{(i)} \quad \Pr\{T < \infty\} = 1,$$

and for some $K < \infty$,

$$\text{(ii)} \quad E[X_{T \wedge n}^2] \le K, \quad \textit{for all } n,$$

then $E[X_T] = E[X_0]$.

Proof. Since $X_{T \wedge n}^2 \ge 0$, condition (ii) implies

$$\begin{aligned} K &\ge E[X_{T \wedge n}^2 I_{\{T \le n\}}] \\ &= \sum_{k=0}^{n} E[X_T^2 | T = k] \Pr\{T = k\} \\ &\xrightarrow[n \to \infty]{} \sum_{k=0}^{\infty} E[X_T^2 | T = k] \Pr\{T = k\} \\ &= E[X_T^2]. \end{aligned}$$

It follows from Schwarz' inequality that $E[|X_T|] \le (E[X_T^2])^{1/2} < \infty$, which verifies condition (ii) of Theorem 3.2. For (iii) we use Schwarz' inequality again to conclude that

$$\begin{aligned}\{E[X_n I_{\{T>n\}}]\}^2 &= \{E[X_{T\wedge n} I_{\{T>n\}}]\}^2 \\ &\le E[X_{T\wedge n}^2]E[I_{\{T>n\}}^2] \\ &\le \mathrm{K}\Pr\{T>n\} \to 0, \qquad \text{as} \quad n\to\infty. \quad \blacksquare\end{aligned}$$

Corollary 3.3. *Suppose $Y_0 = 0$ and $Y_1, Y_2, \ldots$ are independent identically distributed random variables for which $E[Y_k] = \mu$ and $\operatorname{Var}[Y_k] = \sigma^2 < \infty$. Set $X_n = S_n - n\mu$, where $S_n = Y_0 + \cdots + Y_n$. If T is a Markov time for which $E[T] < \infty$, then $E[|X_T|] < \infty$ and $E[X_T] = E[S_T] - \mu E[T] = 0$.*

Proof. We apply the theorem to the martingale $\{S_n - n\mu\}$. Let $Y_0' = 0$ and $Y_k' = Y_k - \mu$, $k = 1, 2, \ldots$. To show $E[|X_T|] < \infty$, we have

$$\begin{aligned}E[|X_T|] &\le E\left[\sum_{k=1}^{T} |Y_k'|\right] \\ &= E\left[\sum_{n=1}^{\infty}\sum_{k=1}^{n} |Y_k'| I_{\{T=n\}}\right] \\ &= E\left[\sum_{k=1}^{\infty} |Y_k'| I_{\{T\ge k\}}\right].\end{aligned}$$

Now $I_{\{T\ge k\}} = I_{\{T>k-1\}}$ depends only on $\{Y_0, \ldots, Y_{k-1}\}$ and thus is independent of Y_k'. Hence

$$\begin{aligned}E\left[\sum_{k=1}^{\infty} |Y_k'| I_{\{T\ge k\}}\right] &= E[|Y_1'|]\sum_{k=1}^{\infty}\Pr\{T\ge k\} \\ &= E[|Y_1'|]E[T] < \infty.\end{aligned}$$

To confirm condition (iii) of Theorem 3.2, we have, using Schwarz' inequality,

$$\begin{aligned}(E[X_n I_{\{T>n\}}])^2 &\le E[X_n^2]E[I_{\{T>n\}}] \\ &\le n\sigma^2 \Pr\{T\ge n\}.\end{aligned}$$

But $\infty > E[T] = \sum_{k=0}^{\infty} k\Pr\{T=k\}$, so that

$$\begin{aligned}0 &= \lim_{n\to\infty} \sum_{k\ge n} k\Pr\{T=k\} \\ &\ge \lim_{n\to\infty} n\Pr\{T\ge n\} \ge 0. \quad \blacksquare\end{aligned}$$

4: *Some Applications of the Optional Sampling Theorem*

As we shall see, the optional sampling theorem finds ready use in computing and bounding certain probabilities connected with stochastic processes. More applications relevant to Brownian motion appear in Chapter 7, Section 5.

(a) *Random Walks*

The optional sampling theorem quickly yields a number of important results in connection with random walks. First let us examine one of the examples that opened this chapter. Let $Y_0 = 0$ and, for $i = 1, 2, \ldots,$ let Y_i be independent identically distributed random variables with $\Pr\{Y_i = 1\} = p$ and $\Pr\{Y_i = -1\} = q = 1 - p$. Let $S_0 = 0$ and $S_n = Y_1 + \cdots + Y_n$, $n \geq 1$.

Suppose first that $p = q = \frac{1}{2}$. Then $\{S_n\}$ is a martingale. If $T = \min\{n : S_n = 1\}$, then $\Pr\{T < \infty\} = 1$, since S_n is recurrent. But $S_T \equiv 1$, so $E[S_T] \neq E[S_0] = 0$, which contradicts the result of Corollary 3.3. Thus the hypothesis of this corollary cannot hold, and in particular $E[T] = \infty$.

Continue assuming $p = q = \frac{1}{2}$, but now let

$$T = \min\{n : S_n = -a \quad \text{or} \quad S_n = b\} \qquad (a,\ b \text{ positive integers}).$$

Let v_a be the probability that S_n reaches $-a$ before reaching b. Then, from Theorem 3.1,

$$0 = E[S_T] = v_a(-a) + (1 - v_a)b$$

or

$$v_a = \frac{b}{a + b},$$

which was determined by other means in Chapter 3.

$Z_n = S_n^2 - n$ also defines a martingale, and

$$E[Z_T] = 0 = [v_a a^2 + (1 - v_a)b^2] - E[T],$$

which reduces to give

$$E[T] = ab.$$

Now suppose $p > q$, and set $\mu = E[Y_k] = p - q > 0$. Then

$$X_n = S_n - n\mu, \tag{4.1}$$

and

$$X_n' = (q/p)^{S_n}, \tag{4.2}$$

are martingales. From (4.1) and Corollary 3.1, we extract the identity

$$E[S_T] = \mu E[T],$$

applicable for any Markov time T satisfying $E[T] < \infty$.

To use (4.2) let

$$T = \min\{n : S_n = -a \qquad \text{or} \quad S \ = b\}.$$

Then

$$1 = E[X_T'] = v_a\left(\frac{q}{p}\right)^{-a} + (1 - v_a)\left(\frac{q}{p}\right)^{b},$$

or

$$v_a = \frac{1 - (q/p)^b}{(q/p)^{-a} - (q/p)^b},$$

where, as before, v_a is the probability that S_n reaches $-a$ before b. Again, this agrees with a formula derived in Chapter 3 through other means.

(b) *Wald's Identity*

Let $Y_0 = 0$ and $Y_1, Y_2, \ldots$ be nondegenerate independent identically distributed random variables having the *moment generating function*

$$\phi(\theta) = E[\exp\{\theta Y_1\}],$$

defined and finite for θ in some open interval containing the origin. Set $S_0 = 0$ and $S_n = Y_1 + \cdots + Y_n$. Finally, fix values $-a < 0$ and $b > 0$ and set

$$T = \min\{n : S_n \leq -a \qquad \text{or} \quad S_n \geq b\}.$$

The fundamental identity of Wald is

$$E[\phi(\theta)^{-T} \exp\{\theta S_T\}] = 1, \tag{4.3}$$

valid for any θ satisfying $\phi(\theta) \geq 1$. This identity bears numerous applications throughout applied probability and statistics.

We will use Corollary 3.1 to establish (4.3). Recall from Example (g) of Section 1 that $X_0 = 1$, and

$$X_n = \phi(\theta)^{-n} \exp\{\theta S_n\}, \qquad n \geq 1,$$

defines a martingale with respect to $\{Y_n\}$. Then

$$E[|X_{n+1} - X_n| \,|\, Y_0, \ldots, Y_n] = X_n E[|\phi(\theta)^{-1} \exp(\theta Y_{n+1}) - 1|].$$

By assumption, $\phi(\theta)^{-n} \leq 1$, and, for $n < T$, $\exp\{\theta S_n\} \leq e^b$. Thus $X_n \leq e^b$ for $n < T$. In addition,

$$E[|\phi(\theta)^{-1} \exp(\theta Y_{n+1}) - 1|] \leq \phi(\theta)^{-1}\{E[\exp \theta Y_{n+1}] + \phi(\theta)\} = 2.$$

Thus

$$E[|X_{n+1} - X_n| | Y_0, \ldots, Y_n] \leq 2e^b, \qquad \text{for} \quad n < T,$$

and we need only verify that $E[T] < \infty$ in order to apply Corollary 3.1. Let $c = a + b$. Since Y_k is stipulated nondegenerate, there exists an integer N and a $\delta > 0$ such that $\Pr\{|S_N| > c\} > \delta$. Define $S_1' = S_N$, $S_2' = S_{2N} - S_N, \ldots$, and $S_k' = S_{kN} - S_{(k-1)N}$. Then

$$\begin{aligned}\Pr\{T \geq kN\} &\leq \Pr\{|S_1'| \leq c\} \cdots \Pr\{|S_k'| \leq c\} \\ &\leq (1 - \delta)^k,\end{aligned}$$

and also bringing in the fact that $\Pr\{T \geq n\}$ decreases in n, we secure

$$\begin{aligned}E[T] &= \sum_{n=1}^{\infty} \Pr\{T \geq n\} \\ &\leq N \sum_{k=0}^{\infty} \Pr\{T \geq kN\} \leq N/\delta < \infty.\end{aligned}$$

To see how Wald's identity is commonly applied, let us suppose there exists a value $\theta_0 \neq 0$ for which $\phi(\theta_0) = 1$. Then (4.3) becomes

$$E[\exp\{\theta_0 S_T\}] = 1.$$

Setting

$$E_a = E[\exp\{\theta_0 S_T\} | S_T \leq -a],$$

and

$$E_b = E[\exp\{\theta_0 S_T\} | S_T \geq b],$$

we conclude that

$$\begin{aligned}1 &= E_a \Pr\{S_T \leq -a\} + E_b \Pr\{S_T \geq b\} \\ &= E_a + (E_b - E_a) \Pr\{S_T \geq b\},\end{aligned}$$

or

$$\Pr\{S_T \geq b\} = \frac{1 - E_a}{E_b - E_a}.$$

One might expect $E_a \cong \exp\{-\theta_0 a\}$ and $E_b \cong \exp\{\theta_0 b\}$, provided that when S_n leaves the interval $[-a, b]$, it does so without jumping too far from the boundary. This is the intuition underlying Wald's approximation

$$\Pr\{S_T \geq b\} \cong \frac{1 - \exp\{-\theta_0 a\}}{\exp\{\theta_0 b\} - \exp\{-\theta_0 a\}}.$$

Return to identity (4.3) and formally differentiate it with respect to θ to obtain

$$0=\frac{d}{d\theta}E[\phi(\theta)^{-T}\exp\{\theta S_T\}]$$

$$=E[(-T\phi(\theta)^{-T-1}\phi'(\theta)+\phi(\theta)^{-T}S_T)\exp\{\theta S_T\}]$$
$$=-\phi'(\theta)E[T\phi(\theta)^{-T-1}\exp\{\theta S_T\}]+E[\phi(\theta)^{-T}S_T\exp\{\theta S_T\}].$$

Set $\theta=0$, using $\phi(0)=1$ and $\phi'(0)=E[Y_1]$. Then

$$0=-E[Y_1]E[T]+E[S_T],$$

or

$$E[S_T]=E[Y_1]E[T].$$

OPTIONAL STOPPING FOR SUPERMARTINGALES

Let $\{X_n\}$ be a supermartingale with respect to $\{Y_n\}$. According to Lemma 3.2, $E[X_0]\geq E[X_{T\wedge n}]$ for any Markov time T, and we may infer $E[X_0]\geq E[X_T]$ provided we can justify the interchange of limit and expectation as $n\to\infty$, just as in the case with martingales. The following two theorems are important cases.

Theorem 4.1. *Let $\{X_n\}$ be a supermartingale and T a Markov time. If $\Pr\{T<\infty\}=1$ and there exists a random variable $W\geq 0$ for which $E[W]<\infty$ and $X_{T\wedge n}>-W$ for all n, then*

$$E[X_0]\geq E[X_T].$$

Proof. Let $c>0$ be fixed and define $X_n^c=\min\{c, X_n\}$, for $n=0, 1, \ldots$. Then $\{X_n^c\}$ is also a supermartingale with respect to $\{Y_n\}$ (in this connection consult p. 250), so that

$$E[X_0^c]\geq E[X_{T\wedge n}^c],$$

and since

$$|X_{T\wedge n}^c|\leq \max\{c, W\},$$

for all n, we may interchange the limit as $n\to\infty$ and expectation as in Theorem 3.1, and deduce that

$$E[X_0^c]\geq E[X_T^c].$$

But clearly $E[X_0]\geq E[X_0^c]$, while

$$\lim_{c\to\infty}E[X_T^c]=\lim_{c\to\infty}\int_{-\infty}^{c}x\,d\Pr\{X_T\leq x\}=E[X_T].$$

Thus $E[X_0] \geq E[X_T]$ is achieved as forecast. ∎

Theorem 4.2. *Let $\{X_n\}$ be a supermartingale and T a Markov time. If $X_n \geq 0$ for all n, then*

$$E[X_0] \geq E[X_T I_{\{T<\infty\}}].$$

Proof. As usual,

$$E[X_0] \geq E[X_{T\wedge n}].$$

Since $X_n \geq 0$, $X_{T\wedge n} = X_T I_{\{T\leq n\}} + X_n I_{\{T>n\}} \geq X_T I_{\{T\leq n\}}$, so that $E[X_0] \geq E[X_T I_{\{T\leq n\}}]$, and

$$\begin{aligned} E[X_0] &\geq \lim_{n\to\infty} E[X_T I_{\{T\leq n\}}] \\ &= \lim_{n\to\infty} \sum_{k=0}^{n} E[X_T | T=k] \Pr\{T=k\} \\ &= \sum_{k=0}^{\infty} E[X_T | T=k] \Pr\{T=k\} \\ &= E[X_T I_{\{T<\infty\}}]. \quad ∎ \end{aligned}$$

BOUNDS ON THE VALUE OF AN OPTION

Let W_n be the price on day n of an asset, say a share of stock, that is traded in a public market. Let Y_n be the ratio of the price on day n to the price on day $n-1$, so that $W_n = w \times Y_1 \times \cdots \times Y_n$, where $W_0 = w$ is today's price. In this context, the historically famous and controversial "random walk hypothesis" asserts that $Y_1, Y_2, \ldots$ are independent and identically distributed positive random variables. It can be shown that certain assumptions characterizing a "perfect market" lead to this behavior. Recently interest has centered in replacing the random walk assumption by a weaker assumption phrased in terms of martingales. Let us recognize a long-term growth and inflation rate $\alpha \geq 0$ and assume that $e^{-\alpha n} W_n$ is a martingale with respect to Y_n. Then $E[e^{-\alpha n} W_n] = E[W_0] = w$ or $E[W_n] = we^{\alpha n}$, so that α represents the mean growth rate of the market price of the asset.

Consider now an *option contract* that entitles the holder to purchase the asset at any time he pleases at a fixed stated price, regardless of what the market price might be. In the stock market such options are called "warrants" and "calls." By changing our scale of values, if necessary, we may suppose that the fixed stated price is one. Then if $W_n > 1$, the option holder may "exercise" his option, purchase at the stated price of one, and resell in the market at W_n for a profit of $W_n - 1$. If $W_n \le 1$, no such profit is possible. Thus the potential profit to the option holder is

$$r(W_n) = (W_n - 1)^+ = \max\{W_n - 1, 0\}.$$

An alternative to holding the option is to hold the asset itself, and the rate of return here, on the average, is α. Since this alternative is always available, one could justify holding the option only if it provided a greater rate of return $\beta > \alpha$. Equivalently, we discount the potential return $r(W_n)$ on day n by the factor $e^{-\beta n}$. Let T be the time the option is exercised. In this general martingale model we seek a bound on the mean discounted profit $E[e^{-\beta T} r(W_T)]$ as a function of the current price w, under the moment condition that there exists a $\theta > 1$ for which

$$E[Y_n^\theta | Y_1, \ldots, Y_{n-1}] \le e^\beta, \qquad \text{for} \quad n = 1, 2, \ldots. \tag{4.4}$$

In fact, (4.4) is the sole assumption needed for what follows. Our results do not depend on either the random walk model or the martingale model for market prices but are compatible with both these models. Note, we interpret $e^{-\beta T} r(W_T) = 0$ if $T = \infty$ so that no profit is made if the option is never exercised.

Example. Suppose $Y_1, Y_2, \ldots$ are independent identically distributed log normal random variables, i.e., $V_k = \ln Y_k$ is normally distributed with mean μ and variance σ^2. Then

$$E[Y_n | Y_1, \ldots, Y_{n-1}] = E[Y_n] = E[\exp\{V_n\}] = \exp\{\mu + \tfrac{1}{2}\sigma^2\},$$

so that $\alpha = \mu + \frac{1}{2}\sigma^2$, while

$$E[Y_n^\theta | Y_1, \ldots, Y_{n-1}] = E[\exp\{\theta V_n\}] = \exp\{\theta\mu + \tfrac{1}{2}\theta^2\sigma^2\}.$$

We solve $\theta\mu + \frac{1}{2}\theta^2\sigma^2 = \beta$ to see that (4.4) holds as an equality for

$$\theta = \frac{(\mu^2 + 2\sigma^2\beta)^{1/2} - \mu}{\sigma^2}.$$

Since $\beta > \alpha = \mu + \frac{1}{2}\sigma^2$,

$$\theta > \frac{(\mu^2 + 2\sigma^2\alpha)^{1/2} - \mu}{\sigma^2} = 1,$$

as required.

To return to the general case, we will show that $E[e^{-\beta T} r(W_T)] \le f(w)$ for all $w \ge 0$, where

$$f(w) = \begin{cases} w^\theta(\theta - 1)^{\theta - 1}/\theta^\theta, & \text{if} \quad w \le \theta/(\theta - 1), \\ w - 1, & \text{if} \quad w > \theta/(\theta - 1). \end{cases}$$

Notice that $f(w) \leq w^{\theta}(\theta - 1)^{\theta - 1}/\theta^{\theta}$ for all $w > 0$.
This bound holds no matter what strategy the option owner uses in deciding when, if ever, to exercise his option. Thus the bound might be used by sellers of options to limit their mean loss. Note also that if today's price $W_0 = w$ exceeds $\theta/(\theta - 1)$, then the value of the option is at most $f(w) = w - 1$, the amount that could be obtained by exercising immediately, and thus the option should be exercised if the market price is this high. This conclusion requires only the moment assumption (4.4) and subject to this, holds regardless of the form of the probability distribution for daily price changes!

To verify the bound, set $X_n = e^{-\beta n} f(W_n)$. We claim $\{X_n\}$ is a nonnegative supermartingale with respect to $\{Y_n\}$. It suffices to show

$$f(w) \geq e^{-\beta} E[f(w \times Y)], \qquad \text{for all} \quad w \geq 0, \tag{4.5}$$

whenever

$$E[Y^{\theta}] \leq e^{\beta}, \tag{4.6}$$

since once (4.5) is established then using (4.4) we obtain

$$\begin{aligned} E[X_n | Y_0, \ldots, Y_{n-1}] &= e^{-\beta n} E[f(W_{n-1} \times Y_n) | Y_0, \ldots, Y_{n-1}] \\ &\leq e^{-\beta(n-1)} f(W_{n-1}) = X_{n-1}. \end{aligned}$$

It remains to prove (4.5). For a fixed $t > 1$, define

$$v(t, w) = w^t (t - 1)^{t-1}/t^t, \qquad w \geq 0.$$

Then

$$v(t, w) \geq f(w), \quad 1 < t \leq \theta, \quad w \geq 0. \tag{4.7}$$

We leave to the reader the exercise of verifying (4.7). [With $g_t(w) = v(t, w) - (w - 1)$ and $w_0 = t/(t - 1) > \theta/(\theta - 1)$ he should first check that both $g_t(w_0) = 0$ and $g_t'(w_0) = 0$, where prime denotes the derivative with respect to w. Then, after verifying the positive second derivative $g_t''(w) > 0$ he knows $g_t(w) \geq 0$ or $v(t, w) \geq w - 1$, for all w. Second, he should compute the derivative of $\log v(t, w)$ with respect to t and simplify it to get

$$\frac{d \log v(t, w)}{dt} = \log\left\{\frac{w}{t/(t - 1)}\right\}$$

which is negative when $w < \theta/(\theta - 1) < t/(t - 1)$. That is $v(t, w)$ increases as t decreases from θ for $w \leq \theta/(\theta - 1)$. Therefore $v(t, w) > v(\theta, w) = f(w)$ for w in this region.]

To continue we next consider two cases. Suppose first that $w \leq \theta/(\theta-1)$. Then

$$\begin{aligned} f(w) &= v(\theta, w) \\ &\geq e^{-\beta} v(\theta, w) E[Y^{\theta}] && \text{[because of (4.6)]} \\ &= e^{-\beta} E[v(\theta, w \times Y)] && \text{[by the definition of } v(\theta, w)] \qquad (*) \\ &\geq e^{-\beta} E[f(w \times Y)] && \text{[by (4.7)].} \end{aligned}$$

The second case is $w > \theta/(\theta-1)$. Now $E[Y^{a}]$ is a convex function of $a \in [0, \theta]$, and $E[Y^{0}] = 1 < e^{\beta}$. It follows using Jensen's inequality and the hypothesis (4.6) that $E[Y^{w/(w-1)}] \leq e^{\beta}$ for $w/(w-1) < \theta$. Now consider

$$\begin{aligned} f(w) &= w - 1 \\ &= v(w/(w-1), w) \\ &\geq e^{-\beta} E[v(w/(w-1), w \times Y)] && [\text{since } E(Y^{w/w-1}) \leq e^{\beta}] \qquad (**) \\ &\geq e^{-\beta} E[f(w \times Y)] && \text{[by (4.7)].} \end{aligned}$$

The deliberations of (*) and (**) verify (4.5). Thus $X_n = e^{-\beta n} f(W_n)$ forms a nonnegative supermartingale, and so

$$X_0 = f(w) \geq E[e^{-\beta T} f(W_T)], \tag{4.8}$$

for any Markov time T. Lastly, we check that $f(w) \geq r(w) = (w-1)^{+}$, and then (4.8) will imply

$$f(w) \geq E[e^{-\beta T} r(W_T)],$$

as asserted earlier. Manifestly, $f(w) \geq 0$ for all w, and $f(w) = w - 1$ for $w \geq \theta/(\theta-1)$. Furthermore,

$$df/dw = [(\theta-1)/\theta]^{\theta-1} w^{\theta-1} < 1, \qquad \text{for} \quad w < \theta/(\theta-1).$$

It follows by integration that

$$f\left(\frac{\theta}{\theta-1}\right) - f(w) < \frac{\theta}{\theta-1} - w,$$

and therefore $f(w) > w - 1$ for $w < \theta/(\theta-1)$. This completes the verification of the inequality $f(w) \geq (w-1)^{+}$.

BOUNDS IN A RESERVOIR MODEL

Let Z_t be the water level at time t in a dam of finite capacity b. Let I_t be the random inflow in the time interval $(t, t+1]$ and O_t the outflow. The balance equation

$$Z_{t+1} = \min\{(Z_t + I_t - O_t)^{+}, b\}$$

expresses the fact that the water level cannot be negative nor can it exceed the capacity b. (We use "x^+" to denote "$\max\{x, 0\}$".)

Let us suppose that it is desirable for navigation, recreation, or emergency supply purposes always to maintain a water level above some minimal acceptable level a. Then

$$T = \min\{t : Z_t \le a\}$$

is the first time that this requirement is not met. The demands $\{O_t\}$ and the capacity b are controllable or design parameters. For various values of these parameters the performance of the dam might be compared using the mean time $E[T]$ as a criterion, the longer mean times being the better.

A common approach is to make exact assumptions concerning the inflows and outflows and then to compute $E[T]$ exactly. However, it is often difficult to justify exact assumptions for water reservoir systems because of seasonal effects and upstream surface water storage, which may affect inflows for several successive time periods. It is also true that little information is generally available concerning the distribution of inflows. Moreover, where past information does exist, it often bears little relevance to present conditions because of the topographical changes that are constantly occurring in any watershed system.

In this example, we will obtain a bound on the mean time $E[T]$ under the rather weak general assumption that the conditional distribution of the net inflow

$$Y_{t+1} = I_{t+1} - O_{t+1}$$

given the past satisfies

$$E[Y_{t+1} | Y_1, \ldots, Y_t] \le m, \tag{4.9}$$

and

$$E[\exp\{-\lambda Y_{t+1}\} | Y_1, \ldots, Y_t] \le 1 \tag{4.10}$$

where m and λ are known positive constants. We then show $E[T] \ge f(z)$, where

$$f(z) = \frac{1}{m}\left\{e^{\lambda(b-a)} \frac{1 - e^{-\lambda(z-a)}}{\lambda} - (z-a)\right\}, \qquad \text{for} \quad a \le z \le b,$$

and $Z_0 = z$ is the initial dam content. A conservative designer might plan with $f(z)$ as his criterion, since this represents the worst case or earliest mean time in which the critical level a could be reached.

We claim

$$X_n = f(Z_n) + n$$

forms a submartingale with respect to $\{Y_n\}$. Extend the domain of f by setting $f(z)=0$ for $z<a$, and $f(z)=f(b)$ for $z>b$. Then $f(Z_{n+1})=f(Z_n+Y_{n+1})$. Set

$$g(z)=\frac{1}{m}\left\{e^{\lambda(b-a)}\frac{1-e^{-\lambda(z-a)}}{\lambda}-(z-a)\right\},\qquad \text{for all}\quad z.$$

Since $g(z)$ is increasing up to $z=b$ and decreasing thereafter, we find that $f(z)\geq g(z)$ for all z, and

$$\begin{aligned}E[X_{n+1}|Y_0,\ldots,Y_n]&=E[f(Z_{n+1})|Y_0,\ldots,Y_n)]+(n+1)\\&=E[f(Z_n+Y_{n+1})|Y_0,\ldots,Y_n]+(n+1)\\&\geq E[g(Z_n+Y_{n+1})|Y_0,\ldots,Y_n]+(n+1).\end{aligned}$$

Now, if U is a random variable for which $E[U]\leq m$ and $E[e^{-\lambda U}]\leq 1$, then

$$\begin{aligned}E[g(z+U)]&=\frac{1}{m}\left\{e^{\lambda(b-a)}\frac{1-E[e^{-\lambda(z+U-a)}]}{\lambda}-(z+E[U]-a)\right\}\\&\geq f(z)-1,\qquad \text{for}\quad a\leq z\leq b.\end{aligned}$$

By virtue of the foregoing analyses and in view of the stipulations of (4.9) and (4.10), we infer that

$$E[X_{n+1}|Y_0,\ldots,Y_n]\geq f(Z_n)+n=X_n,$$

establishing that X_n is a submartingale as claimed. Now let $T=\min\{n:Z_n\leq a\}$ be the first time the water level ever reaches the critical height a. From the optional stopping theorem for submartingales, we have

$$E[f(Z_{T\wedge n})+(T\wedge n)]\geq f(z),$$

where $z=Z_0$ is the initial dam content. Since f is a bounded function, we may appeal to Lemma 3.3, validating the results

$$\lim_{n\to\infty}E[f(Z_{T\wedge n})]=E[f(Z_T)]=0,\qquad (\text{since } Z_T\leq a)$$

and

$$\begin{aligned}\lim_{n\to\infty}E[T\wedge n]&=\lim_{n\to\infty}\sum_{k=1}^{n}\Pr\{T\geq k\}\\&=\sum_{k=1}^{\infty}\Pr\{T\geq k\}=E[T].\end{aligned}$$

Hence

$$\begin{aligned}f(z)&\leq\lim_{n\to\infty}\{E[f(Z_{T\wedge n})]+E[T\wedge n]\}\\&=E[T],\end{aligned}$$

as desired to be shown.

The conditions (4.9) and (4.10) are certainly satisfied where $Y_1, Y_2, \ldots, Y_i, \ldots$ are independent normal random variables having means $\mu_i \leq m$ and variances $\sigma_i^2 \leq 2\mu_i/\lambda$.

THE CROSSINGS INEQUALITY

Given a submartingale $\{X_n\}$ with respect to a sequence $\{Y_n\}$, real numbers $a < b$, and a positive integer N, define $V_{a,b}$ to be the number of pairs (i, j) with $0 \leq i < j \leq N$, for which $X_i \leq a$, $a < X_k < b$, for $i < k < j$ and $X_j \geq b$. Then $V_{a,b}$ counts the number of times X_n upcrosses the interval (a, b) for $n = 0, 1, \ldots, N$, i.e., the number of crosses from a level below a to a level above b. We will prove the fundamental *upcrossings inequality*

$$E[V_{a,b}] \leq \frac{E[(X_N - a)^+] - E[(X_0 - a)^+]}{b - a}. \tag{4.11}$$

The upcrossings inequality indicates limits on the oscillations permissible for a submartingale and suggests that the paths or sample trajectories behave rather regularly. The inequality, its extensions and variations are used widely in probability analysis to prove convergence theorems and to investigate the growth and continuity properties of sample paths for continuous parameter stochastic processes.

We will need the following extension of Lemma 3.2, which covers two Markov times simultaneously in the submartingale case. This is a special circumstance of a more general optional sampling theorem that compares several, or even denumerably many, Markov times.

Lemma 4.1. *Let $\{X_n\}$ be a submartingale and S, T Markov times with respect to $\{Y_n\}$. Suppose $0 \leq S \leq T \leq N$, where N is a fixed positive integer. Then*

$$E[X_S] \leq E[X_T].$$

Proof. Let k be fixed. For $k \leq n \leq N$, since $I_{\{T>n\}}$ depends only on $Y_0, \ldots, Y_n$, using obvious properties of conditional probabilities we have

$$\begin{aligned} &E[X_{n+1}\, I_{\{T>n\}}\, I_{\{S=k\}}] \\ &\quad = E[E\{X_{n+1} | Y_0, \ldots, Y_n\} I_{\{T>n\}}\, I_{\{S=k\}}] \\ &\quad \geq E[X_n\, I_{\{T>n\}}\, I_{\{S=k\}}]. \end{aligned}$$

Thus

$$\begin{aligned} E[X_{T\wedge n}\, I_{\{S=k\}}] &= E[X_T\, I_{\{T\leq n\}}\, I_{\{S=k\}}] + E[X_n\, I_{\{T>n\}}\, I_{\{S=k\}}] \\ &\leq E[X_T\, I_{\{T\leq n\}}\, I_{\{S=k\}}] + E[X_{n+1}\, I_{\{T>n\}}\, I_{\{S=k\}}] \\ &= E[X_{T\wedge(n+1)}\, I_{\{S=k\}}] \end{aligned}$$

is a monotonic increasing function of n. Setting $n=k$ and then $n=N$, using the hypothesis $S\le T\le N$ leads to the relation

$$E[X_k I_{\{S=k\}}]\le E[X_T I_{\{S=k\}}].$$

Now

$$\begin{aligned} E[X_S] &= \sum_{k=0}^{N} E[X_S I_{\{S=k\}}] \\ &= \sum_{k=0}^{N} E[X_k I_{\{S=k\}}] \\ &\le \sum_{k=0}^{N} E[X_T I_{\{S=k\}}] \\ &= E[X_T], \end{aligned}$$

as required to be shown. ∎

We apply the lemma to obtain the upcrossings inequality. Define

$$\hat{X}_n=(X_n-a)^+.$$

Since $g(x)=(x-a)^+=\max\{(x-a),\ 0\}$ is a convex increasing function of x, Lemma 2.2 tells us that $\{\hat{X}_n\}$ is also a submartingale with respect to $\{Y_n\}$. Define $T_1\equiv 0$, and, for $k=1,\ \ldots,\ N$, set

$$T_k=\begin{cases} N, & \text{if } \hat{X}_j\neq 0, \quad \text{for } j>T_{k-1}, \\ \min\{j:j>T_{k-1},\ \hat{X}_j=0\}, & \text{otherwise,} \end{cases}$$

if k is even, and

$$T_k=\begin{cases} N, & \text{if } \hat{X}_j<b-a, \quad \text{for all } j>T_{k-1}, \\ \min\{j:j>T_{k-1},\ \hat{X}_j\ge b-a\}, & \text{otherwise,} \end{cases}$$

if k is odd. Set $T_{N+1}=N$. Then each T_k is a Markov time (validate this rigorously) and $T_k\le T_{k+1}$, so that, using the lemma just obtained,

$$E[\hat{X}_{T_k}]\le E[\hat{X}_{T_{k+1}}]. \tag{4.12}$$

Now

$$\begin{aligned} \hat{X}_N-\hat{X}_0 &= \sum_{k=1}^{N} (\hat{X}_{T_{k+1}}-\hat{X}_{T_k}) \\ &= \sum_{k=2,4,\ldots} (\hat{X}_{T_{k+1}}-\hat{X}_{T_k}) + \sum_{k=1,3,\ldots} (\hat{X}_{T_{k+1}}-\hat{X}_{T_k}). \end{aligned}$$

Now, if k is even, $\hat{X}_{T_{k+1}} - \hat{X}_{T_k}$ is nonzero only if an upcrossing occurs and then is at least $(b-a)$, while the expected value of the second sum is nonnegative by (4.12). Thus

$$E[\hat{X}_N - \hat{X}_0] \geq (b-a)E[V_{a,b}],$$

or

$$E[V_{a,b}] \leq \frac{E[(X_N - a)^+] - E[(X_0 - a)^+]}{b-a},$$

as was to be shown. ■

AN INEQUALITY FOR PARTIAL SUMS

Let $X_1, X_2, \ldots$ be random variables having finite conditional moments

$$M_k = E[X_k | X_1, \ldots, X_{k-1}],$$

and

$$V_k = E[(X_k - M_k)^2 | X_1, \ldots, X_{k-1}].$$

Let $S_n = X_1 + \cdots + X_n$ $(S_0 = 0)$. Under the condition

$$M_k \leq -\alpha V_k, \qquad \text{for all} \quad k, \tag{4.13}$$

for some ***fixed positive*** α, we will show

$$\Pr\left\{\sup_{n \geq 0}[x + S_n] > l\right\} \leq \frac{1}{1 + \alpha(l - x)}, \qquad \text{for} \quad x < l. \tag{4.14}$$

For example, if the summands are independent and identically distributed with mean $\mu < 0$ and variance σ^2, then, by the law of large numbers, $S_n \to -\infty$ as $n \to \infty$ and $M = \max_{n \geq 0} S_n < \infty$ is defined (see Chapter 17). The inequality (4.14) with the choice $\alpha = |\mu|/\sigma^2$ then says

$$\Pr\{M > l\} \leq \sigma^2/[\sigma^2 + |\mu| l].$$

We return to the general case in which independence of the summands is not assumed. Define

$$f(z) = \begin{cases} \dfrac{1}{1 + \alpha(l - z)}, & \text{for} \quad z < l, \\ 1, & \text{for} \quad z \geq l. \end{cases}$$

Our program is to show that, subject to condition (4.13), $\{f(x + S_n)\}$ determines a nonnegative supermartingale. Assuming this fact for the moment, the application of Theorem 4.2 yields

$$\begin{aligned} f(x) &\geq E[f(x+S_T)I_{\{T<\infty\}}] \\ &= \Pr\left\{\sup_{n\geq 0}[x+S_n]>l\right\}, \end{aligned}$$

when T is the first n, if any, for which $x+S_n>l$.

For later use, record the derivatives

$$f'(y)=\frac{\alpha}{[1+\alpha(l-y)]^2}=\alpha[f(y)]^2, \qquad \text{for} \quad y<l, \tag{4.15}$$

and

$$f''(y)=2\alpha f(y)f'(y), \qquad \text{for} \quad y<l, \tag{4.16}$$

which implies, because $0\leq f(y)<1$,

$$f''(y)<2\alpha f'(y), \qquad \text{for} \quad y<l. \tag{4.17}$$

Fix an arbitrary point $z<l$. Let $g(y)$ be a quadratic in y, tangent to $f(y)$ at $y=z$. Specifically, $g(y)$ has the form

$$g(y)=f(z)+f'(z)(y-z)+a(y-z)^2,$$

where a is a suitable constant. We also want $g(l)=f(l)=1$, and accordingly select

$$a=\alpha f'(z)$$

This achieves

$$\begin{aligned} g(l) &= f(z)+f'(z)(l-z)+\alpha f'(z)(l-z)^2 \\ &= f(z)\{1+\alpha(l-z)[1+\alpha(l-z)]f(z)\} \qquad [\text{by } (4.15)] \\ &= f(z)\{1+\alpha(l-z)\} \\ &= 1, \end{aligned}$$

as desired.

Specified thus, we get

$$g(y)\geq f(y), \qquad \text{for all} \quad y. \tag{4.18}$$

The key to seeing this is contained in (4.17), whence

$$g''(z)=2a=2\alpha f'(z)>f''(z)$$

Since $g(z)=f(z)$ and $g'(z)=f'(z)$, it follows that (4.18) prevails in some neighborhood of z. Now (4.18) holds if and only if

$$h(y)=\frac{g(y)}{f(y)}-1\geq 0, \qquad \text{for all} \quad y\leq l$$

But $h(y)$ is a cubic and therefore admits at most three real roots, two of which are located at the point of tangency z, and the third at l. Since (4.18) holds in a neighborhood of z, the only possibility is $g(y) \geq f(y)$ for all $y \leq l$. It is easy to check that $g(y) \geq f(y) = 1$ for $y \geq l$. Thus (4.18) is established. With these preliminaries complete, we turn to the task of proving that $f(x + S_n)$ generates a supermartingale. Let X be an arbitrary random variable having a mean m and a variance v^2, which together satisfy

$$m \leq -\alpha v^2. \tag{4.19}$$

Let $\xi \leq l$ be an arbitrary point and apply the preceding analysis with $z = \xi + m \leq l$ [by (4.19) m is negative]. Using (4.18) for the first inequality,

$$\begin{aligned}
E[f(\xi + X)] &= E[f(z + X - m)] \\
&\leq E[g(z + X - m)] \\
&= f(z) + \alpha f'(z) v^2 \\
&\leq f(z) - m f'(z) \qquad &&[\text{since } f'(z) > 0 \text{ by (4.15),} \\
& &&\text{and then use (4.19)}] \\
&\leq f(z - m) &&[\text{since } f''(y) \geq 0 \text{ for } y < l] \\
&= f(\xi).
\end{aligned}$$

Thus, $f(\xi) \geq E[f(\xi + X)]$ for any $\xi \leq l$ [it trivially holds for $\xi > l$ since $f(z) \leq 1$ everywhere], provided X is a random variable satisfying (4.19). With this fact and recalling (4.13), we obtain immediately

$$\begin{aligned}
E[f(x + S_{n+1}) | X_1, \ldots, X_n] &= E[f(x + S_n + X_{n+1}) | X_1, \ldots, X_n] \\
&\leq f(x + S_n),
\end{aligned}$$

which verifies the supermartingale inequality. The validation of (4.14) is now complete.

Here is an alternative form or equivalent result, from which a number of important inequalities can be obtained.

Let $X_1, X_2, \ldots$ be jointly distributed random variables having finite conditional moments

$$M_k = E[X_k' | X_1', \ldots, X_{k-1}'],$$

and

$$V_k = E[(X_k' - M_k)^2 | X_1', \ldots, X_{k-1}'].$$

Then

$$\Pr\{X_1' + \cdots + X_n' - (M_1 + \cdots + M_n) \geq a(V_1 + \cdots + V_n) + b, \quad \text{for some } n \geq 1\}$$

$$\leq \frac{1}{1 + ab}, \qquad a, b \geq 0.$$

The desired conclusion is equivalent to

$$\Pr\{X_1 + \cdots + X_n \geq b, \text{ for some } n \geq 1\} \leq \frac{1}{1+ab},$$

with

$$X_k = X_n' - M_k - aV_k,$$

and the conditional mean of X_k is $-aV_k$, while the conditional variance remains V_k. Thus the new inequality is immediate from the old.

5: *Martingale Convergence Theorems*

Under quite general conditions, a martingale X_n will converge to a limit random variable X as n increases. Precise statements of these results form some of the most far reaching and powerful theorems in probability theory. We highlight immediately the *basic martingale convergence theorem*. (Chapter 1 reviewed several notions for the convergence of a sequence of random variables.)

Theorem 5.1. (a) *Let $\{X_n\}$ be a submartingale satisfying*

$$\sup_{n \geq 0} E[|X_n|] < \infty. \tag{5.1}$$

Then there exists a random variable X_∞ to which $\{X_n\}$ converges with probability one,

$$\Pr\left\{\lim_{n\to\infty} X_n = X_\infty\right\} - 1. \tag{5.2}$$

(b) *If $\{X_n\}$ is a martingale and is uniformly integrable (see later Remark* 5.3) *then, in addition to* (5.2), *$\{X_n\}$ converges in the mean, that is,*

$$\lim_{n\to\infty} E[|X_n - X_\infty|] = 0, \tag{5.3}$$

and

$$E[X_\infty] = E[X_n], \qquad \textit{for all} \quad n.$$

Remark 5.1. If $E[|X_0|] < \infty$ for a submartingale $\{X_n\}$, then the condition

$$\sup_{n\geq 1} E[|X_n|] < \infty \qquad \text{holds if and only if} \quad \sup_{n \geq 1} E[X_n^+] < \infty$$

also is maintained, where $X^+ = \max\{X, 0\}$. This equivalence emanates from the elementary inequality $X_n^+ \le |X_n|$ and the relation $|X_n| = 2X_n^+ - X_n$, yielding thereby

$$E[|X_n|] = 2E[X_n^+] - E[X_n] \le 2E[X_n^+] - E[X_0].$$

The theorem informs us that, in particular, *every nonpositive submartingale converges with probability one, and so does a nonnegative supermartingale, or a martingale that is uniformly bounded from above or from below.*

Remark 5.2. Convergence with probability one, (5.2), does not entail convergence in the mean, (5.3), nor vice versa. However, both these modes of convergence do imply convergence in probability,

$$\lim_{n\to\infty} \Pr\{|X_n - X_\infty| > \varepsilon\} = 0, \qquad \text{for every} \quad \varepsilon > 0.$$

Indeed, Chebyshev's inequality (consult Chapter 1, Section 1), in the form

$$\Pr\{|X_n - X_\infty| \ge \varepsilon\} \le \frac{E[|X_n - X_\infty|]}{\varepsilon}, \qquad \varepsilon > 0,$$

shows that convergence in the mean implies convergence in probability.

Remark 5.3. Recall from Section 3 that, by definition, a sequence X_n is *uniformly integrable if*

$$\lim_{c\to\infty} \sup_{n\ge 0} E[|X_n| I\{|X_n| > c\}] = 0. \tag{5.4}$$

(The notation $I\{|X_n| > c\}$ stands for the indicator function of the event where $|X_n| > c$). Specifically,

$$I\{|X_n| > c\} = \begin{cases} 1, & \text{if} \quad |X_n| > c, \\ 0, & \text{if} \quad |X_n| \le c. \end{cases}$$

Henceforth, generally I of a relation means the indicator function corresponding to the relation. We write also (see Section 2) $I_{\{|X_n|>c\}}$ to signify $I\{|X_n| > c\}$.

Stipulation (5.4) is implied by either of the following conditions:

$$\text{(i)} \quad |X_n| \le W, \qquad \text{for all} \quad n, \tag{5.5}$$

where W is a random variable satisfying $E[W] < \infty$;

$$\text{(ii)} \quad E[|X_n|^{1+\rho}] \le K < \infty, \qquad \text{for all} \quad n \tag{5.6}$$

where K and ρ are constants with $\rho > 0$. (The student should prove these statements.)

We will not prove Theorem 5.1 in its full generality as it requires extensive measure theoretic considerations. We refer the reader to Doob [1953, Chapter 7], or Neveu [1965]. The upcrossings inequality of the last section is the key tool. We will secure, however, a convergence theorem whose proof parallels and illustrates the general approach but is somewhat simpler in conception. Specifically, the convergence Theorem 5.2 concerns martingales satisfying the stronger condition (5.6) for $\rho = 1$. Concomitantly, under this strengthened hypothesis, is the sharper conclusion to the effect that besides convergence of X_n to X_∞ with probability one, convergence in mean square also prevails. The maximal inequality discussed next is a basic tool for this end and also serves in numerous other capacities.

THE MAXIMAL INEQUALITY

Let $\xi_1, \xi_2, \xi_3, \ldots$ be independent and identically distributed random variables obeying the moment conditions $E[\xi_i] = 0$ and $E[\xi_i^2] = \sigma^2 < \infty$. Define

$$S_0 = 0, \quad \text{and} \quad S_n = \xi_1 + \cdots + \xi_n,$$

for $n \geq 1$. Noting that the variance of S_n is $n\sigma^2$, Chebyshev's inequality gives

$$\varepsilon^2 \Pr\{|S_n| > \varepsilon\} \leq n\sigma^2, \qquad \varepsilon > 0.$$

A finer inequality is available:

$$\varepsilon^2 \Pr\left\{\max_{0 \leq k \leq n} |S_k| > \varepsilon\right\} \leq n\sigma^2, \tag{5.7}$$

known as *Kolmogorov's inequality*. The generalization to submartingales is the simple, yet powerful, *maximal inequality for submartingales*. (See Problem 5 for a strengthened version.)

Lemma 5.1. *Let $\{X_n\}$ be a submartingale for which $X_n \geq 0$ for all n. Then for any positive λ.*

$$\lambda \Pr\left\{\max_{0 \leq k \leq n} X_k > \lambda\right\} \leq E[X_n]. \tag{5.8}$$

Proof. Define the Markov time

$$T = \begin{cases} \min\{k \geq 0;\ X_k > \lambda\}, & \text{if} \quad X_k > \lambda, \quad \text{for some} \quad k = 0, \ldots, n, \\ n, & \text{if} \quad X_k \leq \lambda, \quad \text{for} \quad k = 0, 1, \ldots, n, \end{cases}$$

Applying the submartingale analog of Lemma 3.2, the optional stopping lemma, yields

$$\begin{aligned} E[X_n] &\geq E[X_T] \\ &\geq E\left[X_T \cdot I\left\{\max_{0 \leq k \leq n} X_k > \lambda\right\}\right] \qquad \text{(since } X_i \text{ are all nonnegative)} \\ &\geq \lambda \Pr\left\{\max_{0 \leq k \leq n} X_k > \lambda\right\} \qquad \text{(since on the indicator set, } X_T \geq \lambda\text{),} \end{aligned}$$

the desired inequality. ■

Kolmogorov's inequality ensues immediately, since $\{S_n\}$ is a martingale [Example (a) of Section 1], and, according to Lemma 2.1, $X_n = S_n^2$ determines a submartingale, obviously nonnegative, whence

$$\begin{aligned} n\sigma^2 &= E[S_n^2] \\ &\geq \lambda \Pr\left\{\max_{0 \leq k \leq n} S_k^2 > \lambda\right\} \\ &= \varepsilon^2 \Pr\left\{\max_{0 \leq k \leq n} |S_k| > \varepsilon\right\}, \qquad \text{for} \quad \varepsilon = \sqrt{\lambda}. \end{aligned}$$

Corollary 5.1. *Let $\{X_n\}$ be a martingale. Then for every positive λ*

$$\lambda \Pr\left\{\max_{0 \leq k \leq n} |X_k| > \lambda\right\} \leq E[|X_n|].$$

Proof. If $\{X_n\}$ is a martingale, then Lemma 2.1 assures us that $\{|X_n|\}$ is a nonnegative submartingale. The maximal inequality just proved then applies. ■

The proof of Lemma 5.1 may be readily adapted to yield the *maximal inequality for supermartingales*, whose statement follows. (See Problem 12.)

Lemma 5.2. *If $\{X_n\}$ is a nonnegative supermartingale, then*

$$\lambda \Pr\left\{\max_{0 \leq k \leq n} X_k > \lambda\right\} \leq E[X_0], \qquad \text{for} \quad \lambda > 0.$$

Example. Define $X_0 = 1$ and $X_n = \prod_{i=1}^{n} Y_i$, for $n \geq 1$, where $Y_1, Y_2, \ldots$ are nonnegative independent random variables having a common unit mean, $E[Y_i] = 1$. Then $\{X_n\}$ is a nonnegative martingale, and the maximal inequality says

$$\Pr\left\{\max_{0 \leq k \leq n} X_k > \lambda\right\} \leq 1/\lambda, \qquad \text{for} \quad \lambda > 0. \tag{*}$$

This bound is rather frustrating as the following situation will illustrate. Consider a gambler who risks a fraction q of his fortune, $0 < q < 1$, with each toss of a fair coin. Starting with one dollar, straightforward induction verifies that his fortune X_n after n tosses is $\prod_{j=1}^{n} (1 + \delta_j q)$, where δ_j is a sequence of independent random variables with possible values ± 1, each occurring with probability $\frac{1}{2}$. Now, if our gambler is patient enough, he will see his fortune dwindle to zero. Since $\{X_n\}$ is a martingale, it is a fortiori a submartingale, and, being positive,

$$\sup_{n \geq 1} E[|X_n|] = E[X_n] = 1,$$

so that (5.1) is satisfied. Thus with probability one, X_n tends to a finite limit as $n \to \infty$, which must be zero, since every other state is transient. The inequality of (*) appears rather weak in this context.

THE MARTINGALE MEAN SQUARE CONVERGENCE THEOREM

Let $\{X_n\}$ be a martingale and let A *be the random event that the sequence* $\{X_n\}$ *converges*. A formal characterization of the set A will be forthcoming. A particular realization $X_0, X_1, \ldots$ converges if and only if the Cauchy criterion

$$\lim_{m, n \to \infty} |X_m - X_n| = 0$$

is satisfied, and thus A has the explicit form

$$A = \left\{ \lim_{m, n \to \infty} |X_m - X_n| = 0 \right\}. \tag{5.9}$$

In words, A is the event that the process realization $X_0, X_1, \ldots$ satisfies the Cauchy criterion for convergence. When A occurs, let X_∞ denote the limit. We want to show $\Pr\{A\} = 1$. Then X_∞ will be defined, not always, but at least for a set of realizations $X_0, X_1, \ldots$ having total probability one, and

$$\Pr\left\{ \lim_{n \to \infty} X_n = X_\infty \right\} = 1.$$

Under the assumption that the second moments of $\{X_n\}$ are uniformly bounded, we will indeed prove convergence with probability one and also that convergence in mean square takes place.

Theorem 5.2. *Let* $\{X_n\}$ *be a martingale with respect to* $\{Y_n\}$ *satisfying, for some constant* K,

$$E[X_n^2] \leq K < \infty, \qquad \text{for all } n. \tag{5.10}$$

Then $\{X_n\}$ converges as $n \to \infty$ to a limit random variable X_∞ both with probability one and in mean square. That is,

$$\Pr\left\{\lim_{n\to\infty} X_n = X_\infty\right\} = 1, \tag{5.11}$$

and

$$\lim_{n\to\infty} E[|X_n - X_\infty|^2] = 0, \tag{5.12}$$

prevail. Finally,

$$E[X_0] = E[X_n] = E[X_\infty], \qquad \text{for all} \quad n. \tag{5.13}$$

Proof. Temporarily fix N, and for $k \geq 0$ set

$$\tilde{X}_k = X_{N+k} - X_N.$$

Now, the law of total probability and appropriate conditioning gives

$$\begin{aligned} E[X_{N+k} X_N] &= E\{E[X_{N+k} X_N | Y_0, \ldots, Y_N]\} \\ &= E\{X_N E[X_{N+k} | Y_0, \ldots, Y_N]\} \\ &= E[X_N^2], \end{aligned}$$

so that

$$\begin{aligned} 0 < E[\tilde{X}_k^2] &= E[(X_{N+k} - X_N)^2] \\ &= E[X_{N+k}^2 - 2X_{N+k} X_N + X_N^2] \\ &= E[X_{N+k}^2] - E[X_N^2]. \end{aligned} \tag{5.14}$$

Lemma 2.1 tells us that $\{X_n^2\}$ is a submartingale, $\{X_n\}$ being a martingale, and (5.14) indicates that $E[X_n^2]$ is a monotone nondecreasing sequence, bounded above by K, and hence convergent. Accordingly, the Cauchy criterion applies to give

$$\begin{aligned} 0 &= \lim_{N,k\to\infty} \{E[X_{N+k}^2] - E[X_N^2]\} \\ &= \lim_{N,k\to\infty} E[\tilde{X}_k^2]. \end{aligned} \tag{5.15}$$

We will use this in a minute.

Let A be the event that $\{X_n\}$ converges. Explicitly,

$$\begin{aligned} A &= \text{set of all realizations where } \lim_{m,n\to\infty} |X_m - X_n| = 0 \\ &= \text{set of realizations } \{X_n\} \text{ for which, for every } \varepsilon > 0, \text{ there} \\ &\quad\ \text{exists } N > 0 \text{ satisfying } |X_{N+m} - X_{N+n}| \leq \varepsilon \\ &\qquad\qquad\qquad\qquad\qquad\qquad \text{for all} \quad m, n \geq 1. \end{aligned}$$

From the triangle inequality

$$|X_{N+m} - X_{N+n}| \le |X_{N+m} - X_N| + |X_{N+n} - X_N|,$$

we see that A may be described equivalently in the terms

$$\begin{aligned} A = \{&\text{For every } \varepsilon > 0 \text{ there exists } N \ge 0 \\ &\text{for which } |X_{N+k} - X_N| \le \varepsilon \text{ for all } k \ge 0\}. \end{aligned}$$

Let B denote the complementary event to A consisting of the realizations where $\{X_n\}$ does not converge. Then

$$\begin{aligned} B = \{&\text{for some } \varepsilon > 0, \text{ for every } N \ge 0, \\ &\text{there exists } k \ge 0 \text{ depending on } \varepsilon, N \text{ and the realization} \\ &\text{for which } |X_{N+k} - X_N| > \varepsilon\} \\ = \bigcup_{\varepsilon>0} &\{\text{for every } N \ge 0 \text{ there exists } k \ge 0 \\ &\text{for which } |X_{N+k} - X_N| > \varepsilon\} \\ = \bigcup_{\varepsilon>0} &\bigcap_{N=0}^{\infty} B_N(\varepsilon), \end{aligned}$$

where

$$\begin{aligned} B_N(\varepsilon) = &\text{ event described by the conditions} \\ &\{|X_{N+k} - X_N| > \varepsilon \text{ for some } k = 0, 1, \ldots\}. \end{aligned}$$

We wish to prove the equation $\Pr\{B\} = 0$. For this objective it suffices to establish

$$\lim_{N\to\infty} \Pr\{B_N(\varepsilon)\} = 0, \qquad \text{for every} \quad \varepsilon > 0, \tag{5.16}$$

since in that case

$$\begin{aligned} \Pr\{B\} &= \Pr\left\{\bigcup_{\varepsilon>0} \bigcap_{N=0}^{\infty} B_N(\varepsilon)\right\} \\ &= \lim_{\varepsilon\downarrow 0} \Pr\left\{\bigcap_{N=0}^{\infty} B_N(\varepsilon)\right\} \\ &= \lim_{\varepsilon\downarrow 0} \lim_{N\to\infty} \Pr\{B_N(\varepsilon)\} = 0. \end{aligned}$$

To validate (5.16) we will employ the maximal inequality. Fix N and put

$$\tilde{X}_k = X_{N+k} - X_N, \qquad k = 0, 1, \ldots,$$

$$\tilde{Y}_0 = (Y_0, \ldots, Y_N),$$

and

$$\tilde{Y}_k = Y_{N+k}, \qquad k = 1, 2, \ldots.$$

From Jensen's inequality, or more specifically Schwarz' inequality, and with the stipulation of (5.14), we obtain

$$E[|\tilde{X}_k|] \le (E[\tilde{X}_k^2])^{1/2} \le \sqrt{K} < \infty,$$

and

$$\begin{aligned} E[\tilde{X}_{k+1} | \tilde{Y}_0, \ldots, \tilde{Y}_k] &= E[X_{N+k+1} - X_N | Y_0, \ldots, Y_{N+k}] \\ &= X_{N+k} - E[X_N | Y_0, \ldots, Y_{N+k}] \\ &= X_{N+k} - X_N = \tilde{X}_k, \end{aligned}$$

so that $\{\tilde{X}_k\}$ is a martingale with respect to $\{\tilde{Y}_k\}$. Again, Lemma 2.1 tells us that $\{\tilde{X}_k^2\}$ is a submartingale, and the maximal inequality yields

$$\varepsilon^2 \Pr\left\{\max_{0 \le k \le n} |\tilde{X}_k^2| > \varepsilon^2\right\} \le E[\tilde{X}_n^2],$$

or

$$\varepsilon^2 \Pr\left\{\max_{0 \le k \le n} |X_{N+k} - X_N| > \varepsilon\right\} \le E[\tilde{X}_n^2].$$

But in (5.15) we showed that the right-hand side goes to zero as $N, n \to \infty$. It follows that

$$\begin{aligned} 0 &= \lim_{N\to\infty} \lim_{n\to\infty} \Pr\left\{\max_{0 \le k \le n} |X_{N+k} - X_N| > \varepsilon\right\} \\ &= \lim_{N\to\infty} \Pr\left\{\sup_{0 \le k < \infty} |X_{N+k} - X_N| > \varepsilon\right\} \\ &= \lim_{N\to\infty} \Pr\{B_N(\varepsilon)\}. \end{aligned}$$

The preceding considerations complete the proof for the convergence of $\{X_n\}$ with probability one.

Let X_∞ denote the limit random variable. It remains to verify that $\{X_n\}$ converges to X_∞ in mean square. This requires only justification of the second inequality in

$$\begin{aligned} 0 &\le \lim_{n\to\infty} E[|X_n - X_\infty|^2] \\ &= \lim_{n\to\infty} E[\lim_{m\to\infty} |X_n - X_m|^2] \\ &\le \lim_{n\to\infty} \lim_{m\to\infty} E[|X_n - X_m|^2] = 0. \end{aligned}$$

The last limit is zero, of course, owing to (5.15). Fix n and let $Z_m = |X_n - X_m|^2$, so that we want to prove

$$\lim_{m\to\infty} E[Z_m] \ge E\left[\lim_{m\to\infty} Z_m\right]. \tag{5.17}$$

We begin with the representation

$$\begin{aligned}
E[Z_m] &= \int_0^\infty \Pr\{Z_m \ge t\}\, dt \\
&= \sum_{k=1}^{\infty} \int_{(k-1)\varepsilon}^{k\varepsilon} \Pr\{Z_m \ge t\}\, dt \\
&\ge \sum_{k=1}^{\infty} \int_{(k-1)\varepsilon}^{k\varepsilon} \Pr\{Z_m \ge k\varepsilon\}\, dt \\
&\ge \sum_{k=1}^{N} \varepsilon \Pr\{Z_m \ge k\varepsilon\},
\end{aligned} \tag{5.18}$$

where $\varepsilon > 0$, $N > 0$ are arbitrary.

Remark 5.2 recalled the property that convergence with probability one entails convergence in probability, whence, for $\delta > 0$,

$$\begin{aligned}
\lim_{m\to\infty} \Pr\{Z_m \ge k\varepsilon\} &\ge \lim_{m\to\infty} [\Pr\{Z \ge k\varepsilon + \delta\} - \Pr\{|Z_m - Z| > \delta\}] \\
&= \Pr\{Z \ge k\varepsilon + \delta\},
\end{aligned}$$

where $Z = \lim_{m\to\infty} Z_m$.

Since $\delta > 0$ is arbitrary,

$$\lim_{m\to\infty} \Pr\{Z_m \ge k\varepsilon\} \ge \Pr\{Z > k\varepsilon\}.$$

Now returning to (5.18), we have

$$\begin{aligned}
\lim_{m\to\infty} E[Z_m] &\ge \lim_{m\to\infty} \sum_{k=1}^{N} \varepsilon \Pr\{Z_m \ge k\varepsilon\} \\
&\ge \sum_{k=1}^{N} \varepsilon \Pr\{Z > k\varepsilon\} \\
&\ge \sum_{k=0}^{N} \varepsilon \Pr\{Z > k\varepsilon\} - \varepsilon \\
&\ge \sum_{k=0}^{N} \int_{k\varepsilon}^{(k+1)\varepsilon} \Pr\{Z > t\}\, dt - \varepsilon \\
&\ge \int_0^{(N+1)\varepsilon} \Pr\{Z > t\}\, dt - \varepsilon.
\end{aligned}$$

Keep $\varepsilon > 0$ fixed, and let $N \to \infty$ to deduce

$$\lim_{m\to\infty} E[Z_m] \ge \int_0^\infty \Pr\{Z > t\}\, dt - \varepsilon = E[Z] - \varepsilon.$$

Since $\varepsilon > 0$ is arbitrary, (5.17) is verified, and $\{X_n\}$ converges to X_∞ in mean square. This implies convergence in the mean, by Schwarz' inequality, viz.,

$$0 \le E[|X_n - X_\infty|] \le \{E[|X_n - X_\infty|^2]\}^{1/2} \to 0, \qquad \text{as} \quad n \to \infty.$$

And, in the same vein, we obtain

$$\begin{aligned} 0 &\leqq |E[X_n] - E[X_\infty]| \\ &= |E[X_n - X_\infty]| \le E[|X_n - X_\infty|] \to 0, \qquad \text{as} \quad n \to \infty, \end{aligned}$$

so that $E[X_n] \to E[X_\infty]$ But $E[X_n] = E[X_0]$, for all n. Therefore,

$$E[X_0] = E[X_n] = E[X_\infty]$$

This completes the proof of the martingale mean square convergence theorem ■

6: *Applications and Extensions of the Martingale Convergence Theorems*

Here are some sample implications of the convergence theorems of Section 5.

(a) *Bounded Solutions of $y = Py$, where $P = \|P_{ij}\|$ is the Transition Matrix of an Irreducible Recurrent Markov Chain $\{Y_n\}$.* The martingale convergence theorem can be invoked to establish that every bounded solution $y = \{y(i)\}$ to

$$y(i) = \sum_{j=0}^{\infty} P_{ij}\, y(j), \qquad \text{for all} \quad i, \quad \text{is constant,}$$

i.e., $y(i) = y(j)$ for all i, j. (Compare with Chapter 3, Theorem 4.1.) Because $X_n = y(Y_n)$ is a bounded martingale [cf. Example (d) of Section 1], we have $\lim_{n\to\infty} X_n = \lim_{n\to\infty} y(Y_n)$ exists with probability one. Since the chain is recurrent, all states are visited infinitely often (see Chapter 2), and so

$$\{X_n = y(i)\}, \qquad \text{and} \qquad \{X_n = y(j)\},$$

necessarily both occur for infinitely many n. However, $\lim_{n\to\infty} X_n$ exists, so we must have $y(i) = y(j)$.

(b) *Solutions to $f(y) = \int f(y+z)p(z)\,dz$.* Let $p(z)$ be a continuous probability density function. Every constant function $f(y) \equiv a$ is a solution to the integral equation

$$f(y) = \int f(y+z)p(z)\,dz, \qquad \text{for all} \quad y. \tag{6.1}$$

The martingale convergence theorem can be used to show that, in fact, the only *bounded and continuous solutions to* (6.1) are constant functions. To see this, suppose $f(y)$ is bounded, continuous, and solves (6.1). Then, for every x, $\{f(x+S_n)\}$ constitutes a martingale sequence, where $\{S_n\}$ designates the sequence of partial sums generated by the independent identically distributed random variables $X_1, X_2, \ldots,$ whose common probability density function is p. Since $f(y)$ is bounded, the conditions for the mean square convergence theorem are satisfied, and for each x we infer the existence of a random variable U_x satisfying

$$\Pr\left\{\lim_{n\to\infty} f(x+S_n) = U_x\right\} = 1,$$

and

$$\lim_{n\to\infty} E[|f(x+S_n) - U_x|^2] = 0.$$

We prove first that U_x is not random, but a constant $U_x = u(x)$, and subsequently we will prove that $u(x)$ is actually independent of x.

It is a trivial fact that $f(x+S_m - S_n)$ has the same distribution as $f(x+S_{m-n})$ for $m \geq n$. It is a more recondite property that the pair of random variables

$$\{f(x+S_m), \qquad f(x+S_m-S_n)\},$$

shares the identical joint distribution as the pair

$$\{f(x+S_m), \qquad f(x+S_{m-n})\}, \qquad m \geq n.$$

(Why?) Using these facts, we have

$$\begin{aligned}\lim_{n\to\infty}\lim_{m\to\infty} & E[|f(x+S_m) - f(x+S_m-S_n)|^2] \qquad (6.2)\\ &= \lim_{n\to\infty}\lim_{m\to\infty} E[|f(x+S_m) - f(x+S_{m-n})|^2] = 0.\end{aligned}$$

This is the crucial step, as will be seen imminently.

On the basis of Schwarz' inequality, we have

$$\begin{aligned}\{E[U_x^2 - f(x+S_n)U_x]\}^2 &= \{E[U_x\{U_x - f(x+S_n)\}]\}^2\\ &\leq E[U_x^2]\cdot E[|U_x - f(x+S_n)|^2].\end{aligned}$$

But the right-hand side goes to zero as n increases, implying

$$E[U_x^2] = \lim_{n\to\infty} E[f(x+S_n)U_x]$$

Analogously, we deduce

$$E[f(x+S_n)U_x] = \lim_{m\to\infty} E[f(x+S_n)f(x+S_m)].$$

Putting these relations together,

$$\begin{aligned}E[U_x^2] &= \lim_{n\to\infty}\lim_{m\to\infty} E[f(x+S_n)f(x+S_m)]\\ &= \lim_{n\to\infty}\lim_{m\to\infty} E[f(x+S_n)f(x+S_m-S_n)]\\ &\quad+\lim_{n\to\infty}\lim_{m\to\infty} E[f(x+S_n)\{f(x+S_m)-f(x+S_m-S_n)\}].\end{aligned}$$

For the first term on the right, since S_n and $S_m - S_n$ are independent and $E[f(x+S_n)] = E[U_x]$ for all n, by the martingale convergence theorem, we have

$$E[f(x+S_n)f(x+S_m-S_n)] = E[f(x+S_n)]E[f(x+S_m-S_n)] = \{E[U_x]\}^2.$$

Examining the second term, we employ Schwarz' inequality to obtain

$$\begin{aligned}&\{E[f(x+S_n)\{f(x+S_m)-f(x+S_m-S_n)\}]\}^2\\ &\quad\le E[\{f(x+S_n)\}^2]\cdot E[|f(x+S_m)-f(x+S_m-S_n)|^2],\end{aligned}$$

and since $f(y)$ is bounded, the last factor goes to zero as $m\to\infty$, utilizing the crucial observation (6.2).

Combining all these relations leads to the equation

$$E[U_x^2] = \{E[U_x]\}^2,$$

which says that the variance of U_x is zero, and this means that U_x is a nonrandom constant, say $u(x)$.

A martingale has a constant mean, and, because the martingale mean square convergence theorem applies, this mean value is maintained for the limit random variable. Accordingly,

$$f(x) = E[f(x+S_0)] = E[U_x] = u(x).$$

At this stage we have established that, with probability one,

$$\lim_{n\to\infty} f(x+S_n) = u(x) = f(x).$$

But we also necessarily have

$$\lim_{n\to\infty} f(x+X_1+S_n-X_1) = f(x+X_1),$$

so that

$$\Pr\{f(x) = f(x+X_1)\} = 1,$$

and, by induction,

$$\Pr\{f(x) = f(x+S_n)\} = 1.$$

This fact in conjunction with the assumption that X_1 is a continuous random variable having probability density function $p(x)$ may be exploited to prove the identity $f(x)=f(y)$ for all x, y. For example, the desired inference is immediate if $p(z)>0$ for all z, since

$$\begin{aligned}0&=E[|f(x+X_1)-f(x)|]\\&=\int|f(x+z)-f(x)|p(z)\,dz\end{aligned}$$

requires $|f(x+z)-f(x)|=0$ for all z, as $f(x)$ is continuous, by hypothesis.

It follows that $f(x)=a$ for all x, and every bounded continuous solution to (6.1) is constant.

If $f(x)$ is assumed to achieve its maximum at a point x_0, a much simpler proof is possible. With this added assumption, (6.1) gives

$$\begin{aligned}0&=\int\{f(x_0)-f(x_0+y)\}p(y)\,dy\\&=\int|f(x_0)-f(x_0+y)|p(y)\,dy,\end{aligned}$$

which easily implies $f(x_0)=f(x_0+y)$ for all y, when $p(y)>0$ for all y. In contrast, such a simple proof is not possible in the general case.

(c) *An Urn Model.* Consider the urn scheme of Example (i), Section 1, where the urn contains n red balls and m green balls at stage 0. As before, X_k, the fraction of red balls in the urn at stage $k=0,1,\ldots$, determines a bounded martingale, so that $X_\infty=\lim_{k\to\infty}X_k$ exists with probability one.

The limit random variable X_∞ has a Beta distribution. We will sketch the derivation. Let $Y_k=(n+m+k)X_k$ be the total number of red balls in the urn at stage k. A straightforward induction on k validates the formula

$$\Pr\{Y_k=i\}=\frac{\binom{i-1}{n-1}\binom{N-i-1}{m-1}}{\binom{N-1}{n+m-1}},\qquad n\le i\le n+k,\qquad N=n+m+k.$$

Use Stirling's approximation $M!\sim e^{-M}M^M(2\pi M)^{1/2}$ to show that $\binom{M}{j}\sim(M-j)^j/j!$ for M large and j fixed. Then

$$\begin{aligned}\Pr\{X_k\le x\}&=\Pr\{Y_k\le Nx\}\\&=\sum_{i=0}^{[Nx]}\binom{i-1}{n-1}\binom{N-i-1}{m-1}\Big/\binom{N-1}{n+m-1}\\&\cong\frac{(n+m-1)!}{(n-1)!\,(m-1)!}\sum_{i=0}^{[Nx]}\left(\frac{i-n}{k}\right)^{n-1}\left(\frac{k-i+n}{k}\right)^{m-1}\frac{1}{k}\\&=\frac{\Gamma(m+n)}{\Gamma(m)\Gamma(n)}\sum_{i/k=0}^{[Nx]/k}\left(\frac{i}{k}-\frac{n}{k}\right)^{n-1}\left(1-\frac{i}{k}+\frac{n}{k}\right)^{m-1}\Delta\!\left(\frac{i}{k}\right),\end{aligned}$$

where $\Delta(i/k) = (i+1)/k - i/k = 1/k$. When N and k are large, n/k becomes negligible, and the sum is approximated by the integral in which $z = i/k$, $dz \approx \Delta(i/k)$, and $[Nx]/k \sim x$. Thus, as $k \to \infty$,

$$\Pr\{X_k \le x\} \to \frac{\Gamma(m+n)}{\Gamma(m)\Gamma(n)} \int_0^x z^{n-1}(1-z)^{m-1}\,dz$$

$$= \Pr\{X_\infty \le x\}, \qquad \text{for} \quad 0 \le x \le 1.$$

This is the Beta distribution, as asserted.

(d) *Branching Processes.* Example (f) of Section 1 indicated that $X_n = m^{-n}Y_n$ is a martingale, where $m < \infty$ is the mean of the offspring distribution of a branching process $\{Y_n\}$. The basic martingale convergence theorem, amplified by Remark 5.1, tells us that $X_\infty = \lim_{n\to\infty} X_n$ exists with probability one. Roughly speaking, Y_n behaves asymptotically like $X_\infty m^n$, and it is remarkable that the entire asymptotic behavior is captured in the single random variable X_∞.

In Chapter 8 we will show that whenever $m \le 1$, $Y_n \to 0$ with probability one. Since the possible values for Y_n are $\{0, 1, \ldots\}$, this means in almost every realization of the process, $Y_n = 0$ for sufficiently large n, and therefore

$$X_\infty = \lim_{n\to\infty} m^{-n} Y_n = 0.$$

Thus, here is a case in which

$$1 = E[m^{-n}Y_n] \ne E[X_\infty] = 0,$$

so that the sequence $X_n = m^{-n}Y_n$ cannot be uniformly integrable when $m \le 1$.

When $m > 1$, and the progeny distribution has a finite variance σ^2, from Section 2 of Chapter 8 we obtain the variance

$$\operatorname{Var}[Y_n] = \frac{\sigma^2}{m}\left(\frac{m^{2n} - m^n}{m-1}\right)$$

and use this to get

$$E[X_n^2] = \{\operatorname{Var}[Y_n] + (E[Y_n])^2\}/m^{2n}$$

$$= \frac{\sigma^2}{m}\left(\frac{1-m^{-n}}{m-1}\right) + 1$$

$$\le \frac{\sigma^2}{m(m-1)} + 1 \qquad \text{for all } n.$$

We see that the conditions for the martingale mean square convergence theorem are satisfied. Thus $1 = X_0 = E[X_\infty]$, and with positive probability X_∞ is strictly positive, and then $Y_n \sim X_\infty m^n$ which shows that Y_n asymptotically grows exponentially fast at rate m.

(e) *Split Times in Branching Processes.* Consider a population of particles having independent random lifetimes, at the end of which each particle splits into a random number of new particles that independently exhibit the same life behavior as the parent. Suppose specifically that the lifetimes are all independent exponentially distributed random variables with *the same parameter a.*

Let $X(t)$ be the number of particles in the population at time t. Let τ_n be the time of the nth split in the population ($\tau_0 = 0$). The random variable $\xi_n = X(\tau_n + 0) - X(\tau_n - 0)$ counts the number of progeny contributed at the nth split. Let

$$X(0) = 1$$
$$S_i = X(\tau_i) = X(\tau_i + 0) = \xi_1 + \cdots + \xi_i + 1,$$

and define $T_i = \tau_i - \tau_{i-1}$ as the time between the $(i-1)$th and ith splits. We claim that the sequence of random variables

$$Y_n = \sum_{i=1}^{n} \left(T_i - \frac{1}{aS_{i-1}}\right), \qquad n = 1, 2, \ldots,$$

is a martingale with respect to $\{(\tau_n, \xi_n)\}$. We need only check [cf. Example (b) of Section 1] that

$$E\left[T_n - \frac{1}{aS_{n-1}} \,\middle|\, \tau_0, \ldots, \tau_{n-1}, \xi_0, \ldots, \xi_{n-1}\right] = 0. \tag{6.3}$$

The memoryless character of the exponential distribution and the definitions involved imply that T_n is the minimum of S_{n-1} independent lifetimes, which are all exponentially distributed with parameter a, and thus T_n is itself exponentially distributed with parameter aS_{n-1} (cf. Elementary Problem 1, Chapter 4). Equation (6.3) immediately ensues from these considerations.

The next calculation also exploits the martingale character of the sum and the exponential distribution underlying each summand. We get $Y_0 = 0$, and then

$$\begin{aligned} E[Y_n^2] &= \sum_{k=1}^{n} E[(Y_k - Y_{k-1})^2] \qquad \text{(see Problem 3)} \\ &= \sum_{k=1}^{n} E\left[\left(T_k - \frac{1}{aS_{k-1}}\right)^2\right] \\ &= \sum_{k=1}^{n} E\left\{E\left[\left(T_k - \frac{1}{aS_{k-1}}\right)^2 \middle| S_{k-1}\right]\right\} \end{aligned}$$

$$= \sum_{k=1}^{n} E\left[\left(\frac{1}{aS_{k-1}}\right)^2\right]$$

$$\leq \frac{1}{a^2}\left\{1 + \sum_{k=1}^{\infty} \frac{1}{k^2} E\left[\left(\frac{k}{S_k}\right)^2\right]\right\}.$$

In a moment we will show that $E[(k/S_k)^2]$ is uniformly bounded, say by C, and then

$$E[Y_n^2] \leq a^{-2}\left[1 + C\sum_{k=1}^{\infty} k^{-2}\right] < \infty, \qquad n = 1, 2, \ldots,$$

obtains, thereby verifying the conditions of the martingale mean square convergence theorem.

To obtain the bound C, let $V_k = \tilde{\xi}_1 + \tilde{\xi}_2 + \cdots + \tilde{\xi}_k$, where

$$\tilde{\xi}_i = \begin{cases} 0, & \text{if } \xi_i = 0, \\ 1, & \text{if } \xi_i \geq 1. \end{cases}$$

Then V_k has a binomial distribution with parameters k and $p = \Pr\{\xi_i > 0\} > 0$, for which we know

$$E[s^{V_k}] = [1 - p + ps]^k, \qquad 0 \leq s \leq 1,$$

and $1 + V_k \leq S_k$, whence

$$E\left[\frac{k}{S_k}\right] \leq kE\left[\frac{1}{1 + V_k}\right]$$

$$= k \int_0^1 E[s^{V_k}]\, ds$$

$$= k \int_0^1 [1 - p + ps]^k\, ds$$

$$= [k/(k+1)][1 - (1-p)^{k+1}]/p$$

$$\leq p^{-1} < \infty.$$

Note also that for $0 < c \leq 1$,

$$E\left[\frac{k}{c + \xi_1 + \cdots + \xi_k}\right] \leq \frac{1}{c} E\left[\frac{k}{1 + \xi_1 + \cdots + \xi_k}\right]$$

$$\leq (cp)^{-1} < \infty.$$

Next, using the elementary inequality $(a+b)^2 \geq 4ab$, together with the independence of $\xi_1, \xi_2, \ldots$, we obtain

$$E\left[\left(\frac{2k}{S_{2k}}\right)^2\right] = E\left[\left\{\frac{2k}{(\frac{1}{2}+\xi_1+\cdots+\xi_k)+(\frac{1}{2}+\xi_{k+1}+\cdots+\xi_{2k})}\right\}^2\right]$$

$$\leq E\left[\frac{k}{\frac{1}{2}+\xi_1+\cdots+\xi_k}\cdot\frac{k}{\frac{1}{2}+\xi_{k+1}+\cdots+\xi_{2k}}\right]$$

$$\leq \left\{E\left[\frac{k}{\frac{1}{2}+\xi_1+\cdots+\xi_k}\right]\right\}^2 \leq \left(\frac{2}{p}\right)^2.$$

This bounds $E[(n/S_n)^2]$ when n is even. When n is odd,

$$E\left[\left(\frac{n+1}{S_{n+1}}\right)^2\right] \leq \left(\frac{n+1}{n}\right)^2 E\left[\left(\frac{n}{S_n}\right)^2\right]$$

$$\leq 4\left(\frac{2}{p}\right)^2.$$

Thus $E[(k/S_k)^2] \leq C$ for all k if we take $C = 16/p^2$.

We apply the martingale mean square convergence theorem to conclude $Y_\infty = \lim_{n\to\infty} Y_n$ exists, with probability one. Since $\sum_{i=1}^{n} T_i = \tau_n$,

$$\tau_n - a^{-1}\sum_{i=1}^{n} S_{i-1}^{-1} \to Y_\infty, \qquad \text{as} \quad n\to\infty. \tag{6.4}$$

Further consequences can be drawn after we analyze the behavior of the series $\sum_{i=1}^{n} 1/(S_{i-1})$. Let $\mu = E[\xi_i] > 0$. From the strong law of large numbers we know that

$$\frac{1}{n}S_n \to \mu, \qquad \text{as} \quad n\to\infty,$$

with probability one. We write

$$\frac{1}{\log n}\sum_{i=1}^{n}\frac{1}{S_{i-1}} = \frac{1}{\log n}\sum_{i=1}^{N}\frac{1}{S_{i-1}} + \frac{1}{\log n}\sum_{i=N}^{n-1}\frac{1}{i}\frac{i}{S_i}.$$

For any $\varepsilon > 0$ we choose N so large that $|i/S_i - \mu^{-1}| \leq \varepsilon$ for all $i \geq N$. On the other hand, for any fixed N, the first term on the right goes to zero as $n\to\infty$. These estimates lead to the result

$$\limsup_{n\to\infty}\frac{1}{\log n}\left|\sum_{i=1}^{n}\frac{1}{S_{i-1}} - \sum_{i=N}^{n}\frac{1}{\mu i}\right| \leq \varepsilon,$$

and since ε is arbitrary, we infer

$$\lim_{n\to\infty} \frac{1}{\log n} \sum_{i=1}^{n} \frac{1}{S_{i-1}} = \frac{1}{\mu}, \tag{6.5}$$

with probability one. Combining the limits (6.4) and (6.5) we find that

$$\tau_n - \frac{\log n}{a\mu} \to Y_\infty, \qquad \text{as} \quad n \to \infty.$$

Again, the limit is in the probability one sense. In contrast, it appears remarkable that

$$\tau_{2n} - \tau_n \cong (a\mu)^{-1} \log 2$$

is asymptotically constant.

(f) *Doob's Process.* We will show that Doob's process [Example (k) of Section 1] is uniformly integrable and thus satisfies the full conditions of the basic martingale convergence theorem. Let Z, Y_0, Y_1, ... be joint random variables with $E[|Z|] < \infty$. We have shown (see p. 246) that

$$X_n = E[Z | Y_0, \ldots, Y_n], \qquad n = 0, 1, \ldots,$$

determines a martingale satisfying

$$E[|X_n|] \leq E[|Z|], \qquad \text{for all} \quad n. \tag{6.6}$$

The maximal inequality for martingales yields that

$$\Pr\left\{\max_{0\leq k\leq n} |X_k| > \lambda\right\} \leq \lambda^{-1} E[|X_n|] \leq \lambda^{-1} E[|Z|],$$

and thus for $U = \sup_{k\geq 0} |X_k|$

$$\Pr\{U > \lambda\} \leq \lambda^{-1} E[|Z|].$$

What is important is that

$$\lim_{\lambda\to\infty} \Pr\{U > \lambda\} = 0, \tag{6.7}$$

establishing that U is a finite-valued random variable. Now as $N \to \infty$,

$$\begin{aligned} E[|Z|] &\geq E[|Z| I\{0 \leq U < N\}] \qquad \text{(concerning the notation } I\{\ \} \text{ see p. 279)} \\ &= \sum_{k=0}^{N-1} E[|Z| | k \leq U < k+1] \Pr\{k \leq U < k+1\} \\ &\to \sum_{k=0}^{\infty} E[|Z| | k \leq U < k+1] \Pr\{k \leq U < k+1\} \\ &= E[|Z|], \end{aligned}$$

implying that

$$\lim_{N\to\infty} E[|Z|I\{U \geq N\}] = 0. \tag{6.8}$$

We next verify the uniform integrability requirement of Remark 5.3. Consider

$$\begin{aligned} |E[X_n I\{|X_n| > c\}]| &\leq E[(I\{|X_n| > c\})(E[|Z||Y_0, \ldots, Y_n])] \\ &\leq E[|Z|I\{|X_n| > c\}] \\ &\leq E[|Z|I\{U > c\}] \to 0, \qquad \text{as} \quad c \to \infty, \end{aligned}$$

by (6.8). Thus, $\{X_n\}$ is uniformly integrable, and we may conclude that

$$\lim_{n\to\infty} X_n = X_\infty,$$

for some random variable X_∞. Moreover, the relations

$$E[X_\infty] = E[X_0]$$

and

$$E[|X_n - X_\infty|] \to 0, \qquad \text{as} \quad n \to \infty,$$

also prevail. It is correct that

$$X_\infty = E[Z|Y_0, Y_1, \ldots], \tag{6.9}$$

although the exact meaning of the conditional expectation in (6.9) is beyond our present scope. (See Section 7.)

For an application relevant to mathematical analysis, suppose W is a uniformly distributed random variable on $[0, 1)$, and define Y_n by

$$Y_n = k2^{-n}, \qquad \text{for} \quad k2^{-n} \leq W < (k+1)2^{-n}$$

As noted in Example (1) of Section 1, $Y_0, \ldots, Y_n$ determine the first n bits in the terminating binary expansion of W.

Let f be an arbitrary function defined on $[0, 1]$, for which

$$\int_0^1 |f(w)|\, dw < \infty.$$

Set $Z = f(W)$ and observe that

$$\begin{aligned} X_n &= E[Z|Y_0, \ldots, Y_n] \\ &= 2^n \int_{k/2^n}^{(k+1)/2^n} f(w)\, dw, \qquad \text{if} \quad k/2^n \leq W < (k+1)/2^n. \end{aligned}$$

From what we just proved about Doob's process, $\lim_{n\to\infty} X_n = X_\infty$ exists, and, since $Y_0, Y_1, Y_2, \ldots$ give the full binary expansion of W, it is natural to suppose

$$\begin{aligned} X_\infty &= E[Z \mid Y_0, Y_1, \ldots] \\ &= E[f(W) \mid W] \\ &= f(W). \end{aligned}$$

While this is well beyond our scope, it is indeed valid, provided one adds the qualification "with probability one." We have then shown, with probability one,

$$f(W) = \lim_{n\to\infty} f_n(W),$$

where

$$f_n(w) = 2^n \int_{k(w)/2^n}^{[k(w)+1]/2^n} f(z)\, dz,$$

in which $k(w)$ is determined uniquely by the inequalities

$$k(w)/2^n \leq w < [k(w)+1]/2^n.$$

Each approximating function f_n is a step function, constant on each interval $[k/2^n, (k+1)/2^n)$. Thus we have shown that an arbitrary integrable function f can be approximated by a sequence of step functions f_n in the sense that $f(w) = \lim_{n\to\infty} f_n(w)$ for "almost every" w, i.e., for every w in a set having probability one.

Finally the convergence $E[|f(W) - f_n(W)|] \to 0$ gives

$$\lim_{n\to\infty} \int_0^1 |f(z) - f_n(z)|\, dz = 0.$$

7: *Martingales with Respect to σ-Fields*

Until now we have always considered conditional expectations to be expectations computed under conditional distributions. This is mostly satisfactory for expressions of the form $E[X \mid Y_0, \ldots, Y_n]$, where $X, Y_0, \ldots, Y_n$ possess a joint continuous density or are jointly discrete random variables. However, the analysis extended to the more complex expressions like $E[X \mid Y_0, Y_1, \ldots]$ or $E[X \mid Y(u), 0 \leq u \leq t]$ becomes more delicate.

The alternative and more modern approach is to define and evaluate conditional expectation, not with respect to a finite family of random variables, as we have done so far, but with respect to certain collections, called σ-fields, of events. This suggests in a natural way a definition of a martingale with respect to a sequence of σ-fields. We will now sketch this formulation, so pervasive in contemporary writing.

REVIEW OF AXIOMATIC PROBABILITY THEORY

For the most part, this book has studied random variables only through their distributions. For example, at the very outset we considered a stochastic process $\{X(t); t \in T\}$ to be defined once all the finite-dimensional distributions

$$F(x_1, \dots, x_n, t_1, \dots, t_n) = \Pr\{X(t_1) \leq x_1, \dots, X(t_n) \leq x_n\}$$

were specified. A little more precision and structure is now needed.

Recall that the basic elements of probability theory are:

(1) The *sample space*, a set Ω whose elements ω correspond to the possible outcomes of an experiment;

(2) The *family of events*, a collection $\mathscr{F}$ of subsets A of Ω. We say that the event A *occurs* if the outcome ω of the experiment is an element of A; and

(3) The *probability measure*, a function P defined on $\mathscr{F}$ and satisfying

$$\text{(a)} \quad 0 = P[\varnothing] \leq P[A] \leq P[\Omega] = 1, \qquad \text{for } A \in \mathscr{F} \quad (\varnothing = \text{the empty set}),$$

$$\text{(b)} \quad P[A_1 \cup A_2] = P[A_1] + P[A_2] - P[A_1 \cap A_2], \quad \text{for } A_i \in \mathscr{F}, \quad i = 1, 2, \tag{7.1}$$

and

$$\text{(c)} \quad P\left[\bigcup_{n=1}^{\infty} A_n\right] = \sum_{n=1}^{\infty} P[A_n],$$

if $A_n \in \mathscr{F}$, are mutually disjoint ($A_i \cap A_j = \varnothing$, $i \neq j$).

The triple $(\Omega, \mathscr{F}, P)$ is called a *probability space*.

Example. When there are only a denumerable number of possible outcomes, say $\Omega = \{\omega_1, \omega_2, \dots\}$, we may take $\mathscr{F}$ to be the collection of all subsets of Ω. If $p_1, p_2, \dots$ are nonnegative numbers with $\sum_n p_n = 1$, the assignment

$$P[A] = \sum_{\omega_i \in A} p_i$$

determines a probability measure defined on $\mathscr{F}$.

It is not always desirable, consistent, or feasible to take the family of events as the collection of *all* subsets of Ω. Indeed, when Ω is non-denumerably infinite, it may not be possible to define a probability measure on the collection of all subsets maintaining the properties of (7.1). In whatever way we prescribe $\mathscr{F}$ such that (7.1a)–(7.1c) hold, the family of events $\mathscr{F}$ should satisfy

(a) $\varnothing \in \mathscr{F}, \Omega \in \mathscr{F}$;
(b) $A^c \in \mathscr{F}$, whenever $A \in \mathscr{F}$, where $A^c = \{\omega \in \Omega; \omega \notin A\}$ is the complement of A; and (7.2)
(c) $\bigcup_{n=1}^{\infty} A_n \in \mathscr{F}$, whenever $A_n \in \mathscr{F}$, $n = 1, 2, \ldots$.

A collection $\mathscr{F}$ of subsets of a set Ω satisfying (7.2a)–(7.2c) is called a *σ-field*. If $\mathscr{F}$ is a *σ-field*, then

$$\bigcap_{n=1}^{\infty} A_n = \left(\bigcup_{n=1}^{\infty} A_n^c\right)^c \in \mathscr{F},$$

whenever $A_n \in \mathscr{F}$, $n = 1, 2, \ldots$. Manifestly, as a consequence we find that finite unions and finite intersections of members of $\mathscr{F}$ are maintained in $\mathscr{F}$.

In this framework, a real random variable X is a real-valued function defined on Ω fulfilling certain "measurability" conditions given below. The distribution function of the random variable X is formally given by

$$\Pr\{a < X \le b\} = P[\{\omega : a < X(\omega) \le b\}]. \tag{7.3}$$

In words, the probability that the random variable X takes a value in $(a, b]$ is calculated as the probability of the set of outcomes ω for which $a < X(\omega) \le b$. If relation (7 3) is to have meaning, X cannot be an arbitrary function on Ω, but must satisfy the condition that

$$\{\omega : a < X(\omega) \le b\} \in \mathscr{F}, \qquad \text{for all real} \quad a < b,$$

since $\mathscr{F}$ embodies the only sets A for which $P[A]$ is defined. In fact, by exploiting the properties (7.2a)–(7.2c) of the σ-field $\mathscr{F}$, it is enough to require

$$\{\omega : X(\omega) \le x\} \in \mathscr{F}, \qquad \text{for all} \quad x.$$

Let $\mathscr{A}$ be any σ-field of subsets of Ω. We say that X is *measurable with respect to $\mathscr{A}$*, or more briefly $\mathscr{A}$-measurable, if

$$\{\omega : X(\omega) \le x\} \in \mathscr{A} \qquad \text{for all real} \quad x.$$

Thus, every real random variable is by definition $\mathscr{F}$-measurable. There may, in general, be smaller σ-fields with respect to which X is also measurable.

The σ-field *generated* by a random variable X is defined to be the smallest σ-field with respect to which X is measurable. It is denoted by $\mathscr{F}(X)$ and consists exactly of those sets A that are in every σ-field $\mathscr{A}$ for which X is $\mathscr{A}$-measurable. For example, if X has only denumerably many possible values $x_1, x_2, \ldots$ the sets

$$A_i = \{\omega : X(\omega) = x_i\} \qquad i = 1, 2, \ldots$$

form a countable *partition* of Ω, i.e.,

$$\Omega = \bigcup_{i=1}^{\infty} A_i,$$

and

$$A_i \cap A_j = \varnothing \qquad \text{if} \quad i \neq j,$$

and then $\mathscr{F}(X)$ includes precisely $\varnothing$, Ω, and every set that is the union of some of the A_i's.

Example. For the reader completely unfamiliar with this framework, the following simple example will help set the concepts. The experiment consists in tossing a nickel and a dime and observing "heads" or "tails." We take Ω to be

$$\Omega = \{(\mathrm{H, H}), (\mathrm{H, T}), (\mathrm{T, H}), (\mathrm{T, T})\},$$

where for example, (H, T) stand for the outcome "nickel = heads, and dime = tails." We will take the collection of all subsets of Ω as the family of events. Assuming each outcome in Ω to be equally likely, we arrive at the probability measure:

$A \in \mathscr{F}$	$P[A]$	$A \in \mathscr{F}$	$P[A]$
ϕ	0	Ω	1
{(H, H)}	$\frac{1}{4}$	{(H, T), (T, H), (T, T)}	$\frac{3}{4}$
{(H, T)}	$\frac{1}{4}$	{(H, H), (T, H), (T, T)}	$\frac{3}{4}$
{(T, H)}	$\frac{1}{4}$	{(H, H), (H, T), (T, T)}	$\frac{3}{4}$
{(T, T)}	$\frac{1}{4}$	{(H, H), (H, T), (T, H)}	$\frac{3}{4}$
{(H, H), (H, T)}	$\frac{1}{2}$	{(T, H), (T, T)}	$\frac{1}{2}$
{(H, H), (T, H)}	$\frac{1}{2}$	{(H, T), (T, T)}	$\frac{1}{2}$
{(H, H), (T, T)}	$\frac{1}{2}$	{(H, T), (T, H)}	$\frac{1}{2}$

The event "the nickel is heads" is {(H, H), (H, T)} and has, according to the table, probability $\frac{1}{2}$, as it should.

Let X_n be 1 if the nickel is heads, and 0 otherwise, let X_d be the corresponding random variable for the dime, and let $Z = X_n + X_d$ be the total number of heads. As functions on Ω, we have

$\omega \in \Omega$	$X_n(\omega)$	$X_d(\omega)$	$Z(\omega)$
(H, H)	1	1	2
(H, T)	1	0	1
(T, H)	0	1	1
(T, T)	0	0	0

Finally, the σ-fields generated by X_n and Z are:

$$\mathscr{F}(X_n) = \phi, \Omega, \{(\text{H}, \text{H}), (\text{H}, \text{T})\}, \{(\text{T}, \text{H}), (\text{T}, \text{T})\},$$

and

$$\begin{aligned}\mathscr{F}(Z) = \phi, \Omega, &\{(\text{H}, \text{H})\}, \{(\text{H}, \text{T}), (\text{T}, \text{H})\}, \{(\text{T}, \text{T})\},\\ &\{(\text{H}, \text{T}), (\text{T}, \text{H}), (\text{T}, \text{T})\}, \{(\text{H}, \text{H}), (\text{T}, \text{T})\},\\ &\{(\text{H}, \text{H}), (\text{H}, \text{T}), (\text{T}, \text{H})\}.\end{aligned}$$

$\mathscr{F}(X_n)$ contains 4 sets and $\mathscr{F}(Z)$ contains 8. Is X_n measurable with respect to $\mathscr{F}(Z)$, or vice versa?

Every pair X, Y of random variables determines a σ-field called the σ-field generated by X, Y. It is the smallest σ-field with respect to which both X and Y are measurable. This field comprises exactly those sets A that are in every σ-field $\mathscr{A}$ for which X and Y are both $\mathscr{A}$-measurable. If both X and Y assume only denumerably many possible values, say $x_1, x_2, \ldots$ and $y_1, y_2, \ldots$, respectively, then the sets

$$A_{ij} = \{\omega : X(\omega) = x_i,\ Y(\omega) = y_j\}, \qquad i, j = 1, 2, \ldots,$$

present a countable partition of Ω and $\mathscr{F}(X, Y)$ consists precisely of ϕ, Ω, and every set that is the union of some of the A_{ij}'s. Observe that X is measurable with respect to $\mathscr{F}(X, Y)$, and thus $\mathscr{F}(X) \subset \mathscr{F}(X, Y)$.

More generally, let $\{X(t); t \in T\}$ be any family of random variables. Then the σ-field generated by $\{X(t); t \in T\}$ is the smallest σ-field with respect to which every random variable $X(t)$, $t \in T$, is measurable. It is denoted by $\mathscr{F}\{X(t); t \in T\}$.

A special role is played by a distinguished σ-field of sets of real numbers. The σ-field of *Borel sets* is the σ-field generated by the identity function $f(x) = x$, for $x \in (-\infty, \infty)$. Alternatively, the σ-field of Borel sets is the smallest σ-field containing every interval of the form $(a, b]$, $-\infty \le a \le b < +\infty$. A real-valued function of a real variable is said to be *Borel measurable* if it is measurable with respect to the σ-field of Borel sets.

In n-dimensional Euclidean space, the σ-field of Borel sets is the σ-field generated by the set of functions

$$\{f_i(x_1, \ldots, x_n) = x_i;\ i = 1, \ldots, n\}.$$

CONDITIONAL EXPECTATION WITH RESPECT TO A σ-FIELD

While every random variable Y generates a σ-field $\mathscr{F}(Y)$, it is not true that every σ-field arises in this manner. Thus, the concept of conditional expectation with respect to a σ-field, our next topic, is a strict extension of the concept of conditional expectation with respect to random variables.

We begin with the formal definition.

Definition 7.1. *Let X be a random variable on a probability space $(\Omega, \mathscr{F}, P)$ for which $E[|X|] < \infty$. Let $\mathscr{B}$ be a σ-field contained in $\mathscr{F}$, i.e., every set $B \in \mathscr{B}$ is also a member of $\mathscr{F}$. The conditional expectation of X with respect to $\mathscr{B}$ is defined to be any random variable $E[X|\mathscr{B}]$ having the properties:*

(i) *$E[X|\mathscr{B}]$ is a measurable function with respect to $\mathscr{B}$; and*

(ii) *$E[XI_B] = E\{E[X|\mathscr{B}]I_B\}$, for all $B \in \mathscr{B}$, where I_B is the indicator function for the event B. Alternatively,* (ii) *may be replaced by the equivalent*

(ii′) *$E[XZ] = E\{E[X|\mathscr{B}]Z\}$ for every bounded random variable Z that is $\mathscr{B}$-measurable.*

Several remarks are in order. First, it can be shown that a random variable $E[X|\mathscr{B}]$ satisfying (i) and (ii) exists whenever $E[|X|] < \infty$, so that the definition is nonvoid. In fact, a meaningful definition results as long as not both $E[X^+]$ and $E[X^-]$ are infinite. On the other hand, the definition is ambiguous in that there may be more than one conditional expectation $E[X|\mathscr{B}]$ satisfying (i) and (ii). Thus we speak of different "versions" of the conditional expectation. Fortunately, any two versions are equal, with probability one. That is, if $E^{(1)}[X|\mathscr{B}]$ and $E^{(2)}[X|\mathscr{B}]$ satisfy (i) and (ii), then

$$P\{E^{(1)}[X|\mathscr{B}] = E^{(2)}[X|\mathscr{B}]\} = 1.$$

Thus, in probability terms, the ambiguity causes no difficulty. Finally, let us mention the equivalence of (ii) and (ii′). Clearly (ii′) implies (ii), since we may always take Z to be the bounded $\mathscr{B}$-measurable function

$$Z(\omega) = I_B(\omega) = \begin{cases} 1, & \text{if } \omega \in B, \\ 0, & \text{if } \omega \notin B. \end{cases}$$

The converse implication is validated by suitably approximating an arbitrary Z by step functions of the form

$$Z_n(\omega) = \sum_{i=1}^{n} \alpha_{in} 1_{B_i}(\omega),$$

where $\{B_1, \ldots, B_n\}$ is a finite partition of Ω with $B_i \in \mathscr{B}$. Then (ii′) holds for such Z_n, and by passing to the limit, we can infer (ii′) for arbitrary bounded $\mathscr{B}$-measurable random variables.

In Chapter 1 we expressed the conditional expectation of X given a random variable $Y = y$ as

(I) Any function $E[X|Y=y]$ of y which satisfies

(II) $E[Xg(Y)] = \int E[X|Y=y]g(y)\,dF_Y(y)$, for every bounded function g.

One would hope that our current definition extends the earlier one, that is, coincides with it when $\mathscr{B} = \mathscr{F}(Y)$ is the σ-field generated by the random variable Y. This is indeed the case. One can show that a random variable Z is measurable with respect to $\mathscr{B} = \mathscr{F}(Y)$ if and only if one can write $Z = f(Y)$ for some Borel measurable function f. (Problem 13 asks for a proof of this statement when $\mathscr{B}$ is the σ-field of unions of some countable partition $\mathscr{B}_0$.) Then (I) states that $E[X|Y]$ is measurable with respect to $\mathscr{B} = \mathscr{F}(Y)$ and (II) yields (ii′), $E[XZ] = E\{E[X|Y]Z\}$ for all bounded $Z = f(Y)$. Thereby, Definition 7.1 extends the concept of conditional expectation with respect to a random variable.

Last, let us work out what Definition 7.1 means in the case that $\Omega = \{\omega_1, \omega_2, \ldots\}$ is denumerable, $\mathscr{F}$ consists of all subsets of Ω, and P is evaluated by the formula

$$P[A] = \sum_{\omega_i \in A} p_i, \qquad A \in \mathscr{F}, \tag{7.4}$$

where $p_1, p_2, \ldots$ are nonnegative numbers summing to one. The expectation of a random variable X is defined by

$$E[X] = \sum_{j=1}^{\infty} X(\omega_j)p_j,$$

provided the sum converges absolutely. Let $\mathscr{B}_0 = \{B_1, B_2, \ldots\}$ be a denumerable partition of Ω, and let $\mathscr{B}$ be the σ-field consisting of ϕ, Ω and all possible unions of sets in $\mathscr{B}_0$. For each B_j in $\mathscr{B}_0$, define the elementary conditional expectation

$$E[X|B_j] = \sum_{\omega_k \in B_j} X(\omega_k)P[\{\omega_k\}|B_j],$$

where

$$P[A|B_j] = P[A \cap B_j]/P[B_j], \qquad A \in \mathscr{F}. \tag{7.5}$$

The definition breaks down when $P[B_j]=0$, since then the right-hand side of (7.5) is 0/0. Arbitrarily set $E[X|B_j]=17$ whenever $P[B_j]=0$, which completes the definition and, incidentally, indicates where the lack of uniqueness in Definition 7.1 arises. The next step is to make the collection of numbers $E[X|B_j]_{j=1}^{\infty}$ into a random variable $E[X|\mathscr{B}]$ by the formula

$$\begin{aligned} E[X|\mathscr{B}](\omega) &= E[X|B_j], \qquad \text{if} \quad \omega \in B_j, \\ &= \sum_{j=1}^{\infty} E[X|B_j] I_{B_j}(\omega), \end{aligned}$$

where

$$I_{B_j}(\omega) = \begin{cases} 1, & \text{if} \quad \omega \in B_j, \\ 0, & \text{if} \quad \omega \notin B_j. \end{cases}$$

Then, the random variable $E[X|\mathscr{B}]$, being constant on each of the sets B_j, is $\mathscr{B}$-measurable. We check (ii) of Definition 7.1. Let $B \in \mathscr{B}$ be prescribed, say $B = \bigcup_{n=1}^{\infty} B_n'$, where $B_n' \in \mathscr{B}_0$, $n=1, 2 \ldots$. On the one hand,

$$E[XI_B] = \sum_{n=1}^{\infty} \sum_{\omega_k \in B_n'} X(\omega_k) p_k,$$

while at the same time,

$$\begin{aligned} E\{E[X|\mathscr{B}]I_B\} &= \sum_{n=1}^{\infty} E[X|B_n'] P[B_n'] \\ &= \sum_{n=1}^{\infty} \sum_{\omega_k \in B_n'} X(\omega_k) p_k. \end{aligned}$$

The equality of the two right-hand sides verifies (ii).

Let us show that the elementary definition for $E[X|B_j]$ can be recovered from Definition 7.1 by taking $B=B_j$, provided $P[B_j]>0$. Then (ii) becomes

$$\sum_{\omega_k \in B_j} X(\omega_k) p_k = \sum_{\omega_k \in B_j} E[X|\mathscr{B}](\omega_k) p_k. \tag{7.6}$$

Now $E[X|\mathscr{B}]$ is $\mathscr{B}$-measurable if and only if it has a constant value, say a_j, on each of the sets B_j. Then (7.6) becomes

$$\sum_{\omega_k \in B_j} X(\omega_k) p_k = a_j P[B_j],$$

and the constant value a_j must be

$$\begin{aligned} a_j &= \sum_{\omega_k \in B_j} X(\omega_k) p_k / P[B_j] \\ &= E[X|B_j], \end{aligned}$$

whenever $P[B_j]>0$.

Thus, one can recover our intuitive concept of conditional expectation from Definition 7.1 whenever $\mathscr{B}$ is the σ-field of unions of a countable partition $\mathscr{B}_0$.

The definition of conditional expectation given a random variable was expectation computed under a conditional distribution. Conditional expectations with respect to σ-fields inherit most of the familiar properties, provided we interpret "equal" as meaning "equal with probability one." For reference, we list some of these properties, corresponding to (1.6), (1.7), and (1.10)–(1.14) of Chapter 1. There is no satisfactory analog of (1.8). We suppose X, X_1, and X_2 are random variables having finite expectations, a_1, a_2 real numbers, and $\mathscr{A}$ and $\mathscr{B}$ are sub-σ-fields of $\mathscr{F}$. Then

$$E[a_1X_1 + a_2X_2|\mathscr{B}] = a_1E[X_1|\mathscr{B}] + a_2E[X_2|\mathscr{B}]; \tag{7.7}$$

$$X \geq 0 \quad \text{implies} \quad E[X|\mathscr{B}] \geq 0; \tag{7.8}$$

$$E[XZ|\mathscr{B}] = ZE[X|\mathscr{B}], \quad \text{for every bounded } \mathscr{B}\text{-measurable } Z; \tag{7.9}$$

$$E[XZ] = E\{Z \cdot E[X|\mathscr{B}]\}, \quad \text{for every bounded } \mathscr{B}\text{-measurable } Z; \tag{7.10}$$

$$E[Z|\mathscr{B}] = Z, \quad \text{for every } \mathscr{B}\text{-measurable } Z \text{ satisfying } E[|Z|] < \infty; \tag{7.11}$$

$$E[X|\mathscr{A}] = E\{E[X|\mathscr{B}]|\mathscr{A}\}, \quad \text{if } \mathscr{A} \subset \mathscr{B}; \tag{7.12}$$

$$E[X] = E\{E[X|\mathscr{B}]\} \quad \text{(the law of total probability)}. \tag{7.13}$$

The style of proof used in validating these properties is typified by examining (7.7). We show that $a_1E[X_1|\mathscr{B}] + a_2E[X_2|\mathscr{B}]$ satisfies the defining conditions for $E[a_1X_1 + a_2X_2|\mathscr{B}]$. First, it can be checked that a linear combination of two $\mathscr{B}$-measurable random variables is also $\mathscr{B}$-measurable. (Problem 14 requests a proof of this statement, where $\mathscr{B}$ is the σ-fields of unions of a countable partition $\mathscr{B}_0$.) Thus, $a_1E[X_1|\mathscr{B}] + a_2E[X_2|\mathscr{B}]$ satisfies stipulation (i) of Definition 7.1. Substitute $a_1E[X_1|\mathscr{B}] + a_2E[X_2|\mathscr{B}]$ into what is required, for $E[a_1X_1 + a_2X_2|\mathscr{B}]$ in condition (ii′) and see if it is satisfied. Consider any bounded $\mathscr{B}$-measurable Z. The justification of the succeeding steps is routine:

$$\begin{aligned} E[\{a_1X_1 + a_2X_2\}Z] &= a_1E[X_1Z] + a_2E[X_2Z] \\ &= a_1E\{E[X_1|\mathscr{B}]Z\} + a_2E\{E[X_2|\mathscr{B}]Z\} \\ &= E\{(a_1E[X_1|\mathscr{B}] + a_2E[X_2|\mathscr{B}])Z\}. \end{aligned}$$

This completes the validation of (7.7).

MARTINGALES WITH RESPECT TO AN INCREASING FAMILY OF σ-FIELDS

Let $\{X_n\}_0^\infty$ be a sequence of real random variables on a probability space $(\Omega, \mathscr{F}, P)$. Let $\{\mathscr{F}_n\}$ be a sequence of sub-σ-fields of $\mathscr{F}$ with

$$\mathscr{F}_0 \subset \mathscr{F}_1 \cdots \subset \mathscr{F}_n \subset \cdots \subset \mathscr{F}.$$

We say that $\{X_n\}$ is adapted to $\{\mathscr{F}_n\}$ if, for every n, *X_n is $\mathscr{F}_n$-measurable.* For example, suppose $Y_0, Y_1, \ldots$ are also defined on $(\Omega, \mathscr{F}, P)$ and $\mathscr{F}_n$ is the σ-field generated by $\{Y_0, Y_1, \ldots, Y_n\}$. Then

$$\mathscr{F}_n \subset \mathscr{F}_{n+1} \subset \mathscr{F}, \qquad \text{for all} \quad n,$$

and if $X_n = g_n(Y_0, \ldots, Y_n)$ for a sequence of Borel measurable functions $g_n(\cdot, \ldots, \cdot)$, then $\{X_n\}$ is adapted to $\{\mathscr{F}_n\}$.

We again think of $\mathscr{F}_n$ as containing the information available at stage n, just as we did earlier with $(Y_0, \ldots, Y_n)$. Then X_n is measurable with respect to $\mathscr{F}_n = \mathscr{F}(Y_0, \ldots, Y_n)$ if and only if, in our earlier usage, X_n is *determined* by $(Y_0, \ldots, Y_n)$.

The relation $\mathscr{F}_n \subset \mathscr{F}_{n+1}$ expresses the increase in information as n progresses.

Definition 7.2. *Let $\{X_n\}$ be a sequence of random variables defined on a probability space $(\Omega, \mathscr{F}, P)$. Let $\{\mathscr{F}_n\}$ be a sequence of sub-σ-fields of $\mathscr{F}$ with*

$$\mathscr{F}_n \subset \mathscr{F}_{n+1} \subset \mathscr{F}, \qquad \textit{for all} \quad n.$$

Then $\{X_n\}$ is called a submartingale with respect to $\{\mathscr{F}_n\}$ if:

(i) *$\{X_n\}$ is adapted to $\{\mathscr{F}_n\}$ (that is each X_n is $\mathscr{F}_n$-measurable),*
(ii) *$E[X_n^+] < \infty$, for all n, and*
(iii) *$E[X_{n+1} | \mathscr{F}_n] \geq X_n$, for all n.*

If $\{-X_n\}$ is a submartingale, then $\{X_n\}$ is called a supermartingale. If both $\{X_n\}$ and $\{-X_n\}$ are submartingales, then $\{X_n\}$ is called a martingale with respect to $\{\mathscr{F}_n\}$.

A few remarks may be helpful. If $\{X_n\}$ is a martingale, then

$$X_n = E[X_{n+1} | \mathscr{F}_n]. \tag{7.14}$$

The right-hand side, and hence the left, is $\mathscr{F}_n$-measurable by the definition of conditional expectation. Hence the representation (7.14) implies (i) for a martingale. Requirement (iii) can be stated in an equivalent form by using the properties of conditional expectation. We get

(iii′) $E[X_{n+1} Z] \geq E[X_n Z]$, for all bounded $\mathscr{F}_n$-measurable $Z \geq 0$.

To infer (iii′) from (iii), use the definition of conditional expectation with respect to σ-fields and properties (7.7) and (7.8) to obtain

$$E[X_{n+1}Z] = E\{E[X_{n+1}|\mathscr{F}_n]Z\} \geq E[X_n Z].$$

To deduce (iii) from (iii′), use

$$E\{E[X_{n+1}|\mathscr{F}_n]Z\} = E[X_{n+1}Z]$$

to obtain

$$E\{(E[X_{n+1}|\mathscr{F}_n] - X_n)Z\} \geq 0, \qquad \text{for all bounded } \mathscr{F}_n\text{-measurable } Z \geq 0.$$

Now $Y = E[X_{n+1}|\mathscr{F}_n] - X_n$ is $\mathscr{F}_n$-measurable, and if $E[YZ] \geq 0$ for all bounded $\mathscr{F}_n$-measurable $Z \geq 0$, then $Y \geq 0$. (Problem 15 asks for a verification of this statement, where $\mathscr{B}$ is the σ-field consisting of unions of sets in a denumerable partition $\mathscr{B}_0$.) Of course, the relation

$$Y = E[X_{n+1}|\mathscr{F}_n] - X_n \geq 0$$

is the desired (iii).

All of the results concerning martingales with respect to random variables that were developed earlier in this chapter carry over to martingales with respect to increasing σ-fields, with only technical modifications required. More explicitly, once we produce a definition for a Markov time with respect to a sequence of σ-fields, the optional sampling theorems and the martingale convergence theorems will persist. We will not repeat the entire development, but only the early part of it in the martingale case, and this mainly for the pedagogical practice it provides in manipulating conditional expectations with respect to σ-fields.

Proposition 7.1. *Let $\{X_n\}$ be a martingale with respect to $\{\mathscr{F}_n\}$. Then $E[X_n] = E[X_0]$ for all n.*

Proof. Applying the law of total probability (7.13) in the form $E[X] = E\{E[X|\mathscr{B}]\}$ to the martingale equality $X_n = E[X_{n+1}|\mathscr{F}_n]$, we obtain

$$\begin{aligned} E[X_n] &= E\{E[X_{n+1}|\mathscr{F}_n]\} \\ &= E[X_{n+1}]. \end{aligned}$$

An induction completes the proof. ■

Proposition 7.2. *Let $\{X_n\}$ be a martingale with respect to $\{\mathscr{F}_n\}$. If Z is a bounded $\mathscr{F}_n$-measurable random variable, then*

$$E[ZX_{n+k}|\mathscr{F}_n] = ZX_n, \qquad n = 0, 1, \ldots; \qquad k \geq 1$$

Proof. We appeal to property (7.9),

$$E[ZX_{n+k}|\mathscr{F}_n] = ZE[X_{n+k}|\mathscr{F}_n], \text{ for } \quad Z \text{ bounded and } \mathscr{F}_n\text{-measurable.} \tag{7.15}$$

Now on the basis of (7.12), we obtain

$$\begin{aligned} E[X_{n+k}|\mathscr{F}_n] &= E\{E[X_{n+k}|\mathscr{F}_{n+k-1}]|\mathscr{F}_n\} \\ &= E[X_{n+k-1}|\mathscr{F}_n], \end{aligned}$$

which continues by induction until

$$E[X_{n+k}|\mathscr{F}_n] = E[X_{n+1}|\mathscr{F}_n] = X_n.$$

This together with (7.15) completes the proof. ∎

Let $\{\mathscr{F}_n\}$ be a sequence of sub-σ-fields of $\mathscr{F}$ satisfying $\mathscr{F}_n \subset \mathscr{F}_{n+1} \subset \mathscr{F}$, for all n. *A random variable T taking values in* $\{0, 1, \ldots, \infty\}$ is called a *Markov time* with respect to $\{\mathscr{F}_n\}$, if for every $n = 0, 1, 2, \ldots$, the event $\{T = n\}$ is in $\mathscr{F}_n$. Recall that every random variable is a function defined on the sample space Ω. Thus we require

$$\{\omega : T(\omega) = n\} \in \mathscr{F}_n, \qquad \text{for all} \quad n. \tag{7.16}$$

Alternatively, using the facts that each $\mathscr{F}_n$ is a σ-field and $\mathscr{F}_n \subset \mathscr{F}_{n+1}$ for all n, requirement (7.16) may be replaced by either of the equivalent conditions

$$\{\omega : T(\omega) \le n\} \in \mathscr{F}_n, \qquad \text{for all} \quad n, \tag{7.17}$$

or

$$\{\omega : T(\omega) > n\} \in \mathscr{F}_n, \qquad \text{for all} \quad n. \tag{7.18}$$

For example, to conclude (7.17) from (7.16), observe

$$\{\omega;\ T(\omega) \le n\} = \bigcup_{k=0}^{n} \{\omega;\ T(\omega) = k\}.$$

Now each $\{\omega : T(\omega) = k\} \in \mathscr{F}_k \subset \mathscr{F}_n$, so the union belongs to $\mathscr{F}_n$, and (7.17) is satisfied.

Alternatively, we can require that every indicator random variable

$$I_{\{T=n\}} = \begin{cases} 1, & \text{if} \quad T = n, \\ 0 & \text{if} \quad T \ne n, \end{cases}$$

be measurable with respect to $\mathscr{F}_n$.

If $\mathscr{F}_n = \mathscr{F}(Y_0, Y_1, \ldots, Y_n)$ is the σ-field generated by the random variables $Y_0, \ldots, Y_n$, then $I_{\{T=n\}}$ is measurable with respect to $\mathscr{F}_n$ if and only if

$$I_{\{T=n\}} = g_n(Y_0, \ldots, Y_n),$$

for some appropriately measurable function $g_n(\cdot, \ldots, \cdot)$. Thus, the latest definition of Markov time is an extension of the earlier one.

Every constant $T \equiv n$ is a Markov time. If T and S are Markov times, so are $T+S$, $T \wedge S = \min\{T, S\}$, and $T \vee S = \max\{T, S\}$. A sample proof is

$$\{\omega : T \wedge S > n\} = \{\omega : T > n\} \cap \{\omega : S > n\} \in \mathscr{F}_n.$$

Lemma 7.1. *Let $\{X_n\}$ be a martingale and T a Markov time with respect to $\{\mathscr{F}_n\}$. Then for all $n \geq k$,*

$$E[X_n I_{\{T=k\}}] = E[X_k I_{\{T=k\}}].$$

($I_{\{\cdot\}}$ is the indicator function of the event described in $\{\cdot\}$.)

Proof. We use the fact that $I_{\{T=k\}}$ is $\mathscr{F}_k$-measurable. Then,

$$\begin{aligned} E[X_n I_{\{T=k\}}] &= E\{E[X_n I_{\{T=k\}} | \mathscr{F}_k]\} && \text{(by the law of total probability)} \\ &= E\{I_{\{T=k\}} E[X_n | \mathscr{F}_k]\} && \text{[by (7.10)]} \\ &= E[X_k I_{\{T=k\}}]. \quad \blacksquare \end{aligned}$$

From this point on, the study of martingales with respect to σ-fields paraphrases that carried out in Sections 1–6, for example, as in the following lemma.

Lemma 7.2. *Let $\{X_n\}$ be a martingale and T a Markov time with respect to $\{\mathscr{F}_n\}$. Then for all $n = 0, 1, \ldots,$*

$$E[X_0] = E[X_{T \wedge n}] = E[X_n].$$

Proof. As in Lemma 3.2, mutatis mutandis, relying on Lemma 7.1 rather than Lemma 3.1. $\blacksquare$

The crossings inequality, maximal inequality, optional sampling theorems, and martingale convergence theorems all follow from Lemma 7.2 *just as they did earlier from Lemma* 3.2. We proceed to an example.

Example. Let $\{Y_n\}$ be random variables on some probability space $(\Omega, \mathscr{F}, P)$, and for each n let $\mathscr{F}_n$ be the σ-field generated by $(Y_0, \ldots, Y_n)$. If Z satisfies $E[|Z|] < \infty$, we pointed out in Example (k) of Section 1 that

$$X_n = E[Z | \mathscr{F}_n], \qquad n = 0, 1, \ldots,$$

constitutes a martingale, and we established in Example (f) of Section 6 that this martingale was uniformly integrable. The martingale convergence theorem affirms that

$$\lim_{n\to\infty} X_n = X_\infty$$

exists, with probability one and, moreover,

$$\lim_{n\to\infty} E[|X_n - X_\infty|] = 0$$

holds. We mentioned that X_∞ could be represented as

$$X_\infty = E[Z|Y_0, Y_1, \ldots].$$

Now interpreting the right-hand side as an expectation of Z under a conditional distribution is rather delicate. However, if we prescribe $\mathscr{F}_\infty$ as the σ-field generated by $(Y_0, Y_1, \ldots)$ it is not hard to motivate the formula

$$X_\infty = E[Z|\mathscr{F}_\infty].$$

In accordance with Definition 7.1, we need to show first that X_∞ is $\mathscr{F}_\infty$-measurable and second that for every bounded $\mathscr{F}_\infty$-measurable random variable W, the equation

$$E[X_\infty W] = E[ZW] \tag{7.19}$$

obtains. Each X_n is $\mathscr{F}_n$-measurable, and hence $\mathscr{F}_\infty$-measurable, since $\mathscr{F}_n \subset \mathscr{F}_\infty$ for all n. It follows that $X_\infty = \lim_{n\to\infty} X_n$ is $\mathscr{F}_\infty$-measurable. Another way to view this is that each $X_n = E[Z|Y_0, \ldots, Y_n]$ is a function of $Y_0, \ldots, Y_n$, so that $X_\infty = \lim X_n$ is an appropriately measurable function of the entire sequence $Y_0, Y_1, \ldots$, and hence measurable with respect to $\mathscr{F}_\infty$.

To prove (7.19), it suffices to consider a bounded $\mathscr{F}_m$-measurable W_m for arbitary m. The general case follows by suitably approximating the $\mathscr{F}_\infty$-measurable W by random variables W_m with m increasing. But if W_m is $\mathscr{F}_m$-measurable,

$$\begin{aligned} E[X_n W_m] &= E\{E[Z|\mathscr{F}_n]W_m\} \\ &= E\{E[ZW_m|\mathscr{F}_n]\} \text{ if } n \geq m \qquad &&\text{(since } W_m \text{ is } \mathscr{F}_m \subset \mathscr{F}_n \text{ measurable)} \\ &= E[ZW_m] &&\text{(by the law of total probabilities).} \end{aligned}$$

Passing to the limit with n yields

$$E[X_\infty W_m] = \lim_{n\to\infty} E[X_n W_m] = E[ZW_m],$$

and (7.19) is proved.

We pause in the example to bring out an observation. Since $X_\infty = \lim_{n\to\infty} X_n$ is $\mathscr{F}_\infty$-measurable, we know from (7.11)

$$X_\infty = E[X_\infty | \mathscr{F}_\infty].$$

On the other hand, we have just validated the representation

$$X_\infty = E[Z | \mathscr{F}_\infty],$$

and by virtue of property (7.12) and the fact of $\mathscr{F}_n \subset \mathscr{F}_\infty$, we have

$$\begin{aligned} X_n &= E[Z | \mathscr{F}_n] \\ &= E\{E[Z | \mathscr{F}_\infty] | \mathscr{F}_n\} \\ &= E[X_\infty | \mathscr{F}_n]. \end{aligned}$$

That is, $X_n = E[X_\infty | \mathscr{F}_n]$, where $X_\infty = \lim_{n\to\infty} X_n$. That this is correct for every uniformly integrable martingale is worth highlighting as a lemma.

Lemma 7.3. *Let $\{X_n\}$ be a uniformly integrable martingale (see p. 258) with respect to $\{\mathscr{F}_n)$. Then*

$$X_n = E[X_\infty | \mathscr{F}_n]$$

where

$$X_\infty = \lim_{n\to\infty} X_n.$$

Proof. The basic martingale convergence theorem guarantees the existence of $X_\infty = \lim_{n\to\infty} X_n$ and the fact of

$$\lim_{n\to\infty} E[|X_n - X_\infty|] = 0 \tag{7.20}$$

We now show that X_n possesses the properties required of $E[X_\infty | \mathscr{F}_n]$ in line with Definition 7.1. Note, first, since $\{X_n\}$ is a martingale that X_n is $\mathscr{F}_n$-measurable. Let W be a bounded $\mathscr{F}_n$-measurable random variable. Then

$$\begin{aligned} E[X_\infty W] &= E\left[\lim_{m\to\infty} X_m W\right] \\ &= \lim_{m\to\infty} E[X_m W] \qquad \text{(the justification of interchange of limit and expectation is given below)} \\ &= E[X_n W]. \end{aligned}$$

That is, X_n satisfies the requirements for $E[X_\infty|\mathscr{F}_n]$. The interchange of limits is legitimate in view of the inequalities

$$\begin{aligned}|E[X_\infty W]-E[X_n W]| &\le E[|X_\infty W - X_n W|]\\ &\le AE[|X_n - X_\infty|],\end{aligned}$$

where $A<\infty$ is such that $|W|\le A$, and now appeal to (7.20). ■

We have established the important result that *every* uniformly integrable martingale $\{X_n\}$ has the form of a Doob's process $X_n = E[Z|\mathscr{F}_n]$ for $Z = X_\infty = \lim_{n\to\infty} X_n$.

An Application to Mathematical Analysis. Let f be a real-valued function on $[0, 1]$ that is Lipschitz continuous, i.e., f satisfies

$$|f(x)-f(y)|\le C|x-y|, \qquad \text{for all} \quad x, y\in[0, 1],$$

where $C<\infty$ is a constant. For $n = 1, 2, \ldots$, specify $\mathscr{P}_n$ as the partition of $[0, 1)$ given by

$$\mathscr{P}_n = \{[k/2^n, [k+1]/2^n);\ k=0, \ldots, 2^n-1\}.$$

Determine $\mathscr{F}_n$ as the σ-field consisting of ϕ, $\Omega=[0, 1)$ and unions of sets in $\mathscr{P}_n$.

Let Z have a uniform distribution on $[0, 1)$ and define the sequence

$$X_n = 2^n\{f(k/2^n)-f((k-1)/2^n)\}, \qquad \text{if} \quad (k-1)/2^n\le Z<k/2^n.$$

Then $\{X_n\}$ is a martingale with respect to $\{\mathscr{F}_n\}$. In fact, $\mathscr{F}_n$ is the σ-field generated by $Y_0, \ldots, Y_n$, where

$$Y_n = k/2^n, \qquad \text{for } k \text{ satisfying} \quad k/2^n\le Z<(k+1)/2^n,$$

and we verified the martingale property in Example (l) of Section 1.

Observe that X_n is approximately the derivative of f at the (randomly chosen) point Z. Of course, f may not be differentiable, but being Lipschitz continuous, $|X_n|\le C$ for all n, hence $\{X_n\}$ is uniformly integrable, and consequently

$$X_\infty = \lim_{n\to\infty} X_n$$

exists for a set of $Z\in[0, 1)$ having probability one. By Lemma 7.3, we have

$$X_n = E[X_\infty|\mathscr{F}_n]. \tag{7.21}$$

We make explicit the fact that X_∞ is some function g of the random variable Z, by writing $X_\infty = g(Z)$.

Take $B = [0, k/2^n) \in \mathscr{F}_n$. Then from (7.21),

$$\begin{aligned} E[X_n I_B] &= f(k/2^n) - f(0) \\ &= E[X_\infty I_B] \\ &= \int_0^{k/2^n} g(x)\, dx. \end{aligned}$$

By passing to the limit in a sequence of binary rationals converging to an arbitrary $z \in [0, 1)$, it follows that

$$f(z) - f(0) = \int_0^z g(x)\, dx.$$

In this sense, g is a derivative of f, the so-called Radon–Nikodym derivative.

8: Other Martingales

The martingale concept requires only that the index set T of the process $\{X(t);\, t \in T\}$ have some notion of ordering. In particular, T may be any subset of the real line.

Definition 8.1. *Let T be a set in $(-\infty, +\infty)$, and let $\{X(t);\, t \in T\}$ be a stochastic process defined on a probability space $(\Omega, \mathscr{F}, P)$. For each $t \in T$, suppose $\mathscr{F}_t$ is a sub-σ-field of $\mathscr{F}$ and*

$$\mathscr{F}_t \subset \mathscr{F}_s, \qquad \text{if} \quad t < s, \quad t, s \in T.$$

Then $\{X(t)\}$ is called a submartingale with respect to $\{\mathscr{F}_t\}$ if for all $t \in T$,

(i) *$X(t)$ is $\mathscr{F}_t$-measurable,*
(ii) *$E[X(t)^+] < \infty$, and*
(iii) *$E[X(t+u)|\mathscr{F}_t] \geq X(t)$, $u > 0$, $t + u \in T$.*

To continue, $\{X(t)\}$ is called a supermartingale if $\{-X(t)\}$ is a submartingale, and a martingale if it is both a supermartingale and a submartingale.

A number of cases commonly arise:

$T = \{\ldots, -2, -1, 0\}$,	the set of negative integers,
$T = \{\ldots, -1, 0, 1, \ldots\}$,	the set of all integers,
$T = [0, \infty)$,	the positive real line,
$T = (-\infty, \infty)$,	the total real line,

and even

$T = Q$,	the set of rational numbers.

BACKWARD MARTINGALES

Let $\{X_n;\ n=0, -1, -2, \ldots\}$ be a submartingale with respect to $\{\mathscr{F}_n;\ n=0, -1, -2, \ldots\}$. For a concrete example, one might suppose $\mathscr{F}_n$ to be the σ-field generated by some jointly distributed random variables $\{Y_n, Y_{n-1}, Y_{n-2}, \ldots\}$, but other situations are, of course, possible.

The maximal inequality, Lemma 3.1, becomes

$$\lambda \Pr\left\{\max_{n\le k\le 0} X_k > \lambda\right\} \le E[X_0], \qquad \lambda > 0, \tag{8.1}$$

provided every $X_n \ge 0$, and, in view of the independence of the right-hand side on n,

$$\lambda \Pr\left\{\sup_{k\le 0} X_k > \lambda\right\} \le E[X_0], \qquad \lambda > 0.$$

We discover the same improvement in the upcrossings inequality (4.11) of Section 4. Given real numbers $a < b$ and a negative integer N, define $V_{a,b}(N)$ to be the number of pairs (i, j), $N \le i < j \le 0$, for which the inequalities $X_i \le a$, $a < X_k < b$, for $i < k < j$, and $X_j \ge b$ take place. That is, $V_{a,b}(N)$ counts the number of times X_n upcrosses the interval (a, b) for $N \le n \le 0$, with n traversing from N to 0. Then from Eq. (4.11)

$$\begin{aligned} E[V_{a,b}(N)] &\le (b-a)^{-1}\{E[(X_0-a)^+] - E[(X_N-a)^+]\} \\ &\le (b-a)^{-1}E[(X_0-a)^+]. \end{aligned}$$

Again, the right-hand side does not depend on N, so that

$$E[V_{a,b}] \le (b-a)^{-1}E[(X_0-a)^+],$$

where $V_{a,b} = V_{a,b}(-\infty)$ is the number of upcrossings of (a, b) by X_n for all $n \le 0$.

As a consequence of these strengthened inequalities, a martingale $\{X_n\}$ whose index set is $\{\ldots, -2, -1, 0\}$ *always* possesses a limit as $n \to -\infty$: needing no additional assumptions,

$$X_{-\infty} = \lim_{n\to-\infty} X_n$$

exists with probability one. But even more is true. If

$$\{X_n;\ n=0, -1, -2, \ldots\}$$

is a martingale, $\{|X_n|\}$ is a submartingale, and by (8.1)

$$\Pr\{W > \lambda\} \to 0, \qquad \text{as} \quad \lambda \to \infty,$$

where $W = \sup|X_n|$. Using the submartingale property, in the form $E[|X_n|I(A_n)] \leq E[|X_0|I(A_n)]$ for any event A_n that is $\mathscr{F}_n$-measurable, to justify the first inequality, we get

$$\sup_{n \leq 0} E[|X_n|I\{|X_n| > c\}] \leq \sup_{n \leq 0} E[|X_0|I\{|X_n| > c\}]$$
$$\leq E[|X_0|I\{W > c\}].$$

The same reasoning as in Eq. (6.8) shows that the last term goes to zero as $c \to \infty$. Thus, the martingale $\{X_n;\ n = 0, -1, -2 \ldots\}$ is uniformly integrable, and

$$\lim_{n \to -\infty} E[|X_n - X_{-\infty}|] = 0.$$

Naturally, this reasoning applies instantly to a martingale

$$\{X_n;\ n = \ldots, -1, 0, +1, \ldots\}$$

indexed by the set of all integers. For such a martingale,

$$X_{-\infty} = \lim_{n \to -\infty} X_n$$

always exists,

$$E[|X_n - X_{-\infty}|] \to 0, \qquad \text{as} \quad n \to -\infty,$$

and, furthermore,

$$E[X_{-\infty}] = E[X_n] = E[X_0], \qquad \text{for all} \quad n.$$

In striking contrast, following the basic martingale convergence theorem, something additional, say,

$$\sup_{n \geq 0} E[X_n^+] < \infty,$$

is essential in order to secure the existence of

$$X_{+\infty} = \lim_{n \to +\infty} X_n,$$

and the equation

$$E[X_{+\infty}] = E[X_0]$$

requires even more hypotheses, e.g., that the sequence $\{X_n;\ n \geq 0\}$ be uniformly integrable.

Let $\{Z_n;\ n = 0, 1, \ldots\}$ be random variables on a probability space $(\Omega, \mathscr{F}, P)$ and let $\{\mathscr{G}_n; n = 0, 1, \ldots\}$ be a *decreasing* sequence of sub-σ-fields of $\mathscr{F}$, viz.,

$$\mathscr{F} \supset \mathscr{G}_n \supset \mathscr{G}_{n+1}, \qquad \text{for all} \quad n.$$

Then $\{Z_n\}$ is called a *backward martingale with respect to* $\{\mathscr{G}_n\}$ if for $n = 0, 1, \ldots$

(i) Z_n is $\mathscr{G}_n$-measurable,
(ii) $E[|Z_n|] < \infty$, and
(iii) $E[Z_n | \mathscr{G}_{n+1}] = Z_{n+1}$.

Thus $\{Z_n\}$ is a backward martingale, if and only if

$$X_n = Z_{-n}, \qquad n = 0, -1, -2, \ldots,$$

forms a martingale with respect to

$$\mathscr{F}_n = \mathscr{G}_{-n}, \qquad n = 0, -1, -2, \ldots.$$

On the basis of our preceding disucssion, the following *backward martingale convergence theorem* is established.

Theorem 8.1. *Let* $\{Z_n\}$ *be a backward martingale with respect to a decreasing sequence of* σ*-fields* $\{\mathscr{G}_n\}$. *Then with probability one*

$$Z = \lim_{n\to\infty} Z_n$$

exists,

$$\lim_{n\to\infty} E[|Z - Z_n|] = 0,$$

and

$$E[Z_n] = E[Z], \qquad \textit{for all} \quad n.$$

Example: The Law of Large Numbers. Let $X_1, X_2, \ldots$ be independent identically distributed random variables for which $E[|X_1|] < \infty$. Let $\mu = E[X_1]$, $S_0 = 0$, and introduce the partial sum $S_n = X_1 + \cdots + X_n$ for $n \geq 1$. Let $\mathscr{G}_n$ be the σ-field generated by $\{S_n, S_{n+1}, \ldots\}$. We will derive the strong law of large numbers from the observation that

$$Z_n = n^{-1} S_n \qquad (Z_0 = \mu)$$

forms a backward martingale with respect to $\mathscr{G}_n$. Clearly, $E[|Z_n|] < \infty$ and Z_n is $\mathscr{G}_n$-measurable.

We start with the trivial identity

$$\begin{aligned} S_n &= E[S_n | S_n, S_{n+1} \ldots] \\ &= \sum_{k=1}^{n} E[X_k | \mathscr{G}_n] \\ &= nE[X_k | \mathscr{G}_n], \qquad 1 \leq k \leq n, \end{aligned}$$

the last equality resulting in view of the symmetry of the summands. It is convenient to write this relation in the form

$$E[X_k|\mathscr{G}_n] = n^{-1}S_n = Z_n, \qquad 1 \le k \le n.$$

It follows that

$$\begin{aligned} E[Z_{n-1}|\mathscr{G}_n] &= (n-1)^{-1}E[S_{n-1}|\mathscr{G}_n] \\ &= (n-1)^{-1}\sum_{k=1}^{n-1} E[X_k|\mathscr{G}_n] \\ &= Z_n, \end{aligned}$$

which verifies the backward martingale property. [The full independence is not required in order that $\{Z_n\}$ be a backward martingale. A weaker sufficient condition is that $\{X_k\}$ be *exchangeable* (also called *symmetric* or *interchangeable*) random variables, meaning that $(X_1, \ldots, X_n)$ have the same joint distribution as $(X_{\sigma(1)}, \ldots, X_{\sigma(n)})$ for every integer $n \ge 0$ and every permutation σ of the indices $(1, \ldots, n)$ into themselves.]

Invoking the backward martingale convergence theorem, we find that

$$Z = \lim_{n\to\infty} Z_n \qquad \text{exists with probability one,}$$

and $E[Z] = E[Z_n] = \mu$. The independence of $X_1, X_2, \ldots$ is vital in order to conclude that Z is nonrandom, so that, in fact, $Z \equiv \mu$. The proof follows. For any $m = 1, 2, \ldots,$

$$Z = \lim_{n\to\infty} \frac{X_m + X_{m+1} + \cdots + X_{n+m}}{n},$$

since any finite number of terms bears no influence in the limit. It follows that Z and $Z_m = m^{-1}S_m$ are independent for any finite $m = 1, 2, \ldots$. Hence, for any real a,

$$\Pr\{Z \ge a \text{ and } Z_m \ge a\} = \Pr\{Z \ge a\} \Pr\{Z_m \ge a\},$$

$$\Pr\{Z \ge a \text{ and } \max_{n\le k\le m} Z_k \ge a\} = \Pr\{Z \ge a\} \Pr\{\max_{n\le k\le m} Z_k \ge a\},$$

and

$$\Pr\{Z \ge a \text{ and } \limsup Z_n \ge a\} = \Pr\{Z \ge a\} \Pr\{\limsup Z_n \ge a\}.$$

But $Z = \lim Z_n = \limsup Z_n$, and therefore

$$\Pr\{Z \ge a\} = [\Pr\{Z \ge a\}]^2.$$

It follows that $\Pr\{Z \ge a\}$ can only attain the values 0 or 1, for every real a, and this property implies that Z is constant (why?). Moreover, in view of $E[Z] = \mu$, the constant value of Z must be μ. We have completed the proof of the strong law of large numbers

$$\lim_{n\to\infty} n^{-1}S_n = \mu$$

with probability one.

CONTINUOUS PARAMETER MARTINGALES

Let $\{X(t);\ t \geq 0\}$ be a continuous parameter stochastic process on a probability space $(\Omega, \mathscr{F}, P)$. For each $t \geq 0$, let $\mathscr{F}_t$ be a sub-σ-field of $\mathscr{F}$ with

$$\mathscr{F}_s \subset \mathscr{F}_t, \qquad \text{if} \quad s \leq t.$$

A random variable T, having possible values in $[0, \infty]$, is called a Markov time relative to $\{\mathscr{F}_t\}$ if, for every $t \geq 0$, the event $\{T \leq t\}$ is in $\mathscr{F}_t$. We may think of $\mathscr{F}_t$ as the information available up to time t. From this viewpoint, the event that a Markov time is less than or equal to t is completely decidable by the information available up to time t.

Since a σ-field includes the complement set of each of its members, an equivalent requirement is

$$\{T > t\} \in \mathscr{F}_t, \qquad \text{for all} \quad t > 0. \tag{8.2}$$

For continuous parameter processes, it is not sufficient to require $\{T = t\}$ to be an event in $\mathscr{F}_t$ for each t. However, as before, every constant time $T \equiv \tau$ is a Markov time, and if S and T are Markov times, so are

$$S + T, \qquad S \wedge T = \min\{S, T\}, \qquad \text{and} \qquad S \vee T = \max\{S, T\}.$$

Thus, if T is a Markov time, so is $T \wedge t = \min\{T, t\}$ for every fixed $t > 0$.

Of fundamental importance are the times T_a where the process values first reach a given level a or beyond,

$$T_a = \inf\{t \geq 0;\ X(t) \geq a\}.$$

Let us suppose that every path $X(t)$ is a continuous function of t. This will be the case, for example, if $X(t)$ is Brownian motion. Let $\mathscr{F}_t = \mathscr{F}(X(s);\ 0 \leq s \leq t)$ be the σ-field generated by $\{X(s);\ 0 \leq s \leq t\}$. Then each $X(s)$ is $\mathscr{F}_s$-measurable and $\mathscr{F}_s \subset \mathscr{F}_t$ for $s < t$. In this context, T_a is a Markov time with respect to $\{\mathscr{F}_t\}$. To verify (8.2), observe that, $X(t)$ being continuous, $\{T > t\}$ is synonymous with the occurrence, for some $k = 1, 2 \ldots$, of the event $\{\min_{0 \leq u \leq t}(a - X(u)) \geq 1/k\}$, which, again using the continuity, is equivalent to the simultaneous occurrence of $\{(a - X(r)) \geq 1/k\}$ for every rational r, $0 \leq r \leq t$. That is,

$$\{T > t\} = \bigcup_{k=1}^{\infty} \bigcap_{\substack{r,\ \text{rational} \\ 0 \leq r \leq t}} \{(a - X(r)) \geq 1/k\}.$$

Each event $\{(a - X(r)) \geq 1/k\} \in \mathscr{F}_t$ as $r \leq t$. Since $\mathscr{F}_t$ is a σ-field, and there are only denumerably many rationals r in $[0, t]$.

$$\bigcap_{0 \leq r \leq t} \{(a - X(r)) \geq 1/k\} \in \mathscr{F}_t .$$

Again the union of denumerably many sets in $\mathscr{F}_t$ is itself in $\mathscr{F}_t$, and thus $\{T > t\} \in \mathscr{F}_t$ as we wished to show.

Let A be a closed set and define $T(A)$, the *entry time to* A, to be the random time

$$T(A) = \inf\{t \geq 0 ; X(t) \in A\}.$$

The parallel reasoning reveals that $T(A)$ is a Markov time with respect to $\mathscr{F}_t = \mathscr{F}(X(u); 0 \leq u \leq t)$, provided $X(t)$ is a continuous function of t.

Unfortunately, for several technical reasons, the entry time to a set A is not necessarily a Markov time with respect to $\{\mathscr{F}_t\}$ if $X(t)$ is not continuous or A not closed. It is possible to repair this defect however, by enlarging the σ-fields $\mathscr{F}_t$. Suppose that every realization $X(t)$, as a function of t, is continuous from the right and possesses a limit from the left. That is, suppose

$$X(t) = \lim_{s \downarrow t} X(s), \qquad \text{for all} \quad t \geq 0,$$

and

$$X(t-) = \lim_{s \uparrow t} X(s) \qquad \text{exists for all} \quad t > 0.$$

Continuing with $\mathscr{F}_t = \mathscr{F}(X(u); 0 \leq u \leq t)$, let $\mathscr{F}_{t+}$ consist exactly of those events that are in every σ-field $\mathscr{F}_{t+\varepsilon}$ for every $\varepsilon > 0$. In set-theoretic terms, $\mathscr{F}_{t+}$ is the intersection

$$\mathscr{F}_{t+} = \bigcap_{\varepsilon > 0} \mathscr{F}_{t+\varepsilon} .$$

Each $\mathscr{F}_{t+}$ is a σ-field, each $X(t)$ is $\mathscr{F}_{t+}$-measurable, and

$$\mathscr{F}_{s+} \subset \mathscr{F}_{t+}, \qquad \text{if} \quad s < t.$$

Finally, let $\overline{\mathscr{F}}_{t+}$ be the smallest σ-field containing every set in $\mathscr{F}_{t+}$ together with every set in Ω that is a subset of a set $A \in \mathscr{F}$ for which $P[A] = 0$. Roughly speaking, $\overline{\mathscr{F}}_{t+}$ consists of all events that are probabilistically equivalent to events in $\mathscr{F}_{t+}$.

Then for every Borel set A, the entry time

$$T(A) = \begin{cases} \inf\{t \geq 0 : X(t) \in A\}, & \text{if} \quad X(t) \in A \quad \text{for some } t \geq 0, \\ \infty, & \text{if} \quad X(t) \notin A \quad \text{for all} \quad t, \end{cases}$$

is a Markov time with respect to $\{\overline{\mathscr{F}}_{t+}\}$.

Both the martingale optional sampling and convergence theorems are valid in continuous time. If $\{X(t); t \geq 0\}$ is a submartingale with respect to $\{\mathscr{F}_t\}$, then

$$E[X(0)] \leq E[X(T \wedge t)] \leq E[X(t)], \qquad t \geq 0, \tag{8.3}$$

for all Markov times T. The inequalities are reversed for a supermartingale and equality obtains for a martingale. If $\Pr\{T < \infty\} = 1$, then

$$X(T \wedge t) \to X(T), \qquad \text{as} \quad t \to \infty.$$

The optional sampling theorem results when we justify the interchange of this limit with the expectation in (8.3).

Theorem 8.1. *Let $\{X(t); t \geq 0\}$ be a submartingale and T a Markov time with respect to $\{\mathscr{F}_t\}$. If $\Pr\{T < \infty\} = 1$ and the random variables $\{X(t \wedge T)^+; t \geq 0\}$ are uniformly integrable, then*

$$E[X(0)] \leq E[X(T)].$$

Corollary 8.1. *Let $\{X(t); t \geq 0\}$ be a martingale and T a Markov time. If $\Pr\{T < \infty\} = 1$ and $E[\sup_{t \geq 0} |X(t)|] < \infty$, then*

$$E[X(0)] = E[X(T)].$$

We use these results to derive a number of important properties of Brownian motion in Chapter 7. If $\{X(t); t \geq 0\}$ is a Brownian motion process with mean zero and variance parameter σ^2, then all of

(i) $X(t)$,
(ii) $Y(t) = X^2(t) - \sigma^2 t$, and
(iii) $Z(t) = \exp\{\theta X(t) - \frac{1}{2}\theta^2\sigma^2 t\}$, real θ,

are martingales with respect to $\mathscr{F}_t = \mathscr{F}(X(u); 0 \leq u \leq t)$. This is proved in Section 5 of Chapter 7 where these martingales are used to derive a number of probabilistic quantities associated with Brownian motion.

It is also true, but much more difficult to show, that

$$W(t) = \exp\left\{\theta f[X(t)] - \frac{\sigma^2}{2} \int_0^t \{\theta^2 (f'[X(u)])^2 + \theta f''[X(u)]\}\, du\right\}$$

is a martingale for every real θ and every strictly increasing function f having continuous first and second derivatives f' and f'', respectively, provided, as usual, $E[W(t)] < \infty$.

Poisson Processes

If $\{X(t);\ t \geq 0\}$ is a Poisson process with parameter λ, then all of

$$Y(t) = X(t) - \lambda t \tag{8.4}$$

$$U(t) = Y^2(t) - \lambda t, \tag{8.5}$$

and

$$V(t) = \exp\{-\theta X(t) + \lambda t(1 - e^{-\theta})\}, \qquad -\infty < \theta < \infty, \tag{8.6}$$

are martingales [with respect to $\mathscr{F}_t = \mathscr{F}(X(u);\ 0 \leq u \leq t)$].

Fix a positive integer a and let T_a be the first time $X(t)$ reaches a. Applying the optional sampling theorem to (8.4)–(8.6) under the assumption $X(0) = 0$ and with the observation $X(T_a) = a$ (since a Poisson process varies by unit jumps), we obtain $a = \lambda E[T_a)]$,

$$E[(a - \lambda T_a)^2] = \lambda E[T_a] = a, \qquad \text{or} \qquad \text{variance}(T_a) = a/\lambda^2,$$

and with

$$\beta = -\lambda(1 - e^{-\theta}),$$
$$e^{\theta a} = E[\exp\{-\beta T_a\}],$$

or

$$E[\exp\{-\beta T_a\}] = \left(\frac{\lambda}{\lambda + \beta}\right)^a.$$

This last expression is the Laplace transform of the distribution of T_a. It shows, as we already knew, that T_a has a gamma distribution with parameters a and λ.

Birth Processes

Suppose $\{X(t);\ t \geq 0\}$ is a pure birth process having birth parameters $\lambda(i) \geq 0$ for $i \geq 0$. Assume, for convenience only, $X(0) = 0$. We claim that

$$Y(t) = X(t) - \int_0^t \lambda[X(u)]\, du,$$

and

$$V(t) = \exp\left\{\theta X(t) + [1 - e^{\theta}] \int_0^t \lambda[X(u)]\, du\right\}, \tag{8.7}$$

where θ is fixed, are both martingales, provided their expectations are finite. There are a number of ways to verify these assertions. One of the best is to reduce the problem to an equivalent assertion concerning Poisson processes.

Let $\tau_0, \tau_1, \ldots$ denote the times between successive births in the given process. The τ_i's are independent, and τ_k has an exponential distribution with parameter $\lambda(k)$. The variables $\sigma_k = \lambda(k)\tau_k$, $k = 0, 1, \ldots$, remain independent and in addition have a common exponential distribution with parameter one. They can serve as interoccurrence times in a standard Poisson process $\{N(t), t \geq 0\}$. The relation between $X(t)$ and $N(t)$ is illustrated in Fig. 1.

From what was stated earlier,

$$W(T) = \exp\{\theta N(T) + T(1 - e^{\theta})\}, \qquad T \geq 0,$$

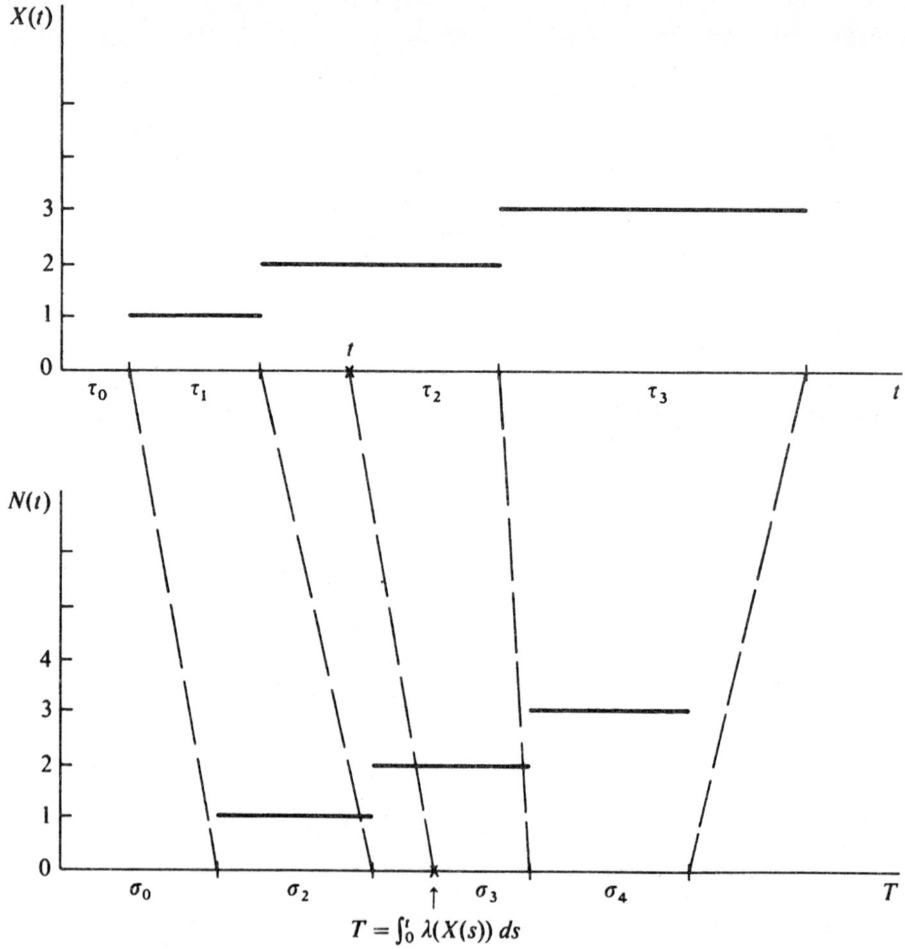

FIG. 1. The interoccurrence times $\sigma_k = \lambda(k)\tau_k$ all have mean one and thus define a Poisson process.

is a martingale with respect to $\mathscr{G}_T = \mathscr{F}(N(u); 0 \le u \le T)$. Thus for $T \ge S$,

$$E[W(T)|N(u); 0 \le u \le S] = W(S).$$

Fix a point t and let $T = T(t)$ be the corresponding point on the T scale. The relation is

$$T = T(t) = \int_0^t \lambda[X(u)]\, du; \tag{8.8}$$

and

$$N(T) = X(t). \tag{8.9}$$

Fix a point $s < t$ and let $S = S(s)$ correspond to it in a similar manner. Conditioning with respect to $\{N(u);\ 0 \le u \le S\}$ is equivalent to conditioning with respect to $\{X(u);\ 0 \le u \le s\}$. Thus

$$E[W(T)|X(u); 0 \le u \le s] = W(S). \tag{8.10}$$

But $W(T) = V(t)$ and $W(S) = V(s)$, through the substitution of (8.8) and (8.9). Thus

$$E[V(t)|\mathscr{F}_s] = V(s),$$

where $\mathscr{F}_s = \mathscr{F}(X(u); 0 \le u \le s)$ and $\{V(t)\}$ is a martingale.

The cautious reader will have noted a lacuna in our argument. For a fixed t, $T = T(t)$ is not fixed, but is random. However, T is a Markov time with respect to $\{\mathscr{G}_T\}$, and an application of an extended version of the optional sampling theorem works to verify (8.10).

Formally, we may show that $Y(t) = X(t) - \int_0^t \lambda[X(u)]\, du$ is a martingale by letting θ vanish in the martingale

$$\theta^{-1}[V(t) - 1] - Y(t) + o(\theta),$$

where $o(\theta)$ are (random) remainder terms. The left-hand side is a martingale for every $\theta \ne 0$; hence $Y(t)$ is a martingale.

Birth and Death Processes

Let $\{X(t);\ t \ge 0\}$ be a birth and death process with birth parameters $\lambda_i = \lambda(i)$, $i \ge 0$, and death parameters $\mu_i = \mu(i)$, $i \ge 1$. Assume $\lambda(0) = 0$, so that 0 is an absorbing state, but suppose $\lambda(i) > 0$ for $i \ge 1$. Define

$$f(0) = 0, \qquad f(1) = 1,$$

and

$$f(j) = 1 + \frac{\mu_1}{\lambda_1} + \frac{\mu_1\mu_2}{\lambda_1\lambda_2} + \cdots + \frac{\mu_1 \cdots \mu_{j-1}}{\lambda_1 \cdots \lambda_{j-1}}, \qquad \text{for} \quad j \ge 2. \tag{8.11}$$

Then $Z(t) = f[X(t)]$ is a martingale whenever its mean is finite. (Compare to Elementary Problem 25). To see this, fix $s < t$ and a state $i \geq 1$, and consider

$$\begin{aligned} g_i(t) &= E[Z(t)|X(u); 0 \leq u \leq s, X(s) = i] \\ &= E[Z(t)|X(s) = i], \end{aligned}$$

the last equation resulting by the Markov property. Then for small $h > 0$, on examining the transitions that can occur over the time interval $(t, t+h)$, we obtain the equation

$$\begin{aligned} g_i(t+h) &= \sum_{k=0}^{\infty} E[Z(t+h)|X(t) = k] \Pr\{X(t) = k|X(s) = i\} \\ &= g_i(t) + h \sum_{k=0}^{\infty} \{\lambda_k[f(k+1) - f(k)] - \mu_k[f(k) - f(k-1)]\} \\ &\quad \cdot \Pr\{X(t) = k|X(s) = i\} + o(h). \end{aligned}$$

Thus

$$\begin{aligned} g_i'(t) &= \lim_{h \downarrow 0} \frac{g_i(t+h) - g_i(t)}{h} \\ &= \sum_{k=0}^{\infty} \{\lambda_k[f(k+1) - f(k)] - \mu_k[f(k) - f(k-1)]\} \Pr\{X(t) = k|X(s) = i\} \\ &= \sum_{k=0}^{\infty} \left\{\lambda_k \left[\frac{\mu_1 \cdots \mu_k}{\lambda_1 \cdots \lambda_k}\right] - \mu_k \left[\frac{\mu_1 \cdots \mu_{k-1}}{\lambda_1 \cdots \lambda_{k-1}}\right]\right\} \Pr\{X(t) = k|X(s) = i\} = 0. \end{aligned}$$

Since $g_i'(t) = 0$, $g_i(t) = E[Z(t)|X(s) = i]$ is a constant function of t, for $t > s$. Letting $t \downarrow s$, we conclude

$$\begin{aligned} g_i(s) &= E[Z(s)|X(s) = i] \\ &= g_i(t) = E[Z(t)|X(s) = i], \end{aligned}$$

and $Z(t)$ is a martingale.

Fix states $i < m$ and let $v(i)$ be the probability that the process is absorbed at 0 before reaching state m conditioned on $X(0) = i$. Formally,

$$T_{0,m} = \inf\{t \geq 0 : X(t) = 0 \quad \text{or} \quad X(t) = m\}.$$

We apply the optional sampling theorem to conclude that

$$f(i) = E[Z(T_{0,m})] = v(i) \cdot 0 + (1 - v(i))f(m),$$

and subsequently

$$v(i) = \frac{f(m) - f(i)}{f(m)},$$

where f is given in (8.11).

A different approach produced a similar result in Theorem 7.1 of Chapter 4.

There are numerous other martingales associated with a birth and death process. We mention two:

(a) Let $g(i)$, $i=0, 1, \ldots,$ be arbitrary, provided the expectation of

$$Y(t)=g[X(t)]-\int_0^t \{\lambda[X(u)][g(X(u)+1)-g(X(u))] - \mu[X(u)][g(X(u))-g(X(u)-1)]\}\,du,$$

is finite. Then $\{Y(t)\}$ is a martingale.

Observe that the integral greatly simplifies when $g(i)$ is a solution to

$$\lambda(i)[g(i+1)-g(i)]-\mu(i)[g(i)-g(i-1)]\equiv 1, \qquad i\geq 1.$$

(b) Let $g(i)$, $i=0, 1, \ldots,$ be arbitrary provided the expectation of

$$V(t)=\exp\left(-\theta g[X(t)]-\int_0^t [\lambda(X(u))\{1-e^{-\theta[g(X(u)+1)-g(X(u))]}\} + \mu(X(u))\{1-e^{+\theta[g(X(u))-g(X(u)-1)]}\}]\,du\right)$$

is finite for some fixed real parameter θ. Then $\{V(t)\}$ is a martingale.

Elementary Problems

1. Consider a random walk on the integer lattice of the positive quadrant in two dimensions. If at any step the process is at (m, n), it moves at the next step to $(m+1, n)$ or $(m, n+1)$ with probability $\frac{1}{2}$ each. Let the process start at $(0, 0)$. Let Γ be any curve connecting neighboring lattice points (extending from the Y axis to the X axis) in the first quadrant. Show that $EY_1=EY_2$, where Y_1 and Y_2 denote the number of steps to the right and up, respectively, before hitting the boundary Γ. The diagram describes an example of Γ.

Hint: Use an optional stopping theorem for partial sums to show $E[Y_1]=E[Y_2]=\frac{1}{2}E[T]$, where T is the number of steps it takes to reach the boundary.

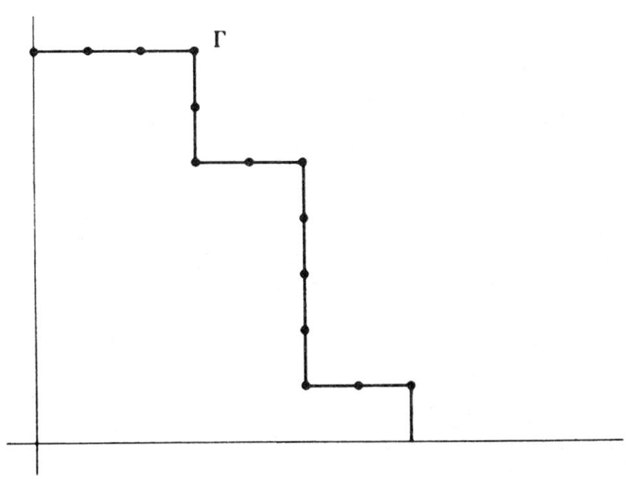

2. Consider the following discrete time Markov process with the unit interval as state space. If the process is at p $(0<p<1)$ at the present, it will jump to $\alpha+\beta p$ with probability p and to βp with probability $1-p$ after the next trial, where $\alpha, \beta>0$ and $\alpha+\beta=1$. In symbols, the process is defined by the transformation law

$$X_{n+1}=\begin{cases}\alpha+\beta X_n, & \text{with probability } X_n,\\ \beta X_n, & \text{with probability } 1-X_n.\end{cases}$$

Show that this process is a martingale.

3. Let $W(n)$ be a branching process with immigration:

$$W(n+1)=Y_n+X_{n,1}+\cdots+X_{n,W(n)},$$

where Y_n is the immigration in generation n and $X_{n,j}$ is the number of offspring of the jth individual in generation n, all independent. Suppose $E[Y_n]=\lambda$ and $E[X_{n,j}]=m\neq 1$. Show that

$$Z_n=m^{-n}\left[W(n)-\lambda\left\{\frac{1-m^n}{1-m}\right\}\right]$$

is a martingale.

4. Let X_n be the number of males and Y_n the number of females in the nth generation of a population. Permanent pairs are formed. Thus $Z_n=\min\{X_n, Y_n\}$ pairs produce offspring, and they do so independently according to the generating function $g(t, s)=E[t^{\xi}s^{\eta}]$, where ξ is the number of male, and η the number of female offspring of a single parental pair. Show that Z_n is a supermartingale if either $E[\xi]\leq 1$ or $E[\eta]\leq 1$ holds.

5. Assume $Y_1, Y_2, \ldots$ are independent and identically distributed with $\Pr\{Y_1=+1\}=p$, and $\Pr\{Y_1=-1\}=q=1-p$. Fix positive integers a and b. With $S_0=0$, and $S_n=Y_1+\cdots+Y_n$, $n\geq 1$, let

$$T=\min\{n:\quad S_n=-a \text{ or } S_n=b\}.$$

Establish the formula

$$E[T]=\frac{b}{p-q}-\frac{a+b}{p-q}\cdot\frac{1-(p/q)^b}{1-(p/q)^{a+b}}\qquad \text{when } p\neq q.$$

(The equation $E[T]=ab$ when $p=q=\frac{1}{2}$ was derived in Example (a) of Section 4.)

6. Let $Y_1, Y_2, \ldots$ be the independent and identically distributed with $\Pr\{Y_1=+1\}=p$, and $\Pr\{Y_1=-1\}=q=1-p$. Suppose $p>\frac{1}{2}>q$. With $S_0=0$ and $S_n=Y_1+\cdots+Y_n$ for $n\geq 1$ let

$$T=\min\{n:\quad S_n\geq b\}$$

for some fixed positive integer b. Deduce the generating function

$$E[s^T] = \left(\frac{1-\{1-4pqs^2\}^{1/2}}{2qs}\right)^b, \qquad 0 < s \leq 1,$$

Hint: Use Wald's identity.

7. Under the conditions of Elementary Problem 6, derive the mean $E[T] = b/(p-q)$ and the variance $\mathrm{Var}[T] = b[1-(p-q)^2]/(p-q)^3$.

8. Let $Y(0)$, $Y(1)$, ... be the success-runs Markov chain in which $P_{00} = 1$, so 0 is an absorbing state, and $P_{i,i+1} = p$, $P_{i0} = q = 1 - p$ for $i = 1, 2, \ldots$. Let a and b be arbitrary real constants. Show that

$$X_n = \begin{cases} b & \text{if } Y(n) = 0, \\ a\left(\dfrac{1}{p}\right)^{Y(n)-1} + b\left[1 - \left(\dfrac{1}{p}\right)^{Y(n)-1}\right], & \text{if } Y(n) > 0 \end{cases}$$

is a martingale.

9. Consider a family of r.v.'s $\{X_n\}_0^\infty$, each having finite absolute expectation and satisfying

$$E[X_{n+1} | X_0, X_1, \ldots, X_n] = \alpha X_n + \beta X_{n-1}, \qquad n > 0,$$

with $\alpha > 0$, $\beta > 0$, and $\alpha + \beta = 1$. Find an appropriate value of a such that the sequence

$$Y_n = aX_n + X_{n-1}, \qquad n \geq 1, \quad Y_0 = X_0,$$

constitutes a martingale with respect to $\{X_n\}$.

10. Let $\{X_n; n \geq 0\}$ be a martingale with respect to $\{Y_n\}$. Prove for any set of integers $k \leq l < m$ that the difference $X_m - X_l$ is uncorrelated with X_k, that is,

$$E[(X_m - X_l)X_k] = 0.$$

Hint: Evaluate the expectation by conditioning on $Y_1, \ldots, Y_k$.

11. Let $\{\xi_i\}$ be a sequence of r.v.'s such that the partial sums

$$X_n = \xi_0 + \xi_1 + \cdots + \xi_n, \qquad n \geq 1,$$

determine a martingale. Show that the summands are mutually uncorrelated, i.e., $E[\xi_i \xi_j] = 0$ for $i \neq j$.

12. Let $S_n = X_1 + \cdots + X_n$ be a martingale satisfying $E[X_k^2] \leq K < \infty$, for all k. Show that S_n obeys the weak law of large numbers:

$$\Pr\{|S_n/n| > \varepsilon\} \to 0, \qquad \text{as } n \to \infty,$$

for any positive ε.

Hint: Use the maximal inequality and the orthogonality result of Elementary Problem 11.

13. Let $\{\xi_i\}_{i=0}^{\infty}$ be a sequence of real valued jointly distributed random variables that satisfy $E[\xi_i|\xi_0, \xi_1, \ldots, \xi_{i-1}] = 0$, $i = 1, 2, \ldots$. Define

$$X_0 = \xi_0, \qquad X_{n+1} = \sum_{i=0}^{n} \xi_{i+1} f_i(\xi_0, \xi_1, \ldots, \xi_i),$$

where f_i are a prescribed sequence of functions of $i+1$ real variables. Show that $\{X_n\}$ form a martingale.

14. Consider a game of tossing repeatedly and independently a fair coin where the result ξ_k at round k has $\Pr\{\xi_k = 1\} = \Pr\{\xi_k = -1\} = \frac{1}{2}$. Suppose a player stakes in the first round a unit and doubles the stake each time he loses and returns to the unit stake each time he wins. Assume the player has unlimited funds (or credit). Let X_n be the net gain after the nth round. Show that $\{X_n\}_1^{\infty}$ determines a martingale with respect to $\{\xi_n\}_1^{\infty}$.

Hint: Establish that X_n can be represented in the form

$$X_n = \sum_{k=1}^{n} \xi_k f_k(\xi_1, \ldots, \xi_{k-1})$$

for suitable f_k, and consult Elementary Problem 13.

15. (a) Consider a Markov chain $\{X_n;\ n > 0\}$ on the state space $\{0, 1, 2, \ldots, N\}$ with transition probability matrix

$$(*) \qquad P_{ij} = \binom{N}{j} \left(\frac{i}{N}\right)^j \left(1 - \frac{i}{N}\right)^{N-j}.$$

Establish that $\{X_n;\ n \geq 0\}$ and $\left\{V_n = \dfrac{X_n(N - X_n)}{(1 - N^{-1})^n},\ n \geq 0\right\}$ constitute martingales with respect to $\{X_n\}$.

(b) Replace (*) by

$$(**) \qquad P_{ij} = \frac{\binom{2i}{j}\binom{2N-2i}{N-j}}{\binom{2N}{N}}.$$

In this case determine λ such that

$$W_n = \frac{X_n(N - X_n)}{\lambda^n}, \qquad n \geq 0,$$

is a martingale with respect to $\{X_n\}$.

16. Suppose Y_0 is uniformly distributed on $(0, 1]$, and given Y_n, suppose Y_{n+1} is uniformly distributed on $(1 - Y_n, 1]$. Show $X_0 = Y_0$, and

$$X_n = 2^n \prod_{k=1}^{n} \left[\frac{1 - Y_k}{Y_{k-1}}\right], \qquad n = 1, 2, \ldots$$

is a martingale.

17. From an urn that initially contains one red and one green ball, a ball is drawn at random and it and one more of the same color are returned. This process is repeated indefinitely. Let X_n be the fraction of red balls at stage n. (a) Use the maximal inequality to show $\Pr\{X_n \geq 3/4 \text{ for some } n = 1, 2, \ldots\} \leq 2/3$. In words, there is 2/3 or less chance of ever there being more than 3/4 of the balls red. (b) Using the limit distribution found in Example (c) of Section 6, show $\lim_{n\to\infty} \Pr\{X_n \geq 3/4\} = 1/4$. In words, the probability is 1/4 that, in the limit, 3/4 or more of the balls will be red.

18. Let $P_{ij} = e^{-i} i^j / j!$, $i, j = 0, 1, \ldots$ be the transition probabilities for a Markov chain X_n. We consider $P_{00} = 1$. (a) Verify that X_n is a martingale. (b) Derive the inequality

$$\Pr\{\max_{0 \leq n < \infty} X_n \geq a | X_0 = i\} \leq i/a$$

for $i, a = 1, 2, \ldots$. (c) Prove that $\lim_{n\to\infty} X_n = 0$ with probability one.

Hint: Apply the optional sampling theorem with T being the first time n that $X_n = 0$ or $X_n \geq a$.

19. Let X_n be a Markov chain whose transition probabilities are $P_{i,j} = 1/[e(j-i)!]$ for $i = 0, 1, \ldots$ and $j = i, i+1, \ldots$.

Verify the martingale property for:

$$\begin{aligned} &\text{(a)} \quad Y_n = X_n - n; \\ &\text{(b)} \quad U_n = Y_n^2 - n; \\ &\text{(c)} \quad V_n = \exp\{X_n - n(e-1)\}. \end{aligned}$$

20. Let $\{X_n\}_1^\infty$ be a submartingale. Show that the sequence

$$U_1 = 0, \qquad U_n = \sum_{i=2}^{n} \{E[X_i | X_1, X_2, X_3, \ldots, X_{i-1}] - X_{i-1}\}, \qquad n \geq 2,$$

is an increasing process, i.e., $U_n \geq U_{n-1}$.

21. Consider a Markov chain $\{X_n;\ n \geq 0\}$ on the state space of the nonnegative integers with transition probability matrix $P = \| P_{ij} \|$. Let $u(i, n)$ be a function defined on the integers $i, n \geq 0$ and satisfying the functional equation

$$u(i, n) = \sum_{k=0}^{\infty} u(k, n+m) P_{ik}^{(m)}$$

where $P_{ik}^{(m)}$ is the m step transition probability from state i to k. Show that

$$U_n = u(X_n, n)$$

is a martingale with respect to $\{X_n\}$.

22. Consider a Markov chain $\{X_n;\ n \geq 0\}$ involving N states whose possible state values are $x_0 < x_1 < \cdots < x_N$ with transition possibility matrix $P_{ij} = \Pr\{X_{n+1} = x_j | X_n = x_i\}$. Suppose $\{X_n\}$ is also a martingale. Show that states x_0 and x_N are absorbing, i.e., $P_{0,0} = P_{N,N} = 1$.

23. Consider a Markov chain $\{X_n;\ n \geq 0\}$ of N states $\{0, 1, 2, \dots N\}$ and transition probabilities

$$P_{ij} = \binom{N}{j} \pi_i^j (1 - \pi_i)^{N-j},$$

where

$$\pi_i = \frac{1 - e^{-2ai/N}}{1 - e^{-2a}}.$$

Show that $Z_n = e^{-2aX_n}$ is a Martingale.

24. Let $\{X_n,\ n \geq 0\}$ describe a transient Markov chain on the non-negative integers with transition probability matrix $P = \| P_{ij} \|$. Define

$$u(i) = \sum_{n=0}^{\infty} P_{i0}^{(n)}.$$

Show that

$$U_n = u(X_n) \text{ is a supermartingale.}$$

25. Consider a finite birth and death process $\{X(t),\ t \geq 0\}$ with infinitesimal parameters λ_i and μ_i, $0 \leq i \leq N$ $(\mu_0 = 0)$. The infinitesimal matrix is

$$A = \begin{pmatrix} -\lambda_0 & \lambda_0 & 0 & 0 & 0 \\ \mu_1 & -(\lambda_1 + \mu_1) & \lambda_1 & 0 & 0 \\ 0 & \mu_2 & -(\lambda_2 + \mu_2) & \lambda_2 & 0 \\ \vdots & \vdots & \vdots & \vdots & \vdots \\ \cdot & \cdot & \cdot & \mu_N & -\mu_N \end{pmatrix}$$

Consider any solution $y = (y_0, y_1, \dots)$ of the linear system

$$Ay = 0.$$

Establish that $Y(t) = y_{X(t)}$, $t > 0$, is a martingale with respect to $\mathscr{F}_t = \sigma(X(u);\ u \leq t)$.

Hint: Show that if $Ay = 0$, then

$$y_i = \sum_{j=0}^{N} P_{ij}(t) y_j, \qquad i = 0, 1, \dots, N,$$

holds for all $t > 0$, where $P_{ij}(t)$ represents the transition probability matrix of the process $\{X(t),\ t \geq 0\}$.

Problems

1. Prove: if $\{X_n\}$ is a submartingale and $\varphi(x)$ is a convex, increasing function, then $\{\varphi(X_n)\}$ is a submartingale whenever $E|\varphi^+(X_n)| < \infty$ for all n (cf. Lemma 2.2).

2. Suppose $P = \|P_{ij}\|$ is the transition probability matrix of an irreducible recurrent Markov chain $\{X_n\}$. Use the supermartingale convergence theorem (see Remark 5.1) to show that every nonnegative solution $y = \{y(i)\}$ to the system of inequalities

$$y(i) \geq \sum_{j=0}^{\infty} P_{ij} y(j), \qquad \text{for all} \quad i,$$

is constant.

Hint: Paraphrase Example (a) of Section 6.

3. Let $\{U_n\}$ and $\{V_n\}$ be martingales with respect to the same process $\{Y_n\}$. Suppose $U_0 = V_0 = 0$ and $E[U_n^2] < \infty$, $E[V_n^2] < \infty$ for all n. Show

$$E[U_n V_n] = \sum_{k=1}^{n} E[(U_k - U_{k-1})(V_k - V_{k-1})].$$

As a special case,

$$E[U_n^2] = \sum_{k=1}^{n} E[(U_k - U_{k-1})^2].$$

Hint: Because $U_n V_n = \sum_{k=1}^{n} (U_k V_k - U_{k-1} V_{k-1})$, it is enough to show $E[U_k V_k - U_{k-1} V_{k-1}] = E[(U_k - U_{k-1})(V_k - V_{k-1})]$. But $E[(U_k - U_{k-1})(V_k - V_{k-1})] = E[U_k V_k] - E[U_{k-1} V_k] - E[(U_k - U_{k-1}) V_{k-1}]$. Now evaluate the last two expectations by first conditioning on $Y_0, \ldots, Y_{k-1}$ and using the martingale property.

4. Suppose $\{X_n\}$ is a martingale satisfying, for some $\alpha > 1$,

$$E[|X_n|^\alpha] < \infty, \qquad \text{for all} \quad n.$$

Show

$$E\left[\max_{0 \leq k \leq n} |X_k|\right] \leq \frac{\alpha}{\alpha - 1} E[|X_n|^\alpha]^{1/\alpha}.$$

Hint: $E[\max_{0 \leq k \leq n} |X_k|] = \int_0^\infty \Pr\{\max_{0 \leq k \leq n} |X_k| > t\}\, dt$. Now use the maximal inequality on the submartingale $|X_n|^\alpha$.

5. Let $\{X_n\}$ be a submartingale. Strengthen the maximal inequality, Lemma 5.1., to

$$\lambda \Pr\left\{\max_{0 \leq k \leq n} X_k > \lambda\right\} \leq E\left[X_n I\left\{\max_{0 \leq k \leq n} X_k > \lambda\right\}\right]$$

$$\leq E[X_n^+] \leq E[|X_n|], \qquad \lambda > 0.$$

(*Note:* Lemma 5.1 requires $X_k \geq 0$ for all k. The above does not.) Consequently, for a martingale $\{X_n\}$,

$$\lambda \Pr\left\{\max_{0 \leq k \leq n} |X_k| > \lambda\right\} \leq E\left[|X_n| I\left\{\max_{0 \leq k \leq n} |X_k| > \lambda\right\}\right], \qquad \lambda > 0.$$

6. The result of Problem 5 can be used to strengthen the inequality in Problem 4 to the form

$$E\left[\max_{0\le k\le n}|X_k|^\alpha\right]\le\left(\frac{\alpha}{\alpha-1}\right)^\alpha E[|X_n|^\alpha].$$

Prove this when $\alpha=2$.

7. *Extinction of populations.* Consider a population of organisms living in some bounded environment, say the Earth. Let X_n be the number of organisms alive at time n and observe that $\{0\}$ is an absorbing state, $X_n=0$ implies $X_{n+m}=0$ for all m. It is reasonable to suppose that for every N there exists $\delta>0$ satisfying

$$\Pr[X_{n+1}=0|X_1,\ldots,X_n]\ge\delta,\qquad\text{if}\quad X_n\le N,$$

$n=1,2,\ldots$. Let $\mathscr{E}$ be the event of eventual extinction

$$\mathscr{E}=\{X_k=0\text{ for some }k=1,2,\ldots\}.$$

Show that with probability one, either $\mathscr{E}$ occurs or else $X_n\to\infty$ as $n\to\infty$. Since the latter cannot occur in a bounded environment, eventual extinction is certain.

8. Let Z, Y_0, Y_1, ... be jointly distributed random variables and assume $E[|Z|^2]<\infty$. Show that $X_n=E[Z|Y_0,\ldots,Y_n]$ satisfies the conditions for the martingale mean square convergence theorem.

9. Let $\{X_n\}$ be a martingale satisfying $E[X_n^2]\le K<\infty$ for all n. Suppose

$$\lim_{n\to\infty}\sup_{m\ge1}|E[X_nX_{n+m}]-E[X_n]E[X_{n+m}]|=0.$$

Show that $X=\lim_{n\to\infty}X_n$ is a constant, i.e., nonrandom.

10. Let $\{X_n\}$ be a martingale for which $E[X_n]=0$ and $E[X_n^2]<\infty$ for all n. Show that

$$\Pr\left\{\max_{0\le k\le n}X_k>\lambda\right\}\le\frac{E[X_n^2]}{E[X_n^2]+\lambda^2},\qquad\lambda>0.$$

Hint: For every $c>0$, $(X_n+c)^2$ is a submartingale, and for $\lambda>0$ we may apply the maximal inequality to get

$$\begin{aligned}\Pr\left\{\max_{0\le k\le n}X_k>\lambda\right\}&\le\Pr\left\{\max_{0\le k\le n}(X_k+c)^2>(\lambda+c)^2\right\}\\&\le\frac{E[(X_n+c)^2]}{(\lambda+c)^2},\qquad\text{for all }c>0.\end{aligned}$$

Now determine the value c which gives the best bound, i.e., minimizes the right-hand side.

11. Let $\{X_n\}$ be a submartingale. Show that

$$\lambda \Pr\left\{\min_{0\le k\le n} X_k < -\lambda\right\} \le E[X_n^+] - E[X_0], \qquad \lambda > 0.$$

12. Prove: If $\{X_n\}$ is a nonnegative supermartingale, then

$$\lambda \Pr\left\{\max_{0\le k\le n} X_k \ge \lambda\right\} \le E[X_0], \qquad \lambda > 0.$$

(Cf. Lemma 5.2.)

Problems 13–16 all occur in the same context. Let $\mathscr{B}_0 = \{B_1, B_2, \ldots\}$ be a denumerable partition of a set Ω. That is, $\Omega = \bigcup_{n=1}^{\infty} B_n$ and $B_i \cap B_j = \varnothing$ if $i \ne j$. Let $\mathscr{B}$ be the σ-field consisting of $\varnothing$, Ω and all sets that are unions of sets in $\mathscr{B}_0$, i.e., of the form

$$B = \bigcup_{k=1}^{j} B_{n(k)}, \qquad 1 \le j \le \infty, \quad \text{with} \quad B_{n(k)} \in \mathscr{B}_0.$$

13. Suppose $\mathscr{B}$ is the σ-field generated by some random variable Y (having, then, at most a denumerable number of possible values). Show that a random variable X is $\mathscr{B}$-measurable if and only if $X = f(Y)$ for some real-valued function f.

14. Suppose X_1 and X_2 are $\mathscr{B}$-measurable random variables. Show that $a_1 X_1 + a_2 X_2$ is $\mathscr{B}$-measurable for all real a_1, a_2.

15. Suppose Y is $\mathscr{B}$-measurable, and $E[|Y|] < \infty$. Show that $E[YZ] \ge 0$ for all bounded nonnegative $\mathscr{B}$-measurable random variables Z implies $P[\{\omega: Y(\omega) \ge 0\}] = 1$.

16. Show that X is $\mathscr{B}$-measurable if and only if

$$X(\omega) = \sum_{k=1}^{\infty} \alpha_k I_{B_k}(\omega),$$

for some real sequence $\{\alpha_k\}$, where

$$I_{B_j}(\omega) = \begin{cases} 1, & \text{if } \omega \in B_j, \\ 0, & \text{if } \omega \notin B_j. \end{cases}$$

In particular, observe that $X(\omega)$ is constant on each of the sets B_j.

17. Fix $\lambda > 0$. Suppose $X_1, X_2, \ldots$ are jointly distributed random variables whose joint distributions satisfy

$$E[\exp\{\lambda X_{n+1}\} | X_1, \ldots, X_n] \le 1, \qquad \text{for all } n.$$

Let $S_n = X_1 + \cdots + X_n$ $(S_0 = 0)$. Establish

$$\Pr\left\{\sup_{n\ge 0} (x + S_n) > l\right\} \le e^{-\lambda(l-x)}, \qquad \text{for } x \le l.$$

Hint: Use an optional sampling theorem on the nonnegative supermartingale $\exp\{-\lambda(l - x - S_n)\}$.

18. Let X be a random variable for which

$$\Pr\{-\varepsilon \leq X \leq +\varepsilon\} = 1, \tag{A}$$

and

$$E[X] \leq -\rho\varepsilon, \tag{B}$$

where $\varepsilon > 0$ and $\rho > 0$ are given. Show that

$$E[e^{\lambda X}] \leq 1,$$

for $\lambda = \varepsilon^{-1} \log[(1+\rho)/(1-\rho)]$. Apply the result of Problem 17 to bound

$$\Pr\left\{\sup_{n \geq 0} (x + S_n) > l\right\}, \qquad \text{for} \quad x < l,$$

where $S_n = X_1 + \cdots + X_n$, and the conditional distribution of X_{n+1} given $X_1, \ldots, X_n$ satisfies (A) and (B).

19. Let X be a random variable satisfying

(a) $E[X] \leq m < 0$, and
(b) $\Pr\{-1 \leq X \leq +1\} = 1$.

Suppose $X_1, X_2, \ldots$ are jointly distributed random variables for which the conditional distribution of X_{n+1} given $X_1, \ldots, X_n$ always satisfies (a) and (b). Let $S_n = X_1 + \cdots + X_n$ ($S_0 = 0$) and for $a < x$ let

$$T_a = \min\{n: x + S_n \leq a\}.$$

Establish the inequality

$$E[T_a] \leq (1 + x - a)/|m|, \qquad a < x.$$

20. Let $T, Y_0, Y_1, \ldots$ be random variables. Suppose the possible values for T are $\{0, 1, \ldots\}$ and, for every $n \geq 0$, the event $\{T \geq n\}$ is determined by $(Y_0, \ldots, Y_n)$. Is T necessarily a Markov time with respect to $\{Y_n\}$? Provide a proof or counterexample to support your claim.

21. Let $S_n = \xi_1 + \cdots + \xi_n$, where $\{\xi_k\}$ are independent identically distributed positive random variables ($\Pr\{\xi_k > 0\} = 1$). Prove that

$$\sup_{n \geq 1} E\left[\frac{n}{a + S_n}\right] < \infty, \qquad \text{for any} \quad a > 0.$$

[The case where ξ_k assumes only integer values was treated in Example (e) of Section 6].

22. Let $Y_1, Y_2, \ldots$ be independent random variables with $\Pr\{Y_k = +1\} = \Pr\{Y_k = -1\} = 1/2$. Put $S_k = Y_1 + \cdots + Y_k$. Show that

$$\Pr\{S_k < k \qquad \text{for all } k = 1, \ldots, N | S_N = a\} = 1 - \frac{a}{N}.$$

23. Let ξ_n be nonnegative random variables satisfying

$$E[\xi_{n+1}|\xi_1, \ldots, \xi_n] \leq \delta_n + \xi_n,$$

where $\delta_n \geq 0$ are constants and $\Delta = \sum_{n=1}^{\infty} \delta_n < \infty$. Show that with probability one, ξ_n converges to a finite random variable ξ as $n \to \infty$.

24. The Haar functions on $[0, 1)$ are defined by

$$H_1(t) \equiv 1,$$

$$H_2(t) = \begin{cases} 1, & 0 \leq t < \frac{1}{2}, \\ -1, & \frac{1}{2} \leq t < 1, \end{cases}$$

$$H_{2^n+1}(t) = \begin{cases} 2^{n/2}, & 0 \leq t < 2^{-(n+1)}, \\ -2^{n/2} & 2^{-(n+1)} \leq t < 2^{-n}, \quad n = 1, 2, \ldots, \\ 0, & \text{otherwise}, \end{cases}$$

$$H_{2^n+j}(t) = H_{2^n+1}\left(t - \frac{j-1}{2^n}\right). \qquad j = 1, \ldots, 2^n.$$

It helps to plot the first five.

Let $f(z)$ be an arbitrary function on $[0, 1]$ but satisfying

$$\int_0^1 |f(z)|\, dz < \infty.$$

Define $a_k = \int_0^1 f(t) H_k(t)\, dt$. Let Z be uniformly distributed on $[0, 1]$. Show that

$$f(Z) = \lim_{n \to \infty} \sum_{k=1}^{n} a_k H_k(Z) \qquad \text{with probability one,}$$

and

$$\lim_{n \to \infty} \int_0^1 \left| f(t) - \sum_{k=1}^{n} a_k H_k(t) \right| dt = 0.$$

25. Suppose $X_1, X_2, \ldots$ are independent random variables having finite moment generating functions $\varphi_k(t) = E[\exp\{tX_k\}]$. Show, if $\Phi_n(t_0) = \prod_{k=1}^{n} \varphi_k(t_0) \to \Phi(t_0)$ as $n \to \infty$, $t_0 \neq 0$ and $0 < \Phi(t_0) < \infty$, then $S_n = X_1 + \cdots + X_n$ converges with probability one.

26. Let 0 be an absorbing state in a success runs Markov chain $\{X_n\}$ having transition probabilities $P_{00} = 1$ and $P_{i,\, i+1} = p_i = 1 - P_{i,0}$ for $i = 1, 2, \ldots$. Suppose $p_i \geq p_{i+1} \geq \cdots$, and let a be the unique value for which $ap_{a-1}/(a-1) > 1 \geq (a+1)p_a/a$. Define

$$f(i) = \begin{cases} 0, & \text{for } i = 0, \\ ap_i p_{i+1} \cdots p_{a-1}, & \text{for } 1 \leq i < a, \\ i, & \text{for } i \geq a. \end{cases}$$

(a) Show that $f(i) \geq i$ for all $i = 0, 1, \ldots$.

(b) Show that $f(i) \geq E[f(X_{n+1})|X_n = i]$ for all i, so that $\{f(X_n)\}$ is a nonnegative supermartingale.

(c) Use (a) and (b) to verify that $f(i) \geq E[X_T|X_0 = i]$ for all Markov times T.

(d) Prove $f(i) = E[X_{T^*}|X_0 = i]$, where $T^* = \min\{n \geq 0\colon X_n \geq a \text{ or } X_n = 0\}$.

Thus, T^* maximizes $E[X_T|X_0 = i]$ over all Markov times T.

27. Let $\Omega = \{\omega_1, \omega_2, \ldots\}$ be a countable set and $\mathscr{F}$ the σ-field of all subsets of Ω. For a fixed N, let $X_0, X_1, \ldots, X_N$ be random variables defined on Ω and let T be a Markov time with respect to $\{X_n\}$ satisfying $0 \leq T \leq N$. Let $\mathscr{F}_n$ be the σ-field generated by $X_0, X_1, \ldots, X_n$ and define $\mathscr{F}_T$ to be the collection of sets A in $\mathscr{F}$ for which $A \cap \{T = n\}$ is in $\mathscr{F}_n$ for $n = 0, \ldots, N$. That is,

$$\mathscr{F}_T = \{A\colon A \in \mathscr{F} \quad \text{and} \quad A \cap \{T = n\} \in \mathscr{F}_n, \quad n = 0, \ldots, N\}.$$

Show:

(a) $\mathscr{F}_T$ is a σ-field,

(b) T is measurable with respect to $\mathscr{F}_T$,

(c) $\mathscr{F}_T$ is the σ-field generated by $\{X_0, \ldots, X_T\}$, where $\{X_0, \ldots, X_T\}$ is considered to be a variable-dimensional vector-valued function defined on Ω.

28. Suppose $S_k = X_1 + \cdots + X_n$ is a zero-mean martingale for which $E[X_n^2] < \infty$ for all n. Show that $S_n/b_n \to 0$ with probability one for any monotonic real sequence $b_1 \leq \cdots \leq b_n \leq b_{n+1} \uparrow \infty$, provided $\sum_{n=1}^{\infty} E[X_n^2]/b_n^2 < \infty$.

29. Let X_n be the total assets of an insurance company at the end of year n. In each year, n, premiums totaling $b > 0$ are received, and claims A_n are paid, so $X_{n+1} = X_n + b - A_n$. Assume $A_1, A_2, \ldots$ are independent random variables, each normally distributed with mean $\mu < b$ and variance σ^2. The company is ruined if its assets ever drop to zero or less. Show

$$\Pr\{\text{ruin}\} < \exp\{-2(b - \mu)X_0/\sigma^2\}.$$

30. Let $Y_1, Y_2, \ldots$ be independent identically distributed positive random variables having finite mean μ. For fixed $0 < \beta < 1$, let a be the smallest value u for which $u \geq \beta E[u \vee Y_1] = \beta E[\max\{u, Y_1\}]$. Set $f(x) = a \vee x$. Show that $\{\beta^n f(M_n)\}$ is a nonnegative supermartingale, where $M_n = \max\{Y_1, \ldots, Y_n\}$ whence $a = f(0) \geq E[\beta^T f(M_T)]$ for all Markov times T. Finally establish that $a = E[\beta^{T^*} M_{T^*}]$ for $T^* = \min\{n \geq 1\colon Y_n \geq a\}$. Thus, T^* maximizes $E[\beta^T M_T]$ over all Markov times T.

31. Let $X, X_1, X_2, \ldots$ be independent identically distributed random variables having negative mean μ and finite variance σ^2. With $S_0 = 0$ and $S_n = X_1 + \cdots + X_n$, set $M = \max_{n \geq 0} S_n$. In view of $\mu < 0$, we know that $M < \infty$. Assume $E[M] < \infty$. (In fact, it can be shown that this is a consequence of $\sigma^2 < \infty$.) Define $r(x) = x^+ = \max\{x, 0\}$ and $f(x) = E[(x + M - E[M])^+]$.

(a) Show $f(x) \geq r(x)$ for all x.

(b) Show $f(x) \geq E[f(x+X)]$ for all x, so that $\{f(x+S_n)\}$ is a nonnegative supermartingale [*Hint*: Verify and use the fact that M and $(X+M)^+$ have the same distribution.]

(c) Use (a) and (b) to show $f(x) \geq E[(x+S_T)^+]$ for all Markov times T. $[(x+S_\infty)^+ = \lim_{n\to\infty}(X+S_n)^+ = 0.]$

32. (Continuation). Let T^* be the Markov time

$$T^* = \begin{cases} \min\{n \geq 0 : x + S_n \geq E[M]\}, & \text{if } x + S_n \geq E[M] \text{ for some } n, \\ \infty, & \text{if } x + S_n < E[M], \text{ for all } n. \end{cases}$$

Show that $f(x) = E[(x+S_{T^*})^+]$, so that T^* maximizes $E[r(S_T)]$ over all Markov times T.

33. Let $\{X_n\}$ be a success runs Markov chain having transition probabilities $P_{i,\,i+1} = p_i = 1 - P_{i,0}$, for $i = 0, 1, \ldots$. Suppose $0 < p_i < 1$ and $p_i \geq p_{i+1} \geq \cdots$. Fix $0 < \beta < 1$, and let a be the unique value for which $a\beta p_{a-1}/(a-1) > 1 \geq (a+1)\beta p_a/a$. Define

$$f(i) = \begin{cases} a\beta^{a-i} p_i \cdot p_{i+1} \cdots p_{a-1}, & \text{for } i < a, \\ i, & \text{for } i \geq a. \end{cases}$$

(a) Show that $f(i) \geq i$ for all i.

(b) Show that $f(i) \geq \beta E[f(X_n) | X_{n-1} = i]$, so that $\{\beta^n f(X_n)\}$ is a nonnegative supermartingale.

(c) Use (a) and (b) to verify that $f(i) \geq E[\beta^T X_T | X_0 = i]$ for all Markov times T.

(d) Finally, prove $f(i) = E[\beta^{T^*} X_{T^*} | X_0 = i]$, where $T^* = \min\{n \geq 0 : X_n \geq a\}$. Thus, T^* maximizes $E[\beta^T X_T | X_0 = i]$ over all Markov times T.

34. Let Z_n be a Markov chain having transition matrix $P(i,j)$. Let $f(i)$ be a bounded function and define $F(i) = \sum_j P(i,j) f(j) - f(i)$ for all i. Show that

$$\frac{F(Z_1) + \cdots + F(Z_n)}{n} \to 0, \quad \text{as} \quad n \to \infty,$$

with probability one.

Hint: Use the results of Problem 28.

35. Let $\{X_n\}$ be a martingale satisfying $\sup_n E[|X_n|] < \infty$. Derive the representation $X_n = X_n^{(1)} - X_n^{(2)}$, where $\{X_n^{(i)}\}$ are nonnegative martingales having bounded means.

Hint: $Z_n^N = E[|X_{N+1}| \mid Y_0, \ldots, Y_n]$ is increasing in N, so $Z_n = \lim_{N\to\infty} Z_n^N$ exists, is nonnegative, and $E[|Z_n|] \leq \sup_n E[|X_n|] < \infty$. Prove that $\{Z_n\}$ is a martingale, and then use $X_n^{(1)} = Z_n$ and $X_n^{(2)} = Z_n - X_n$.

36. Let $\{X_n\}$ be a submartingale having a finite mean and for which $X_0 = 0$. Derive the representation $X_n = X_n' + X_n''$, where $\{X_n'\}$ is a martingale and $X_n'' \leq X_{n+1}''$ is a nondecreasing process.

Hint: See Elementary Problem 20.

37. Let $\{X_n\}$ be a martingale for which $Y = \sup_n |X_{n+1} - X_n|$ has a finite mean. Let A_1 be the event that $\{X_n\}$ converges and A_2 the event that $\limsup X_n = +\infty$ and $\liminf X_n = -\infty$. Show that $\Pr\{A_1\} + \Pr\{A_2\} = 1$. In words, $\{X_n\}$ either converges, or oscillates very greatly indeed.

Hint: For every k, $\tilde{X}_n = X_{T \wedge n}$ converges, where $T = \min\{n: X_n \geq k\}$, because $\tilde{X}_n \leq k + Y$, so $\sup_n E[\tilde{X}_n] < \infty$. Thus the alternative to $\{X_n\}$ converging is included in the event $\limsup X_n > k$ for every k. The same analysis applies to $\{-X_n\}$.

38. Let $\varphi(\xi)$ be a symmetric function, nondecreasing in $|\xi|$, with $\varphi(0) = 0$, and such that $\{\varphi(Y_j)\}_{j=0}^n$ is a submartingale. Fix $0 = u_0 \leq u_1 \leq \cdots \leq u_n$. Show that

$$\Pr\{|Y_j| \leq u_j;\ 1 \leq j \leq n\} \geq 1 - \sum_{j=1}^{n} \frac{E[\varphi(Y_j)] - E[\varphi(Y_{j-1})]}{\varphi(u_j)}.$$

(If $\varphi(\xi) = \xi^2$, $u_1 = \cdots = u_n = \lambda$, we obtain Kolmogorov's inequality.)

Hint: Let I_j be 1 if $\{|Y_j| \leq u_j\}$ and 0 otherwise. Then

$$\Pr\{|Y_j| \leq u_j;\ 1 \leq j \leq n\} = E\left[\prod_{j=1}^{n} I_j\right]$$

$$\geq E\left[\prod_{j=1}^{n-1} I_j\left(1 - \frac{\varphi(Y_n)}{\varphi(u_n)}\right)\right]$$

$$\geq E\left[\prod_{j=1}^{n-1} I_j\left(1 - \frac{\varphi(Y_{n-1})}{\varphi(u_{n-1})}\right)\right] - \frac{E[\varphi(Y_n)] - E[\varphi(Y_{n-1})]}{\varphi(u_n)},$$

using successively that $\{\varphi(Y_n)\}$ is a submartingale, and $\{u_n\}$ increasing. Repeat.

39. Let $\{Y_n\}$ be a nonnegative submartingale and suppose b_n is a nonincreasing sequence of positive numbers. Suppose $\sum_{n=1}^{\infty}(b_n - b_{n+1})E[Y_n] < \infty$. Prove that

$$\lambda \Pr\{\sup_{k \geq 1} b_k Y_k > \lambda\} < \sum_{k=1}^{\infty} (b_k - b_{k+1})E[Y_k].$$

40. Let $\{X_n\}$ be a family of r.v.'s and let $\varphi(\xi)$ be a positive function defined for $\xi > 0$ satisfying

$$\frac{\varphi(\xi)}{\xi} \to \infty \quad \text{as} \quad \xi \to \infty.$$

Suppose that

$$\sup_{m \geq 1} E[\varphi(|X_m|)] \leq K < \infty.$$

Show that $\{X_n\}$ is uniformly integrable.

41. Let $R_k(x)$ be a Rademacher functions $R_k(x) = \text{sign}\sin(2^{k+1}\pi x)$. Define

$$L_n(x) = \prod_{k=1}^{n} (1 + a_k R_k(x)) \qquad \text{for} \quad 0 \leq x \leq 1,$$

where a_k are constants.

Let $\mathscr{F}_n$, $n = 0, 1, \ldots$ be the field of sets induced by the partition of the unit interval, viz.,

$$\left(\frac{k}{2^{n+1}}, \frac{k+1}{2^{n+1}}\right) \qquad k = 0, 1, \ldots, 2^{n+1}.$$

Let $\mu(dx)$ be a probability measure which assigns probability $1/2^{n+1}$ to each basic subinterval of $\mathscr{F}_n$. Show that

(1) L_n is a r.v. measurable $\mathscr{F}_n$.
(2) L_n is a martingale adapted to the σ-fields $\mathscr{F}_n$.

NOTES

Doob [1] developed martingale theory and demonstrated the broad usefulness of the concept.

REFERENCES

1. J. L. Doob, "Stochastic Processes." Wiley, New York, 1953.
2. Paul-Andre Meyer, "Martingales and Stochastic Integrals." Springer-Verlag, Berlin, New York, 1972 (Lecture Notes in Mathematics No. 284).
3. J. Neveu, "Mathematical Foundations of the Calculus of Probability." Holden-Day, San Francisco, 1965.
4. J. Neveu, "Martingales a Temps Discret." Masson, Paris, 1972.

Chapter 7

BROWNIAN MOTION

R. Brown, in 1827, observed that small particles immersed in a liquid exhibit ceaseless irregular motions. Historically, the Brownian motion process that is the subject of this chapter arose as an early attempt to explain this phenomenon. Today, the Brownian motion process and its many generalizations and extensions arise in numerous and diverse areas of pure and applied science such as economics, communication theory, biology, management science, and mathematical statistics.

The first four sections of this chapter provide an introduction that should be included in every first course in stochastic processes. The next section uses martingale methods to compute a number of expectations and probabilities associated with Brownian motion. It requires Section 5 of Chapter 6 as a prerequisite. The last sections treat more specialized topics.

1: *Background Material*

Certain special classes of stochastic processes have undergone extensive mathematical development. The Brownian motion process is the most renowned and historically the first which was thoroughly investigated. We will present a bare introduction to some of its salient features and hope thereby to whet the appetite of the reader for the elegant and elaborate theory of this process.

As a physical phenomenon the Brownian motion was discovered by the English botanist Brown in 1827. A mathematical description of this phenomenon was first derived from the laws of physics by Einstein in 1905. Since then the subject has made considerable progress. The physical theory was further perfected by Smoluchowski, Fokker, Planck, Burger, Furth, Ornstein, Uhlenbeck, Chandrasekhar, Kramers, and others. The mathematical theory was slower in developing because the exact mathematical description of the model posed difficulties, whereas some of the questions to which the physicists sought answers on the basis of this model were quite simple and intuitive. Many of the answers were obtained in a heuristic way by Bachelier in his 1900 dissertation[1] whereas the first

[1] Louis Bachelier, "Théorie de la spéculation" (doctoral dissertation in mathematics, University of Paris, March 29, 1900), *Annales de l'Ecole Normale Supérieure*, *Ser.* 3, 17, 21–86 (1900). English translation: pp. 17–75 of P. H. Cootner (ed.) The Random Character of Stock Market Prices, MIT Press, Cambridge, Massachusetts, 1964.

concise mathematical formulation of the theory was given by Wiener in his 1918 dissertation and later papers. (See the References at the close of the chapter.)

In terms of our general framework of stochastic processes, the Brownian motion process is an example of a continuous time, continuous state space, Markov process.

Let $X(t)$ be the x component (as a function of time) of a particle in Brownian motion (cf. p. 21). Let x_0 be the position of the particle at time t_0, i.e., $X(t_0) = x_0$. Let $p(x, t|x_0)$ represent the conditional probability density of $X(t + t_0)$, given that $X(t_0) = x_0$. We postulate that the probability law governing the transitions is stationary in time and therefore $p(x, t|x_0)$ does not depend on the initial time t_0.

Since $p(x, t|x_0)$ is a density function in x, we have the properties

$$p(x, t|x_0) \geq 0, \qquad \int_{-\infty}^{\infty} p(x, t|x_0)\, dx = 1. \tag{1.1}$$

Further, we stipulate that, for small t, $X(t + t_0)$ is likely to be near $X(t_0) = x_0$. This is done formally by requiring

$$\lim_{t \to 0} p(x, t|x_0) = 0, \qquad \text{for } x \neq x_0. \tag{1.2}$$

From physical principles Einstein showed that $p(x, t|x_0)$ must satisfy the partial differential equation

$$\frac{\partial p}{\partial t} = D \frac{\partial^2 p}{\partial x^2}. \tag{1.3}$$

This is called the diffusion equation, and D is the diffusion coefficient. Small particles execute Brownian motion owing to collisions with the molecules in the gas or liquid in which they are suspended. The evaluation of D is based on the formula $D = 2RT/Nf$, where R is the gas constant, T is the temperature, N is Avogadro's number, and f is a coefficient of friction. By choosing the proper scale we may take $D = \frac{1}{2}$. Then we can verify directly that

$$p(x, t|x_0) = \frac{1}{\sqrt{2\pi t}} \exp\left(-\frac{1}{2t}(x - x_0)^2\right) \tag{1.4}$$

is a solution of (1.3), in fact, the unique solution under the boundary conditions (1.1) and (1.2). (The problem of the uniqueness of solutions of (1.3) needs to be formulated precisely and its analysis entails considerable care beyond the scope of this book.

Another approach to (1.3) is an approximation by means of a discrete random walk. Consider the symmetric random walk on the integers (see Example B, Section 2 of Chapter 2). Let $p_k(n)$ be the probability that a particle in this random walk finds itself k steps to the right of its starting point at time n. The Chapman–Kolmogorov relation [formula (3.2) of Chapter 2] for this process becomes

$$p_k(n+1) = \tfrac{1}{2}p_{k+1}(n) + \tfrac{1}{2}p_{k-1}(n),$$

which we may write as

$$p_k(n+1) - p_k(n) = \tfrac{1}{2}[p_{k+1}(n) - 2p_k(n) + p_{k-1}(n)]. \tag{1.5}$$

We recognize on the left the discrete version of the time derivative and on the right one half of the discrete version of the second derivative in the spatial variable. By an appropriate limiting process where the time between transitions shrinks to zero and simultaneously the size of the steps contracts appropriately to zero we may pass from (1.5) to (1.3).

Specifically, let the length of time between transitions be Δ, and the length of each step η. Then the analog of (1.5) is

$$\frac{p_{k\eta}((n+1)\Delta) - p_{k\eta}(n\Delta)}{\Delta} = \frac{\tfrac{1}{2}[p_{(k+1)\eta}(n\Delta) - 2p_{k\eta}(n\Delta) + p_{(k-1)\eta}(n\Delta)]}{\Delta}. \tag{1.6}$$

Now let Δ and η shrink to zero, preserving the relationship $\Delta = \eta^2$, and at the same time let n and k increase to ∞ so that $k\eta \to x$ while $n\Delta \to t$. Then $p_{k\eta}(n\Delta) \to p(x, t|0)$ and (1.6) passes formally into (1.3).

We will not attempt to rigorize this procedure. It is simple in concept, but requires rather delicate analysis to make it precise.

Another kind of limiting process for $p_k(n)$ requires the central limit theorem. We write

$$p_k(n) = \Pr\{X_1 + X_2 + \cdots + X_n = k\},$$

where $\{X_i\}$ represent the successive outcomes of tossing a fair coin, (i.e., $X_i = 1$ if heads and $X_i = -1$ if tails, each occurring with probability $\frac{1}{2}$). By the central limit theorem (see Section 1, Chapter 1).

$$\lim_{n\to\infty} \sum_{k=-\infty}^{\sqrt{n}x} p_k(n) = \frac{1}{\sqrt{2\pi}} \int_{-\infty}^{x} \exp(-u^2/2)\, du. \tag{1.7}$$

The limiting relation of (1.6) and that of (1.7) are essentially the same and are connected by the "invariance principle of stochastic processes." These heuristics can be made precise but are beyond the scope of this book.

2: *Joint Probabilities for Brownian Motion*

The transition probability density function (1.4) gives merely the probability distribution of $X(t)-X(0)$. The complete description of the Brownian motion process is furnished by the following definition.

Definition 2.1. *Brownian motion is a stochastic process* $\{X(t);\ t\geq 0\}$ *with the following properties:*

(a) *Every increment* $X(t+s)-X(s)$ *is normally distributed with mean* 0 *and variance* $\sigma^2 t$; σ *is a fixed parameter.*

(b) *For every pair of disjoint time intervals* $[t_1, t_2]$, $[t_3, t_4]$, *say* $t_1<t_2\leq t_3<t_4$, *the increments* $X(t_4)-X(t_3)$ *and* $X(t_2)-X(t_1)$ *are independent random variables with distributions given in* (a), *and similarly for* n *disjoint time intervals where* n *is an arbitrary positive integer.*

(c) $X(0)=0$ *and* $X(t)$ *is continuous at* $t=0$.

This means that we postulate that a displacement $X(t+s)-X(s)$ is independent of the past, or alternatively, if we know $X(s)=x_0$, then no further knowledge of the values of $X(\tau)$ for $\tau<s$ has any effect on our knowledge of the probability law governing $X(t+s)-X(s)$. Written formally, this says that if $t>t_0>t_1>\cdots>t_n$,

$$\begin{aligned}\Pr[X(t)\leq x|X(t_0)=x_0, X(t_1)=x_1, \cdots, X(t_n)=x_n]\\ =\Pr[X(t)\leq x|X(t_0)=x_0].\end{aligned}\tag{2.1}$$

This is a statement of the Markov character of the process. We emphasize, however, that the independent increment assumption (b) is actually more restrictive than the Markov property.

Under the condition that $X(0)=0$, the variance of $X(t)$ is $\sigma^2 t$. Hence σ^2 is sometimes called the variance parameter of the process. The process $\tilde{X}(t)=X(t)/\sigma$ is a Brownian motion process having a variance parameter of one, called *standard Brownian motion*. By this device we may always reduce an arbitrary Brownian motion to a standard Brownian motion; for the most part we derive results only for the latter.

By part (a) of the definition with $\sigma^2=1$, we have

$$\begin{aligned}\Pr[X(t)\leq x|X(t_0)=x_0]&=\Pr[X(t)-X(t_0)\leq x-x_0]\\ &=\frac{1}{\sqrt{2\pi(t-t_0)}}\int_{-\infty}^{x-x_0}\exp\left[-\frac{\alpha^2}{2(t-t_0)}\right]d\alpha.\end{aligned}\tag{2.2}$$

The consistency of part (b) of the definition with part (a) follows from well-known properties of the normal distribution, e.g., if $t_1 \le t_2 \le t_3$ then

$$X(t_3) - X(t_1) = [X(t_3) - X(t_2)] + [X(t_2) - X(t_1)].$$

On the right we have independent normal random variables with means 0 and variances $t_3 - t_2$ and $t_2 - t_1$, respectively. Hence their sum is normal with mean 0 and variance $t_3 - t_1$ as it should be.

It is not difficult using (2.1) and (2.2) to derive the joint density of $X(t_1), X(t_2), \ldots, X(t_n)(t_1 < t_2 < \cdots < t_n)$ subject to the condition $X(0) = 0$. Indeed, we only have to know the probability density of $X_1 = X(t_1) = x_1$, of $X_2 - X_1 = x_2 - x_1$, etc., and finally that of $X_n - X_{n-1} = x_n - x_{n-1}$. By part (b) of the definition we get at once the following expression for the density function:

$$f(x_1, \ldots, x_n) = p(x_1, t_1)p(x_2 - x_1, t_2 - t_1) \cdot \cdots \cdot p(x_n - x_{n-1}, t_n - t_{n-1}), \tag{2.3}$$

where

$$p(x, t) = \frac{1}{\sqrt{2\pi t}} \exp(-x^2/2t). \tag{2.4}$$

With the explicit formula (2.3) in hand we can compute in principle any set of conditional probabilities desired.

According to the Markov property, we know that, if $t_1 < t_2 < t_3$, the conditional density of $X(t_3)$, given $X(t_1)$ and $X(t_2)$, is the same as that of $X(t_3)$ given just $X(t_2)$.

However, the density of $X(t_2)$ given $X(t_1)$ and $X(t_3)$ is also of interest. Suppose, for definiteness, $X(t_1) = X(t_3) = 0$ and say specifically that $t_1 = 0$, $t_3 = 1$, and $t_2 = t(0 < t < 1)$.

By (2.3) the joint density of $X(t)$ and $X(1)$ is

$$f(x, y) = \frac{1}{2\pi\sqrt{t(1-t)}} \exp\left[-\frac{1}{2}\left\{\frac{x^2}{t} + \frac{(y-x)^2}{1-t}\right\}\right].$$

It follows that the conditional density of $X(t)$ given $X(0) = X(1) = 0$, denoted by $f_t(x|X(0) = X(1) = 0)$ is

$$\frac{1}{\sqrt{2\pi t(1-t)}} \exp\left[-\frac{1}{2}\frac{x^2}{t(1-t)}\right] \qquad -\infty < x < \infty.$$

In particular $E_c(X(t)) = 0$ and $E_c(X^2(t)) = t(1-t)$, where E_c refers to expectations taken under the conditions $X(0) = X(1) = 0$. The same methods yield the more general interpolation result.

Theorem 2.1. *The conditional density of $X(t)$ for $t_1 < t < t_2$ given $X(t_1) = A$ and $X(t_2) = B$ is a normal density with mean*

$$A + \frac{B - A}{t_2 - t_1}(t - t_1) \qquad \textit{and variance} \quad \frac{(t_2 - t)(t - t_1)}{t_2 - t_1}.$$

This can be reduced to the preceding case as follows. The conditional random variable $X(t)$ as indicated, i.e., the r.v. $X(t)$ subject to the conditions $X(t_1) = A$ and $X(t_2) = B$, has the same density as the random variable $A + X(t - t_1)$ under the condition $X(0) = 0$, $X(t_2 - t_1) = B - A$. This clearly has the same density as the random variable

$$A + X(t - t_1) + \frac{(t - t_1)}{t_2 - t_1}(B - A)$$

under the conditions $X(0) = 0$ and $X(t_2 - t_1) = 0$.

3: Continuity of Paths and the Maximum Variables

The physical origins of the Brownian motion process suggest that the possible realizations $X(t)$, as the graphs of the x coordinate of the position of a particle (i.e., the sample paths) whose movements result from continuous collisions in the surrounding medium are continuous functions. This fact is correct but a rigorous proof requires rather delicate analysis and is deferred until Section 7.

The sample paths $X(t)$, although continuous, are very kinky and their derivative exists nowhere. This fact is also rather deep. A complete description of the path structure of the Brownian motion process can be found in P. Lévy and in Ito and McKean (see References at the end of this chapter).

Using the property of the continuity of paths we will show how to calculate various interesting probability expressions of the Brownian motion. The first computation illustrates the use of the so-called *reflection principle.*

Bearing in mind the continuity of $X(t)$, we consider the collection of sample paths $X(t)$, $0 \le t \le T$, $X(0) = 0$, with the property that $X(T) > a$ $(a > 0)$. Since $X(t)$ is continuous and $X(0) = 0$ there exists a time τ (itself a random variable depending on the particular sample path) at which $X(t)$ first attains the value a.

For $t > \tau$, we reflect $X(t)$ about the line $x = a$ to obtain

$$\tilde{X}(t) = \begin{cases} X(t) & \text{for } \ t < \tau, \\ a - [X(t) - a] & \text{for } \ t > \tau \end{cases}$$

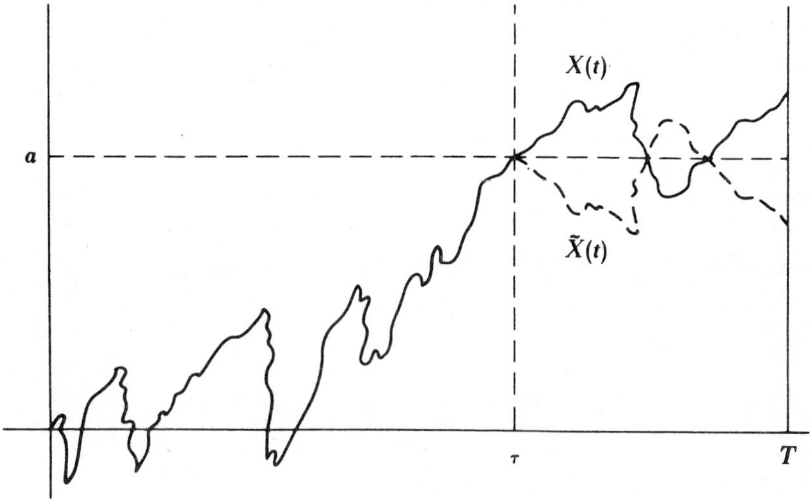

FIG. 1

(see Fig. 1). Note that $\tilde{X}(T) < a$ since $X(T) > a$. Because the probability law of the path for $t > \tau$, given $X(\tau) = a$, is symmetrical with respect to the values $x > a$ and $x < a$ and independent of the history prior to time τ, the reflection argument displays for every sample path with $X(T) > a$ two sample paths $X(t)$ and $\tilde{X}(t)$ with the same probability of occurrence such that

$$\max_{0 \le u \le T} X(u) \ge a \qquad \text{and} \qquad \max_{0 \le u \le T} \tilde{X}(u) \ge a.$$

Conversely, by the nature of this correspondence every sample function $X(t)$ for which $\max_{0 \le u \le T} X(u) \ge a$ results from either of two sample functions $X(t)$ with equal probability, one of which is such that $X(T) > a$, unless $X(T) = a$. But $\Pr\{X(T) = a\} = 0$. Thus, we may conclude, under the condition $X(0) = 0$, that

$$\Pr\left\{\max_{0 \le u \le T} X(u) \ge a\right\} = 2 \Pr\{X(T) > a\} = \frac{2}{\sqrt{2\pi T}} \int_a^\infty \exp(-x^2/2T)\, dx. \tag{3.1}$$

The above argument cannot be considered complete although the method is typical of a great deal of the analysis underlying the study of Markov processes with continuous paths. (Such processes are called diffusion processes.) A rigorous treatment would involve using the strong Markov property on the Markov time (see Section 4, Chapter 14) corresponding to the event of first passage from the value 0 to the value a.

With the help of (3.1) we may determine the distribution of the first time of reaching $a > 0$ subject to the condition $X(0) = 0$. Let T_a denote the time at which $X(t)$ first attains the value a where $X(0) = 0$. Then clearly

$$\Pr\{T_a \le t\} = \Pr\left\{\max_{0\le u\le t} X(u) \ge a \,|\, X(0) = 0\right\}. \tag{3.2}$$

But according to (3.1)

$$\Pr\left\{\max_{0\le u\le t} X(u) \ge a \,|\, X(0) = 0\right\} = 2\Pr\{X(t) > a\} = \frac{2}{\sqrt{2\pi t}} \int_a^\infty \exp\left[-\frac{1}{2}\frac{x^2}{t}\right] dx$$

and so

$$\Pr\{T_a \le t\} = \sqrt{\frac{2}{\pi t}} \int_a^\infty \exp\left[-\frac{1}{2}\frac{x^2}{t}\right] dx.$$

The change of variable $x = y\sqrt{t}$ leads to

$$\Pr\{T_a \le t\} = \sqrt{\frac{2}{\pi}} \int_{a/\sqrt{t}}^\infty \exp\left[-\frac{y^2}{2}\right] dy. \tag{3.3}$$

The density function of the random variable T_a is obtained by differentiating (3.3) with respect to t. Thus

$$f_{T_a}(t \,|\, X(0) = 0)\, dt = \frac{a}{\sqrt{2\pi}} t^{-3/2} \exp\left[-\frac{a^2}{2t}\right] dt. \tag{3.4}$$

Because of the symmetry and spatial homogeneity of the Brownian motion process we infer for the distribution (3.4) that

$$\begin{aligned}
&\Pr\left\{\min_{0\le u\le t} X(u) \le 0 \,|\, X(0) = a\right\} \\
&= \Pr\left\{\max_{0\le u\le t} X(u) \ge 0 \,|\, X(0) = -a\right\} && \text{(by symmetry)} \\
&= \Pr\left\{\max_{0\le u\le t} X(u) \ge a \,|\, X(0) = 0\right\} = \Pr\{T_a \le t\} && \text{(by homogeneity)} \\
&= \frac{a}{\sqrt{2\pi}} \int_0^t u^{-3/2} \exp\left[-\frac{a^2}{2u}\right] du, && a > 0.
\end{aligned} \tag{3.5}$$

Another way to express the result of (3.5) is as follows: If $X(t_0) = a$ then the probability $P(a)$ that $X(t)$ has at least one zero between t_0 and t_1 is

$$P(a) = \frac{|a|}{\sqrt{2\pi}} \int_0^{t_1 - t_0} \exp\left[-\frac{a^2}{2u}\right] u^{-3/2}\, du. \tag{3.6}$$

With this in hand we can calculate the probability α that if $X(0)=0$ then $X(t)$ vanishes at least once in the interval (t_0, t_1).

In fact, we condition on the possible values of $X(t_0)$. Thus, if $X(t_0)=a$ then the probability that $X(t)$ vanishes in the interval (t_0, t_1) is $P(a)$. By the law of total probabilities

$$\alpha=\int_0^\infty P(a)\Pr\{|X(t_0)|=a \,|\, X(0)=0\}\,da=\sqrt{\frac{2}{\pi t_0}}\int_0^\infty P(a)\exp\left[-\frac{a^2}{2t_0}\right]da. \tag{3.7}$$

Substituting from (3.6) and then interchanging the order of integration yields

$$\begin{aligned}\alpha&=\sqrt{\frac{2}{\pi t_0}}\int_0^\infty \exp\left[-\frac{a^2}{2t_0}\right]\frac{a}{\sqrt{2\pi}}\left(\int_0^{t_1-t_0}\exp\left[-\frac{a^2}{2u}\right]u^{-3/2}\,du\right)da\\ &=\frac{1}{\pi\sqrt{t_0}}\int_0^{t_1-t_0}u^{-3/2}\left(\int_0^\infty a\exp\left[-\frac{a^2}{2}\left(\frac{1}{u}+\frac{1}{t_0}\right)\right]da\right)du.\end{aligned} \tag{3.8}$$

The inner integral can be integrated exactly and after simplifying we get

$$\alpha=\frac{\sqrt{t_0}}{\pi}\int_0^{t_1-t_0}\frac{du}{(t_0+u)\sqrt{u}}.$$

The change of variables $u=t_0v^2$ produces

$$\alpha=\frac{2}{\pi}\int_0^{\sqrt{(t_1-t_0)/t_0}}\frac{dv}{1+v^2}=\frac{2}{\pi}\arctan\sqrt{\frac{t_1-t_0}{t_0}},$$

which we may write by virtue of some standard trigonometric relations in the form

$$\sqrt{\frac{t_0}{t_1}}=\cos\frac{\pi\alpha}{2}\qquad\text{or}\qquad\alpha=\frac{2}{\pi}\arccos\sqrt{\frac{t_0}{t_1}}.$$

To sum up, we have

Theorem 3.1. *The probability that $X(t)$ has at least one zero in the interval (t_0, t_1), given $X(0)=0$, is*

$$\alpha=\frac{2}{\pi}\arccos\sqrt{\frac{t_0}{t_1}}.$$

With the aid of the same "reflection principle" we now solve the following problem: Determine

$$A_t(x,y)=\Pr\left\{X(t)>y,\ \min_{0\le u\le t}X(u)>0 \,\middle|\, X(0)=x\right\} \tag{3.9}$$

for $x > 0$ and $y > 0$. To determine (3.9), we start with the obvious relation

$$\Pr\{X(t) > y | X(0) = x\}$$
$$= A_t(x, y) + \Pr\left\{X(t) > y, \min_{0 \le u \le t} X(u) \le 0 | X(0) = x\right\}. \tag{3.10}$$

The reflection principle is applied to the last term.

Figure 2 is the appropriate picture to guide the analysis; we may deduce that

$$\Pr\{X(t) > y, \min_{0 \le u \le t} X(u) \le 0 | X(0) = x\}$$
$$= \Pr\left\{X(t) < -y, \min_{0 \le u \le t} X(u) \le 0 | X(0) = x\right\} \tag{3.11}$$
$$= \Pr\{X(t) < -y | X(0) = x\}.$$

The reasoning behind (3.11) goes as follows: Consider a path starting at $x > 0$ satisfying $X(t) > y$ which reaches 0 at some intermediate time τ.

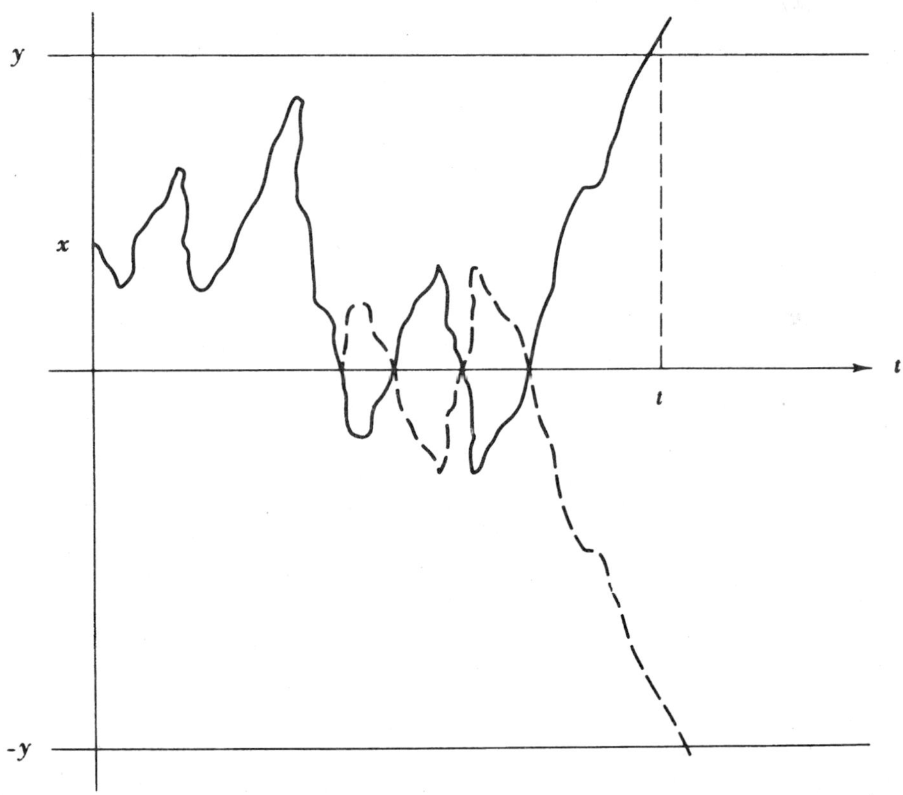

FIG. 2

By reflecting such a path about zero after time τ we obtain a path starting from x and reaching a value smaller than $-y$ at time t. This implies the equality of the first two terms of (3.11). The equality of the last two terms is clear from their meaning since the condition $\min_{0\le u\le t} X(u) \le 0$ is superfluous in view of the requirement $X(t) < -y$ $(y > 0)$. Inserting (3.11) in (3.10) yields

$$\begin{aligned} A_t(x, y) &= \Pr\{X(t) > y | X(0) = x\} - \Pr\{X(t) < -y | X(0) = x\} \\ &= \Pr\{X(t) > y - x | X(0) = 0\} - \Pr\{X(t) < -(y + x) | X(0) = 0\} \\ &\qquad \text{(by spatial homogeneity)} \\ &= \Pr\{X(t) > y - x | X(0) = 0\} - \Pr\{X(t) > y + x | X(0) = 0\} \\ &\qquad \text{(by symmetry)} \\ &= \int_{y-x}^{y+x} p(u, t)\, du, \end{aligned} \tag{3.12}$$

where $p(u, t) = (2\pi t)^{-1/2} \exp\{-u^2/2t\}$ is the transition probability density function for the Brownian motion process.

As a final application of the reflection principle we now derive the joint probability density function for

$$M(t) = \max_{0\le u\le t} X(u), \qquad \text{and} \qquad Y(t) = M(t) - X(t).$$

The reflection principle, with Fig. 3 as an aid, implies

$$\begin{aligned} \Pr\{M(t) \ge m,\ X(t) \le x\} &= \Pr\{X(t) \ge 2m - x\} \\ &= 1 - \Phi\left(\frac{2m - x}{\sqrt{t}}\right), \qquad m \ge 0, \quad m \ge x, \end{aligned}$$

where $\Phi(x)$ is the distribution function of the standard normal density $\phi(x) = (1/\sqrt{2\pi}) \exp(-x^2/2)$. Differentiate with respect to x and then with respect to m, changing the sign, to get the joint density function for $M(t)$ and $X(t)$.

The calculations are:

$$\begin{aligned} -\frac{d}{dm}\frac{d}{dx}\left\{1 - \Phi\left(\frac{2m - x}{\sqrt{t}}\right)\right\} &= -\frac{d}{dm}\left\{\frac{1}{\sqrt{t}}\phi\left(\frac{2m - x}{\sqrt{t}}\right)\right\} \\ &= \frac{2m - x}{t}\frac{2}{\sqrt{t}}\phi\left(\frac{2m - x}{\sqrt{t}}\right), \end{aligned}$$

using the elementary relation

$$\frac{d}{dx}\phi(x) = -x\phi(x).$$

Denoting this joint density by $f(m, x)$, we have explicitly

$$f(m, x)=\sqrt{\frac{2}{\pi t^3}}\,(2m-x)\exp[-(2m-x)^2/2t], \qquad \begin{cases}0\le m,\\ x\le m.\end{cases} \tag{3.13}$$

To obtain the joint density $g(m, y)$ of $M(t)$, $Y(t)=M(t)-X(t)$, we have

$$\Pr\{M(t)\le a,\ Y(t)\le b\}=\int\limits_{m\le a}\int\limits_{y\le b} f(m, m-y)\,dy\,dm,$$

so the desired joint density is $g(m, y)=f(m, m-y)$ or

$$g(m, y)=\sqrt{\frac{2}{\pi t^3}}\,(m+y)\exp[-(m+y)^2/2t], \qquad m\ge 0,\quad y\ge 0. \tag{3.14}$$

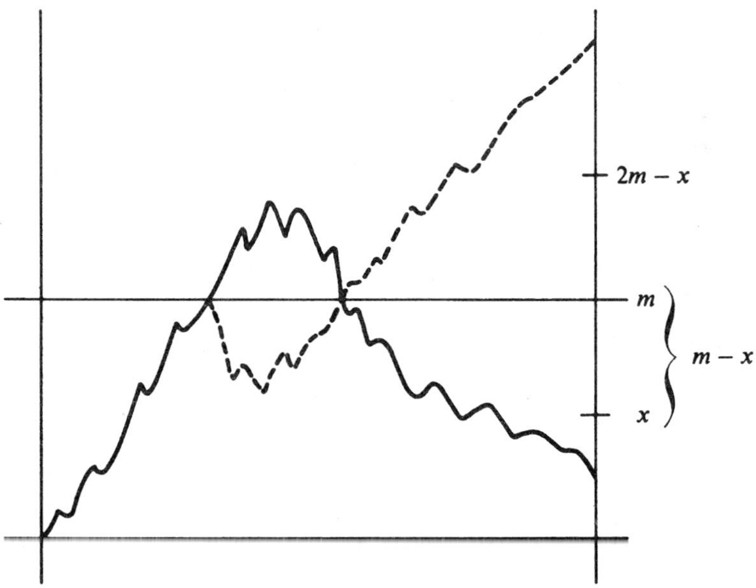

FIG. 3

4: Variations and Extensions

We claim that if $X(t)$ is a standard Brownian motion process, then the processes

$$X_1(t)=cX(t/c^2), \qquad \text{for fixed}\quad c>0,$$

$$X_2(t)=\begin{cases}tX(1/t), & \text{for}\quad t>0,\\ 0, & \text{for}\quad t=0,\end{cases}$$

and

$$X_3(t)=X(t+h)-X(h), \qquad \text{for fixed}\quad h>0.$$

are each a version of standard Brownian motion.

We check the requirements of Definition 2.1. Manifestly, every increment $X_i(t+s)-X_i(t)$ in these processes is normally distributed with zero mean, and the increments over disjoint time intervals manifestly determine independent r.v's. To continue the verification that these are Brownian motions we need the variance $E[\{X_i(s+t)-X_i(s)\}^2]$ in each case. We have

$$\begin{aligned}
E[\{X_1(t+s)-X_1(s)\}^2] &= c^2E[\{X((t+s)/c^2)-X(s/c^2)\}^2] \\
&= c^2\{(t+s)/c^2 - s/c^2\} = t,
\end{aligned}$$

$$\begin{aligned}
E[\{X_2(t+s)-X_2(s)\}^2] &= E\left[\left\{sX\left(\frac{1}{s}\right)-(t+s)X\left(\frac{1}{t+s}\right)\right\}^2\right] \\
&= s^2E\left[\left\{X\left(\frac{1}{s}\right)-X\left(\frac{1}{t+s}\right)\right\}^2\right]+t^2E\left[\left\{X\left(\frac{1}{t+s}\right)\right\}^2\right] \\
&= s^2\left\{\frac{1}{s}-\frac{1}{t+s}\right\}+t^2\frac{1}{t+s} \\
&= t,
\end{aligned}$$

and

$$E[\{X_3(t+s)-X_3(s)\}^2] = E[\{X(t+h+s)-X(h+s)\}^2] = t.$$

To complete the analysis, it is necessary to check that each $X_i(t)$ is continuous at the origin. This property is obvious for $X_1(t)$ and $X_3(t)$ but needs some arguments for $X_2(t)$. Equivalently, in the latter case it is enough to show that

$$\Pr\left\{\lim_{t\to\infty}\frac{X(t)}{t}=0 \middle| X(0)=0\right\}=1.$$

(See Problems 14 and 15.)

Other modifications of Brownian motion lead to new and important stochastic processes. Here are some examples.

A. BROWNIAN MOTION REFLECTED AT THE ORIGIN

Let $\{X(t),\ t\geq 0\}$ be a Brownian motion process. A stochastic process having the distribution of

$$\begin{aligned}
Y(t) &= |X(t)|, \qquad t\geq 0 \\
&= \begin{cases} X(t), & \text{if } X(t)\geq 0, \\ -X(t), & \text{if } X(t)<0, \end{cases}
\end{aligned}$$

is called *Brownian motion reflected at the origin*, which we abbreviate to *reflected Brownian motion*.

Because of the spatial symmetry of Brownian motion, reflected Brownian motion is Markov. Indeed, in the case of standard Brownian motion ($\sigma^2 = 1$),

$$
\begin{aligned}
\Pr\{Y(t_n+s) \le z \mid Y(t_0)=x_0, \ldots, Y(t_n)=x_n\} \\
&= \Pr\{-z \le X(t_n+s) \le +z \mid X(t_0) = \pm x_0, \ldots, X(t_n) = \pm x_n\} \\
&= \Pr\{-z \le X(t_n+s) \le +z \mid X(t_0) = x_0, \ldots, X(t_n) = x_n\} \\
&\qquad\qquad\qquad\qquad \text{by symmetry} \\
&= \Pr\{-z \le X(t_n+s) \le +z \mid X(t_n) = x_n\} \\
&= \int_{-z}^{+z} p(y - x_n, s)\, dy, \qquad (4.1)
\end{aligned}
$$

where

$$p(x, t) = \frac{1}{\sqrt{2\pi t}} \exp\{-x^2/2t\}, \qquad (4.2)$$

and $0 \le t_0 < t_1 < \cdots < t_n$, $s > 0$. Thus reflected Brownian motion furnishes an example of another continuous time Markov process whose sample paths $Y(t)$ are continuous. The state space consists of the set of nonnegative real numbers.

Since the moments of $Y(t)$ are the same as the moments of $|X(t)|$, the mean and variance of reflected Brownian motion may be computed easily. Under the condition $Y(0) = 0$, for example, we have,

$$
\begin{aligned}
E[Y(t)] &= \int_{-\infty}^{+\infty} |x| p(x, t)\, dx \\
&= 2\int_0^\infty \frac{x}{\sqrt{2\pi t}} \exp\{-x^2/2t\}\, dx \\
&= \sqrt{\frac{2t}{\pi}}.
\end{aligned}
$$

The integral was evaluated through the change of variable $y = x/\sqrt{t}$. Also,

$$
\begin{aligned}
\text{variance of } Y(t) &= E[Y(t)^2] - E[Y(t)]^2 \\
&= E[|X(t)|^2] - 2t/\pi \\
&= (1 - 2/\pi)t.
\end{aligned}
$$

By changing variables in (4.1) it is easily seen that, for $t > 0$, $Y(t)$ is a continuous random variable with transition probability density function

$$p_t(x, y) = p(y - x, t) + p(y + x, t), \tag{4.3}$$

for which

$$\Pr\{\alpha \le Y(t) \le \beta \mid Y(0) = x\} = \int_\alpha^\beta p_t(x, y)\, dy,$$

where $p(x, t)$ is given in (4.2).

B. BROWNIAN MOTION ABSORBED AT THE ORIGIN

Suppose the initial value $X(0) = x$ of a Brownian motion process is positive† and let τ be the first time the process reaches zero. A stochastic process having the distribution of

$$Z(t) = \begin{cases} X(t), & \text{for } t \le \tau, \\ 0 & \text{for } t > \tau, \end{cases} \tag{4.4}$$

is called ***Brownian motion absorbed at the origin***, which we will shorten to ***absorbed Brownian motion.***

Again, absorbed Brownian motion is a continuous time Markov process. We verify the Markov property in the form,

$$\begin{aligned} &\Pr\{Z(t_n + s) > y \mid Z(t_0) = x_0, \ldots, Z(t_{n-1}) = x_{n-1}, Z(t_n) = x\} \\ &\qquad = \Pr\{Z(t_n + s) > z \mid Z(t_n) = x\}, \end{aligned}$$

where $x > 0$ and $0 < t_0 < \cdots < t_n$, $s > 0$. (The easier case, when $x = 0$ is left to the reader.) We compute this by way of a Brownian motion process $X(t)$ related to $Z(t)$ as in (4.1). The condition $x > 0$ entails

$$\min_{0 \le u \le t_n} X(u) > 0.$$

Hence

$$\begin{aligned} &\Pr\{Z(t_n + t) > y \mid Z(t_0) = x_0, \ldots, Z(t_{n-1}) = x_{n-1}, Z(t_n) = x\} \\ &\quad = \Pr\{Z(t_n + t) > y \mid Z(t_0) = x_0, \ldots, Z(t_{n-1}) = x_{n-1}, Z(t_n) \\ &\qquad\qquad = x, \min_{0 \le v \le t_n} X(u) > 0\} \\ &\quad = \Pr\{X(t_n + t) > y, \min_{0 \le u \le t} X(t_n + u) > 0 \mid X(t_0) = x_0, \ldots, X(t_{n-1}) \\ &\qquad\qquad = x_{n-1}, X(t_n) = x\} \\ &\quad = \Pr\{X(t) > y, \min_{0 \le u \le t} X(u) > 0 \mid X(0) = x\} \\ &\quad = A_t(x, y), \end{aligned}$$

† To define Brownian motion conditioned on $X(0) = x$, or "Brownian motion starting from x," replace "$X(0) = 0$" by "$X(0) = x$" in Part (c) of Definition 2.1.

where $A_t(x, y)$ was defined in (3.9) and computed in (3.12) to be

$$A_t(x, y) = \int_y^\infty [p(u - x, t) - p(u + x, t)]\, du$$
$$= \int_y^{y+2x} p(u - x, t)\, du.$$

Under the condition $Z(0) = x > 0$, $Z(t)$ is a random variable whose distribution has both discrete and continuous parts. The discrete part is

$$\Pr\{Z(t) = 0 | Z(0) = x\} = 1 - A_t(x, 0)$$
$$= 1 - \int_0^{2x} p(u - x, t)\, du.$$
$$= 1 - \int_{-x}^{x} p(u, t)\, du$$
$$= 2 \int_x^\infty p(u, t)\, du$$
$$= 2 \int_0^\infty p(u + x, t)\, du.$$

In the region $z > 0$, $Z(t)$ is a continuous random variable and for $0 < a < b$

$$\Pr\{a < Z(t) < b | Z(0) = x\} = A_t(x, a) - A_t(x, b)$$
$$= \int_a^b [p(u - x, t) - p(u + x, t)]\, du.$$

Thus the transition probability density function for the continuous part of absorbed Brownian motion is

$$p_t(x, y) = p(y - x, t) - p(y + x, t).$$

C. BROWNIAN MOTION WITH DRIFT

Let $\{\tilde{X}(t), t \geq 0\}$ be a Brownian motion process. *Brownian motion with drift* is a stochastic process having the distribution of

$$X(t) = \tilde{X}(t) + \mu t, \qquad t \geq 0,$$

where μ is a constant, called the *drift parameter*. Alternatively, we may describe Brownian motion with drift in a manner that parallels Definition 2.1.

Definition 4.1. *Brownian motion with drift is a stochastic process* $\{X(t); t \geq 0\}$ *with the following properties:*

(a) *Every increment* $X(t+s) - X(s)$ *is normally distributed with mean* μt *and variance* $\sigma^2 t$; μ, σ *being fixed constants.*

(b) *For every pair of disjoint time intervals* $[t_1, t_2]$, $[t_3, t_4]$, *say,* $t_1 < t_2 \leq t_3 < t_4$, *the increments* $X(t_4) - X(t_3)$ *and* $X(t_2) - X(t_1)$ *are independent random variables with distributions given in* (a), *and similarly for n disjoint time intervals, where n is an arbitrary positive integer.*

(c) $X(0) = 0$ *and* $X(t)$ *is continuous at* $t = 0$.

As before, it follows that a displacement $X(t+s) - X(s)$ is independent of the past, or alternatively, if we know $X(s) = x_0$, then no further knowledge of the values of $X(\tau)$ for $\tau < s$ affects the conditional probability law governing $X(t+s) - X(s)$. Written formally, this says that if $t > t_0 > t_1 > \cdots > t_n$,

$$\begin{aligned} &\Pr\{X(t) \leq x | X(t_0) = x_0, X(t_1) = x_1, \ldots, X(t_n) = x_n\} \\ &\quad = \Pr\{X(t) \leq x | X(t_0) = x_0\}. \end{aligned} \tag{4.5}$$

This is a statement of the Markov character of the process. We emphasize, however, that the independent increment assumption (b) is actually more restrictive than the Markov property. By part (a) of the definition, we have

$$\begin{aligned} \Pr\{X(t) \leq x | X(t_0) = x_0\} &= \Pr\{X(t) - X(t_0) \leq x - x_0\} \\ &= \int_{-\infty}^{x-x_0} \frac{1}{\sqrt{2\pi(t-t_0)}\sigma} \exp\left\{-\frac{(y - \mu(t-t_0))^2}{2(t-t_0)\sigma^2}\right\} dy \\ &= \int_{-\infty}^{\{x-x_0-\mu(t-t_0)\}/\sigma} p(t-t_0, y)\, dy, \end{aligned}$$

where

$$p(t, x) = \frac{1}{\sqrt{2\pi t}} \exp\{-x^2/2t\}.$$

When $\mu \neq 0$, the process is no longer symmetric, and the reflection argument may not be used to compute the distribution of the maximum of the process. We will compute this distribution in the next section using facts of martingale theory.

D. GEOMETRIC BROWNIAN MOTION

Let $\{X(t),\ t \geq 0\}$ be a Brownian motion process with drift μ and diffusion coefficient σ^2. The process defined by

$$Y(t) = e^{X(t)}, \qquad t \geq 0,$$

is sometimes called *geometric Brownian motion*. The state space is the interval $(0, \infty)$.

Since $Y(t) = Y(0)e^{X(t)-X(0)}$, using the characteristic function for the normal distribution, we compute

$$\begin{aligned} E[Y(t) \mid Y(0) = y] &= yE[e^{X(t)-X(0)}] \\ &= y \exp\{t(\mu + \tfrac{1}{2}\sigma^2)\}, \end{aligned}$$

and

$$\begin{aligned} E[Y(t)^2 \mid Y(0) = y] &= y^2 E[e^{2[X(t)-X(0)]}] \\ &= y^2 \exp\{t[2\mu + \tfrac{1}{2}4\sigma^2]\}, \end{aligned}$$

so that the variance of $Y(t)$ is

$$\begin{aligned} \operatorname{Var}[Y(t) \mid Y(0) = y] &= E[Y(t)^2 \mid Y(0) = y] - \{E[Y(t) \mid Y(0) = y]\}^2 \\ &= y^2\{\exp[2t(\mu + \tfrac{1}{2}2\sigma^2)] - \exp[2t(\mu + \tfrac{1}{2}\sigma^2)]\} \\ &= y^2 \exp[2t(\mu + \tfrac{1}{2}\sigma^2)][\exp(t\sigma^2) - 1]. \end{aligned}$$

5: *Computing Some Functionals of Brownian Motion by Martingale Methods*

A number of important quantities can be expeditiously calculated by applying the optional sampling theorem to martingales associated with Brownian motion. We remarked in Chapter 1 that a standard Brownian motion process $\{X(t);\ t \geq 0\}$ is a martingale, but this is by no means the only martingale of interest in this context. Both of the processes

$$U(t) = X^2(t) - t,$$

and (5.1)

$$V(t) = \exp\{\lambda X(t) - \tfrac{1}{2}\lambda^2 t\},$$

where λ is an arbitrary real constant, are martingales with respect to standard Brownian motion $\{X(t)\}$. We present direct validation. Indeed, we have, for $0 \le t_1 \le \cdots \le t_n = t$, and $s > 0$,

$$\begin{aligned} E[U(t+s)|X(t_1), \ldots, X(t_n)] &= E[X^2(t+s)|X(t)] - (t+s) \\ &= E[\{X(t+s) - X(t)\}^2|X(t)] \\ &\quad + 2E[X(t)\{X(t+s) - X(t)\}|X(t)] \\ &\quad + E[X^2(t)|X(t)] - (t+s) \\ &= s + 2 \times 0 + X^2(t) - (t+s) \\ &= U(t). \end{aligned}$$

Similarly,

$$\begin{aligned} E[V(t+s)|X(t_1), \ldots, X(t_n)] &= V(t) \times E[\exp\{\lambda[X(t+s) - X(t)] - \tfrac{1}{2}\lambda^2 s\}] \\ &= V(t). \end{aligned}$$

Digression. It is useful to place the martingale examples of (5.1) in a more facile framework. A general construction of martingales associated with a Markov process $\{X(t);\ t \ge 0\}$ having stationary transition probability density

$$p(t, x|y)\,dx = \Pr\{x \le X(t) < x + dx | X(0) = y\}$$

runs as follows. Let $u(x, t)$ solve the functional equation

$$u(x, s) = \int p(t, \xi|x) u(\xi, t+s)\, d\xi, \qquad s, t > 0. \tag{5.2}$$

We claim that $Z(t) = u(X(t), t)$ determines a martingale adapted to the sigma fields $\mathscr{F}_t = \sigma\{X(u);\ 0 \le u \le t\}$ generated by the history of $X(t)$ up to time t, provided $E[|Z(t)|] < \infty$.

Proof. We compute

$$\begin{aligned} E[Z(t+s)|\mathscr{F}(s)] &= E[Z(t+s)|X(s)] \qquad \text{(by the Markov property)} \\ &= E[u(X(t+s), t+s)|X(s)] \\ &= \int p(t, \xi|X(s)) u(\xi, t+s) d\xi \\ &= u(X(s), s) \qquad \text{(using the functional equation)} \\ &= Z(s). \end{aligned}$$

Thus, the martingale property for $\{Z(t)\}$ is fully corroborated.

A direct calculation reveals that

$$u(x, t) = x^2 - t \qquad \text{and} \qquad v(x, t) = \exp\{\lambda x - \tfrac{1}{2}\lambda^2 t\}$$

obey the functional relation (5.2) with

$$p(t, x|y) = \frac{1}{\sqrt{2\pi t}} \exp\{-(x-y)^2/2t\}.$$

In the case of the Brownian motion process it can be shown further that if $u(x, t)$ is sufficiently differentiable and fulfills the relation (5.2), then $u(x, t)$ also satisfies

$$\frac{\partial u}{\partial t} + \frac{1}{2} \frac{\partial^2 u}{\partial x^2} = 0. \tag{5.3}$$

In Chapter 15 on diffusion processes we provide a fuller proof of this last assertion. The converse is also correct, affirming that where (5.3) prevails, (5.2) also ensues.

Here are some sample calculations involving the martingales of (5.1). Let $a < 0 < b$ be given and let $T = T_{ab}$ be the first time the process reaches a or b:

$$T_{ab} = \inf\{t \geq 0 : X(t) = a \quad \text{or} \quad X(t) = b\},$$

and let $T \wedge n = \min\{T, n\}$.

Since $\{U(t)\}$ is a martingale, $E[U(T \wedge n)] = E[U(0)] = 0$, which gives

$$E[T \wedge n] = E[X^2(T \wedge n)] \leq (|a| + b)^2.$$

Thus

$$\begin{aligned} E[T] &= \lim_{n\to\infty} \int_0^n \Pr\{T > t\}\, dt \\ &= \lim_{n\to\infty} E[T \wedge n] \leq (|a| + b)^2. \end{aligned}$$

The important point is that $T = T_{ab}$ is finite. Even more, T_{ab} has a finite mean.

Let u be the probability that the $\{X(t)\}$ process reaches b before it reaches a, or

$$u = \Pr\{X(T_{ab}) = b\}.$$

Now $\{X(t)\}$ is a martingale, $T = T_{ab}$ is finite, and $\{X(t \wedge T)\}$ is bounded. Thus the optional stopping theorem applies and

$$\begin{aligned} 0 &= E[X(T)] \\ &= a \Pr\{X(T) = a\} + b \Pr\{X(T) = b\} \\ &= a[1 - u] + bu, \end{aligned}$$

so that

$$u = \Pr\{X(T_{ab}) = b\} = \frac{|a|}{|a| + b}.$$

We now return to the martingale $\{U(t)\}$, noticing $E[U(T)] = 0$, to compute

$$
\begin{aligned}
E[T_{ab}] &= E[X^2(T_{ab})] \\
&= a^2[1-u] + b^2 u \\
&= a^2 \frac{b}{|a|+b} + b^2 \frac{|a|}{|a|+b} \\
&= |a|b.
\end{aligned}
$$

By changing the origin and scale of a given process we may compute analogous quantities for a Brownian motion with variance parameter σ^2 and starting position $X(0) = x$. The result is:

Theorem 5.1. *Let $\{X(t); t \geq 0\}$ be a Brownian motion process with variance σ^2 and $X(0) = x$. Let a, b with $a < x < b$ be given, and let T be the first time the process reaches a or b. Then*

$$
\Pr\{X(T) = b | X(0) = x\} = (x-a)/(b-a),
$$

and

$$
E[T | X(0) = x] = \frac{1}{\sigma^2}(b-x)(x-a).
$$

Let us turn to a Brownian motion process $\{X(t); t \geq 0\}$ with drift $\mu \neq 0$ and variance σ^2. Then, for any real λ,

$$
V(t) = \exp\{\lambda X(t) - (\lambda\mu + \tfrac{1}{2}\lambda^2\sigma^2)t\} \tag{5.4}
$$

defines a martingale. Let us choose

$$
\lambda_0 = -2\mu/\sigma^2,
$$

so that the second term in the exponent of (5.4) vanishes. Then $V_0(t) = \exp\{\lambda_0 X(t)\}$ is a martingale. We apply the optional stopping theorem, with T_{ab} being the first time the process reaches $a < 0$ or $b > 0$, to learn

$$
\begin{aligned}
1 &= E[V_0(T_{ab})] \\
&= \Pr\{X(T_{ab}) = a\} \exp\{\lambda_0 a\} + \Pr\{X(T_{ab}) = b\} \exp\{\lambda_0 b\},
\end{aligned}
$$

and

$$
\Pr\{X(T_{ab}) = b\} = \frac{1 - \exp\{\lambda_0 a\}}{\exp\{\lambda_0 b\} - \exp\{\lambda_0 a\}},
$$

where $\lambda_0 = -2\mu/\sigma^2$. Again, we may translate the origin to treat the case $X(0) = x$.

Theorem 5.2. *Let $\{X(t);\ t \geq 0\}$ be a Brownian motion process with drift $\mu \neq 0$ and variance σ^2, and suppose $X(0) = x$. The probability that the process reaches the level $b > x$ before hitting $a < x$ is given by*

$$\Pr\{X(T_{ab}) = b | X(0) = x\} = \frac{\exp(-2\mu x/\sigma^2) - \exp(-2\mu a/\sigma^2)}{\exp(-2\mu b/\sigma^2) - \exp(-2\mu a/\sigma^2)}.$$

Corollary 5.1. *Let $X(t)$ be a Brownian motion process with drift $\mu < 0$. Let*

$$W = \max_{0 \leq t < \infty} X(t) - X(0).$$

Then W has the exponential distribution

$$\Pr\{W \geq w\} = e^{-\lambda w}, \qquad w \geq 0,$$

where $\lambda = 2|\mu|/\sigma^2$.

Proof. We let $a \to -\infty$ in the formula of Theorem 5.2. Since $\mu < 0$, $\exp(-\mu a/\sigma^2) \to 0$. Thus

$$\lim_{a \to -\infty} \Pr\{X(T_{ab}) = b | X(0) = x\} = \exp[2\mu(b - x)/\sigma^2].$$

But as $a \to -\infty$, the left-hand side becomes the probability that the process ever reaches b, that is, the probability that the maximum of the process ever exceeds b. Thus, for $w = b - x$,

$$\Pr\{W \geq w\} = \Pr\left\{\max_{0 \leq t < \infty} X(t) > b | X(0) = x\right\}$$
$$= e^{-\lambda w},$$

with $\lambda = 2|\mu|/\sigma^2$, as claimed. ■

As a last example, we calculate the Laplace transform of the first passage time to a single barrier. We let $z > 0$ be fixed and $T = T_z$ be the first time, if any, the process reaches the level z:

$$T = T_z = \begin{cases} \inf\{t : X(t) \geq z\}, & \text{if } X(t) \geq z, \text{ for some } t \geq 0, \\ \infty, & \text{if } X(t) < z, \text{ for all } t \geq 0. \end{cases}$$

Set $\theta = \lambda\mu + \frac{1}{2}\lambda^2\sigma^2$. Then $V(t) = \exp\{\lambda X(t) - \theta t\}$ is a martingale, and, if $X(0) = 0$,

$$1 = E[V(T \wedge t)],$$

or

$$1 = E[\exp\{\lambda X(T \wedge t) - \theta(T \wedge t)\}].$$

Let us suppose $\lambda \geq 0$ is sufficiently large to ensure $\theta \geq 0$. Then

$$0 \leq V(T \wedge t) \leq e^{\lambda z},$$

so that, using Lemma 3.3 of Chapter 6, we may pass to the limit as $t \to \infty$. We obtain

$$\lim_{t\to\infty} V(t \wedge T) = \begin{cases} \exp\{\lambda z - \theta T\}, & \text{if} \quad T < \infty, \\ 0, & \text{if} \quad T = \infty, \end{cases}$$

so that

$$\begin{aligned} 1 &= \lim_{t\to\infty} E[V(T \wedge t)] \\ &= e^{\lambda z} E[e^{-\theta T}], \end{aligned}$$

or

$$E[e^{-\theta T}] = e^{-\lambda z}.$$

It remains only to relate θ and λ. We have

$$\tfrac{1}{2}\sigma^2\lambda^2 + \mu\lambda - \theta = 0,$$

or

$$\lambda = \frac{-\mu \pm \sqrt{\mu^2 + 2\sigma^2\theta}}{\sigma^2}.$$

We require $\lambda \geq 0$, which implies

$$\lambda = \frac{1}{\sigma^2}(\sqrt{\mu^2 + 2\sigma^2\theta} - \mu).$$

When $\mu < 0$, T has a defective probability distribution, that is, T is infinite with positive probability, and

$$\begin{aligned} \Pr\{T < \infty\} &= \lim_{\theta\to 0} E[e^{-\theta T}] \\ &= \lim_{\theta\to 0} \exp\left[-\frac{z}{\sigma^2}(\sqrt{\mu^2 + 2\sigma^2\theta} - \mu)\right] \\ &= \exp(-2z|\mu|/\sigma^2), \end{aligned}$$

which agrees with Corollary 5.1. When $\mu \geq 0$, $T < \infty$ with certainty, and the Laplace transform is

$$E[e^{-\theta T}] = \exp\left[-\frac{z}{\sigma^2}(\sqrt{\mu^2 + 2\sigma^2\theta} - \mu)\right]. \tag{5.5}$$

For Brownian motion with drift $\mu \geq 0$, it is possible to invert the transform (5.5) and obtain an explicit expression for the probability density function of T_z. We satisfy ourselves with quoting the result.

Theorem 5.3. *Let $X(t)$ be a Brownian motion with drift $\mu \geq 0$. Let $z > X(0) = x$ be given and let T_z be the first time the process reaches the level z. Conditioned on $X(0) = x$, T_z has the probability density function*

$$f(t; x, z) = \frac{(z-x)}{\sigma\sqrt{2\pi t^3}} \exp\left[-\frac{(z-x-\mu t)^2}{2\sigma^2 t}\right], \qquad t > 0.$$

Example. Geometric Brownian motion (Example D of Section 4) is often used to model prices of assets, say shares of stock, that are traded in a perfect market. Such prices are nonnegative and usually exhibit oscillatory behavior comprised of exponential growth intermittent with exponential decay over the long run, two properties possessed by geometric Brownian motion. More importantly, if $t_0 < t_1 < \cdots < t_n$ are time points, the successive ratios

$$Y(t_1)/Y(t_0), \ldots, Y(t_n)/Y(t_{n-1}),$$

are independent random variables, so that, crudely speaking, the percentage changes over nonoverlapping time intervals are independent. Here, in a rough form, is the reasoning that supports the geometric Brownian motion as an appropriate model in a perfect market. If a ratio $Y(t+s)/Y(t)$ of a future price to a current price could be anticipated or predicted as being favorable, a number of buyers would enter the market, and their demand would tend to raise the current price $Y(t)$. Similarly, if the ratio $Y(t+s)/Y(t)$ could be predicted as being unfavorable, a number of sellers would appear and tend to depress the current price. Equilibrium obtains where the ratio cannot be predicted as being either favorable or unfavorable, that is, where price ratios over nonoverlapping time intervals are independent.

We will give an example in which the geometric Brownian motion model is used to evaluate the worth of a perpetual warrant in a stock. A warrant is an option to buy a fixed number of shares in a given stock at a stated price at any time during a specified time period. The profit to a holder of such an option is the excess of the market price over the option price. The assumption is that the holder can purchase at the stated price and resell at the market price and thus realize the potential profit.

We consider only perpetual warrants, options having no expiration dates. For such a warrant, a reasonable strategy would be to exercise the option the first time the stock price reaches some specified level we will denote by a. By an appropriate choice of units, we may assume that the stated price in the warrant is one, so that the potential profit upon exercising the option at a market price of a is $a-1$. Of course, we need only consider $a>1$, since one would not purchase at the stated price of one if the current market price were lower.

In owning such an option, one is foregoing, in part at least, direct ownership of the stock, which is increasing at a rate of $\alpha=\mu+\frac{1}{2}\sigma^2$ per unit time, since

$$E[Y(t)|\,Y(0)=y]=y\exp\{t(\mu+\tfrac{1}{2}\sigma^2)\}.$$

One requires a higher rate of return, $\theta>\alpha$, from the option, or equivalently, discounts the potential profit of $(a-1)$ at a rate of $-\theta$ per unit time.

Let $T(a)$ be the first time the stock price reaches the level a. Then the discounted potential profit to the option holder is

$$e^{-\theta T(a)}[Y(T(a))-1]=e^{-\theta T(a)}(a-1).$$

We want to compute the expected discounted profit and then choose a to maximize this expected profit. In terms of the Brownian motion, $T(a)$ is the first time that $X(t)=\ln Y(t)$ reaches the level $\ln a$. We computed the probability density function for $T(a)$ in Theorem 5.3, and the Laplace transform in Eq. (5.5). Using (5.5) with $z=\ln a$ and $x=\ln y$, we have (see Fig. 4)

$$E[e^{-\theta T(a)}|\,Y(0)=y]=\left(\frac{y}{a}\right)^{\rho},$$

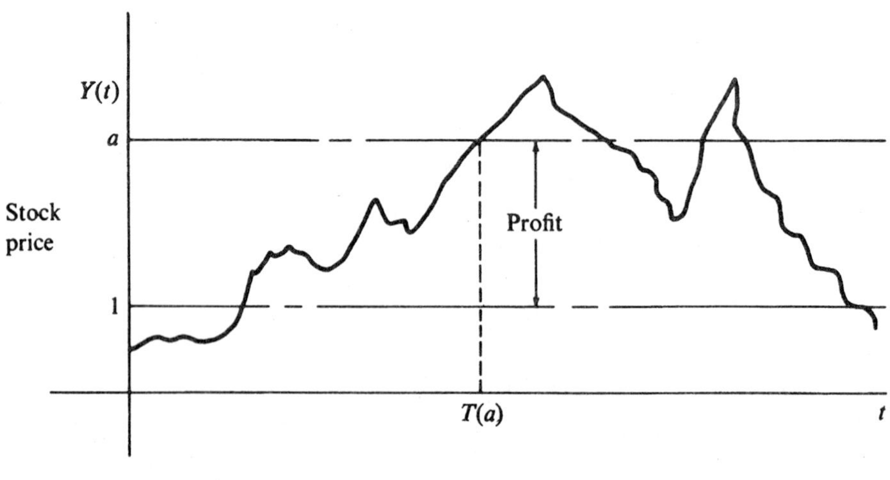

FIG. 4.

where

$$\rho = \sqrt{\frac{\mu^2}{\sigma^4} + \frac{2\theta}{\sigma^2}} - \frac{\mu}{\sigma^2}.$$

Letting $g(y, a)$ be the expected discounted profit, we have

$$\begin{aligned} g(y, a) &= (a-1)E[e^{-\theta T(a)} \mid Y(0) = y] \\ &= (a-1)\left(\frac{y}{a}\right)^{\rho}. \end{aligned}$$

We differentiate with respect to a and equate to zero to find the profit maximizing level $a = a^*$:

$$\frac{\partial g}{\partial a} = 0 = -\rho(a^* - 1)\left(\frac{y}{a^*}\right)^{\rho+1}\frac{1}{y} + \left(\frac{y}{a^*}\right)^{\rho},$$

and

$$a^* = \frac{\rho}{\rho - 1}.$$

The condition $\theta > \mu + \frac{1}{2}\sigma^2$ ensures $1 < a^* < \infty$. Given a current stock price y, the warrant has value

$$\begin{aligned} g(y, a^*) &= (a^* - 1)(y/a^*)^{\rho} \\ &= \frac{1}{\rho - 1}\left[\frac{y(\rho - 1)}{\rho}\right]^{\rho}. \end{aligned}$$

6: Multidimensional Brownian Motion

Let $\{X_1(t);\ t \geq 0\}, \ldots, \{X_N(t);\ t \geq 0\}$, be standard Brownian motion processes, statistically independent of one another in the sense that, for any finite set of time points

$$\begin{array}{l} t_{11}, t_{12}, \ldots, t_{1,n_1}, \\ t_{21}, t_{22}, \ldots, t_{2,n_2}, \\ \vdots \\ t_{N,1}, t_{N,2}, \ldots, t_{N,n_N}, \end{array}$$

the N vectors

$$\begin{aligned} \mathbf{X}_1 &= (X_1(t_{11}), \ldots, X_1(t_{1,n_1})), \\ \mathbf{X}_2 &= (X_2(t_{21}), \ldots, X_2(t_{2,n_2})), \\ &\vdots \\ \mathbf{X}_N &= (X_N(t_{N1}), \ldots, X_N(t_{N,n_N})), \end{aligned}$$

are independent. The vector-valued process defined by

$$\mathbf{X}(t) = (X_1(t), \ldots, X_N(t)), \qquad t \geq 0,$$

is called N-dimensional Brownian motion. The motion of a particle undergoing Brownian motion in the plane and in space are described by two-dimensional and three-dimensional Brownian motions, respectively.

Consider a two-dimensional Brownian motion $\mathbf{X}(t) = (X_1(t), X_2(t))$, and let us compute the distribution of the second coordinate at the random time the first coordinate first reaches a given level $z > 0$. We let T_z be the first time t at which $X_1(t) = z$, and we then want the distribution of $Y(z) = X_2(T_z)$.

Figure 5 describes the path traced in the plane by the two-dimensional Brownian motion and displays the value $Y(z) = X_2(T_z)$.

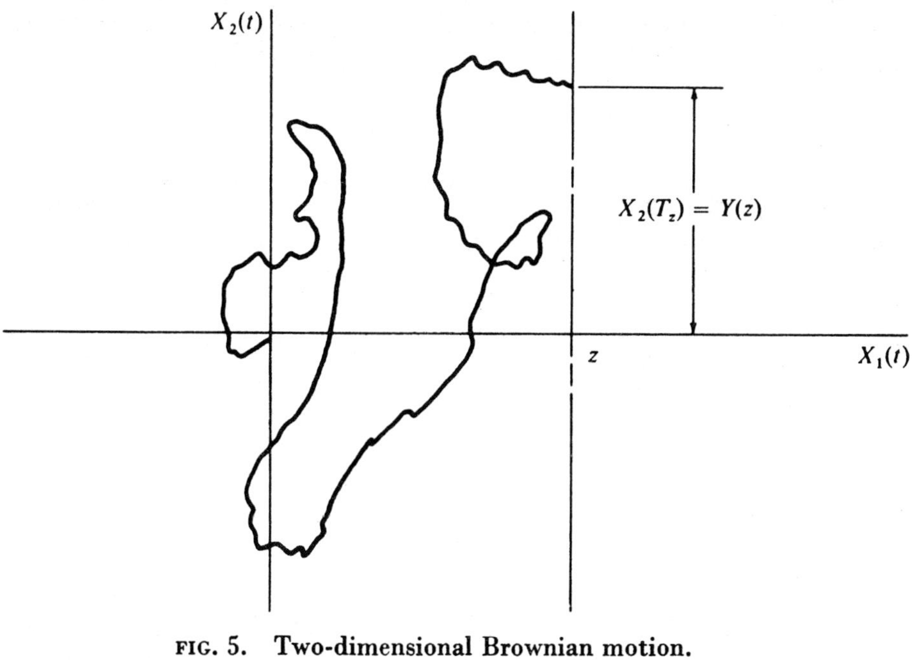

FIG. 5. Two-dimensional Brownian motion.

Fix $z > 0$. We will compute the characteristic function $\phi(u) = E[\exp\{iuY(z)\}]$. Since T is determined by the X_1 process, T and the X_2 process are independent. Hence, by the law of total probability

$$\phi(u) = \int_0^\infty E[\exp\{iuX_2(t)\}]\, dF(t),$$

where

$$F(t) = \Pr\{T_z \leq t\}$$

is the cumulative distribution function of T_z, computed explicitly just prior to Eq. (3.3). Since $X_2(t)$ is normally distributed with mean zero and variance t,

$$E[\exp\{iuX_2(t)\}] = \exp(-\tfrac{1}{2}u^2t).$$

Clearly

$$\begin{aligned}\phi(u) &= \int_0^\infty \exp(-\tfrac{1}{2}u^2t)\, dF(t) \\ &= E[\exp(-\tfrac{1}{2}u^2 T_z)] \\ &= \exp(-|u|z), \qquad -\infty < u < \infty.\end{aligned}$$

using (5.5), the Laplace transform for T_z, with $\theta = \frac{1}{2}u^2$, $\mu = 0$, and $\sigma^2 = 1$.

This is the characteristic function of the Cauchy probability density function

$$p(x) = \frac{1}{\pi z[1 + (x/z)^2]}, \qquad -\infty < x < \infty.$$

Even more can be said. Elementary Problem 5 is the first step in proving that the stochastic process $\{T_z;\ z \geq 0\}$ has stationary independent increments. From this it follows that

$$Y(z) = X_2(T_z) \tag{6.1}$$

also has stationary independent increments. In general, given any Markov process $\{X(t),\ t \geq 0\}$ and a process $\{T_z;\ z \geq 0\}$ having stationary independent increments and increasing sample paths, with $T_0 = 0$, it is possible to derive a new process

$$Y(z) = X[T_z], \qquad z \geq 0.$$

The process of forming Y from X is called *subordination*, and the process $\{T_z;\ z \geq 0\}$ is called the *subordinator*. Under the conditions given, $\{Y(z);\ z \geq 0\}$ will be a Markov process. If, in addition, $\{X(t);\ t \geq 0\}$ has stationary independent increments, then so will $\{Y(z);\ z \geq 0\}$.

Radial Brownian Motion.

Let $\{\mathbf{X}(t);\ t \geq 0\}$ be an N-dimensional Brownian motion process. The stochastic process defined by

$$R(t) = [X_1(t)^2 + \cdots + X_N(t)^2]^{1/2}, \qquad t \geq 0,$$

is called *Radial Brownian motion* or the *Bessel process* with parameter $\frac{1}{2}N - 1$. It is a Markov process having continuous sample paths in the state space $[0, \infty)$. The transition probability density function from x to y is

$$p_t(x, y) = t^{-1} \exp\left\{-\frac{x^2+y^2}{2t}\right\}(xy)^{1-(N/2)} I_{(N/2)-1}\left(\frac{xy}{t}\right) y^{N-1},$$

$$t > 0, \quad x, y > 0, \qquad (6.2)$$

where $I_\nu(z)$ is the modified Bessel function

$$I_\nu(z) = \sum_{k=0}^{\infty} \frac{(z/2)^{2k+\nu}}{k!\Gamma(k+\nu+1)}. \qquad (6.3)$$

For $N = 1$, we use

$$I_{-1/2}(z) = \sqrt{\frac{2}{\pi z}} \cosh z$$

to get

$$p_t(x, y) = \sqrt{\frac{2}{\pi t}} \exp\left\{-\frac{x^2+y^2}{2t}\right\} \cosh\left(\frac{xy}{t}\right).$$

Comparison of this formula with (4.3) reveals that the Bessel process for $N = 1$ reduces to reflected Brownian motion.

We will investigate the case $N = 2$ shortly. When $N = 3$, the relation

$$I_{1/2}(z) = \sqrt{\frac{2}{\pi z}} \sinh z$$

produces

$$p_t(x, y) = \sqrt{\frac{2}{\pi t}} \exp\left\{-\frac{x^2+y^2}{2t}\right\} \frac{y}{x} \sinh\left(\frac{xy}{t}\right).$$

We obtain the density corresponding to $x = 0$ through continuity, letting $x \to 0$. This gives

$$p_t(0, y) = \sqrt{\frac{2}{\pi t^3}}\, y^2 \exp(-y^2/2t),$$

the marginal density of $R(t)$ when $N = 3$ and $R(0) = 0$.

Let us now consider the case $N = 2$, showing that the corresponding Bessel process is Markov and computing the transition density. We change to polar coordinates by defining

$$R(t) = \sqrt{X_1(t)^2 + X_2(t)^2},$$
$$\Theta(t) = \arctan[X_2(t)/X_1(t)].$$

Since Brownian motion is Markov,

$$\begin{aligned}\Pr\{R(t_n+t)\le b \mid \mathbf{X}(t_0)=\mathbf{x}_0, \ldots, \mathbf{X}(t_{n-1})=\mathbf{x}_{n-1}, \mathbf{X}(t_n)=\mathbf{x}\}\\ = \Pr\{R(t_n+t)\le b \mid \mathbf{X}(t_n)=\mathbf{x}\} = \Pr\{R(t)\le b \mid \mathbf{X}(0)=\mathbf{x}\}, \qquad (6.4)\end{aligned}$$

where $0<t_0<\cdots<t_n$, $t>0$, and $\mathbf{x}_1, \ldots, \mathbf{x}_n$ are arbitrary points in the plane, $\mathbf{x}=(x_1, x_2)$. Then

$$\begin{aligned}\Pr\{R(t)\le b \mid \mathbf{X}(0)=\mathbf{x}\}\\ &= \iint\limits_{y_1^2+y_2^2\le b^2} \frac{1}{2\pi t}\exp\left\{-\frac{(y_1-x_1)^2+(y_2-x_2)^2}{2t}\right\} dy_1\, dy_2\\ &= \int_0^b \left[\int_0^{2\pi} \frac{1}{2\pi t}\exp\left\{-\frac{(r\sin\theta-x_1)^2+(r\cos\theta-x_2)^2}{2t}\right\} d\theta\right] r\, dr,\end{aligned}$$

where we have changed variables according to $y_1=r\sin\theta$, $y_2=r\cos\theta$, recalling from advanced calculus that $dy_1 dy_2 = r\,dr\,d\theta$. Since

$$(r\sin\theta-x_1)^2+(r\cos\theta-x_2)^2 = r^2-2r(x_1\sin\theta+x_2\cos\theta)+\|\mathbf{x}\|^2$$

where $\|\mathbf{x}\|^2 = x_1^2+x_2^2$,

$$\Pr\{R(t)\le b \mid X(0)=x\} = \int_0^b \frac{r}{2\pi t}\exp\left\{\frac{\mathbf{r}^2+\|\mathbf{x}\|^2}{2t}\right\} I(r, \mathbf{x})\, dr$$

where

$$I(r, \mathbf{x}) = \int_0^{2\pi} \exp\left\{\frac{r}{t}(x_1\sin\theta+x_2\cos\theta)\right\} d\theta.$$

Define an angle ϕ by writing

$$\sin\phi = x_1/\|\mathbf{x}\|, \qquad \cos\phi = x_2/\|\mathbf{x}\|,$$

where $\|\mathbf{x}\| = \sqrt{x_1^2+x_2^2}$. Using the trigonometric identity $\sin\phi\sin\theta + \cos\phi\cos\theta = \cos(\phi+\theta)$,

$$\begin{aligned}I(r, \mathbf{x}) &= \int_0^{2\pi} \exp\left\{\frac{r\|\mathbf{x}\|}{t}\cos(\phi+\theta)\right\} d\theta\\ &= \int_0^{2\pi} \exp\left\{\frac{r\|\mathbf{x}\|}{t}\cos\theta\right\} d\theta,\end{aligned}$$

since the integral is over the interval $\theta \in [0, 2\pi]$, over which, $\cos(\phi + \theta)$ is periodic. Now

$$\int_0^{2\pi} \exp\{\alpha \cos \theta\}\, d\theta = \int_0^{2\pi} \sum_{k=0}^{\infty} \frac{(\alpha \cos \theta)^k}{k!}\, d\theta$$
$$= \sum_{k=0}^{\infty} \frac{\alpha^k}{k!} \int_0^{2\pi} \cos^k \theta\, d\theta.$$

But

$$\int_0^{2\pi} \cos^k \theta\, d\theta = \begin{cases} 0, & \text{if } k = 1, 3, \ldots, \\ \dfrac{k!\,2\pi}{2^k[(k/2)!]^2}, & \text{if } k = 0, 2, \ldots. \end{cases}$$

Thus, in terms of the modified Bessel function,

$$\int_0^{2\pi} \exp\{\alpha \cos \theta\}\, d\theta = 2\pi \sum_{k=0,2,\ldots} \frac{\alpha^k}{k!} \left\{\frac{\alpha^k}{2^k[(k/2)!]^2}\right\}$$
$$= 2\pi \sum_{j=0}^{\infty} \frac{\alpha^{2j}}{2^{2j}(j!)^2}$$
$$= 2\pi\, I_0(\alpha)$$

We have computed, then,

$$\Pr\{R(t) \le b \mid \mathbf{X}(0) = \mathbf{x}\} = \int_0^b \frac{r}{2\pi t} \exp\left\{\frac{r^2 + \|\mathbf{x}\|^2}{2t}\right\} 2\pi I_0\left\{\frac{r\|\mathbf{x}\|}{t}\right\} dr$$
$$= \int_0^b p_t(\|\mathbf{x}\|, r)\, dr, \tag{6.5}$$

where we take $N = 2$ in Eq. (6.2) defining p_t. We have thus shown

$$\Pr\{R(t_n + t) \le b \mid \mathbf{X}(t_0) = \mathbf{x}_0, \ldots, \mathbf{X}(t_n) = \mathbf{x}\} = \int_0^b p_t(\|\mathbf{x}\|, r)\, dr. \tag{6.6}$$

Let $r_j = (x_{1j}^2 + x_{2j}^2)^{1/2}$, $j = 0, \ldots, n$, where $\mathbf{x}_j = (x_{1j}, x_{2j})$. Similarly, let $\theta_j = \arctan(x_{2j}/x_{1j})$. The conditions $\mathbf{X}(t_0) = \mathbf{x}_0, \ldots, \mathbf{X}(t_n) = \mathbf{x}_n$, are equivalent to the conditions $R(t_0) = r_0$, $\Theta(t_0) = \theta_0, \ldots, R(t_n) = r_n$, $\Theta(t_n) = \theta_n$. Using this in (6.6), we will establish both the Markov property and determine the transition density function for $\{R(t), t \ge 0\}$. Beginning with the law of total probability, where $p(\theta_0, \ldots, \theta_n)$ is the joint probability density function for $(\Theta(t_0), \ldots, \Theta(t_n))$, we have

$$\begin{aligned}
&\Pr\{R(t_n + t) \le b | R(t_0) = r_0, \ldots, R(t_n) = r_n\} \\
&= \int_0^{2\pi} \cdots \int_0^{2\pi} \Pr\{R(t_n + t) \le b | R(t_0) = r_0, \Theta(t_0) = \theta_0, \ldots, \\
&\qquad R(t_n) = r_n, \Theta(t_n) = \theta_n\} p(\theta_0, \ldots, \theta_n)\, d\theta_0, \ldots, d\theta_n \\
&= \int_0^{2\pi} \cdots \int_0^{2\pi} \left\{\int_0^b p_t(r_n, r)\, dr\right\} p(\theta_0, \ldots, \theta_n)\, d\theta_0, \ldots, d\theta_n \\
&= \int_0^b p_t(r_n, r)\, dr.
\end{aligned}$$

This verifies the Markov property and establishes (6.2) as the transition density for the two-dimensional Bessel process.

7: *Brownian Paths*

Considered as randomly chosen functions (as opposed to collections of random variables) the trajectories or sample paths of Brownian motion are quite remarkable. Were you asked to exhibit a continuous function that was nowhere differentiable, you might expend a considerable amount of effort to discover an example. Yet a Brownian path is "certain" (meaning the probability is one) to be such a function! This is but one example of numerous striking features of Brownian paths.

A. CONTINUITY OF PATHS

There are several ways in which a stochastic process $X(t)$, whose index set is a real interval, can be considered continuous. Three of these correspond to the different notions of *limit* for random sequences introduced in Chapter 1. We say $\{X(t)\}$ is:

(a) *Continuous in mean square* if, for every t,

$$\lim_{s \to t} E[|X(s) - X(t)|^2] = 0.$$

(b) *Continuous in probability* if, for every t and positive ε,

$$\lim_{s \to t} \Pr\{|X(s) - X(t)| > \varepsilon\} = 0.$$

(c) *Continuous almost surely* if, for every t,

$$\Pr\left\{\lim_{s\to t} X(s) = X(t)\right\} = 1.$$

The first two of these notions are decidable in terms of the finite-dimensional distributions of the process. Indeed, a process whose second moments are finite is continuous in mean square if and only if the mean value function $m(t) = E[X(t)]$ is continuous and the covariance function $\Gamma(s, t) = E[\{X(s) - m(s)\}\{X(t) - m(t)\}]$ is continuous at the diagonal $t = s$, as can be discerned readily from the expansion

$$E[|X(s) - X(t)|^2] = \Gamma(s, s) - 2\Gamma(s, t) + \Gamma(t, t) + [m(s) - m(t)]^2.$$

Chebyshev's inequality in the form

$$\Pr\{|X(s) - X(t)| > \varepsilon\} \le \frac{1}{\varepsilon^2} E[|X(s) - X(t)|^2], \qquad \varepsilon > 0,$$

shows that every mean square continuous process is continuous in probability.

Although these are reasonable, and quite useful, concepts of continuity for many contexts, they are not adequate for all situations. Indeed, a Poisson process $N(t)$ is continuous according to all three criteria. In fact, note first that the mean value function $m(t) = \lambda t$ and covariance $\Gamma(s, t) = \lambda \min\{s, t\}$, are manifestly continuous. Moreover, for every fixed t, the event $\lim_{s\to t} X(s) \ne X(t)$ occurs only if one of the jump times of the process is at t. Since these jump times have a continuous (gamma) distribution, this event has zero probability. Thus, for every $t \ge 0$,

$$\Pr\left\{\lim_{s\to t} N(s) = N(t)\right\} = 1,$$

and a Poisson process is, according to our definition, continuous almost surely at every specified t.

But one never sees a graph of a Poisson process that shows it as a continuous function! Clearly, a more stringent criterion for continuity of random functions is called for. We say that a stochastic process $X(t)$ *almost surely has continuous paths* if, with probability one, $X(t)$ is a continuous function of t. A number of technical difficulties arise with this definition. In Chapter 1 we defined a stochastic process by specifying all its finite-dimensional distributions. Whether or not a process almost surely has continuous paths cannot be answered in terms of these distributions alone. Indeed, if $X(t)$ almost surely has continuous paths, and we define

$$\tilde{X}(t) = \begin{cases} X(t), & \text{if } \ t \ne \tau, \\ 0, & \text{if } \ t = \tau, \end{cases}$$

for some random variable τ, then, typically $\tilde{X}(t)$ does not exhibit continuous paths. Yet $X(t)$ and $\tilde{X}(t)$ have the same finite-dimensional distributions whenever τ has a continuous distribution and is independent of $\{X(t)\}$. Thus we weaken our requirement. We will say that a stochastic process, defined through its finite-dimensional distributions, almost surely has continuous paths if there is a concrete representation $\{X(t)\}$ of the process that is certain (with probability one) to be a continuous function of t.

We will now give such a representation for Brownian motion $\{X(t);\ 0 \le t \le 1\}$. Note that only time indices t in $[0, 1]$ are considered.

The Haar functions on $[0, 1]$ are defined by

$$H_1(t) = 1, \qquad 0 \le t \le 1,$$

$$H_2(t) = \begin{cases} 1, & 0 \le t < \frac{1}{2}, \\ -1, & \frac{1}{2} \le t \le 1, \end{cases}$$

$$H_{2^n+1}(t) = \begin{cases} 2^{n/2}, & 0 \le t < 2^{-(n+1)}, \\ -2^{n/2}, & 2^{-(n+1)} \le t \le 2^{-n}, \\ 0, & \text{otherwise.} \end{cases}$$

$$H_{2^n+j}(t) = H_{2^n+1}\left(t - \frac{j-1}{2^n}\right), \qquad j = 1, \ldots, 2^n.$$

The first six are shown in Fig. 6.

The Schauder functions are the integrals of the Haar functions, $S_k(t) = \int_0^t H_k(\tau)\, d\tau$. Their graphs are little tents, and if they are drawn, one can see

$$\max_{0 \le t \le 1} S_{2^n+j}(t) = (\tfrac{1}{2})^{(n+2)/2}, \qquad n = 0, 1, \ldots, \qquad 0 \le j \le 2^n - 1, \tag{7.1}$$

and

$$S_{2^n+j}(t) S_{2^n+k}(t) = 0, \qquad 1 \le k < j \le 2^n. \tag{7.2}$$

Now let $a(j)$, $j = 1, 2, \ldots$, be a real sequence, and set

$$b_n = \max\{|a(2^n + k)|;\ k = 1, \ldots, 2^n\}. \tag{7.3}$$

We claim the following fact. If

$$\sum_{n=0}^{\infty} b_n (\tfrac{1}{2})^{n/2} < \infty, \tag{7.4}$$

then the series

$$x(t) = \sum_{k=1}^{\infty} a(k) S_k(t)$$

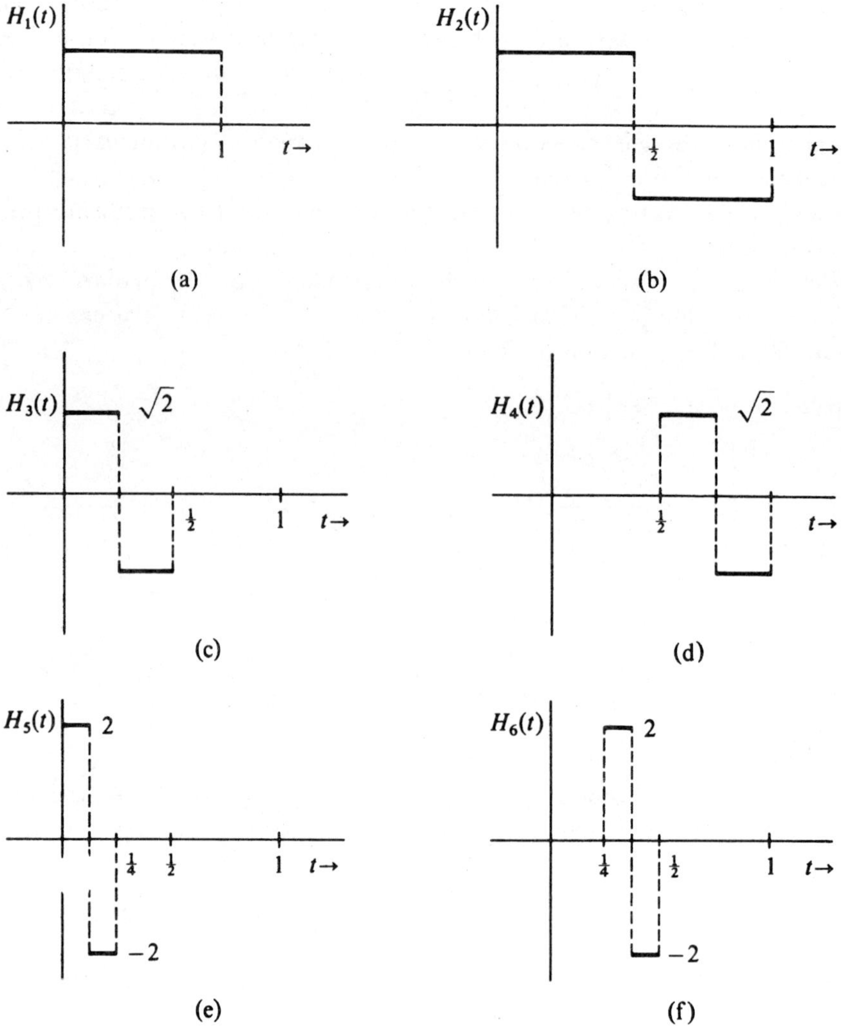

FIG. 6

converges uniformly to a continuous function of t. To validate this claim, it suffices to check the condition

$$\lim_{m,\, n\to\infty} \left| \sum_{k=m}^{m+n} a(k) \max_{0\le t\le 1} S_k(t) \right| = 0. \tag{7.5}$$

Now (7.1)–(7.3) tell us

$$\left| \sum_{k=2^j+1}^{2^{j+1}} a(k) \max_{0\le t\le 1} S_k(t) \right| \le b_j 2^{-(j+2)/2}, \tag{7.6}$$

so by grouping the summands in (7.5) according to indices $k=2^j$, $2^j+1, \ldots, 2^{j+1}$, we see that whenever $m>2^N$, the Cauchy sum in (7.5) is smaller than $\sum_{j=N}^{\infty} b_j 2^{-(j+2)/2}$, which converges to zero under (7.4). Then $x(t)$ is a continuous function of t whenever the coefficients satisfy (7.4), as claimed.

Now let $A_1, A_2, A_3, \ldots$ be independent normally distributed random variables having zero means and unit variances. Let

$$B_n=\max\{|A_k| : 2^n<k\leq 2^{n+1}\}. \tag{7.7}$$

Then

$$X(t)=\sum_{k=1}^{\infty} A_k S_k(t) \tag{7.8}$$

is a continuous function of t whenever $\sum_{n=0}^{\infty} B_n(\frac{1}{2})^{n/2}<\infty$. We claim

$$\Pr\left\{\sum_{n=0}^{\infty} B_n(\tfrac{1}{2})^{n/2}<\infty\right\}=1,$$

so that, with "certainty," (7.8) defines a continuous function. To validate this claim, we first implement integration by parts on the normal integral to get

$$\begin{aligned}\Pr\{|A_k|\geq x\}&=\frac{2}{\sqrt{2\pi}}\int_x^{\infty}\exp(-u^2/2)\,du\\&=\frac{2}{\sqrt{2\pi}}\left\{\frac{\exp(-x^2/2)}{x}-\int_x^{\infty}\frac{\exp(-u^2/2)}{u^2}\,du\right\}\\&\leq\frac{2}{\sqrt{2\pi}}\frac{\exp(-x^2/2)}{x}.\end{aligned}$$

Thus

$$\sum_{n=2}^{\infty}\Pr\{|A_n|>2\sqrt{\log n}\}\leq K\sum_{n=2}^{\infty}\frac{1}{n^2\sqrt{\log n}},$$

where K is a constant. The sum on the right converges, so the Borel–Cantelli lemma (Chapter 1) implies that only finitely many values of $|A_n|$ exceed $2\sqrt{\log n}$. This means, that only finitely many values of $B_j=\max\{|A_n| : 2^j<n\leq 2^{j+1}\}$ exceed $2\sqrt{\log 2}\sqrt{j}$. Since $\sum\sqrt{j}(\frac{1}{2})^{j/2}<\infty$, this verifies the convergence, with probability one, of $\sum B_n(\frac{1}{2})^{n/2}$, and consequently the continuity of $X(t)=\sum A_k S_k(t)$.

We have yet to show that $X(t)$ is Brownian motion. If every finite-dimensional vector $\{X(t_1), \ldots, X(t_k)\}$ of a process has a multivariate normal distribution, we call the process *Gaussian*. A Gaussian process is determined by its mean value and covariance functions, because these parameters uniquely specify all the finite-dimensional multivariate normal distributions. Thus, to complete our endeavor, we need only show that: (1) $X(t)$ is Gaussian; (2) $E[X(t)] = 0$; and (3) $E[X(t)X(s)] = \min\{s, t\}$.

The first two properties are easy to check. Each partial sum $X_n(t) = \sum_{k=0}^{n} A_k S_k(t)$ is Gaussian (why?), and this property is preserved in the limit. Indeed, it is easy to ascertain that $X_n(t)$ converges to $X(t)$ in mean square, which will justify the interchange of limit and expectation in

$$E[X(t)] = \lim_{n\to\infty} \sum_{k=1}^{n} E[A_k]S_k(t) = 0.$$

All that remains is to determine the covariance between $X(t)$ and $X(s)$ and see if it is identical with the covariance of standard Brownian motion, namely $\min\{s, t\}$. That is, we wish to verify the equation

$$\begin{aligned}\min\{s, t\} &\stackrel{?}{=} E[X(s)X(t)] \\ &= \sum_{j=1}^{\infty} \sum_{k=1}^{\infty} E[A_j A_k] S_j(s) S_k(t) \\ &= \sum_{k=1}^{\infty} S_k(s) S_k(t).\end{aligned}$$

This is a question purely in classical analysis. But to keep our treatment self-contained, and to demonstrate the power of our methods and the content of our theorems, we will use a martingale argument. In Problem 24 of Chapter 6, we asserted

$$\sum_{k=1}^{n} a_k H_k(Z) = E[f(Z) | Y_1, \ldots, Y_n],$$

where $f(\tau)$ was an arbitrary function satisfying

$$\int_0^1 |f(\tau)| \, d\tau < \infty, \qquad a_k = \int_0^1 f(\tau) H_k(\tau) \, d\tau, \qquad \text{and} \qquad Y_k = H_k(Z),$$

for Z uniformly distributed on $[0, 1]$. Thus these partial sums form a Doob's martingale that converges. If $\int_0^1 |f(\tau)|^2 \, d\tau < \infty$, the martingale is actually square integrable and

$$\sum_{k=1}^{n} a_k H_k(Z) \to E[f(Z) | Y_1, Y_2, \ldots] = f(Z),$$

the convergence occurring in mean square as $n \to \infty$. The last equality is a consequence of Z being determined by the infinite sequence $Y_1, Y_2, \ldots$. Evaluate the mean square to see

$$\int_0^1 |f(\tau) - \sum_{k=1}^{n} a_k H_k(\tau)|^2 \, d\tau = \int_0^1 \{f(\tau)\}^2 \, d\tau - 2 \sum_{k=1}^{n} a_k \int_0^1 f(\tau) H_k(\tau) \, d\tau$$

$$+ \int_0^1 \left\{\sum_{k=1}^{n} a_k H_k(\tau)\right\}^2 d\tau$$

$$= \int_0^1 \{f(\tau)\}^2 \, d\tau - \sum_{k=1}^{n} a_k^2.$$

Since this converges to zero as $n \to \infty$, we deduce $\int_0^1 \{f(\tau)\}^2 \, d\tau = \sum_{k=1}^{\infty} a_k^2$. Applying this formula first to $[f(\tau) + g(\tau)]$ and then to $f(\tau)$ and $g(\tau)$ and subtracting leads to the (so-called) Parseval relation

$$\int_0^1 f(\tau) g(\tau) \, d\tau = \sum_{k=1}^{\infty} a_k b_k, \tag{7.9}$$

where $b_k = \int_0^1 g(\tau) H_k(\tau) \, d\tau$. Fix $s < t$ and let

$$f(\tau) = \begin{cases} 1, & 0 \leq \tau \leq s, \\ 0, & s < \tau \leq 1, \end{cases}$$

and

$$g(\tau) = \begin{cases} 1, & 0 \leq \tau \leq t, \\ 0, & t < \tau \leq 1. \end{cases}$$

Then $a_k = \int_0^1 f(\tau) H_k(\tau) \, d\tau = S_k(s)$, and $b_k = S_k(t)$, while $\int_0^1 f(\tau) g(\tau) \, d\tau = s$ whenever $s < t$. Substitution into (7.9) gives $s = \sum_{k=0}^{\infty} S_k(s) S_k(t)$. The same argument works when $t < s$ to give our desired

$$\min\{s, t\} = \sum_{k=1}^{\infty} S_k(s) S_k(t).$$

This completes our proof that $X(t) = \sum_{k=1}^{\infty} A_k S_k(t)$ is a Brownian motion process whose paths are continuous functions of t with probability one.

If a Brownian motion $B(t)$ whose index set is $0 \leq t < \infty$ is desired, first set $W(t) = tX(1/t)$, for $1 \leq t < \infty$, and then set $B(t) = W(1 + t) - W(1)$, $t \geq 0$. We leave it to the reader to check that this is indeed the desired process. (It is Gaussian and has the required mean and covariance functions.)

A final curiosity that emanates from the construction: Array the digits in the decimal expansion of a uniform (0, 1) random variable $U = Z_1 Z_2 Z_3 \cdots$ diagonally in an infinite matrix as shown:

$$\begin{array}{lllll} Z_1 & Z_3 & Z_6 & Z_{10} & \cdots \\ Z_2 & Z_5 & Z_9 & \cdots & \\ Z_4 & Z_8 & \cdots & & \\ Z_7 & \cdots & & & \end{array}$$

The rows give the decimal expansion for

$$U_1 = \cdot\, Z_1 Z_3 Z_6 Z_{10} \cdots,$$
$$U_2 = \cdot\, Z_2 Z_5 Z_9 Z_{14} \cdots,$$
$$U_3 = \cdot\, Z_4 Z_8 Z_{13} Z_{19} \cdots,$$

which are independent and also uniformly distributed over (0, 1). Let Φ^{-1} be the inverse function to the normal integral

$$\Phi(x) = \frac{1}{\sqrt{2\pi}} \int_{-\infty}^{x} \exp(-t^2/2)\, dt,$$

and set $A_k = \Phi^{-1}(U_k)$. These random variables are independent and, being inverse probability transforms, are normally distributed with zero means and unit variances. Use them in formula (7.8) to construct a Brownian motion process. We have then formed an entire Brownian motion process using as our sole source of "randomness" a single uniform random variable U! In this sense, Brownian motion has no more "randomness" than the experiment of drawing a single number by chance!

B. THE SQUARED VARIATION

Let $X(t)$ be a standard Brownian motion. We will not show that $X(t)$ is nowhere differentiable, although, as mentioned earlier, this is indeed true. What we will do, however, will lend support to this conclusion. We will establish that, for every fixed $t > 0$,

$$\lim_{n\to\infty} \sum_{k=1}^{2^n} \left[X\left(\frac{k}{2^n} t\right) - X\left(\frac{k-1}{2^n} t\right) \right]^2 = t. \tag{7.10}$$

This convergence takes place both in mean square and with probability one, or almost surely.

An elementary calculus approach to the limit on the left suggests the formula

$$\int_0^t [dX(\tau)]^2 = t = \int_0^t d\tau.$$

The same formula expressed in differentials reads $[dX(t)]^2 = dt$! A typical feeling on seeing this for the first time is disbelief accompanied by a strong desire to check the analysis carefully and preclude the possibility of error. No error has been made, as we invite you to check for yourself shortly. In fact, the differential formula $dX(t)^2 = dt$ can be endowed with a precise meaning in which it is not only true, but highly useful, but this development is deferred to Chapter 15 on diffusion processes.

Before proceeding to the proof, let us draw an easy corollary of (7.10):

$$\lim_{n\to\infty} \sum_{k=1}^{2^n} \left| X\left(\frac{k}{2^n} t\right) - X\left(\frac{k-1}{2^n} t\right) \right| = \infty. \tag{7.11}$$

In words, the total variation of a Brownian path is infinite (with probability one). This suggests, but does not imply, the nondifferentiable nature of the paths mentioned earlier. The infinite total variation results from the inequality

$$\sum_{k=1}^{2^n} \left| X\left(\frac{k}{2^n} t\right) - X\left(\frac{k-1}{2^n} t\right) \right| \ge \frac{\sum_{k=1}^{2^n} \left[X\left(\frac{k}{2^n} t\right) - X\left(\frac{k-1}{2^n} t\right) \right]^2}{\max_{j=1,\ldots,2^n} \left| X\left(\frac{j}{2^n} t\right) - X\left(\frac{j-1}{2^n} t\right) \right|}.$$

The numerator on the right converges to t, while the denominator vanishes because Brownian paths are continuous and thus uniformly continuous over bounded intervals. Thus the left hand side must become infinite which validates (7.11).

The proof of the squared variation formula is greatly eased if we introduce some briefer notation. Let

$$\Delta_{nk} = X\left(\frac{k}{2^n} t\right) - X\left(\frac{k-1}{2^n} t\right), \qquad k = 1, \ldots, 2^n,$$

and

$$W_{nk} = \Delta_{nk}^2 - t/2^n, \qquad k = 1, \ldots, 2^n.$$

We wish to show that $\sum_{k=1}^{2^n} \Delta_{nk}^2 \to t$, or what is the same, $\sum_{k=1}^{2^n} W_{nk} \to 0$. For each n, the random variables in $\{W_{nk}\}_{k=1}^{2^n}$ are independent, identically distributed, and

$$E[W_{nk}] = E[\Delta_{nk}^2] - t/2^n = 0, \qquad E[W_{nk}^2] = 2t^2/4^n.$$

The last computation is the fourth moment of the normally distributed Δ_{nk}. In fact, if Δ is normally distributed with mean zero and variance σ^2, then $E[\Delta^{2m}] = 1 \cdot 3 \cdots (2m-1)\sigma^{2m}$, which is readily confirmed inductively by differentiating the normal characteristic function. Then, $E[W_{kn} W_{jn}] = 0$ if $j \neq k$, and squaring the sum leads to

$$E\left[\left\{\sum_{k=1}^{2^n} W_{kn}\right\}^2\right] = \sum_{k=1}^{2^n} E[W_{nk}^2] = 2^{n+1}t^2/4^n = 2t^2/2^n.$$

Since $2t^2/2^n \to 0$ as $n \to \infty$, this immediately shows our desired squared variation formula holds when the limit is understood in the mean square sense. To get convergence with probability one let $\varepsilon > 0$ be given and apply Chebyshev's inequality to see

$$\Pr\left\{\left|\sum_{k=1}^{2^n} W_{nk}\right| > \varepsilon\right\} \leq \frac{2t^2}{\varepsilon^2}\left(\frac{1}{2}\right)^n.$$

Since $\sum (\frac{1}{2})^n < \infty$, the Borel–Cantelli lemma implies that $\left|\sum_{k=1}^{2^n} W_{nk}\right| > \varepsilon$ can occur for only finitely many values of n. Since $\varepsilon > 0$ is arbitrary, we must have (with probability one)

$$\lim_{n\to\infty} \sum_{k=1}^{2^n} W_{nk} = 0.$$

This is equivalent to the squared variation relation (7.10).

While $X(t)$ is not differentiable, in Section 8 of Chapter 9 we will attach a meaning to expressions like $\int_0^t f(\tau)\, dX(\tau)$ by defining the integral to be the mean square limit of the approximating sums. A more general stochastic integral will be developed in Chapter 15.

C. THE LAW OF THE ITERATED LOGARITHM

The principal form of the celebrated law of the iterated logarithm for Brownian motion $X(t)$ states that

$$\limsup_{t\downarrow 0} \frac{X(t)}{\sqrt{2t \log\log(1/t)}} = 1 \tag{7.12}$$

is a certain event or, equivalently, is an event of probability one. There are many variations and generalizations. For example, since $tX(1/t)$ is also a Brownian motion, we have

$$\limsup_{t\downarrow 0} \frac{tX(1/t)}{\sqrt{2t \log\log(1/t)}} = 1,$$

or, with $s = 1/t$,

$$\limsup_{s\uparrow\infty} \frac{X(s)}{\sqrt{2s \log\log s}} = 1.$$

Given a positive ε, on the one hand this means that no matter how large a value s we take, there are values $t > s$ for which

$$\frac{1}{\sqrt{t}} X(t) > (1-\varepsilon)\sqrt{2 \log\log t},$$

while on the other hand, we may guarantee for each sample path

$$\frac{1}{\sqrt{t}} X(t) < (1+\varepsilon)\sqrt{2 \log\log t}, \qquad \text{for all} \quad t > s,$$

by choosing s sufficiently large. In this form, we see that the law of the iterated logarithm furnishes a remarkable answer to what is basically a simple question. For any fixed t, $X(t)/\sqrt{t}$ is normally distributed with mean zero and variance one, and so

$$\Pr\left\{\frac{1}{\sqrt{t}} X(t) > K\sqrt{2 \log\log t}\right\} = 1 - \Phi(K\sqrt{2 \log\log t}),$$

where $\Phi(x)$ is the normal integral. For $K = 1$ and $t = 10^{10}$, this probability is quite small, approximately 0.006. On the other hand, it is conceivable that the probability of

$$\frac{1}{\sqrt{t}} X(t) > K\sqrt{2 \log\log t},$$

for *some* $t > 10^{10}$ could be much larger. The law of the iterated logarithm says "no" if $K > 1$ but "yes," with the probability approaching one, if $K < 1$.

We content ourselves with proving only half of the law, namely

$$\limsup_{t\downarrow 0} \frac{X(t)}{\sqrt{2t \log\log(1/t)}} \le 1, \tag{7.13}$$

with probability one. We begin by applying the maximal inequality to the nonnegative martingale

$$Z(s) = \exp\{\alpha X(s) - \tfrac{1}{2}\alpha^2 s\}, \qquad \alpha > 0,$$

to deduce, for $\alpha > 0$, $\beta > 0$,

$$\begin{aligned}\Pr\left\{\max_{k=1,\ldots,2^n} \exp\left\{\alpha X\left(\frac{k}{2^n}t\right) - \frac{1}{2}\alpha^2\frac{k}{2^n}t\right\} > e^{\alpha\beta}\right\} &\le e^{-\alpha\beta}E[Z(t)] \\ &= e^{-\alpha\beta}E[Z(0)] \\ &= e^{-\alpha\beta}.\end{aligned}$$

This holds for every $n = 1, 2, \ldots$, and since the paths of $X(s)$ are continuous, we may let $n \to \infty$ to see

$$\begin{aligned}e^{-\alpha\beta} &\ge \Pr\left\{\sup_{0\le s\le t} \exp\{\alpha X(s) - \tfrac{1}{2}\alpha^2 s\} > e^{\alpha\beta}\right\} \\ &= \Pr\left\{\sup_{0\le s\le t}\{X(s) - \tfrac{1}{2}\alpha s\} > \beta\right\}, \qquad \alpha > 0.\end{aligned}$$

Fix a value θ, with $0 < \theta < 1$, set

$$h(t) = \sqrt{2t \log\log(1/t)},$$

and for $\varepsilon > 0$, choose

$$\alpha = \alpha_n = (1 + 2\varepsilon)\theta^{-n}h(\theta^n), \qquad \beta = \beta_n = \tfrac{1}{2}h(\theta^n).$$

We get

$$\alpha\beta = (1 + 2\varepsilon)\log\log\theta^{-n} = (1 + 2\varepsilon)\log nc, \qquad \text{for} \quad c = \log(1/\theta) > 0.$$

Thus $e^{-\alpha\beta} = (nc)^{-(1+2\varepsilon)}$. Since $\sum_{n=1}^{\infty}(nc)^{-(1+2\varepsilon)} < \infty$, the Borel–Cantelli lemma applies, and we conclude that

$$\sup_{0\le s\le t}\{X(s) - \tfrac{1}{2}\alpha_n s\} \le \beta_n, \tag{7.14}$$

holds for all but finitely many values of n. In particular, we may assume there is some integer N, random since it depends on the particular path being studied, but for which (7.14) holds whenever $n > N$. If $t < \theta^N$, then when covered by the interval $\theta^n < t \le \theta^{n-1}$, we have $n > N$, so that

$$\begin{aligned}\beta_n &\ge \sup_{0\le s\le t}\{X(s) - \tfrac{1}{2}\alpha_n s\} \\ &\ge X(t) - \tfrac{1}{2}\alpha_n t,\end{aligned}$$

and

$$\begin{aligned}X(t) &\le \tfrac{1}{2}\alpha_n t + \beta_n \\ &\le \tfrac{1}{2}\alpha_n\theta^{n-1} + \beta_n \\ &= \tfrac{1}{2}(1 + 2\varepsilon)\theta^{-1}h(\theta^n) + \tfrac{1}{2}h(\theta^n) \\ &= \frac{1}{2}\left\{\frac{1 + 2\varepsilon}{\theta} + 1\right\}h(\theta^n).\end{aligned}$$

Since $h(t)$ is an increasing function for t near zero, $h(\theta^n) \le h(t)$, and

$$X(t) \le \frac{1}{2}\left\{\frac{1+2\varepsilon}{\theta} + 1\right\} h(t).$$

This inequality holds for all t sufficiently near the origin. To be precise, it holds for all $t \le \theta^N$. Thus, with probability one,

$$\limsup_{t \downarrow 0} \frac{X(t)}{h(t)} \le \frac{1}{2}\left\{\frac{1+2\varepsilon}{\theta} + 1\right\}.$$

Since we have placed no restrictions on θ other than $0 < \theta < 1$, let $\theta \to 1$ to conclude

$$\limsup_{t \downarrow 0} \frac{X(t)}{h(t)} \le 1 + \varepsilon,$$

with probability one.

Since ε is an arbitrary positive number, we have proved the half of the law of the iterated logarithm that is stated in (7.13).

Elementary Problems

In these problems, $X(t)$ is standard Brownian motion.

1. Let T_0 be the largest zero of $X(\tau)$ not exceeding t. Establish the formula

$$\Pr\{T_0 < t_0\} = \frac{2}{\pi} \arcsin\sqrt{t_0/t}.$$

Hint: Use Theorem 3.1.

2. Let T_1 be the smallest zero of $X(\tau)$ exceeding t. Show that:

(a) $\Pr\{T_1 < t_1\} = \dfrac{2}{\pi} \arccos\sqrt{t/t_1}$.

(b) $\Pr\{T_0 < t_0, T_1 > t_1\} = \dfrac{2}{\pi} \arcsin\sqrt{t_0/t_1}$.

3. Verify that $E(X(t)X(s) | X(0) = 0) = \min(t, s)$.

4. Show that the density

$$p(t, x, y) = \frac{1}{\sqrt{2\pi t}} \exp[-(x-y)^2/2t]$$

satisfies the heat equation

$$\frac{\partial p}{\partial t} = \frac{1}{2} \frac{\partial^2 p}{\partial x^2}.$$

5. Let $T(\lambda)$ be the first passage time for reaching $\lambda > 0$ when $X(0) = 0$. Prove that the distribution of $T(\lambda_1 + \lambda_2)$ is the same as the distribution of the sum of $T(\lambda_1)$ and $T(\lambda_2)$, where $T(\lambda_1)$ and $T(\lambda_2)$ are regarded as independent random variables, $\lambda_1, \lambda_2 > 0$.

Hint: Verify $\phi_{\lambda_1+\lambda_2}(\theta) = \phi_{\lambda_1}(\theta)\phi_{\lambda_2}(\theta)$, where $\phi_\lambda(\theta)$ is the Laplace transform of $T(\lambda)$, given in Eq. (5.3).

6. Determine the covariance functions for

$$U(t) = e^{-t}X(e^{2t}), \qquad t \geq 0,$$

and

$$V(t) = X(t) - tX(1), \qquad 0 \leq t \leq 1.$$

Solution:

$$E[U(t)U(s)] = \exp\{-|t-s|\},$$

and

$$E[V(t)V(s)] = t(1-s), \qquad \text{for} \quad t \leq s.$$

7. For a standard Brownian motion $X(t)$ and constants $\alpha > 0$, $\beta > 0$, establish

$$\Pr\{X(t) \leq \alpha t + \beta \quad \text{for all} \quad t \geq 0 | X(0) = w\} = 1 - e^{-2\alpha(\beta - w)}, \qquad \text{for} \quad w \leq \beta.$$

Hint: Apply Corollary 5.1 to the Brownian motion with drift $W(t) = X(t) - \alpha t - w$.

8. Let $W = \int_0^t X(s)\, ds$. Verify that $E[W] = 0$ and $E[W^2] = t^3/3$.

Hint: Validate and complete the computation

$$\begin{aligned} E[W^2] &= E\left[\left\{\int_0^t X(s)\,ds\right\}^2\right] \\ &= E\left[\left\{\int_0^t X(u)\,du\right\}\left\{\int_0^t X(v)\,dv\right\}\right] \\ &= \int_0^t\int_0^t E[X(u)X(v)]\,du\,dv \\ &= 2\int_0^t\left\{\int_0^v u\,du\right\}dv. \end{aligned}$$

9. Derive the conditional distribution of $W = \int_0^t X(s)\, ds$ given that $X(t) = x$.

Hint: W and $X(t)$ have a joint normal distribution.

Solution: Given $X(t) = x$, W is normally distributed with mean $E[W|X(t) = x] = \frac{1}{2}tx$ and variance $E[(W - \frac{1}{2}tx)^2|X(t) = x] = t^3/12$.

10. Let T be the first time the Brownian motion process crosses the line $l(t) = \alpha + \beta t$, $(\alpha > 0, \beta > 0)$. Determine the Laplace transform of T.

Hint: Use the second martingale of (5.1) yielding

$$E[\exp\{\lambda(\alpha + \beta T) - \tfrac{1}{2}\lambda^2 T\}] = 1$$

and then a change of variable $\lambda\beta - \frac{1}{2}\lambda^2 = z$.

11. Let $Y(t) = e^{X(t)}$ be geometric Brownian motion. Determine the diffusion coefficients

$$\lim_{h\downarrow 0} \frac{E[Y(t+h) - Y(t) | Y(t) = y]}{h} = b(y), \qquad 0 < y < \infty,$$

and

$$\lim_{h\downarrow 0} \frac{E[\{Y(t+h) - Y(t)\}^2 | Y(t) = y]}{h} = a(y), \qquad 0 < y < \infty.$$

12. Use relation (5.5) to evaluate the integrals

$$\int_0^\infty \frac{1}{\sqrt{t}} \exp\left\{-\left(at + \frac{b}{t}\right)\right\} dt, \qquad a, b > 0;$$

$$\int_0^\infty \frac{1}{t^{3/2}} \exp\left\{-\left(at + \frac{b}{t}\right)\right\} dt.$$

13. Prove that $\Pr\{M(t) > \xi | X(t) = M(t)\} = \exp(-\xi^2/2t)$, where $M(t) = \max_{0 \le u \le t} X(u)$.

Hint: Let $Y(t) = M(t) - X(t)$. Find the conditional distribution of $M(t)$ given $Y(t) = 0$.

14. Validate the identities

$$\text{(i)} \qquad E[\exp\{\lambda \int_0^t X(s)\, ds\}] = \exp(\lambda^2 t^3/6), \qquad -\infty < \lambda < \infty,$$

and

$$\text{(ii)} \qquad E[\exp\{\lambda \int_0^t sX(s)\, ds\}] = \exp(\lambda^2 t^5/15), \qquad -\infty < \lambda < \infty.$$

15. Let $R(t) = [X_1(t)^2 + \cdots + X_m(t)^2]^{1/2}$ be the radial Brownian motion or Bessel process in m dimensions. (a) Validate that $R(t)^2 - mt$ is a martingale. (b) Use the martingale optional sampling theorem to establish that $E[T] = r^2/m$, where $T = \inf\{t \ge 0;\ R(t) \ge r\}$ is the first time the m-dimensional Brownian motion $[X_1(t), \ldots, X_m(t)]$ reaches a distance r from the origin.

Problems

We use the notation

$$M(t) = \max_{0 \le u \le t} X(u),$$

and

$$Y(t) = M(t) - X(t),$$

where $X(t)$ is standard Brownian motion.

1. Prove that $Y(t) = M(t) - X(t)$ is a continuous-time Markov process.

Hint: Note that for $t' < t$,

$$Y(t) = \max\{\max_{t' \le u \le t} (X(u) - X(t')),\ Y(t')\} - (X(t) - X(t')).$$

2. Show that the stochastic process $Y(t) = M(t) - X(t)$ and the stochastic process $|X(t)|$ are equivalent. (Two processes are said to be equivalent if the finite-dimensional distributions are the same.)

Hint: Since $|X(t)|$ and $Y(t)$ are both Markov processes, it is enough to prove that the density functions of

$$\Pr\{Y(t) < y \mid Y(t_0) = y_0,\ t_0 < t\} \qquad \text{and} \qquad \Pr\{|X(t)| < y \mid |X(t_0)| = y_0,\ t_0 < t\}$$

are identical.

To compute the left-hand side, use the representation of $Y(t)$ in Problem 1.

3. Prove that the probability of at least one zero of $Y(t)$ in the interval (t_0, t_1) is $(2/\pi) \arccos\sqrt{t_0/t_1}$.

4. Let $T_1^*(T_0^*)$ be the smallest (largest) zero of $Y(\tau) = M(\tau) - X(\tau)$ exceeding (not exceeding) t. Show that T_0^* and T_1^* possess the same distribution as T_0 and T_1, respectively, as defined in Elementary Problems 1 and 2.

5. For $a \cdot b > 0$, prove

$$\Pr\{X(\tau) \text{ is not zero in } (0, t) \mid X(0) = a,\ X(t) = b\} = 1 - e^{-2ab/t}.$$

Hint: Use the function $A_t(x, y)$ of (3.9).

6. Prove that, for $\alpha, \beta > 0$,

$$\Pr\{X(u) < \alpha u + \beta,\ 0 \le u \le 1 \mid X(0) = X(1) = 0\} = 1 - e^{-2\beta(\beta+\alpha)}.$$

Hint: Use Theorem 2.1 to establish the identity

$$\begin{aligned}
&\Pr\{X(u) < \alpha u + \beta,\ 0 \le u \le 1 \mid X(0) = X(1) = 0\} \\
&\quad = \Pr\{X(u) < 0,\ 0 \le u \le 1 \mid X(0) = -\beta,\ X(1) = -\beta - \alpha\},
\end{aligned}$$

and then consult Problem 5.

7. Find the conditional probability that $X(t)$ is not zero in the interval (t_0, t_2), given that it is not zero in the interval (t_0, t_1), $0 < t_0 \le t_1 \le t_2$.

Answer:

$$\frac{\arcsin\sqrt{t_0/t_2}}{\arcsin\sqrt{t_0/t_1}}.$$

8. Show that the probability that $X(t)$ is not zero in $(0, t_2)$, given that it is not zero in the interval $(0, t_1)$, $0 < t_1 < t_2$, is $\sqrt{t_1/t_2}$.

Hint: Compute

$$\Pr\{X(t) \ne 0,\ 0 < t_0 \le t \le t_2 | X(t) \ne 0,\ 0 < t_0 \le t \le t_1\},$$

and then let $t_0 \to 0$.

9. Show that the probability of the event $|X(t_1) - X(t_0)| > \xi$, given that $X(t)$ takes on an extreme value [$X(t)$ has two extreme values] over the interval (t_0, t_1) at either t_0 or t_1, is $\exp(-\xi^2/2(t_1 - t_0))$, $t_0 > 0$.

Hint: Prove the following statements:

(i) The event of the problem can take place in any one of four ways: (A) $X(t_0)$ is a minimum, (B) $X(t_0)$ is a maximum, (C) $X(t_1)$ is a minimum, (D) $X(t_1)$ is a maximum.

(ii) The conditional probability, given any one of (A), (B), (C), (D) that any other one of (A), (B), (C), (D) occurs is zero.

(iii)

$$\begin{aligned}
&\Pr\{|X(t_1) - X(t_0)| > \xi | \text{(A), (B), (C), or (D) occurs}\} \\
&= \sum_{\alpha = \text{(A), (B), (C), (D)}} \Pr\{|X(t_1) - X(t_0)| > \xi | \alpha\} \\
&\quad \times \Pr\{\alpha | \text{(A), (B), (C), or (D) occurs}\} \\
&= \exp[-\xi^2/2(t_1 - t_0)].
\end{aligned}$$

(Use Elementary Problem 13 and the reflection principle.)

10. Prove that

$$\begin{aligned}
&\Pr\{X(\tau) \ne 0 \quad \text{in} \quad 0 < t < \tau < u < 1 | X(0) = X(1) = 0\} \\
&= \frac{2}{\pi} \arccos \sqrt{\frac{u - t}{u(1 - t)}}.
\end{aligned}$$

Hint: Compute the quantity

$$\begin{aligned}
2 &\int_{\alpha=0}^{\infty} \int_{\tau=u}^{1} \Pr\{X(t) = \alpha,\ T(\alpha) = \tau - t,\ X(1 - \tau) = 0 | X(0) = 0\} \\
&\quad \times [\Pr\{X(1) = 0 | X(0) = 0\}]^{-1}\, d\alpha\, d\tau,
\end{aligned}$$

where $T(\alpha)$ denotes the time at which the Brownian particle first becomes 0 starting from $X(0)=\alpha$ [see (3.7)], and

$$\begin{aligned}\frac{d}{du}&\left[\frac{2}{\pi}\arccos\sqrt{\frac{u-t}{u(1-t)}}\right]\\&=-\frac{2}{\pi}\frac{1}{\sqrt{1-(u-t)/u(1-t)}}\left(\frac{1}{\sqrt{1-t}}\right)\frac{t}{2\sqrt{1-(t/u)}u^2}\\&=-\frac{\sqrt{t}}{\pi}\frac{1}{(\sqrt{1-u})(\sqrt{u-t})u},\end{aligned}$$

which proves the result.

11. Establish the identity

$$E\left[\exp\left\{\lambda\int_0^t f(s)\,X(s)\,ds\right\}\right]=\exp\left\{\lambda^2\int_0^t f(v)\left[\int_0^v uf(u)\,du\right]dv\right\},\qquad -\infty<\lambda<\infty$$

for any continuous function $f(s)$, $0\le s<\infty$.

12. Prove that $\Pr\{X(1)\le x|X(u)\ge 0,\ 0\le u\le 1\}=1-\exp(-x^2/2)$.

Hint: $X'(t)=X(1)-X(1-t)$ is also a Brownian motion. The desired probability, in terms of $X'(t)$, is

$$\Pr\{X'(1)\le x|M'(1)=X'(1)\},$$

where $M'(t)=\max_{0\le x\le t}X'(x)$. Now consult Elementary Problem 13.

13. For $a>0$, $b<a$, show

$$\Pr\left\{\sup_{t\ge 0}\frac{b+X(t)}{1+t}\ge a\right\}=e^{-2a(a-b)}.$$

Then show that the left-hand side, hence also the right, equals

$$\Pr\left\{\sup_{0\le u\le 1}X(u)\ge a|X(1)=b\right\}.$$

14. Prove Kolmogorov's inequality for Brownian motion:

$$\Pr\left\{\sup_{0\le u\le t}|X(u)|>\varepsilon\right\}\le t/\varepsilon^2,\qquad \varepsilon>0.$$

15. (Continuation). Use Kolmogorov's inequality to show

$$\lim_{t\to\infty}\frac{1}{t}X(t)=0.$$

Hint: Set $\varepsilon=2^{2n/3}$ and $t=2^n$, and apply the Borel–Cantelli lemma.

16. For $n = 1, 2, \ldots$ and $k = 1, \ldots, 2^n$, set

$$\Delta_{nk} = X\left(\frac{k}{2^n}\right) - X\left(\frac{k-1}{2^n}\right)$$

where $X(t)$ is standard Brownian motion.

Show $E[S_{n+1}|S_n] = \frac{1}{2}(S_n + 1)$, where $S_n = \sum_{k=1}^{2^n} \Delta_{nk}^2$.

Hint: Use Theorem 2.1 to establish

$$E[\Delta_{n+1,2k-1}^2 + \Delta_{n+1,2k}^2 | X(j/2^n), \quad j = 1, \ldots, 2^n] = \tfrac{1}{2}(\Delta_{nk}^2 + 1).$$

Then sum both sides.

17. Using the notation of Problem 16, show $E[S_n|S_{n+1}] = S_{n+1}$.

Hint: Use symmetry to argue

$$\begin{aligned} E[\Delta_{nk}^2|\Delta_{n+1,2k-1}^2, \quad \Delta_{n+1,2k}^2] &= E[(\Delta_{n+1,2k-1} + \Delta_{n+1,2k})^2 | \Delta_{n+1,2k-1}^2, \quad \Delta_{n+1,2k}^2] \\ &= \tfrac{1}{2}(\Delta_{n+1,2k-1} + \Delta_{n+1,2k})^2 + \tfrac{1}{2}(\Delta_{n+1,2k-1} - \Delta_{n+1,2k})^2 \\ &= \Delta_{n+1,2k-1}^2 + \Delta_{n+1,2k}^2. \end{aligned}$$

18. Let $X(t)$ be standard Brownian motion, and for $\varepsilon > 0$ and $T > 1$ let $g_{\varepsilon, T}(x)$ be the conditional probability density for $X(1)$, given $X(t) \geq -\varepsilon$ for all $t \leq T$. Show

$$\lim_{\substack{\varepsilon \downarrow 0 \\ T \to \infty}} g_{\varepsilon, T}(x) = \sqrt{\frac{2}{\pi}}\, x^2 \exp(-x^2/2).$$

Remark: This is the distribution of $R(1)$ in a 3-dimensional Bessel process.

19. $\{f_\theta(X(t), t)\}$ is a martingale for any real parameter θ, where $f_\theta(x, t) = \exp\{\theta x - \frac{1}{2}\theta^2 t\}$. Use the martingale $f_\theta(X(t), t) + f_{-\theta}(X(t), t)$, where $\theta = \sqrt{2\lambda}$ to show

$$E[e^{-\lambda T}] = \frac{1}{\cosh(\sqrt{2\lambda}\, a)},$$

where $T = \min\{t: X(t) = +a \text{ or } X(t) = -a\}$.

20. Set

$$p(x, t) = \frac{1}{\sqrt{t}} \exp(x^2/2t), \qquad t > 0.$$

Show that $p(X(t), a + t)$ is a martingale for $a > 0$.

Hint: Verify

$$p(x, t) = \int_{-\infty}^{+\infty} \frac{1}{\sqrt{2\pi}} f_\theta(x, t)\, d\theta,$$

where $f_\theta(x, t) = \exp\{\theta x - \frac{1}{2}\theta^2 t\}$. Consult also (5.2).

21. Use the martingale in Problem 20 and the maximal inequality for martingales to show

$$\Pr\{|X(t)| \geq \sqrt{2(a+t)\log\sqrt{a+t}}, \quad \text{for some} \quad t \geq 0\} \leq \frac{1}{\sqrt{a}}.$$

22. Fix $a < 0 < b$ and let $T(a)$ [respectively, $T(b)$] be the first time the process reaches a (respectively, b). Let $I_a = 1$ if $T(a) < T(b)$, and zero otherwise. Similarly, let I_b be the indicator of the event that b is reached before a. Show that

$$\exp(-\sqrt{2\lambda}\, b) = E\{I_b \exp[-\lambda T(b)]\} + E\{I_a \exp[-\lambda T(a)]\} \exp[-\sqrt{2\lambda}\,(b-a)],$$

and

$$\exp(\sqrt{2\lambda}\, a) = E\{I_a \exp[-\lambda T(a)]\} + E\{I_b \exp[-\lambda T(b)]\} \exp[-\sqrt{2\lambda}\,(b-a)].$$

Hint: The first equation dichotomizes paths to b according to whether a is hit first or not. If a is hit first, a move to a without hitting b is followed by a move from a to b. Finally, recall

$$\exp(-\sqrt{2\lambda}\, b) = E[\exp[-\lambda T(b)] | X(0) = 0],$$

and

$$\exp[-\sqrt{2\lambda}\,(b-a)] = E[\exp[-\lambda T(b)] | X(0) = a].$$

23. (Continuation). Solve the equations derived in Problem 22 simultaneously for $E\{I_a \exp[-\lambda T(a)]\}$ and $E\{I_b \exp[-\lambda T(b)]\}$. Let $T = \min\{T(a), T(b)\}$ be the first time either a or b is reached. Find

$$E[\exp(-\lambda T)] = E\{I_a \exp[-\lambda T(a)]\} + E\{I_b \exp[-\lambda T(b)]\}.$$

24. Let $W(t)$ be a Brownian motion with positive drift $\mu > 0$ and variance σ^2. Let $M(t) = \max_{0 \leq u \leq t} W(u)$ and $Y(t) = M(t) - W(t)$. Fix $a > 0$ and $y > 0$, and let

$$T(a) = \min\{t\colon M(t) = a\}, \qquad S(y) = \min\{t\colon Y(t) = y\}.$$

Establish that

$$\Pr\{T(a) < S(y)\} = \exp\left\{\frac{-2\mu a}{\sigma^2[\exp(2\mu y/\sigma^2) - 1]}\right\}.$$

Hint: Let $f(a) = \Pr\{T(a) < S(y)\}$. Argue first, that $f(a_1 + a_2) = f(a_1)f(a_2)$, and thus $f(a) = e^{-ka}$ for some constant k.

With $\lambda = -2\mu/\sigma^2$, $e^{\lambda X(t)} = e^{\lambda[M(t) - Y(t)]}$ is a martingale. Set

$$T = \min\{T(a), S(y)\}$$

and apply the optional stopping theorem. Observe $M(T) = a$, $Y(T) = 0$, if $T(a) < S(y)$, and $Y(T) = y$ if $T(a) > S(y)$. Disect $1 = E[e^{\lambda[M(T) - Y(T)}]$ according as $T(a) < S(y)$ or $T(a) > S(y)$. Let $a \to 0$ to determine the unknown constant k.

25. Let $\{X(t); t \geq 0\}$ be a Brownian motion process. By formally differentiating the martingale

$$\mathscr{X}_\theta(t) = \exp\{\theta X(t) - (1/2)\theta^2 t\},$$

with respect to θ, show that, for each n, $H_n(X(t), t)$ is a martingale, where

$$H_0(x, t) \equiv 1,$$
$$H_1(x, t) = x,$$

and

$$H_n(x, t) = xH_{n-1}(x, t) - (n-1)tH_{n-2}(x, t).$$

An alternative approach is to show that (5.2) applies.

26. Consider any continuous integrable function f defined on the real line satisfying

$$\int_{-\infty}^{\infty} f(\delta)\, d\delta = a > 0.$$

Form the process

$$Y(t) = \frac{1}{\sqrt{t}} \int_0^t f(X(u))\, du.$$

Show that

$$\lim_{t\to\infty} E[Y(t)] \qquad \text{and} \qquad \lim_{t\to\infty} E[Y^2(t)]$$

exist and determine their values.

27. (Continuation.)
Show that

$$\lim_{t\to\infty} E[\{Y(t)\}^k] = \mu_k a^k$$

where μ_k is the kth moment of the one-sided normal distribution. (The one sided normal is the distribution of $|Z|$ where Z follows a standard normal distribution.)

NOTES

For applications of Brownian motion to statistical mechanics and mathematical analysis we recommend the delightful monograph by Kac [2].

An outstanding treatise on diffusion processes, which completes and profoundly extends the work of Lévy, is that of Ito and McKean [3].

REFERENCES

1. P. Lévy, "Processus Stochastiques et Mouvement Brownien." Gauthier-Villars, Paris, 1948.
2. M. Kac, "Probability and Related Topics in Physical Sciences." Wiley, New York, 1959.
3. K. Ito and H. P. McKean, "Diffusion Processes and Their Sample Paths." Springer-Verlag, Berlin, 1965.

Chapter 8

BRANCHING PROCESSES

The first four sections of this chapter provide a basic introduction to branching processes and their applications. Sections 5 through 11 provide generalizations and extensions and should not be attempted until after the earlier material has been mastered. In a one semester course, where time is scarce, these later sections might be omitted.

1: *Discrete Time Branching Processes*

Branching processes were introduced as examples of Markov chains in Section 2 of Chapter 2. There are numerous examples of Markov branching processes that arise naturally in various scientific disciplines. We list some of the more prominent ones.

(a) *Electron Multipliers*
An electron multiplier is a device that amplifies a weak current of electrons. A series of plates are set up in the path of electrons emitted by a source. Each electron, as it strikes the first plate, generates a random number of new electrons, which in turn strike the next plate and produce more electrons, etc. Let X_0 be the number of electrons initially emitted, X_1 the number of electrons produced on the first plate by the impact due to the X_0 initial electrons; in general let X_n be the number of electrons emitted from the nth plate due to electrons emanating from the $(n-1)$st plate. The sequence of random variables $X_0, X_1, X_2, \ldots, X_n, \ldots$ constitutes a branching process.

(b) *Neutron Chain Reaction*
A nucleus is split by a chance collision with a neutron. The resulting fission yields a random number of new neutrons. Each of these secondary

neutrons may hit some other nucleus producing a random number of additional neutrons, etc. In this case the initial number of neutrons is $X_0 = 1$. The first generation of neutrons comprises all those produced from the fission caused by the initial neutron. The size of the first generation is a random variable X_1. In general the population X_n at the nth generation is produced by the chance hits of the X_{n-1} individual neutrons of the $(n-1)$st generation.

(c) *Survival of Family Names*

The family name is inherited by sons only. Suppose that each individual has probability p_k of having k male offspring. Then from one individual there result the 1st, 2nd, ..., nth, ... generations of descendants. We may investigate the distribution of such random variables as the number of descendants in the nth generation, or the probability that the family name will eventually become extinct. Such questions will be dealt with in the general analysis of branching processes of this chapter.

(d) *Survival of Mutant Genes*

Each individual gene has a chance to give birth to k offspring, $k = 1, 2, \ldots$, which are genes of the same kind. However, any individual has a chance to transform into a different type or mutant gene. This gene may become the first in a sequence of generations of a particular mutant gene. We may inquire about the chances of survival of the mutant gene within the population of the original genes.

All of the above examples possess the following structure. Let X_0 denote the size of the initial population. Each individual gives birth, *independently of the others*, with probability p_k to k new individuals, where

$$p_k \geq 0, \qquad k = 0, 1, 2, \ldots, \qquad \text{and} \qquad \sum_{k=0}^{\infty} p_k = 1. \tag{1.1}$$

The totality of all the direct descendants of the initial population constitutes the first generation whose size we denote by X_1. Each individual of the first generation independently bears a progeny whose size is governed by the probability distribution (1.1). The descendants produced constitute the second generation of size X_2. In general the nth generation is composed of descendants of the $(n-1)$st generation each of whose members independently produces k progeny with probability p_k, $k = 0, 1, 2, \ldots$. The population size of the nth generation is denoted by X_n. The X_n form a sequence of integer-valued random variables which generate a Markov chain.

2: *Generating Function Relations for Branching Processes*

We will develop some relations for the probability generating functions of the X_n. Assume first that the initial population consists of one individual, i.e., assume $X_0 = 1$. Clearly we can write for every $n = 0, 1, 2, \ldots$

$$X_{n+1} = \sum_{r=1}^{X_n} \xi_r,$$

where ξ_r $(r \geq 1)$ are independently identically distributed random variables with distribution

$$\Pr\{\xi_r = k\} = p_k, \qquad k = 0, 1, 2, \ldots, \qquad \sum_{k=0}^{\infty} p_k = 1.$$

We introduce the probability generating function

$$\varphi(s) = \sum_{k=0}^{\infty} p_k s^k$$

and

$$\varphi_n(s) = \sum_{k=0}^{\infty} \Pr\{X_n = k\} s^k, \qquad \text{for} \quad n = 0, 1, 2, \ldots.$$

Manifestly,

$$\varphi_0(s) \equiv s \qquad \text{and} \qquad \varphi_1(s) = \varphi(s).$$

Further,

$$\begin{aligned}
\varphi_{n+1}(s) &= \sum_{k=0}^{\infty} \Pr\{X_{n+1} = k\} s^k \\
&= \sum_{k=0}^{\infty} \sum_{j=0}^{\infty} \Pr\{X_{n+1} = k | X_n = j\} \Pr\{X_n = j\} s^k \\
&= \sum_{k=0}^{\infty} s^k \sum_{j=0}^{\infty} \Pr\{X_n = j\} \cdot \Pr\{\xi_1 + \cdots + \xi_j = k\} \\
&= \sum_{j=0}^{\infty} \Pr\{X_n = j\} \cdot \sum_{k=0}^{\infty} \Pr\{\xi_1 + \cdots + \xi_j = k\} s^k. \qquad (2.1)
\end{aligned}$$

Since ξ_r $(r = 1, 2, \ldots, j)$ are independent, identically distributed random variables with common probability generating function $\varphi(s)$, the sum $\xi_1 + \cdots + \xi_j$ has the probability generating function $[\varphi(s)]^j$. Thus,

$$\varphi_{n+1}(s) = \sum_{j=0}^{\infty} \Pr\{X_n = j\} [\varphi(s)]^j.$$

But the right-hand side is just the generating function $\varphi_n(\cdot)$ evaluated at $\varphi(s)$. Thus,

$$\varphi_{n+1}(s) = \varphi_n(\varphi(s)). \tag{2.2}$$

Iterating this relation we obtain

$$\begin{aligned}\varphi_{n+1}(s) &= \varphi_n(\varphi(s)) = \varphi_{n-1}(\varphi(\varphi(s))) = \varphi_{n-1}(\varphi_2(s))\\ &= \varphi_{n-2}(\varphi_2(\varphi(s))) = \varphi_{n-2}(\varphi_3(s)).\end{aligned}$$

It follows, by induction, that for any $k = 0, 1, \ldots, n$

$$\varphi_{n+1}(s) = \varphi_{n-k}(\varphi_{k+1}(s)).$$

In particular, with $k = n - 1$,

$$\varphi_{n+1}(s) = \varphi(\varphi_n(s)). \tag{2.3}$$

If instead of $X_0 = 1$ we assume $X_0 = i_0$ (constant), then

$$\varphi_0(s) \equiv s^{i_0} \qquad \text{and} \qquad \varphi_1(s) = [\varphi(s)]^{i_0}$$

because

$$X_1 = \sum_{j=1}^{i_0} \xi_j.$$

We still have

$$\varphi_{n+1}(s) = \varphi_n(\varphi(s))$$

but (2.3) no longer holds.

With the help of (2.2), we will now compute the expectation and variance of X_n. It is assumed henceforth, unless explicitly stated to the contrary, that $X_0 = 1$. We postulate that

$$m = EX_1 \qquad \text{and} \qquad \sigma^2 = \operatorname{Var} X_1 = E(X_1^2) - [E(X_1)]^2$$

exist and are finite.

Obviously, $EX_n = \varphi_n'(1)$. Then differentiating (2.2) and setting $s = 1$ yields [since $\varphi(1) = 1$] $\varphi_{n+1}'(1) = \varphi_n'(1)\varphi'(1)$. Iteration produces

$$\varphi_{n+1}'(1) = \varphi'(1)\varphi_n'(1) = [\varphi'(1)]^2\varphi_{n-1}'(1) = [\varphi'(1)]^3\varphi_{n-2}'(1)$$

and by induction

$$\varphi_{n+1}'(1) = [\varphi'(1)]^n\varphi_1'(1) = [\varphi'(1)]^{n+1}.$$

But $\varphi'(1) = \varphi_1'(1) = EX_1 = m$. Thus

$$EX_{n+1} = m^{n+1}. \tag{2.4}$$

To compute $\operatorname{Var} X_{n+1}$, first note that

$$\varphi_n''(1) = \sum_{k=2}^{\infty} k(k-1)\Pr\{X_n = k\} = EX_n^2 - EX_n = EX_n^2 - \varphi_n'(1)$$

and so

$$\operatorname{Var} X_n = \varphi_n''(1) + \varphi_n'(1) - [\varphi_n'(1)]^2.$$

But differentiating (2.3) twice and setting $s = 1$ yields

$$\varphi_{n+1}''(1) = \varphi''(1)[\varphi_n'(1)]^2 + \varphi'(1)\varphi_n''(1).$$

Since $\varphi'(1) = m$ and $\varphi''(1) = EX_1^2 - EX_1 = \sigma^2 + m^2 - m$, we have

$$\varphi_{n+1}''(1) = Mm^{2n} + m\varphi_n''(1),$$

where $M = \sigma^2 + m^2 - m$. By induction,

$$\varphi_{n+1}''(1) = M\{m^{2n} + m^{2n-1}\} + m^2\varphi_{n-1}''(1) = \cdots = M\{m^{2n} + m^{2n-1} + \cdots + m^n\}.$$

Thus

$$\begin{aligned}\operatorname{Var} X_{n+1} &= (\sigma^2 + m^2 - m)\{m^{2n} + m^{2n-1} + \cdots + m^n\} + m^{n+1} - m^{2n+2} \\ &= \sigma^2\{m^{2n} + m^{2n-1} + \cdots + m^n\} \\ &= \sigma^2 m^n \frac{m^{n+1} - 1}{m - 1} \qquad \text{if} \quad m \neq 1\end{aligned}$$

and

$$\operatorname{Var} X_{n+1} = (n+1)\sigma^2 \qquad \text{if} \quad m = 1.$$

We have hereby verified the formulas $EX_n = m^n$ and

$$\operatorname{Var} X_n = \begin{cases} \sigma^2 m^{n-1} \dfrac{m^n - 1}{m - 1} & \text{if} \quad m \neq 1, \\ n\sigma^2 & \text{if} \quad m = 1. \end{cases}$$

Thus, the variance increases (decreases) geometrically if $m > 1$ $(m < 1)$, and linearly if $m = 1$. This behavior is characteristic of many results for branching processes.

3: Extinction Probabilities

We want to determine the probability that the population will eventually die out, i.e., $\Pr\{X_n = 0 \text{ for some } n\}$. Obviously whenever $X_n = 0$, $X_k = 0$ for all $k > n$.

Note first that extinction never occurs if the probability that an individual gives birth to no offspring is zero, i.e., when $p_0 = 0$. Thus in investigating the probability of extinction we will assume $0 < p_0 < 1$. Let

$$q_n = \Pr\{X_n = 0\} = \varphi_n(0).$$

Then by formula (2.3)

$$q_{n+1} = \varphi_{n+1}(0) = \varphi(\varphi_n(0)) = \varphi(q_n). \tag{3.1}$$

Since $\varphi(s)$ is a strictly increasing function (it is a power series with non-negative coefficients and $p_0 < 1$) and $q_1 = \varphi_1(0) = p_0 > 0$, $q_2 = \varphi(q_1) > \varphi(0) = q_1$. Assume that $q_n > q_{n-1}$; then $q_{n+1} = \varphi(q_n) > \varphi(q_{n-1}) = q_n$. This shows inductively that $q_1, q_2, \ldots, q_n, \ldots$ is a monotone increasing sequence bounded by 1. Hence

$$\pi = \lim_{n\to\infty} q_n$$

exists and $0 < \pi \leq 1$. Since $\varphi(s)$ is continuous, for $0 \leq s \leq 1$ [at $s = 1$, by Abel's lemma (Lemma 5.1, Chapter 2)], letting $n \to \infty$ in (3.1) yields

$$\pi = \varphi(\pi). \tag{3.2}$$

Since q_n is defined as the probability of extinction at or prior to the nth generation, we infer that π is the probability of eventual extinction and (3.2) shows that π is a root of the equation

$$\varphi(s) = s. \tag{3.3}$$

We now establish the result that π is the smallest positive root of (3.3). Let s_0 be a positive root of (3.3). Then $q_1 = \varphi(0) < \varphi(s_0) = s_0$. Assume $q_n < s_0$. Then by (3.1) $q_{n+1} = \varphi(q_n) < \varphi(s_0) = s_0$. Thus we infer by induction that $q_n < s_0$ holds for all n. It follows that $\pi = \lim q_n \leq s_0$, validating the assertion that π is the smallest positive root of (3.3).

Now, assume also that $p_0 + p_1 < 1$. Then $\varphi(s)$ is a convex function in $0 < s \leq 1$, as $\varphi''(s) = \sum_{k=2}^{\infty} k(k-1)p_k s^{k-2} > 0$. Therefore, the graph of $\varphi(s)$ can intersect the 45° line in at most two points. We know that $\varphi(1) = 1$ and so there certainly is an intersection at (1, 1). Clearly we have one of the two cases represented by Figs. 1 and 2. If $m = \varphi'(1) > 1$, then the slope of the tangent to the graph of $\varphi(s)$ at $s = 1$ exceeds 1 and the case represented by Fig. 1 is germane. In this case $0 < \pi < 1$. If $m = \varphi'(1) \leq 1$, then the slope of the tangent at $s = 1$ is smaller than or equal to one and we are in the situation of Fig. 2. Then necessarily $\pi = 1$. Thus, we have proved that the probability of extinction is 1 if $m \leq 1$ and is less than 1 if $m > 1$. In other words, extinction is certain if and only if the mean number of offspring per individual does not exceed one.

Further, note that for $0 \leq s \leq \pi$, $\varphi(s) \leq \varphi(\pi)$ (see Fig. 2). By induction we have $\varphi_n(s) \leq \pi$ $(0 \leq s \leq \pi)$ for all n. But $\varphi_n(s) \geq \varphi_n(0) = q_n$ and thus, $q_n \leq \varphi_n(s) \leq \pi$. Let $n \to \infty$. Then

$$\lim_{n\to\infty} \varphi_n(s) = \pi \qquad \text{for} \quad 0 \leq s \leq \pi.$$

Further, for the case $m > 1$, when $\pi < s < 1$ we have $\pi < \varphi(s) < s < 1$ (consult Fig. 1). By induction

$$\pi < \varphi_n(s) < \varphi_{n-1}(s) < \cdots \qquad (\pi < s < 1).$$

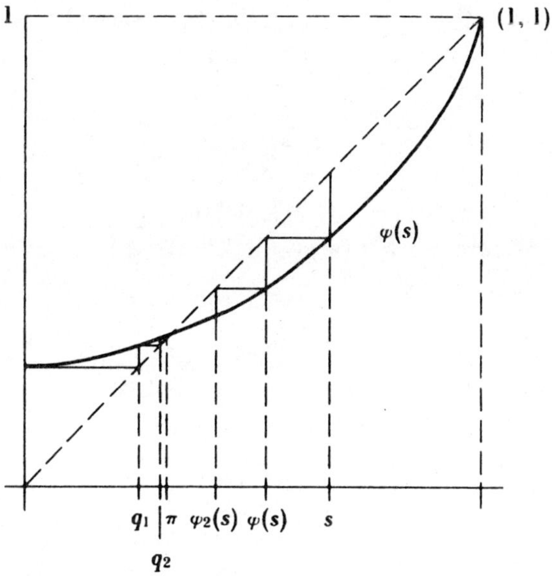

FIG. 1

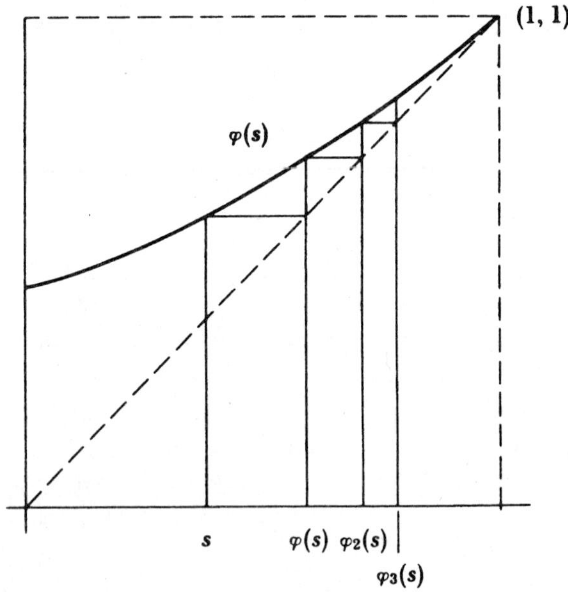

FIG. 2

It follows that

$$\lim_{n\to\infty} \varphi_n(s) \geq \pi. \tag{3.4}$$

The limit has to equal π for if $\lim_{n\to\infty} \varphi_n(s) = \alpha > \pi$, then $\varphi(\alpha) < \alpha$ and the convergence in (3.4) is impossible in view of the relation $\lim_{n\to\infty} \varphi_{n+1}(s) = \lim_{n\to\infty} \varphi(\varphi_n(s))$. The above analysis shows that

$$\lim_{n\to\infty} \varphi_n(s) = \pi \qquad \text{for} \quad 0 \leq s < 1.$$

The fact that $\varphi_n(s)$ converge to the constant function π on $0 \leq s < 1$ implies that in the series

$$\varphi_n(s) = \sum_{k=0}^{\infty} \Pr\{X_n = k\} s^k$$

the first coefficient

$$\Pr\{X_n = 0\} \quad \text{converges to} \quad \pi \qquad \text{as} \quad n \to \infty,$$

and all the other coefficients

$$\Pr\{X_n = k\} \quad \text{converge to} \quad 0 \qquad \text{as} \quad n \to \infty \quad \text{for} \quad k = 1, 2, \ldots.$$

Hence, regardless of the actual value of $m = EX_1 > 1$, the probability that the nth generation will consist of any positive finite number of individuals tends to zero as $n \to \infty$, while the probability of extinction tends to π. In this circumstance we say that $X_n \to \infty$ as $n \to \infty$ with probability $1 - \pi$.

This result is also a consequence of the general theory of Markov chains in that the Markov chain determined by the sequence $X_0, X_1, X_2, \ldots$ has a single absorbing state $\{0\}$ and so $\lim_{n\to\infty} P_{ij}^n = 0$, $1 \leq i, j < \infty$, since i and j are automatically transient.

We close this section by noting the interesting property that the conditional expectation of X_{n+r} (r a positive integer), given X_n, is $m^r \cdot X_n$, i.e., $E(X_{n+r} | X_n) = m^r X_n$. To prove this we first consider the case $r = 1$:

$$E\left\{X_{n+1} \middle| X_n\right\} = E\left\{\sum_{j=1}^{X_n} \xi_j \middle| X_n\right\} = X_n E\xi_j = mX_n.$$

We now assume the stated relation for r and prove the formula for $r + 1$. Thus

$$E\{X_{n+r+1} | X_n\}$$
$$= E\{E[X_{n+r+1} | X_{n+r}, X_{n+r-1}, \ldots, X_n] | X_n\} = E\{E[X_{n+r+1} | X_{n+r}] | X_n\},$$

where we use the Markov nature of $\{X_n\}$. But $E[X_{n+r+1} | X_{n+r}] = X_{n+r} \cdot m$ and by the induction hypothesis, $E(mX_{n+r} | X_n) = m^{r+1} X_n$. Thus we have

$$E\{X_{n+r} | X_n\} = X_n m^r \qquad \text{for} \quad r = 0, 1, 2, \ldots, \quad n = 0, 1, 2, \ldots. \tag{3.5}$$

Now consider the random variables

$$W_n = \frac{X_n}{m^n} \qquad n = 0, 1, 2, \ldots.$$

Then on the basis of (3.5) , we have

$$E\{W_{n+r}|W_n\} = \frac{1}{m^{n+r}} E\{X_{n+r}|X_n\} = \frac{1}{m^{n+r}} \cdot X_n \cdot m^r = W_n.$$

We may write for $r, n = 0, 1, 2, \ldots$

$$E\{W_{n+r}|W_n, W_{n-1}, \ldots, W_1, W_0\} = W_n, \tag{3.6}$$

which shows that $\{W_n\}_{n=0}^{\infty}$ is a martingale.

4: Examples

(i) Let $\varphi(s) = p_0 + p_1 s$, $0 < p_0 < 1$. The associated branching process is a pure death process. In each period each individual independently dies with probability p_0 and survives with probability $1 - p_0 = p_1$.

(ii) Let $\varphi(s) = p_0 + p_2 s^2$ $(0 < p_0 < 1,\ p_0 + p_2 = 1)$. This is the probability-generating function corresponding to a branching process in which in each generation an individual either dies or is replaced by two progeny.

(iii) Consider the example where each individual produces N or 0 direct descendants with probabilities p or q respectively. Thus $p_0 = q$, $p_N = p$, and $p_k = 0$ for $k \neq 0, N$. Then

$$\varphi(s) = q + ps^N. \tag{4.1}$$

(iv) Each individual may have k offspring where k has a binomial probability distribution with parameters N and p. Then

$$\varphi(s) = (q + ps)^N. \tag{4.2}$$

(v) In connection with Example (d) described at the beginning of this chapter it is frequently assumed that the probability of a mutant gene having k direct descendants $(k = 0, 1, 2, \ldots)$ is governed by a Poisson distribution with mean $\lambda = 1$. Then $\varphi(s) = e^{s-1}$ and $\pi = 1$.

The rationale behind this choice of distribution is as follows. In many populations a large number of zygotes (fertilized eggs) are produced, only a small number of which grow to maturity. The events of fertilization and maturation of different zygotes obey the law of independent binomial trials. The number of trials (i.e., number of zygotes) is large so that the actual number of mature progeny follows the Poisson distribution. This is a corollary of the principle of rare events commonly invoked to justify the Poisson approximation. It seems quite appropriate in the model of population growth of a rare mutant gene. If the mutant gene carries a biological advantage (or disadvantage), then the probability distribution is taken to be the Poisson distribution with mean $\lambda > 1$ or (< 1). Specifically,

$$\varphi(s) = e^{\lambda(s-1)} \tag{4.3}$$

and $0 < \pi < 1$ if and only if $\lambda > 1$.

In a heterogeneous population of mutant genes we may assume that the probability distribution of the number of offspring is a Poisson distribution, but with the mean also a random variable.

For example, we may have a large geographical area in which for each subarea a branching process characterized by the probability generating function of a Poisson distribution with parameter λ is taking place. We assume, furthermore, that the value of λ varies depending on the subarea and its distribution over the whole area is that of a gamma. Formally we postulate that the probability of a mutant gene having exactly k direct descendants is given by

$$p_k = e^{-\lambda}\frac{\lambda^k}{k!}, \qquad k = 0, 1, 2, \ldots,$$

where λ itself is a random variable distributed according to a gamma distribution with the density function

$$\begin{aligned} f(\lambda) &= \frac{(q/p)^{\alpha}\lambda^{\alpha-1}}{\Gamma(\alpha)} \exp\left(-\frac{q}{p}\lambda\right) \qquad && \text{for} \quad \lambda \geq 0, \\ &= 0 && \text{otherwise,} \end{aligned}$$

where q, p, α are positive constants and $q + p = 1$. The probability of an individual having k offspring, if we average with respect to the values of the parameter λ, is

$$\Pr\{\xi = k\} = \int_0^\infty \Pr\{\xi = k | \lambda\} f(\lambda)\, d\lambda.$$

Thus the generating function is

$$\begin{aligned} \varphi(s) &= \sum_{k=0}^{\infty} \Pr\{\xi = k\} s^k = \sum_{k=0}^{\infty} \int_0^\infty \exp(-\lambda)\frac{\lambda^k}{k!}\frac{(q/p)^{\alpha}\lambda^{\alpha-1}}{\Gamma(\alpha)} \exp\left(-\frac{q}{p}\lambda\right) d\lambda \cdot s^k \\ &= \int_0^\infty \exp(-\lambda)\frac{(q/p)^{\alpha}\lambda^{\alpha-1}}{\Gamma(\alpha)} \exp\left(-\frac{q}{p}\lambda\right)\left(\sum_{k=0}^{\infty}\frac{(\lambda s)^k}{k!}\right) d\lambda \\ &= \int_0^\infty \exp\left\{-\left(\frac{q}{p} + 1 - s\right)\lambda\right\}\frac{(q/p)^{\alpha}\lambda^{\alpha-1}}{\Gamma(\alpha)}\, d\lambda \\ &= \left(\frac{q/p}{(q/p) + 1 - s}\right)^{\alpha} = \left(\frac{q}{1 - ps}\right)^{\alpha}. \end{aligned}$$

This we recognize as the probability generating function of the negative binomial distribution.

(vi) In Examples (ii)–(iv) no closed-form expressions are known for the nth-generation probability generating function $\varphi_n(s)$. The final example studied below is amenable to a rather complete analysis. Specifically, we will compute the nth-generation probability generating function. Let

$$p_k = bc^{k-1}, \qquad k = 1, 2, \dots,$$

and

$$p_0 = 1 - \sum_{k=1}^{\infty} p_k,$$

where $b, c > 0$ and $b + c < 1$. Then

$$p_0 = 1 - b \sum_{k=1}^{\infty} c^{k-1} = 1 - \frac{b}{1-c} = \frac{1-b-c}{1-c}$$

and the corresponding probability generating function is

$$\varphi(s) = 1 - \frac{b}{1-c} + bs \sum_{k=1}^{\infty} (cs)^{k-1} = \frac{1-(b+c)}{1-c} + \frac{bs}{1-cs}. \tag{4.4}$$

Notice that $\varphi(s)$ has the form of a linear fractional transformation

$$f(s) = \frac{\alpha + \beta s}{\gamma + \delta s}, \qquad \alpha\delta - \beta\gamma \neq 0. \tag{4.5}$$

We now record several elementary properties of linear fractional transformations needed below:

(i) Iterates of linear fractional transformations are again linear fractional transformations, for if $f(s)$ is defined by (4.5) simple algebra gives

$$f(f(s)) = \frac{\alpha(\gamma + \beta) + (\alpha\delta + \beta^2)s}{\alpha\delta + \gamma^2 + \delta(\gamma + \beta)s}.$$

(ii) There always exist two finite (possibly identical) solutions to the equation $f(s) = s$. The solutions are called fixed points of $f(\cdot)$. If $f(s)$ is a probability-generating function then $s_1 = 1$ is one of the fixed points and we shall see that the other fixed point s_0 is less than one, equal to one, or greater than one, according to whether $f'(1)$ is greater than, equal to, or less than one.

For the generating function given by (4.4), one can verify by straightforward algebra that the second fixed point, for $c > 0$, and $b + c < 1$, is

$$s_0 = \frac{1-b-c}{c(1-c)}.$$

(iii) For any two points s_i, $i = 0, 1$, it is easily seen that

$$\frac{f(s)-f(s_i)}{s-s_i} = \frac{\gamma\beta-\alpha\delta}{(\gamma+\delta s)(\gamma+\delta s_i)}.$$

Hence

$$\frac{f(s)-f(s_0)}{f(s)-f(s_1)} = \left(\frac{\gamma+\delta s_1}{\gamma+\delta s_0}\right)\left(\frac{s-s_0}{s-s_1}\right). \tag{4.6}$$

If we now let s_0 and s_1 be the two (nonidentical) fixed points of $f(\cdot)$ and write $w = f(s)$, (4.6) becomes

$$\frac{w-s_0}{w-s_1} = \kappa\frac{s-s_0}{s-s_1}, \tag{4.7}$$

where κ can be calculated from (4.6) or more simply from (4.5) by setting $s = 0$.

Using (4.7) we easily obtain the iterates $f_n(s) = w_n$ of $f(s)$:

$$\frac{w_2-s_0}{w_2-s_1} = \kappa\frac{w_1-s_0}{w_1-s_1} = \kappa\left(\kappa\frac{s-s_0}{s-s_1}\right),$$

and in general

$$\frac{w_n-s_0}{w_n-s_1} = \kappa^n\frac{s-s_0}{s-s_1}. \tag{4.8}$$

For the generating function of the geometric distribution given by (4.4), noting that the fixed points are $s_0 = (1-b-c)/c(1-c)$ and $s_1 = 1$, we obtain

$$\kappa = \frac{(1-c)^2}{b} = \frac{1}{m},$$

where m is the mean of the geometric distribution. For $m \neq 1$ the two fixed points s_0 and 1 are different; hence, solving for w_n in (4.8) gives

$$w_n = \frac{s_0-(1/m^n)[(s-s_0)/(s-1)]}{1-(1/m^n)[(s-s_0)/(s-1)]}, \qquad m \neq 1, \tag{4.9}$$

which may be written in the form

$$\varphi_n(s) = 1-m^n\left(\frac{1-s_0}{m^n-s_0}\right)+\frac{m^n[(1-s_0)/(m^n-s_0)]^2 s}{1-[(m^n-1)/(m^n-s_0)]s} \tag{4.10}$$

Then the probabilities of extinction at the nth generation are

$$\Pr\{X_n = 0\} = \varphi_n(0) = 1-m^n\left(\frac{1-s_0}{m^n-s_0}\right).$$

Note that this expression converges to s_0 as $n \to \infty$ if $m > 1$ and to 1 if $m < 1$. The probability of a given population size in the nth generation, $\Pr\{X_n = k\}$, $k = 1, 2, \ldots$, can be computed by simply expanding (4.10) as a power series in s. If we define the time to extinction T as the smallest subscript n such that $X_n = 0$, i.e., the first passage time into state 0, then

$$\Pr\{T \le n\} = \Pr\{X_n = 0\} = \varphi_n(0)$$

and

$$\Pr\{T = n\} = \Pr\{T \le n\} - \Pr\{T \le n - 1\} = \varphi_n(0) - \varphi_{n-1}(0).$$

In the case $m \ne 1$, we have

$$\Pr\{T = n\} = 1 - m^n \left(\frac{1 - s_0}{m^n - s_0}\right) - 1 + m^{n-1} \left(\frac{1 - s_0}{m^{n-1} - s_0}\right)$$

$$= m^{n-1} s_0 \frac{(m - 1)(1 - s_0)}{(m^n - s_0)(m^{n-1} - s_0)} \qquad \text{for} \quad n = 1, 2, \ldots.$$

If $m = 1$, then $b = (1 - c)^2$ and the equation $\varphi(s) = s$ has the double root $s = 1$ and no other root. In fact,

$$\varphi(s) = c + \frac{(1 - c)^2 s}{1 - cs} = \frac{c - (2c - 1)s}{1 - cs}.$$

Then

$$\varphi_2(s) = \varphi(\varphi(s)) = \frac{c - (2c - 1)[(c - (2c - 1)s)/(1 - cs)]}{1 - c[(c - (2c - 1)s)/(1 - cs)]} = \frac{2c - (3c - 1)s}{1 + c - 2cs}$$

and by induction

$$\varphi_n(s) = \frac{nc - [(n + 1)c - 1]s}{1 + (n - 1)c - ncs}. \tag{4.11}$$

In the case $m = 1$ we have the extinction probabilities

$$\Pr\{X_n = 0\} = \varphi_n(0) = \frac{nc}{1 + (n - 1)c} \qquad \text{for} \quad n = 1, 2, \ldots.$$

Further, the time to extinction T has the distribution

$$\Pr\{T = n\} = \frac{nc}{1 + (n - 1)c} - \frac{(n - 1)c}{1 + (n - 2)c} = \frac{c(1 - c)}{[1 + (n - 1)c]\,[1 + (n - 2)c]}$$

5: Two-Type Branching Processes

We generalize the previous developments to two dimensions. Consider a population of organisms or objects where two different types may be distinguished. Individuals of either type will produce offspring of possibly both types independently. Let U_n and V_n be the number of individuals of types I and II, respectively, in the nth generation. We may write

$$U_{n+1} = \sum_{j=1}^{U_n} \xi_j^{(1)} + \sum_{j=1}^{V_n} \xi_j^{(2)},$$

$$V_{n+1} = \sum_{j=1}^{U_n} \zeta_j^{(1)} + \sum_{j=1}^{V_n} \zeta_j^{(2)},$$

where $(\xi_j^{(i)}, \zeta_j^{(i)})$ are independent, identically distributed, random vectors with distribution

$$\Pr\{\xi_j^{(i)} = k, \zeta_j^{(i)} = l\} = p_i(k, l), \qquad k, l = 0, 1, 2, \ldots,$$
$$\text{for} \quad j = 1, 2, \ldots \quad \text{and} \quad i = 1, 2.$$

Here $p_i(k, l) \geq 0$ and $\sum_{k,l=0}^{\infty} p_i(k, l) = 1$ for $i = 1, 2$.

In other words $p_1(k, l)$ and $p_2(k, l)$ are the probabilities that a single individual of type I and type II, respectively, produces $k + l$ direct descendants of which k are of type I and l are of type II.

We assume the process begins with a single individual, i.e., we assume either

$$U_0 = 1 \quad \text{and} \quad V_0 = 0 \tag{5.1}$$

or

$$U_0 = 0 \quad \text{and} \quad V_0 = 1. \tag{5.2}$$

We introduce the pair of two-dimensional probability generating functions

$$\varphi^{(i)}(s, t) = \sum_{k,l=0}^{\infty} p_i(k, l) s^k \cdot t^l, \qquad i = 1, 2,$$

that is,

$$\varphi_n^{(1)}(s, t) = \sum_{k,l=0}^{\infty} \Pr\{U_n = k, V_n = l | U_0 = 1, V_0 = 0\} s^k \cdot t^l,$$

$$\varphi_n^{(2)}(s, t) = \sum_{k,l=0}^{\infty} \Pr\{U_n = k, V_n = l | U_0 = 0, V_0 = 1\} s^k \cdot t^l.$$

The generating function of (5.1) is

$$\varphi_0^{(1)}(s, t) \equiv s,$$

and that of (5.2) is

$$\varphi_0^{(2)}(s, t) \equiv t.$$

Also

$$\varphi_1^{(i)}(s, t) = \varphi^{(i)}(s, t) \qquad \text{for} \quad i = 1, 2.$$

It can be shown by generalizing the method used for the one-dimensional process that

$$\varphi_{n+m}^{(i)}(s, t) = \varphi_m^{(i)}(\varphi_n^{(1)}(s, t), \varphi_n^{(2)}(s, t)), \tag{5.3}$$
$$\text{for} \quad i = 1, 2 \quad \text{and} \quad n, m = 0, 1, 2, \ldots.$$

This is the two-dimensional equivalent of formula (2.3).

To generalize formula (3.5) we introduce the following notation. Let $\mathbf{X}_n = (U_n, V_n)$ be the two-dimensional vector with components U_n and V_n. Let

$$m_{11} = E\{U_1 | U_0 = 1, V_0 = 0\} = E\xi^{(1)},$$

$$m_{12} = E\{V_1 | U_0 = 1, V_0 = 0\} = E\zeta^{(1)},$$

$$m_{21} = E\{U_1 | U_0 = 0, V_0 = 1\} = E\xi^{(2)}$$

$$m_{22} = E\{V_1 | U_0 = 0, V_0 = 1\} = E\zeta^{(2)}$$

and introduce the matrix of expectations

$$\mathbf{M} = \begin{Vmatrix} m_{11} & m_{12} \\ m_{21} & m_{22} \end{Vmatrix}.$$

Thus m_{11} and m_{12} are the expected numbers of offspring of type I or type II, respectively, produced by a single parent of type I. Then as a generalization of (3.5) we have the matrix identity

$$E[\mathbf{X}_{n+r} | \mathbf{X}_n] = \mathbf{X}_n \mathbf{M}^r \qquad \text{for} \quad r, n = 0, 1, 2, \ldots. \tag{5.4}$$

The proof for $r = 1$ proceeds directly. Thus

$$E[\mathbf{X}_{n+1} | \mathbf{X}_n] =$$

$$\left(E\left[\sum_{j=1}^{U_n} \xi_j^{(1)} + \sum_{j=1}^{V_n} \xi_j^{(2)} | U_n, V_n) \right], \; E\left[\sum_{j=1}^{U_n} \zeta_j^{(1)} + \sum_{j=1}^{V_n} \zeta_j^{(2)} | (U_n, V_n) \right] \right)$$

$$= (m_{11} U_n + m_{21} V_n, m_{12} U_n + m_{22} V_n)$$

$$= (U_n, V_n) \begin{Vmatrix} m_{11} & m_{12} \\ m_{21} & m_{22} \end{Vmatrix}$$

$$= \mathbf{X}_n \cdot \mathbf{M}.$$

We now assume that relation (5.4) holds for r and prove it for $r + 1$. By the Markov property for $\{\mathbf{X}_n\}$, we have

$$\begin{aligned} E[\mathbf{X}_{n+r+1} | \mathbf{X}_n] &= E\{E[\mathbf{X}_{n+r+1} | \mathbf{X}_{n+r}, \ldots, \mathbf{X}_n] | \mathbf{X}_n\} \\ &= E\{E[\mathbf{X}_{n+r+1} | \mathbf{X}_{n+r}] | \mathbf{X}_n\} = E\{\mathbf{X}_{n+r} \mathbf{M} | \mathbf{X}_n\} \\ &= E\{\mathbf{X}_{n+r} | \mathbf{X}_n\} \cdot \mathbf{M} \qquad \text{(using the induction hypothesis)} \\ &= \mathbf{X}_n \mathbf{M}^{r+1}. \end{aligned}$$

This completes the induction step.

For the two-dimensional branching process we may introduce the extinction probabilities

$$\pi^{(1)} = \Pr\{U_n = V_n = 0 \quad \text{for some} \quad n | U_0 = 1,\ V_0 = 0\},$$
$$\pi^{(2)} = \Pr\{U_n = V_n = 0 \quad \text{for some} \quad n | U_0 = 0,\ V_0 = 1\}.$$

The one-dimensional theory extends to this case with the remark that the role of the expectation m is played here by the largest eigenvalue ρ of the expectation matrix $\mathbf{M}$.

We direct the reader to the Appendix and particularly to the Frobenius theorem concerning matrices with nonnegative elements. It is proved there that if $\mathbf{M}$ is a matrix with positive elements (symbolically written here as $\mathbf{M} \gg 0$) then the eigenvalue of largest magnitude is positive and real. This eigenvalue is designated as $\rho(\mathbf{M}) = \rho$.

It is convenient to introduce the vector notations

$$\begin{aligned}
\mathbf{u} &= (s, t),\\
\boldsymbol{\phi}(\mathbf{u}) &= (\varphi^{(1)}(s, t), \varphi^{(2)}(s, t)),\\
\boldsymbol{\phi}_n(\mathbf{u}) &= (\varphi_n^{(1)}(s, t), \varphi_n^{(2)}(s, t)),\\
\boldsymbol{\pi} &= (\pi^{(1)}, \pi^{(2)}),\\
\mathbf{1} &= (1, 1).
\end{aligned}$$

Then we may state

Theorem 5.1. *Assume that the components of $\boldsymbol{\phi}(\mathbf{u})$ are not linear functions of s and t and that $\mathbf{M} \gg \mathbf{0}$ (every element of $\mathbf{M}$ is positive). Then $\boldsymbol{\pi} = \mathbf{1}$ if the largest eigenvalue ρ of $\mathbf{M}$ does not exceed one and $\boldsymbol{\pi} \ll \mathbf{1}$ if $\rho > 1$. (The notation $\mathbf{u} \ll \mathbf{v}$ ($\mathbf{u} \leq \mathbf{v}$) signifies that $\mathbf{v} - \mathbf{u}$ has positive (nonnegative) components.) In the case $\rho > 1$, $\boldsymbol{\pi}$ is the smallest nonnegative solution of*

$$\mathbf{u} = \boldsymbol{\phi}(\mathbf{u}), \qquad \mathbf{u} \ll \mathbf{1}. \tag{5.5}$$

Proof. Consider the case $\rho \leq 1$. According to the general theory of Markov chains we know that if a chain has a single absorbing state then all states from which the absorbing state may be reached are transient. The two-dimensional process $\mathbf{X}_n = (U_n, V_n)$ is just such a process: the origin is the only absorbing state and it may be reached from all other states. This is a consequence of the fact that $\boldsymbol{\phi}(\mathbf{u})$ has no linear components and $\rho \leq 1$. Thus every state with the exception of the origin is transient. Therefore, if $|\mathbf{X}_n| = U_n + V_n$, then

$$\Pr\{0 < |\mathbf{X}_n| < N \text{ for infinitely many } n\} = 0 \qquad \text{for any positive } N$$

(cf. Theorem 7.1 of Chapter 2). This means that

$$\Pr\{|\mathbf{X}_n| \to 0\} + \Pr\{|\mathbf{X}_n| \to \infty\} = 1.$$

From formula (5.4) $E[\mathbf{X}_n|\mathbf{X}_0] = \mathbf{X}_0\mathbf{M}^n$. But Theorem 2.3 of the Appendix asserts that $(1/\rho^n)\mathbf{M}^n$ converges componentwise as $n \to \infty$. Consequently, in the case $\rho \le 1$, the components of $E[\mathbf{X}_n|\mathbf{X}_0]$ stay bounded as $n \to \infty$. It follows from this that the event $|\mathbf{X}_n| \to \infty$ occurs with probability zero. Hence $\Pr\{|\mathbf{X}_n| \to 0\} = 1$ or, what is the same, $U_n \to 0$ and $V_n \to 0$ as $n \to \infty$ with probability one. Thus if $\rho \le 1$,

$$\pi^{(1)} = \pi^{(2)} = 1$$

holds.

Next consider the case $\rho > 1$. From formula (5.3) we have with $s = t = 0$

$$\varphi_{n+1}^{(i)}(0, 0) = \varphi^{(i)}(\varphi_n^{(1)}(0, 0), \varphi_n^{(2)}(0, 0)), \qquad i = 1, 2. \tag{5.6}$$

Let

$$q_n^{(1)} = \varphi_n^{(1)}(0, 0) = \Pr\{U_n = V_n = 0 | U_0 = 1, V_0 = 0\},$$
$$q_n^{(2)} = \varphi_n^{(2)}(0, 0) = \Pr\{U_n = V_n = 0 | U_0 = 0, V_0 = 1\}.$$

Then (5.6) is the same as

$$q_{n+1}^{(i)} = \varphi^{(i)}(q_n^{(1)}, q_n^{(2)}), \qquad i = 1, 2. \tag{5.7}$$

Since $\varphi^{(i)}(s, t)$ is increasing in the variables s and t, strictly so if both increase, and since $q_1^{(i)} = \varphi_1^{(i)}(0, 0) > 0$, $i = 1, 2$, we plainly have

$$q_2^{(i)} = \varphi^{(i)}(q_1^{(1)}, q_1^{(2)}) > \varphi^{(i)}(0, 0) = q_1^{(i)}, \qquad i = 1, 2.$$

Then by induction

$$q_{n+1}^{(i)} = \varphi^{(i)}(q_n^{(1)}, q_n^{(2)}) > \varphi^{(i)}(q_{n-1}^{(1)}, q_{n-1}^{(2)}) = q_n^{(i)}, \qquad i = 1, 2.$$

Hence, $q_n^{(i)}$, $n = 1, 2, 3, \ldots$, for each $i = 1, 2$, form a monotone increasing sequence bounded above by 1, and

$$\lim_{n \to \infty} q_n^{(i)} = \pi^{(i)} \le 1, \qquad i = 1, 2.$$

Let $n \to \infty$ in (5.7). Then

$$\pi^{(i)} = \varphi^{(i)}(\pi^{(1)}, \pi^{(2)}), \qquad i = 1, 2,$$

or in vector notation $\boldsymbol{\pi} = \boldsymbol{\phi}(\boldsymbol{\pi})$. We will now prove that $\boldsymbol{\pi} \ll \mathbf{1}$ and that this is the unique solution of (5.5) under the conditions stated. Expanding $\varphi_n^{(i)}(\cdot,\cdot)$ according to Taylor's theorem about (1, 1) we have

$$\varphi_n^{(i)}(1 - s, 1 - t) = \varphi_n^{(i)}(1, 1) - \left(\frac{\partial \varphi_n^{(i)}(s, t)}{\partial s}\bigg|_{s=t=1}\right)s$$
$$- \left(\frac{\partial \varphi_n^{(i)}(s, t)}{\partial t}\bigg|_{s=t=1}\right)t + o(|s| + |t|), \tag{5.8}$$

which is valid for $|1-s| \leq 1$, $|1-t| \leq 1$, and s and t sufficiently small. The $o(\cdot)$ symbol signifies that $[o(|s|+|t|)]/(|s|+|t|) \to 0$ whenever $|s|+|t| \to 0$. Moreover,

$$\left.\frac{\partial \varphi_n^{(1)}(s, t)}{\partial s}\right|_{s=t=1} = E[U_n | U_0 = 1, V_0 = 0] = m_{11}^{(n)},$$

$$\left.\frac{\partial \varphi_n^{(1)}(s, t)}{\partial t}\right|_{s=t=1} = E[V_n | U_0 = 1, V_0 = 0] = m_{12}^{(n)},$$

$$\left.\frac{\partial \varphi_n^{(2)}(s, t)}{\partial s}\right|_{s=t=1} = E[U_n | U_0 = 0, V_0 = 1] = m_{21}^{(n)},$$

$$\left.\frac{\partial \varphi_n^{(2)}(s, t)}{\partial t}\right|_{s=t=1} = E[V_n | U_0 = 0, V_0 = 1] = m_{22}^{(n)}.$$

We may write (5.8) in vector form as

$$\boldsymbol{\varphi}_n(\mathbf{1}-\mathbf{u}) = \mathbf{1} - \mathbf{M}^{(n)}\mathbf{u} + \mathbf{o}(|s|+|t|), \tag{5.9}$$

where

$$\mathbf{M}^{(n)} = \begin{Vmatrix} m_{11}^{(n)} & m_{12}^{(n)} \\ m_{21}^{(n)} & m_{22}^{(n)} \end{Vmatrix}$$

and $|\mathbf{u}| < \varepsilon$. Of course $\mathbf{M}^{(n)} = \mathbf{M}^n$ as is evident from the relation $E[\mathbf{X}_n | \mathbf{X}_0] = \mathbf{X}_0 \mathbf{M}^n$. Let the absolute value of a vector $\mathbf{v} = (v_1, v_2)$ be defined as the sum of the absolute values of its coordinates: $|\mathbf{v}| = |v_1| + |v_2|$. We will now prove that for n sufficiently large

$$|\mathbf{M}^n \mathbf{u}| > 2|\mathbf{u}|, \qquad \mathbf{u} = (s, t), \tag{5.10}$$

provided $\mathbf{u} \geq \mathbf{0}$. In fact, according to Theorem 2.3 of the Appendix we know that

$$\mathbf{M}^n \mathbf{u} = \rho^n \begin{Vmatrix} x_1^0 y_1^0 & x_1^0 y_2^0 \\ x_2^0 y_1^0 & x_2^0 y_2^0 \end{Vmatrix} \cdot \mathbf{u} + \mathbf{o}(\rho^n)\mathbf{u},$$

where ρ is the largest eigenvalue of $\mathbf{M}$ and $\mathbf{x}^0 = (x_1^0, x_2^0)$ and $\mathbf{y}^0 = (y_1^0, y_2^0)$ represent the unique (modulo a multiplicative factor) left and right positive eigenvectors normalized so that $x_1^0 y_1^0 + x_2^0 y_2^0 = 1$. The meaning ascribed to the term $\mathbf{o}(\rho^n)$ is an extension of the traditional one. When dividing by ρ^n and letting $n \to \infty$ the quantity $(\mathbf{o}(\rho^n))/\rho^n$ is a matrix each element of which tends to zero. The $\mathbf{o}(\rho^n)$ factor does not depend on $\mathbf{u}$. It represents the error term in the convergence of $\mathbf{M}^n/\rho^n$ to its limit. We rewrite the above expression in the form

$$\mathbf{M}^n \mathbf{u} = \rho^n (y_1^0 s + y_2^0 t)\mathbf{x}^0 + o(\rho^n)\mathbf{u}, \qquad \mathbf{u} = (s, t),$$

and if $\mathbf{u} \geq \mathbf{0}$ we obtain the obvious estimate

$$|\mathbf{M}^n \mathbf{u}| \geq \rho^n [x_1^0 + x_2^0] \min(y_1^0, y_2^0) \cdot |\mathbf{u}| + o(\rho^n)|\mathbf{u}|.$$

Since $\rho > 1$, a sufficiently large choice of n implies (5.10). Combining (5.9) and (5.10) we deduce

$$|\mathbf{1} - \boldsymbol{\varphi}_n(\mathbf{1} - \mathbf{u})| > 2|\mathbf{u}|,$$

provided $\mathbf{1} \geq \mathbf{u} \geq \mathbf{0}$, $|\mathbf{u}|$ is sufficiently small, and n is sufficiently large, say $n \geq n_0$. Let $\mathbf{v} = \mathbf{1} - \mathbf{u}$; then

$$|\mathbf{1} - \boldsymbol{\varphi}_n(\mathbf{v})| > 2|\mathbf{1} - \mathbf{v}| \tag{5.11}$$

for all $\mathbf{0} \leq \mathbf{v} \leq \mathbf{1}$ satisfying $|\mathbf{1} - \mathbf{v}| < \varepsilon$ and $n \geq n_0$. We now utilize (5.11) in order to demonstrate that $\boldsymbol{\pi} \ll 1$. Suppose $\boldsymbol{\pi} = \mathbf{1}$, i.e., $\pi^{(i)} = 1$ for $i = 1, 2$. Then $q_n^{(i)} = \varphi_n^{(i)}(0) \geq 0$ approaches 1 $(n \to \infty)$. Now referring to (5.3) we know that

$$\boldsymbol{\phi}_{n+N}(\mathbf{0}) = \boldsymbol{\phi}_n(\boldsymbol{\phi}_N(\mathbf{0})).$$

Using (5.11) with $\mathbf{v} = \boldsymbol{\phi}_N(\mathbf{0})$ we have

$$|\mathbf{1} - \boldsymbol{\phi}_{n+N}(\mathbf{0})| = |\mathbf{1} - \boldsymbol{\phi}_n(\boldsymbol{\phi}_N(\mathbf{0}))| > 2|\mathbf{1} - \boldsymbol{\phi}_N(\mathbf{0})| \tag{5.12}$$

only if $|\mathbf{1} - \boldsymbol{\phi}_N(\mathbf{0})| < \varepsilon$, and this can be achieved by taking N large enough. However, relation (5.12) contradicts the assumption that $\varphi_n^{(i)}(0)$ tends to 1 as $n \to \infty$. Thus $\pi^{(1)} = \pi^{(2)} = 1$ is impossible. Assume now that $\pi^{(1)} < 1$ and $\pi^{(2)} = 1$. Then

$$\pi^{(1)} = \varphi^{(1)}(\pi^{(1)}, 1)$$

and

$$1 = \pi^{(2)} = \varphi^{(2)}(\pi^{(1)}, 1).$$

Thus, we have

$$\varphi^{(2)}(1, 1) = 1 \qquad \text{and} \qquad \varphi^{(2)}(\pi^{(1)}, 1) = 1,$$

where $\pi^{(1)} < 1$. Since $\varphi^{(2)}(s, t)$ is monotone in s, $\varphi^{(2)}(s, 1)$ must be constant on the interval $\pi^{(1)} \leq s \leq 1$;

$$\frac{\partial \varphi^{(2)}(s, 1)}{\partial s} = 0 \qquad \text{in} \qquad \pi^{(1)} \leq s \leq 1$$

and also

$$m_{21}^{(2)} = \left.\frac{\partial \varphi^{(2)}(s, t)}{\partial s}\right|_{s=t=1} = 0,$$

which clearly contradicts our assumption that $\mathbf{M} \gg \mathbf{0}$. In a similar manner, we deduce that $\pi^{(1)} = 1$, $\pi^{(2)} < 1$ is impossible. Thus $\boldsymbol{\pi} \ll \mathbf{1}$ is established. The verification that $\boldsymbol{\pi}$ is smaller than any other positive fixed point proceeds as follows. Let $\boldsymbol{\pi}^* > \mathbf{0}$ satisfy $\boldsymbol{\phi}(\boldsymbol{\pi}^*) = \boldsymbol{\pi}^*$. By monotonicity, we have $\boldsymbol{\pi}^* = \boldsymbol{\phi}(\boldsymbol{\pi}^*) \geq \boldsymbol{\phi}_1(0, 0)$. Iteration produces $\boldsymbol{\pi}^* \geq \boldsymbol{\phi}_n(0, 0)$ and passing to the limit leads to the desired result: $\boldsymbol{\pi}^* \geq \boldsymbol{\pi}$. ■

We can strengthen the result of Theorem 5.1 and prove

Theorem 5.2. *Under the assumptions of Theorem* 5.1, *if* $\mathbf{q}$ *is any vector in the unit square other than* $\mathbf{1}$ *then* $\lim_{n\to\infty} \boldsymbol{\phi}_n(\mathbf{q}) = \boldsymbol{\pi}$.

Proof. Suppose first that $0 \le q^i < 1$ $(i = 1, 2)$. If N is a positive integer then the Taylor expansion of $\varphi_n^{(1)}(\mathbf{q})$ has the form

$$\begin{aligned}\varphi_n^{(1)}(\mathbf{q}) = \Pr\{|\mathbf{X}_n| = 0 \,|\, U_0 = 1,\ V_0 = 0\} \\ + \sum_{0<|\mathbf{x}|\le N} \Pr\{\mathbf{X}_n = \mathbf{x} \,|\, U_0 = 1,\ V_0 = 0\}(q^1)^{x_1}(q^2)^{x_2} \\ + \sum_{|\mathbf{x}|>N} \Pr\{\mathbf{X}_n = \mathbf{x} \,|\, U_0 = 1,\ V_0 = 0\}(q^1)^{x_1}(q^2)^{x_2}.\end{aligned}$$

The last sum is bounded by $(\max(q^1, q^2)^N \Pr\{|\mathbf{X}_n| > N\} \le (\max(q^1, q^2))^N$ and as $N \to \infty$ this quantity goes to zero since $\max(q^1, q^2) < 1$.

Each coefficient of the first sum goes to zero when $n \to \infty$ since $|\mathbf{X}_n|$ approaches either 0 or ∞. This fact rests on the property that all finite nonzero states are transient. It follows that as $n \to \infty$ with N fixed the first sum tends to zero. This argument proves that

$$\begin{aligned}\lim_{n\to\infty} \varphi_n^{(1)}(\mathbf{q}) &= \lim_{n\to\infty} \Pr\{|\mathbf{X}_n| = 0 \,|\, U_0 = 1,\ V_0 = 0\} \\ &= \lim_{n\to\infty} \varphi_n^{(1)}(\mathbf{0}) = \pi^{(1)}\end{aligned}$$

as asserted in the theorem. Similarly

$$\lim_{n\to\infty} \varphi_n^{(2)}(\mathbf{q}) = \pi^{(2)}.$$

If one of the $q^{(i)}$ $(i = 1, 2)$ is equal to 1 but not both, then $\boldsymbol{\phi}_1(\mathbf{q}) = (\varphi^1(\mathbf{q}),\ \varphi^2(\mathbf{q}))$ determines a nonnegative vector with each component strictly smaller than 1. We apply the preceding analysis to $\boldsymbol{\phi}_1(\mathbf{q})$ and deduce that

$$\lim_{n\to\infty} \boldsymbol{\phi}_n(\boldsymbol{\phi}_1(\mathbf{q})) = \pi = \lim_{n\to\infty} \boldsymbol{\phi}_{n+1}(\mathbf{q}). \quad \blacksquare$$

Corollary 5.1. *The only nonnegative solutions of* (5.5) *are* 1 *and* π.

6: Multi-Type Branching Processes

The generalization of the theory of the preceding section to the case of more than two types proceeds *mutatis mutandis* as in the case of two types. The proofs involve no new ideas or techniques. We merely list the results. The industrious student should supply the detailed proofs.

We will consider a branching growth process consisting of p types. The different types may correspond to actual different mutant forms of an organism or may refer to a single organism where the type distinguishes age or some other like property. The restriction to a finite number of types has the interpretation, for example, that we have specified a finite set of age classifications.

In the case of the production of photons arising in cosmic ray cascades of electrons the type may represent the energy level associated with a photon.

Associated with type i is the probability generating function

$$f^{(i)}(s_1, \ldots, s_p) = \sum_{r_1,\ldots,r_p=0}^{\infty} p^{(i)}(r_1, \ldots, r_p) s_1^{r_1}, \ldots, s_p^{r_p}, \qquad |s_1| \le 1, \ldots, |s_p| \le 1, \quad i = 1, \ldots, p,$$

where $p^{(i)}(r_1, \ldots, r_p)$ is the probability that a single object of type i has r_1 children of type 1, r_2 children of type 2, ..., r_p of type p.

We introduce the vector notation $\mathbf{s} = (s_1, \ldots, s_p)$.

Let $f_n^{(i)}(\mathbf{s})$ denote the nth-generation probability generating function arising from one individual of type i. Analogous to (5.3) we have

$$f_{n+1}^{(i)}(\mathbf{s}) = f^{(i)}(f_n^{(1)}(\mathbf{s}), f_n^{(2)}(\mathbf{s}), \ldots, f_n^{(p)}(\mathbf{s})), \qquad f_0^{(i)}(\mathbf{s}) = s_i, \quad n = 0, 1, \ldots, \quad i = 1, \ldots, p.$$

Let $\mathbf{Z}_n = (Z_n^{(1)}, \ldots, Z_n^{(p)})$ denote the vector representing the population size of p types in the nth generation. The analog of (5.4) is

$$E(\mathbf{Z}_{n+m} | \mathbf{Z}_n) = \mathbf{Z}_n \mathbf{M}^m,$$

where $\mathbf{M} = \| m_{ij} \|_{i,j=1}^{p}$ is the matrix of first moments:

$$m_{ij} = E(Z_1^{(j)} | \mathbf{Z}_0 = \mathbf{e}_i) = \frac{\partial f^{(i)}}{\partial s_j}(1, 1, \ldots, 1), \qquad i, j = 1, \ldots, p,$$

and $\mathbf{e}_i$ denotes the vector with 1 for the ith component and zero otherwise.

We now state the analog of Theorem 5.1 for p types. We will assume $m_{ij} > 0$ for all i, j. (It suffices to have $m_{ij}^{(n)} > 0$ for some n and all i, j.) Let $\pi^{(i)}$ be the extinction probability if initially there is one object of type i ($i = 1, \ldots, p$); that is,

$$\pi^{(i)} = \Pr\{\mathbf{Z}_n = \mathbf{0} \quad \text{for some} \quad n | \mathbf{Z}_0 = \mathbf{e}_i\}.$$

The vector $(\pi^1, \ldots, \pi^p)$ is denoted by $\boldsymbol{\pi}$. Let $\mathbf{1}$ denote the vector $(1, 1, \ldots, 1)$.

Theorem 6.1 *Let $m_{ij} > 0$ for all $i, j = 1, \ldots, p$ and let ρ denote the eigenvalue of largest absolute value of the matrix $\mathbf{M}$. If $\rho \le 1$ then $\boldsymbol{\pi} = \mathbf{1}$. If $\rho > 1$ then $\mathbf{0} \le \boldsymbol{\pi} \ll \mathbf{1}$ and $\boldsymbol{\pi}$ satisfies the equation*

$$\pi^{(i)} = f^{(i)}(\boldsymbol{\pi}), \qquad i = 1, \ldots, p.$$

7: Continuous Time Branching Processes

The branching processes dealt with in Sections 1–6 are limited in that generation times are fixed. Although some phenomena, particularly experimental trials, fit this situation, most natural reproductive processes occur continuously in time. It is therefore of interest to formulate a continuous time version of branching processes.

In the present section we explore the structure of *time-homogeneous Markov branching processes*; in Section 11 the Markov restriction will be dropped. We determine a continuous time Markov branching process with state variable $X(t) = \{\text{number of particles at time } t, \text{ given } X(0) = 1\}$ by specifying the infinitesimal probabilities of the process. Let

$$\delta_{1k} + a_k h + o(h), \qquad k = 0, 1, 2, \ldots, \tag{7.1}$$

(see Section 4 of Chapter 4 and Chapter 14 of Volume II) represent the probability that a single particle will split producing k particles (or objects) during a small time interval $(t, t+h)$ of length h. In (7.1) δ_{1k} denotes, as customary, the Kronecker delta symbol, and we assume that $a_1 \leq 0$, $a_k \geq 0$ for $k = 0, 2, 3, \ldots$, and

$$\sum_{k=0}^{\infty} a_k = 0. \tag{7.2}$$

We further postulate that individual particles act independently of each other, always governed by the infinitesimal probabilities (7.1). Note that we are effectively assuming time homogeneity for the transition probabilities since a_k is not a function of the time at which the conversion or splitting occurs.

Another way to express the infinitesimal transitions is to differentiate between the time until a split occurs and the nature of the split. Thus each object lives a random length of time following an exponential distribution with mean $\lambda^{-1} = a_0 + a_2 + a_3 + \cdots$. On completion of its lifetime, it produces a random number D of descendants of like objects, where the probability distribution of D is

$$\Pr\{D = k\} = \frac{a_k}{a_0 + a_2 + a_3 + \cdots}, \qquad k = 0, 2, 3, \ldots.$$

The lifetime and progeny distribution of separate individuals are independent and identically distributed. Taking account of the independence assumptions, particularly the property that individuals act independently, we can write (7.1) equivalently in terms of the infinitesimal transition probability matrix as

$$\Pr\{X(t+h) = n + k - 1 | X(t) = n\} = n a_k h + o(h) \tag{7.3}$$

(since in a small time interval one particle on the average will split) and

$$\Pr\{X(t+h) = n | X(t) = n\} = 1 + n a_1 h + o(h), \tag{7.4}$$

where $o(h)/h$ tends to zero as $h \to 0+$.

We have already encountered an example of a continuous time branching process in the guise of a birth and death process. In fact, if we put $a_2 = \lambda$, $a_0 = \mu$, $a_1 = -(\lambda + \mu)$, and $a_k = 0$ otherwise, then $(\lambda + \mu)^{-1}$ can be interpreted as the probability of a birth or death event; $\lambda/(\lambda + \mu)$ $((\mu/(\lambda + \mu)))$ is the probability of a birth (death) under the condition that an event has happened. The stochastic process so obtained whose state variable is population size can now be recognized as a linear growth birth and death process (see Chapter 4, Section 6).

As explained in Chapter 14, it is not a simple matter to construct a Markov process corresponding to a prescribed matrix of infinitesimal probabilities. It is an even more recondite task to assure that the constructed process possesses realizations conforming to the laws of a branching process, i.e., individual particles generate independent families and the descendents act independently, etc. We do not enter the analysis of this construction as it is beyond the scope of this text. The more advanced reader can consult Harris on this point (see the references at the close of this chapter). We further direct attention to Chapter 14 of Volume II for additional discussion on the relations between Markov processes and matrices of infinitesimal probabilities.

Let $P_{ij}(t)$, assumed henceforth well defined, denote the probability that the population of size i at time zero will be of size j at time t, or in symbols $P_{ij}(t) = \Pr\{X(t+s) = j | X(s) = i\}$. As the notation indicates, this probability depends only on the elapsed time, i.e., the process has stationary transition probabilities. We introduce the generating function

$$\phi(t; s) = \sum_{j=0}^{\infty} P_{1j}(t)s^j. \tag{7.5}$$

Since individuals act independently, we have the fundamental relation (cf. page 289)

$$\sum_{j=0}^{\infty} P_{ij}(t)s^j = [\phi(t; s)]^i. \tag{7.6}$$

The formula (7.6) characterizes and distinguishes branching processes from other continuous time Markov chains. It expresses the property that different individuals (i.e., particles) give rise to independent realizations of the process uninfluenced by the pedigrees evolving owing to the other individuals present. In other words the population $X(t; i)$ evolving in time t from i initial parents is the same, probabilistically, as the combined sum of i populations each with one initial parent.

In view of the time homogeneity, the Chapman–Kolmogorov equations take the form

$$P_{ij}(t + \tau) = \sum_{k=0}^{\infty} P_{ik}(t)P_{kj}(\tau). \tag{7.7}$$

With the aid of (7.5), (7.6), and (7.7), we obtain

$$\begin{aligned}[\phi(t+\tau;s)]^i &= \sum_{j=0}^{\infty} P_{ij}(t+\tau)s^j = \sum_{j=0}^{\infty}\sum_{k=0}^{\infty} P_{ik}(t)P_{kj}(\tau)s^j \\ &= \sum_{k=0}^{\infty} P_{ik}(t)\sum_{j=0}^{\infty} P_{kj}(\tau)s^j = \sum_{k=0}^{\infty} P_{ik}(t)[\phi(\tau;s)]^k \\ &= [\phi(t;\phi(\tau;s))]^i,\end{aligned}$$

and in particular

$$\phi(t+\tau;s) = \phi(t;\phi(\tau;s)). \tag{7.8}$$

The relation (7.8) is the continuous time analog of the functional iteration formula of Section 2, fundamental in the case of discrete time branching processes. Next we introduce the generating function of the infinitesimal probabilities defined in (7.1). Specifically, let

$$u(s) = \sum_{k=0}^{\infty} a_k s^k.$$

The following analysis is formal. Consider

$$\begin{aligned}\phi(h;s) &= \sum_{j=0}^{\infty} P_{1j}(h)s^j = \sum_{j=0}^{\infty} (\delta_{1j} + a_j h + o(h))s^j \\ &= s + h\sum_{j=0}^{\infty} a_j s^j + o(h) = s + hu(s) + o(h).\end{aligned} \tag{7.9}$$

From (7.8) with $\tau = h$

$$\phi(t+h;s) = \phi(t;\phi(h;s)) = \phi(t;s+hu(s)+o(h))$$

and expanding the right-hand side with respect to the second variable, by Taylor's theorem, yields

$$\phi(t+h;s) = \phi(t;s) + \frac{\partial\phi(t;s)}{\partial s}hu(s) + o(h).$$

Then

$$\frac{\phi(t+h;s)-\phi(t;s)}{h} = \frac{\partial\phi(t;s)}{\partial s}u(s) + \frac{o(h)}{h}.$$

Letting h decrease to 0 leads to

$$\frac{\partial\phi(t;s)}{\partial t} = \frac{\partial\phi(t;s)}{\partial s}u(s). \tag{7.10}$$

This is a partial differential equation for the function of two variables $\phi(t;s)$, subject to the initial condition

$$\phi(0;s) \equiv \sum_{j=0}^{\infty} P_{1j}(0)s^j \equiv s. \tag{7.11}$$

When $u(s)$ is known, the partial differential equation (7.10) in the presence of (7.11) can be solved for $\phi(t; s)$.

The differential equation (7.10) is merely a form of the forward Kolmogorov differential equations which has been converted into an equivalent differential equation satisfied by the generating function of the transition probability function.

We may derive a second differential equation satisfied by ϕ corresponding to the backward Kolmogorov differential equation. To this end, we substitute $t = h$ in (7.8), which becomes

$$\phi(h+\tau; s) = \phi(h; \phi(\tau; s)),$$

and then use (7.9) with Taylor's expansion as before. This gives

$$\phi(h+\tau; s) = \phi(\tau; s) + hu(\phi(\tau; s)) + o(h).$$

This expression can be written more suggestively as

$$\frac{\phi(\tau+h; s) - \phi(\tau; s)}{h} = u(\phi(\tau; s)) + \frac{o(h)}{h}. \tag{7.12}$$

Letting $h \to 0+$ and replacing τ by t, we obtain

$$\frac{\partial \phi(t; s)}{\partial t} = u(\phi(t; s)). \tag{7.13}$$

This is an ordinary differential equation. The initial condition is again (7.11). Later on we will show how to effectively solve (7.13).

8: Extinction Probabilities for Continuous Time Branching Processes

We first carry out the easier task of computing the mean of $X(t)$. To this end, differentiate (7.10) with respect to s and interchange the order of differentiation on the left side. The result is

$$\frac{\partial}{\partial t}\frac{\partial \phi(t; s)}{\partial s} = \frac{\partial^2 \phi(t; s)}{\partial s^2} u(s) + \frac{\partial \phi(t; s)}{\partial s} u'(s). \tag{8.1}$$

Set $s = 1$. Then, since $u(1) = 0$ [Condition (7.2)], we have

$$\frac{\partial m(t)}{\partial t} = u'(1)m(t), \tag{8.2}$$

where

$$m(t) = EX(t) = \left.\frac{\partial \phi(t; s)}{\partial s}\right|_{s=1}$$

The solution of (8.2) is

$$m(t) = \exp[u'(1)t], \tag{8.3}$$

since the initial condition is $m(0) = 1$ if we assume $X(0) \equiv 1$.

Next we deal with the problem of extinction. In this connection, we assume for the remainder of this section that $a_0 > 0$, as otherwise extinction is impossible. It is enough to consider the case where we start with a single individual at time zero. In fact, from (7.6) we know that

$$\sum_{j=0}^{\infty} P_{ij}(t)s^j = \left[\sum_{j=0}^{\infty} P_{1j}(t)s^j\right]^i.$$

Hence,

$$P_{i0}(t) = [P_{10}(t)]^i.$$

But $P_{i0}(t)$ is the probability of a population of size i dying out by time t. By intuitive considerations we can infer that $P_{i0}(t)$ is nondecreasing in t. We prove this formally by using (7.8). Indeed,

$$P_{i0}(t+\tau) = [\phi(t+\tau;\, 0)]^i = [\phi(t;\, \phi(\tau, 0))]^i \geq [\phi(t, 0)]^i = P_{i0}(t),$$

where we used the fact that $\phi(t, s)$ is a power series in s with nonnegative coefficients and is, therefore, an increasing function of s.

The extinction probability may be defined as the probability that the "family" originating from a single individual will eventually die out, i.e.,

$$q = \lim_{t \to \infty} P_{10}(t).$$

Utilizing the theory of discrete time branching processes (Section 3) we can easily determine the probability of extinction in the continuous case. Let t_0 be any fixed positive number and consider the discrete time process

$$X(0), \quad X(t_0), \quad X(2t_0), \ldots, \quad X(nt_0), \ldots,$$

where $X(t)$ is the population size at time t corresponding to the original continuous time branching process that starts with a single individual at time $t = 0$. Since $X(t)$ was assumed to be a Markov process, the discrete time process $Y_n = X(nt_0)$ will obviously be a Markov chain. Moreover, it describes a discrete time branching process. Indeed, by the hypothesis of homogeneity of the probability function of $X(t)$ and by virtue of (7.6), we obtain

$$\begin{aligned}
\sum_{k=0}^{\infty} \Pr\{Y_{n+1} = k \mid Y_n = i\}s^k &= E[s^{Y_{n+1}} \mid Y_n = i] \\
&= E[s^{X((n+1)t_0)} \mid X(nt_0) = i] = E[s^{X(t_0)} \mid X(0) = i] \\
&= [\phi(t_0;\, s)]^i = \{E[s^{X(t_0)} \mid X(0) = 1]\}^i \\
&= \{E[s^{Y_1} \mid Y_0 = 1]\}^i.
\end{aligned}$$

This shows that Y_n constitutes a branching process. The generating function of the number of offspring of a single individual in this process is $\phi(t_0; s)$. Hence, we know that the probability of extinction for the Y_n process is the smallest nonnegative root of the equation

$$\phi(t_0; s) = s, \tag{8.4}$$

as was proved in Section 3. But

$$\begin{aligned}\Pr\{Y_n = 0 \quad \text{for some} \quad n\} &= \lim_{n\to\infty} \Pr\{Y_n = 0\} \\ &= \lim_{n\to\infty} \Pr\{X(nt_0) = 0\} \\ &= \lim_{t\to\infty} \Pr\{X(t) = 0\} = q.\end{aligned}$$

Hence, *the extinction probability q of the continuous time branching process $X(t)$ is the smallest nonnegative root of Eq.* (8.4), *where t_0 is any positive number.*

Since q is a root of Eq. (8.4) for any t_0, we expect that we should also be able to calculate q from an equation that does not depend on time. This is indeed the case and we assert the following theorem.

Theorem 8.1. *The probability of extinction q is the smallest nonnegative root of the equation*

$$u(s) = 0. \tag{8.5}$$

Hence, $q = 1$ if and only if $u'(1) \leq 0$. (Recall that $u(s) = \sum_{k=0}^{\infty} a_k s^k = a_1 s + [a_0 + a_2 s^2 + \cdots] = a_1 s + g(s)$.)

Proof. Since q satisfies (8.4) for any t_0, we see on the basis of Eq. (7.12) that

$$0 = u(q) + \frac{o(h)}{h} \qquad \text{for any} \quad h > 0.$$

Letting $h \to 0+$, we obtain $u(q) = 0$.

Since $u''(s) = \sum_{k=2}^{\infty} a_k k(k-1) s^{k-2} \geq 0$, $u(s)$ is convex in the interval $[0, 1]$. As $u(1) = 0$ and $u(0) = a_0 > 0$, $u(s)$ may have at most one zero in $(0, 1)$. According to whether $u'(1) \leq 0$ or $u'(1) > 0$ holds, we have the case represented by Fig. 3 or 4. Notice that $E(X(t_0)) = E(Y) > 1$ if and only if $u'(1) > 0$. This means that for the discrete time branching process $X(nt_0)$, $n = 0, 1, 2, \ldots$ ($t_0 > 0$ fixed), extinction occurs with probability < 1 and therefore the same is true for the process $X(t)$. The probability of extinction q is in this case necessarily the smaller zero of $u(s)$ in $[0, 1]$. In a similar manner we conclude that if $u'(1) \leq 0$, q must equal one. In either case q is the smallest nonnegative root of (8.5).

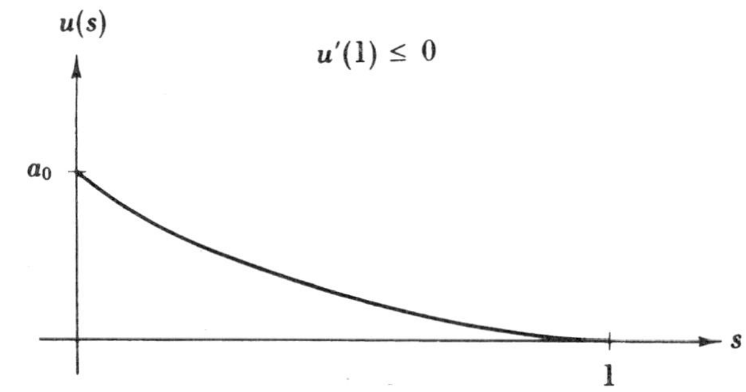

FIG. 3

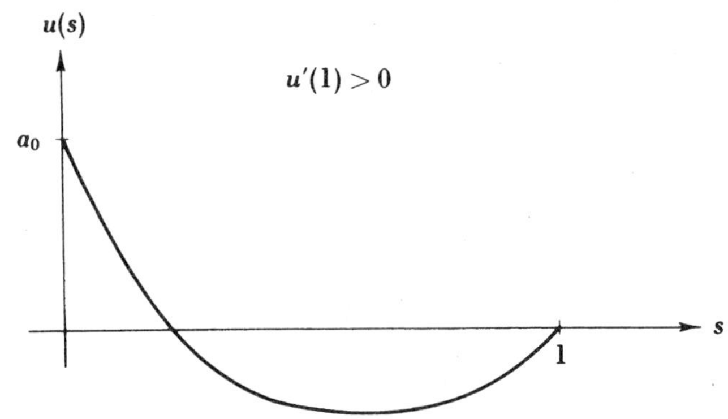

FIG. 4

9: Limit Theorems for Continuous Time Branching Processes

We turn to the task of solving the ordinary differential equation (7.13) and analyzing and interpreting its growth properties as $t \to \infty$. Since $\exp[u'(1)t]$ is the expected number of particles at time t we anticipate different behavior according to whether $u'(1)$ is negative, zero, or positive. We will only discuss the case when $u'(1) < 0$ under the additional assumption that $u''(1) < \infty$. First we prove that the function

$$B(s) = \frac{1}{u(s)} - \frac{1}{u'(1)(s-1)}$$

is bounded and hence integrable in $0 \leq s < 1$. Indeed, expanding $u(s)$ in the neighborhood of $s = 1$ leads to the formula

$$u(s) = u(1) + u'(1)(s-1) + R(s)(s-1)^2, \qquad s \leq 1,$$

where

$$\lim_{s \to 1-} R(s) = \frac{u''(1)}{2!} < \infty. \tag{9.1}$$

Then, recalling that $u(q) = u(1) = 0$, we have

$$\frac{1}{u(s)} = \frac{1}{u'(1)(s-1) + R(s)(s-1)^2} = \frac{1}{u'(1)(s-1)} \cdot \frac{1}{1 + [R(s)(s-1)/u'(1)]}$$

$$= \frac{1}{u'(1)(s-1)} \left\{1 - \frac{R(s)(s-1)/u'(1)}{1 + [R(s)(s-1)/u'(1)]}\right\}.$$

Hence,

$$B(s) = -\frac{R(s)/[u'(1)]^2}{1 + [R(s)(s-1)/u'(1)]} \tag{9.2}$$

and we can now infer as a direct consequence of (9.1) that $B(s)$ is bounded in the neighborhood of $s = 1-$. Certainly $B(s)$ is bounded for s away from $s = 1$, i.e., for $0 \le s \le 1 - \delta$, as is evident from its definition, since $u(s)$ vanishes only at $s = 1$ in the case under consideration $[u'(1) < 0]$. Thus, $B(s)$ is bounded in $0 \le s < 1$ under the conditions $u''(1) < \infty$, and $u'(1) < 0$. Now we may define, for $0 \le s < 1$,

$$K(s) = \int_1^s \left[\frac{1}{u(x)} - \frac{1}{u'(1)(x-1)}\right] dx + \frac{\log(1-s)}{u'(1)}, \tag{9.3}$$

as the integral exists and is finite.

Notice, further, that

$$K'(s) = \frac{1}{u(s)} > 0 \qquad \text{for} \quad 0 \le s < 1,$$

again owing to the assumption $u'(1) < 0$. This means that $K(s)$ is strictly increasing and continuous; hence, the mapping

$$w = K(s) \tag{9.4}$$

possesses a continuous strictly increasing inverse function

$$s = K^{-1}(w) = L(w), \qquad L(K(s)) = s, \tag{9.5}$$

with the property that as s traverses $[0, 1)$, w traverses $[K(0), \infty)$, and observe that $K(0) < 0$. We are now in possession of the ingredients needed to exhibit the desired solution of (7.13) under the initial condition (7.11). Separation of variables in (7.13) and integration lead to an implicit formula for $\phi(t, s)$:

$$\int_s^{\phi(t;s)} \frac{dx}{u(x)} = t.$$

Performing obvious rearrangements and using the definition of $K(\cdot)$, we obtain

$$t = \int_s^{\phi(t;s)} \frac{dx}{u(x)} = \int_s^{\phi(t;s)} \left[\frac{1}{u(x)} - \frac{1}{u'(1)(x-1)}\right] dx + \frac{1}{u'(1)} \log(1-x)\Big|_s^{\phi(t;s)}$$

$$= \int_1^{\phi(t;s)} \left[\frac{1}{u(x)} - \frac{1}{u'(1)(x-1)}\right] dx + \frac{\log(1-\phi(t;s))}{u'(1)}$$

$$- \int_1^{s} \left[\frac{1}{u(x)} - \frac{1}{u'(1)(x-1)}\right] dx - \frac{\log(1-s)}{u'(1)}$$

$$= K(\phi(t;s)) - K(s).$$

Equivalently, we have the relation

$$K(\phi(t;s)) = t + K(s).$$

Since the inverse function exists, this becomes

$$\phi(t;s) = K^{-1}(t+K(s)) \quad \text{for} \quad 0 \leq s < 1 \quad \text{and} \quad t \geq 0. \tag{9.6}$$

Under the assumptions $u'(1) < 0$, $u''(1) < \infty$ we may also derive some asymptotic results for the probability of extinction in time t ($t \to \infty$). Because $B(s)$ is bounded in $0 \leq s < 1$ and $\lim_{s\to 1-} B(s)$ exists we may write [see (9.3)]

$$K(s) = \frac{\log(1-s)}{u'(1)} - C\cdot(1-s) + o(1-s) \tag{9.7}$$

in the neighborhood of $s = 1$. Here C is a negative constant; in fact, $\lim_{x\to 1-} [1/u(x) - (1/(x-1)u'(1))] = C = (-u''(1)/2[u'(1)]^2)$. The $o(1-s)$ term has the usual interpretation, i.e., $[o(1-s)]/(1-s) \to 0$ as $s \to 1-$. Rearranging the last expression in the form

$$\log(1-s) = u'(1)K(s) - Cu'(1)(1-s) + o(1-s)$$

and taking exponentials yields

$$1-s = \exp[u'(1)K(s)] \exp[-Cu'(1)(1-s)] \exp[o(1-s)].$$

But

$$\exp[o(1-s)] = 1 + o(1-s)$$

and

$$\exp[-Cu'(1)(1-s)] = 1 - Cu'(1)(1-s) + o(1-s).$$

It follows that

$$1-s = \exp[u'(1)K(s)][1 - Cu'(1)(1-s) + o(1-s)]. \tag{9.8}$$

Consequently

$$\lim_{s\to 1-} \frac{1-s}{\exp[u'(1)K(s)]} = 1.$$

By virtue of this limit relation we can write (9.8) in the form

$$1-s = \{\exp[u'(1)K(s)]\}(1 - Cu'(1)\exp[u'(1)K(s)] + o(\exp[u'(1)K(s)]).$$

Replacing s throughout by $K^{-1}(w)$ [see (9.5)] we get

$$1 - K^{-1}(w) = \exp[u'(1)w][1 - Cu'(1)\exp[u'(1)w] + o(\exp[u'(1)w])\}, \tag{9.9}$$

where $s \to 1-$ is equivalent to $w \to \infty$. Now with the aid of (9.6) and (9.9), we can calculate the probability of no extinction in time t. Thus

$$\begin{aligned}
1 - P_{10}(t) &= 1 - \phi(t;0) = 1 - K^{-1}(t + K(0)) \\
&= [\exp\{u'(1)(t + K(0))\}] \\
&\qquad \times \{1 - Cu'(1)(\exp[u'(1)(t + K(0)]) + o(\exp[u'(1)(t + K(0))])\}] \\
&= \exp\{u'(1)K(0)\}\exp\{u'(1)t\} + O(\exp\{2u'(1)t\}) + o(\exp[u'(1)t])
\end{aligned}$$

or, equivalently,

$$1 - P_{10}(t) = \exp[u'(1)K(0)]m(t) + o(\exp[u'(1)t]). \tag{9.10}$$

Another asymptotic result, as $t \to \infty$, may be obtained as follows. The conditional probability generating function of $X(t)$, given that $X(t) \neq 0$, is defined as

$$g(z, t) = \sum_{k=0}^{\infty} \Pr\{X(t) = k | X(t) \neq 0\} z^k, \qquad 0 \le z < 1.$$

But

$$\begin{aligned}
\Pr\{X(t) = k | X(t) \neq 0\} &= \frac{\Pr\{X(t) = k, X(t) \neq 0\}}{\Pr\{X(t) \neq 0\}} \\
&= \begin{cases} 0 & \text{if } k = 0, \\ \dfrac{\Pr\{X(t) = k\}}{1 - \Pr\{X(t) = 0\}} & \text{if } k \neq 0. \end{cases}
\end{aligned}$$

Thus

$$\begin{aligned}
g(z;t) &= \sum_{k=1}^{\infty} \frac{\Pr\{X(t) = k\}}{1 - \Pr\{X(t) = 0\}} z^k = \frac{\phi(t;z) - \phi(t;0)}{1 - \phi(t;0)} \\
&= \frac{K^{-1}(t + K(z)) - K^{-1}(t + K(0))}{1 - K^{-1}(t + K(0))} \\
&= \frac{[1 - K^{-1}(t + K(0))] - [1 - K^{-1}(t + K(z))]}{1 - K^{-1}(t + K(0))}
\end{aligned}$$

where formula (9.6) is used for $\phi(t;s)$.

Substituting the expression for $K^{-1}(w)$ given by (9.9) yields

$$g(z;t)=\frac{e^{u'(1)(t+K(0))}[1+O(e^{u'(1)(t+K(0))})]-e^{u'(1)(t+K(z))}[1+O(e^{u'(1)(t+K(z))})]}{e^{u'(1)(t+K(0))}[1+O(e^{u'(1)(t+K(0))})]}$$

$$=1-e^{u'(1)[K(z)-K(0)]}\frac{1+O(e^{u'(1)(t+K(z))})}{1+O(e^{u'(1)(t+K(0))})}.$$

Now let $t\to\infty$. Then the fraction on the right-hand side reduces to 1 by the assumption $u'(1)<0$. Hence

$$\lim_{t\to\infty} g(z;t)=g(z)=1-\exp\{u'(1)[K(z)-K(0)]\}.$$

By (9.3), however,

$$K(z)-K(0)=\int_0^z\left[\frac{1}{u(x)}-\frac{1}{u'(1)(x-1)}\right]dx+\frac{\log(1-z)}{u'(1)}$$

$$=\int_0^z\frac{dx}{u(x)}-\frac{\log(1-x)}{u'(1)}\bigg|_0^z+\frac{\log(1-z)}{u'(1)}=\int_0^z\frac{dx}{u(x)}.$$

Hence, as $t\to\infty$ we have the limit probability generating function

$$g(z)=1-\exp\left[u'(1)\int_0^z\frac{dx}{u(x)}\right]=\sum_{k=1}^{\infty}\lim_{t\to\infty}\Pr\{X(t)=k|X(t)\neq 0\}z^k.$$

We summarize the preceding discussion in the statement of the following theorem:

Theorem 9.1. *Consider a continuous time branching process $X(t)$ determined by the infinitesimal generating function*

$$u(s)=\sum_{k=0}^{\infty}a_ks^k, \tag{9.11}$$

where the $\{a_k\}$ possesses the interpretation given in (7.1) *and is subject to the conditions* (7.2). *Suppose that $u''(1)<\infty$. Suppose further that $u'(1)<0$ so that the extinction probability $q=1$* (see Theorem 8.1). *Then*

$$\phi(t,s)=\sum_{k=0}^{\infty}\Pr\{X(t)=k|X(0)=1\}s^k \tag{9.12}$$

$$=K^{-1}(t+K(s)),\qquad t\geq 0\qquad |s|<1,$$

where $K(s)$ is defined in (9.3). *The probability of no extinction by time t tends to zero at an exponential rate according to*

$$\lim_{t\to\infty}\frac{1-P_{10}(t)}{\exp[u'(1)K(0)]\exp[u'(1)t]}=1.$$

Moreover, the random variable $X(t)$ conditioned by $X(t)>0$ has a limit distribution whose probability generating function is given by

$$g(z,t)=\frac{\sum_{k=1}^{\infty}\Pr\{X(t)=k|X(0)=1\}z^k}{1-\Pr\{X(t)=0\}}$$

$$\to 1-\exp\left[u'(1)\int_0^z\frac{dx}{u(x)}\right]\qquad \text{as}\quad t\to\infty. \tag{9.13}$$

We state without proof the following limit theorem which corresponds to the case $u'(1)=0$ and $u'(1)>0$. Their proofs are more complicated although similar in substance.

Theorem 9.2. (i) *Suppose $u'(1)=0$, $u''(1)<\infty$. Then*

$$\Pr\{X(t)>0|X(0)=1\}\sim\frac{2}{u''(t)}\frac{1}{t},\qquad t\to\infty,$$

and

$$\lim_{t\to\infty}\Pr\left\{\frac{2X(t)}{u''(1)t}>\lambda|X(t)>0\right\}=e^{-\lambda},\qquad \lambda>0.$$

(ii) *If $u'(1)>0$ and $u''(1)<\infty$, then*

$$Z(t)=\frac{X(t)}{\exp[u'(1)t]}$$

has a limit distribution as $t\to\infty$.

10: Two-Type Continuous Time Branching Process

Consider two different types of particles which we will call type 1 and type 2 particles, respectively. A continuous time branching Markov process for two types of particles will be determined by appropriately specifying the infinitesimal probabilities [(7.3) and (7.4)]. Explicitly, we postulate that each particle of type $i(i=1,2)$ may at any time, independent of its past and independent of the history or present state of any of the other particles of either type, convert during a small time interval $(t,t+h)$ into k_1 and k_2 particles of types 1 and 2, respectively, with probabilities

$$\delta_{1k_1}\delta_{0k_2}+a_{k_1,k_2}^{(1)}h+o(h)$$

(δ_{ij} denotes the familiar Kronecker delta symbol) for a single parent of type 1 and

$$\delta_{0k_1}\delta_{1k_2}+a_{k_1,k_2}^{(2)}h+o(h)$$

for a single parent of type 2 ($k_1, k_2 = 0, 1, 2, \ldots$). Note that we are again postulating time homogeneity for the transition probabilities in that the constants $a_{k_1,k_2}^{(i)}$ are time independent. The parameters obey the restrictions

$$
\begin{aligned}
&a_{1,0}^{(1)} \leq 0, && a_{0,1}^{(2)} \leq 0, \\
&a_{k_1,k_2}^{(1)} \geq 0 && \text{for all } k_1, k_2 = 0, 1, 2, \ldots \\
& && \text{except } k_1 = 1, k_2 = 0, \\
&a_{k_1,k_2}^{(2)} \geq 0 && \text{for all } k_1, k_2 = 0, 1, 2, \ldots \\
& && \text{except } k_1 = 0, k_2 = 1,
\end{aligned}
$$

and

$$\sum_{k_1,k_2=0}^{\infty} a_{k_1,k_2}^{(i)} = 0, \qquad i = 1, 2.$$

We introduce the pair of infinitesimal generating functions

$$u^{(i)}(s_1, s_2) = \sum_{k_1,k_2=0}^{\infty} a_{k_1,k_2}^{(i)} s_1^{k_1} s_2^{k_2}, \qquad i = 1, 2 \qquad (|s_1| \leq 1, |s_2| \leq 1).$$

Let $P_{k_1,k_2;j_1,j_2}(t)$ be the probability that a population of k_1 objects of type 1 and k_2 objects of type 2 present at time 0 will be transformed into a population consisting of j_1 objects of type 1 and j_2 objects of type 2 over a time period of length t. Since the infinitesimal probabilities $a_{k_1,k_2}^{(i)}$ were defined to be independent of time, the transition probabilities are necessarily time homogeneous. We define the probability generating functions

$$\phi^{(1)}(t; s_1, s_2) = \sum_{j_1,j_2=0}^{\infty} P_{1,0;j_1j_2}(t) s_1^{j_1} s_2^{j_2},$$

$$\phi^{(2)}(t; s_1, s_2) = \sum_{j_1,j_2=0}^{\infty} P_{0,1;j_1j_2}(t) s_1^{j_1} s_2^{j_2}.$$

Then it follows analogously as in the model of the one-type branching process that

$$\sum_{j_1,j_2=0}^{\infty} P_{k_1,k_2;j_1j_2}(t) s_1^{j_1} s_2^{j_2} = [\phi^{(1)}(t; s_1, s_2)]^{k_1} [\phi^{(2)}(t; s_1, s_2)]^{k_2}$$
$$(k_1, k_2 = 0, 1, 2, \ldots). \qquad (10.1)$$

In fact, (10.1) can be regarded as the defining relation of a continuous time two-type branching process. In other words any transition probability matrix function satisfying (10.1) is said to generate a two-type continuous time Markov branching process. The Markov character of the process is summarized in the Chapman–Kolmogorov equations

$$P_{k_1,k_2,j_1,j_2}(t + \tau) = \sum_{l_1,l_2=0}^{\infty} P_{k_1,k_2,;l_1,l_2}(t)\, P_{l_1,l_2;j_1,j_2}(\tau). \qquad (10.2)$$

Then from (10.1) and (10.2)

$$\begin{aligned}
\phi^{(1)}(t+\tau; s_1, s_2) &= \sum_{j_1, j_2=0}^{\infty} P_{1,0;j_1,j_2}(t+\tau) s_1^{j_1} s_2^{j_2} \\
&= \sum_{j_1, j_2=0}^{\infty} \sum_{l_1, l_2=0}^{\infty} P_{1,0;l_1,l_2}(t) P_{l_1,l_2;j_1,j_2}(\tau)\, s_1^{j_1} s_2^{j_2} \\
&= \sum_{l_1, l_2=0}^{\infty} P_{1,0;l_1,l_2}(t) \sum_{j_1, j_2=0}^{\infty} P_{l_1,l_2;j_1,j_2}(\tau)\, s_1^{j_1} s_2^{j_2} \\
&= \sum_{l_1, l_2=0}^{\infty} P_{1,0;l_1,l_2}(t)\, [\phi^{(1)}(\tau; s_1, s_2)]^{l_1} [\phi^{(2)}(\tau; s_1, s_2)]^{l_2} \\
&= \phi^{(1)}(t; \phi^{(1)}(\tau; s_1, s_2), \phi^{(2)}(\tau; s_1, s_2)).
\end{aligned}$$

The same procedure applied to the generating function $\phi^{(2)}(t; s_1, s_2)$ yields

$$\phi^{(i)}(t+\tau; s_1, s_2) = \phi^{(i)}(t; \phi^{(1)}(\tau; s_1, s_2), \phi^{(2)}(\tau; s_1, s_2)) \quad \text{for} \quad i = 1, 2. \tag{10.3}$$

Moreover,

$$\begin{aligned}
\phi^{(1)}(h; s_1, s_2) &= \sum_{j_1, j_2=0}^{\infty} P_{1,0;j_1,j_2}(h)\, s_1^{j_1} s_2^{j_2} \\
&= \sum_{j_1, j_2=0}^{\infty} [\delta_{1j_1}\delta_{0j_2} + a_{j_1 j_2}^{(1)} h + o(h)]\, s_1^{j_1} s_2^{j_2} \\
&= s_1 + h u^{(1)}(s_1, s_2) + o(h)
\end{aligned}$$

and similarly for $\phi^{(2)}(h; s_1, s_2)$. Thus we have

$$\phi^{(i)}(h; s_1, s_2) = s_i + h u^{(i)}(s_1, s_2) + o(h), \qquad i = 1, 2. \tag{10.4}$$

We now derive a pair of partial differential equations satisfied by $\phi^{(i)}(t; s_1, s_2)$ $(i = 1, 2)$, analogous to (7.10) and (7.13). To this end, we start by setting $\tau = h$ and substituting (10.4) in (10.3). Using Taylor's expansion, we obtain

$$\begin{aligned}
\phi^{(i)}(t+h; s_1, s_2) &= \\
&\phi^{(i)}(t; s_1 + h u^{(1)}(s_1, s_2) + o(h), s_2 + h u^{(2)}(s_1, s_2) + o(h)) \\
&= \phi^{(i)}(t; s_1, s_2) + \frac{\partial \phi^{(i)}(t; s_1, s_2)}{\partial s_1} h u^{(1)}(s_1, s_2) \\
&\quad + \frac{\partial \phi^{(i)}(t; s_1, s_2)}{\partial s_2} h u^{(2)}(s_1, s_2) + o(h)
\end{aligned}$$

Dividing both sides by h and letting $h \to 0$ we formally obtain the differential equations

$$\frac{\partial \phi^{(i)}(t; s_1, s_2)}{\partial t} = \frac{\partial \phi^{(i)}(t; s_1, s_2)}{\partial s_1} u^{(1)}(s_1, s_2)$$
$$+ \frac{\partial \phi^{(i)}(t; s_1, s_2)}{\partial s_2} u^{(2)}(s_1, s_2), \qquad i = 1, 2. \tag{10.5}$$

We start again with (10.3), this time setting $t = h$ and using (10.4); this leads to the formula

$$\begin{aligned}\phi^{(i)}(h + \tau; s_1, s_2) &= \phi^{(i)}\ (h; \phi^{(1)}(\tau; s_1, s_2), \phi^{(2)}(\tau; s_1, s_2)) \\ &= \phi^{(i)}(\tau; s_1, s_2) + hu^{(i)}(\phi^{(1)}(\tau; s_1, s_2), \phi^{(2)}(\tau; s_1, s_2)) + o(h).\end{aligned}$$

Then dividing by h, letting $h \to 0$, and finally writing t in place of τ, we obtain a second system of differential equations:

$$\frac{\partial \phi^{(i)}(t; s_1, s_2)}{\partial t} = u^{(i)}(\phi^{(1)}(t; s_1, s_2), \phi^{(2)}(t; s_1, s_2)), i = 1,2. \tag{10.6}$$

The initial conditions for both (10.5) and (10.6) are

$$\phi^{(i)}(0; s_1, s_2) = s_i, \qquad i = 1, 2.$$

With the aid of (10.5) and (10.6) we can derive systems of ordinary differential equations satisfied by the moments of the random variables of the process. We will not enter into details of these calculations here.

We next offer some applications and examples of two-type continuous time branching processes.

Example 1. Our first example involves a branching process with immigration. We consider the one-type continuous time branching process and enlarge its scope by allowing, in addition to branching, some migration of particles into the system. Recall that

$$\delta_{1k} + a_k h + o(h), \qquad k = 0, 1, 2, \ldots,$$

represents the probability that a particle will convert into k particles during a small time interval $(t, t + h)$ independent of its past and of all other particles. Let us superimpose immigration into the population as follows. Specifically, let

$$\delta_{0k} + b_k h + o(h), \qquad k = 0, 1, 2, \ldots,$$

denote the probability, independent of the present or past history of the population, that k particles of the same kind immigrate and merge with the population during the time interval $(t, t+h)$. Note that the parameters a_k as well as the parameters b_k are assumed to be independent of the precise time t that the conversion or the immigration takes place. In other words the associated infinitesimal transition probabilities per individual are time homogeneous. For the a_k and b_k we impose the conditions

$$\begin{aligned} &a_1 \le 0, \qquad b_0 \le 0, \\ &a_k \ge 0 \qquad \text{for} \quad k = 0, 2, 3, \ldots, \\ &b_k \ge 0 \qquad \text{for} \quad k = 1, 2, 3, \ldots, \\ &\sum_{k=0}^{\infty} a_k = \sum_{k=0}^{\infty} b_k = 0. \end{aligned}$$

Let

$$\begin{aligned} P_k(t) &= \Pr\left\{\begin{matrix}\text{population at time } t \text{ is of size } k \text{ if} \\ \text{there were no particles at time } t = 0\end{matrix}\right\} \\ &= \Pr\{X(t) = k \mid X(0) = 0\} \qquad k = 0, 1, 2, \ldots, \end{aligned} \tag{10.7}$$

and denote its generating function by

$$\phi(t; s) = \sum_{k=0}^{\infty} P_k(t) s^k. \tag{10.8}$$

Our objective is to evaluate $P_k(t)$ or, if this is not feasible, to ascertain some of its properties.

We introduce the infinitesimal generating functions

$$u(s) = \sum_{k=0}^{\infty} a_k s^k \qquad \text{and} \qquad v(s) = \sum_{k=0}^{\infty} b_k s^k.$$

It is possible to cast the one-type continuous time branching process with immigration in the form of a two-type continuous time branching process. This is done as follows. Assume that we have two different types of particles, types 1 and 2, wit[illegible]finitesimal probabilities of conversion which we will now specialize, as described at the start of this section.

The idea underlying the identification runs as follows. We have available two types of particles: the first is real, while the second is of a fictitious nature. Real particles upon termination of their lifetime (which is of random duration distributed according to an exponential law with parameter $\lambda^{-1} = a_0 + a_2 + a_3 + \cdots$) create k new real particles with probability $\lambda \cdot a_k$ $(k = 0, 2, 3, \ldots)$. A fictitious particle also lives a random length of time (exponentially distributed with parameter $\bar{\lambda}^{-1} = b_1 + b_2 + \cdots$) and at the end of its life produces l real particles and one further fictitious particle with probability $\bar{\lambda} \cdot b_l$ $(l = 1, 2, 3, \ldots)$. Notice that $\sum_{l=1}^{\infty} \bar{\lambda} b_l = 1$.

The progeny of fictitious particles account for the immigration factor. Thus, we set

$$a^{(1)}_{k_1,k_2} = \begin{cases} a_{k_1} & \text{if } k_2 = 0, \\ 0 & \text{if } k_2 \neq 0, \end{cases}$$

$$a^{(2)}_{k_1,k_2} = \begin{cases} b_{k_1} & \text{if } k_2 = 1, \\ 0 & \text{if } k_2 \neq 1. \end{cases}$$

Then in accordance with the notation of the beginning of this section we have

$$u^{(1)}(s_1, s_2) = \sum_{k_1,k_2=0}^{\infty} a^{(1)}_{k_1,k_2} s_1^{k_1} s_2^{k_2} = \sum_{k_1=0}^{\infty} a_{k_1} s_1^{k_1},$$

$$u^{(2)}(s_1, s_2) = \sum_{k_1,k_2=0}^{\infty} a^{(2)}_{k_1,k_2} s_1^{k_1} s_2^{k_2} = s_2 \sum_{k_1=0}^{\infty} b_{k_1} s_1^{k_1}.$$

Thus

$$u^{(1)}(s_1, s_2) = u(s_1), \qquad u^{(2)}(s_1, s_2) = s_2 v(s_1).$$

In the special case under consideration the differential equation (10.5) reduces to

$$\frac{\partial \phi^{(i)}(t; s_1, s_2)}{\partial t} = \frac{\partial \phi^{(i)}(t; s_1, s_2)}{\partial s_1} u(s_1) + \frac{\partial \phi^{(i)}(t; s_1, s_2)}{\partial s_2} s_2 v(s_1), \qquad i = 1, 2, \tag{10.9}$$

and the differential equation (10.6) becomes

$$\frac{\partial \phi^{(1)}(t; s_1, s_2)}{\partial t} = u(\phi^{(1)}(t; s_1, s_2)) \tag{10.10}$$

and

$$\frac{\partial \phi^{(2)}(t; s_1, s_2)}{\partial t} = [\phi^{(2)}(t; s_1, s_2)] v(\phi^{(1)}(t; s_1, s_2)). \tag{10.11}$$

Now we will relate the probabilities $P_{0,1;j_1,j_2}(t)$ of the two-type process to the probabilities defined in (10.7). In accordance with the meaning ascribed to the two types of particles the initial state (0, 1) signifies that we start at time 0 with no real particles but with the presence of a potential immigrant signified by a fictitious particle. By the very meaning of the symbols we obviously have

$$P_{0,1;j_1,j_2}(t) = \begin{cases} P_{j_1}(t) & \text{if } j_2 = 1, \\ 0 & \text{if } j_2 \neq 1, \end{cases}$$

and hence

$$\phi^{(2)}(t; s_1, s_2) = s_2 \phi(t; s_1). \tag{10.12}$$

Then from (10.9) we obtain

$$\frac{\partial \phi(t; s)}{\partial t} = \frac{\partial \phi(t; s)}{\partial s} u(s) + \phi(t; s)v(s), \tag{10.13}$$

where we have written s in place of s_1. The initial condition here is

$$\phi(0; s) = 1. \tag{10.14}$$

Instead of solving this differential equation, it is easier to solve the system (10.10) and (10.11) with appropriate initial conditions. Equation (10.10) can be dealt with by methods paraphrasing the analysis of (7.13). The solution of (10.10) can be represented as in (9.6). We denote the solution of (10.10) by $f(t; s)$, where s has taken the place of s_1 and s_2 is suppressed. Because of (10.12), (10.11) becomes

$$\frac{\partial \phi(t; s)}{\partial t} = \phi(t; s)v(f(t; s)), \tag{10.15}$$

with initial condition (10.14). The solution of (10.15) is

$$\phi(t; s) = \exp\left[\int_0^t v(f(\tau; s))\, d\tau\right].$$

Example 2. We close this section by describing a simple, binary-fission, *non*-Markov, one-type, continuous time, branching process that can be reduced to a two-type, continuous time, Markov branching process. Assume that a particle has a lifetime distribution with density

$$\frac{\lambda^2}{2} te^{-\lambda t}, \tag{10.16}$$

i.e., a gamma distribution of order 2. When the particle dies it is replaced by two particles of the same kind, each independent of the other and of the original particle, and each following the lifetime distribution (10.16).

Markov processes are generally characterized by the property that the waiting time in any given state is exponentially distributed. In the present context the waiting time in a given state is determined by the lifetime of the particle. If this is exponential then the population process of these particles constitutes a Markov process. In the growth model introduced above, lifetime does not follow an exponential distribution but that of a convolution of two exponentials.

Let $X(t)$ represent the number of particles at time t and assume that $X(0) = 1$. Since (10.16) is the density of the sum of two independent exponentially distributed r.v's each with parameter λ, we may regard each particle as going through two separate phases of life each with an exponentially distributed lifetime of parameter λ. This may easily be reduced to the two-type, continuous time, Markov branching process. Instead of referring to two phases of life for the same particle, we will talk about two different types of particles. A particle of type 1 has an exponential distribution lifetime with parameter λ and then converts into a particle of type 2. A particle of type 2 has an exponential distribution lifetime with parameter λ and then converts into two particles of type 1. Thus, conforming to the notation of the beginning of this section we have

$$a_{k_1,k_2}^{(1)} = \begin{cases} -1 & \text{if } k_1 = 1 \text{ and } k_2 = 0, \\ +1 & \text{if } k_1 = 0 \text{ and } k_2 = 1, \\ 0 & \text{otherwise,} \end{cases}$$

$$a_{k_1,k_2}^{(2)} = \begin{cases} +1 & \text{if } k_1 = 2 \text{ and } k_2 = 0, \\ -1 & \text{if } k_1 = 0 \text{ and } k_2 = 1, \\ 0 & \text{otherwise,} \end{cases}$$

where, for simplicity, we have assumed $\lambda = 1$. Then,

$$u^{(1)}(s_1, s_2) = -s_1 + s_2$$

and

$$u^{(2)}(s_1, s_2) = s_1^2 - s_2 .$$

The relations (10.5) and (10.6) will take special forms. The generating function of $X(t)$, given $X(0) = 1$, can be obtained from $\phi^{(1)}(t; s_1, s_2)$ by setting $s_1 = s_2 = s$.

11: Branching Processes with General Variable Lifetime

In this section we will discuss a branching process model where each object (or particle or individual) lives a random length of time following a general lifetime distribution and at the culmination of its life produces its progeny. This process should be compared with branching processes of fixed lifetime or of exponentially distributed lifetime. We assume that an individual object has a lifetime of random length T with probability density function $f(t)$; that is, the probability that this organism will die during the time interval $(t, t + dt)$ is $f(t)\, dt$. We further assume that at the time of its death the object splits into two, thus creating two new objects of like kind. These will have independently distributed random lifetimes with the same density function $f(t)$. At the end of its life each object splits again into two new objects of the same kind and this process continues indefinitely. Let $N(t)$ denote the number of objects existing at time t, and represent its probability distribution by

$$p_k(t) = \Pr\{N(t) = k\} \qquad \text{for} \quad k = 0, 1, 2, \ldots.$$

Clearly $p_0(t) = 0$ for all $t \geq 0$, as we will always have at least one object. In fact, we will have exactly one before the first split occurs and at least two after the first split. Thus

$$p_1(t) = \Pr\{N(t) = 1\} = \Pr\{T > t\} = 1 - F(t),$$

where

$$F(t) = \Pr\{T \leq t\} = \int_0^t f(\tau)\, d\tau$$

is the cumulative distribution function of T.

Generally, let $G(s, t)$ be the probability generating function of $N(t)$, i.e.,

$$G(s, t) = \sum_{k=0}^{\infty} p_k(t) s^k = \sum_{k=1}^{\infty} p_k(t) s^k.$$

We will now obtain an integral equation for $G(s, t)$. The probability of having exactly k ($k = 2, 3, \ldots$) objects at time t, $p_k(t)$, can be evaluated as follows. Assume that the first fission occurs between time τ and $\tau + d\tau$ ($0 \leq \tau \leq t$) with probability $f(\tau)\, d\tau$, and that each of the two new objects independently undergoing the same branching process will produce a total number k of descendants during the remaining time of length $t - \tau$. Naturally the time, τ, of the first split may take any value in the interval $[0, t]$. Thus, from the law of total probabilities we obtain

$$p_k(t) = \int_0^t d\tau\, f(\tau) \sum_{l=1}^{k} p_l(t - \tau) p_{k-l}(t - \tau), \qquad k = 2, 3, \ldots,$$

and

$$p_1(t) = 1 - F(t).$$

Then from the definition of $G(s, t)$, we have

$$G(s, t) = [1 - F(t)]s + \sum_{k=2}^{\infty} s^k \int_0^t d\tau\, f(\tau) \sum_{l=1}^{k} p_l(t - \tau) p_{k-l}(t - \tau)$$

$$= [1 - F(t)]s + \sum_{k=0}^{\infty} s^k \int_0^t d\tau\, f(\tau) \sum_{l=0}^{k} p_l(t - \tau) p_{k-l}(t - \tau).$$

Since all quantities involved are nonnegative, the summations and the integral sign may be interchanged, and

$$G(s, t) = \int_0^t d\tau\, f(\tau) \sum_{k=0}^{\infty} s^k \sum_{l=0}^{k} p_l(t - \tau) p_{k-l}(t - \tau) + [1 - F(t)]s.$$

We recognize the sum as a convolution, each factor of which is $\sum_{k=0}^{\infty} s^k p_k(t-\tau) = G(s, t-\tau)$. Thus,

$$G(s, t) = \int_0^t [G(s, t-\tau)]^2 f(\tau)\, d\tau + [1 - F(t)]s. \tag{11.1}$$

Unfortunately, this integral equation cannot be solved in general. We will solve it, however, in the special case when T has the exponential distribution with density

$$f(t) = \lambda e^{-\lambda t} \qquad \text{for} \quad t \geq 0. \tag{11.2}$$

The process corresponding to this special case is equivalent to the Yule pure birth process. In fact, if there are n initial objects then the time interval until the first split is the random variable $Z = \min(X_1, X_2, \ldots, X_n)$, where the X_i are independent and possess the distribution law (11.2). The distribution of Z is exponential with parameter $n\lambda$. Therefore, the chance of a split during the next h units of time is $n\lambda h + o(h)$. When this occurs the population increases to $n+1$ and now the time interval until the next split is exponentially distributed with parameter $(n+1)\lambda$, etc. The study of this example from the point of view of pure birth processes was given in Section 1 of Chapter 4. The following alternative method is of independent interest.

When $1 - F(t) = e^{-\lambda t}$ Eq. (11.1) becomes

$$G(s, t)\, e^{\lambda t} = \lambda \int_0^t [G(s, t-\tau)]^2 e^{\lambda(t-\tau)}\, d\tau + s.$$

After executing the change of variables $u = t - \tau$ we get

$$G(s, t) e^{\lambda t} = \lambda \int_0^t [G(s, u)]^2 e^{\lambda u}\, du + s.$$

Now differentiate with respect to t. There results the equation

$$e^{\lambda t} G'(s, t) + \lambda e^{\lambda t} G(s, t) = \lambda [G(s, t)]^2 e^{\lambda t},$$

where

$$G'(s, t) = \frac{d}{dt} G(s, t).$$

Canceling the factor $e^{\lambda t}$ the differential equation reduces to a Bernoulli-type differential equation:

$$G'(s, t) = \lambda [G(s, t)]^2 - \lambda G(s, t). \tag{11.3}$$

To solve this differential equation we may simply separate variables:

$$\frac{dG(s, t)}{G(s, t)[G(s, t) - 1]} = \lambda\, dt.$$

Then the solution is

$$\frac{G(s, t) - 1}{G(s, t)} = C(s)e^{\lambda t},$$

or explicitly

$$G(s, t) = \frac{1}{1 - C(s)e^{\lambda t}}, \tag{11.4}$$

where $C(s)$ is a constant in t, but may be a function of s. To determine $C(s)$, let $t = 0$ in (11.4). Since

$$p_k(0) = \begin{cases} 0 & \text{if} \quad k \neq 1, \\ 1 & \text{if} \quad k = 1, \end{cases} \qquad s \equiv G(s, 0) = \frac{1}{1 - C(s)},$$

it follows that

$$C(s) = \frac{s - 1}{s}.$$

Thus, the solution of (11.3) and also the solution of (11.1) in the case of exponential lifetime is

$$G(s, t) = \frac{se^{-\lambda t}}{1 - (1 - e^{-\lambda t})s}. \tag{11.5}$$

To obtain explicit formulas for $p_k(t)$ we expand (11.5) in powers of s; i.e.,

$$G(s, t) = e^{-\lambda t}s \sum_{k=0}^{\infty} (1 - e^{-\lambda t})^k s^k.$$

Visibly, we have

$$p_k(t) = e^{-\lambda t}(1 - e^{-\lambda t})^{k-1} \qquad \text{for} \quad k = 1, 2, \ldots.$$

Although we cannot solve the integral equation (11.1) in the general case, we may obtain from it an equation for the mean function $m(t) = EN(t)$. Recall that

$$\left.\frac{dG(s, t)}{ds}\right|_{s=1} = \sum_{k=1}^{\infty} kp_k(t) = m(t).$$

Differentiating (11.1) with respect to s leads to

$$\frac{dG(s, t)}{ds} = 2\int_0^t G(s, t - \tau)\frac{dG(s, t - \tau)}{ds} f(\tau)\, d\tau + 1 - F(t).$$

Now, set $s = 1$ on both sides, remembering that

$$G(1, t - \tau) = \textstyle\sum_{k=1}^{\infty} p_k(t - \tau) = 1.$$

Then

$$m(t) = 2\int_0^t m(t-\tau)f(\tau)\,d\tau + 1 - F(t).$$

This integral equation is an example of what is called a renewal equation. Its characteristic feature is the appearance of the unknown function under the integral sign in the convolution form. There is much classical theory available concerning the renewal equation which describes the asymptotic growth properties of the solution $m(t)$.

An obvious generalization of the above model is obtained by allowing an object at the time of its death to split into exactly r new objects of the same kind, where r is a fixed integer greater than 2. It is easy to see that the integral equation (11.1) will then be replaced by

$$G(s,t) = \int_0^t [G(s,t-\tau)]^r f(\tau)\,d\tau + [1-F(t)]s.$$

A further generalization of this model is the case in which any object may split into a random number of new objects of the same kind at the time of its death; e.g., we may assume that an object produces l new objects at the time of its death with probability q_l, $l = 0, 1, 2, \ldots$. Let

$$h(s) = \sum_{l=0}^{\infty} q_l s^l$$

be the corresponding generating function. Then we may derive the integral equation in the following way. Assume that the first split occurs at time τ $(0 \le \tau \le t)$ and l new objects are created. This event has probability $f(\tau)\,d\tau\, q_l$. Then during the remaining $t-\tau$ units of time each of the l objects may produce any number of descendants such that the total number of objects at time t totals k. By the law of total probabilities, we have

$$p_k(t) = \int_0^t d\tau\, f(\tau) \sum_{l=0}^{\infty} q_l \sum_{k_1+k_2+\cdots+k_l=k} p_{k_1}(t-\tau)p_{k_2}(t-\tau)\cdot \cdots \cdot p_{k_l}(t-\tau)$$

$$\text{for} \quad k = 2, 3, \ldots$$

and $p_1(t) = 1 - F(t)$ as before. Then the generating function

$$G(s,t) = [1-F(t)]s + \sum_{k=2}^{\infty} s^k \int_0^t d\tau\, f(\tau) \sum_{l=0}^{\infty} q_l \sum_{k_1+\cdots+k_l=k} p_{k_1}(t-\tau)\cdots p_{k_l}(t-\tau)$$

$$= [1-F(t)]s + \int_0^t d\tau\, f(\tau) \sum_{l=0}^{\infty} q_l \sum_{k=1}^{\infty} s^k \sum_{k_1+\cdots+k_l=k} p_{k_1}(t-\tau)\cdot \cdots \cdot p_{k_l}(t-\tau).$$

But the inner sum of

$$\sum_{k=0}^{\infty} s^k \sum_{k_1+\cdots+k_l=k} p_{k_1}(t-\tau)\cdot \cdots \cdot p_{k_l}(t-\tau)$$

is recognized as an l-fold convolution (the student should prove this) where each factor corresponds to

$$\sum_{k=0}^{\infty} s^k p_k(t-\tau) = G(s, t-\tau)$$

and the full sum is $[G(s, t-\tau)]^l$. Thus,

$$G(s, t) = [1-F(t)]s + \int_0^t d\tau\, f(\tau) \sum_{l=0}^{\infty} q_l[G(s, t-\tau)]^l.$$

But the summation inside the integral on the right-hand side gives the generating function $h(s)$ evaluated at $x = G(s, t-\tau)$. Finally, in this case the integral equation takes the form

$$G(s, t) = \int_0^t h(G(s, t-\tau)) f(\tau)\, d\tau + [1-F(t)]s.$$

Elementary Problems

1. Let X_n be a branching process where $X_0 \equiv 1$. For an arbitrary but fixed positive integer k define the sequence

$$Y_r = X_{rk}, \qquad r = 0, 1, 2, \ldots.$$

Show that $\{Y_r, r = 0, 1, 2, \ldots\}$ generates a branching process. Moreover, prove that if $\varphi(s)$ denotes the generating function of the number of direct descendants of a single individual in the X_n process and $\varphi_n(s)$ its nth iterate, then $\varphi_k(s)$ is the generating function in the Y_r process of the number of direct descendants of a single individual.

2. Let $f(s) = 1 - p(1-s)^\beta$, where p and β are constants and $0 < p < 1$, $0 < \beta < 1$. Prove that $f(s)$ is a probability generating function and its iterates are

$$f_n(s) = 1 - p^{1+\beta+\cdots+\beta^{n-1}}(1-s)^{\beta^n} \qquad \text{for} \quad n = 1, 2, \ldots.$$

3. Suppose $f(s)$ is a probability generating function and $h(s)$ is a function such that

$$g(s) = h^{-1}[f(h(s))]$$

is a probability generating function. Verify that

$$g_n(s) = h^{-1}[f_n(h(s))]$$

is a probability generating function, where f_n and g_n denote the functional iterates of f and g, respectively.

4. As an example of Elementary Problem 3, take

$$f(s) = \frac{s}{m-(m-1)s} \qquad (m>1)$$

and

$$h(s) = s^k \qquad (k \text{ a positive integer}).$$

Prove that $g(s) = h^{-1}f(h(s))$ is a generating function and establish that the nth iterate of g is

$$g_n(s) = \frac{s}{(m^n - (m^n - 1)s^k)^{1/k}}.$$

5. Show that $E(\sum_{n=1}^{\infty} X_n) = m/(1-m)$ when $m = E(X_1) < 1$ in a branching process.

6. At time 0, a blood culture starts with one red cell. At the end of one minute, the red cell dies and is replaced by one of the following combinations with probabilities as indicated:

2 red cells	$\frac{1}{4}$
1 red, 1 white	$\frac{2}{3}$
2 white	$\frac{1}{12}$

Each red cell lives for one minute and gives birth to offspring in the same way as the parent cell. Each white cell lives for one minute and dies without reproducing. Assume the individual cells behave independently.

(a) At time $n + \frac{1}{2}$ minutes after the culture began, what is the probability that no white cells have yet appeared?

(b) What is the probability that the entire culture dies out eventually?

Solution: (a) $(\frac{1}{4})^{2^n-1}$; (b) $\frac{1}{3}$.

7. Let $f(s) = as^2 + bs + c$, where a, b, c are positive and $f(1) = 1$. Assume that the probability of extinction is d $(0 < d < 1)$. Prove that

$$d = \frac{c}{a}.$$

8. Suppose that in a branching process the number of offspring of an initial particle has a distribution whose generating function is $f(s)$. Each member of the first generation has a number of offspring whose distribution has generating function $g(s)$. The next generation has generating function f, the next g, and the functions continue to alternate in this way from generation to generation.

Arguing from basic principles (i.e., without using any general results from multi-type theory of Sections 5 and 6, determine extinction probability of the process, and the mean number of particles in the nth generation (n even, say). Would either of these quantities change if we started the process with the g function, and then continued to alternate?

9. Consider a discrete time branching process X_n with $X_0 = 1$. Establish the simple inequality

$$\Pr\{X_n > L \quad \text{for some} \quad 0 \le n \le m | X_m = 0\} \le [\Pr\{X_m = 0\}]^L.$$

10. Consider a branching process with initial size N and probability generating function

$$\varphi(s) = q + ps, \qquad q, p > 0, \quad q + p = 1.$$

Determine the probability distribution of the time T when the population first becomes extinct.

Solution: $\Pr\{T = n\} = (1 - p^n)^N - (1 - p^{n-1})^N.$

11. Compute Var $X(t)$, where $X(t)$ is a continuous time branching process and $X(0) = 1$.

Solution:

$$\operatorname{Var} X(t) = \begin{cases} \left[\dfrac{u''(1) - u'(1)}{u'(1)}\right] e^{u'(1)t}(e^{u'(1)t} - 1) & \text{if } u'(1) \neq 0, \\ u''(1)t & \text{if } u'(1) = 0. \end{cases}$$

12. A population consists of two types of individuals, males and females. We assume that all the females can produce offspring, according to a generating function $f(x)$, provided that the population contains at least one male. If the probability that an offspring is female is α, what is the p.g.f. for the number of females produced in the next generation given that at least one male is produced as well.

Solution: $\dfrac{f(\alpha s + (1 - \alpha)) - f(\alpha s)}{1 - f(\alpha)}.$

Problems

1. The following model has been introduced to study a urological process. Suppose bacteria grow according to a Yule process of parameter λ (see Section 1, Chapter 4). At each unit of time each bacterium present is eliminated with probability p. What is the probability generating function of the number of bacteria existing at time n?

Hint: This is the probability generating function of the nth iterate of a branching process.

Answer: $f_n(s)$ is the nth iterate of

$$f(s) = \frac{e^{-\lambda}(p + qs)}{1 - (1 - e^{-\lambda})(p + qs)}.$$

2. (a) A mature individual produces offspring according to the probability-generating function $f(s)$. Suppose we have a population of k immature individuals, each of which grows to maturity with probability p and then reproduces independently of the other individuals. Find the probability generating function of the number of (immature) individuals at the next generation.

(b) Find the probability generating function of the number of mature individuals at the next generation, given that there are k mature individuals in the parent generation.

Answer: (a) $(1-p+pf(s))^k$; (b) $(f(1-p+ps))^k$.

3. Show that the distributions in (a) and (b) of Problem 2 have the same mean, but not necessarily the same variance.

4. Consider a discrete time branching process $\{X_n\}$ with probability generating function

$$\varphi(s)=\frac{1-(b+c)}{1-c}+\frac{bs}{1-cs}, \qquad 0<c<b+c<1,$$

where $(1-b-c)/c(1-c)>1$. Assume $X_0=1$. Determine the conditional limit distribution:

$$\lim_{n\to\infty} \Pr\{X_n=k|X_n>0\}.$$

Answer:

$$\left(1-\frac{1}{s_0}\right)\left(\frac{1}{s_0}\right)^{k-1}, \qquad s_0=\frac{1-b-c}{c(1-c)}.$$

5. In the previous problem suppose $1-b-c=c(1-c)$. Determine $\Pr\{X_n>0\}$.

Answer: $(1-c)/[1+(n-1)c]$.

6. Under the same conditions as in Problem 5 prove that $\Pr\{X_n\le nx|X_n>0\}$ converges to an exponential distribution.

Hint: Compute the Laplace transform of X_n/n conditioned on the event $X_n>0$ and determine its limit as $n\to\infty$.

Answer: Exponential with parameter $(1-c)/c$.

7. Find the generating function $\varphi(t;s)$ of the continuous time branching process with infinitesimal generating function

$$u(s)=s^k-s \qquad (k\ge 2, \text{ integer}).$$

Hint: Solve

$$\frac{\partial\varphi(t;s)}{\partial t}=u(\varphi(t;s)) \qquad \text{with} \quad \varphi(0;s)=s.$$

Answer: $\varphi(t;s)=s[e^{(k-1)t}-(e^{(k-1)t}-1)s^{k-1}]^{-1/(k-1)}$.

8. Find the generating function $\varphi(t;s)$ of the continuous time branching process if the infinitesimal generating function is

$$u(s)=1-s-\sqrt{1-s}.$$

Answer: $\varphi(t;s)=1-[1-e^{-t/2}+e^{-t/2}\sqrt{1-s}]^2$.

9. Consider a multiple birth Yule process where each member in a population has a probability $\beta h+o(h)$ of giving birth to k new members and probability

$(1-\beta h+o(h))$ of no birth in an interval of time length h ($\beta>0$, k positive integer). Assume that there are N members present at time 0.

(a) Let $X(t)$ be the number of splits up to time t. Determine the growth behavior of $E(X(t))$.

(b) Let τ_n be the time of the nth split. Find the density function of τ_n.

Hint: (a) Note that

$$\Pr\{\tau_n\le t|\tau_{n-1}=\xi\}=\begin{cases}1-\exp\{-[(n-1)k+N]\beta(t-\xi)\}, & \xi\le t\\ 0, & \xi>t\end{cases}$$

and obtain a recursion formula for the density function of τ_n in terms of the density function of τ_{n-1}.

Answer:

(a) $$\frac{E(X(t))}{e^{k\beta t}}\to\frac{N}{k}\qquad \text{as}\quad t\to\infty.$$

(b) Let $f_n(t)$ be the probability density function of τ_n:

$$f_n(t)=\frac{N(N+k)\cdots[N+(n-1)k]}{(n-1)!k^{n-1}}\beta e^{-N\beta t}(1-e^{-k\beta t})^{n-1}.$$

10. Let X_n, $n\ge0$, describe a branching process with associated probability generating function $\varphi(s)$.

Define Y_n as the total number of individuals in the first n generations, i.e.,

$$Y_n=X_0+X_1+\cdots+X_n,\qquad n=0,1,2,\ldots,\qquad X_0=1,$$

Let $F_n(s)$ be the probability generating function of Y_n. Establish the functional relation

$$F_{n+1}(s)=s\varphi(F_n(s)),\qquad \text{for}\quad n=0,1,2,\ldots.$$

11. Let $\varphi(s)$ be the generating function of the number of progeny of a single individual in a branching process that starts with one individual at time zero, and let $\varphi_n(s)$ denote its nth iterate.

Suppose in addition to the ordinary branching process there also exists some immigration into the population during a single generation described by the probability generating function $h(s)$. Consider the branching process with immigration whose transition probability matrix is defined by

$$\sum_{j=0}^{\infty}P_{ij}s^j=[\varphi(s)]^i\cdot h(s).$$

Prove that the n-step transition probability matrix is determined by the relation

$$\sum_{j=0}^{\infty}P_{ij}^ns^j=[\varphi_n(s)]^ih(\varphi_{n-1}(s))h(\varphi_{n-2}(s))\cdot\cdots\cdot h(\varphi(s))h(s).$$

12. In the branching process with immigration (Problem 11) assume that $\varphi'(1)=m<1$. Prove that the associated Markov chain has a stationary probability distribution with probability generating function $\pi(s)=\sum_{r=0}^{\infty}\pi_rs^r$

that satisfies the functional equation

$$\pi(\varphi(s))h(s) = \pi(s).$$

13. Under the set-up of Problem 12 for the specification $\varphi(s) = q + ps$ $(0 < p < 1, q + p = 1)$ and $h(s) = e^{s-1}$ determine the stationary probability distribution.

14. Consider the simple birth and death process (linear growth without immigration), i.e., $\lambda_n = \lambda n$ and $\mu_n = \mu n$ with $\lambda > 0$, $\mu > 0$, and $\mu > \lambda$. Let $Z(t)$ be the population size at time t. By appropriate identifications, show that the busy period of a single server queueing process with the interarrival distribution $1 - e^{-\lambda t}$ and the service time distribution $1 - e^{-\mu t}$ has the same distribution as that of $\int_0^\infty Z(t)\,dt$ under the initial condition $Z(0) = 1$.

15. Let X_n be a discrete branching process with associated probability generating function $\varphi(s)$ and let $\varphi_n(s) = \sum_{k=0}^\infty \Pr\{X_n = k\}\, s^k$. Assume that $\varphi'(1) > 1$. Let

$\tilde{X}_n$ denote the number of all the particles in the nth generation which have an infinite line of descent.

Show that the probability generating function for $\tilde{X}_n$ is

$$\sum_{k=0}^{\infty} \Pr\{\tilde{X}_n = k \mid \tilde{X}_0 = X_0 = 1\}\, s^k = \frac{\varphi_n(s(1-q)+q) - q}{1-q}$$

where q is the probability of extinction.

Hint: Note that for $k \geq 1$

$$\Pr\{\tilde{X}_n = k \mid \tilde{X}_0 = 1, X_0 = 1\} = \frac{\sum_{l=k}^{\infty} \Pr\{\tilde{X}_n = k, X_n = l \mid X_0 = 1\}}{\Pr\{\tilde{X}_0 = 1 \mid X_0 = 1\}}.$$

16. The purpose of this next problem is to determine the effects that different forms of mortality have on the stability of a population. We define *stability* as the probability of indefinite survivorship = 1 − probability of eventual extinction.

In the absence of the additional mortality we'll consider momentarily, the offspring X of a single individual has the probability distribution

$$\Pr\{X = k\} = p_k, \quad k = 0, 1, \ldots.$$

Suppose that the mean of the distribution is m and that all offspring in the population are independent and identically distributed.

We consider 3 types of mortality. In each case, the probability of an individual surviving is p, but the form the survivorship takes differs among the cases. Assume

$$mp > 1.$$

(a) *Mortality on Individuals:* Independent of what happens to others, each individual survives with probability p. That is, given an actual litter size or number of offspring of X, the effective litter size has a binomial distribution with parameters (X, p). This type of mortality might reflect predation on adults.

(b) *Mortality on Litters:* Independent of what happens to other litters, each litter survives with probability p and is wiped out with probability $q = 1 - p$. That is, given an actual litter size of X, the effective litter size is X with probability p and 0 with probability q. This type of mortality might reflect predation on juveniles, or on nests and eggs in the case of birds.

(c) *Mortality on Generations:* An entire generation survives with probability p and is wiped out with probability q. This type of mortality might represent environmental catastrophies such as forest fire, flood, etc.

Give the equations for determining 1 — Stability = Pr {Eventual Extinction} in each of these cases.

Which population is the most stable? Which is least stable? Can you prove this?

NOTES

The source of inspiration for this chapter is the treatise on branching processes by T. Harris [1], which also contains a comprehensive bibliography of the subject and its applications.

REFERENCE

1. T. Harris, "The Theory of Branching Processes." Springer-Verlag, Berlin, 1963.

Chapter 9

STATIONARY PROCESSES

A stationary process is a stochastic process whose probabilistic laws remain unchanged through shifts in time (sometimes in space). The concept captures the very natural notion of a physical system that lacks an inherent time (space) origin. It is an appropriate assumption for a variety of processes in communication theory, astronomy, biology, ecology, and economics.

The stationary property leads to a number of important conclusions in a rich theory. In this chapter we focus on the prediction problem, the ergodic behavior, the spectral representation of a stationary process, stationary point processes, and the level-crossing problem. Sections 1 and 2 are prerequisite to the later sections. However, the section pairs 3 and 4, on prediction; 5 and 6, on ergodic theory; 7 and 8, on spectral analysis; and 9 and 10 on point processes and the level-crossing problem may be read in any order one desires.

1: *Definitions and Examples*

Let T be an abstract index set having the property that the sum of any two points in T is also in T. Often T will be the set $\{0, 1, \dots\}$ of non-negative integers, but it just as well could be the positive half or whole real line, the plane, finite-dimensional space, the surface of a sphere, or perhaps even an infinite-dimensional space.

Definition 1.1. *A stationary process is a stochastic process* $\{X(t),\ t \in T\}$ *with the property that for any positive integer k and any points $t_1, \dots, t_k$ and h in T, the joint distribution of*

$$\{X(t_1), \dots, X(t_k)\}$$

is the same as the joint distribution of

$$\{X(t_1 + h), \dots, X(t_k + h)\}.$$

Here are some short examples.

(a) Electrical pulses in communication theory are often postulated to describe a stationary process. Of course, in any physical system there is a transient period at the beginning of a signal. Since typically this has a short duration compared to the signal length, a stationary model may be appropriate. In electrical communication theory, often both the electrical potential and the current are often represented as complex variables. Here we may encounter complex-valued stationary processes.

(b) The spatial and/or planar distributions of stars or galaxies, plants, and animals, are often stationary. Here T might be Euclidean space, the surface of a sphere, or the plane.

A stationary distribution may be postulated for the height of a wave and T taken to be a set of longitudes and latitudes, again two dimensional.

(c) Economic time series, such as unemployment, gross national product, national income, etc., are often assumed to correspond to a stationary process, at least after some correction for long-term growth has been made.

As these examples show, stationary processes appear in an abundance of shapes and sizes. To treat the most general situation would counter our purpose of providing an introduction. Having alerted the reader to the vast scope of possibilities, henceforth we concentrate mostly on the simplest case of a real-valued process for which $T = \{0, 1, 2, \ldots\}$.

Let $\{X(t),\ t \in T\}$ be a stationary process. If the mean $m(t) = E[X(t)]$ exists, it follows that this quantity must be a constant, $m(t) = m$ for all t. Similarly, if the second moment $E[X(t)^2]$ is finite, then the variance $\sigma^2 = E[(X(t) - m)^2]$ is a constant, independent of time. Let t and s be time points, and suppose, without loss in generality, that $t > s$. Using the stationary property, we compute the covariance

$$E[(X(t) - m)(X(s) - m)] = E[(X(t - s) - m)(X(0) - m)],$$

such that the right-hand side depends only on the time difference $t - s$. If we define the *covariance function*,

$$R(h) = E[(X(h) - m)(X(0) - m)],$$

then

$$E[(X(t) - m)(X(s) - m)] = R(|t - s|).$$

Of course, $\sigma^2 = R(0)$. Sometimes it is convenient to standardize the covariance producing what is called the *correlation function* or *autocorrelation function*, defined by

$$\rho(v) = \frac{1}{\sigma^2} R(v) = R(v)/R(0).$$

Then $\rho(0) = 1$, and it can be shown (using Schwarz' inequality) that $-1 \leq \rho(v) \leq 1$ for all v.

The concept of stationarity introduced in Definition 1.1 involves all finite-dimensional distributions of the process. For many purposes it is desirable to have available a weaker concept, involving only the first two moments.

Definition 1.2. *A covariance stationary process is a stochastic process $\{X(t),\ t \in T\}$ having finite second moments, $E[X(t)^2] < \infty$, a constant mean $m = E[X(t)]$, and a covariance $E[(X(t) - m)(X(s) - m)]$ that depends only on the time difference $|t - s|$.*

Other terms used in the literature synonymously with covariance stationary are *weakly stationary* or *wide-sense stationary*, and what we have called a stationary process is often termed *strictly stationary* to emphasize the distinction.

A stationary process that has finite second moments is covariance stationary (but, of course, a stationary process may have no finite moments whatsoever). It is quite possible that a covariance stationary process will not be stationary, but there is an important exception to this general rule. A stochastic process $\{X(t),\ t \in T\}$ for which, for every k and every finite set $\{t_1, \ldots, t_k\}$ of time points, the random vector

$$(X(t_1), \ldots, X(t_k))$$

has a multivariate normal distribution (Chapter 1) is called a *Gaussian process*. Since the multivariate normal distribution is determined by its first two moments, the mean value vector and the covariance matrix, a Gaussian process which is covariance stationary will be strictly stationary.

Examples

Several of the examples that follow will be developed further in the sequel.

A. *Two Contrasting Stationary Processes*

(i) A sequence $Y_0, Y_1, \ldots$ of independent and identically distributed random variables is a stationary process. If the common distribution of $Y_0, Y_1, \ldots$ has a finite variance σ^2 then the process is covariance stationary, and the covariance function is

$$R(v) = \begin{cases} \sigma^2, & \text{for} \quad v = 0, \\ 0, & \text{for} \quad v \neq 0. \end{cases}$$

(ii) To consider a quite different stationary process, let Z be a single random variable with known distribution and set $Z_0 = Z_1 = Z_2 = \cdots = Z$. The process $\{Z_n\}$ is easily seen to be stationary. If the random variable Z has a finite variance σ^2, then the process is covariance stationary, and the covariance function is

$$R(v) = \sigma^2, \qquad \text{for all} \quad v.$$

In many ways $\{Y_n\}$ and $\{Z_n\}$ are extremes and may be used to exemplify contrasting behavior of stationary processes. For example, assuming that the common distribution is known, observing $Y_0, Y_1, \ldots, Y_n$ provides no information that could be used to predict Y_{n+1}, while observing only Z_0 enables $Z_1, Z_2, \ldots$ to be predicted exactly. Here is a second way that the processes are opposites. Suppose the Y_n process has a finite mean value function m. Then by the law of large numbers, the sample averages

$$\frac{1}{n}(Y_0 + \cdots + Y_{n-1})$$

converge to the constant $m = E[Y_0]$. No such convergence takes place in the $\{Z_n\}$ process. Indeed

$$\frac{1}{n}\{Z_0 + \cdots + Z_{n-1}\} = Z_0 = Z,$$

and there is just as much "randomness" in the nth sample average as there is in the first observation.

The behavior in which sample averages formed from a process converge to some underlying parameter of the process is termed *ergodic*. To make inferences about the underlying laws governing an ergodic process, one need not observe separate independent replications of entire processes or sample paths. Instead, one need only observe a single realization of the process, but over a sufficiently long span of time. Thus, it is an important practical problem to determine conditions that lead to a stationary process being ergodic.

Perhaps surprisingly, these two examples of opposite behavior have related causes. For covariance stationary processes, the crux of the matter in both situations is whether or not the covariance function $R(|t-s|)$ converges to zero as the time difference $|t-s|$ becomes large, and if it does so vanish, the rate at which this convergence takes place has relevance. For the $\{Y_n\}$ process, the convergence is very fast indeed, since the covariance is exactly zero for lags or time differences of one or more, while for the $\{Z_n\}$ process, the correlation function is one at all time differences.

The theory of stationary processes has as a prime goal the clarification of ergodic behavior and the prediction problem for processes falling in the vast range between the two extreme examples just exhibited. The general problem of prediction for stationary processes is studied in Sections 3 and 4 of this chapter, and the convergence of sample averages is elaborated in Sections 5 and 6.

B. *Trigonometric Polynomials*

Some interesting examples of stationary processes can be obtained by considering certain trigonometric expressions having random amplitudes. Let A and B be identically distributed random variables having a mean of zero and variance σ^2. We suppose A and B are uncorrelated, i.e., $E[AB]=0$. Fix a frequency $\omega \in [0, \pi]$ and for $n=0, \pm 1, \pm 2, \ldots$ define

$$X_n = A\cos(\omega n) + B\sin(\omega n).$$

Then $E[X_n]=0$ for all n, and, using the trigonometric identity

$$\cos(\alpha-\beta) = \cos\alpha\cos\beta + \sin\alpha\sin\beta,$$

and the fact that $E[AB]=0$, we compute the covariance

$$\begin{aligned} E[X_n X_{n+v}] &= E[\{A\cos\omega n + B\sin\omega n\}\{A\cos\omega(n+v) + B\sin\omega(n+v)\}] \\ &= E[A^2\cos\omega n\cos\omega(n+v) + B^2\sin\omega n\sin\omega(n+v)] \\ &= \sigma^2\cos\omega v. \end{aligned}$$

Since the covariance between X_n and X_{n+v} plainly depends only on the time difference v, we conclude that the process is covariance stationary. If A and B have a normal distribution with mean zero and variance σ^2, then the process is Gaussian and thus strictly stationary.

For the particular frequency $\omega=0$, we have $\cos n\omega = 1$ and $\sin n\omega = 0$, so that $X_n = A$ for all n. Thus the $\{Z_n\}$ process in the previous example falls within this framework.

More generally, let $A_0, A_1, \ldots, A_m$ and $B_0, B_1, \ldots, B_m$ be uncorrelated random variables having zero means. Assume that A_i and B_i have a common variance σ_i^2, and let $\sigma^2 = \sigma_0^2 + \cdots + \sigma_m^2$. Take $\omega_0, \omega_1, \ldots, \omega_m$ as distinct frequencies in $[0, \pi]$, and for $n=0, \pm 1, \pm 2, \ldots$ set

$$X_n = \sum_{k=0}^{m} \{A_k\cos n\omega_k + B_k\sin n\omega_k\}.$$

Since the coefficients $\{A_k\}$ and $\{B_k\}$ are uncorrelated with zero means, we have $E[A_i B_j] = 0$ and $E[A_i A_k] = E[B_i B_k] = 0$ for $k \neq i$. We compute the covariance

$$\begin{aligned} E[X_n X_{n+v}] &= E\left[\left(\sum_{k=0}^{m} \{A_k \cos n\omega_k + B_k \sin n\omega_k\}\right)\right. \\ &\qquad \left.\left(\sum_{j=0}^{m} \{A_j \cos(n+v)\omega_j + B_j \sin(n+v)\omega_j\}\right)\right] \\ &= \sum_{k=0}^{m} E[A_k^2 \cos n\omega_k \cos(n+v)\omega_k + B_k^2 \sin n\omega_k \sin(n+v)\omega_k] \\ &= \sum_{k=0}^{m} \sigma_k^2 \cos v\omega_k . \end{aligned}$$

Again, the process is covariance stationary.

To go on, it is helpful to let $p_k = \sigma_k^2/\sigma^2$ and write the covariance function as

$$R(v) = \sigma^2 \sum_{k=0}^{m} p_k \cos v\omega_k . \tag{1.1}$$

Then p_k represents the contribution of frequency ω_k in the covariance. Observe that $\{p_k\}$ is a discrete probability distribution, that is, $p_k \geq 0$ and $\sum p_k = 1$, which suggests the possibility of generalizing (1.1) to a continuum of frequencies, something of the form

$$R(v) = \sigma^2 \int_0^{\pi} \cos(v\omega)\, dF(\omega), \tag{1.2}$$

where $F(\omega)$ is a cumulative distribution function of a random variable having possible values in $[0, \pi]$. In Section 7, we shall see that such a generalization is indeed possible and that the most general covariance stationary process has a representation of this form. In the special case in which F corresponds to a uniform distribution on $[0, \pi]$, meaning all frequencies are equally represented, we calculate

$$\begin{aligned} R(v) &= \sigma^2 \frac{1}{\pi} \int_0^{\pi} \cos(v\omega)\, d\omega \\ &= \begin{cases} \sigma^2, & \text{if } v = 0, \\ 0, & \text{if } v \neq 0. \end{cases} \end{aligned}$$

This is the covariance function of the independent and identically distributed sequence $\{Y_n\}$ in the previous example. Again $\{Y_n\}$ and $\{Z_n\}$

are opposites in some sense, $\{Z_n\}$ corresponding to a single frequency $\omega = 0$, and $\{Y_n\}$ corresponding to all frequencies in $[0, \pi]$ given equal weight.

C. *Moving Average Processes*

Let $\{\xi_n : n = 0, \pm 1, \pm 2, \ldots\}$ be uncorrelated random variables having a common mean μ and variance σ^2. Let $a_1, a_2, \ldots, a_m$ be arbitrary real numbers and consider the process defined by

$$X_n = a_1 \xi_n + a_2 \xi_{n-1} + \cdots + a_m \xi_{n-m+1}.$$

We have

$$E[X_n] = \mu(a_1 + \cdots + a_m),$$

and

$$\operatorname{Var}[X_n] = \sigma^2(a_1^2 + \cdots + a_m^2),$$

for the mean and variance, respectively. Let $\hat{\xi}_k = \xi_k - \mu$. For the covariance, we have

$$\begin{aligned} E&\left[\left(X_n - \mu \sum_{i=1}^m a_i\right)\left(X_{n+v} - \mu \sum_{i=1}^m a_i\right)\right] \\ &= E\left[\left(\sum_{i=1}^m a_i \hat{\xi}_{n-i+1}\right)\left(\sum_{j=1}^m a_j \hat{\xi}_{n+v-j+1}\right)\right] \\ &= \begin{cases} E[a_m a_{m-v} \hat{\xi}^2_{n+v-m+1} + a_{m-1} a_{m-v-1} \hat{\xi}^2_{n+v-m+2} + \cdots \\ \qquad + a_{v+1} a_1 \hat{\xi}_n^2], & \text{if } v \le m-1, \\ 0, & \text{if } v \ge m. \end{cases} \\ &= \begin{cases} \sigma^2(a_m a_{m-v} + \cdots + a_{v+1} a_1), & \text{if } v \le m-1, \\ 0, & \text{if } v \ge m. \end{cases} \end{aligned}$$

Since the covariance between X_n and X_{n+v} depends only on the lag v, and not on n, the process is covariance stationary.

A common case is the "moving average" with a standardized variance in which $a_k = 1/\sqrt{m}$ for $k = 1, \ldots, m$. The covariance function becomes

$$R(v) = \begin{cases} \sigma^2\left(1 - \dfrac{v}{m}\right), & v \le m-1, \\ 0, & \text{for } v \ge m. \end{cases}$$

The case $m = 1$ corresponds to the uncorrelated random variables in the $\{Y_n\}$ process of Example A, and, at the other extreme, roughly speaking, $m = \infty$ corresponds to the $\{Z_n\}$ process.

D. *A Stationary Process on the Circle*

Let U, V be independent normally distributed random variables having zero mean and unit variance. Let T be the circumference of the unit circle, represented by $T=[0, 2\pi]$, and for $t \in T$ define the bivariate process $X(t) = (Y(t), Z(t))$, where

$$Y(t) = U \sin t + V \cos t,$$
$$Z(t) = -U \cos t + V \sin t.$$

Then $(X(t), t \in T)$ is a stationary process. Clearly, $E[Y(t)] = E[Z(t)] = 0$, and since $\sin^2 t + \cos^2 t = 1$ for all t, $E[Y(t)^2] = E[Z(t)^2] = 1$. Since $Y(t)$ and $Z(t)$ have a joint normal distribution, to complete the specification of their distribution, we need only compute their covariance. But, easily

$$E[Y(t)Z(t)] = 0.$$

Thus the distribution of $X(t)$ is the same as the distribution of $X(t+\theta)$ for any θ. Since one can verify the same property for any vector $(X(t_1), \ldots, X(t_k))$, the process is stationary.

E. *Stationary Markov Chains*

In Chapter 3 we showed that, under quite general conditions a Markov chain $\{X_n\}$ would evolve towards an equilibrium regime of statistical fluctuations in which the importance of the period n and initial state X_0 would have faded into the past. To be more precise, we gave conditions under which, as n became large, the distribution $\Pr\{X_n = j | X_0 = i\}$ would approach a constant π_j not depending on i. Let us suppose we are observing such a system, but one which began its evolution indefinitely far in the past and is now evolving in its equilibrium regime. Then for any $n = 0, \pm 1, \pm 2, \ldots$, the probability distribution of X_n does not depend on n. Indeed, $\Pr\{X_n = j\} = \pi_j$, so that this probability, or marginal distribution for X_n, is *stationary* in the sense that it does not depend on n. Similarly, the joint distribution of (X_n, X_{n+1}) does not depend on n, but is given by

$$\Pr\{X_n = i, X_{n+1} = j\} = \Pr\{X_n = i\} \Pr\{X_{n+1} = j | X_n = i\} = \pi_i P_{ij},$$

where $\mathbf{P} = \|P_{ij}\|$ is the transition matrix for the Markov chain. Quite obviously we may continue and state that for any fixed $k = 0, 1, \ldots$ the joint distribution of $(X_n, X_{n+1}, \ldots, X_{n+k})$ does not depend on n.

Similarly, let $\{X_n, n = 0, 1, \ldots\}$ be a Markov chain for which the initial state X_0 is chosen according to the stationary distribution π_j. The same reasoning shows that $\{X_n\}$ is a stationary process.

2: Mean Square Distance

Since "covariance stationarity" is a property defined using only the first two moments of a stochastic process, it is desirable to have a measure of dissimilarity or "distance" between random variables Y, Z, that also is defined in terms of only the first two moments. A natural choice for such a measure is the mean of the squared difference, $E[(Y-Z)^2]$, or what is even better, since it resumes the original units of measurement, the square root of this mean square difference. To enhance the suggestion of distance, we introduce the notation

$$\|Z\| = \sqrt{E[Z^2]}, \qquad \text{and} \qquad \|Y-Z\| = \sqrt{E[(Y-Z)^2]}.$$

Thus, for example, we would measure the ability of a predictor $\hat{X}_{t+k}$ to predict a random variable X_{t+k} by the root mean square difference $\|\hat{X}_{t+k} - X_{t+k}\|$. Again, using this measure of distance we may introduce a notion of convergence for sequences of random variables. Accordingly, a sequence $\{X_n\}$ of random variables will be said to converge to a random variable X if the mean square difference $E[(X_n - X)^2]$ tends to zero as n increases indefinitely. A formal definition follows:

Definition 2.1. *Let $X, X_1, X_2, \ldots$ be random variables. We say $\{X_n\}$ converges in mean square to X, written $X_n \to X$ (ms) or $\lim_{n\to\infty} X_n = X$ (ms) if*

(i) $E[X_n^2] < \infty$ for all n, and
(ii) $\lim_{n\to\infty} E[(X_n - X)^2] = 0$ (or equivalently $\lim_{n\to\infty} \|X_n - X\| = 0$).

Here are some elementary properties of mean square distance and mean square convergence. In this list, Y, Z is an arbitrary pair of random variables having finite second moments, and y, z are arbitrary real numbers.

Schwarz' Inequality

Observe

$$2|yz| \le y^2 + z^2. \tag{2.1}$$

Since this inequality is true for arbitrary y, z, it must hold when these values are chosen randomly, i.e.,

$$2|YZ| \le |Y|^2 + |Z|^2.$$

By taking the expectation of both sides, we conclude

$$2E[|YZ|] \leq E[|Y|^2] + E[|Z|^2].$$

In particular, $E[|YZ|] < \infty$. If instead we substitute

$$Y/\sqrt{E[|Y|^2]} = Y/\|Y\|, \qquad \text{for} \quad y,$$

and

$$Z/\sqrt{E[|Z|^2]} = Z/\|Z\|, \qquad \text{for} \quad z,$$

in (2.1) and take expectations, we conclude

$$2E\left\{\frac{|YZ|}{\|Y\| \cdot \|Z\|}\right\} \leq E\left\{\frac{Y^2}{\|Y\|^2}\right\} + E\left\{\frac{Z^2}{\|Z\|^2}\right\} = 2$$

Hence

$$E[|YZ|] \leq \sqrt{E[Y^2]E[Z^2]} = \|Y\| \, \|Z\|.$$

This is known as *Schwarz' inequality.*

The Parallelogram Law

We compute

$$E[(Y+Z)^2] = E[Y^2 + 2YZ + Z^2] = E[Y^2] + 2E[YZ] + E[Z^2],$$

and

$$E[(Y-Z)^2] = E[Y^2 - 2YZ + Z^2] = E[Y^2] - 2E[YZ] + E[Z^2],$$

which added together give the parallelogram law

$$E[(Y+Z)^2] + E[(Y-Z)^2] = 2E[Y^2] + 2E[Z^2],$$

or

$$\|Y+Z\|^2 + \|Y-Z\|^2 = 2\{\|Y\|^2 + \|Z\|^2\}. \tag{2.2}$$

The name results from the similarity of this equation with the result in geometry, where Y, Z are vectors, that the sum of squares of the two diagonals in a parallelogram is equal to the sum of squares of the four sides.

The Triangle Inequality

We compute

$$E[(Y+Z)^2] = E[Y^2] + 2E[YZ] + E[Z^2].$$

From Schwarz' inequality,

$$E[YZ] \leq E[|YZ|] \leq \sqrt{E[Y^2]E[Z^2]}.$$

Hence

$$\|Y+Z\|^2 \le E[Y^2] + 2\sqrt{E[Y^2]}\sqrt{E[Z^2]} + E[Z^2]$$
$$= (\|Y\| + \|Z\|)^2,$$

or

$$\|Y+Z\| \le \|Y\| + \|Z\|. \tag{2.3}$$

The name results from the similarity to the geometric inequality that states that the sum of lengths of two sides of a triangle always exceeds the length of the third side. Observe the parallel between $\|Z\|$ and the usual notion of length of a vector in space. There is an alternative form that is sometimes more useful:

$$|(\|Y\| - \|X\|)| \le \|Y - X\|. \tag{2.4}$$

This is obtained from (2.3) in the same way that $|(|a| - |b|)| \le |a - b|$ is obtained from $|a + b| \le |a| + |b|$ for real a, b.

Uniqueness of ms Limit

If we set $Y = X_n - X'$ and $Z = X - X_n$ in the triangle inequality (2.3), we get

$$\|X - X'\| \le \|X_n - X'\| + \|X_n - X\|.$$

Thus, if $X_n \to X(\text{ms})$ and $X_n \to X'(\text{ms})$, then $E[(X - X')^2] = \|X - X'\|^2 = 0$. Applying Chebyshev's inequality, we have

$$\Pr\{|X - X'| > \varepsilon\} \le \frac{1}{\varepsilon^2} E[(X - X')^2], \qquad \varepsilon > 0,$$

yielding $\Pr\{|X - X'| > \varepsilon\} = 0$ for all positive ε, and thus,

$$\Pr\{X = X'\} = 1. \tag{2.5}$$

Hence the limit of a sequence of random variables converging in mean square is unique in the sense of (2.5).

Convergence in Probability

Again using Chebyshev's inequality

$$\Pr\{|X_n - X| > \varepsilon\} \le \frac{1}{\varepsilon^2} E[(X_n - X)^2], \qquad \varepsilon > 0,$$

we see that $X_n \to X(\text{ms})$ implies

$$\lim_{n\to\infty} \Pr\{|X_n - X| > \varepsilon\} = 0,$$

for any positive ε. Hence convergence in mean square implies convergence in probability. Warning! The converse is *not* true.

Convergence of Second Moments

Let us apply the triangle inequality (2.4) with $Y = X_n$. We have

$$| \|X\| - \|X_n\|| \leq \|X - X_n\| \to 0.$$

Hence

$$\lim_{n \to \infty} \|X_n\| = \|X\|. \tag{2.6}$$

The Cauchy Criterion for Convergence

If we set $Y = X_n - X$ and $Z = X - X_m$ in (2.2), we get

$$E[(X_n - X_m)^2] \leq 2E[(X_n - X)^2] + 2E[(X_m - X)^2].$$

Hence, if $X_n \to X(\text{ms})$ then

$$\lim_{m, n \to \infty} E[(X_n - X_m)^2] = 0, \qquad \text{or} \qquad \lim_{m, n \to \infty} \|X_n - X_m\| = 0.$$

Conversely, it can be shown that if $\{X_n\}$ is a sequence of random variables for which

$$\lim_{m, n \to \infty} E[(X_n - X_m)^2] = 0,$$

then there exists a random variable X for which

$$X_n \to X(\text{ms}).$$

This result parallels the Cauchy criterion for convergence of sequences of real numbers.

Convergence of Means

We have

$$E[|Y|] = E[|Y \cdot 1|] \leq \sqrt{E[Y^2] \cdot 1} = \|Y\|,$$

by using Schwarz' inequality with $Z \equiv 1$. Thus $E[|Y|] < \infty$ if $E[Y^2] < \infty$. In a similar manner, setting $Y = X_n - X$, we compute

$$|E[X_n] - E[X]| \leq E[|X_n - X|] \leq \|X_n - X\|.$$

Thus $X_n \to X(\text{ms})$ as $n \to \infty$ implies

$$\lim_{n \to \infty} E[X_n] = E[X].$$

Convergence of Covariances

Let $\{X_n\}$ be a sequence of random variables converging in mean square to a random variable X. Let Y be a random variable having a finite second moment. We want to show $\lim_{n\to\infty} E[YX_n] = E[YX]$, or, equivalently, $\lim_{n\to\infty} |E[YX_n] - E[YX]| = 0$. We use Schwarz' inequality:

$$|E[YX_n] - E[YX]| = |E[Y(X_n - X)]| \le \|Y\| \; \|X_n - X\|.$$

Since $E[Y^2] < \infty$ and $\|X_n - X\| \to 0$, the proof is complete.

AUTOREGRESSIVE AND MOVING AVERAGE PROCESSES

Let $\{X_n;\ n = 0, \pm 1, \pm 2, \ldots\}$ be a covariance stationary process. Suppose that for some real number λ, satisfying $|\lambda| < 1$, that the random variables defined by

$$\xi_n = X_n - \lambda X_{n-1}$$

are uncorrelated with zero means and a common variance σ^2. Such a process is called an *autoregressive process of order one*. We may write

$$\begin{aligned} X_n &= \lambda X_{n-1} + \xi_n \\ &= \lambda\{\lambda X_{n-2} + \xi_{n-1}\} + \xi_n \\ &= \lambda^2 X_{n-2} + \lambda \xi_{n-1} + \xi_n \end{aligned}$$

and inductively

$$= \lambda^k X_{n-k} + \sum_{j=0}^{k-1} \lambda^j \xi_{n-j}. \tag{2.7}$$

We rearrange terms and compute the mean square difference between X_n and $\sum_{j=0}^{k-1} \lambda^j \xi_{n-j}$. This yields

$$\begin{aligned} E\left[\left(X_n - \sum_{j=0}^{k-1} \lambda^j \xi_{n-j}\right)^2\right] &= E[(\lambda^k X_{n-k})^2] \\ &= \lambda^{2k} E[X_{n-k}^2]. \end{aligned}$$

Since the process is stationary, $E[X_{n-k}^2]$ is a constant, independent of n and k, and since $|\lambda| < 1$, the right-hand side decreases to zero at a geometric rate. Thus

$$\begin{aligned} X_n &= \lim_{k\to\infty} \sum_{j=0}^{k-1} \lambda^j \xi_{n-j} \ (\text{ms}) \\ &= \sum_{j=0}^{\infty} \lambda^j \xi_{n-j}. \end{aligned} \tag{2.8}$$

It is to be remembered that $\sum_{j=0}^{\infty}$ signifies the limit *in mean square* of the sequence of partial sums $\sum_{j=0}^{k-1}$. Equation (2.8) provides a representation of the original process as a *moving average* (Example C, earlier in this section).

Since mean square convergence implies convergence of the means and second moments, we have

$$E[X_n] = \lim_{k\to\infty} E\left[\sum_{j=0}^{k-1} \lambda^j \xi_{n-j}\right] = 0,$$

and

$$\begin{aligned} E[X_n^2] &= \lim_{k\to\infty} E\left[\left(\sum_{j=0}^{k-1} \lambda^j \xi_{n-j}\right)^2\right] \\ &= \lim_{k\to\infty} \left\{E\left[\sum_{j=0}^{k-1} \lambda^{2j} \xi_{n-j}^2\right] + E\left[\sum_{i\neq j} \lambda^{i+j} \xi_{n-i}\xi_{n-j}\right]\right\}. \end{aligned}$$

The expectation of the second term vanishes since the $\{\xi_m\}$ sequence is uncorrelated. Since $E[\xi_{n-j}^2] = \sigma^2$ and $|\lambda| < 1$, we get

$$\begin{aligned} E[X_n^2] &= \lim_{k\to\infty} \sum_{j=0}^{k-1} \lambda^{2j}\sigma^2 \\ &= \sigma^2/(1-|\lambda|^2). \end{aligned}$$

Let us compute the covariance between X_n and X_{n+k}. We have from (2.7)

$$X_{n+k} = \lambda^k X_n + \sum_{j=0}^{k-1} \lambda^j \xi_{n+k-j},$$

so that

$$E[X_n X_{n+k}] = \lambda^k E[X_n^2] + E\left[X_n \cdot \sum_{j=0}^{k-1} \lambda^j \xi_{n+k-j}\right].$$

The first term on the right is $\lambda^k \sigma^2$. Using the convergence of covariances, the second term is evaluated routinely, viz.,

$$\begin{aligned} E\left[X_n \sum_{j=0}^{k-1} \lambda^j \xi_{n+k-j}\right] &= \lim_{l\to\infty} E\left[\sum_{m=0}^{l-1} \lambda^m \xi_{n-m} \cdot \sum_{j=0}^{k-1} \lambda^j \xi_{n+k-j}\right] \\ &= \lim_{l\to\infty} \sum_{m=0}^{l-1} \sum_{j=0}^{k-1} \lambda^{m+j} E[\xi_{n-m}\xi_{n+k-j}] \\ &= 0, \end{aligned}$$

where the fact that $\{\xi_m\}$ are uncorrelated is heavily exploited. Thus

$$E[X_n X_{n+k}] = \sigma^2 \lambda^k/(1-|\lambda|^2), \qquad k = 0, 1, 2, \ldots.$$

To move on, writing the process in the form

$$X_n = \lambda X_{n-1} + \xi_n$$

suggests the natural generalization to covariance stationary processes that have the form

$$X_n = \lambda_1 X_{n-1} + \lambda_2 X_{n-2} + \cdots + \lambda_p X_{n-p} + \xi_n, \tag{2.9}$$

where $\{\xi_n\}$ is a sequence of zero mean uncorrelated random variables having a common variance. Such a process is called a pth *order autoregressive process.* For such a process, linear regression theory suggests that a natural predictor for X_n given the past $X_{n-1}, X_{n-2}, \ldots$ would be given by the formula

$$\hat{X}_n = \lambda_1 X_{n-1} + \cdots + \lambda_p X_{n-p}.$$

This is not necessarily the case. The crucial point concerns the correlation between ξ_n and the past $(X_{n-1}, \ldots, X_{n-p})$. Such prediction problems are the subject of the next section. Here we content ourselves with the preliminary work of determining when a pth order autoregressive process has a moving average representation.

One time unit earlier, (2.9) is

$$X_{n-1} = \lambda_1 X_{n-2} + \lambda_2 X_{n-3} + \cdots + \lambda_p X_{n-p-1} + \xi_{n-1},$$

which inserted back in (2.9) gives

$$\begin{aligned} X_n &= \lambda_1[\lambda_1 X_{n-2} + \cdots + \lambda_p X_{n-p-1} + \xi_{n-1}] \\ &\quad + \lambda_2 X_{n-2} + \cdots + \lambda_p X_{n-p} + \xi_n \\ &= \xi_n + \lambda_1 \xi_{n-1} + (\lambda_1^2 + \lambda_2) X_{n-2} \\ &\quad + \cdots + (\lambda_1 \lambda_{p-1} + \lambda_p) X_{n-p} + \lambda_1 \lambda_p X_{n-p-1}. \end{aligned}$$

Following this procedure m times brings us to

$$\begin{aligned} X_n &= \xi_n + \delta_1 \xi_{n-1} + \cdots + \delta_m \xi_{n-m} + \beta_{m1} X_{n-m-1} \\ &\quad + \beta_{m2} X_{n-m-2} + \cdots + \beta_{mp} X_{n-m-p}, \end{aligned} \tag{2.10}$$

for certain constants δ_i and β_{mi}. (Each substitution leaves p consecutive X_n's on the right.) Then, substitution of

$$X_{n-m-1} = \xi_{n-m-1} + \lambda_1 X_{n-m-2} + \cdots + \lambda_p X_{n-m-p-1}$$

into (2.10) gives

$$\begin{aligned} X_n &= \xi_n + \delta_1 \xi_{n-1} + \cdots + \delta_m \xi_{n-m} + \beta_{m1} \xi_{n-m-1} \\ &\quad + (\beta_{m1} \lambda_1 + \beta_{m2}) X_{n-m-2} + \cdots \\ &\quad + (\beta_{m1} \lambda_{p-1} + \beta_{mp}) X_{n-m-p} + \beta_{m1} \lambda_p X_{n-m-p-1}, \end{aligned}$$

from which we deduce the recurrence relations

$$\delta_{m+1} = \beta_{m1},$$
$$\beta_{m+1,j} = \beta_{m1}\lambda_j + \beta_{m,j+1}, \qquad j = 1, \ldots, p-1,$$

and

$$\beta_{mp} = \beta_{m1}\lambda_p.$$

Continuation of this procedure leads to the moving average representation

$$X_n = \sum_{k=0}^{\infty} \delta_k \xi_{n-k}, \qquad \delta_0 = 1, \tag{2.11}$$

provided the remainder terms $R_m = (\beta_{m1}X_{n-m-1} + \cdots + \beta_{mp}X_{n-m-p})$ *become negligible in mean square as* $m \to \infty$. We will derive momentarily the proper conditions to insure formula (2.11).

The procedure becomes neater when formulated in a more abstract setting. Let T be the *shift operator* which takes the real sequence $\{x_n\} = (\ldots, x_{-1}, x_0, x_1, \ldots)$ into the sequence $T(\{x_n\}) = (\ldots, x_0, x_1, x_2, \ldots)$ (i.e., x_1 is the zeroth coordinate). Each time index has been advanced by one. Of course, T^{-1} works in the opposite direction:

$$T^{-1}(\{x_n\}) = (\ldots, x_{-2}, x_{-1}, x_0, \ldots),$$

and

$$T^{-k}(\{x_n\}) = (\ldots, x_{-k-1}, x_{-k}, x_{-k+1}, \ldots).$$

In this notation, (2.9) becomes

$$\{X_n\} = \lambda_1 T^{-1}(\{X_n\}) + \cdots + \lambda_p T^{-p}(\{X_n\}) + \{\xi_n\}$$
$$= \sum_{k=1}^{p} \lambda_k T^{-k}(\{X_n\}) + \{\xi_n\},$$

or

$$\left(I - \sum_{k=1}^{p} \lambda_k T^{-k}\right)(\{X_n\}) = \{\xi_n\},$$

where $I = T^0$ is the identity operator. Now we see that what is needed is an inverse to the operator $\left(I - \sum_{k=1}^{p} \lambda_k T^{-k}\right)$ such that we are permitted to write

$$\{X_n\} = \left(I - \sum_{k=1}^{p} \lambda_k T^{-k}\right)^{-1}(\{\xi_n\}).$$

That is, if

$$X_n = \sum_{i=0}^{\infty} \delta_i \xi_{n-i}, \qquad \text{or} \qquad \{X_n\} = \left(\sum_{i=0}^{\infty} \delta_i T^{-i}\right)(\{\xi_n\}),$$

then the δ_i's are the coefficients in

$$\left(1-\sum_{k=1}^{p}\lambda_k z^k\right)^{-1}=\sum_{k=0}^{\infty}\delta_k z^k.$$

As such, they can be determined by formal long division. For example, the case $\lambda_1=\lambda$, $\lambda_k=0$, for $k\geq 2$, which immediately preceded this general discussion, is solved by

$$\frac{1}{1-\lambda z}=1+\lambda z+\lambda^2 z^2+\lambda^3 z^3+\cdots,$$

or

$$X_n=\sum_{j=0}^{\infty}\lambda^j \xi_{n-j},$$

which was obtained in (2.8).

A tedious but straightforward computation reveals that

$$\frac{1}{1-\lambda_1 z-\cdots-\lambda_p z^p}=1+\delta_1 z+\cdots+\delta_m z^m+r_m(z),$$

where

$$r_m(z)=\frac{\beta_{m1}z^{m+1}+\cdots+\beta_{mp}z^{m+p}}{1-\lambda_1 z-\cdots-\lambda_p z^p}.$$

That is, the formal division yields exactly the same recursion as we obtained earlier through direct substitution. It follows that if $r_m(z)\to 0$ as $m\to\infty$, then each $\beta_{mk}\to 0$, $k=1,\ldots,p$, and the random remainder term $R_m=\beta_{m1}X_{n-m-1}+\cdots+\beta_{mp}X_{n-m-p}$ vanishes in mean square, so that the infinite moving average representation (2.11) is valid. We give the conditions. The equation

$$x^p-\lambda_1 x^{p-1}-\cdots-\lambda_p=0 \tag{2.12}$$

has p roots, $x_1,\ldots,x_p$. If $|x_i|<1$, $i=1,\ldots,p$, then the roots of

$$1-\lambda_1 z-\cdots-\lambda_p z^p=0$$

are $z_i=1/x_i$, provided $\lambda_p\neq 0$, and $|z_i|>1$. For any z satisfying $|z|<\min_i|z_i|$, the series

$$\frac{1}{1-\lambda_1 z-\cdots-\lambda_p z^p}=\frac{1}{\prod_{i=1}^{p}\left(1-\dfrac{z}{z_i}\right)}=\prod_{i=1}^{p}\sum_{\nu=0}^{\infty}\left(\frac{z}{z_i}\right)^{\nu}$$

$$=\sum_{r=0}^{\infty}\delta_r z^r,$$

converges absolutely. Hence $r_m(z) \to 0$ as $m \to \infty$ for $|z| < \min_i |z_i|$, and in particular for $|z| = 1$. This implies $\beta_{mk} \to 0$ as $m \to \infty$ for $k = 1, 2, \ldots, p$, and, easily, R_m converges to zero in mean square so that the infinite moving average representation (2.11) holds.

For future reference, we highlight an important conclusion emanating from the preceding analysis.

Remark 2.1. Suppose $\{X_n\}$ is a zero-mean covariance stationary process satisfying

$$X_n = \lambda_1 X_{n-1} + \cdots + \lambda_p X_{n-p} + \xi_n, \qquad n = 0, \pm 1, \ldots,$$

where $\{\xi_n\}$ is a sequence of zero-mean uncorrelated random variables, and $\lambda_1, \ldots, \lambda_p$ are fixed. If every root x_i, $i = 1, \ldots, p$, of

$$x^p - \lambda_1 x^{p-1} - \cdots - \lambda_p = 0$$

has magnitude $|x_i| < 1$, then ξ_n and $(X_{n-1}, \ldots, X_{n-p})$ are uncorrelated. This follows since the terms in $X_{n-k} = \sum_{j=0}^{\infty} \delta_j \xi_{n-k-j}$ $(k \geq 1)$ and ξ_n are uncorrelated by assumption.

To glimpse at the alternative, involving a moving average in the opposite direction, look at

$$X_n = \eta_n + \rho \eta_{n+1} + \rho^2 \eta_{n+2} + \cdots, \tag{2.13}$$

where $|\rho| < 1$ and $\{\eta_n\}$ are zero mean and uncorrelated. Then

$$\rho X_n = X_{n-1} - \eta_{n-1}, \qquad \text{or} \qquad X_n = \lambda X_{n-1} + \xi_n,$$

where $\lambda = 1/\rho$ and $\xi_n = -\rho^{-1} \eta_{n-1}$. Since $\{\xi_n\}$ are uncorrelated, $\{X_n\}$ is an autoregressive process, but $|\lambda| > 1$ precludes a moving average representation of the form (2.11). Our construction of the process in (2.13) is as a moving average in the forward direction, and this exhibits typical behavior when the roots of (2.12) all exceed one in magnitude. When the sizes of the roots of (2.12) lie on both sides of one, a doubly infinite moving average $\sum_{k=-\infty}^{+\infty} \delta_k \xi_{n-k}$ is required to represent $\{X_n\}$. Finally, if any root has magnitude exactly one, the autoregressive process satisfying (2.9) cannot be stationary (except in the trivial case $\xi_n \equiv 0$).

The autoregressive and moving average models may be combined to generate more complex stationary processes. One might suppose

$$X_n = \lambda_1 X_{n-1} + \cdots + \lambda_p X_{n-p} + \eta_n,$$

where

$$\eta_n = \alpha_1 \xi_n + \alpha_2 \xi_{n-1} + \cdots + \alpha_m \xi_{n-m+1},$$

is a moving average. More generally, one can also consider

$$Z_n = X_n + \varepsilon_n,$$

where $\{\varepsilon_n\}$ is an uncorrelated "noise" process. The analysis of these more complex models is quite difficult.

3: Mean Square Error Prediction

A problem that arises in many, many contexts is the problem of predicting the value of a given random variable that will be observed in the future. The newspapers often contain predictions for future values of Gross National Product, employment, consumer prices, and other economic quantities. The problem of control, say process control, implicitly involves prediction. If the predicted output of a process is not satisfactory, a control or change is implemented to bring the process more in line with what is desired.

This section considers the prediction problem in the context of stationary random processes. We suppose we are concerned with a quantity whose values at times $n = \ldots, -2, -1, 0, 1, 2, \ldots$ form a stationary process $\{X_n\}$. We want to predict the value X_{n+1}, or more generally X_{n+k}, based on the values observed in the past, $X_n, X_{n-1}, X_{n-2}, \ldots$. This is the *prediction* or *extrapolation* problem for stationary processes.

GENERAL PREDICTION THEORY

Let X denote the outcome of some "experiment." We suppose that X is unknown, to be observed in the future, and that it is desired to predict the value for X that will occur. Let $\hat{X}$ be our prediction for X. Our prediction error will be $X - \hat{X}$, and it is desired to make this as small as possible, in some sense. A problem arises immediately: What is meant by "small"? In general, $X - \hat{X}$ will be a random quantity, so that we must mean small *on the average*, or that the expected value of some function of the error should be small. Whatever function of the error we choose, it seems reasonable to suppose that it has a minimum at an error of zero and increases as the error deviates from zero. In this section, we measure the performance of a predictor by its *mean squared error* $E[(X - \hat{X})^2] = \|X - \hat{X}\|^2$. This criterion reflects a reasonable requirement that large errors are more serious than small ones. However, perhaps even more important is the mathematical tractability of this criterion which, as we will see, enables a general theory to be developed that leads to explicit formulas for optimal predictors in a number of specific situations.

Thus our problem is to find a predictor that minimizes over all predictors $\hat{X}$ the mean square error $E[(X-\hat{X})^2]$. To complete the description we must specify the class of allowable predictors over which the minimization takes place. In general, this class is determined by the knowledge concerning the experiment or the distribution of X that is available. To bring this explicitly into the general formulation, let us denote the class of allowable predictors by **H**.

Examples. (i) We suppose X, the outcome of an experiment, has known mean μ and variance σ^2. The best predictor for X, in the sense of mean square error and in the absence of further information, is $\hat{X}=\mu$. Since no further information concerning X is available, we take our space of predictors **H** to be the set of real numbers. We may choose any real number a as our predicted value for X. We compute

$$\begin{aligned}E[(X-\hat{X})^2] &= E[(X-\mu+\mu-\hat{X})^2]\\ &= E[(X-\mu)^2]+2E[(X-\mu)(\mu-\hat{X})]+E[(\mu-\hat{X})^2].\end{aligned}$$

Then $E[(X-\mu)^2]=\sigma^2$, and since $\hat{X}$ is a fixed real number, $E[(\mu-\hat{X})^2] = (\mu-\hat{X})^2$ and $E[(X-\mu)(\mu-\hat{X})]=(\mu-\hat{X})E[X-\mu]=0$. Thus,

$$E[(X-\hat{X})^2]=\sigma^2+(\mu-\hat{X})^2.$$

It follows immediately that the mean square error is minimized by setting $\hat{X}=\mu$. Thus, in the absence of further information, the minimum mean square error predictor for a random variable X is its mean $\mu=E[X]$.

(ii) Now let X, Y be jointly distributed random variables having finite variances and a known joint distribution. We suppose that X is to be predicted from an observation on Y. Common examples are the prediction of tensile strength of a specimen of steel from a reading of its hardness and the prediction of the true value of a physical quantity such as pressure, temperature, etc., based on a measurement subject to random error.

Since we suppose Y is observable and no further information on the outcome for X is available (other than knowing the joint distribution), we allow any function $\hat{X}=f(Y)$ having finite variance as a predictor.

We might argue that, after observing $Y=y$, we are in the same situation as Example (i) except that in this second case the appropriate distribution is the conditional distribution for X given $Y=y$. Therefore the minimum mean square error predictor would be the mean of X computed under this conditional distribution, $\mu_{X|Y}=E[X|Y]$. This is indeed the case. We compute

$$\begin{aligned}&E[(X-\hat{X})^2]\\ &= E[(X-\mu_{X|Y})^2]+2E[(X-\mu_{X|Y})(\mu_{X|Y}-\hat{X})]+E[(\mu_{X|Y}-\hat{X})^2].\end{aligned}$$

We show that the expectation of the middle term on the right vanishes by conditioning on Y, and recalling that $\mu_{X|Y}$ and $\hat{X}$ are functions of Y. We have

$$\begin{aligned} E[(X-\mu_{X|Y})(\mu_{X|Y}-\hat{X})] &= E\{E[(X-\mu_{X|Y})(\mu_{X|Y}-\hat{X})|Y]\} \\ &= E\{(\mu_{X|Y}-\hat{X})E[(X-\mu_{X|Y})|Y]\} \\ &= 0, \end{aligned}$$

since $E[(X-\mu_{X|Y})|Y]=E[X|Y]-\mu_{X|Y}=0$. Thus

$$E[(X-\hat{X})^2]=E[(X-\mu_{X|Y})^2]+E[(\mu_{X|Y}-\hat{X})^2],$$

and the right-hand side is minimized by setting $\hat{X}=E[X|Y]$.

(iii) The computation of $\hat{X}=E[X|Y]$ requires full knowledge of the joint distribution of X, Y. Even when this knowledge is available, the resulting formulas are often too complicated to be of practical value. In the study of covariance stationary processes we assume knowledge of the first two moments of the process only, and no further information on the joint distribution is assumed available. Therefore, it is desirable to have a prediction theory that both leads to simple predictor formulas and requires knowledge of the first two moments only. This is the theory of *linear predictors*. Let X, Y be jointly distributed random variables having known means μ_X, μ_Y, respectively, variances σ_X^2, σ_Y^2, respectively, and covariance $\sigma_{X,Y}=E[(X-\mu_X)(Y-\mu_Y)]$. We allow as predictors only those formulas that are linear functions of Y, say $\hat{X}=a+bY$, or, what is equivalent and more convenient, $\hat{X}=a+b(Y-\mu_Y)$, where a and b are arbitrary real numbers. Since the class of allowable predictors is smaller in this example than in Example (ii), the resulting minimum mean square prediction error cannot be smaller and quite possibly might be larger. However the predictor formula, being linear, is simple, and we will show that the optimal coefficients can be determined without knowing the full joint distribution, but knowing only the given moments. The assertion is that the optimal linear predictor of X based on Y is

$$\hat{X}^*=\mu_X+\frac{\sigma_{XY}}{\sigma_Y^2}(Y-\mu_Y).$$

We proceed to validate this claim. Let

$$\hat{X}=a+b(Y-\mu_Y),$$

and note that

$$\hat{X}^*-\hat{X}=a'+b'(Y-\mu_Y),$$

where $a' = \mu_X - a$ and $b' = (\sigma_{XY}/\sigma_Y^2) - b$. As before, we compute

$$E[(X-\hat{X})^2] = E[(X-\hat{X}^*)^2] + 2E[(X-\hat{X}^*)(\hat{X}^*-\hat{X})] + E[(\hat{X}^*-\hat{X})^2].$$

We again determine that the second term on the right vanishes. Indeed,

$$\begin{aligned}
E[(X-\hat{X}^*)(\hat{X}^*-\hat{X})] &= E\left[\left\{(X-\mu_X) - \frac{\sigma_{XY}}{\sigma_Y^2}(Y-\mu_Y)\right\}\right. \\
&\qquad \left.\times \{a' + b'(Y-\mu_Y)\}\right] \\
&= a'E\left[(X-\mu_X) - \frac{\sigma_{XY}}{\sigma_Y^2}(Y-\mu_Y)\right] \\
&\quad + b'E\left[(X-\mu_X)(Y-\mu_Y) - \frac{\sigma_{XY}}{\sigma_Y^2}(Y-\mu_Y)^2\right] \\
&= 0 + b'\left(\sigma_{XY} - \frac{\sigma_{XY}}{\sigma_Y^2}\sigma_Y^2\right) \\
&= 0.
\end{aligned}$$

Thus we have

$$E[(X-\hat{X})^2] = E[(X-\hat{X}^*)^2] + E[(\hat{X}^*-\hat{X})^2],$$

and the right-hand side is minimized over linear predictors $\hat{X}$ by setting $\hat{X} = \hat{X}^*$. Thus $\hat{X}^*$ is the minimum mean square error linear predictor, as stated.

There is an important special case in which the restriction to linear predictor formulas results in no loss of prediction efficiency. If X and Y have a joint normal distribution, then, as shown in Chapter 1, the conditional mean of X given $Y = y$ is

$$E[X|Y=y] = \mu_X + \frac{\sigma_{XY}}{\sigma_Y^2}(y-\mu_Y).$$

We observe that this best predictor is linear in y. Thus, if X and Y have a joint normal distribution, the minimum mean square error *linear* predictor of X given Y is, in fact, the minimum mean square error predictor.

A pattern emerges in these examples. In each case, to show that a given predictor $\hat{X}^*$ was optimal, the crux of the matter lay in showing that a cross product, $E[(X-\hat{X}^*)(\hat{X}^*-\hat{X})]$, vanished. We formalize the pattern into *the prediction theorem for minimum mean square error predictors.*

Theorem 3.1. *Let X be a random variable having a finite second moment and let $\mathbf{H}$ be a space of allowable predictors $\hat{X}$, that is, a set of random variables $\hat{X}$ having finite second moments. Assume that $\mathbf{H}$ is a linear space in the sense that $a\hat{X}_1 + \hat{X}_2$ is allowed as a predictor whenever $\hat{X}_1$ and $\hat{X}_2$ are predictors and a is a real number. Then:*

(i) *A predictor $\hat{X}^*$ has minimum mean square error if and only if $E[(X - \hat{X}^*)U] = 0$ for every predictor U;*

(ii) *If a minimum mean square error predictor exists, it is unique in the sense of mean square distance. That is, if $\hat{X}_1^*$ and $\hat{X}_2^*$ are minimum mean square error predictors, then $E[(\hat{X}_1^* - \hat{X}_2^*)^2] = 0$;*

(iii) *To assure the existence of a minimum mean square error predictor, it is sufficient to assume that $\mathbf{H}$ is closed in the sense that, if $\hat{X}_n$, $n = 0, 1, \ldots$, is a sequence of predictors converging in mean square to a random variable $\hat{X}$, then $\hat{X}$ is also allowed as a predictor.*

Proof. (i) For the first part we suppose that $\hat{X}^*$ is a predictor for which

$$E[(X - \hat{X}^*)U] = 0,$$

for every predictor U. We will show that $\hat{X}^*$ represents the minimum mean square prediction error. Let $\hat{X}$ be an arbitrary allowable predictor and compute

$$E[(X - \hat{X})^2] = E[(X - \hat{X}^*)^2] + 2E[(X - \hat{X}^*)(\hat{X}^* - \hat{X})] + E[(\hat{X}^* - \hat{X})^2].$$

Set $U = \hat{X}^* - \hat{X}$. Then U is a predictor since both $\hat{X}^*$ and $\hat{X}$ are and any linear combination of predictors is an allowable predictor. Thus $E[(X - \hat{X}^*)(\hat{X}^* - \hat{X})] = E[(X - \hat{X}^*)U] = 0$, and

$$E[(X - \hat{X})^2] = E[(X - \hat{X}^*)^2] + E[(\hat{X}^* - \hat{X})^2].$$

Hence

$$E[(X - \hat{X})^2] \geq E[(X - \hat{X}^*)^2],$$

and the mean square error for $\hat{X}^*$ is smaller than that for any other predictor $\hat{X}$. Thus $\hat{X}^*$ achieves minimum mean square prediction error.

On the other hand, suppose for a given predictor $\hat{X}^*$ that $E[(X - \hat{X}^*)U] = a \neq 0$ for some predictor U. We will show that

$$\hat{X} = \hat{X}^* + \frac{a}{E[U^2]}U \tag{3.1}$$

provides a smaller mean square error, and hence $\hat{X}^*$ cannot be optimal.

This will complete the proof of (i). First note that $\hat{X}$ is a predictor since it is a linear combination of predictors. Rewriting (3.1) as

$$\hat{X} - \hat{X}^* = \frac{a}{E[U^2]} U$$

and inserting this twice in

$$\begin{aligned} E[(X-\hat{X})^2] &= E[\{(X-\hat{X}^*) - (\hat{X}-\hat{X}^*)\}^2] \\ &= E[(X-\hat{X}^*)^2] - 2E[(X-\hat{X}^*)(\hat{X}-\hat{X}^*)] \\ &\quad + E[(\hat{X}-\hat{X}^*)^2], \end{aligned}$$

we get

$$\begin{aligned} E[(X-\hat{X})^2] &= E[(X-\hat{X}^*)^2] - 2\frac{a}{E[U^2]} E[(X-\hat{X}^*)U] \\ &\quad + \frac{a^2}{\{E[U^2]\}^2} E[U^2] \\ &= E[(X-\hat{X}^*)^2] - \frac{a^2}{E[U^2]} \\ &< E[(X-\hat{X}^*)^2]. \end{aligned}$$

We conclude that $\hat{X}^*$ cannot provide minimum mean square error since we have exhibited a predictor $\hat{X}$ with smaller error.

(ii) To demonstrate that the minimum mean square error predictor is unique, let us suppose both $\hat{X}_1^*$ and $\hat{X}_2^*$ have minimum mean square error. Then $E[(X-\hat{X}_i^*)U] = E[XU - \hat{X}_i^* U] = E[XU] - E[\hat{X}_i^* U] = 0$, for $i = 1, 2$ and all predictors U. Thus

$$E[\hat{X}_1^* U] = E[XU] = E[\hat{X}_2^* U],$$

and

$$E[(\hat{X}_1^* - \hat{X}_2^*)U] = 0,$$

for all predictors U. We choose $U = \hat{X}_1^* - \hat{X}_2^*$ to conclude

$$E[(\hat{X}_1^* - \hat{X}_2^*)^2] = 0. \tag{3.2}$$

Thus minimum mean square error predictors are unique in the sense that the mean square difference between them is zero. Using Chebyshev's inequality one can show, as was done earlier in this chapter, that (3.2) implies

$$\Pr\{\hat{X}_1^* \neq \hat{X}_2^*\} = 0.$$

(iii) Let d be the infimum of the mean square errors of predictors in $\mathbf{H}$,

$$d = \inf\{E[|X - \hat{X}|^2] : \hat{X} \in \mathbf{H}\}.$$

We may select a sequence $\{\hat{X}_n\}$ of predictors from $\mathbf{H}$ whose mean square errors approach d,

$$\lim_{n\to\infty} E[|X - \hat{X}_n|^2] = d.$$

For an arbitrary m, n, we apply the parallelogram law with

$$Y = X - \hat{X}_n, \qquad Z = X - \hat{X}_m,$$

to conclude

$$E[|\hat{X}_m - \hat{X}_n|^2] + E[|2X - \hat{X}_n - \hat{X}_m|^2] = 2E[|X - \hat{X}_n|^2] + 2E[|X - \hat{X}_m|^2]. \tag{3.3}$$

Since $\frac{1}{2}(\hat{X}_n + \hat{X}_m)$ is a predictor, its mean square error must exceed d. Hence

$$E[|2X - \hat{X}_n - \hat{X}_m|^2] = 4E[|X - \tfrac{1}{2}(\hat{X}_n + \hat{X}_m)|^2] \geq 4d.$$

Inserting this in (3.3) gives

$$E[|\hat{X}_n - \hat{X}_m|^2] + 4d \leq 2E[|\hat{X}_n - X|^2] + 2E[|\hat{X}_m - X|^2].$$

We subtract $4d$ from both sides and let m, n increase indefinitely to conclude

$$\begin{aligned}\lim_{m,n\to\infty} E[|\hat{X}_m - \hat{X}_n|^2] &\leq 2\lim_{n\to\infty} E[|\hat{X}_n - X|^2] + 2\lim_{m\to\infty} E[|\hat{X}_m - X|^2] - 4d \\ &= 0.\end{aligned}$$

Since the Cauchy criterion of mean square convergence is satisfied, we know there exists a random variable, call it $\hat{X}^*$, for which $\hat{X}_n \to \hat{X}^*$(ms). By assumption, $\hat{X}^*$ is a predictor. Then $X - \hat{X}_n \to X - \hat{X}^*$(ms), and by the continuity of the mean square in mean square convergence

$$E[|X - \hat{X}^*|^2] = \lim_{n\to\infty} E[|X - \hat{X}_n|^2] = d.$$

Thus $\hat{X}^*$ is a minimum mean square error predictor and the proof is complete. ■

In Examples (i)–(iii) our approach was to verify that given predictors were optimal. Let us return to those examples and show how, with the aid of the previous theorem, we might derive the optimal predictors. We use part (i), the necessary and sufficient condition for a predictor to have minimum mean square error. In Example (i), **H** is the set of real numbers, and we desire a real number $\hat{X}^*$ for which

$$E[(X-\hat{X}^*)u]=0, \tag{3.4}$$

for all real numbers u. It clearly suffices to take $u=1$. Then

$$E[(X-\hat{X}^*)]=0,$$

and, since $\hat{X}^*$ is nonrandom,

$$\hat{X}^*=E[\hat{X}^*]=E[X]=\mu.$$

Since $\hat{X}^*$ so chosen satisfies (3.4), we know $\hat{X}^*$ is the (unique) minimum mean square error predictor.

For Example (ii), **H** is the set of all functions $\hat{X}=f(Y)$ of Y having finite second moments. The necessary and sufficient condition for $\hat{X}^*$, a function of Y, to be optimal is that

$$E[(X-\hat{X}^*)f(Y)]=0,$$

for all functions of Y having finite second moments, or

$$E[Xf(Y)]=E[\hat{X}^*f(Y)].$$

This is the defining property for $\hat{X}^*$ to be the conditional expectation of X given Y (see Chapter 1). Thus, $\hat{X}^*=E[X|Y]$ is the (unique in the sense of mean square distance) optimal predictor.

The condition in Example (iii) is

$$E[(X-\hat{X}^*)U]=0, \tag{3.5}$$

whenever U is a linear function of Y. We write

$$U=a+b(Y-\mu_Y),$$
$$\hat{X}^*=a^*+b^*(Y-\mu_Y),$$

so that (3.5) becomes

$$E[\{X-(a^*+b^*(Y-\mu_Y))\}\times\{a+b(Y-\mu_Y)\}]=0.$$

This must hold for all choices of a and b. In particular, let us choose first $a=1$ and $b=0$, and then $a=0$ and $b=1$, to conclude

$$E[X-(a^*+b^*(Y-\mu_Y))]=0,$$

or

$$E[X]=a^*+b^*E[Y-\mu_Y]=a^*,$$

and

$$E[\{X-a^*-b^*(Y-\mu_Y)\}(Y-\mu_Y)]=0,$$

or

$$E[(X-\mu_X)(Y-\mu_Y)] = b^*E[(Y-\mu_Y)^2],$$

$$\sigma_{XY} = b^*\sigma_Y^2.$$

Thus $a^* = \mu_X$ and $b^* = \sigma_{XY}/\sigma_Y^2$, so

$$\hat{X}^* = \mu_X + \frac{\sigma_{XY}}{\sigma_Y^2}(Y-\mu_Y).$$

Note. Examining some parallels in finite-dimensional Euclidean geometry leads to a better understanding of why it is possible to develop a nice theory of prediction under the mean square error criterion. Recall that a (real) *vector space* is a set of elements x, y with associated operations of vector addition and scalar multiplication such that $ax + by$ is a vector whenever x and y are vectors, and a and b are real numbers. An *inner product* in a vector space is a real-valued function denoted (x, y) of pairs of vectors x, y satisfying $(x, y) = (y, x)$, $(a_1x_1 + a_2x_2, y) = a_1(x_1, y) + a_2(x_2, y)$, and $(x, x) > 0$ if x is not the zero vector. In an inner product space we can define the *norm* or length of a vector x by $\|x\| = (x, x)^{1/2}$. A *Hilbert space* is an inner product space that is complete in the metric determined by the norm. This means that if $\{x_n\}$ is a sequence of vectors for which $\lim_{m,n\to\infty}\|x_n - x_m\| = 0$, then there exists a vector x for which $\lim_{n\to\infty}\|x_n - x\| = 0$.

Under the full assumptions of Theorem 1, **H**, the space of predictors $\hat{X}$, $\hat{Y}$, is a Hilbert space where the inner product is $(\hat{X}, \hat{Y}) = E[\hat{X}\hat{Y}]$. The space **H**′ consisting of all random variables of the form $aX + b\hat{X}$, where a and b are real and $\hat{X}$ is in **H**, i.e., a predictor, is also a Hilbert space. The mean square error is the square of the norm or length of the difference vector $X - \hat{X}$. That is, it is the square of the distance between X and $\hat{X}$. In Hilbert space terminology, our problem is to find a vector $\hat{X}^*$ in **H** that is nearest to the vector X in **H**′.

Hilbert space is a generalization of d-dimensional Euclidean space having vectors $x = (x_1, \ldots x_d)$, $y = (y_1, \ldots, y_d)$. The inner product is $(x, y) = \sum x_i y_i$, and the norm is the Euclidean distance $\|x\| = \{\sum x_i^2\}^{1/2}$. The cosine of the angle between two vectors x, y is often defined as $(x, y)/(\|x\|\,\|y\|)$. In particular, two vectors x, y are perpendicular if and only if $(x, y) = 0$.

The problem is to find a vector $\hat{x}^*$ in a subspace **H** of a space **H**′ that is nearest to a vector x in **H**′. Theorem 1 states that $\hat{x}^*$ is nearest to x if and only if the difference $x - \hat{x}^*$ is perpendicular to all vectors u in **H**. Figure 1 will help guide the geometric intuition.

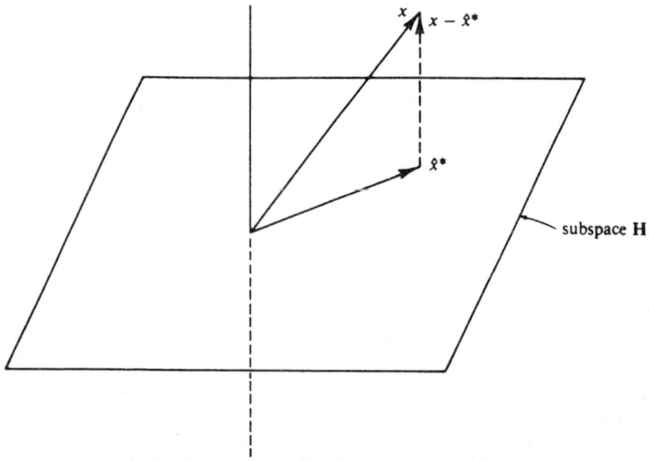

FIG. 1. Diagram showing that a vector $\hat{x}^*$ in a subspace **H** is nearest to a vector x if and only if the difference $x - \hat{x}^*$ is perpendicular to all vectors in **H**.

4: Prediction of Covariance Stationary Processes

Let X_n, $n = 0, \pm 1, \pm 2, \ldots$, be a covariance stationary process having a known covariance function $R(v)$, $v = 0, \pm 1, \ldots$. (Where X_n is a real valued process then $R(-v) = R(v)$.) The mean of the process is constant, assumed known, and thus, after changing the origin if necessary, we may assume the mean is zero. Let us consider the problem of finding the minimum mean square error linear predictor of X_n based on the *finite* past $X_{n-1}, X_{n-2}, \ldots, X_{n-p}$. Thus consider predictors of the form

$$\hat{X}_n = \alpha_1 X_{n-1} + \alpha_2 X_{n-2} + \cdots + \alpha_p X_{n-p}.$$

Using our criterion for optimality, we know that a predictor

$$\hat{X}_n^* = \alpha_1^* X_{n-1} + \alpha_2^* X_{n-2} + \cdots + \alpha_p^* X_{n-p}$$

has minimum mean square error if and only if, for all predictors

$$U = u_1 X_{n-1} + u_2 X_{n-2} + \cdots + u_p X_{n-p},$$

we have

$$E[(X_n - \hat{X}_n^*)U] = 0.$$

Let us consider the p particular choices for U given by

$$U_i = X_{n-i}, \qquad \text{for} \quad i = 1, \ldots, p.$$

Since any predictor U may be written as $U = u_1 U_1 + \cdots + u_p U_p$,

$$E[(X_n - \hat{X}_n^*)U] = 0, \qquad \text{for all} \quad U,$$

if and only if

$$E[(X_n - \hat{X}_n^*)U_i] = 0, \qquad \text{for} \quad i = 1, \ldots, p. \tag{4.1}$$

Substituting in (4.1) we get

$$E[(X_n - \{\alpha_1^* X_{n-1} + \alpha_2^* X_{n-2} + \cdots + \alpha_p^* X_{n-p}\})X_{n-i}] = 0,$$

or

$$E[X_n X_{n-i}] = \alpha_1^* E[X_{n-1}X_{n-i}] + \cdots + \alpha_p^* E[X_{n-p}X_{n-i}].$$

Since these cross products are the covariances, we have

$$R(i) = \alpha_1^* R(i-1) + \cdots + \alpha_p^* R(i-p), \qquad i = 1, \ldots, p.$$

Thus $\alpha^* = (\alpha_1^*, \ldots, \alpha_p^*)$ may be taken as any vector satisfying the p linear equations

$$\begin{aligned}
R(1) &= \alpha_1^* R(0) + \alpha_2^* R(1) + \alpha_3^* R(2) + \cdots + \alpha_p^* R(p-1),\\
R(2) &= \alpha_1^* R(1) + \alpha_2^* R(0) + \alpha_3^* R(1) + \cdots + \alpha_p^* R(p-2),\\
R(3) &= \alpha_1^* R(2) + \alpha_2^* R(1) + \alpha_3^* R(0) + \cdots + \alpha_p^* R(p-3),\\
&\vdots\\
R(p) &= \alpha_1^* R(p-1) + \alpha_2^* R(p-2) + \alpha_3^* R(p-3) + \cdots + \alpha_p^* R(0).
\end{aligned} \tag{4.2}$$

Part (iii) of the basic prediction theorem asserts there is a minimum mean square error predictor in this case. (One can show that the required hypothesis is satisfied.) Thus, there is at least one solution α^* to (4.2), and there may be many. However, by the uniqueness part of the basic prediction theorem, all solutions lead to the same $\hat{X}_n^*$. As an example, consider the extreme $\{Z_n\}$ process of Section 1 in which $Z_n = Z$, $n = 0, \pm 1, \ldots$, and $R(v) = \sigma^2$ for all $v = 0, \pm 1, \ldots$. Then any α^* vector satisfying $\alpha_1^* + \cdots + \alpha_p^* = 1$ will solve (4.2). All such α^* vectors lead to $\hat{Z}_n^* = Z$, however.

We can compute the minimum mean square error σ_p^2 by

$$\begin{aligned}
\sigma_p^2 &= E[|X_n - \hat{X}_n^*|^2]\\
&= E[(X_n - \hat{X}_n^*)(X_n - \hat{X}_n^*)]\\
&= E[(X_n - \hat{X}_n^*)X_n] - E[(X_n - \hat{X}_n^*)\hat{X}_n^*].
\end{aligned}$$

The second term vanishes by the necessary and sufficient condition for a predictor to be optimal. Keeping the first term,

$$\begin{aligned}
\sigma_p^2 &= E[X_n^2] - E[\hat{X}_n^* X_n]\\
&= R(0) - E\left[\sum_{k=1}^{p} \alpha_k^* X_{n-k} X_n\right]\\
&= R(0) - \sum_{k=1}^{p} \alpha_k^* R(k).
\end{aligned}$$

Let us now consider the problem of linearly predicting X_n based on the entire past $X_{n-1}, X_{n-2}, \ldots$. We allow as predictors all random variables of the form

$$\hat{X}_n = \alpha_1 X_{n-1} + \cdots + \alpha_p X_{n-p},$$

where p is any positive integer and $\alpha_1, \ldots, \alpha_p$ are real numbers, and also all limits, in the mean square sense, of such random variables. The space **H** of such predictors satisfies all conditions in the basic prediction theorem. Clearly every random variable of the form

$$\hat{X}_n = \sum_{k=1}^{\infty} \alpha_k X_{n-k} \tag{4.3}$$

is a predictor, provided the α's are chosen so that the infinite sum converges in the mean square sense. By applying the Cauchy criterion to the sequence of partial sums, it can be be shown that the infinite sum will converge whenever $\sum_{k,l} \alpha_k \alpha_l R(|k-l|) < \infty$. No matter how counterintuitive it may seem, it is unfortunately true that *not* every limit of finite predictors can be represented in the manner of (4.3).

Examples are easy. Let $Z, \ldots, \zeta_{-1}, \zeta_0, \zeta_1, \ldots$ be independent identically distributed random variables having zero mean and unit variance. Let $X_n = Z + \zeta_n$. By the mean square law of large numbers,

$$Z = Z + \lim_{m\to\infty} \frac{1}{m}(\zeta_n + \cdots + \zeta_{n-m+1}) = \lim_{m\to\infty} \frac{1}{m}(X_n + \cdots + X_{n-m+1}),$$

so that Z is an allowable predictor, given the entire past, and clearly is the best predictor. But Z cannot be represented in the form of (4.3). However, we know a minimal mean square error predictor $\hat{X}^*$ exists. In most situations of practical interest, such a predictor will have a representation in the form

$$\hat{X}_n^* = \sum_{k=1}^{\infty} \alpha_k^* X_{n-k}, \tag{4.4}$$

and thus it is worthwhile to examine this case in some detail. Since $E[(X_n - \hat{X}_n^*)U] = 0$ for every U that is a finite linear combination of variables in $X_{n-1}, X_{n-2}, \ldots$, we must have

$$E[(X_n - \hat{X}_n^*)X_{n-k}] = 0, \qquad k = 1, 2, \ldots. \tag{4.5}$$

This then will imply that

$$E[(X_n - \hat{X}_n^*)U] = 0, \tag{4.6}$$

for every U of the form $U = u_1 X_{n-1} + u_2 X_{n-2} + \cdots + u_p X_{n-p}$, and, by continuity of the cross product, (4.6) will hold for all allowable predictors

U. Thus (4.5) provides a necessary and sufficient condition for a predictor of the form (4.4) to be optimal.

Let us apply this criterion to the autoregressive processes of Section 2. Suppose that $\{X_n\}$ is a covariance stationary process satisfying

$$X_n = \lambda_1 X_{n-1} + \cdots + \lambda_p X_{n-p} + \xi_n, \tag{4.7}$$

where $\lambda_1, \ldots, \lambda_p$ are fixed and $\{\xi_n\}$ is a sequence of zero mean uncorrelated random variables having a common variance. Write (4.7) in the form

$$X_n = \hat{X}_n + \xi_n,$$

where

$$\hat{X}_n = \lambda_1 X_{n-1} + \cdots + \lambda_p X_{n-p}.$$

We pointed out in Remark 2.1 that ξ_n is uncorrelated with X_{n-k} for $k \geq 1$, *provided all roots* $x_1, \ldots, x_p$ *of*

$$x^p - \lambda_1 x^{p-1} - \cdots - \lambda_p = 0$$

have magnitude $|x_i| < 1$. It follows that, under this condition, $\hat{X}_n$ is a minimum mean square linear predictor for X_n given the entire past, since

$$E[(X_n - \hat{X}_n)X_{n-k}] = E[\xi_n X_{n-k}] = 0, \qquad k = 1, 2, \ldots,$$

and the condition (4.5) is satisfied.

Return to the general case, and suppose there exists an optimal predictor of the form

$$\hat{X}_n^* = \sum_{k=1}^{\infty} \alpha_k^* X_{n-k}. \tag{4.8}$$

As mentioned earlier, this need not be the case. However since the cross product is continuous in the mean square limit, we substitute into (4.5) and interchange the expectation and sum. The result is

$$R(k) = \sum_{l=1}^{\infty} \alpha_l^* R(k-l), \qquad k = 1, 2, \ldots. \tag{4.9}$$

If these equations have a solution $(\alpha_1^*, \alpha_2^*, \ldots)$ for which the series in (4.8) converges in mean square, then, in fact, (4.8) will define a minimum mean square error predictor.

Example. Suppose $\{X_n, n = 0, \pm 1, \ldots\}$ is a covariance stationary process having the covariance function

$$R(v) = \begin{cases} 1, & v = 0, \\ \lambda/(1+\lambda^2), & |v| = 1, \\ 0, & |v| > 1, \end{cases}$$

where $0 < \lambda < 1$. Equations (4.9) become

$$\lambda = (1+\lambda^2)\alpha_1^* + \lambda\alpha_2^*,$$
$$0 = \lambda\alpha_{k-1}^* + (1+\lambda^2)\alpha_k^* + \lambda\alpha_{k+1}^*, \qquad k = 2, 3, \ldots.$$

It is easy to verify that a solution is given by

$$\alpha_k^* = -(-\lambda)^k, \qquad k = 1, 2, \ldots,$$

and the minimum mean square error linear predictor is

$$\hat{X}_n^* = +\lambda X_{n-1} - \lambda^2 X_{n-2} + \lambda^3 X_{n-3} - \cdots.$$

An interesting point is that, although X_n and X_{n-k} are uncorrelated for $k \geq 2$, the optimal linear predictor for X_n involves the entire past of the process.

5: *Ergodic Theory and Stationary Processes*

An ergodic theorem gives conditions under which an average over time

$$\bar{X}_n = \frac{1}{n}(X_1 + \cdots + X_n)$$

of a stochastic process will converge as the number n of observed periods becomes large. A most important ergodic theorem is the strong law of large numbers which, for independent and identically distributed random variables $X_1, X_2, \ldots$ having finite means $m = E[X_k]$, asserts that the sample averages $\bar{X}_n$ will converge to the mean m on a set of outcomes having probability one. In symbols,

$$\Pr\left\{\lim_{n\to\infty} \bar{X}_n = m\right\} = 1.$$

Stationary processes provide a natural setting for generalizations of the law of large numbers, since for such processes, the mean value is a constant $m = E[X_n]$, independent of time.

Let us consider, for the moment, the problem of estimating an unknown mean value function $m(n) = E[X_n]$ of an arbitrary process. In general, we must take a large number N of separate realizations of the process, say

$$\{X_n^1; n = 1, 2, \ldots\},$$
$$\{X_n^2; n = 1, 2, \ldots\},$$
$$\vdots$$
$$\{X_n^N; n = 1, 2, \ldots\},$$

and then calculate the arithmetic means

$$\bar{X}(n) = \frac{1}{N}\{X_n^1 + \cdots + X_n^N\},$$

which we would use as estimates for $m(n)$. Of course, if $m(n)$ were constant, as would be the case for a stationary process, we might additionally average over n time points and calculate a grand mean

$$\bar{\bar{X}} = \frac{1}{n}\{\bar{X}(1) + \cdots + \bar{X}(n)\}.$$

However, the point remains that, in general, to estimate a mean value of a process, separate independent realizations of the entire process are needed. For comparison, let us consider the same estimation problem for a stationary process $\{X_n\}$ that obeys an ergodic theorem

$$\bar{X}_n = \frac{1}{n}(X_1 + \cdots + X_n) \to m, \qquad \text{as} \quad n \to \infty. \tag{5.1}$$

In view of (5.1), we now need observe only a single realization of the process, but over a sufficiently long time duration. We then use $\bar{X}_n$ as our estimate of the constant mean m. The practical value of the ergodic theory for stationary processes is due, to a considerable extent, to this fact. For such processes the mean value (and correlation function) often can be estimated from just a single realization of the process.

In this section we will present two ergodic theorems for stationary processes. Just as there are strong and weak laws of large numbers, there are a variety of ergodic theorems, differing in their assumptions and in the modes of convergence. Our first theorem generalizes the weak law, as it is often stated, to cover covariance stationary processes. Here the natural mode of convergence is in mean square. The second theorem generalizes the strong law and requires strict stationarity. Here the convergence is with probability one.

THE MEAN SQUARE ERGODIC THEOREM

Let $\{X_n\}$ be a covariance stationary process with mean m and covariance function

$$R(v) = E[\{X_{n+v} - m\} \cdot \{X_n - m\}].$$

Let

$$\bar{X}_n = \frac{1}{n}(X_1 + \cdots + X_n).$$

One form of the weak law of large numbers states that $\bar{X}_n$ converges to m in the mean square sense whenever the sequence $\{X_n\}$ is uncorrelated.

The mean square ergodic theorem draws the same conclusion assuming only that the sequence X_n is asymptotically uncorrelated, in the sense that the covariance $R(v)$ has a Cesaro limit of zero as the lag v increases.

Theorem 5.1. *Suppose $\{X_n\}$ is a covariance stationary process having covariance function $R(v)$. Then*

$$\lim_{N\to\infty} \frac{1}{N} \sum_{v=0}^{N-1} R(v) = 0, \tag{5.2}$$

if and only if

$$\lim_{N\to\infty} E[(\bar{X}_N - m)^2] = 0. \tag{5.3}$$

Proof. Since $m = E[X_n]$, we recognize (5.3) as the limit of the variance of $\bar{X}_N$, and (5.2) as the limit of the covariance between $\bar{X}_N$ and X_1. Thus the theorem states that the variance of $\bar{X}_N$ converges to zero if and only if the covariance between X_1 and $\bar{X}_N$ converges to zero.

Let

$$Y_n = X_n - m, \qquad \text{and} \qquad \bar{Y}_N = \frac{1}{N}(Y_1 + \cdots + Y_N).$$

Then, using Schwarz' inequality,

$$\begin{aligned}\left\{\frac{1}{N}\sum_{v=0}^{N-1} R(v)\right\}^2 &= \{E[Y_1\ \bar{Y}_N]\}^2\\ &\le E[Y_1^2]\cdot E[\bar{Y}_N^2]\\ &= R(0)\cdot E[(\bar{X}_N - m)^2].\end{aligned}$$

Thus (5.3) entails (5.2). To establish the opposite implication, let us suppose that (5.2) holds. We calculate the variance of

$$\bar{Y}_N = \frac{1}{N}(Y_1 + \cdots + Y_N),$$

obtaining

$$\begin{aligned}E[\bar{Y}_N^2] &= \frac{1}{N^2} E\left[\left(\sum_{k=1}^{N} Y_k\right)^2\right]\\ &= \frac{1}{N^2}\left\{E\left[\sum_{k=1}^{N} Y_k^2 + 2\sum_{k<l} Y_k Y_l\right]\right\}\\ &= \frac{1}{N^2}\left\{NR(0) + 2\sum_{l=1}^{N}\sum_{k=1}^{l-1} R(l-k)\right\}\\ &= \frac{1}{N^2}\left\{2\sum_{l=1}^{N}\sum_{v=0}^{l-1} R(v) - NR(0)\right\}.\end{aligned}$$

Observe that

$$\frac{1}{N} R(0) \to 0, \qquad \text{as} \quad N \to \infty,$$

so that we need concentrate only on the first term. For it we have, for any $M < N$,

$$\frac{2}{N^2} \sum_{l=1}^{N} \sum_{v=0}^{l-1} R(v) = \frac{2}{N^2} \left\{ \sum_{l=1}^{M} \sum_{v=0}^{l-1} R(v) + \sum_{l=M+1}^{N} \sum_{v=0}^{l-1} R(v) \right\}.$$

Let $\varepsilon > 0$ be given and, using assumption (5.2), choose M so that

$$\left| \frac{1}{l} \sum_{v=0}^{l-1} R(v) \right| \leq \varepsilon, \qquad \text{if} \quad l \geq M.$$

Then

$$\left| \frac{2}{N^2} \sum_{l=M+1}^{N} l \times \frac{1}{l} \sum_{v=0}^{l-1} R(v) \right| \leq \frac{2}{N^2} \sum_{l=M+1}^{N} l\varepsilon \leq 2\varepsilon.$$

Thus

$$\left| \frac{2}{N^2} \sum_{l=1}^{N} \sum_{v=0}^{l-1} R(v) \right| \leq \frac{2}{N^2} \left| \sum_{l=1}^{M} \sum_{v=0}^{l-1} R(v) \right| + 2\varepsilon.$$

Let $N \to \infty$. Since M is fixed, the first term on the right vanishes. Since ε is an arbitrary positive number, we must have

$$\lim_{N \to \infty} \frac{2}{N^2} \sum_{l=1}^{N} \sum_{v=0}^{l-1} R(v) = 0,$$

and so $E[\bar{Y}_N^2] \to 0$. This completes the proof. ■

Using Chebyshev's inequality

$$\Pr\{|\bar{X}_N - m| > \varepsilon\} \leq \frac{E[(\bar{X}_N - m)^2]}{\varepsilon^2}, \qquad \varepsilon > 0,$$

we see that (5.3) implies

$$\lim_{N \to \infty} \Pr\{|\bar{X}_N - m| > \varepsilon\} = 0, \tag{5.4}$$

for all $\varepsilon > 0$. Thus, for sufficiently large N, (5.4) furnishes grounds for believing that the time average $\bar{X}_N$ is approximately m, and thus provides an estimate for this unknown mean.

If the correlation becomes negligible for sufficiently large lags, viz.,

$$\lim_{v \to \infty} R(v) = 0, \tag{5.5}$$

then (5.2) will hold, since for any $M < N$ we may write

$$\frac{1}{N} \sum_{v=0}^{N-1} R(v) = \frac{1}{N} \sum_{v=0}^{M-1} R(v) + \frac{1}{N} \sum_{v=M}^{N-1} R(v),$$

and, in view of (5.5), the second term on the right may be made smaller in absolute value than any preassigned ε by choosing M sufficiently large, and for any fixed M, the first term on the right vanishes as N approaches infinity. Thus (5.5) is a sufficient condition to insure that the time averages $\bar{X}_N$ converge to the mean m.

Suppose $\{X_n\}$ is a covariance stationary process having a mean of zero. The same theorem may be used to obtain conditions under which the sample average covariance

$$\hat{R}_N(v) = \frac{1}{N} \sum_{k=0}^{N-1} X_k X_{k+v} \tag{5.6}$$

will converge to the covariance

$$R(v) = E[X_n X_{n+v}]. \tag{5.7}$$

If we write $W_k = X_k X_{k+v}$, then (5.6) becomes

$$\hat{R}_N(v) = \frac{1}{N} \sum_{k=0}^{N-1} W_k = \bar{W}_N .$$

Thus, if $\{W_k\}$ forms a covariance stationary process for which

$$\lim_{T \to \infty} \frac{1}{T} \sum_{l=0}^{T-1} E[\{W_n - R(v)\} \cdot \{W_{n+l} - R(v)\}] = 0, \tag{5.8}$$

then

$$\lim_{N \to \infty} E[(\hat{R}_N(v) - R(v))^2] = 0.$$

Of course, the conditions required on the covariance of $\{W_k\}$ are conditions on the fourth product moments of the original $\{X_n\}$ process, which limits the general applicability of this result. However, a Gaussian process is determined by its mean and covariance functions, and thus, for a Gaussian process, (5.8) can be stated in terms of the covariance. Condition (5.8) requires

$$\lim_{T\to\infty} \frac{1}{T} \sum_{l=0}^{T-1} E[\{X_n X_{n+v} - R(v)\} \cdot \{X_{n+l} X_{n+l+v} - R(v)\}] = 0,$$

which reduces to

$$\lim_{T\to\infty} \frac{1}{T} \sum_{l=0}^{T-1} \{E[X_n X_{n+v} X_{n+l} X_{n+l+v}] - R(v)^2\} = 0.$$

The fourth product moment of joint normally distributed random variables having zero mean is given by

$$E[X_i X_j X_k X_l] = \sigma_{ij}\sigma_{kl} + \sigma_{ik}\sigma_{jl} + \sigma_{il}\sigma_{jk},$$

where σ_{ij} is the covariance between X_i and X_j. Relevant to this case, we have

$$E[X_n X_{n+v} X_{n+l} X_{n+l+v}] = R(v)^2 + R(l)^2 + R(l-v)R(l+v).$$

Thus, in the case of a Gaussian process, (5.8) requires

$$\lim_{T\to\infty} \frac{1}{T} \sum_{l=0}^{T-1} \{R(l)^2 + R(l-v)R(l+v)\} = 0. \tag{5.9}$$

For any real numbers a, b, we have $|ab| \le a^2 + b^2$. Thus

$$|R(l-v)R(l+v)| \le R(l-v)^2 + R(l+v)^2.$$

Now

$$\lim_{T\to\infty} \frac{1}{T} \sum_{l=0}^{T-1} R(l)^2 = 0 \tag{5.10}$$

implies

$$\lim_{T\to\infty} \frac{1}{T} \sum_{l=0}^{T-1} R(l \pm v)^2 = 0,$$

since the two sums differ by at most a finite number of terms. In view of the inequality, (5.9) will hold provided only that (5.10) is assumed. We have thus demonstrated the following theorem.

Theorem 5.2. *Let $\{X_n\}$ be a Gaussian covariance stationary process having covariance function $R(v)$ and a mean of zero. If*

$$\lim_{T\to\infty} \frac{1}{T} \sum_{v=0}^{T-1} R(v)^2 = 0,$$

then, for any fixed $v = 0, \pm 1, \ldots,$

$$\lim_{T\to\infty} E[|\hat{R}_T(v) - R(v)|^2] = 0,$$

where $\hat{R}_T(v)$ *is the sample covariance function*

$$\hat{R}_T(v) = \frac{1}{T}\sum_{l=0}^{T-1} X_l X_{l+v}.$$

As a last topic before proceeding to the strong convergence theorem we will prove a general mean square ergodic theorem.

Theorem 5.3. *Let* $\{X_n\}$ *be a covariance stationary process and let*

$$\bar{X}_n = \frac{1}{n}(X_1 + \cdots + X_n)$$

define the sequence of time averages. Then there exists a random variable $\bar{X}$ *that is the mean square limit of* $\{\bar{X}_n\}$,

$$\lim_{n\to\infty} \|\bar{X}_n - \bar{X}\| = 0.$$

Proof. Before commencing the proof let us remark that, in general, the limit $\bar{X}$ will be random. Theorem 5.1 gives the necessary and sufficient additional assumptions needed if it is to be concluded that $\bar{X}$ is, in fact, not random, but is the constant $m = E[X_1]$.

According to the Cauchy criterion for mean square convergence, to prove the theorem it suffices to show

$$\lim_{m,n\to\infty} \|\bar{X}_n - \bar{X}_m\| = 0.$$

Set

$$\mu_N = \inf\|\lambda_1 X_1 + \cdots + \lambda_N X_N\|,$$

where the infimum is over all nonnegative λ_i satisfying $\lambda_1 + \cdots + \lambda_N = 1$. Notice that $\mu_{N+1} \le \mu_N$, and set

$$\mu = \lim_{N\to\infty} \mu_N = \inf \mu_N.$$

Suppose, for the moment, that $m < n$ and calculate as follows:

$$\|\bar{X}_m + \bar{X}_n\| = \left\|\left(\frac{1}{m}+\frac{1}{n}\right)X_1 + \cdots + \left(\frac{1}{m}+\frac{1}{n}\right)X_m + \frac{1}{n}X_{m+1} + \cdots + \frac{1}{n}X_n\right\|$$

$$= 2\|\lambda_1 X_1 + \cdots + \lambda_n X_n\| \ge 2\mu,$$

where

$$\lambda_i = \frac{1}{2}\left(\frac{1}{m} + \frac{1}{n}\right), \qquad i = 1, \ldots, m,$$

$$\lambda_i = \frac{1}{2n}, \qquad i = m+1, \ldots, n.$$

Of course, the same inequality obtains if $m > n$. Now, the key to the proof of the theorem is to show

$$\lim_{n\to\infty} \|\bar{X}_n\| = \mu, \tag{5.11}$$

because, if we can do this, from the parallelogram law and the inequality just shown,

$$\begin{aligned}\|\bar{X}_n - \bar{X}_m\|^2 &= 2\|\bar{X}_n\|^2 + 2\|\bar{X}_m\|^2 - \|\bar{X}_n + \bar{X}_m\|^2\\ &\le 2\|\bar{X}_n\|^2 + 2\|\bar{X}_m\|^2 - (2\mu)^2\\ &\le 2\{|\,\|\bar{X}_n\|^2 - \mu^2| + |\,\|\bar{X}_m\|^2 - \mu^2|\},\end{aligned}$$

and (5.11) implies that the right-hand side vanishes.

Thus we concentrato on verifying (5.11). Let a positive ε be given and choose N and $\lambda_1, \ldots, \lambda_N$ satisfying

$$\|\lambda_1 X_1 + \cdots + \lambda_N X_N\| \le \mu + \varepsilon,$$

where, of course, $\lambda_i \ge 0$ and $\lambda_1 + \cdots + \lambda_N = 1$. Let

$$Y_k = \lambda_1 X_k + \cdots + \lambda_N X_{k+N-1}.$$

Then $\{Y_k\}$ is a covariance stationary process and

$$\|Y_k\| \le \mu + \varepsilon, \qquad k = 1, 2, \ldots.$$

We compute

$$\begin{aligned}\bar{Y}_n &= \frac{1}{n}(Y_1 + \cdots + Y_n)\\ &= \frac{1}{n}(\lambda_1 X_1 + \lambda_2 X_2 + \cdots + \lambda_N X_N\\ &\quad + \lambda_1 X_2 + \lambda_2 X_3 + \cdots + \lambda_N X_{N+1} + \cdots\\ &\quad + \lambda_1 X_n + \lambda_2 X_{n+1} + \cdots + \lambda_N X_{N+n-1})\\ &= \lambda_1 \bar{X}_{1,n} + \lambda_2 \bar{X}_{2,n} + \cdots + \lambda_N \bar{X}_{N,n}\end{aligned}$$

where

$$\bar{X}_{k,n} = \frac{1}{n}(X_k + X_{k+1} + \cdots + X_{k+n-1}).$$

Since $\bar{X}_n = \bar{X}_{1,n}$ and $\lambda_1 - 1 = -(\lambda_2 + \cdots + \lambda_N)$, we may write

$$\bar{Y}_n - \bar{X}_n = \lambda_2(\bar{X}_{2,n} - \bar{X}_{1,n}) + \cdots + \lambda_N(\bar{X}_{N,n} - \bar{X}_{1,n}).$$

Then, using the triangle inequality

$$\|\bar{Y}_n - \bar{X}_n\| \le \lambda_2 \|\bar{X}_{2,n} - \bar{X}_{1,n}\| + \cdots + \lambda_N \|\bar{X}_{N,n} - \bar{X}_{1,n}\|.$$

But

$$\begin{aligned}
\|\bar{X}_{k,n} - \bar{X}_{1,n}\| &= \frac{1}{n} \|(X_k + \cdots + X_{k+n-1}) - (X_1 + \cdots + X_n)\| \\
&= \frac{1}{n} \|X_{n+1} + \cdots + X_{n+k-1} - X_1 - \cdots - X_{k-1}\| \\
&\le \frac{1}{n} \{\|X_{n+1}\| + \cdots + \|X_{n+k-1}\| + \|X_1\| + \cdots + \|X_{k-1}\|\} \\
&= \frac{2k-2}{n} \|X_1\|, \qquad \text{for} \quad k = 2, \ldots, N.
\end{aligned}$$

Thus

$$\begin{aligned}
\|\bar{Y}_n - \bar{X}_n\| &\le \sum_{k=2}^{N} \lambda_k \frac{2k}{n} \|X_1\| \\
&\le \frac{2N\|X_1\|}{n}.
\end{aligned}$$

It follows that

$$\lim_{n\to\infty} \|\bar{Y}_n - \bar{X}_n\| = 0.$$

To conclude the proof of (5.11),

$$\begin{aligned}
\mu \le \|\bar{X}_n\| &\le \|\bar{X}_n - \bar{Y}_n\| + \|\bar{Y}_n\| \\
&\le \|\bar{X}_n - \bar{Y}_n\| + \mu + \varepsilon
\end{aligned}$$

Since $\|\bar{X}_n - \bar{Y}_n\| \to 0$ as $n \to \infty$ and ε is arbitrary, we must have

$$\lim_{n\to\infty} \|\bar{X}_n\| = \mu.$$

This validates (5.11) and completes the proof of the theorem. ■

THE STRONG ERGODIC THEOREM

Theorem 5.4. *Let $\{X_n; n = 0, 1, 2, \ldots\}$ be a strictly stationary process having finite mean $m = E[X_n]$ Let*

$$\bar{X}_n = \frac{1}{n}(X_0 + \cdots + X_{n-1})$$

be the sample time average. Then, with probability one, the sequence $\{\bar{X}_n\}$ converges to some limit random variable, denoted $\bar{X}$. That is,

$$\Pr\left\{\lim_{n\to\infty} \bar{X}_n = \bar{X}\right\} = 1.$$

Proof. Let

$$\bar{X}^* = \limsup_{n\to\infty} \bar{X}_n, \qquad \text{and} \qquad \bar{X}_* = \liminf_{n\to\infty} \bar{X}_n.$$

The event that the sequence $\{\bar{X}_n\}$ converges is, of course, the event that $\bar{X}^* = \bar{X}_*$, and the complementary event, the event that $\{\bar{X}_n\}$ does not converge, is the event $\bar{X}^* > \bar{X}_*$. Let K denote this latter event. We want to show

$$\Pr\{K\} = 0.$$

Consider for the moment a particular realization $X_0 = x_0$, $X_1 = x_1$, $\ldots$, for which the event K occurs. Then $\bar{X}^* = \bar{x}^* > \bar{X}_* = \bar{x}_*$, and for some rationals $\alpha < \beta$ we must have

$$\bar{x}^* > \beta > \alpha > \bar{x}_*.$$

Since there are only denumerably many pairs of rationals we may let $(\alpha_1, \beta_1), (\alpha_2, \beta_2), \ldots$ be an enumeration of all such pairs for which $\alpha_k < \beta_k$. Let K_k be the event

$$\bar{X}^* > \beta_k > \alpha_k > \bar{X}_*.$$

If the event K occurs, then for some k, the event K_k must occur. We showed this just above. Conversely, if some K_k occurs, then so does the event K. Thus $K = \bigcup_{k=1}^{\infty} K_k$, and

$$\Pr\{K\} \le \sum_{k=1}^{\infty} \Pr\{K_k\}.$$

It follows that, to prove $\Pr\{K\} = 0$, it suffices to show that for every k, $\Pr\{K_k\} = 0$. That is, if α and β are arbitrary rational numbers with $\alpha < \beta$, we need only show

$$\Pr\{\bar{X}^* > \beta > \alpha > \bar{X}_*\} = 0.$$

Let A denote the event $\bar{X}^* > \beta > \alpha > \bar{X}_*$ and let $I(A)$ be the indicator random variable of the event A:

$$I(A) = \begin{cases} 1, & \text{if } A \text{ occurs,} \\ 0, & \text{if } A \text{ does not occur.} \end{cases}$$

To show $\Pr\{A\} = E[I(A)] = 0$, we first prove the inequalities

$$E[(X_0 - \beta)I(A)] \geq 0, \tag{5.12}$$

and

$$E[(\alpha - X_0)I(A)] \geq 0. \tag{5.13}$$

These, added together, give

$$E[(\alpha - \beta)I(A)] \geq 0,$$

or

$$(\alpha - \beta) \Pr\{A\} \geq 0.$$

Since $\alpha < \beta$, this will imply $\Pr\{A\} = 0$, which will complete the proof. Our objective will be to establish the inequalities (5.12) and (5.13).

Certainly $I(A) = I(\limsup \bar{X}_n > \beta$ and $\liminf \bar{X}_n < \alpha)$ is a function of the entire sequence $X_0, X_1, \ldots$. Recall that the limits superior and inferior of a real sequence $a_1, a_2, \ldots$ coincide with the corresponding limits on any shifted sequence $a_{k+1}, a_{k+2}, \ldots$. It follows that

$$I(A) = I(\limsup \bar{X}_{k+n} > \beta \text{ and } \liminf \bar{X}_{k+n} < \alpha), \tag{5.14}$$

for any fixed k, and $I(A)$ is invariant under time shifts in this sense. This will be important later.

Introduce the notation $Y_i = X_i - \beta$, $i = 0, 1, \ldots$, and

$$S_{i,k} = Y_i + Y_{i+1} + \cdots + Y_{i+k-1}, \qquad k \geq 1.$$

There are k summands in $S_{i,k}$, the initial one being Y_i. Let

$$M_{i,n} = \max\{0, S_{i,1}, \ldots, S_{i,n}\}.$$

Of course,

$$\begin{aligned} 0 < S_{0,n} &= Y_0 + \cdots + Y_{n-1} \\ &= (X_0 + \cdots + X_{n-1}) - n\beta, \end{aligned}$$

when and only when

$$\bar{X}_n = n^{-1}(X_0 + \cdots + X_{n-1}) > \beta.$$

The event A entails that the inequality $\bar{X}_n > \beta$ takes place for some positive integer, which in turn implies that the event $\{M_{0,n} > 0\}$ must occur for n sufficiently large. Consequently, we have

$$A \subset \bigcup_{n=1}^{\infty} \{M_{0,n} > 0\},$$

and in view of the monotone nature of $M_{0,n}$

$$I(A) = \lim_{n\to\infty} I(A)I\{M_{0,n} > 0\},$$

where, as usual, $I\{M_{0,n} > 0\}$ denotes the indicator random variable of the event $\{M_{0,n} > 0\}$. Finally, by virtue of the hypothesis $E[|Y_0|] < \infty$, we are permitted to interchange limit and expectation and thereby achieve the formula

$$E[Y_0 I(A)] = \lim_{n\to\infty} E[Y_0 I\{M_{0,m} > 0\}I(A)].$$

We can now proceed to the verification of the two inequalities (5.12) and (5.13).

Obviously,

$$\begin{aligned} M_{1,n} &= \max\{0, S_{1,1}, \ldots, S_{1,n}\} \\ &\geq S_{1,k}, \qquad \text{for} \quad k = 1, \ldots, n-1, \end{aligned}$$

and so

$$Y_0 + M_{1,n} \geq Y_0 + S_{1,k} = S_{0,k+1}, \qquad k = 1, \ldots, n-1.$$

We write this as

$$Y_0 \geq S_{0,k} - M_{1,n}, \qquad \text{for} \quad k = 2, \ldots, n.$$

Trivially, since $M_{1,n} \geq 0$,

$$Y_0 \geq Y_0 - M_{1,n},$$

which, combined with the previous inequality, gives

$$Y_0 \geq \max\{S_{0,1}, \ldots, S_{0,n}\} - M_{1,n},$$

and, since $M_{0,n} = \max\{0, S_{0,1}, \ldots, S_{0,n}\}$,

$$Y_0 \geq M_{0,n} - M_{1,n}, \qquad \text{if} \quad M_{0,n} > 0.$$

Thus

$$\begin{aligned} E[Y_0 I\{M_{0,n} > 0\}I(A)] &\geq E[(M_{0,n} - M_{1,n})I\{M_{0,n} > 0\}I(A)] \\ &= E[M_{0,n} I(A)] - E[M_{1,n} I\{M_{0,n} > 0\} I(A)] \\ &\geq E[M_{0,n} I(A)] - E[M_{1,n} I(A)], \end{aligned}$$

where the last inequality is a consequence of $M_{1,n} \geq 0$. Recall that the event A is invariant under shifts in time [see (5.14)]. Also since the process is stationary, $M_{0,n}$ and $M_{1,n}$ share the same distribution. Thus $E[M_{0,n} I(A)] = E[M_{1,n} I(A)]$, and the last right-hand side in the above string of inequalities is zero. Hence

$$E[Y_0 I(A)] = \lim_{n\to\infty} E[Y_0 I\{M_{0,n} > 0\} I(A)] \geq 0.$$

Since $Y_0 = X_0 - \beta$, we have demonstrated (5.12), that $E[(X_0 - \beta)I(A)] \geq 0$. The proof of (5.13) is accomplished by applying exactly parallel reasoning to $\tilde{Y}_k = \alpha - X_k$. As these inequalities were all that was needed, the proof of the theorem is complete. ■

Remark 5.1. Under the conditions of the strong ergodic theorem, it is true in addition that

$$\lim_{n\to\infty} E[|\bar{X}_n - \bar{X}|] = 0. \tag{5.15}$$

Hence

$$E[\bar{X}] = E[X_n] = m. \tag{5.16}$$

Remark 5.2. Further elementary considerations show that

$$\bar{X} = \lim_{n\to\infty} \frac{1}{n}(X_k + \cdots + X_{k+n-1}), \tag{5.17}$$

for every $k = 1, 2, \ldots$. Suppose the random variables $X_0, X_1, \ldots$ are, in addition, independent. In view of (5.17), $\bar{X}$ is then independent of $X_0, \ldots, X_{k-1}$ for every k, and consequently independent of $\bar{X}_k$. Since $\bar{X} = \lim \bar{X}_k$, we must have $\bar{X}$ independent of itself. The only possibility, then, is for $\bar{X}$ to be constant (why?), and (5.16) tells us that constant must be m. Thus $\lim_{n\to\infty} \bar{X}_n = m$ for every sequence of independent identically distributed random variables having finite mean m. We have thus verified the strong law of large numbers.

The strong law motivates a desire to find general conditions under which the limit random variable $\bar{X}$ is constant. In the mean square ergodic theorem, this was the result if and only if $\bar{X}_n$ and X_1 were asymptotically uncorrelated. The situation is not this simple under the weaker assumption of the strong ergodic theorem. Nonetheless, some principles can be laid down.

If $x = (x_0, x_1, \ldots)$ is a real sequence, let Tx denote the shifted sequence $(x_1, x_2, \ldots)$. We call T the *shift operator*. A set A of real sequences is called *shift invariant* when Tx is an element of A if and only if x is in A. Several examples will kindle the imagination:

$$A_1 = \{x : \text{for some } k = 1, 2, \ldots, x_k = x_{k+1} = \cdots = 0\},$$
$$A_2 = \{x : \lim\sup x_n = a\},$$
$$A_3 = \{x : \lim n^{-1}(x_1 + \cdots + x_n) = b\}.$$

The student should verify that A_1, A_2 and A_3 are shift invariant sets.

A stationary process is said to be *ergodic* if $\Pr\{(X_0, X_1 \ldots) \in A\}$ is either zero or one whenever A is shift invariant.

Theorem 5.5. *Let $\{X_n\}$ be an ergodic stationary process having a finite mean m. Then, with probability one,*

$$\lim_{n\to\infty} \frac{1}{n}(X_1 + \cdots + X_n) = m,$$

Proof. For each real a define

$$A = \{x = (x_0, x_1 \ldots); \lim_{n\to\infty} n^{-1}(x_1 + \cdots + x_n) \le a\}.$$

Then A is shift invariant. It follows that

$$\begin{aligned}\Pr\{(X_0, X_1, \ldots) \in A\} &= \Pr\{\lim n^{-1}(X_1 + \cdots + X_n) \le a\}\\ &= \Pr\{\bar{X} \le a\} = 0 \quad \text{or} \quad 1,\end{aligned}$$

for every constant a. Hence $\bar{X}$ is necessarily a constant random variable. In view of (5.16), that constant can only be m. ■

It is obviously desirable to have some equivalent and more accessible formulations of ergodicity. Unfortunately not much can be done here. We state some results, without proof, in the next theorem.

Theorem 5.6. *Let $\{X_n\}$ be a stationary process. The following conditions are equivalent:*

(a) *$\{X_n\}$ is ergodic;*

(b) *For every shift invariant set A,*

$$\Pr\{(X_0, X_1, \ldots) \in A\} = 0 \quad \text{or} \quad 1;$$

(c) *For every set A of real sequences $(x_0, x_1, \ldots)$,*

$$\lim_{n\to\infty} \frac{1}{n} \sum_{j=1}^{n} I\{(X_j, X_{j+1}, \ldots) \in A\} = \Pr\{(X_0, X_1, \ldots) \in A\};$$

(d) *For every $k = 1, 2, \ldots$ and every set A of real vectors $(x_0, \ldots, x_k)$,*

$$\lim_{n\to\infty} \frac{1}{n} \sum_{j=1}^{n} I\{(X_j, \ldots, X_{j+k}) \in A\} = \Pr\{(X_0, \ldots, X_k) \in A\};$$

(e) *For every k and every function ϕ of $k+1$ variables,*

$$\lim_{n\to\infty} \frac{1}{n} \sum_{j=1}^{n} \phi(X_j, \ldots, X_{j+k}) = E[\phi(X_0, \ldots, X_k)],$$

provided the expectation exists;

(f) *For every function ϕ of a real sequence $(x_0, x_1, \ldots)$.*

$$\lim_{n\to\infty} \frac{1}{n} \sum_{j=1}^{n} \phi(X_j, X_{j+1}, \ldots) = E[\phi(X_0, X_1, \ldots)],$$

provided the expectation exists.

In these conditions, the existence of the limits is a consequence of the strong ergodic theorem. For example, if ϕ is a function of $k+1$ variables for which $E[|\phi(X_0, \ldots, X_k)|] < \infty$, then

$$Y_n = \phi(X_n, \ldots, X_{n+k}), \qquad n = 0, 1, \ldots,$$

determines a stationary process to which the strong ergodic theorem applies. Hence, $\lim_{n\to\infty} n^{-1} \sum_{j=1}^{n} Y_j$ exists. What is asserted in condition (e) of Theorem 5.6 is that this limit is constant.

Remark 5.3. It is obvious from the equivalent condition of Theorem 5.6 that, for any function ϕ, the sequence

$$Y_n = \phi(X_n, X_{n+1}, \ldots)$$

generates an ergodic stationary process whenever $\{X_n\}$ is ergodic and stationary.

A stationary process $\{X_n\}$ is said to be *mixing* (or *strong mixing*) if for all sets A and B of real sequences

$$\lim_{n\to\infty} \Pr\{(X_1, X_2, \ldots) \in A \text{ and } (X_{n+1}, X_{n+2}, \ldots) \in B\}$$
$$= \Pr\{(X_1, X_2, \ldots) \in A\} \Pr\{(X_1, X_2, \ldots) \in B\}.$$

Mixing is a form of asymptotic independence, and therefore that every mixing process is ergodic is perhaps not surprising. We now validate this statement. Suppose $A = B$ is an invariant set. Then $(X_n, X_{n+1}, \ldots) \in B$ if and only if $(X_1, X_2, \ldots) \in B$. The mixing property applies, yielding

$$\Pr\{(X_1, X_2, \ldots) \in A\} = \Pr\{(X_1, X_2, \ldots) \in A, (X_n, X_{n+1}, \ldots) \in A\}$$
$$\to [\Pr\{(X_1, X_2 \ldots) \in A\}]^2, \qquad \text{as} \quad n \to \infty.$$

The only possibilities are $\Pr\{(X_1, X_2, \ldots) \in A\} = 0$ or 1, so the process is ergodic. There are other equivalent formulations for mixing. For example, it is enough to check that, for arbitrary $k = 1, 2, \ldots$ and sets A, B in k-space, that

$$\lim_{n \to \infty} \Pr\{(X_1, \ldots, X_k) \in A \text{ and } (X_{n+1}, \ldots, X_{n+k}) \in B\}$$
$$= \Pr\{(X_1, \ldots, X_k) \in A\} \Pr\{(X_1, \ldots, X_k) \in B\}.$$

We would be remiss in our duties if we did not at least indicate that what we have exposed heretofore is not ergodic theory, but mostly the application of ergodic theory to stationary processes. The modern view is much more general. Let L be an abstract space of functions f for which some notion of integral $\int f$ is defined. Let T be an operator that carries a function f in L into the function Tf in L. Ergodic theory is the study of iterates T^n of the operators T that satisfy:

(i) If f is a nonnegative function then so is Tf, and

(ii) $\int |Tf| \le \int |f|$.

In the context of a stationary process $\{X_n\}$, L consists of all functions $f(\{X_n\}) = \phi(X_0, X_1, \ldots)$ for which $E[|\phi(X_0, X_1, \ldots)|] < \infty$, the notion of integral is the expectation, $\int f(\{X_n\}) = E[\phi(X_0, X_1, \ldots)]$, and T is related to the shift operator by

$$T\phi(X_0, X_1, X_2, \ldots) = \phi(X_1, X_2, \ldots).$$

6: *Applications of Ergodic Theory*

At the start of Section 5 mention was made of the ergodic theorem used to justify time averages such as $\bar{X}_n = n^{-1}(X_0 + \cdots + X_{n-1})$ as estimators of the corresponding process expectations, in this case $m = E[X_0]$. There are numerous other applications. We develop three examples.

A. BRANCHING PROCESSES IN RANDOM ENVIRONMENTS

A key feature of the branching processes introduced in Example F of Chapter 2 and thoroughly discussed in Chapter 8 is the invariance over time of the offspring distribution. But there are a multitude of situations in which the offspring distribution depends on a changing environment. As an introduction to recent work in this area, we treat the extinction problem in an environment that varies randomly according to a stationary ergodic process.

We postulate a stationary ergodic process $\zeta = \{\zeta_n\}_{n=0}^{\infty}$, called the *environmental process.* To each value ζ_n there corresponds an offspring distribution $p_{\zeta_n} = \{p_n(i)\}_{i=0}^{\infty}$. Of course, $p_n(i) \geq 0$ and $\sum_{i=0}^{\infty} p_n(i) = 1$. Then $\{p_{\zeta_n}\}_{n=0}^{\infty}$ is again a stationary ergodic process, albeit one whose values are discrete probability distributions.

Let $Z_n(=Z(n))$ count the number of particles existing in the nth generation, and take $Z_0 = 1$. Conditional on a prescribed environment $\zeta = \{\zeta_n\}$, we postulate that $\{Z_n\}$ evolves as an ordinary branching process excepting only that the offspring distribution in generation n is p_{ζ_n}. To be precise, we assume

$$E[s^{Z(n+1)} | \zeta_0, \ldots, \zeta_n; Z_0, \ldots, Z_n] = [\phi_{\zeta_n}(s)]^{Z(n)}, \qquad n = 0, 1, 2, \ldots, |s| \leq 1,$$

where

$$\phi_{\zeta_n}(s) = \sum_{j=0}^{\infty} p_n(j) s^j$$

is the probability generating function corresponding to p_{ζ_n}. In other words, conditioned on the past environment and population levels, $Z(n+1)$ is the sum of $Z(n)$ litters (or broods) of offspring, where the sizes of each brood are independent and identically distributed random variables, following the common distribution p_{ζ_n}.

Let B_n be the event that $Z_n = 0$, and clearly $B = \bigcup_{n=1}^{\infty} B_n$ connotes the event of (ultimate) extinction. It is useful to introduce the notation

$$q(\zeta) = \Pr\{B | \zeta\}$$

and

$$q = \Pr\{B\} = E[q(\zeta)].$$

Conditioned on the environmental process ζ, $\{Z_n\}$ behaves as an ordinary, although *time-inhomogeneous*, branching process, and the techniques of Chapter 8 lead us easily to the following formula*:

$$E[s^{Z(n+1)} | \zeta] = [\phi_{\zeta_0}(\phi_{\zeta_1}(\cdots(\phi_{\zeta_n}(s))\cdots))].$$

* We assume throughout that for any Z, the associated $\phi_{\zeta_i}(s)$ are never constant functions.

We frequently write ϕ_i for brevity in place of ϕ_{ζ_i} if no ambiguity is likely in the interpretation. Obviously

$$q(\zeta) = \lim_{n\to\infty} \phi_0(\phi_1(\cdots(\phi_n(0))\cdots))$$

$$= \phi_{\zeta_0}\left[\lim_{n\to\infty} \phi_1\phi_2(\cdots(\phi_n(0)))\cdots)\right],$$

or

$$q(\zeta) = \phi_{\zeta_0}[q(T\zeta)], \tag{6.1}$$

where $T\zeta$ denotes the shifted environmental sequence $\{\zeta_1, \zeta_2, \ldots\}$. The important functional equation $q(\zeta) = \phi_{\zeta_0}[q(T\zeta)]$ is the stochastic analog of the equation $s = \phi(s)$ of Chapter 8.

Consider the event $\{q(\zeta) = 1\}$. In words, this event occurs whenever the random environment leads to sure (i.e., certain) extinction of the population. We may clearly exploit the properties of the probability generating function ϕ_{ζ_0} in the basic equation $q(\zeta) = \phi_{\zeta_0}[q(T\zeta)]$ to conclude that $q(T\zeta) = 1$ whenever $q(\zeta) = 1$. That is, the event $\{q(\zeta) = 1\}$ is shift invariant. By assumption, the environmental process $\zeta = \{\zeta_n\}$ is ergodic, and therefore we have

$$\Pr\{q(\zeta) = 1\} = 0 \quad \text{or} \quad 1. \tag{6.2}$$

Let $m_{\zeta_n} = \sum_{j=0}^{\infty} jp_n(j)$ be the conditional mean, given the environment, of the nth generation's offspring distribution. The $\{m_{\zeta_n}\}$ is again a stationary ergodic process, and if

$$E[|\log m_{\zeta_0}|] < \infty, \tag{6.3}$$

the strong ergodic theorem tells us

$$\lim_{n\to\infty} n^{-1} \sum_{k=1}^{n} \log m_{\zeta_k} = E[\log m_{\zeta_0}].$$

Let us assume (6.3) and, in addition,

$$\Pr\{q(\zeta) < 1\} = 1, \tag{6.4}$$

and see where this leads us. Probability generating functions are increasing and convex so that

$$m_{\zeta_0} = \phi_{\zeta_0}'(1) \geq \frac{1 - \phi_{\zeta_0}(s)}{1 - s}, \qquad \text{for any} \quad s \in [0, 1). \tag{6.5}$$

According to (6.4), $q(\zeta) < 1$, and added to the basic functional equation $q(\zeta) = \phi_{\zeta_0}[q(T\zeta)]$, we stipulated equivalent to (6.4) that $q(T\zeta) < 1$ (see the footnote on p. 490). This allows the substitution $q(\zeta) = q(T\zeta)$ from (6.1) in (6.5) to obtain

$$m_{\zeta_0} \geq \frac{1 - \phi_{\zeta_0}[q(T\zeta)]}{1 - q(T\zeta)} = \frac{1 - q(\zeta)}{1 - q(T\zeta)}.$$

The stationary property extends this to

$$m_{\zeta_n} \geq \frac{1 - q(T^n\zeta)}{1 - q(T^{n+1}\zeta)},$$

where $T^n\zeta$ is the sequence $(\zeta_n, \zeta_{n+1}, \ldots)$. A collapsing sum appears in

$$\begin{aligned}\frac{1}{n}\sum_{k=0}^{n-1} \log m_{\zeta_k} &\geq \frac{1}{n}\sum_{k=0}^{n-1} \log\left\{\frac{1 - q(T^k\zeta)}{1 - q(T^{k+1}\zeta)}\right\} \\ &= \frac{1}{n}[\log(1 - q(\zeta)) - \log(1 - q(T^n\zeta))] \\ &\geq \frac{1}{n}\log[1 - q(\zeta)].\end{aligned}$$

If $E[|\log m_{\zeta_0}|] < \infty$, as we have assumed, then the left-hand side converges to $E[\log m_{\zeta_0}]$ by the strong ergodic theorem, while the right vanishes. Thus

$$E[\log m_{\zeta_0}] \geq 0.$$

It is possible to strengthen the conclusion by ruling out the possibility $E[\log m_{\zeta_0}] = 0$. To avoid a more technical proof, let us assume

$$E[|\log[1 - q(\zeta)] - \log[1 - q(T\zeta)]|] < \infty.$$

Then

$$Y_n = \log[1 - q(T^n\zeta)] - \log[1 - q(T^{n+1}\zeta)]$$

forms an ergodic stationary process to which the ergodic theorem applies. Thus

$$\begin{aligned}E\left[\log\frac{1 - q(\zeta)}{1 - q(T\zeta)}\right] &= \lim_{n\to\infty}\frac{1}{n}\sum_{k=0}^{n-1}\log\left(\frac{1 - q(T^k\zeta)}{1 - q(T^{k+1}\zeta)}\right) \\ &= \lim_{n\to\infty}\frac{1}{n}\{\log[1 - q(\zeta)] - \log[1 - q(T^n\zeta)]\} \qquad (6.6) \\ &\geq 0.\end{aligned}$$

Now from (6.5) we know that

$$\log \phi'_{\zeta_0}(1) - \log\left\{\frac{1 - \phi_{\zeta_0}[q(T\zeta)]}{1 - q(T\zeta)}\right\} \geq 0.$$

If we assume $0 = E[\log m_{\zeta_0}] = E[\log \phi'_{\zeta_0}(1)]$, then the inequality

$$0 \leq -E\left[\log\left\{\frac{1-\phi_{\zeta_0}[q(T\zeta)]}{1-q(T\zeta)}\right\}\right]$$

ensues. Comparing to (6.6), we conclude that

$$E\left[\log\left\{\frac{1-\phi_{\zeta_0}[q(T\zeta)]}{1-q(T\zeta)}\right\}\right] = 0,$$

and consequently the only consistent value is $q(T\zeta) = 1$ in violation of the stipulation $\Pr\{q(\zeta) < 1\} = 1$. Therefore, $E[\log m_{\zeta_0}] > 0$ must hold.

To sum up, if $E[\log m_{\zeta_0}] < \infty$, then $\Pr\{q(\zeta) < 1\} = 1$ implies $E[\log m_{\zeta_0}] > 0$. Conversely, $E[\log m_{\zeta_0}] \leq 0$, entails $\Pr\{q(\zeta) = 1\} = 1$. [Use (6.2).]

B. THE RANGE OF A RANDOM WALK

Let $X_1, X_2, \ldots$ be independent identically distributed random variables whose possible values are the integers $0, \pm 1, \pm 2, \ldots$. Consider the partial sum process $S_n = X_1 + \cdots + X_n$, $n \geq 1$, and $S_0 = 0$. Define the range R_n involving the first n sums to be the number of distinct values in $\{S_1, \ldots, S_n\}$. We may write

$$R_n = \sum_{k=1}^{n} I_k$$

where

$$I_k = \begin{cases} 1, & \text{if } S_j \neq S_k, \quad \text{for } j = 1, \ldots, k-1, \\ 0, & \text{otherwise.} \end{cases}$$

Now

$$\begin{aligned} E[I_k] &= \Pr\{S_k - S_{k-1} \neq 0, S_k - S_{k-2} \neq 0, \ldots, S_k - S_1 \neq 0\} \\ &= \Pr\{X_k \neq 0, X_k + X_{k-1} \neq 0, \ldots, X_k + \cdots + X_2 \neq 0\} \\ &= \Pr\{S_1 \neq 0, S_2 \neq 0, \ldots, S_{k-1} \neq 0\} \end{aligned}$$

(since the X_i are independent identically distributed). We obtain

$$\lim_{k\to\infty} E[I_k] = \Pr\{S_n \neq 0 \text{ for all } n \geq 1\}. \tag{6.7}$$

Observe that $\{S_n \neq 0 \text{ for all } n \geq 1\}$ is the event that the $\{S_n\}$ process never returns to its origin $S_0 = 0$. But every convergent sequence also converges in the Cesaro mean sense. From (6.7) then,

$$\lim_{n\to\infty} \frac{E[R_n]}{n} = \lim_{n\to\infty} \frac{1}{n} \sum_{k=1}^{n} E[I_k] = \Pr\{S_n \neq 0 \text{ for all } n \geq 1\}. \tag{6.8}$$

It is a deeper fact that this limit holds even if expectations are not taken on the left. That is, with probability one,

$$\lim_{n\to\infty} \frac{R_n}{n} = \Pr\{S_n \neq 0 \text{ for all } n \geq 1\}. \tag{6.9}$$

We verify this by proving the equivalent pair of inequalities for the limit superior and limit inferior. First, designate m as any positive integer and let Z_k be the number of distinct points visited by the sequence of sums $\{S_i\}$ during the times $(k-1)m+1$ to km. Equivalently, Z_k is the range involved in the collection $\{S_{(k-1)m+1}, \ldots, S_{km}\}$. Note that Z_k depends only on X_n for n between $(k-1)m+1$ and km, so that the Z_k are mutually independent random variables, $|Z_k| \leq m$, and, manifestly, the Z_k are identically distributed. Verify the inequality $R_{km} \leq Z_1 + \cdots + Z_k$ and apply the law of large numbers to obtain

$$\limsup_{k\to\infty} \frac{R_{km}}{km} \leq \limsup_{k\to\infty} \frac{Z_1 + \cdots + Z_k}{mk} = \frac{E[Z_1]}{m}.$$

With $[n/m]$ denoting the largest integer not exceeding n/m, we have $R_n \leq R_{([n/m]+1)m}$, whence

$$\begin{aligned}\limsup_{n\to\infty} \frac{1}{n} R_n &\leq \limsup_{n\to\infty} \frac{([n/m]+1)m}{n} \frac{R_{([n/m]+1)m}}{([n/m]+1)m}\\ &= \frac{E[Z_1]}{m}.\end{aligned}$$

This holds for any m. But $Z_1 = R_m$, so by (6.8)

$$\limsup_{n\to\infty} \frac{1}{n} R_n \leq \limsup_{n\to\infty} \frac{E[R_n]}{n} = \Pr\{S_n \neq 0 \text{ for all } n \geq 1\}. \tag{6.10}$$

The reverse inequality is the deeper one, and for it we invoke the strong ergodic theorem.

Define

$$V_k = \begin{cases} 1, & \text{if } S_j \neq S_k, \quad \text{for all } j > k, \\ 0, & \text{otherwise.} \end{cases}$$

V_k is one, if S_k is a state never visited after time k, and zero, otherwise, and $V_1 + \cdots + V_n$ is the number of states visited up to time n that are never revisited. Since R_n is the number of states visited in time n that are not revisited prior to $n+1$, manifestly $R_n \geq V_1 + \cdots + V_n$. Now

$\{X_k\}$ is a stationary ergodic process (see Problem 21) and by Remark 5.3 so is $\{V_k\}$, since

$$V_k = \begin{cases} 1, & \text{if} \quad X_{k+1} \neq 0, \quad X_{k+1} + X_{k+2} \neq 0, \ldots, \\ 0, & \text{otherwise,} \end{cases}$$

$$= \phi(X_{k+1}, X_{k+2}, \ldots),$$

where

$$\phi(x_1, x_2, \ldots) = \begin{cases} 1, & \text{if} \quad x_1 \neq 0, \quad x_1, + x_2 \neq 0, \quad x_1 + x_2 + x_3 \neq 0, \cdots \\ 0, & \text{otherwise.} \end{cases}$$

The ergodic theorem implies

$$\liminf_{n \to \infty} \frac{R_n}{n} \geq \liminf_n \frac{V_1 + \cdots + V_n}{n} = E[V_1]. \tag{6.11}$$

Of course,

$$E[V_1] = \Pr\{S_k \neq 0, \text{ for all } k \geq 1\}.$$

Combining (6.10) and (6.11), we see that the proof of (6.9) is done.

C. ENTROPY

Probability measures uncertainty about the *occurrence* of a single event. Entropy measures the uncertainty of a collection of events. Let X be a random variable assuming the value i with probability p_i, $i = 1, \ldots, n$. The *entropy of* X, (or of the events $\{X = i\}$ $i = 1, \ldots, n$) is computed according to

$$H(X) = -\sum_{i=1}^{n} p_i \log p_i \tag{6.12}$$

(with the understanding that $0 \cdot \log 0 = 0$). The reader should verify that the definition possesses the following three desirable properties: (i) The entropy of a constant random variable is zero; (ii) If we add the possible value $i + 1$, assigning it probability $p_{i+1} = 0$, the entropy is unchanged; and (iii) The entropy is maximized, with maximum value $\log n$, when $p_1 = \cdots = p_n = 1/n$. This last property agrees with our intuition about uncertainty, e.g., the random variable

$$X_1 = \begin{cases} 1, & \text{with probability } 0.999, \\ 0, & \text{with probability } 0.001, \end{cases}$$

is far more predictable or ascertainable than

$$X_2 = \begin{cases} 1, & \text{with probability } \frac{1}{2} \\ 0, & \text{with probability } \frac{1}{2} \end{cases}$$

It is natural to extend this definition to a pair of random variables X, Y, where $\Pr\{X=i,\ Y=j\}=p_{ij}$, through the formula

$$H(X,\ Y)=-\sum_{i,\ j}p_{ij}\log p_{ij}.$$

Define the *conditional entropy of X given Y* by

$$H(X|Y)=-\sum_{j}\Pr\{Y=j\}\sum_{i}p(i|j)\log p(i|j),$$

where $p(i|j)=\Pr\{X=i|Y=j\}$. Substituting $p(i|j)=p_{ij}/\Pr\{Y=j\}$ gives

$$\begin{aligned}H(X|Y)&=-\sum_{i,\ j}p_{ij}\log[p_{ij}/\Pr\{Y=j\}]\\&=H(X,\ Y)-H(Y).\end{aligned}\tag{6.13}$$

What is important here is that

$$H(X,\ Y)\geq H(Y).\tag{6.14}$$

In words, the uncertainty in a pair of random variables exceeds that of either one.

It is a little harder to show that X given Y has less uncertainty than X unconditionally. Let $q_j=\Pr\{Y=j\}$. Observe that the function $\Gamma(t)=-t\log t$ is concave for $t>0$, and use Jensen's inequality (i.e., the extended definition of convexity, see page 249) to obtain

$$\begin{aligned}H(X|Y)&=\sum_{i}\sum_{j}q_j\Gamma[p(i|j)]\\&\leq\sum_{i}\Gamma\left[\sum_{j}q_jp(i|j)\right]\\&=H(X).\end{aligned}\tag{6.15}$$

It follows from this and (6.13) that

$$H(X,\ Y)\leq H(X)+H(Y).\tag{6.16}$$

We continue to extend the definition of entropy. If $X_1,\ \ldots,\ X_m$ are jointly distributed random variables and $\Pr\{X_1=i_1,\ \ldots,\ X_m=i_m\}=p(i_1,\ \ldots,\ i_m)$, set

$$H(X_1,\ \ldots,\ X_m)=-\sum_{i_1,\ldots,i_m}p(i_1,\ \ldots,\ i_m)\log p(i_1,\ \ldots,\ i_m).$$

We have the results analogous to (6.13) and (6.15),

$$\begin{aligned}&H(X_1,\ \ldots,\ X_m)\\&=H(X_1)+H(X_2|X_1)+H(X_3|X_1,\ X_2)+\cdots+H(X_m|X_1,\ \ldots,\ X_{m-1}),\end{aligned}\tag{6.17}$$

and

$$H(X_k|X_1,\ \ldots,\ X_{k-1})\leq H(X_k|X_2,\ \ldots,\ X_{k-1}).\tag{6.18}$$

Now let $\{X_n\}$ be a stationary process where the possible values of each X_k are the numbers 1, ..., N. The stationary property in conjunction with (6.18) implies

$$H(X_{k-1}|X_1, \dots, X_{k-2}) = H(X_k|X_2, \dots, X_{k-1}) \\ \geq H(X_k|X_1, \dots, X_{k-1}).$$

Since the sequence is monotone decreasing and nonnegative, we may define the entropy of the process $\{X_n\}$ by

$$H(\{X_n\}) = \lim_{k\to\infty} H(X_k|X_1, \dots, X_{k-1}). \tag{6.19}$$

Alternatively, we may write

$$H(\{X_n\}) = \lim_{l\to\infty} \frac{1}{l} H(X_1, \dots ,X_l),$$

since according to (6.17), $(1/l)H(X_1, \dots, X_l)$ is the Cesaro average of $H(X_k|X_1, \dots, X_{k-1})$.

Let $p(i_1, \dots, i_m) = \Pr\{X_1 = i_1, \dots, X_m = i_m\}$. The remarkable result we have been leading to is, with probability one,

$$\lim_{n\to\infty}\left[-\frac{1}{n}\log p(X_0, \dots, X_{n-1})\right] = H(\{X_n\}), \tag{6.20}$$

provided $\{X_n\}$ is ergodic. The right member of (6.20) is constant, computed according to (6.19). The left is a limit taken along a random sequence $X_1, X_2, \dots$. The result says that, for large n, the probability $p(X_1, \dots, X_n)$ of the observed sequence $X_1, X_2, \dots$ is bound to be near $\exp(-nH(\{X_n\}))$.

We continue this example by verifying (6.20) in the special case that $\{X_n\}$ is a stationary ergodic finite Markov chain. Later we will state and prove the general result as a theorem.

Suppose $P = \|P(i, j)\|_{i,j=1}^N$ is the transition matrix of an irreducible finite state Markov chain $\{X_n\}$. We assume $\Pr\{X_0 = i\} = \pi(i)$, where $\{\pi(i)\}_1^N$ is the stationary distribution associated with P. Compute

$$H(X_n|X_0, \dots, X_{n-1}) \\ = -\sum \pi(i_0)P(i_0, i_1) \cdots P(i_{n-2}, i_{n-1}) \sum_{i_n} P(i_{n-1}, i_n) \log P(i_{n-1}, i_n)$$

(by virtue of the Markov chain character of the process and using the fact that $\pi(i)$ is a stationary distribution)

$$= -\sum_{i,j} \pi(i)P(i, j) \log P(i, j),$$

and so

$$H(\{X_n\}) = -\sum_{i,j} \pi(i)P(i, j) \log P(i, j).$$

On the other hand,

$$-\frac{1}{n}\log p(X_0,\dots,X_{n-1}) = -\frac{1}{n}\log\{\pi(X_0)P(X_0,X_1)\cdots P(X_{n-2},X_{n-1})\}$$

$$=\frac{1}{n}\sum_{i=0}^{n-2} W_i - \frac{1}{n}\log\pi(X_0),$$

where

$$W_i = -\log P(X_i, X_{i+1}).$$

An irreducible finite-state Markov chain started with its stationary distribution generates an ergodic stationary process. Since there are only a finite number of states, W_i is bounded. The ergodic theorem applies to yield

$$\lim_{n\to\infty}\left[-\frac{1}{n}\log p(X_0,\dots,X_{n-1})\right]$$

$$=\lim_{n\to\infty}\left[-\frac{1}{n}\sum_{k=0}^{n-2} W_k\right]$$

$$=E[W_0] = -\sum_{i,j}\pi(i)P(i,j)\log P(i,j)$$

$$=H(\{X_n\}),$$

as desired. Here is the general case.

Theorem 6.1. *Let $\{X_n\}$ be an ergodic stationary process having a finite state space $\{1,\dots,N\}$. Let $p(i_1,\dots,i_m)=\Pr\{X_1=i_1,\dots,X_m=i_m\}$, and*

$$H(\{X_n\}) = \lim_{n\to\infty}\left(-\frac{1}{n}\sum_{k=1}^{n}\sum_{i_1,\dots,i_k} p(i_1,\dots,i_k)\log p(i_1,\dots,i_k)\right).$$

Then, with probability one,

$$\lim_{n\to\infty}\left[-\frac{1}{n}\log p(X_1,\dots,X_n)\right] = H(\{X_n\}).$$

Proof. Note first, imposing no limitations on the analysis, we may as well assume $n=\dots,-1,0,+1,\dots$. Indeed, given any one-sided stationary process $\{\tilde{X}_n;\ n=0,1,\dots\}$, a consistent collection of finite-dimensional distributions for a two-sided stationary process is given by

$$\Pr\{X_m=i_m,\dots,X_{m+k}=i_{m+k}\} = \Pr\{\tilde{X}_1=i_m,\dots,\tilde{X}_{k+1}=i_{m+k}\},$$

for any $m=\dots,-1,0,+1,\dots$ and $k=1,2,\dots$.

Set

$$f_k(i; i_1, \ldots, i_k) = \Pr\{X_k = i | X_0 = i_k, \ldots, X_{k-1} = i_1\}$$
$$= \Pr\{X_0 = i | X_{-k} = i_k, \ldots, X_{-1} = i_1\}$$

(by stationarity). The backward martingale convergence theorem (Theorem 8.1 of Chapter 6), assures us of the existence of

$$f(i; i_1, i_2, \ldots) = \lim_{k \to \infty} f_k(i; i_1, \ldots, i_k)$$
$$= \Pr\{X_0 = i | X_{-1} = i_1, X_{-2} = i_2, \ldots\}$$
$$= \Pr\{X_n = i | X_{n-1} = i_1, X_{n-2} = i_2, \ldots\}.$$

Set

$$g_0(i) = -\log \Pr\{X_0 = i\},$$

$$g_k(i_0, i_1, \ldots, i_k) = -\log f_k(i_0; i_1, \ldots, i_k)$$
$$= -\log \Pr\{X_0 = i_0 | X_{-k} = i_k, \ldots, X_{-1} = i_1\}$$
$$= -\log \frac{\Pr\{X_{-k} = i_k, \ldots, X_{-1} = i_1, X_0 = i_0\}}{\Pr\{X_{-k} = i_k, \ldots, X_{-1} = i_1\}},$$

and

$$g(i, i_1, i_2, \ldots) = -\log f(i; i_1, i_2, \ldots).$$

Direct computation produces the equation

$$-\frac{1}{n} \log p(X_0, \ldots, X_{n-1}) = \frac{1}{n} \sum_{k=0}^{n-1} g_k(X_k, \ldots, X_0).$$

If we could replace $g_k(X_k, \ldots, X_0)$ by $g(X_k, X_{k-1}, \ldots)$, the right member would be the type of average to which the ergodic theorem applies, $W_k = g(X_k, X_{k-1}, \ldots)$ being stationary since $\{X_k\}$ is stationary. This adjustment was immediate in the Markov case since there ipso facto $g_k(X_k, \ldots, X_0) = g(X_k, X_{k-1}, \ldots)$ whenever $k \geq 1$.

In our present situation our first task will be to establish

$$E\left[\sup_{n \geq 1} g_n(X_n, \ldots, X_0)\right] < \infty. \tag{6.21}$$

Fix $\lambda > 0$ and decompose the event as indicated:

$$\left\{\sup_{n \geq 1} g_n(X_n, \ldots, X_0) > \lambda\right\} = \bigcup_{n=1}^{\infty} \{g_k(X_k, \ldots, X_0) \leq \lambda \text{ for } k = 1, \ldots, n-1$$
$$\text{and } g_n(X_n, \ldots, X_0) > \lambda\}.$$
$$= \bigcup_{n=1}^{\infty} \{(X_0, \ldots, X_n) \in E_n\},$$

where

$$E_n = \{(i_0, \ldots, i_n); g_k(i_k, \ldots, i_0) \le \lambda \quad \text{for} \quad k = 1, \ldots, n-1 \quad \text{and} \quad g_n(i_n, \ldots, i_0) > \lambda\}.$$

We have partitioned the event on the left on the basis of the first time n for which $g_n(X_n, \ldots, X_0) > \lambda$. As this is a disjoint union

$$\Pr\left\{\sup_{n \ge 1} g_n(X_n, \ldots, X_0) > \lambda\right\} = \sum_{n=1}^{\infty} \Pr\{(X_0, \ldots, X_n) \in E_n\}.$$

Let us partition further by specifying the final state. Let

$$E_n^{(i)} = \{(i_0, \ldots, i_{n-1}); (i_0, \ldots, i_{n-1}, i) \in E_n\}.$$

Consider now

$$\Pr\{(X_0, \ldots, X_n) \in E_n\} = \sum_i \Pr\{(X_0, \ldots, X_{n-1}) \in E_n^{(i)} \quad \text{and} \quad X_n = i\}. \tag{6.22}$$

By the definition of conditional probability, we have

$$\begin{aligned} &\Pr\{X_n = \mathrm{i} \quad \text{and} \quad (X_0, \ldots, X_{n-1}) \in E_n^{(i)}\} \\ &= \sum_{(i_0, \ldots, i_{n-1}) \in E_n^{(i)}} \Pr\{X_n = i | X_0 = i_0, \ldots, X_{n-1} = i_{n-1}\} \\ &\quad \cdot \Pr\{X_0 = i_0, \ldots, X_{n-1} = i_{n-1}\}. \end{aligned} \tag{6.23}$$

The process is stationary, so the conditional probability may be shifted to read

$$\begin{aligned} \Pr\{X_n = i | X_0 = i_0, \ldots, X_{n-1} = i_{n-1}\} &= \Pr\{X_0 = i | X_{-n} = i_0, \ldots, X_{-1} = i_{n-1}\} \\ &= \exp[-g_n(i, i_{n-1}, \ldots, i_0)]. \end{aligned}$$

Manifestly, $g_n(i, i_{n-1}, \ldots, i_0)$ exceeds λ whenever $(i_0, \ldots, i_{n-1})$ is in $E_n^{(i)}$. Thus the probability in (6.23) is bounded by

$$\begin{aligned} &\Pr\{X_n = i \quad \text{and} \quad (X_0, \ldots, X_{n-1}) \in E_n^{(i)}\} \\ &\le \sum_{(i_0, \ldots, i_{n-1}) \in E_n^{(i)}} e^{-\lambda} \Pr\{X_0 = i_0, \ldots, X_{n-1} = i_{n-1}\} \\ &\le e^{-\lambda} \Pr\{(X_0, \ldots, X_{n-1}) \in E_n^{(i)}\}. \end{aligned}$$

For each fixed i, the sets $E_1^{(i)}, E_2^{(i)}, \ldots$ are disjoint for the same reasons that $E_1, E_2, \ldots$ are disjoint. We sum (6.22) over n and use our bound to deduce

$$\begin{aligned}\sum_{n=1}^{\infty} \Pr\{(X_0, \ldots, X_n) \in E_n\} &= \sum_i \sum_{n=1}^{\infty} \Pr\{(X_0, \ldots, X_{n-1}) \in E_n^{(i)} \text{ and } X_n = i\} \\ &\le e^{-\lambda} \sum_i \left\{\sum_{n=1}^{\infty} \Pr\{(X_0, \ldots, X_{n-1}) \in E_n^{(i)}\}\right\} \\ &\le e^{-\lambda} \sum_i 1 \\ &\le Ne^{-\lambda},\end{aligned}$$

where N is the number of distinct states (i values) of the process. We have thus shown

$$\Pr\left\{\sup_{n \ge 1} g_n(X_n, \ldots, X_0) > \lambda\right\} \le Ne^{-\lambda}.$$

With this estimate the validation of (6.21) follows readily.

Since, with probability one,

$$g_k(X_0, X_{-1}, \ldots, X_{-k}) \to g(X_0, X_{-1}, \ldots),$$

as $k \to \infty$, and the expectations of the left functions are uniformly integrable, we may interchange expectation and limit to conclude

$$\begin{aligned}E[g(X_0, X_{-1}, \ldots)] &= \lim_{k \to \infty} E[g_k(X_0, \ldots, X_{-k})] \\ &= \lim_{n \to \infty} \frac{1}{n} E\left\{\sum_{k=0}^{n-1} g_k(X_k, \ldots, X_0)\right\} = H(\{X_k\}).\end{aligned}$$

The second equation is due to stationarity.

Write

$$\begin{aligned}\frac{1}{n}\sum_{k=0}^{n-1} g_k(X_k, \ldots, X_0) = \frac{1}{n}\sum_{k=0}^{n-1} g(X_k, X_{k-1}, \ldots) + \frac{1}{n}\sum_{k=0}^{n-1} \{g_k(X_k, \ldots, X_0) \\ -g(X_k, X_{k-1}, \ldots)\}. \qquad (6.24)\end{aligned}$$

We have established that $E[g(X_k, X_{k-1}, \ldots)] < \infty$. The ergodic theorem implies

$$\lim_{n \to \infty} \frac{1}{n}\sum_{k=0}^{n-1} g(X_k, X_{k-1}, \ldots) = E[g(X_0, X_{-1}, \ldots)] = H(\{X_n\}). \quad (6.25)$$

Set

$$\phi_N(x_0, x_{-1}, \ldots) = \sup_{k \geq N} |g_k(x_0, \ldots, x_{-k}) - g(x_0, x_{-1}, \ldots)|,$$

and

$$Z_k^N = \phi_N(X_k, X_{k-1}, \ldots).$$

Of course, $\{Z_k^N\}$ is stationary, ergodic, and $E[|Z_k^N|] < \infty$. Then

$$\begin{aligned} &\limsup_{n\to\infty} \left| \frac{1}{n} \sum_{k=0}^{n-1} \{g_k(X_k, \ldots, X_0) - g(X_k, X_{k-1}, \ldots)\} \right| \\ &\leq \limsup_{n\to\infty} \frac{1}{n} \sum_{k=0}^{n-1} |g_k(X_k, \ldots, X_0) - g(X_k, X_{k-1}, \ldots)| \\ &\leq \limsup_{n\to\infty} \frac{1}{n} \sum_{k=0}^{n-1} Z_k^N = E[Z_1^N]. \end{aligned}$$

But as $N \to \infty$, $Z_1^N \to 0$, and the interchange of limit and expectation can be justified to conclude $\lim_{N\to\infty} E[Z_1^N] = 0$. It follows that the second term on the right in (6.24) goes to zero as $n \to \infty$. Combined with (6.25) we have proved

$$\lim_{n\to\infty} \frac{1}{n} \sum_{k=0}^{n-1} g_k(X_k, \ldots, X_0) = H(\{X_n\})$$

as claimed.

7: *Spectral Analysis of Covariance Stationary Processes*

In this section we motivate a canonical representation for zero-mean covariance stationary processes in terms of harmonic functions. Earlier we suggested that an arbitrary such process can be represented as the mean square limit of a sequence of processes of the form of Example B of Section 1, that is, of the form

$$X_n = \sum_{k=0}^{m} \{A_k \cos n\omega_k + B_k \sin n\omega_k\}, \tag{7.1}$$

where $0 \leq \omega_k \leq \pi$, and the coefficients $\{A_k\}$ and $\{B_k\}$ are uncorrelated with zero means and variances $\sigma_k^2 = E[A_k^2] = E[B_k^2]$. In Section 1 we computed the covariance function of (7.1) to be

$$R(v) = \sigma^2 \sum_{k=0}^{m} p_k \cos v\omega_k, \tag{7.2}$$

where $\sigma^2 = \sigma_0^2 + \cdots + \sigma_m^2$, and $p_k = \sigma_k^2/\sigma^2$. At this stage it is more convenient to assume $\omega_0 = 0$ and write (7.2) in the symmetric form

$$R(v) = \sigma^2 \sum_{k=-m}^{m} q_k \cos v\omega_k,$$

where $q_0 = p_0$, and for $k = 1, \ldots, m$, $q_k = \frac{1}{2}p_k$, $q_{-k} = q_k$, $\omega_{-k} = -\omega_k$. As in Section 1 this suggests the generalization to

$$R(v) = \sigma^2 \int_{-\pi}^{\pi} \cos v\omega \, dF(\omega), \tag{7.3}$$

where F is a cumulative distribution function of a symmetric random variable having possible values in $[-\pi, \pi]$. In the first part of this section we will show that every covariance function may be written in the form of (7.3) for some unique probability distribution function $F(\omega)$. This function thus associated with the covariance function is called the *spectral distribution function* of the process.

In general, it is possible to develop from (7.3) a canonical representation for the process $\{X_n\}$. To sketch the thinking, suppose $\{Z^{(1)}(\omega), 0 \le \omega \le \pi\}$ and $\{Z^{(2)}(\omega), 0 \le \omega \le \pi\}$ are two stochastic processes, uncorrelated with each other and having uncorrelated increments. Suppose further that $Z^{(i)}(0) = 0$ and that the $Z^{(i)}$ processes have the common variance function

$$\begin{aligned} E[Z^{(i)}(\omega)^2] &= \sigma^2[F(\omega) - F(-\omega)], \\ &= 2\sigma^2[F(\omega) - F(0)], \qquad 0 \le \omega \le \pi. \end{aligned}$$

For expository convenience in this preliminary sketch we have assumed that $F(\omega)$ is continuous.

Let $0 = \omega_0 < \omega_1 < \cdots < \omega_m < \omega_{m+1} = \pi$ be given, and set $\Delta Z_k^{(i)} = Z^{(i)}(\omega_{k+1}) - Z^{(i)}(\omega_k)$. Since nonoverlapping increments are uncorrelated and the variance function is F, we have

$$E[\Delta Z_k^{(i)} \Delta Z_l^{(j)}] = 0, \qquad \text{if} \quad i \ne j, \quad \text{or} \quad k \ne l,$$

and

$$\frac{1}{\sigma^2} E[(\Delta Z_k^{(i)})^2] = 2\{F(\omega_{k+1}) - F(\omega_k)\} = 2\Delta F_k.$$

With $A_k = \Delta Z_k^{(1)}$ and $B_k = \Delta Z_k^{(2)}$, Eq. (7.1) becomes

$$\sum_{k=0}^{m} \cos n\omega_k \Delta Z_k^{(1)} + \sum_{k=0}^{m} \sin n\omega_k \Delta Z_k^{(2)},$$

the Riemann–Stieltjes approximating sum for the integral

$$\int_0^\pi \cos n\omega \, dZ^{(1)}(\omega) + \int_0^\pi \sin n\omega \, dZ^{(2)}(\omega).$$

The approximating sums converge in the mean square sense yielding the required representation. The corresponding development for Gaussian processes is given in the next section.

SPECTRAL REPRESENTATION OF THE COVARIANCE FUNCTION

Let $\{X_n; n = 0, \pm 1, \pm 2, \ldots\}$ be a covariance stationary process having a mean of zero and a known covariance function. By multiplying each observation by a constant, if necessary, we may assume the constant variance of the process is one. Thus we are studying a covariance stationary process $\{X_n\}$ whose covariance function

$$R(v) = E[X_n X_{n+v}], \qquad v = 0, \pm 1, \pm 2, \ldots,$$

satisfies $R(0) = 1$.

Before presenting the first theorem, we give two brief definitions. First, a real-valued function $R(v)$, $v = 0, \pm 1, \pm 2, \ldots$, is called *positive semi-definite* if for all $k = 1, 2, \ldots$ and all real numbers $\alpha_1, \ldots, \alpha_k$,

$$\sum_{i=1}^{k} \sum_{j=1}^{k} \alpha_i \alpha_j R(i-j) \geq 0. \tag{7.4}$$

Second, a random variable W, or its distribution function F, is said to be *symmetric* if W has the same distribution as $-W$. Thus, F is symmetric if $F(\omega) = 1 - F(-\omega)$ at all points of continuity ω.

Theorem 7.1. *Let $R(v)$, $v = 0, \pm 1, \pm 2, \ldots$, be given. The following statements are equivalent:*

(a) *$R(v)$ is the covariance function of a real-valued covariance stationary process having mean zero and variance one;*

(b) *$R(0) = 1$, $R(v) = R(-v)$, for $v = 0, 1, \ldots$, and $R(v)$ is positive semi-definite;*

(c) *There exists a symmetric probability distribution F on $[-\pi, \pi]$ for which*

$$R(v) = \int_{-\pi}^{\pi} \cos v\omega \, dF(\omega), \qquad v = 0, 1, \ldots. \tag{7.5}$$

Proof. (a) $\Rightarrow$ (b). Let us suppose $R(v)$ is the covariance function of a covariance stationary process $\{X_n\}$ having mean zero and variance one. Clearly, $R(0) = E[X_n^2] = 1$, and $R(v) = E[X_n X_{n+v}] = E[X_{n+v} X_n] = R(-v)$.
To show $R(v)$ is positive semidefinite, let $\alpha_1, \ldots, \alpha_k$ be given, and compute

$$\begin{aligned} 0 &\le E\left[\left|\sum_{i=1}^{k} \alpha_i X_{n+i}\right|^2\right] \\ &= E\left[\left(\sum_{i=1}^{k} \alpha_i X_{n+i}\right)\left(\sum_{j=1}^{k} \alpha_j X_{n+j}\right)\right] \\ &= E\left[\sum_{i=1}^{k} \sum_{j=1}^{k} \alpha_i \alpha_j X_{n+i} X_{n+j}\right] \\ &= \sum_{i=1}^{n} \sum_{j=1}^{n} \alpha_i \alpha_j E[X_{n+i} X_{n+j}] \\ &= \sum_{i=1}^{n} \sum_{j=1}^{n} \alpha_i \alpha_j R(i-j). \end{aligned}$$

Thus, (a) implies (b).

(b) $\Rightarrow$ (a). Let us suppose we are given a function $R(v)$ having the properties listed in (b), and set

$$a_{ij} = R(i-j).$$

Then, for any $k = 1, 2, \ldots$, the matrix $A = \|a_{ij}\|_{i,j=1}^{k}$ is symmetric and positive semidefinite. According to our remarks on the multivariate normal distribution in Chapter 1, we may associate with any such matrix A a multivariate normal distribution with zero mean and for which A is the covariance matrix. This procedure describes in a consistent way the distribution of any finite set $(X_{n+1}, \ldots, X_{n+k})$ and thus describes a distribution of the process $\{X_n;\, n = 0, \pm 1, \ldots\}$. It is easily seen that R is the covariance function of this process, and thus, for every function R with the properties listed in (b), there is at least one covariance stationary process having R as its covariance function.

(c) $\Rightarrow$ (b). We suppose

$$R(v) = \int_{-\pi}^{\pi} \cos v\omega \, dF(\omega) = E[\cos vW],$$

where W is a symmetric random variable having distribution function F. Easily $R(0) = 1$, and, since $\cos v\omega = \cos(-v\omega)$, $R(v) = R(-v)$. We need only show that $R(v)$ is positive semidefinite. We use the identity $\cos(x-y)=\cos x\cos y+\sin x\sin y$ to write

$$\sum_{i=1}^{k}\sum_{j=1}^{k}\alpha_i\alpha_j R(i-j)=\sum_{i=1}^{k}\sum_{j=1}^{k}\alpha_i\alpha_j E[\cos(i-j)W]$$
$$=E\left[\sum_{i=1}^{k}\sum_{j=1}^{k}\alpha_i\alpha_j\cos(iW-jW)\right]$$
$$=E\left[\left|\sum_{i=1}^{k}\alpha_i\cos iW\right|^2+\left|\sum_{i=1}^{k}\alpha_i\sin iW\right|^2\right]\geq 0.$$

Thus (c) implies (b).

(b) $\Rightarrow$ (c). Let R be given. For any given n and ω, use property (7.4) with $\alpha_j=\cos j\omega$ to conclude

$$0\leq\sum_{i=1}^{n}\sum_{j=1}^{n}R(i-j)\cos i\omega\cos j\omega.$$

Similarly, with $\alpha_i=\sin i\omega$, we have

$$0\leq\sum_{i=1}^{n}\sum_{j=1}^{n}R(i-j)\sin i\omega\sin j\omega.$$

We add these inequalities and use the trigonometric identity $\cos(x-y)=\cos x\cos y+\sin x\sin y$ to infer

$$0\leq\frac{1}{2\pi n}\sum_{i=1}^{n}\sum_{j=1}^{n}R(i-j)\cos(i-j)\omega$$
$$=\frac{1}{2\pi n}\sum_{v=-n+1}^{n-1}(n-|v|)\,R(v)\cos v\omega.$$

Thus, if we define

$$f_n(\omega)=\frac{1}{2\pi n}\sum_{v=-n+1}^{n-1}(n-|v|)\,R(v)\cos v\omega,$$

for $-\pi\leq\omega\leq\pi$, then

$$f_n(\omega)\geq 0.$$

Next we compute,

$$\int_{-\pi}^{\pi}f_n(\omega)\,d\omega=\frac{1}{2\pi n}\sum_{v=-n+1}^{n-1}(n-|v|)\left\{\int_{-\pi}^{\pi}\cos v\omega\,d\omega\right\}R(v)$$
$$=\frac{1}{2\pi n}(n)(2\pi)R(0)=1.$$

Thus, for every n, f_n is a probability density function on $[-\pi, \pi]$. Observe from its definition that f_n is symmetric:

$$f_n(\omega) = f_n(-\omega).$$

Let F_n be the cumulative distribution corresponding to the density function f_n. Using the definition for f_n, we compute

$$\begin{aligned}
\int_{-\pi}^{\pi} \cos v\omega \, dF_n(\omega) &= \int_{-\pi}^{\pi} \cos v\omega \, f_n(\omega) \, d\omega \\
&= \int_{-\pi}^{\pi} \cos v\omega \left\{ \frac{1}{2\pi n} \sum_{k=-n+1}^{n-1} (n - |k|) \cos k\omega R(k) \right\} d\omega \\
&= \sum_{k=-n+1}^{n-1} \left(1 - \frac{|k|}{n}\right) \frac{1}{2\pi} \left\{ \int_{-\pi}^{\pi} \cos v\omega \cos k\omega \, d\omega \right\} R(k) \\
&= \sum_{k=-n+1}^{n-1} \left(1 - \frac{|k|}{n}\right) \delta_{vk} R(k) \\
&= \left(1 - \frac{|v|}{n}\right) R(v),
\end{aligned}$$

where δ_{vk} is one if $v = k$, and zero otherwise. We have thus defined a sequence of distribution functions F_n for which the result (7.5) is "approximately" true, in the sense that

$$\left(1 - \frac{|v|}{n}\right) R(v) = \int_{-\pi}^{\pi} \cos v\omega \, dF_n(\omega).$$

From the Helly–Bray lemma (Chapter 1), there exists a cumulative distribution function F and a subsequence $\{F_{n_k}\}$ such that, for every bounded continuous function h,

$$\lim_{k \to \infty} \int_{-\pi}^{\pi} h(\omega) \, dF_{n_k}(\omega) = \int_{-\pi}^{\pi} h(\omega) \, dF(\omega).$$

We apply this with $h(\omega) = \cos v\omega$ to get

$$\begin{aligned}
\int_{-\pi}^{\pi} \cos v\omega \, dF(\omega) &= \lim_{k \to \infty} \int_{-\pi}^{\pi} \cos v\omega \, dF_{n_k}(\omega) \\
&= \lim_{k \to \infty} \left(1 - \frac{|v|}{n_k}\right) R(v) \\
&= R(v), \qquad \text{for} \quad v = 0, \pm 1, \ldots,
\end{aligned}$$

which completes the proof of the theorem. ■

According to Eq. (7.5), the covariance function $R(v)$ can easily be determined from the spectral distribution function F. In fact,

$$R(v) = \int_{-\pi}^{\pi} \cos v\omega \, dF(\omega)$$

states that $R(v)$ is the Fourier–Stieltjes cosine transformation of the distribution $F(\omega)$. Conversely, in general the spectral distribution function F can be determined from the covariance function $R(v)$ by computing an inverse cosine transformation. We content ourselves with stating without proof the results in an important case in which $F(\omega)$ is differentiable with *spectral density function*

$$f(\omega) = \frac{dF(\omega)}{d\omega}, \qquad \text{for} \quad -\pi < \omega < \pi.$$

In this case,

$$R(v) = \int_{-\pi}^{\pi} \cos v\omega \, f(\omega) \, d\omega$$

is the cosine transformation of the spectral density function $f(\omega)$.

Theorem 7.2. *Let $F(\omega)$ be the spectral distribution function corresponding to a covariance function $R(v)$. If*

$$\sum_{v=0}^{\infty} |R(v)| < \infty,$$

then $F(\omega)$ is differentiable with derivative

$$f(\omega) = F'(\omega), \qquad -\pi < \omega < \pi.$$

In this case,

$$\begin{aligned} f(\omega) &= \frac{1}{\pi}\left\{\frac{1}{2} R(0) + \sum_{v=1}^{\infty} \cos v\omega R(v)\right\} \\ &= \frac{1}{2\pi} \sum_{v=-\infty}^{+\infty} R(v) \cos v\omega \\ &= \frac{1}{2\pi} \sum_{v=-\infty}^{+\infty} e^{iv\omega} R(v). \end{aligned}$$

COMPLEX-VALUED PROCESSES

To further the theory and its applications, it is useful to have a theory covering complex-valued stationary processes. As a particular example, in many areas of communication theory it is natural to represent the instantaneous voltage and current of an alternating current signal by a complex number. Fortunately, it is possible to achieve this desired generality in a very natural way.

Let $X = X_1 + iX_2$, and $Y = Y_1 + iY_2$ be complex random variables. Then we define, as anticipated, the expectation

$$m_X = E[X] = E[X_1] + iE[X_2],$$

but for the covariance, we take

$$\mathrm{cov}[X, Y] = E[(X - m_X)(\overline{Y - m_Y})],$$

where the bar signifies the complex conjugate

$$\bar{Y} = Y_1 - iY_2 .$$

Thus the covariance function of a complex covariance stationary process $\{X_n\}$ having zero mean is the complex-valued function

$$R(v) = E[X_n \bar{X}_{n+v}], \qquad v = 0, \pm 1, \pm 2, \ldots.$$

As with real-valued processes, $R(0)$ is real, and

$$R(0) \geq |R(v)|, \qquad v = 0, \pm 1, \pm 2, \ldots.$$

But symmetry now takes the Hermitian form

$$R(v) = \overline{R(-v)},$$

and positive semidefiniteness is the property

$$\sum_{j=1}^{n} \sum_{k=1}^{n} \alpha_i \bar{\alpha}_j R(i-j) \geq 0,$$

for all $n = 1, 2, \ldots$ and complex numbers $\alpha_1, \ldots, \alpha_n$.

The following theorem is the generalization of Theorem 7.1. The proof parallels that of the earlier theorem in every step and is omitted.

Theorem 7.3. *Let the complex-valued function $R(v)$, $v = 0, \pm 1, \ldots$, be given. The following statements are equivalent:*

(a) *$R(v)$ is the covariance function of a complex-valued covariance stationary stochastic process having zero mean and unit variance;*

(b) *$R(0) = 1$, $R(v) = \overline{R(-v)}$, for $v = 0, 1, \ldots$, and $R(v)$ is positive semidefinite;*

(c) *There exists a probability distribution F (not necessarily symmetric) on $[-\pi, \pi]$ for which*

$$R(v) = \int_{-\pi}^{\pi} e^{iv\omega}\, dF(\omega).$$

8: Gaussian Systems

In this section we will construct a real-valued Gaussian stationary process $\{X_n\}$ having symmetric spectral distribution function $F(\omega)$, $-\pi \leq \omega \leq \pi$, through the formula (We use the notation $Z^{(i)}(d\omega) = dZ^{(i)}(\omega)$ interchangeably.)

$$X_n = \int_0^\pi \cos n\omega Z^{(1)}(d\omega) + \int_0^\pi \sin n\omega Z^{(2)}(d\omega), \tag{8.1}$$

where $\{Z^{(i)}(\omega);\ 0 \leq \omega \leq \pi\}$, $i = 1, 2$, are Gaussian processes, independent of one another and having independent increments, and where

$$E[\{Z^{(i)}(\omega_2) - Z^{(i)}(\omega_1)\}^2] = 2\{F(\omega_2) - F(\omega_1)\},$$
$$\text{for}\quad i = 1, 2, \quad \text{and} \quad 0 \leq \omega_1 \leq \omega_2 \leq \pi.$$

In general, a representation of the form (8.1) exists for every covariance stationary process, although $Z^{(i)}$ will not be Gaussian if $\{X_n\}$ is not. The simple result we present is only a sample of what can be done.

GAUSSIAN SYSTEMS

Let T be an abstract set and $\{X(t); t \in T\}$ a stochastic process. We call $\{X(t); t \in T\}$ a *Gaussian system* or *Gaussian process* if, for every $n = 1, 2, \ldots$ and every finite subset $\{t_1, \ldots, t_n\}$ of T, the random vector $(X(t_1), \ldots, X(t_n))$ has a multivariate normal distribution. Equivalently, we may require for every n that every linear combination

$$\alpha_1 X(t_1) + \cdots + \alpha_n X(t_n), \qquad \alpha_i \quad \text{real},$$

have a univariate normal distribution. Every Gaussian system is described uniquely by its two parameters, the mean and covariance function, given respectively by

$$\mu(t) = E[X(t)], \qquad t \in T,$$

and

$$\Gamma(t_1, t_2) = E[\{X(t_1) - \mu(t_1)\}\{X(t_2) - \mu(t_2)\}], \qquad t_i \in T.$$

The covariance function is positive definite, i.e., for every $n = 1, 2, \ldots$, real numbers $\alpha_1, \ldots, \alpha_n$ and elements $t_1, \ldots, t_n$ in T,

$$\sum_{i,j=1}^{n} \alpha_i \alpha_j \Gamma(t_i, t_j) \geq 0. \tag{8.2}$$

We need only compute the variance of $\sum_{i=1}^{n} \alpha_i\{X(t_i) - \mu(t_i)\}$ to verify this.

In fact,

$$0 \le E\left[\left\{\sum_{i=1}^{n} \alpha_i(X(t_i) - \mu(t_i))\right\}^2\right]$$

$$= \sum_{i,\,j=1}^{n} \alpha_i \alpha_j E[\{X(t_i) - \mu(t_i)\}\{X(t_j) - \mu(t_j)\}]$$

$$= \sum_{i,\,j=1}^{n} \alpha_i \alpha_j \Gamma(t_i, t_j).$$

Conversely, given an arbitrary mean $\mu(t)$ and positive definite covariance function $\Gamma(t_1, t_2)$, there exists a corresponding Gaussian system. To convince yourself of this, associate to every finite set $\{X(t_1), \ldots, X(t_n)\}$, $t_i \in T$, a multivariate normal distribution having mean vector $\{\mu(t_1), \ldots, \mu(t_n)\}$ and covariance matrix $\|\Gamma(t_i, t_j)\|_{i,\,j=1}^{n}$. This prescribes a consistent set of finite-dimensional distributions for the process $\{X(t); t \in T\}$, and according to Chapter 1, p. 32, this is enough.

GAUSSIAN RANDOM MEASURE

Let E be a subset of a finite-dimensional space and $g(x)$ a nonnegative function on E for which $\int_E g(x)\,dx < \infty$. For every subset A of E, define

$$m(A) = \int_A g(x)\,dx.$$

We claim that the expression

$$\Gamma(A, B) = m(A \cap B)$$

defines a positive definite function with parameter index consisting of the subsets of E. Almost exactly as before, we compute

$$0 \le \int_E \left\{\sum_{i=1}^{n} \alpha_i I_{A_i}(x)\right\}^2 g(x)\,dx$$

$$= \sum_{i,\,j=1}^{n} \alpha_i \alpha_j \int_E I_{A_i}(x) I_{A_j}(x) g(x)\,dx \tag{8.3}$$

$$= \sum_{i,\,j=1}^{n} \alpha_i \alpha_j m(A_i \cap A_j),$$

where

$$I_A(x) = \begin{cases} 1, & \text{if } x \in A, \\ 0, & \text{if } x \notin A. \end{cases}$$

The Gaussian system $\{Z(A); A \subset E\}$ having mean zero and covariance $\Gamma(A, B) = m(A \cap B)$, $A, B \subset E$ is called the *Gaussian random measure* induced by m. Even if $\int_E g(x)\,dx = \infty$, we may define $Z(A)$, not for all subsets A of E, but for all sets A for which $\int_A g(x)\,dx < \infty$.

Suppose E comprises all of a certain finite-dimensional space and $g(x) = 1$ for all x. The corresponding Gaussian random measure $\{Z(A)\}$ is a stationary process whose index set is a family of subsets. The constancy of g ensures that $(Z(A_1 + x), \ldots, Z(A_n + x))$ has the same distribution as $(Z(A_1), \ldots, Z(A_n))$, where $A_1 + x$ is the set A_1 translated by x, i.e., $A_1 + x = \{y : y = x + z \text{ for some } z \in A_1\}$.

Let us look at $E = [a, b]$, where $0 \le a \le b < \infty$, and suppose $G(x)$ is a nondecreasing bounded function for $a \le x \le b$. Write

$$G(I) = G(x_2) - G(x_1),$$

whenever $I = (x_1, x_2]$, $a \le x_1 < x_2 \le b$. We have made G into a nonnegative function of half-open intervals $I = (x_1, x_2] \subset E$. Set $\Gamma(I_1, I_2) = G(I_1 \cap I_2)$. We claim $\Gamma(I_1, I_2)$ is positive semidefinite. When G has a derivative g, the proof is exactly as in (8.3). The general case follows the same recipe, provided we replace $g(x)\,dx$ by the increment $dG(x)$ and use the Riemann–Stieltjes theory of integration mentioned in Chapter 1.

Let $Z(I)$ be a Gaussian random measure on intervals $I = (x, y]$, $a \le x < y \le b$, with $E[Z(I)^2] = G(I)$. We will define the integral

$$\int_a^b f(x) Z\,(dx),$$

for continuous functions $f(x)$ by taking a mean square limit of approximating sums

$$\sum_{i=0}^{n-1} f(x_i) Z(I_i),$$

where $I_i = (x_i, x_{i+1}]$, $a = x_0 < x_1 < \cdots < x_n = b$.

Let $\mathscr{P} = \{x_i\}$, $a = x_0 < x_1 < \cdots < x_n = b$, induce a partition of $[a, b]$. We call a partition $\mathscr{P}' = \{x_i'\}$ a *refinement* of $\mathscr{P}$ if every $x_i \in \mathscr{P}$ is also a point in $\mathscr{P}'$. Let

$$\mathscr{I}(f; \mathscr{P}) = \sum_{i=0}^{n-1} f(x_i) Z(I_i), \qquad I_i = (x_i, x_{i+1}].$$

Were $\mathscr{I}(f; \mathscr{P})$ deterministic, we would define an integral by building successive refinements $\mathscr{P}'$ of an arbitrary partition $\mathscr{P}$ and show that the approximating sums $\mathscr{I}(f; \mathscr{P}')$ converge. We follow the same pattern here, but since $\mathscr{I}(f; \mathscr{P})$ is random, we substitute mean square convergence for the ordinary convergence of real numbers. To be precise, we will show that for every preassigned $\varepsilon > 0$ there exists a partition $\mathscr{P}$, such that for all refinements $\mathscr{P}'$

$$\|\mathscr{I}(f; \mathscr{P}) - \mathscr{I}(f; \mathscr{P}')\| < \varepsilon,$$

where $\|\cdot\|$ is the mean square distance of Section 2. Using the *completeness* property of mean square distance discussed in that section, this will imply the existence of a limit in the mean square sense as the partitions are refined. This limit is defined to be the integral

$$\mathscr{I}(f) = \int_a^b f(x) Z(dx).$$

Recall that if f is continuous it is uniformly continuous on $[a, b]$. We thus may choose a partition $\mathscr{P} = \{x_i\}$ for which the range of f on any sub-interval $I_i = (x_i, x_{i+1}]$ is smaller than

$$\delta = \varepsilon / \sqrt{\{G(b) - G(a)\}},$$

for any preassigned $\varepsilon > 0$. Let $\mathscr{P}' = \{x_j'\}$ be a refinement of $\mathscr{P}$. Each interval $I_j' = (x_j', x_{j+1}']$ is contained in some $I_i = (x_i, x_{i+1}]$. Certainly $\varepsilon_j = f(x_i) - f(x_j') < \delta$. Then

$$\begin{aligned}
\|\mathscr{I}(f; \mathscr{P}) - \mathscr{I}(f; \mathscr{P}')\|^2 &= E[\{\mathscr{I}(f; \mathscr{P}) - \mathscr{I}(f; \mathscr{P}')\}^2] \\
&= E\left[\left\{\sum_{i=0}^{n-1} f(x_i) Z(I_i) - \sum_{j=0}^{m-1} f(x_j') Z(I_j')\right\}^2\right] \\
&= E\left[\left\{\sum_{j=0}^{m-1} \varepsilon_j Z(I_j')\right\}^2\right] \\
&= \sum_{i,j=0}^{m-1} \varepsilon_i \varepsilon_j G(I_i' \cap I_j') \\
&\leq \delta^2 \sum_{i=0}^{m-1} G(I_j') = \delta^2 \{G(b) - G(a)\} = \varepsilon^2.
\end{aligned}$$

Since ε is arbitrary, the approximating sums converge in the mean square sense as the partitions are refined. The limit achieved is the definition of the integral

$$\mathscr{I}(f) = \int_a^b f(x) Z(dx).$$

It is a random variable defined as a mean square limit.

The integral $\mathscr{I}(\cdot)$ possesses most of the properties of the usual integral. We mention here linearity:

$$\mathscr{I}(\alpha f_1 + \beta f_2) = \alpha \mathscr{I}(f_1) + \beta \mathscr{I}(f_2),$$

for real α, β and continuous f_i, provided we interpret "$=$" as equal in mean square distance,

$$\|\mathscr{I}(\alpha f_1 + \beta f_2) - \alpha \mathscr{I}(f_1) - \beta \mathscr{I}(f_2)\| = 0.$$

Since $\mathscr{I}(f)$ is random, we may compute its mean and variance. Recall from Section 2 that the expectation and covariance are continuous under mean square convergence. Thus

$$E[\mathscr{I}(f)] = \lim E\left[\sum_i f(x_i) Z(I_i)\right] = 0,$$

and

$$\begin{aligned} E[\mathscr{I}(f)\mathscr{I}(h)] &= \lim E\left[\sum_i f(x_i) Z(I_i) \sum_j h(x_j) Z(I_j)\right] \\ &= \lim \sum_{i,j} f(x_i) h(x_j) G(I_i \cap I_j) \\ &= \lim \sum_{i,j} f(x_i) h(x_j) \int I_{I_i}(x) I_{I_j}(x)\, dG(x) \\ &= \lim \int \left\{\sum_i f(x_i) I_{I_i}(x)\right\}\left\{\sum_j h(x_j) I_{I_j}(x)\right\} dG(x) \\ &= \int_a^b f(x) h(x)\, dG(x), \end{aligned}$$

for any continuous $f(x)$ and $h(x)$.

Deceptively simple,

$$E[\mathscr{I}(f)\mathscr{I}(h)] = \int_a^b f(x) h(x)\, dG(x) \tag{8.4}$$

is the most important property of integration with respect to Gaussian random measures.

SPECTRAL REPRESENTATION OF A GAUSSIAN STATIONARY PROCESS.

Let $Z^{(1)}$ and $Z^{(2)}$ be independent Gaussian random measures on $[0, \pi]$ satisfying

$$E[\{Z^{(i)}(I)\}^2] = 2F(I),$$

where $I=(\omega_1, \omega_2]$, $0 \le \omega_1 < \omega_2 \le \pi$, and $F(\omega)$, $-\pi \le \omega \le \pi$, is a given symmetric distribution function. We assume $F(0)=F(0-)$. The reader may wish to verify that such random measures may be explicitly represented by the formula

$$Z^{(i)}(I)=\sqrt{2}\{B(F(\omega_2))-B(F(\omega_1))\},$$

where $\{B(t);\, t\ge 0\}$ is a standard Brownian motion (see Chapter 7). Using the stochastic integral $\mathscr{I}(\cdot)$, define

$$\begin{aligned} X_n &= \int_0^\pi \cos n\omega Z^{(1)}(d\omega) + \int_0^\pi \sin n\omega Z^{(2)}(d\omega), \qquad n=0, \pm 1, \ldots, \\ &= \mathscr{I}_1(\cos n\omega) + \mathscr{I}_2(\sin n\omega). \end{aligned} \tag{8.5}$$

Then, $E[X_n]=0$, and, following (8.4),

$$\begin{aligned} &E[X_n X_{n+v}] \\ &\quad = E[\{\mathscr{I}_1(\cos n\omega)+\mathscr{I}_2(\sin n\omega)\}\{\mathscr{I}_1(\cos(n+v)\omega)+\mathscr{I}_2(\sin(n+v)\omega)\}] \\ &\quad = E[\mathscr{I}_1(\cos n\omega)\mathscr{I}_1(\cos(n+v)\omega)] + E[\mathscr{I}_2(\sin n\omega)\mathscr{I}_2(\sin(n+v)\omega)] \\ &\quad = 2\int_0^\pi \cos n\omega \cos(n+v)\omega \, dF(\omega) + 2\int_0^\pi \sin n\omega \sin(n+v)\omega \, dF(\omega) \\ &\quad = \int_{-\pi}^{\pi} \cos v\omega \, dF(\omega). \end{aligned}$$

It follows from Theorem 7.1 that $\{X_n\}$ is a covariance stationary process having the symmetric spectral distribution function F.

We remark that a parallel development exists for complex-valued Gaussian stationary processes in terms of a complex-valued Gaussian random measure.

Equation (8.5) represents the stationary Gaussian process $\{X_n\}$ in terms of the Gaussian random measure $Z^{(i)}$. We state without proof the converse. Let $\{X_n\}$ be a stationary Gaussian process having spectral distribution function F. The formulas

$$Z^{(1)}(\lambda)=\frac{1}{2\pi}\left\{\lambda X_0+\sum_{n=1}^{\infty}\frac{1}{n}(X_n-X_{-n})\sin \lambda n\right\},$$

and

$$Z^{(2)}(\lambda)=\frac{1}{2\pi}\sum_{n=1}^{\infty}\frac{1}{n}(X_n+X_{-n})\cos \lambda n,$$

define independent Gaussian processes having independent increments.

The infinite summations are understood in the mean square sense, which suffices to define all finite-dimensional distributions of $Z^{(i)}(\lambda)$. If $I=(\omega_1, \omega_2]$ and $Z^{(i)}(I) = Z^{(i)}(\omega_2) - Z^{(i)}(\omega_1)$, then

$$E[\{Z^{(i)}(I)\}^2] = F(\omega_2) - F(\omega_1).$$

9: Stationary Point Processes

Let $\mathscr{A}$ be a family of subsets of the nonnegative half-line $[0, \infty)$, and suppose that every interval of the form $(t, s]$, $0 \leq t < s$, is a member of $\mathscr{A}$. A point process $\{N(A); A \in \mathscr{A}\}$ is said to be *stationary* if, for every real number h, every positive integer k, and every set of intervals

$$(t_1, s_1], \ldots, (t_k, s_k],$$

the k-dimensional random vector

$$(N(t_1, s_1], \ldots, N(t_k, s_k])$$

has the same joint distribution as the vector

$$(N(t_1 + h, s_1 + h], \ldots, N(t_k + h, s_k + h]).$$

Of course, an analogous definition can be formed when $\mathscr{A}$ is a family of subsets of the whole real line, or even a finite-dimensional Euclidean space.

If $\{N(A), A \in \mathscr{A}\}$ is a stationary point process, then for each fixed $t, s \geq 0$, the integer-valued stochastic process

$$W(h) = N(t + h, s + h], \qquad h \geq 0,$$

is a stationary process and thus amenable to the techniques of the first eight sections of this chapter. However, the special character of point processes merits a separate study.

Suppose $\{X(t); t \geq 0\}$ is a stationary process for which every trajectory $X(t)$ is a continuous function of t. Fix a level u and let $N_u(s, t]$ be the number of times the trajectory $X(t)$ crosses u in the time interval $(s, t]$. Then $\{N_u(s, t]; 0 \leq s < t < \infty\}$ is a stationary point process. In Section 10 we will compute the mean $E[N_u(0, t]]$ for certain Gaussian stationary processes $\{X(t)\}$. In the remainder of this section, we content ourselves with showing that a stationary renewal process (Section 7 of Chapter 5) induces a stationary point process.

Let F be an arbitrary cumulative distribution function of a nonnegative random variable X having a finite mean

$$\mu = E[X] = \int_0^\infty x\,dF(x)$$
$$= \int_0^\infty [1 - F(y)]\,dy,$$

the last formula resulting by integration by parts (see also Problem 9, Chapter 1). Thus, since it is nonnegative and integrates to one, the function

$$g(y) = \mu^{-1}[1 - F(y)], \qquad y \geq 0,$$

is a probability density function.

Now let $X_0, X_1, X_2, \ldots$ be independent random variables, where X_0 is continuous and has the probability density function g, while for $i \geq 1$, X_i has the distribution function F. Construct a point process by placing a "point" at each of the times $S_n = X_0 + \cdots + X_n$, for $n \geq 0$. More precisely, for any interval $A = (t, s]$, we let $N(A)$ be the number of indices n for which $t < S_n \leq s$.

We claim that the point process $\{N(A), A \in \mathscr{A}\}$, constructed in this manner is a stationary point process. Now it is quite hard to exhibit explicitly the joint distribution of an arbitrary vector $\mathbf{N}(0) = (N(t_1, s_1], \ldots, N(t_k, s_k])$. However, we need not determine this distribution but merely show that it is the same as that for the shifted vector $\mathbf{N}(h) = (N(t_1 + h, s_1 + h], \ldots, N(t_k + h, s_k + h])$. Let us write X for the entire infinite-dimensional vector $(X_0, X_1, \ldots)$, and observe that $\mathbf{N}(0)$ is a vector-valued function of X. Let f denote this function, and let f_h be the vector-valued function that carries X into $\mathbf{N}(h)$. Then we want to show that $\mathbf{N}(0) = f(X)$ and $\mathbf{N}(h) = f_h(X)$ have the same distribution. Formulated this way, the problem is quite difficult.

The trick is to express $\mathbf{N}(h)$ involving the same function f used to produce $\mathbf{N}(0)$, but evaluated at a shifted sequence $X' = (X_0', X_1', \ldots)$. We claim

$$\mathbf{N}(h) = f(X'), \tag{9.1}$$

where

$$X_0' = S_M - h, \qquad X_k' = X_{M+k}, \qquad k \geq 1, \tag{9.2}$$

and where M is determined by

$$S_{M-1} < h \leq S_M. \tag{9.3}$$

Then to show $\mathbf{N}(h)=f(X')$ has the same distribution as $\mathbf{N}(0)=f(X)$, one need only show that the infinite-dimensional vector $X'=(X_0', X_1', \ldots)$ has the same distribution as the infinite-dimensional vector $X=(X_0, X_1, \ldots)$, since the function f is the same for both $\mathbf{N}(0)$ and $\mathbf{N}(h)$.

To verify Eq. (9.1) is not hard. We consider only the one-dimensional case in which

$$\mathbf{N}(0)=N(t, s],$$

for some fixed $t<s$. Let $\#\{\ \}$ denote "number of," so that we write

$$\begin{aligned} N(t, s] &= \#\{n : t<S_n \leq s\} \\ &= f(X). \end{aligned}$$

Then

$$\begin{aligned} N(t+h, s+h] &= \#\{n \geq 0 : t+h<S_n \leq s+h\} \\ &= \#\{n \geq M : t+h<S_n \leq s+h\} \\ &= \#\{n \geq M : t<S_n-h \leq s\} \\ &= \#\{m \geq 0 : t<S_{m+M}-h \leq s\} \\ &= \#\{m \geq 0 : t<S_m' \leq s\} \\ &= f(X'), \end{aligned}$$

where, as before, X' and M are given by Eqs. (9.2) and (9.3), and $S_m'= X_0'+\cdots+X_m'$.

Thus, to verify that $\{N(A);\ A \in A\}$ is a stationary point process, we need only show

$$X'=(S_M-h, X_{M+1}, X_{M+2}, \ldots)$$

has the same distribution as

$$X=(X_0, X_1, X_2, \ldots).$$

Now M is determined by the random variables $X_0, \ldots, X_M$, and thus is independent of $X_{M+1}, X_{M+2}, \ldots$. It follows that the distribution of X_{M+k} is the same as the conditional distribution of X_{M+k} given $M=n$, which, using independence, is the same as that of X_{n+k}, which is the same as that of X_k. Similarly, $X_{M+1}, X_{M+2}, \ldots$ are independent, and independent of S_M-h. Thus $X_1', X_2', \ldots$ are independent and identically distributed, with cumulative distribution function F, and independent of $X_0'=S_M-h$. It remains only to show that $X_0'=S_M-h$ has the probability density function $g(y)=\mu^{-1}[1-F(y)]$, $y \geq 0$. But this was shown in Section 7 of Chapter 5, where $X_0'=S_M-h$ was identified as the residual life at time

h. Thus, every stationary renewal process induces an associated stationary point process on the positive real line.

The following is the generalization to the whole real line.

Theorem 9.1. *Let $\{X_n; n=0, \pm 1, \pm 2, \ldots\}$ be independent positive random variables. For $k=\pm 1, \pm 2, \ldots$, we suppose the X_k have the common probability density function $f(x)$ for $x \geq 0$. We suppose X_0 has the distribution of a sum $X_0^+ + X_0^-$, where the joint distribution of X_0^+, X_0^- is given by the density function*

$$\mu^{-1} f(x^+ + x^-), \qquad \text{for} \quad x^+ \geq 0, \quad x^- \geq 0.$$

If "points" are placed on the real line at $S_n = X_0^+ + \cdots + X_n$ and at $S_{-n} = -X_0^- - \cdots - X_{-n}$, for $n = 0, 1, 2, \ldots$, the resulting point process is stationary.

10: The Level-Crossing Problem

In this section we suppose $\{X(t); -\infty < t < \infty\}$ is a zero-mean Gaussian stationary process for which every trajectory $X(t)$ is a continuous function of t. We fix a level a and consider the number of times the trajectory $X(t)$ crosses a in the time interval $(0, T]$. This quantity has considerable importance in communication theory as well as arising in a variety of other fields. It is quite difficult to compute the distribution of this random variable, and, indeed, in many cases an explicit form is not known. We confine ourselves to computing the first moment, or mean, and this under the additional condition that

$$\lambda_2 = -\frac{d^2}{dt^2} R(t)\Big|_{t=0} < \infty, \tag{10.1}$$

where $R(t)$ is the covariance function of the process.

The derivation uses several techniques of rather general applicability, which we display as lemmas.

Use the notation

$$N(I) = N(s, t], \qquad I = (s, t], \qquad 0 \leq s < t,$$

for a point process. Say that $\{N(I)\}$ is without multiple events if

$$\lim_{n \to \infty} N(t - (1/n), t] = 0 \quad \text{or} \quad 1, \qquad \text{for all} \quad t. \tag{10.2}$$

The renewal point process of Section 9 furnishes an example.

Lemma 10.1. *Let* $\{N(I)\}$ *be a point process without multiple events. Fix* $T>0$ *and divide the interval* $(0, T]$ *into* n *subintervals*

$$I_{ni}=((i-1)T/n, iT/n], \qquad i=1, \ldots, n; \quad n=1, 2, \ldots.$$

Then

$$E[N(0, T]]=\lim_{n\to\infty}\sum_{i=1}^{n}\Pr\{N(I_{ni})\geq 1\}. \tag{10.3}$$

Proof. Write

$$\chi_{ni}=\begin{cases}1, & \text{if } N(I_{ni})\geq 1,\\ 0, & \text{otherwise,}\end{cases}$$

and $N_n=\sum_{i=1}^{n}\chi_{ni}$. Then $N_n\leq N_{n+1}\leq N(0, T]$ and, in view of (10.2), $\lim_{n\to\infty}N_n=N(0, T]$. The interchange of limit and expectation may be justified to conclude

$$\lim_{n\to\infty}\sum_{i=1}^{n}\Pr\{N(I_{ni})\geq 1\}=\lim_{n\to\infty}E[N_n]=E[N(0, T]]. \quad \blacksquare$$

Equation (10.3) expresses the mean number of events in $[0, T]$ in terms of the distributions of events in small intervals. We are interested in events defined by the crossings of a level a by a continuous process $X(t)$. Our next step is to relate the number of crossings in an interval to the process $X(t)$, and to do this we need a crisp definition of "crossing." Fix a. Then $X(t)$ is said to have a *crossing* of a at t_0 if for every positive ε there are points t_1 and t_2 satisfying, on the one hand,

$$|t_i-t_0|<\varepsilon, \qquad i=1, 2,$$

and, on the other,

$$[X(t_1)-a]\cdot[X(t_2)-a]<0.$$

Observe, for example, that tangencies are not counted as crossings. Let $N_a(0, T]$ be the number of crossings of a by $X(t)$ during $(0, T]$.

Lemma 10.2. *Let* $\{X(t)\}$ *be a stochastic process for which* $X(t)$ *is a continuous function of* t *and for which* $\Pr\{X(t)=a\}=0$ *for every fixed* t. *Then*

$$E[N_a(0, T]]=\lim_{n\to\infty}\left\{\sum_{i=1}^{n}\Pr\left\{X\left(\frac{(i-1)T}{n}\right)<a<X\left(\frac{iT}{n}\right)\right\}\right.$$
$$\left.+\sum_{i=1}^{n}\Pr\left\{X\left(\frac{(i-1)T}{n}\right)>a>X\left(\frac{iT}{n}\right)\right\}\right\}.$$

Proof. This result is nearly the same as Lemma 10.1. Let

$$\chi'_{ni} = \begin{cases} 1, & \text{if } X\left(\frac{(i-1)T}{n}\right) < a < X\left(\frac{iT}{n}\right) \text{ or } X\left(\frac{(i-1)T}{n}\right) > a > X\left(\frac{iT}{n}\right), \\ 0, & \text{otherwise.} \end{cases}$$

Clearly, $N'_n = \sum_{i=1}^{n} \chi'_{ni} \le N_n$, so that

$$\limsup_{n\to\infty} E[N'_n] \le E[N_a(0, T]],$$

by Lemma 10.1. On the other hand, it is apparent that for each fixed n, $N_n \le N'_m$ when m is sufficiently large, since in that case, for example, $(X(t_1) - a) < 0$, $(X(t_2) - a) > 0$, for some

$$\frac{(i-1)T}{n} < t_1 < t_2 < \frac{iT}{n},$$

will imply

$$X\left(\frac{(j-1)T}{m}\right) < a < X\left(\frac{jT}{m}\right),$$

for some subinterval I_{mj} of I_{ni}. [We have excluded the zero probability event that $X(t)$ crosses a at a point of the form $t = rT$, where r is a rational number in (0, 1].] Thus

$$\liminf_{m\to\infty} E[N'_m] \ge E[N_n],$$

and

$$\liminf_{m\to\infty} E[N'_m] \ge \liminf_{n\to\infty} E[N_n] = E[N_a(0, T)].$$

This completes the proof. ∎

Thus the calculation of the mean number of crossings in an interval may be carried out by studying the simpler events

$$\left\{X\left(\frac{(i-1)T}{n}\right) < a < X\left(\frac{iT}{n}\right)\right\},$$

and

$$\left\{X\left(\frac{(i-1)T}{n}\right) > a > X\left(\frac{iT}{n}\right)\right\}.$$

If the process is stationary, these events have the same probabilities, respectively, as do

$$A(n) = \{X(0) < a < X(T/n)\},$$

and

$$B(n) = \{X(0) > a > X(T/n)\}.$$

Theorem 10.1. *Let $\{X(t);\, t \geq 0\}$ be a zero-mean Gaussian stationary process having every trajectory $X(t)$ continuous in t. Suppose the covariance function $R(t)$ satisfies* (10.1), *and set $\sigma^2 = R(0)$, the variance of $X(t)$. Then the mean number of crossings of level a during* $(0, T]$ *is given by*

$$E[N_a(0, T]] = \frac{T}{\pi} (\lambda_2/\sigma^2)^{1/2} \exp(-a^2/2\sigma^2).$$

Proof. The final result must be proportional to T, by the stationary property, and thus we need only treat $T = 1$. According to the preliminaries, our task is to compute

$$\begin{aligned} E[N_a(0, 1]] &= \lim_{n\to\infty} n[\Pr\{A(n)\} + \Pr\{B(n)\}] \\ &= \lim_{n\to\infty} 2^n[\Pr\{A(2^n)\} + \Pr\{B(2^n)\}]. \end{aligned}$$

Now $A(2^n)$ is determined by $X(0)$ and $X(2^{-n})$, whose joint distribution is normal with mean zero, variance $\sigma^2 = R(0)$, and correlation coefficient $\rho(2^n) = R(2^{-n})/R(0)$. (See Chapter 1 for a review of the bivariate normal distribution.) Let

$$\zeta_n = 2^n[X(2^{-n}) - X(0)].$$

The pair $X(0)$, ζ_n has a bivariate normal distribution, and a straightforward computation shows the mean is zero and the covariance matrix is:

$$\left\| \begin{matrix} R(0) & -2^n[R(0) - R(2^{-n})] \\ -2^n[R(0) - R(2^{-n})] & 2^n\{2^n[R(0) - R(2^{-n})] - 2^n[R(-2^{-n}) - R(0)]\}. \end{matrix} \right\|$$

Observe the use of the symmetry $R(-2^{-n}) = R(2^{-n})$ in deriving the entries of the matrix. Using the assumption (10.1), this matrix converges, as $n \to \infty$, to

$$\left\| \begin{matrix} R(0) & R'(0) \\ R'(0) & R''(0) \end{matrix} \right\| = \left\| \begin{matrix} \sigma^2 & 0 \\ 0 & \lambda_2 \end{matrix} \right\| \tag{10.4}$$

where $R'(t)$ and $R''(t)$ are the first and second derivatives, respectively, of $R(t)$. The symmetry of $R(t)$ and the assumed existence of $R''(0) < \infty$

imply $R'(0) = 0$. Let $p_n(x, z)$ denote this bivariate normal density of $X(0)$ and ζ_n. Note that $B(2^n)$ may be described as

$$B(2^n) = \{X(0) > a > X(2^{-n})\}$$
$$= \{a < X(0) < a - 2^{-n}\zeta_n\}.$$

Now compute

$$2^n \Pr\{B(2^n)\} = 2^n \Pr\{a < X(0) < a - 2^{-n}\zeta_n\}$$
$$= 2^n \int_{-\infty}^{0} \int_{a}^{a-2^{-n}z} p_n(x, z)\, dx\, dz$$
$$= \int_{-\infty}^{0} \int_{0}^{-z} p_n(a + 2^{-n}x, z)\, dx\, dz.$$

Using the explicit form of the bivariate normal distribution given in Chapter 1 and the convergence of the covariance of $X(0)$ and ζ_n to that given in (10.4), we deduce

$$\lim_{n\to\infty} p_n(a + 2^{-n}x, z) = \frac{1}{2\pi\sigma\sqrt{\lambda_2}} \exp\left\{-\frac{1}{2}\left[\left(\frac{a}{\sigma}\right)^2 + \frac{z^2}{\lambda_2}\right]\right\}$$
$$= \frac{1}{\sigma}\phi\left(\frac{a}{\sigma}\right) \cdot \frac{1}{\lambda_2^{1/2}}\phi\left(\frac{z}{\lambda_2^{1/2}}\right),$$

where

$$\phi(x) = \frac{1}{\sqrt{2\pi}} \exp(-x^2/2)$$

is the standard normal density.

Thus

$$\lim_{n\to\infty} 2^n \Pr\{B(2^n)\} = \int_{-\infty}^{0} \int_{0}^{-z} \frac{1}{\sigma}\phi\left(\frac{a}{\sigma}\right) \frac{1}{\sqrt{\lambda_2}}\phi\left(\frac{z}{\sqrt{\lambda_2}}\right) dx\, dz$$
$$= \frac{1}{\sigma}\phi\left(\frac{a}{\sigma}\right) \int_{0}^{\infty} \frac{z}{\sqrt{\lambda_2}}\phi\left(\frac{z}{\sqrt{\lambda_2}}\right) dz$$
$$= \frac{\sqrt{\lambda_2}}{\sigma}\phi\left(\frac{a}{\sigma}\right) \int_{0}^{\infty} y\phi(y)\, dy$$
$$= \frac{\sqrt{\lambda_2}}{\sigma}\phi\left(\frac{a}{\sigma}\right)\frac{1}{\sqrt{2\pi}}$$
$$= \frac{\sqrt{\lambda_2}}{\sigma 2\pi} \exp\left\{-\frac{1}{2}\left(\frac{a}{\sigma}\right)^2\right\}.$$

We obtain the same result when we compute $\lim_{n\to\infty} 2^n \Pr\{A(2^n)\}$.

Hence

$$E[N_a(0, 1)] = 2 \lim_{n\to\infty} 2^n \Pr\{B(2^n)\}$$

$$= \frac{\sqrt{\lambda_2}}{\pi\sigma} \exp\left\{-\frac{1}{2}\left(\frac{a}{\sigma}\right)^2\right\},$$

as claimed. ■

As a refinement, say that $X(t)$ has an upcrossing of the level a at t_0 if, for some $\varepsilon > 0$, $X(t) < a$ for $t_0 - \varepsilon < t < t_0$, and $X(t) > a$ for $t_0 < t < t_0 + \varepsilon$. Let $U_a(0, T]$ be the number of upcrossings during $(0, T]$. Then

$$E[U_a(0, 1]] = \lim_{n\to\infty} 2^n \Pr\{A(2^n)\} = \frac{\sqrt{\lambda_2}}{2\pi\sigma} \exp(-a^2/2\sigma^2).$$

To close this section and this chapter, we state one of the more recent results in this fascinating area of probability. Our aim is to whet the student's appetite for further reading. As the level a increases, the upcrossings become rarer, thus raising the possibility of Poisson-like behavior. Of course, as a increases, $U_a(0, T]$ will tend to become smaller, and thus we require normalization. Let

$$f(a) = \frac{\sqrt{\lambda_2}}{2\pi\sigma} \exp(-a^2/2\sigma^2),$$

and

$$N_a(t) = U_a(0, t/f(a)).$$

Observe that $E[N_a(t)] = t$. Here is the result.

Theorem 10.2. *With the above notation, let $X(t)$ be a stationary Gaussian process, with continuous trajectories, and covariance function $R(t)$, where $\lambda_2 = R''(0) < \infty$. Suppose that either:* (i) *$R(t) \log t \to 0$ as $t \to \infty$, or* (ii) *$\int_0^\infty R(s)^2\, ds < \infty$. Then the distribution of $\{N_a(t);\ t \geq 0\}$ converges to that of a Poisson process as $a \to \infty$.*

In thinking about why this might be so, observe that (i) and (ii) imply an asymptotic independence that will reflect itself in the independent increments of the Poisson process.

Elementary Problems

Exercises 1–5 all fall into the following context. Let $\{X_n\}$ and $\{Y_n\}$ be jointly distributed zero-mean covariance stationary processes having covariance functions $R_X(v)$ and $R_Y(v)$, respectively. Let $R_{XY}(v) = E[X_n Y_{n+v}]$, $v = 0,$

± 1, ..., be the cross covariance function. Finally, let $\{\xi_n\}$ be a zero-mean covariance stationary process having covariance function $R_\xi(v)$ and being uncorrelated with $\{X_n\}$ or $\{Y_n\}$. "Best" predictor, estimator, etc., is in the sense of minimum mean square error.

1. (a) Find the best predictor of X_{n+1} of the form $\hat{X}^{(1)}_{n+1} = aX_n$, where a is a constant to be chosen.

Solution: $a^* = R_X(1)/R_X(0)$.

(b) Find the best predictor of X_{n+1} of the form $\hat{X}^{(2)}_{n+1} = aX_n + bX_{n-1}$, where a, b are constants.

Solution:

$$a^* = \frac{1}{\Delta}[R_X(1)R_X(0) - R_X(1)R_X(2)],$$

$$b^* = \frac{1}{\Delta}[R_X(0)R_X(2) - R_X(1)^2],$$

where $\Delta = R_X(0)^2 - R_X(1)^2$.

(c) Express the improvement in mean square predictor error of $\hat{X}^{(2)}_{n+1}$ over $\hat{X}^{(1)}_{n+1}$ in terms of $R_X(v)$.

Solution:

$$\text{Difference in MSE} = \frac{1}{R_X(0)}\left\{R_X(2) - \frac{R_X(1)^2}{R_X(0)}\right\}^2.$$

2. (a) Find the best estimator of X_n of the form $\hat{X}^{(1)}_n = aY_n$, where a is a constant to be chosen.

Solution: $a^* = R_{XY}(0)/R_Y(0)$.

(b) Find the best estimator of X_n of the form $\hat{X}^{(2)}_n = aY_n + bY_{n-1}$, where a and b are constants.

Solution:

$$a^* = \frac{1}{\Delta}[R_{XY}(0)R_Y(0) - R_{XY}(1)R_Y(1)],$$

$$b^* = \frac{1}{\Delta}[R_Y(0)R_{XY}(1) - R_Y(1)R_{XY}(0)],$$

where $\Delta = R_Y(0)^2 - R_Y(1)^2$.

3. Interpret X_n as a signal and ξ_n as a noise. We observe $Z_n = X_n + \xi_n$. Find the best estimator of X_n of the form $\hat{X}_n = aZ_n + bZ_{n-1}$, where a and b are constants to be chosen.

Solution:

$$a^* = \frac{1}{\Delta}[R_X(0)\{R_X(0) + R_\xi(0)\} - R_X(1)\{R_X(1) + R_\xi(1)\}],$$

$$b^* = \frac{1}{\Delta}[\{R_X(0) + R_\xi(0)\}R_X(1) - \{R_X(1) + R_\xi(1)\}R_X(0)],$$

where $\Delta = \{R_X(0) + R_\xi(0)\}^2 - \{R_X(1) + R_\xi(1)\}^2$.

4. Find the best interpolator for X_{n+k} of the form

$$\hat{X}_{n+k} = aX_n + bX_{n+N},$$

where $1 \le k \le N$ are fixed and a, b are constants to be chosen.

Solution:

$$a^* = \frac{1}{\Delta}[R_X(k)R_X(0) - R_X(N)R_X(N-k)],$$

$$b^* = \frac{1}{\Delta}[R_X(0)R_X(N-k) - R_X(k)R_X(N)],$$

where $\Delta = R_X(0)^2 - R_X(N)^2$.

5. Fix $N \ge 1$ and set $Z_n = \sum_{k=0}^{N} X_{n+k}$. Find the best estimator of Z_n of the form

$$\hat{Z}_n = aX_n + bX_{n+N},$$

where a, b are constants to be chosen.

6. For $n = 1, 2, \ldots$ let $X_n = \cos(nU)$ where U is uniformly distributed over the interval $[-\pi, \pi]$. Verify that $\{X_n\}$ is covariance stationary but not strictly stationary.

Hint: For the first part use the trigonometric identity

$$\cos x \cos y = \tfrac{1}{2}[\cos(x+y) + \cos(x-y)].$$

Evaluate

$$E[\cos vU] = \begin{cases} 1 & \text{if} \quad v = 0 \\ 0 & \text{if} \quad v = 1, 2, \ldots \end{cases}$$

by symmetry. For the second part, use the same approach to determine that the third product moment $E[X_n X_{n+v} X_{n+v+h}]$ depends on n.

7. Suppose $\{B(t);\ t \ge 0\}$ is a standard Brownian motion process. Compute the covariance function for $X(t) = B(t+1) - B(t)$, $t \ge 0$, and establish that $X(t)$ is strictly stationary.

Answer:

$$R(v) = \begin{cases} 1 - |v|, & \text{for} \quad |v| \le 1, \\ 0, & \text{for} \quad |v| > 1. \end{cases}$$

8. Compute the covariance function for $X_n = \sqrt{2}\, A \sin(\omega n + U)$ where A is a random variable with mean zero and variance σ^2, and U, independent of A, is uniformly distributed over the interval $[0, 2\pi)$. Assume ω is a constant satisfying $0 \le \omega < 2\pi$.

9. Suppose $\{X_n;\ \ n = 0, 1, \ldots\}$ is a zero mean stationary process which is both Gaussian and Markov. Demonstrate that the covariance function must be of the form $R(v) = \sigma^2 \lambda^{|v|}$ for some fixed λ satisfying $|\lambda| \le 1$.

10. Find the spectral density function corresponding to the covariance function $R(0) = 1$ and $R(v) = \alpha\gamma^{|v|}$, $\ v = \pm 1, \pm 2, \ldots$, where $0 < \alpha < 1$ and $|\gamma| < 1$.

Hint: Write $R(v) = R_1(v) + R_2(v)$ where

$$R_1(v) = \begin{cases} 1 - \alpha & \text{for} \quad v = 0 \\ 0 & \text{for} \quad v \ne 0. \end{cases}$$

and $R_2(v) = \alpha\gamma^{|v|}$ for all v.

11. Suppose $\hat{X}_n = a_1 X_{n-1} + a_2 X_{n-2}$ is an optimal linear predictor for X_n given the entire past of a covariance stationary process $\{X_n\}$. What is the spectral density function?

Hint:

$$\xi_n = X_n - \hat{X}_n = X_n - a_1 X_{n-1} - a_2 X_{n-2}$$

implies

$$\sigma_\xi^2 f_\xi(\lambda) = \sigma_X^2 |1 - a_1 e^{i\lambda} - a_2 e^{2i\lambda}|^2 f_X(\lambda)$$

But we know, since $\hat{X}_n$ is an optimal predictor, $\{\xi_n\}$ are uncorrelated and $f_\xi(\lambda) = \dfrac{1}{2\pi}$, $-\pi \le \lambda \le \pi$. Solve for f_X.

Problems

1. Let $\{\xi_n\}$ be independent and identically distributed random variables having mean zero and variance σ^2. Let $\{a_n\}$ be a real sequence. Prove that $X = \sum_{n=0}^{\infty} a_n \xi_n$ converges in mean square whenever $\sum_{n=0}^{\infty} a_n^2 < \infty$ [In particular, $\sum (1/n)\xi_n$ converges!]. Let $\{\eta_n\}$ be a zero-mean covariance stationary process having covariance function $R(v)$. Show that $\sum_{n=0}^{\infty} a_n \eta_n$ converges in mean square whenever

$$\sum_{i=0}^{\infty} \sum_{j=0}^{\infty} |a_i a_j R(i-j)| < \infty.$$

2. Let $X, X_1, X_2, \ldots$ be random variables having finite second moments. Show that $\lim_{n\to\infty} ||X_n - X|| = 0$, if and only if both conditions $\lim_{n\to\infty} E[X_n Y] = E[XY]$ for all random variables Y satisfying $E[Y^2] < \infty$, and $\lim_{n\to\infty} ||X_n|| = ||X||$ hold.

3. Suppose

$$W_n = \sum_{j=1}^{q} \sigma_j \sqrt{2} \cos(\lambda_j n - V_j),$$

where σ_j, λ_j are positive constants, $j = 1, \ldots, q$, and $V_1, \ldots, V_q$ are independent, uniformly distributed in the interval $(0, 2\pi)$. Show that $\{W_n\}$ is covariance stationary and compute the covariance function.

4. Let $\rho(v) = R(v)/R(0)$ be the correlation function of a covariance stationary process $\{X_n\}$, where

$$X_{n+1} = a_1 X_n + a_2 X_{n-1} + \xi_{n+1},$$

for constants a_1, a_2 and zero mean uncorrelated random variables $\{\xi_n\}$, for which $E[\xi_n^2] = \sigma^2$ and $E[\xi_n X_{n-k}] = 0$, $k = 1, 2, \ldots$. Establish that $\rho(v)$ satisfies the so-called *Yule–Walker* equations

$$\rho(1) = a_1 + a_2 \rho(1), \qquad \text{and} \qquad \rho(2) = a_1 \rho(1) + a_2 .$$

Determine a_1 and a_2 in terms of $\rho(1)$ and $\rho(2)$.

5. Show that no covariance stationary process $\{X_n\}$ can satisfy the stochastic difference equation $X_n = X_{n-1} + \varepsilon_n$, when $\{\varepsilon_n\}$ is a sequence of zero-mean uncorrelated random variables having a common positive variance $\sigma^2 > 0$.

6. Let $\{X_n\}_{n=-\infty}^{+\infty}$ be a zero-mean covariance stationary process having covariance function $R(v) = \gamma^{|v|}$, $v = 0, \pm 1, \ldots$, where $|\gamma| < 1$. Find the minimum mean square error linear predictor of X_{n+1} given the entire past $X_n, X_{n-1} \ldots$.

7. Let $\{\varepsilon_n\}$ be zero-mean uncorrelated random variables having unit variances. Find the minimum mean square linear predictor for X_{n+1} given the entire past $X_n, X_{n-1}, \ldots$, for the moving average process

$$X_n = \varepsilon_n + \beta[\varepsilon_{n-1} + \gamma \varepsilon_{n-2} + \gamma^2 \varepsilon_{n-3} + \cdots],$$

where β and γ are constants, $|\gamma| < 1$, and $|\alpha| < 1$, where $\alpha = \gamma - \beta$.

8. Let $\{X_n\}$ be a zero-mean covariance stationary process having covariance function $R_X(v)$ and spectral density function $f_X(\omega)$, $-\pi \le \omega \le \pi$. Suppose $\{a_n\}$ is a real sequence for which $\sum_{i,j=0}^{\infty} |a_i a_j R(i-j)| < \infty$, and define

$$Y_n = \sum_{k=0}^{\infty} a_k X_{n-k}.$$

Show that the spectral density function $f_Y(\omega)$ for $\{Y_n\}$ is given by

$$\begin{aligned} f_Y(\omega) &= \frac{\sigma_X^2}{\sigma_Y^2} \left| \sum_{k=0}^{\infty} a_k e^{ik\omega} \right|^2 f_X(\omega), \\ &= \frac{\sigma_X^2}{\sigma_Y^2} \left[\sum_{j,k=0}^{\infty} a_j a_k \cos(j-k)\omega \right] f_X(\omega), \qquad -\pi \le \omega \le \pi. \end{aligned}$$

9. Determine the spectral density function corresponding to the covariance function $R(v) = \gamma^{|v|}$, $\quad v = 0, \pm 1, \ldots$, where $|\gamma| < 1$.

Answer:

$$f(\omega) = \frac{1-\gamma^2}{2\pi |1 - \gamma e^{i\omega}|^2}, \qquad -\pi < \omega < \pi.$$

10. Compute the spectral density function of the autoregressive process $\{X_n\}$ satisfying

$$X_n = \beta_1 X_{n-1} + \cdots + \beta_q X_{n-q} + \xi_n,$$

where $\{\xi_n\}$ are uncorrelated zero-mean random variables having unit variance. Assume the q roots of $x^q - \beta_1 x^{q-1} \cdots - \beta_q = 0$ are all less than one in absolute value.

Answer:

$$f(\omega) = \left\{ 2\pi\sigma_X^2 \left| 1 - \sum_{k=1}^{q} \beta_k e^{ik\omega} \right|^2 \right\}^{-1}, \; -\pi < \omega < \pi.$$

11. Compute the spectral density function of the moving average process

$$X_n = \xi_n + \alpha_1 \xi_{n-1}.$$

Answer:

$$f(\lambda) = \frac{1 + \alpha_1^2 + 2\alpha_1 \cos\lambda}{2\pi(1+\alpha_1^2)},$$

where $\{\xi_n\}$ are uncorrelated zero-mean random variables having unit variance.

12. Let $\{X_n\}$ be the finite moving average process

$$X_n = \sum_{r=0}^{q} \alpha_r \xi_{n-r}, \qquad \alpha_0 = 1,$$

where $\alpha_0, \ldots, \alpha_q$ are real and $\{\xi_n\}$ are zero-mean uncorrelated random variables having unit variance. Show that the spectral density function $f(\lambda)$ may be written

$$f(\lambda) = \frac{1}{2\pi\sigma_X^2} \prod_{j=1}^{q} |e^{i\lambda} - z_j|^2,$$

where $z_1, \ldots, z_q$ are the q roots of

$$\sum_{r=0}^{q} a_r z^{q-r} = 0.$$

13. Show that a predictor

$$\hat{X}_n = \alpha_1 X_{n-1} + \cdots + \alpha_p X_{n-p}$$

is optimal among all linear predictors of X_n given $X_{n-1}, \ldots, X_{n-p}$ if and only if

$$0 = \int_{-\pi}^{\pi} e^{ik\lambda} \left[1 - \sum_{l=1}^{p} \alpha_l e^{-il\lambda}\right] dF(\lambda), \qquad k = 1, \ldots, p,$$

where $F(\omega)$, $-\pi \le \omega \le \pi$, is the spectral distribution function of the covariance stationary process $\{X_n\}$.

14. Let $\{X_n\}$ be a zero-mean covariance stationary process having positive spectral density function $f(\omega)$ and variance $\sigma_X^2 = 1$. Kolmogorov's formula states

$$\sigma_e^2 = \exp\left\{\frac{1}{2\pi} \int_{-\pi}^{\pi} \log 2\pi f(\omega)\, d\omega\right\},$$

where $\sigma_e^2 = \inf E[|\hat{X}_n - X_n|^2]$ is the minimum mean square linear prediction error of X_n given the past. Verify Kolmogorov's formula when

$$R(v) = \gamma^{|v|}, \qquad v = 0, \pm 1, \ldots,$$

with $|\gamma| < 1$.

15. Derive

$$R(v) = \int_{-\pi}^{\pi} (\cos \lambda v) f(\lambda)\, d\lambda,$$

from

$$f(\lambda) = \frac{1}{2\pi} \sum_{k=-\infty}^{+\infty} R(k) \cos \lambda k, \qquad -\pi \le \lambda \le \pi.$$

16. Compute the covariance function and spectral density function for the moving average process

$$X_n = \sum_{k=0}^{\infty} a_k \xi_{n-k},$$

where $\{\xi_n\}$ are zero-mean uncorrelated random variables having unit variance and $a_0, a_1, \ldots$ are real numbers satisfying $\sum a_k^2 < \infty$.

17. Find the minimum mean square error linear predictor of X_{n+1} given X_n, $X_{n-1}, \ldots, X_0$ in the following nonstationary linear model: $\theta_0, \zeta_1, \zeta_2, \ldots$, and $\varepsilon_0, \varepsilon_1, \ldots$ are all uncorrelated with zero means. The variances are $E[\theta_0^2] = v_0^2$, $E[\zeta_k^2] = v^2$, and $E[\varepsilon_k^2] = \sigma^2$, where $v^2 = \alpha v_0^2$, $\alpha = v_0^2/(v_0^2 + \sigma^2)$. Finally, $X_n = \theta_n + \varepsilon_n$, where $\theta_{n+1} = \theta_n + \zeta_{n+1}$, $n = 0, 1, \ldots$. (We interpret $\{X_n\}$ as a noise distorted observation on the θ process.)

Answer:

$$\hat{X}_0 = 0$$
$$\hat{X}_k = \alpha X_{k-1} + (1 - \alpha)\hat{X}_{k-1}, \text{ for } k = 1, 2, \ldots,$$

where $\alpha = v_0^2/(v_0^2 + \sigma^2)$.

18. Let $\{X_k\}$ be a moving average process

$$X_n = \sum_{j=0}^{\infty} \alpha_j \xi_{n-j}, \qquad \alpha_0 = 1, \qquad \sum_{j=0}^{\infty} \alpha_j^2 < \infty,$$

where $\{\xi_n\}$ are zero-mean independent random variables having common variance σ^2. Show that

$$U_n = \sum_{k=0}^{n} X_{k-1}\xi_k, \qquad n = 0, 1, \ldots,$$

and

$$V_n = \sum_{k=0}^{n} X_k \xi_k - (n+1)\sigma^2, \qquad n = 0, 1, \ldots,$$

are martingales with respect to $\{\xi_n\}$.

19. Let $i = \sqrt{-1}$. Define the integral of a complex-valued function with respect to Gaussian random measure as the sum of the integrals of the real and imaginary parts. Similarly, define the integral of a function with respect to a complex random measure

$$\zeta(\mathrm{I}) = \xi(\mathrm{I}) + i\eta(\mathrm{I}), \qquad \mathrm{I} = (s, t], \qquad s < t,$$

as the sum of the real and imaginary parts. Obtain the representation

$$X_n = \int_{-\pi}^{\pi} e^{-in\omega} \zeta(d\omega), \qquad n = 0, \pm 1, \ldots,$$

from the representation

$$X_n = \int_0^{\pi} \cos n\omega Z^{(1)}(d\omega) + \int_0^{\pi} \sin n\omega Z^{(2)}(d\omega),$$

by setting

$$\xi(s) = -\xi(-s) = \tfrac{1}{2}Z^{(1)}(s), \qquad 0 \le s \le \pi,$$

and

$$\eta(s) = \eta(-s) = \tfrac{1}{2}Z^{(2)}(s), \qquad 0 \le s \le \pi.$$

Observe that $\xi(I) = \xi(-I)$ and $\eta(I) = -\eta(-I)$, where $I = (s, t]$, $-I = (-t, -s]$, $0 \le s \le t \le \pi$. Compute $E[\zeta(I_1)\overline{\zeta(I_2)}]$, where $I_i = (s_i, t_i]$ and "bar" denotes complex conjugation.

20. Suppose X_0 has probability density function

$$f(x) = \begin{cases} 2x, & \text{for } 0 \le x \le 1, \\ 0, & \text{elsewhere,} \end{cases}$$

and that X_{n+1} is uniformly distributed on $(1 - X_n, 1]$, given $X_0, \ldots, X_n$. Show that $\{X_n\}$ is a stationary ergodic process.

21. Show that every sequence $X_1, X_2, \ldots$ of independent identically distributed random variables forms an ergodic stationary process.

22. Let Z be a random variable uniformly distributed on $[0, 1)$. Let $X_0 = Z$ and $X_{n+1} = 2X_n \pmod 1$ that is,

$$X_{n+1} = \begin{cases} 2X_n & \text{if } X_n < \frac{1}{2}, \\ 2X_n - 1 & \text{if } X_n \ge \frac{1}{2}. \end{cases}$$

(a) Show that if $Z = .Z_0 Z_1 Z_2 \ldots$ is the terminating binary expansion for $Z = \sum_{k=0}^{\infty} 2^{-(k+1)} Z_k$, then $X_n = .Z_n Z_{n+1} \ldots$. (b) Show that X_n is a stationary process.

(c) Show that $\{X_n\}$ is ergodic. (d) Use the ergodic theorem to show that with probability one

$$\frac{1}{n} \sum_{k=0}^{n-1} \{2^k Z\} \to \frac{1}{2},$$

where $\{x\}$ is the fractional part of $x(\{x\} = x - [x]$ with $[x]$ the largest integer not exceeding x).

23. Let $\{\xi_n\}$ be independent identically distributed random variables having zero means and unit variances. Show that every moving average

$$X_n = \sum_{k=0}^{m} a_k \xi_{n-k}, \qquad n = 0, \pm 1, \ldots,$$

is ergodic. Suppose $\sum a_k^2 < \infty$. Is the same true of

$$Y_n = \sum_{k=0}^{\infty} a_k \xi_{n-k}?$$

24. A stochastic process $\{X_n\}$ is said to be *weakly mixing* if, for all sets A, B of real sequences $(x_1, x_2, \ldots)$,

$$\lim_{n\to\infty} \frac{1}{n} \sum_{k=1}^{n} \Pr\{(X_1, X_2, \ldots) \in A \quad \text{and} \quad (X_k, X_{k+1}, \ldots) \in B\}$$

$$= \Pr\{(X_1, X_2, \ldots) \in A\} \times \Pr\{(X_1, X_2, \ldots) \in B\}.$$

Show that every weakly mixing process is ergodic.

Remark: To verify weakly mixing, it suffices to show, for every $m = 1, 2, \ldots,$ and all sets A,B of vectors $(x_1, \ldots, x_m)$, that

$$\lim_{n\to\infty} \frac{1}{n} \sum_{k=1}^{n} \Pr\{(X_1, \ldots, X_m) \in A \quad \text{and} \quad (X_{k+1}, \ldots, X_{k+m}) \in B\}$$

$$= \Pr\{(X_1, \ldots, X_m) \in A\} \times \Pr\{(X_1, \ldots, X_m) \in B\}.$$

25. Let $\{\xi_n\}$ be a zero-mean covariance stationary process having covariance function

$$E[\xi_n \xi_m] = \begin{cases} 1, & n = m, \\ \rho, & n \neq m, \end{cases}$$

where $0 < \rho < 1$. Show that $\{\xi_n\}$ has the representation $\xi_n = U + \eta_n$, where $U, \eta_1, \eta_2, \ldots$ are zero-mean, uncorrelated random variables, $E[U^2] = \rho$, and $E[\eta_k^2] = 1 - \rho$.

Hint: Use the mean square ergodic theorem to define $U = \lim(\xi_1 + \cdots + \xi_n)/n$. Set $\eta_n = \xi_n - U$ and compute $E[U\xi_n]$, $E[U^2]$, and $E[\eta_n \eta_m]$.

26. Let $\{X_n\}$ be a finite-state irreducible Markov chain having the transition probabilities $\|P_{ij}\|_{i,j=1}^{N}$. There then exists a stationary distribution π, i.e., a vector $\pi(1), \ldots, \pi(N)$ satisfying $\pi(i) \geq 0$, $i = 1, \ldots, N$, $\sum_{i=1}^{N} \pi(i) = 1$, and

$$\pi(j) = \sum_{i=1}^{N} \pi(i) P_{ij}, \qquad j = 1, \ldots, N.$$

Suppose $\Pr\{X_0 = i\} = \pi(i)$, $i = 1, \ldots, N$. Show that $\{X_n\}$ is weakly mixing, hence ergodic.

27. Let $\{B(t), t \geq 0\}$ be a standard Brownian motion process and $B(I) = B(t) - B(s)$, for $I = (s, t]$, $0 \leq s < t$ the associated Gaussian random measure. Show that

$$Y(t) = \int_0^t f(x) B(dx), \qquad t \geq 0,$$

is a martingale for every bounded continuous function $f(u)$, $u \geq 0$.

28. Let $\{B(t), t \geq 0\}$ be a standard Brownian motion process and $B(I) = B(t) - B(s)$, for $I = (s, t]$, $0 \leq s < t$ the associated Gaussian random measure. Let $f(u)$ be a continuous function for $u \in [0, h]$. Show

$$Y(t) = \int_t^{t+h} f(u - t) B(du), \qquad t \geq 0,$$

is a stationary process.

29. Under the conditions of Theorem 10.2, show

$$\lim_{\omega \to \infty} \Pr\left\{ \max_{0 \leq s \leq t/f(\omega)} X(s) < \omega \right\} = e^{-t},$$

where

$$f(\omega) = \frac{\sqrt{\lambda_2}}{2\pi\sigma} \exp(-\omega^2/2\sigma^2).$$

30. Let $\{B(t);\ 0 \leq t \leq 1\}$ be a standard Brownian motion process and let $B(I) = B(t) - B(s)$, for $I = (s, t]$, $0 \leq s \leq t \leq 1$ be the associated Gaussian random measure. Validate the identity

$$E\left[\exp\left\{\lambda \int_0^1 f(s)\, dB(s)\right\}\right] = \exp\left\{\tfrac{1}{2}\lambda^2 \int_0^1 f^2(s)\, ds\right\}, \qquad -\infty < \lambda < \infty$$

where $f(s)$, $0 \leq s \leq 1$ is a continuous function.

31. Let $\{B(t);\ 0 \leq t \leq 1\}$ be a standard Brownian motion process and let $B(I) = B(t) - B(s)$, for $I = (s, t]$, $0 \leq s \leq t \leq 1$ be the associated Gaussian random measure. Validate the assertion that $U = \int_0^1 f(s)\, dB(s)$ and $V = \int_0^1 g(s)\, dB(s)$ are independent random variables whenever f and g are bounded continuous functions satisfying $\int_0^1 f(s)\, g(s)\, ds = 0$.

NOTES

For a good introduction to the spectral theory of stationary processes, see the book by Yaglom [2].

Many aspects of stationary processes, including the level-crossing problem, are treated in the text by Cramer and Leadbetter [1].

REFERENCES

1. Cramer, H, and Leadbetter, M., "Stationary and Related Stochastic Processes." Wiley, New York, 1966.
2. Yaglom, A. M., "An Introduction to the Theory of Stationary Random Functions." Prentice-Hall, Englewood Cliffs, New Jersey, 1962.
3. Anderson, T. W., "Statistical Analysis of Time Series." Wiley, New York, 1973.

Appendix

REVIEW OF MATRIX ANALYSIS

1: The Spectral Theorem

A. INTRODUCTORY CONCEPTS (LINEAR INDEPENDENCE AND BASIS)†

The set of all n-tuples (vectors) $\mathbf{x} = (x_1, \ldots, x_n)$, where the x_i are complex numbers, forms what is called an n-dimensional vector space. The sum of two vectors $\mathbf{x} = (x_1, \ldots, x_n)$ and $\mathbf{y} = (y_1, \ldots, y_n)$ is defined by $\mathbf{x} + \mathbf{y} = (x_1 + y_1, \ldots, x_n + y_n)$, and the product of $\mathbf{x}$ by a complex number λ is defined by $\lambda\mathbf{x} = (\lambda x_1, \ldots, \lambda x_n)$.

A set $\mathbf{x}^{(1)}, \ldots, \mathbf{x}^{(r)}$ of vectors is called *linearly independent* if the relation

$$c_1 \mathbf{x}^{(1)} + c_2 \mathbf{x}^{(2)} + \cdots + c_r \mathbf{x}^{(r)} = \mathbf{0}$$

implies $c_1 = c_2 = \cdots = c_r = 0$. As an example, we exhibit the vectors $(1, 0, \ldots, 0)$, $(0, 1, 0, \ldots, 0)$, etc., whose linear independence is obvious. A linearly independent family of vectors of n-tuples cannot contain more than n vectors.

Let $\boldsymbol{\varphi}_1, \ldots, \boldsymbol{\varphi}_r$, $r < n$, be a linearly independent set. There is some vector $\boldsymbol{\varphi}_{r+1}$ which is not a linear combination of $\boldsymbol{\varphi}_1, \ldots, \boldsymbol{\varphi}_r$, i.e., of the form $c_1 \boldsymbol{\varphi}_1 + \cdots + c_r \boldsymbol{\varphi}_r$. It follows at once that $\boldsymbol{\varphi}_1, \ldots, \boldsymbol{\varphi}_{r+1}$ is a linearly independent set. Proceeding in this fashion, we may obviously augment

† Some statements are made without formal proofs; the industrious student should supply detailed arguments.

the set $\varphi_1, \ldots, \varphi_r$ by vectors $\varphi_{r+1}, \ldots, \varphi_n$ so that $\varphi_1, \ldots, \varphi_n$ is a linearly independent set. Since no linearly independent set can contain more than n elements, we can determine for each vector $\mathbf{y}$ and each linearly independent set $\varphi_1, \ldots, \varphi_n$ constants $c_1, \ldots, c_n$ (necessarily unique) such that $c_1\varphi_1 + \cdots + c_n\varphi_n = \mathbf{y}$.

Analogous results hold for any linear manifold $\mathfrak{W}$, i.e., any set $\mathfrak{W}$ of vectors such that $\mathbf{x}, \mathbf{y} \in \mathfrak{W}$ implies $a\mathbf{x} + b\mathbf{y} \in \mathfrak{W}$ for every complex a, b. Given a linear manifold $\mathfrak{W}$, there is a unique integer m, $0 \le m \le n$, the dimension of $\mathfrak{W}$, such that the largest linearly independent set in $\mathfrak{W}$ contains precisely m elements. If $\varphi_1, \ldots, \varphi_r$, $r < m$, is a linearly independent set lying in $\mathfrak{W}$, there is some vector $\varphi_{r+1} \in \mathfrak{W}$ which is not expressible as a linear combination of $\varphi_1, \ldots, \varphi_r$. As before we infer the existence of $\varphi_{r+1}, \ldots, \varphi_m \in \mathfrak{W}$ such that $\varphi_1, \ldots, \varphi_m$ is a linearly independent set. Moreover, for any $\mathbf{y} \in \mathfrak{W}$ there exist (necessarily unique) constants $c_1, \ldots, c_m$ for which $c_1\varphi_1 + \cdots + c_m\varphi_m = \mathbf{y}$ holds. Notice that $\dim \mathfrak{W} = 0$ implies that $\mathfrak{W}$ consists exclusively of the zero element, while $\dim \mathfrak{W} = n$ implies that it contains every vector. If $\dim \mathfrak{W} = m$, any set of m linearly independent vectors in $\mathfrak{W}$ is called a *basis* of $\mathfrak{W}$. The unqualified term "basis" will be used for any set of n linearly independent vectors.

B. SCALAR PRODUCTS

The scalar (also called inner) product of two vectors $\mathbf{x}, \mathbf{y}$ is defined by $(\mathbf{x}, \mathbf{y}) = \sum_{i=1}^{n} x_i \bar{y}_i$, where $\bar{y}_i$ denotes the complex conjugate of y_i. We note the following easily verified properties of the scalar product:

(i) $(\mathbf{x}, \mathbf{x}) \ge 0$, with equality if and only if $\mathbf{x} = (0, \ldots, 0) = \mathbf{0}$.
(ii) $(\lambda\mathbf{x}, \mathbf{y}) = \lambda(\mathbf{x}, \mathbf{y})$ for λ complex.
(iii) $(\mathbf{x}, \mathbf{y}) = \overline{(\mathbf{y}, \mathbf{x})}$; thus from (ii), $(\mathbf{x}, \lambda\mathbf{y}) = \bar{\lambda}(\mathbf{x}, \mathbf{y})$.

Two vectors $\mathbf{x}, \mathbf{y}$ are called orthogonal if $(\mathbf{x}, \mathbf{y}) = 0$. The norm $\|\mathbf{x}\|$ of a vector $\mathbf{x}$ is defined by $\|\mathbf{x}\| = (\mathbf{x}, \mathbf{x})^{\frac{1}{2}}$.

A set $\{a_{ij}\}$, $i, j = 1, \ldots, n$, of complex numbers defines an n-dimensional (square) matrix, usually denoted by $\mathbf{A} = \|a_{ij}\|$, $i, j = 1, \ldots, n$. An $n \times n$ matrix $\mathbf{A}$ defines a transformation (or operator) in an n-dimensional vector space according to either $\mathbf{A}\mathbf{x} = \mathbf{y}$, where $y_i = \sum_{j=1}^{n} a_{ij} x_j$, $i = 1, \ldots, n$, or $\mathbf{x}\mathbf{A} = \mathbf{z}$, where $z_j = \sum_{i=1}^{n} x_i a_{ij}$, $j = 1, \ldots, n$. It is immediate from these definitions that

$$\mathbf{A}(\alpha\mathbf{x} + \beta\mathbf{y}) = \alpha\mathbf{A}\mathbf{x} + \beta\mathbf{A}\mathbf{y}, \qquad (\alpha\mathbf{x} + \beta\mathbf{y})\mathbf{A} = \alpha\mathbf{x}\mathbf{A} + \beta\mathbf{y}\mathbf{A},$$

for any vectors $\mathbf{x}, \mathbf{y}$ and constants α, β. Further, $(\mathbf{x}, \mathbf{A}\mathbf{y}) = (\mathbf{x}\bar{\mathbf{A}}, \mathbf{y})$ where $\bar{\mathbf{A}}$ is the $n \times n$ matrix with elements $\bar{a}_{ij}$. The two transformations induced by operating on the right or left are appropriately dual to each other. An elaborate geometric and algebraic theory of linear transformations is available; it can be found in most textbooks on matrix theory.

C. EIGENVALUES AND EIGENVECTORS

A complex number λ is called an eigenvalue of the matrix $\mathbf{A}$ if there exists a vector $\mathbf{x}^{(\lambda)} \neq 0$ such that $\mathbf{A}\mathbf{x}^{(\lambda)} = \lambda\mathbf{x}^{(\lambda)}$. If λ is an eigenvalue of $\mathbf{A}$, then the set $\mathfrak{W}_\lambda$ consisting of all vectors which satisfy the equation $\mathbf{A}\mathbf{x} = \lambda\mathbf{x}$ is called the right eigenmanifold of $\mathbf{A}$ corresponding to the eigenvalue λ, and the members of $\mathfrak{W}_\lambda$ are called right eigenvectors for λ. Clearly $\mathbf{y}$ and $\mathbf{z} \in \mathfrak{W}_\lambda$ implies $a\mathbf{y} + b\mathbf{z} \in \mathfrak{W}_\lambda$ for any constants a, b. The dimension of $\mathfrak{W}_\lambda$ is called the geometric multiplicity of λ.

If $\mathfrak{W}_1, \ldots, \mathfrak{W}_r$ are distinct eigenmanifolds of the operator $\mathbf{A}$, and $\boldsymbol{\varphi}_1, \ldots, \boldsymbol{\varphi}_r$ are arbitrary nonzero vectors in $\mathfrak{W}_1, \ldots, \mathfrak{W}_r$, respectively, then $\boldsymbol{\varphi}_1, \ldots, \boldsymbol{\varphi}_r$ are linearly independent. In fact, supposing the contrary, we let m be the smallest integer for which we can find distinct $\mathfrak{W}_1, \ldots, \mathfrak{W}_m$ and associated nonzero vectors $\boldsymbol{\varphi}_1 \in \mathfrak{W}_1, \ldots, \boldsymbol{\varphi}_m \in \mathfrak{W}_m$, with accompanying nonzero constants $c_1, \ldots, c_m$ such that $c_1\boldsymbol{\varphi}_1 + \cdots + c_m\boldsymbol{\varphi}_m = 0$. Trivially, $m \geq 2$. Applying $\mathbf{A}$ to both sides of the last equation, we obtain $\lambda_1 c_1 \boldsymbol{\varphi}_1 + \cdots + \lambda_m c_m \boldsymbol{\varphi}_m = \mathbf{0}$, where λ_i is the eigenvalue corresponding to the eigenmanifold $\mathfrak{W}_i$. If one among the λ_i is zero, we have a linear relationship among $m - 1$ elements, which contradicts the definition of m. Thus, $\lambda_1 \neq 0$; multiplying $c_1\boldsymbol{\varphi}_1 + \cdots + c_m\boldsymbol{\varphi}_m = \mathbf{0}$ by λ_1 and subtracting the result from $\lambda_1 c_1\boldsymbol{\varphi}_1 + \cdots + \lambda_m c_m \boldsymbol{\varphi}_m = \mathbf{0}$, we have

$$(\lambda_2 - \lambda_1)c_2\boldsymbol{\varphi}_2 + \cdots + (\lambda_m - \lambda_1)c_m\boldsymbol{\varphi}_m = \mathbf{0}.$$

This again contradicts the definition of m. It follows at once that if $\mathfrak{W}_1, \ldots, \mathfrak{W}_r$ are distinct eigenmanifolds of $\mathbf{A}$, and $\boldsymbol{\varphi}_1^{(i)}, \ldots, \boldsymbol{\varphi}_{m_i}^{(i)}$ is a basis of $\mathfrak{W}_i$, $i = 1, \ldots, r$, then

$$\boldsymbol{\varphi}_1^{(1)}, \ldots, \boldsymbol{\varphi}_{m_1}^{(1)}, \quad \boldsymbol{\varphi}_1^{(2)}, \ldots, \boldsymbol{\varphi}_{m_2}^{(2)}, \ldots, \quad \boldsymbol{\varphi}_1^{(r)}, \ldots, \boldsymbol{\varphi}_{m_r}^{(r)}$$

form a linearly independent set. Therefore, $\mathbf{A}$ can have only a finite number of eigenvalues and eigenmanifolds. In the important case where the sum of the dimensions of the eigenmanifolds equals n, we can construct a basis (for the entire space) composed of eigenvectors only. A matrix with this property is called *diagonalizable*.

We could just as well have started with the equation $\mathbf{x}\mathbf{A} = \lambda\mathbf{x}$ in place of $\mathbf{A}\mathbf{x} = \lambda\mathbf{x}$. It turns out that the values of λ for which $\mathbf{x}\mathbf{A} = \lambda\mathbf{x}$ has a nontrivial solution are precisely the eigenvalues of $\mathbf{A}$ as defined in the preceding paragraph. Furthermore, the dimension of the manifold of vectors satisfying $\mathbf{x}\mathbf{A} = \lambda\mathbf{x}$ (i.e., *left* eigenvectors) is just the multiplicity of λ. (The reader should prove this fact.) As before, a set consisting of left eigenvectors, each associated with a different eigenvalue, is linearly independent.

It may be noted that the eigenvalues of $\mathbf{A}$ are precisely the roots of the nth-degree algebraic equation

$$\det\|\mathbf{A}-\lambda\mathbf{I}\|=0.$$

From this and the known properties of determinants follows a result which we will need later on, namely, that if

$$\mathbf{A}=\begin{Vmatrix}\mathbf{A}_1 & \mathbf{0}\\ \mathbf{B} & \mathbf{A}_2\end{Vmatrix},$$

where $\mathbf{A}_1$, $\mathbf{A}_2$ are square matrices, then a number λ is an eigenvalue of $\mathbf{A}$ if and only if it is an eigenvalue of (at least) one of the matrices $\mathbf{A}_1$, $\mathbf{A}_2$. In fact, since

$$\det\|\mathbf{A}-\lambda\mathbf{I}\|=\det\|\mathbf{A}_1-\lambda\mathbf{I}\|\det\|\mathbf{A}_2-\lambda\mathbf{I}\|,$$

where the same notation $\mathbf{I}$ is used for identity matrices of varying dimensions, the assertion is obvious.

(a) *Spectral Representation*

For the following discussion we assume that $\mathbf{A}$ is real, i.e., its elements are real. Suppose that we can construct a basis for the whole space using right eigenvectors of $\mathbf{A}$. From the preceding remarks it follows that we can construct a basis for the whole space, using left eigenvectors of $\mathbf{A}$ as well. If in addition the elements a_{ij} of $\mathbf{A}$ are all real, we can choose the two bases to be biorthogonal, i.e., $\boldsymbol{\varphi}_1, \ldots, \boldsymbol{\varphi}_n$ and $\boldsymbol{\psi}_1, \ldots, \boldsymbol{\psi}_n$ are respectively the bases consisting of right and left eigenvectors for which $(\boldsymbol{\varphi}_i, \boldsymbol{\psi}_j)=1$ if $i=j$ and 0 otherwise. To demonstrate the construction of eigenvectors with these properties, we note first that if $\mathbf{A}\mathbf{x}_i=\lambda_i\mathbf{x}_i$ and $\mathbf{y}_j\mathbf{A}=\mu_j\mathbf{y}_j$, then

$$\mu_j(\mathbf{y}_j,\mathbf{x}_i)=(\mu_j\mathbf{y}_j,\mathbf{x}_i)=(\mathbf{y}_j\mathbf{A},\mathbf{x}_i)=(\mathbf{y}_j,\mathbf{A}\mathbf{x}_i)=(\mathbf{y}_j,\lambda_i\mathbf{x}_i)=\bar{\lambda}_i(\mathbf{y}_j,\mathbf{x}_i),$$

so that if $\mu_j\neq\bar{\lambda}_i$ we must have $(\mathbf{y}_j,\mathbf{x}_i)=0$. Next we observe that, because $\mathbf{A}$ is real, it follows directly that when $\mathbf{A}\mathbf{x}=\lambda\mathbf{x}$ holds, $\mathbf{A}\bar{\mathbf{x}}=\bar{\lambda}\bar{\mathbf{x}}$ also holds, where $\bar{\mathbf{x}}=(\bar{x}_1,\ldots,\bar{x}_n)$. We see, therefore, that the eigenvalues of $\mathbf{A}$ occur in conjugate pairs, and λ and $\bar{\lambda}$ have the same multiplicity. Let the eigenvalues of $\mathbf{A}$ be

$$\lambda_1,\bar{\lambda}_1,\lambda_2,\bar{\lambda}_2,\ldots,\lambda_r,\bar{\lambda}_r,\lambda_{r+1},\lambda_{r+2},\ldots,\lambda_m,$$

where $\lambda_1,\ldots,\lambda_r$ are complex and $\lambda_{r+1},\ldots,\lambda_m$ are real. We denote the corresponding right eigenmanifolds by $\mathfrak{M}_1, \overline{\mathfrak{M}}_1, \ldots, \mathfrak{M}_r, \overline{\mathfrak{M}}_r, \mathfrak{M}_{r+1}, \ldots, \mathfrak{M}_m$ and the left eigenmanifolds by $\mathfrak{L}_1, \overline{\mathfrak{L}}_1, \ldots, \mathfrak{L}_r, \overline{\mathfrak{L}}_r, \mathfrak{L}_{r+1}, \ldots, \mathfrak{L}_m$.

Now we have shown that every element in $\mathfrak{L}_1$ is orthogonal to every element in all of the right eigenmanifolds except $\overline{\mathfrak{W}}_1$, and similarly for the other left eigenmanifolds. Our task is, therefore, reduced to selecting a basis $\psi_1, \ldots, \psi_d$ for $\mathfrak{L}_1$ and $\varphi_1, \ldots, \varphi_d$ for $\overline{\mathfrak{W}}_1$ such that $(\psi_i, \varphi_j) = 1$ if $i = j$ and 0 otherwise, where d is the multiplicity of λ_1, and similarly for $\overline{\mathfrak{L}}_1, \overline{\mathfrak{W}}_1, \mathfrak{L}_2, \overline{\mathfrak{W}}_2$. To do this, let $\varphi_1, \ldots, \varphi_d$ be any basis for $\mathfrak{W}_1$, and $\mathbf{y}_1, \ldots, \mathbf{y}_d$ any basis for $\mathfrak{L}_1$. We wish to choose constants $c_1, \ldots, c_d$ such that $\psi_1 = c_1 \mathbf{y}_1 + \cdots + c_d \mathbf{y}_d$, and fullfilling the conditions $(\psi_1, \varphi_1) = 1$ and $(\psi_1, \varphi_i) = 0$ for $i = 2, \ldots, d$; i.e., we wish to satisfy the relations

$$\begin{aligned} c_1(\mathbf{y}_1, \varphi_1) + c_2(\mathbf{y}_2, \varphi_1) + \cdots + c_d(\mathbf{y}_d, \varphi_1) &= 1, \\ c_1(\mathbf{y}_1, \varphi_2) + c_2(\mathbf{y}_2, \varphi_2) + \cdots + c_d(\mathbf{y}_d, \varphi_2) &= 0, \\ \vdots \qquad\qquad \vdots \qquad\qquad\qquad & \vdots \\ c_1(\mathbf{y}_1, \varphi_d) + c_2(\mathbf{y}_2, \varphi_d) + \cdots + c_d(\mathbf{y}_d, \varphi_d) &= 0. \end{aligned}$$

Suppose that this system of linear equations for $c_1, \ldots, c_d$ has no solution. This means that no linear combination of the d vectors

$$\mathbf{f}_1 = ((\mathbf{y}_1, \varphi_1), \ldots, (\mathbf{y}_1, \varphi_d)), \ldots, \mathbf{f}_d = ((\mathbf{y}_d, \varphi_1), \ldots, (\mathbf{y}_d, \varphi_d))$$

yields the vector $(1, 0, \ldots, 0)$, and therefore the vectors $\mathbf{f}_1, \ldots, \mathbf{f}_d$ are not linearly independent. Thus, there exist constants $a_1, \ldots, a_d$, not all zero, such that $a_1\mathbf{f}_1 + \cdots + a_d\mathbf{f}_d = \mathbf{0}$. But this implies the equation

$$(a_1 \mathbf{y}_1 + \cdots + a_d \mathbf{y}_d, \varphi_i) = 0, \qquad i = 1, \ldots, d.$$

But it was proved above that the set $\mathbf{y}_1, \ldots \mathbf{y}_d$ (and hence any linear combination of the $\mathbf{y}_i$) is orthogonal to every manifold of right eigenvectors except $\overline{\mathfrak{W}}_1$. Now we see that $a_1 \mathbf{y}_1 + \cdots + a_d \mathbf{y}_d$ is orthogonal to every right eigenvector, and, of course, every linear combination of right eigenvectors. But by assumption there exists a basis formed of right eigenvectors, so that $a_1 \mathbf{y}_1 + \cdots + a_d \mathbf{y}_d$ is orthogonal to itself, and hence equals $\mathbf{0}$. This contradicts the linear independence of $\mathbf{y}_1, \ldots, \mathbf{y}_d$. Thus ψ_1 having the desired properties exists. We construct $\psi_2, \ldots, \psi_d$ in a similar manner. It remains to show that $\psi_1, \ldots, \psi_d$ are linearly independent. Suppose that $a_1\psi_1 + \cdots + a_d\psi_d = 0$; then

$$\begin{aligned} 0 &= (a_1\psi_1 + \cdots + a_d\psi_d, \varphi_1) = a_1, \\ 0 &= (a_1\psi_1 + \cdots + a_d\psi_d, \varphi_2) = a_2, \\ &\vdots \qquad \vdots \qquad\qquad \vdots \qquad\quad \vdots \\ 0 &= (a_1\psi_1 + \cdots + a_d\psi_d, \varphi_d) = a_d, \end{aligned}$$

and the above implication establishes that the ψ_i are linearly independent.

As we have seen, if $\mathbf{A}$ is a matrix whose elements are all real, and whose right (and therefore left) eigenvectors can be chosen to be a basis for the whole space, we can indeed take the basis $\boldsymbol{\varphi}_1, \ldots, \boldsymbol{\varphi}_n$ of right eigenvectors and $\boldsymbol{\psi}_1, \ldots, \boldsymbol{\psi}_n$ of left eigenvectors to be mutually biorthogonal, i.e., satisfying the relations $(\boldsymbol{\psi}_i, \boldsymbol{\varphi}_j) = 1$ if $i = j$, and 0 otherwise.

We will make use of this result to develop a canonical representation of the matrix $\mathbf{A}$, the so-called spectral representation. Suppose that $\lambda_1, \ldots, \lambda_n$ are the eigenvalues corresponding to $\boldsymbol{\varphi}_1, \ldots, \boldsymbol{\varphi}_n$, respectively; i.e., $\mathbf{A}\boldsymbol{\varphi}_i = \lambda_i \boldsymbol{\varphi}_i$, $i = 1, \ldots, n$, where the λ_i need not be distinct. Let

$$\boldsymbol{\varphi}_i = (\varphi_{i1}, \ldots, \varphi_{in}), \qquad \boldsymbol{\psi}_i = (\psi_{i1}, \ldots, \psi_{in}),$$

$$\mathbf{\Phi} = \left\| \begin{matrix} \varphi_{11} & \cdots & \varphi_{n1} \\ \vdots & & \\ \varphi_{1n} & \cdots & \varphi_{nn} \end{matrix} \right\|, \qquad \mathbf{\Psi} = \left\| \begin{matrix} \psi_{11} & \cdots & \psi_{1n} \\ \vdots & & \\ \psi_{n1} & \cdots & \psi_{nn} \end{matrix} \right\|,$$

$$\mathbf{\Lambda} = \left\| \begin{matrix} \lambda_1 & 0 & \cdot & \cdot & \cdot & 0 \\ 0 & \lambda_2 & & & & \\ \cdot & \cdot & \cdot & & & \\ \cdot & \cdot & & \cdot & & \\ \cdot & \cdot & & & \cdot & \\ 0 & 0 & \cdot & \cdot & \cdot & \lambda_n \end{matrix} \right\|.$$

The biorthogonality of $\boldsymbol{\varphi}_1, \ldots, \boldsymbol{\varphi}_n$ and $\boldsymbol{\psi}_1, \ldots, \boldsymbol{\psi}_n$ shows at once that $\mathbf{\Psi\Phi} = \mathbf{I}$, where $\mathbf{I}$ is the identity matrix. Moreover, by direct computation we readily verify that $\mathbf{\Phi\Lambda\Psi}\boldsymbol{\varphi}_i = \lambda_i \boldsymbol{\varphi}_i$, $i = 1, \ldots, n$. Since $\mathbf{A}\boldsymbol{\varphi}_i = \lambda_i \boldsymbol{\varphi}_i$, $i = 1, \ldots, n$, and the $\boldsymbol{\varphi}_i$ form a basis for the whole space, it follows that

$$\mathbf{A} = \mathbf{\Phi\Lambda\Psi} \qquad \text{and} \qquad \mathbf{\Phi\Psi} = \mathbf{I}.$$

From this we see that $\mathbf{A}^m = \mathbf{\Phi\Lambda\Psi\Phi\Lambda\Psi} \cdots \mathbf{\Phi\Lambda\Psi} = \mathbf{\Phi\Lambda}^m\mathbf{\Psi}$. But

$$\mathbf{\Lambda}^m = \left\| \begin{matrix} \lambda_1^m & 0 & \cdots & 0 \\ 0 & \lambda_2^m & \cdots & 0 \\ \cdot & & \cdot\ \cdot & \\ \cdot & & \cdot & \cdot \\ \cdot & & \cdot & \cdot \\ 0 & 0 & \cdots & \lambda_n^m \end{matrix} \right\|,$$

and so $\mathbf{A}^m$ is relatively easy to compute, once its spectral representation is explicitly known.

(b) ***Convergence***

We will need to have a notion of convergence for sequences of vectors and sequences of matrices.

A sequence $\mathbf{x}^{(1)}, \mathbf{x}^{(2)}, \ldots$ of vectors, in a given (n-dimensional) space, is said to converge to a vector $\mathbf{x}^{(0)}$ if

$$\lim_{j \to \infty} x_i^{(j)} = x_i^{(0)}, \qquad i = 1, \ldots, n.$$

Similarly, a sequence $\mathbf{A}^{(1)}, \mathbf{A}^{(2)}, \ldots$ of n-dimensional square matrices is said to converge to a matrix $\mathbf{A}^{(0)}$ if

$$\lim_{h \to \infty} a_{ij}^{(h)} = a_{ij}^{(0)}, \qquad i, j = 1, \ldots, n.$$

As an elementary consequence of these definitions, we observe that if $\lim_{h \to \infty} \mathbf{A}^{(h)} = \mathbf{A}^{(0)}$ and $\lim_{j \to \infty} \mathbf{x}^{(j)} = \mathbf{x}^{(0)}$, then $\lim_{h \to \infty} \mathbf{A}^{(h)}\mathbf{x}^{(h)} = \mathbf{A}^{(0)}\mathbf{x}^{(0)}$. Furthermore, if $\{\mathbf{A}^{(j)}\}$ is a sequence of matrices for which there exists a matrix $\mathbf{A}^{(0)}$ and a basis $\mathbf{x}^{(1)}, \ldots, \mathbf{x}^{(n)}$ of the whole space, such that

$$\lim_{h \to \infty} \mathbf{A}^{(h)}\mathbf{x}^{(i)} = \mathbf{A}^{(0)}\mathbf{x}^{(i)}, \qquad i = 1, \ldots, n,$$

then $\lim_{h \to \infty} \mathbf{A}^{(h)} = \mathbf{A}^{(0)}$. In fact, it is clear that then $\lim_{h \to \infty} \mathbf{A}^{(h)}\mathbf{y} = \mathbf{A}^{(0)}\mathbf{y}$ whenever $\mathbf{y} = c_1 \mathbf{x}^{(1)} + \cdots + c_n \mathbf{x}^{(n)}$, i.e., for every $\mathbf{y}$, since $\mathbf{x}^{(1)}, \ldots, \mathbf{x}^{(n)}$ form a basis.

D. POSITIVE DEFINITE MATRICES

An $n \times n$ real matrix $A = \|a_{ij}\|$ is said to be *positive definite* if $\sum_{i,j} a_{ij} x_i x_j > 0$ unless every $x_i = 0$. For the most part we consider only symmetric positive definite matrices, those for which $a_{ij} = a_{ji}$.

A real symmetric positive definite matrix is nonsingular, and all its eigenvalues are strictly positive. Every such matrix has a "square root", in the sense that there exists a real nonsingular matrix $P = \|p_{ij}\|$ for which $A = PP^T$. Here P^T denotes the *transpose* of P, the matrix having elements $p_{ij}^T = p_{ji}$.

2: *The Frobenius Theory of Positive Matrices*

The Frobenius theory of positive matrices serves usefully in numerous applications of probability theory, particularly in the analysis of Markov transition matrices. We proceed to the development of several aspects of this theory.

Preliminaries

Suppose that $\mathbf{A} = \|a_{ij}\|$, $i, j = 1, \ldots, n$, is a square matrix. If every a_{ij} is nonnegative, we write $\mathbf{A} \geq \mathbf{0}$; if $\mathbf{A} \geq \mathbf{0}$ and at least one a_{ij} is positive, we write $\mathbf{A} > \mathbf{0}$ and call $\mathbf{A}$ a positive matrix; if every a_{ij} is positive, we write $\mathbf{A} \gg 0$. We use the same notation for a vector $\mathbf{x} = (x_1, \ldots, x_n)$, i.e., $\mathbf{x} \geq \mathbf{0}$ requires that $x_i \geq 0$, $i = 1, \ldots, n$; $\mathbf{x} > \mathbf{0}$ implies that $\mathbf{x} \geq \mathbf{0}$ and $x_i > 0$ for at least one i, and $\mathbf{x} \gg \mathbf{0}$ implies that $x_i > 0$, $i = 1, \ldots, n$. We also write $\mathbf{x} \geq \mathbf{y}$ if $\mathbf{x} - \mathbf{y} \geq \mathbf{0}$, etc. Clearly $\mathbf{A} \geq \mathbf{0}$ and $\mathbf{x} \geq \mathbf{y}$ imply $\mathbf{Ax} \geq \mathbf{Ay}$, while $\mathbf{A} \gg \mathbf{0}$ and $\mathbf{x} > \mathbf{y}$ imply $\mathbf{Ax} \gg \mathbf{Ay}$.

Let $\mathbf{A} \geq \mathbf{0}$, and let Λ be the set consisting of all real numbers λ to each of which corresponds a vector $\mathbf{x} = (x_1, \ldots, x_n)$ such that

$$\sum_{i=1}^{n} x_i = 1, \qquad \mathbf{x} > \mathbf{0}, \qquad \text{and} \qquad \mathbf{Ax} \geq \lambda \mathbf{x}.$$

Let $\lambda_0 = \sup_\Lambda \lambda$; then λ_0 is finite, and it is easy to verify that if $\mathbf{A} \gg \mathbf{0}$ then λ_0 is positive. In fact, if $M = \max_{1 \leq i,j \leq n} a_{ij}$, then $\sum_{i=1}^{n} x_i = 1$ and $\mathbf{x} > \mathbf{0}$ implies that $\sum_{j=1}^{n} a_{ij} x_j \leq M \sum_{j=1}^{n} x_j = M$, $i = 1, \ldots, n$, while $x_j \geq 1/n$ for at least one value of j. It follows that $\lambda_0 \leq nM$. Similarly, if $\mathbf{A} \gg \mathbf{0}$, and $\mathbf{x} > \mathbf{0}$, then $0 < \delta = \min_{1 \leq i,j \leq n} a_{ij}$ and $\sum_{j=1}^{n} a_{ij}(1/n) \geq \delta$, $i = 1, \ldots, n$, from which it follows at once that $\lambda_0 \geq \delta n$.

Suppose that, for a matrix $\mathbf{A} > \mathbf{0}$, we have $\lambda_0 = 0$. If $\mathbf{x} \gg \mathbf{0}$, since $\lambda_0 = 0$ it follows that $\mathbf{Ax}$ cannot be $\gg \mathbf{0}$. Since $\mathbf{Ax} = \mathbf{0}$ for some $\mathbf{x} \gg \mathbf{0}$ evidently requires $\mathbf{A} = \mathbf{0}$. Therefore, there exists some $\mathbf{x} \gg \mathbf{0}$ for which $\mathbf{Ax} > \mathbf{0}$. Let C_1 be the set of indices of the positive components of $\mathbf{Ax}$; obviously C_1 does not depend upon the choice of $\mathbf{x} \gg \mathbf{0}$. Let $\mathbf{y} = (y_1, \ldots, y_n) > 0$ be such that $y_i > 0$ if $i \in C_1$, $y_i = 0$ if $i \notin C_1$, and define C_2 to be the indices of the positive components of $\mathbf{Ay}$. Again C_2 does not depend upon the explicit choice of $\mathbf{y}$, and $C_2 \subseteq C_1$. Since $\lambda_0 = 0$, we may conclude in fact that $C_2 \neq C_1$. Continuing in this manner, we find

$$C_1 \supset C_2 \supset \cdots \supset C_m = C_{m+1} = \cdots = \theta,$$

where the indicated inclusions are all proper. We assert now that $\mathbf{A}^m = \mathbf{0}$. In fact, it is clear that $\mathbf{A}^m \mathbf{x} = \mathbf{0}$ for $\mathbf{x} \gg 0$, and since every vector can be written as the difference of two strictly positive vectors, $\mathbf{A}^m \mathbf{z} = \mathbf{0}$ for every $\mathbf{z}$, which is equivalent to $\mathbf{A}^m = \mathbf{0}$.

The First Frobenius Theorem. We are now in a position to prove the first principal Frobenius theorem.

Theorem 2.1. *If* $\mathbf{A} \gg \mathbf{0}$, *then* (a) *there exists* $\mathbf{x}^0 \gg \mathbf{0}$ *such that* $\mathbf{Ax}^0 = \lambda_0 \mathbf{x}^0$; (b) *if* $\lambda \neq \lambda_0$ *is any other eigenvalue of* $\mathbf{A}$, *then* $|\lambda| < \lambda_0$; (c) *the right eigenvectors of* $\mathbf{A}$ *with eigenvalue* λ_0 *form a one-dimensional subspace, i.e.,* $\dim \mathfrak{W}_{\lambda_0} = 1$.

Proof. (a) By definition of λ_0, there exists a sequence $\gamma_1, \gamma_2, \ldots \to \lambda_0$ and vectors $\mathbf{x}^{(1)}, \mathbf{x}^{(2)}, \ldots$ such that

$$\mathbf{x}^{(i)} > \mathbf{0}, \qquad \mathbf{A}\mathbf{x}^{(i)} \geq \gamma_i \mathbf{x}^{(i)}, \qquad \text{and} \qquad x_1^{(i)} + \cdots + x_n^{(i)} = 1. \quad \text{(A2.1)}$$

Since the components of all the $\mathbf{x}^{(i)}$ lie in the interval $[0, 1]$, we can determine by a diagonalization procedure a sequence of positive integers $n_1 < n_2 < n_3 < \cdots$ and a vector $\mathbf{x}^0 = (x_1^0, \ldots, x_n^0)$ where $x_r^0 \in [0, 1]$ $(r = 1, 2, \ldots)$ such that

$$\lim_{j \to \infty} x_r^{(n_j)} \to x_r^0, \qquad r = 1, \ldots, n. \qquad \text{(A2.2)}$$

It follows from (2.1) that $x_1^0 + \cdots + x_n^0 = 1$ and that $\mathbf{x}^0 > \mathbf{0}$. Furthermore, if we replace i by n_j in the second inequality of (2.1) and let $j \to \infty$, it follows that $\mathbf{A}\mathbf{x}^0 \geq \lambda_0 \mathbf{x}^0$. We claim that in fact $\mathbf{A}\mathbf{x}^0 = \lambda_0 \mathbf{x}$, for otherwise $\mathbf{A}\mathbf{x}^0 > \lambda_0 \mathbf{x}^0$. But then, applying $\mathbf{A}$ to both sides of this last inequality, remembering that $\mathbf{A} \gg \mathbf{0}$, and setting $\mathbf{y}^0 = \mathbf{A}\mathbf{x}^0$, we infer that $\mathbf{A}\mathbf{y}^0 \gg \lambda_0 \mathbf{y}^0$ and $\mathbf{y}^0 \gg \mathbf{0}$. Thus for $\varepsilon > 0$ and sufficiently small we have $\mathbf{A}\mathbf{y}^0 \gg (\lambda_0 + \varepsilon)\mathbf{y}^0$; multiplying $\mathbf{y}^0$ by a suitable positive constant so as to make the sum of its components equal to 1, we see that $\lambda_0 + \varepsilon$ belongs to Λ, which contradicts the definition of λ_0. Hence $\mathbf{A}\mathbf{x}^0 = \lambda_0 \mathbf{x}^0$. Since $\mathbf{x}^0 > \mathbf{0}$ and $\mathbf{A} \gg \mathbf{0}$, we have $\lambda_0 \mathbf{x}^0 \gg \mathbf{0}$, or $\mathbf{x}^0 \gg \mathbf{0}$, which proves (a).

(b) Suppose that $\lambda \neq \lambda_0$ and $\mathbf{A}\mathbf{z} = \lambda \mathbf{z}$, where $\mathbf{z} \neq \mathbf{0}$. In component form $\mathbf{A}\mathbf{z} = \lambda \mathbf{z}$ is just

$$\sum_{j=1}^{n} a_{ij} z_j = \lambda z_i, \qquad i = 1, \ldots, n.$$

Taking the absolute value of both sides, keeping in mind that $a_{ij} > 0$, and using the fact that the absolute value of a sum does not exceed the sum of the absolute values of the summands, we obtain

$$\sum_{j=1}^{n} a_{ij} |z_j| \geq |\lambda|\, |z_i|, \qquad i = 1, \ldots, n,$$

i.e.,

$$\mathbf{A}|\mathbf{z}| \geq |\lambda|\, |\mathbf{z}|, \qquad \text{where} \quad |\mathbf{z}| = (|z_1|, \ldots, |z_n|).$$

Multiplying $|\mathbf{z}|$ by a suitable positive constant so that the sum of the components is equal to 1 (recall that $\mathbf{z} \neq 0$), we see that $|\lambda|$ belongs to Λ. Thus $|\lambda| \leq \lambda_0$ by the definition of λ_0. To show that $|\lambda| < \lambda_0$, consider the matrix $\mathbf{A}_\delta = \mathbf{A} - \delta\mathbf{I}$, where $\mathbf{I}$ is the identity matrix and δ is chosen so small that $\mathbf{A}_\delta \gg \mathbf{0}$. Since λ_0 is the largest positive eigenvalue of $\mathbf{A}$, $\lambda_0 - \delta$ is the largest positive eigenvalue of $\mathbf{A}_\delta$.

We repeat the above argument for $|\lambda| \leq \lambda_0$ with $\mathbf{A}$ and λ replaced by

$\mathbf{A}_\delta$ and $\lambda-\delta$, respectively. It follows that $|\lambda-\delta| \leq \lambda_0-\delta$. But

$$|\lambda| = |\lambda-\delta+\delta| \leq |\lambda-\delta|+\delta \leq \lambda_0,$$

so that $|\lambda| = \lambda_0$ implies $|\lambda| = |\lambda-\delta|+\delta$, which requires that λ be real and positive. Therefore $\lambda = |\lambda| = \lambda_0$, and this contradicts the assumption $\lambda \neq \lambda_0$.

(c) Suppose that $\mathbf{Ay} = \lambda_0\mathbf{y}$ and for no constant c does $\mathbf{y} = c\mathbf{x}^0$. Since $\mathbf{A}$ is a real matrix the vectors $\mathbf{u}$, $\mathbf{v}$ whose components consist of the real and imaginary parts, respectively, of the components of $\mathbf{y}$ are also eigenvectors of $\mathbf{A}$ with eigenvalue λ_0, and since $\mathbf{y} \neq c\mathbf{x}^0$ for any value of c, it follows that at least one of $\mathbf{u}$, $\mathbf{v}$ is not of the form $c\mathbf{x}^0$. Thus, we might just as well assume $\mathbf{y}$ to be real in the first place. As $\mathbf{x}^0 \gg 0$, we can choose μ so that $\mathbf{x}^0-\mu\mathbf{y} > \mathbf{0}$ but *not* $\gg \mathbf{0}$; that is to say, we can take $|\mu| = \min_{y_i \neq 0}\{x_i^0/|y_i|\}$, and of appropriate sign. But $\mathbf{A}(\mathbf{x}^0-\mu\mathbf{y}) = \lambda_0(\mathbf{x}^0-\mu\mathbf{y})$; as in the proof of part (a), necessarily $(\mathbf{x}^0-\mu\mathbf{y}) \gg 0$, which is in contradiction to the choice of μ. ∎

Before continuing, let us make a few simple observations. If $\mathbf{A} \gg \mathbf{0}$, then we can assert the existence of a vector $\mathbf{f}^0 \gg \mathbf{0}$ such that $\mathbf{f}^0\mathbf{A} = \lambda_0\mathbf{f}^0$, and the manifold of left eigenvectors corresponding to λ_0 is one-dimensional. To verify this let $\lambda' = \sup_{\Lambda'}\lambda$ where $\Lambda' = \{\lambda|\mathbf{fA} \geq \lambda\mathbf{f}$ for some $\mathbf{f} > \mathbf{0}\}$, and as in the proof of Theorem 2.1, we conclude the existence of $\mathbf{f}^0 \gg \mathbf{0}$ such that $\mathbf{f}^0\mathbf{A} = \lambda'\mathbf{f}^0$, $|\lambda| < \lambda'$ if λ is any eigenvalue $\neq \lambda'$ and the manifold of the left eigenvectors corresponding to λ' is one-dimensional. But this implies that $|\lambda_0| < \lambda'$ if $\lambda_0 \neq \lambda'$, since λ_0 is an eigenvalue of $\mathbf{A}$. But Theorem 2.1 says that $|\lambda'| < \lambda_0$ if the eigenvalue λ' is different from λ_0. Hence $\lambda' = \lambda_0$.

Theorem 2.2. *If $\mathbf{A} > \mathbf{0}$ and $\mathbf{A}^m \gg \mathbf{0}$ for some integer $m > 0$, then the assertions of the preceding theorem hold.*

Proof. As in the proof of Theorem 2.1, we can find $\mathbf{x}^0 > \mathbf{0}$ such that $\mathbf{Ax}^0 \geq \lambda_0\mathbf{x}^0$. If $\mathbf{Ax}^0 \neq \lambda_0\mathbf{x}^0$, then $\mathbf{Ax}^0 > \lambda_0\mathbf{x}^0$. Applying $\mathbf{A}^m$ to both sides, we find that $\mathbf{A}^{m+1}\mathbf{x}^0 \gg \lambda_0\mathbf{A}^m\mathbf{x}^0$, and $\mathbf{y} = \mathbf{A}^m\mathbf{x}^0 \gg 0$. Thus $\mathbf{Ay} \gg \lambda_0\mathbf{y}$ and, by the proof of Theorem 2.1, this contradicts the definition of λ_0; hence $\mathbf{Ax}^0 = \lambda_0\mathbf{x}^0$. Applying $\mathbf{A}$ successively to both sides of $\mathbf{Ax}^0 = \lambda_0\mathbf{x}^0$, we find $\mathbf{A}^m\mathbf{x}^0 = \lambda_0^m\mathbf{x}^0$. Since $\mathbf{A}^m \gg \mathbf{0}$ and $\mathbf{x}^0 > \mathbf{0}$, we conclude that $\lambda_0^m\mathbf{x}^0 \gg \mathbf{0}$, and hence $\mathbf{x}^0 \gg \mathbf{0}$. For Theorem 2.1(b), the proof that $|\lambda| \leq \lambda_0$ depended only upon $\mathbf{A} > \mathbf{0}$. Suppose then, that $|\lambda| = \lambda_0$, and $\mathbf{Az} = \lambda\mathbf{z}$ for some $\mathbf{z} \neq \mathbf{0}$. Then $\mathbf{A}^m\mathbf{z} = \lambda^m\mathbf{z}$, $\mathbf{A}^m\mathbf{x}^0 = \lambda_0^m\mathbf{x}^0$, and $|\lambda^m| = \lambda_0^m$. If we knew that λ_0^m was the largest positive eigenvalue of $\mathbf{A}^m$, the proof would paraphrase that of Theorem 2.1. Now, since $\mathbf{A}^m \gg \mathbf{0}$ by Theorem 2.1 we know that $\mathbf{A}^m$ has a largest positive eigenvalue with a corresponding eigenvector all of whose components are positive. Thus, if λ_0^m is not the largest positive eigenvalue of $\mathbf{A}^m$, we may conclude that $\mathbf{A}^m$ has two positive eigenvalues $\lambda_1 > \lambda_2$ and corresponding eigenvectors $\mathbf{x}_1, \mathbf{x}_2 \gg 0$. But this is not possible; for, let $\mu > 0$ be such that $\mathbf{x}_2 - \mu\mathbf{x}_1 > 0$ but not $\gg \mathbf{0}$. Then $\mathbf{A}^m(\mathbf{x}_2 - \mu\mathbf{x}_1) \gg 0$. On the other hand, $\mathbf{A}^m(\mathbf{x}_2 - \mu\mathbf{x}_1) = \lambda_2\mathbf{x}_2 - \mu\lambda_1\mathbf{x}_1 = \lambda_2(\mathbf{x}_2 - \mu\mathbf{x}_1) - (\lambda_1 - \lambda_2)\mu\mathbf{x}_1$. Since the first term is *not* $\gg 0$ while the second term is $\gg 0$, we obtain a contradiction. The proof of (c) is identical with that given for Theorem 2.1(c), once one observes that any eigenvector of $\mathbf{A}$ is an eigenvector of $\mathbf{A}^m$. ■

To continue our study of matrices $\mathbf{A} > \mathbf{0}$ for which $\mathbf{A}^m \gg \mathbf{0}$ for some integer $m > 0$, we introduce a matrix of rank 1 of the form

$$\mathbf{P} = \|x_i^0 f_j^0\|,$$

where $\mathbf{x}^0$ is the same as earlier, and $\mathbf{f}^0 \gg \mathbf{0}$ satisfies $\mathbf{f}^0\mathbf{A} = \lambda_0\mathbf{f}^0$ and is normalized by a multiplicative factor so that $\sum_{i=1}^n x_i^0 f_i^0 = 1$. Then $\mathbf{P}$ has the following properties:

(i) For any vectors $\mathbf{x}$ and $\mathbf{f}$, $\mathbf{Px} = (\mathbf{x}, \mathbf{f}^0)\mathbf{x}^0$, $\mathbf{fP} = (\mathbf{f}, \mathbf{x}^0)\mathbf{f}^0$, in particular $\mathbf{Px}^0 = \mathbf{x}^0$, $\mathbf{f}^0\mathbf{P} = \mathbf{f}^0$.

(ii) $\mathbf{P}^2 = \mathbf{P}$.

(iii) $\mathbf{AP} = \mathbf{PA} = \lambda_0\mathbf{P}$.

The first two assertions are verified by direct computation; as for the third, we observe that for any vector $\mathbf{x}$

$$\mathbf{APx} = \mathbf{A}(\mathbf{x}, \mathbf{f}^0)\mathbf{x}^0 = (\mathbf{x}, \mathbf{f}^0)\mathbf{Ax}^0 = (\mathbf{x}, \mathbf{f}^0)\lambda_0\mathbf{x}^0 = \lambda_0\mathbf{Px},$$

so that $\mathbf{AP} = \lambda_0\mathbf{P}$; similarly $\mathbf{fPA} = \mathbf{f}\lambda_0\mathbf{P}$, which implies $\mathbf{PA} = \lambda_0\mathbf{P}$.

We now quote without proof the following fact: Let $\mathbf{B}$ be a (square) matrix; set $\mathbf{B}^n = \|b_{ij}^{(n)}\|$, and

$$r = \max_{i,j} \overline{\lim_{n\to\infty}} \sqrt[n]{|b_{ij}^{(n)}|}.$$

Then $\mathbf{B}$ has an eigenvalue λ^* such that $|\lambda^*| = r$, and if λ is any other eigenvalue of $\mathbf{B}$, then $|\lambda| \le r$. Frequently r is called the spectral radius of $\mathbf{B}$. We are now prepared to prove the following theorem.

Theorem 2.3. *If $\mathbf{A} > \mathbf{0}$, $\mathbf{A}^m \gg \mathbf{0}$ for some integer $m > 0$, and λ_0 and $\mathbf{P}$ are defined as above, then*

$$\frac{1}{\lambda_0^n}\mathbf{A}^n \to \mathbf{P} \qquad \text{as} \quad n \to \infty.$$

Proof. We assert first that if λ is an eigenvalue of $\mathbf{B} = \mathbf{A} - \lambda_0 \mathbf{P}$, then $|\lambda| < \lambda_0$. In fact, suppose that $\mathbf{Bz} = \lambda \mathbf{z}$ for some $\mathbf{z} \neq \mathbf{0}$. Then

$$\lambda \mathbf{Pz} = \mathbf{PBz} = \mathbf{P}(\mathbf{A} - \lambda_0 \mathbf{P})\mathbf{z} = (\lambda_0 \mathbf{P} - \lambda_0 \mathbf{P}^2)\mathbf{z} = \lambda_0(\mathbf{P} - \mathbf{P})\mathbf{z} = \mathbf{0},$$

and so $\mathbf{Bz} = \lambda \mathbf{z}$ reduces to $\mathbf{Az} = \lambda \mathbf{z}$. We know from Theorem 2.2 that either $\lambda = \lambda_0$ or $|\lambda| < \lambda_0$. If $\lambda = \lambda_0$, then $\mathbf{Az} = \lambda_0 \mathbf{z}$, and therefore $\mathbf{z}$ is a multiple of $\mathbf{x}^0$. But as established above, $\lambda \mathbf{Pz} = \lambda \mathbf{z} \neq \mathbf{0}$ is impossible. Hence the spectral radius r of $\mathbf{B}$ satisfies $r < \lambda_0$. Let ρ satisfy $r < \rho < \lambda_0$; since

$$r = \overline{\lim_{n \to \infty}} \sqrt[n]{\max_{i,j} |b_{ij}^{(n)}|} < \rho,$$

it follows that $\max_{i,j} |b_{ij}^{(n)}| < \rho^n$ for n sufficiently large. Using properties (ii) and (iii) of $\mathbf{P}$, we readily verify by induction that

$$\mathbf{B}^m = \mathbf{A}^m - \lambda_0^m \mathbf{P}$$

or

$$\frac{\mathbf{A}^m}{\lambda_0^m} = \frac{\mathbf{B}^m}{\lambda_0^m} + \mathbf{P}.$$

Since $\max_{i,j} |b_{ij}^{(n)}| < \rho^n$ for n sufficiently large,

$$\left| \frac{b_{ij}^{(m)}}{\lambda_0^m} \right| \leq \left(\frac{\rho}{\lambda_0} \right)^m \to 0,$$

and so $\mathbf{B}^m / \lambda^m \to 0$. ■

The Second Frobenius Theorem. The main Frobenius theorem is as follows.

Theorem 2.4. *Assume* $\mathbf{A} > \mathbf{0}$, *and let* λ_0 *be defined as in Theorem 2.1. Then* (a) λ_0 *is an eigenvalue of* $\mathbf{A}$ *with an eigenvector* $\mathbf{x}^0 > \mathbf{0}$; (b) *if* λ *is any other eigenvector of* $\mathbf{A}$, *then* $|\lambda| \leq \lambda_0$; (c)

$$\frac{1}{m} \sum_{i=1}^{m} \frac{\mathbf{A}^i}{\lambda_0^i}$$

converges if $\mathbf{x}^0 \gg \mathbf{0}$; (d) *if* λ *is an eigenvalue of* $\mathbf{A}$ *and* $|\lambda| = \lambda_0$, *then* $\eta = \lambda / \lambda_0$ *is a root of unity and* $\eta^m \lambda_0$ *is an eigenvalue of* $\mathbf{A}$ *for* $m = 0, 1, 2, \ldots$.

Proof. (a) Let $\mathbf{E}$ be the matrix all of whose components equal 1; hence $\mathbf{A} + \delta \mathbf{E} \gg \mathbf{0}$ for every $\delta > 0$. Let $0 < \delta_1 < \delta_2$; and choose $\mathbf{x} = (x_1, \ldots, x_n) > 0$ such that $\sum_{i=1}^{n} x_i = 1$. Then $(\mathbf{A} + \delta_1 \mathbf{E})\mathbf{x} \geq \lambda \mathbf{x}$ implies that

$$\begin{aligned}(\mathbf{A} + \delta_2 \mathbf{E})\mathbf{x} &= (\mathbf{A} + \delta_1 \mathbf{E})\mathbf{x} + (\delta_2 - \delta_1)\mathbf{Ex} \\ &\geq [\lambda + (\delta_2 - \delta_1)]\mathbf{x}.\end{aligned}$$

Thus, if $\lambda_0(\delta)$ is the value of λ_0 corresponding to the matrix $\mathbf{A} + \delta\mathbf{E}$, we see that $\lambda_0(\delta)$ is an increasing function of δ. We note that $\lambda_0(0)$ is the value of λ_0 corresponding to $\mathbf{A}$ itself. Now Theorem 2.1 affirms the existence of a vector $\mathbf{x}(\delta) \gg 0$, normalized so that $\sum_{i=1}^{n} x_i(\delta) = 1$ and satisfying

$$(\mathbf{A} + \delta\mathbf{E})\mathbf{x}(\delta) = \lambda_0(\delta)\mathbf{x}(\delta).$$

Let $\delta_1 > \delta_2 > \cdots$ be a positive sequence whose limit is zero. By the proof of Theorem 2.1, we can find integers $n_1, n_2, \ldots$ such that $\lim_{j\to\infty} \mathbf{x}(\delta_{n_j}) \to \mathbf{x}^0$, where $\mathbf{x}^0$ is some vector > 0 and $\sum_{i=1}^{n} x_i^0 = 1$. Clearly $\mathbf{A} + \delta_{n_j}\mathbf{E} \to \mathbf{A}$ and $\lambda_0(\delta_{n_j}) \to \lambda' \geq \lambda_0$. Since

$$(\mathbf{A} + \delta_{n_j}\mathbf{E})\mathbf{x}(\delta_{n_j}) = \lambda_0(\delta_{n_j})\mathbf{x}(\delta_{n_j}),$$

letting $j \to \infty$ yields $\mathbf{A}\mathbf{x}^0 = \lambda'\mathbf{x}^0$. But according to the characterization of λ_0 established in Theorem 2.1(b), $\lambda_0 \geq \lambda'$; hence $\lambda_0 = \lambda'$ and (a) is proved.

The proof of (b) is identical to that for the case $\mathbf{A} \gg \mathbf{0}$.

For (c) and (d), there is clearly no loss of generality in assuming $\lambda_0 = 1$, since otherwise we could divide every element of $\mathbf{A}$ by λ_0.

(c) Since $\mathbf{A}\mathbf{x}_0 = \mathbf{x}_0$ we have $\mathbf{A}^m\mathbf{x}_0 = \mathbf{x}_0$. Writing this equation in terms of components we find immediately that

$$0 \leq a_{ij}^{(m)} \leq \frac{\max_i x_i^0}{\min_i x_i^0}.$$

Hence the elements of $\mathbf{A}^m$ are uniformly bounded.

Let $\mathbf{L} = \{\mathbf{x} | \mathbf{A}\mathbf{x} = \mathbf{x}\}$ and $\mathbf{K} = \{\mathbf{y} | \mathbf{y} = (\mathbf{I} - \mathbf{A})\mathbf{x} \text{ for some } \mathbf{x}\}$; i.e., $\mathbf{L}$ is the linear space of fixed points of $\mathbf{A}$, and $\mathbf{K}$ is the linear space of the range of the matrix I–A. In addition define

$$\mathbf{S}_m = \frac{\mathbf{A} + \mathbf{A}^2 + \cdots + \mathbf{A}^m}{m}.$$

Clearly $\mathbf{L}$ is a closed linear space such that, for every $\mathbf{x}$ in $\mathbf{L}$,

$$\mathbf{S}_m\mathbf{x} = \frac{\mathbf{A} + \mathbf{A}^2 + \cdots + \mathbf{A}^m}{m}\mathbf{x} = \mathbf{x},$$

and so $\lim_{m\to\infty} \mathbf{S}_m\mathbf{x} = \mathbf{x}$. We will show that $\mathbf{S}_m\mathbf{x}$ also converges for every $\mathbf{x}$ in $\mathbf{K}$ and that every vector $\mathbf{x}$ in n-dimensional coordinate space is in $\mathbf{L} \oplus \mathbf{K}$, (the direct sum of the spaces $\mathbf{L}$ and $\mathbf{K}$). This will complete the proof of (c).

We assert that for $\mathbf{y} \in \mathbf{K}$, $\lim_{m\to\infty} \mathbf{S}_m \mathbf{y} = \mathbf{0}$. In fact, since $\mathbf{y} = (\mathbf{I} - \mathbf{A})\mathbf{x}$ for some $\mathbf{x}$,

$$\mathbf{S}_m \mathbf{y} \equiv \frac{\mathbf{A}\mathbf{y} + \cdots + \mathbf{A}^m \mathbf{y}}{m} = \frac{\mathbf{A}\mathbf{x} - \mathbf{A}^{m+1}\mathbf{x}}{m}$$

tends to $\mathbf{0}$ as $m \to \infty$ by virtue of the fact that the elements of $\mathbf{A}^m$ are uniformly bounded.

To show that every vector $\mathbf{x}$ is the sum of a vector in $\mathbf{L}$ and a vector in $\mathbf{K}$ consider

$$\mathbf{x} = (\mathbf{x} - \mathbf{S}_m \mathbf{x}) + \mathbf{S}_m \mathbf{x} = \mathbf{y}_m + \mathbf{z}_m .$$

Since the elements of $\mathbf{A}^m$ are uniformly bounded we may conclude that the components of $\mathbf{y}_m$ and $\mathbf{z}_m$ are also bounded. Hence there exists a sequence of positive integers $m_1 < m_2 < \cdots$ and a vector $\mathbf{z}^0$ such that

$$\lim_{i\to\infty} \mathbf{z}_{m_i} = \mathbf{z}_0$$

Since

$$\mathbf{z}_{m_i} - \mathbf{A}\mathbf{z}_{m_i} = \frac{\mathbf{A} - \mathbf{A}^{m_i+1}}{m_i} \mathbf{x} \to \mathbf{0} \qquad \text{as} \quad i \to \infty,$$

we have

$$\mathbf{z}_0 = \lim_{i\to\infty} \mathbf{z}_{m_i} = \lim_{i\to\infty} \mathbf{A}\mathbf{z}_{m_i} = \mathbf{A} \lim_{i\to\infty} \mathbf{z}_{m_i} = \mathbf{A}\mathbf{z}_0$$

and $\mathbf{z}_0 \in \mathbf{L}$.

Also

$$\mathbf{y}_m = \mathbf{x} - \mathbf{S}_m \mathbf{x} = \frac{1}{m} [(\mathbf{x} - \mathbf{A}\mathbf{x}) + (\mathbf{x} - \mathbf{A}^2\mathbf{x}) + \cdots + (\mathbf{x} - \mathbf{A}^m \mathbf{x})]$$

$$= (\mathbf{I} - \mathbf{A}) \left[\frac{\mathbf{x}}{m} + \frac{(\mathbf{I} + \mathbf{A})\mathbf{x}}{m} + \frac{(\mathbf{I} + \mathbf{A} + \mathbf{A}^2)\mathbf{x}}{m} + \cdots + \right.$$

$$\left. + \frac{(\mathbf{I} + \mathbf{A} + \cdots + \mathbf{A}^{m-1})\mathbf{x}}{m} \right],$$

which implies that $\mathbf{y}_m \in \mathbf{K}$. Since $\mathbf{K}$ is a closed linear space and the elements of $\mathbf{y}_m$ are uniformly bounded, $\mathbf{y}_{m_i} \to \mathbf{x} - \mathbf{z}_0 \in \mathbf{K}$ as $i \to \infty$. Thus $\mathbf{x} = (\mathbf{x} - \mathbf{z}_0) + \mathbf{z}_0$ where $\mathbf{x} - \mathbf{z}_0 \in \mathbf{K}$, $\mathbf{z}_0 \in \mathbf{L}$, and the proof is complete.

(d) We know that there exists a vector $\mathbf{f}^0 > 0$ such that $\mathbf{f}^0 \mathbf{A} = \mathbf{f}^0$. Let us assume first that $\mathbf{f}^0 \gg \mathbf{0}$. Suppose now that $\lambda \neq 1$, $|\lambda| = 1$, and that $\mathbf{A}\mathbf{x} = \lambda \mathbf{x}$ for some $\mathbf{x} \neq \mathbf{0}$. Then

$$\sum_{j=1}^{n} a_{ij} x_j = \lambda x_i \qquad i = 1, 2, \ldots, n$$

and so

$$\sum_{j=1}^{n} a_{ij}|x_j| \geq |x_i| \qquad \text{or} \qquad \mathbf{A}|\mathbf{x}| \geq |\mathbf{x}|.$$

But if $\mathbf{A}|\mathbf{x}| > |\mathbf{x}|$ then $(\mathbf{f}^0, |\mathbf{x}|) < (\mathbf{f}^0, \mathbf{A}|\mathbf{x}|) = (\mathbf{f}^0\mathbf{A}, |\mathbf{x}|) = (\mathbf{f}^0, |\mathbf{x}|)$. This absurdity implies the result $\mathbf{A}|\mathbf{x}| = |\mathbf{x}|$. Consequently

$$\sum_{j=1}^{n} a_{ij}|x_j| = |x_i| = \Big|\sum_{j=1}^{n} a_{ij}x_j\Big|, \qquad i = 1, 2, \ldots, n$$

and so there exist constants $\mu_1, \ldots, \mu_n$, $|\mu_i| = 1$, such that

(*) $$a_{ij}x_j = a_{ij}|x_j|\mu_i \qquad \text{for all } i, j.$$

Let $\mathbf{x}\cdot\mathbf{y}$ denote the vector $(x_1y_1, \ldots, x_ny_n)$. Multiplying the preceding relation by μ_j^r (the rth power of μ_j) and summing over j, we find that

$$\mathbf{A}(\mathbf{x}\cdot\boldsymbol{\mu}^r) = \boldsymbol{\mu}\cdot\mathbf{A}(|\mathbf{x}|\cdot\boldsymbol{\mu}^r).$$

At the same time, summing over i in (*), we obtain

$$\mathbf{A}\mathbf{x} = \boldsymbol{\mu}\cdot\mathbf{A}|\mathbf{x}|,$$

from which follows

$$\lambda\mathbf{x} = \boldsymbol{\mu}\cdot|\mathbf{x}|.$$

Thus

$$\mathbf{A}(\mathbf{x}\cdot\boldsymbol{\mu}^r) = \boldsymbol{\mu}\cdot\mathbf{A}(\lambda\mathbf{x}\cdot\boldsymbol{\mu}^{r-1}) = \lambda\boldsymbol{\mu}\cdot\mathbf{A}(\mathbf{x}\cdot\boldsymbol{\mu}^{r-1}), \qquad r = 1, 2, \ldots,$$

from which it follows inductively that $\mathbf{A}(\mathbf{x}\cdot\boldsymbol{\mu}^r) = \lambda^{r+1}(\boldsymbol{\mu}^r\cdot\mathbf{x})$. Thus λ^r is an eigenvalue of $\mathbf{A}$ for $r = 1, 2, \ldots$. Since the number of eigenvalues of $\mathbf{A}$ is finite, λ must be a root of unity.

Suppose now that $\mathbf{f}^0 > \mathbf{0}$ but not $\gg \mathbf{0}$. By relabeling, if necessary, the rows and columns of $\mathbf{A}$, we may assume that $\mathbf{f}^0 = (f_1^0, \ldots, f_r^0, 0, \ldots, 0)$, where $f_i^0 > 0$, $i = 1, \ldots, r$. Since $\mathbf{A} > \mathbf{0}$ the relation $\mathbf{f}^0\mathbf{A} = \mathbf{f}^0$ implies the decomposition

$$\mathbf{A} = \left\|\begin{matrix} \mathbf{A}_1 & \mathbf{0} \\ \mathbf{B} & \mathbf{A}_2 \end{matrix}\right\|,$$

where $\mathbf{A}_1$ is an $r \times r$ matrix and $\mathbf{A}_2$ is an $n - r \times n - r$ matrix and also that the vector $(f_1^0, \ldots, f_r^0)$ is a left eigenvector, with eigenvalue 1, of $\mathbf{A}_1$. Let λ be an eigenvalue of $\mathbf{A}$; if λ is an eigenvalue of $\mathbf{A}_1$ we are back to the case considered with $\mathbf{A}_1$ replacing $\mathbf{A}$. If λ is not an eigenvalue of $\mathbf{A}_1$, it must be an eigenvalue of $\mathbf{A}_2$. But the eigenvalues of $\mathbf{A}_2$ are eigenvalues of $\mathbf{A}$ and they do not exceed 1 in absolute value. At the same time, since $\mathbf{A}_2 > \mathbf{0}$ it has a largest positive eigenvalue which is an upper bound for the absolute values of all its other eigenvalues. Since $|\lambda| = 1$, the largest positive eigenvalue of $\mathbf{A}_2$ is precisely 1. We can obviously apply to $\mathbf{A}_2$

the preceding analysis; either it has a left eigenvector $\gg \mathbf{0}$ corresponding to the eigenvalue 1, or else it is of the form (under suitable rearrangement of its rows and columns)

$$\mathbf{A}_2 = \begin{Vmatrix} \mathbf{A}_3 & \mathbf{0} \\ \mathbf{B}_1 & \mathbf{A}_4 \end{Vmatrix}.$$

Continuing in this way we can reduce the problem in a finite number of steps to the situation in which there exists a left eigenvector $\gg \mathbf{0}$ with eigenvalue 1. ∎

The following corollaries yield some useful information concerning the spectral radius $\lambda_0(\mathbf{A})$ of a positive matrix $\mathbf{A}$. The first corollary is simply a restatement of Theorem 2.4, (a) and (b).

Corollary 2.1. *If $\mathbf{A} > \mathbf{0}$, then the eigenvalue of largest magnitude $\lambda_0 = \lambda_0(\mathbf{A})$ is real and nonnegative and is characterized as $\lambda_0 = \max_\Lambda \lambda$, where*

$$\Lambda = \{\lambda | \mathbf{A}\mathbf{x} \geq \lambda\mathbf{x} \quad \text{for some} \quad \mathbf{x} > \mathbf{0}\}.$$

Corollary 2.2. *If $\mathbf{A} > \mathbf{0}$ and there exists $\mathbf{x}^0 \gg \mathbf{0}$ such that $\mathbf{A}\mathbf{x}^0 \leq \mu\mathbf{x}^0$, then μ is an upper bound for $\lambda_0(\mathbf{A})$.*

Proof. Applying $\mathbf{A}$ to both sides of $\mathbf{A}\mathbf{x}^0 \leq \mu\mathbf{x}^0$, we have $\mathbf{A}^2\mathbf{x}^0 \leq \mu\mathbf{A}\mathbf{x}^0 \leq \mu^2\mathbf{x}^0$ and iterating we obtain

$$\mathbf{A}^n\mathbf{x}^0 \leq \mu^n\mathbf{x}^0, \qquad n = 1, 2, \ldots.$$

This readily implies

$$a_{ij}^{(n)} \leq \mu^n \frac{\max\limits_i x_i^0}{\min\limits_i x_i^0},$$

and so

$$\lambda_0(\mathbf{A}) = \overline{\lim_{n\to\infty}} \sqrt[n]{\max_{i,j} |a_{ij}^{(n)}|} \leq \mu. \quad ∎$$

Corollary 2.3. *If $\mathbf{A} \geq \mathbf{B} \geq \mathbf{0}$, then $\lambda_0(\mathbf{B}) \leq \lambda_0(\mathbf{A})$.*

Proof. This can be seen either from Corollary 3.1 or from the relation

$$\lambda_0(\mathbf{A}) = \overline{\lim_{n\to\infty}} \sqrt[n]{\max_{i,j} a_{ij}^{(n)}} \geq \overline{\lim_{n\to\infty}} \sqrt[n]{\max_{i,j} b_{ij}^{(n)}} = \lambda_0(\mathbf{B}),$$

since it is clear that $\mathbf{A} \geq \mathbf{B} \geq \mathbf{0}$ implies $\mathbf{A}^n \geq \mathbf{B}^n \geq \mathbf{0}$, $n = 1, 2, \ldots$. ∎

INDEX

G

H

I

J

K

L

M

版 权 声 明

A First Course in Stochastic Processes, Second Edition by Samuel Karlin and Howard M. Taylor, ISBN: 978-0-12-398552-1.

Authorized English language reprint edition published by the Proprietor.

ISBN: 978-981-259-950-6.

Elsevier (Singapore) Pte Ltd.

3 Killiney Road

#08-01 Winsland House I

Singapore 239519

Tel：(65)6349-0200

Fax：(65)6733-1817

First Published 2007

2007年初版